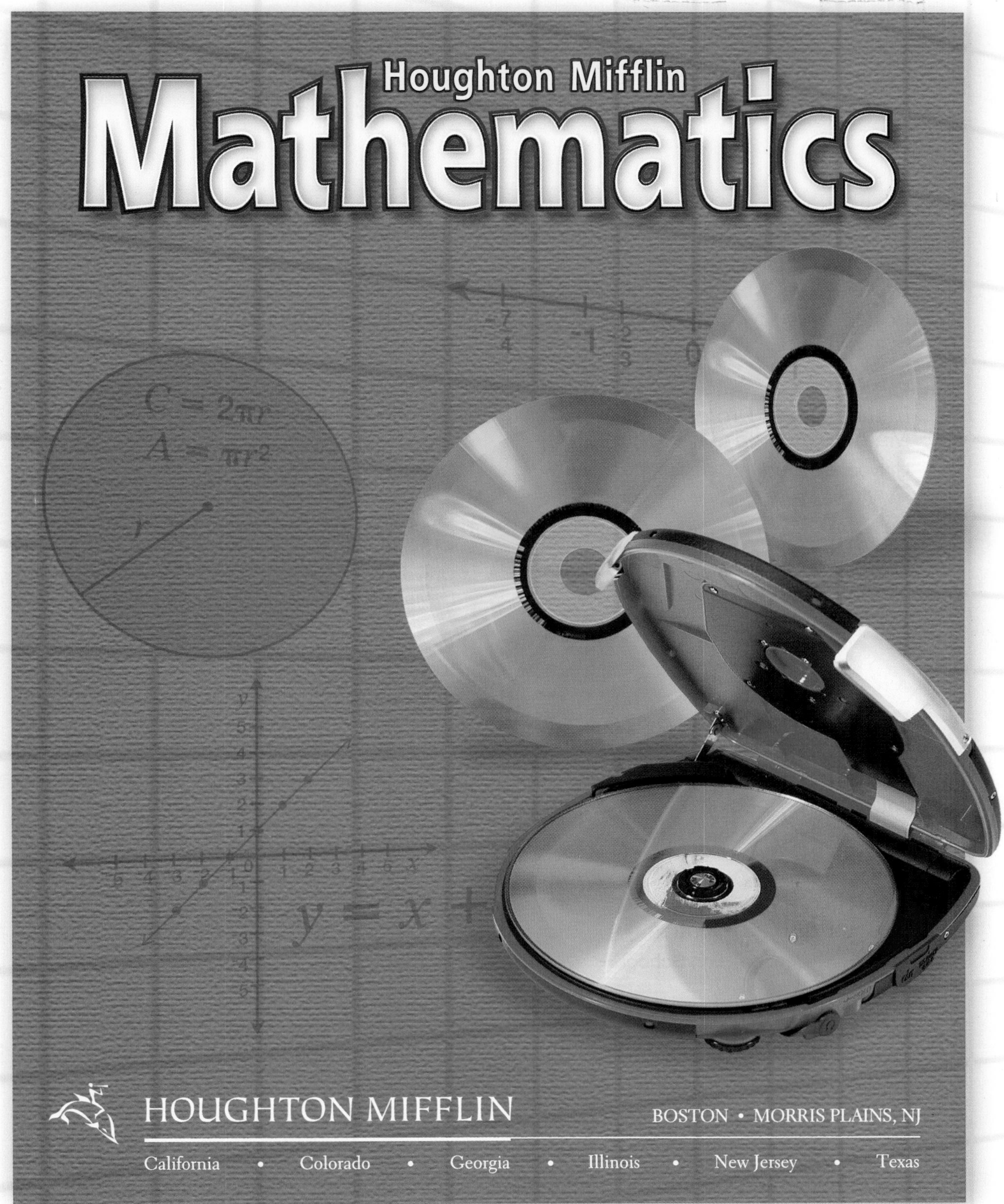

ISBN 0-618-09980-8

6 7 8 9 DW 09 08 07 06 05 04 03

Authors

Senior Authors

Dr. Carole Greenes
Professor of Mathematics Education
Boston University
Boston, MA

Dr. Miriam A. Leiva
Distinguished Professor of Mathematics, Emerita
University of North Carolina
Charlotte, NC

Dr. Bruce R. Vogeli
Clifford Brewster Upton Professor of Mathematics
Teachers College, Columbia University
New York, NY

Program Authors

Dr. Matt Larson
Curriculum Specialist for Mathematics
Lincoln Public Schools
Lincoln, NE

Timothy D. Kanold
Director of Mathematics
Adlai E. Stevenson High School
Lincolnshire, IL

Dr. Jean M. Shaw
Professor of Elementary Education
University of Mississippi
Oxford, MS

Dr. Lee Stiff
Professor of Mathematics Education
North Carolina State University
Raleigh, NC

Content Reviewers

Lawrence Braden (Grades 5–6)
Mathematics Teacher
St. Paul's School
Concord, NH

Dr. Don Chakerian (Grades 3–4)
Emeritus Professor of Mathematics
University of California
Davis, CA

Dr. Kurt Kreith (Grades 3–4)
Emeritus Professor of Mathematics
University of California
Davis, CA

Dr. Liping Ma (Grades K–2)
Independent Scholar
Palo Alto, CA

Dr. David Wright (Grades 5–6)
Professor of Mathematics
Brigham Young University
Provo, UT

Teacher Reviewers

Grade K

Mary Benedetto
John Barry Elementary School
Chicago, IL

Jean Geissinger
Rossville Elementary School
Rossville, GA

Marcia Neuski
Marconi Community Academy
Chicago, IL

Sheila Taylor
West Wortham Elementary School
Saucier, MS

Mary Yoveff
St. James School
Belvidere, IL

Grade 1

Carol Burton
Hernando Elementary School
Hernando, MS

Karen Illyin
Washington Elementary School
Waukegan, IL

Donna Kelly
Emerson School
Maywood, IL

Cris Lee
Little Woods School
St. Charles, IL

Len Mitnaul
Woodrow Wilson Elementary School
Trenton, NJ

Pat Pulido
Stevenson School
Melrose Park, IL

Nancy Turner
Lamar County Primary School
Barnesville, GA

Grade 2

Pat Burns
Maplebrook Elementary School
Naperville, IL

Joan Janopoulos
Garfield School
Maywood, IL

Michelle Kuhn
Melrose Park School
Melrose Park, IL

Diane Maksay
Refkin Elementary School
Glendale Heights, IL

Linda Mallek
Clearview Elementary School
Waukegan, IL

Pam St. Martin
Pass Road Elementary School
Gulfport, MS

Janet Rhodes
Nichols Elementary School
Nichols, NY

Wanda Smith
Louis Frasier Elementary School
Hinesville, GA

Grade 3

Nancy Fister
Reba O. Steck Elementary School
Aurora, IL

Martha Hand
Vine Street Elementary School
Brandon, MS

Margie Henricksen
Andrew Cooke Magnet School
Waukegan, IL

Karen Holly
Robert Healy Elementary School
Chicago, IL

Kathy Ruggerio
Mark Sheridan Academy
Chicago, IL

Joanne Stevens
Nichols Elementary School
Nichols, NY

Veronica Wright
Robert Shaw Theme School
Decatur, GA

Grade 4

Lorraine Bujan
Mark Sheridan Magnet School
Chicago, IL

Billy Dubose
Oak Park Elementary School
Ocean Springs, MS

Robin Gillette
Nichols Elementary School
Nichols, NY

Cheryl Lawrence
Robert Shaw Theme School
Decatur, GA

Ron Metcalf
Barbara B. Rose Elementary School
South Barrington, IL

Mary Mitchell
McKinley School
New Brunswick, NJ

Mary Peterson
Long Beach Elementary School
Montgomery, IL

Grade 5

Wesley Banks
Robert E. Lee Elementary School
Jackson, MS

Nancy Claxton
Alexander II Magnet School
Macon, GA

Chuck Freundt
Meadow Glens Elementary School
Naperville, IL

Patricia Heintz
P.S. 92 Queens
Corona, NY

Kristen Mellish
Whittier Elementary School
Downers Grove, IL

Grade 6

Loyce Holley
Hills Chapel Elementary School
Boonville, MS

Linda Hunt
O. A. Thorp Scholastic Academy
Chicago, IL

Judy O'Neill
Gwynedd Mercy Academy
Spring House, PA

Mary Ryan
Barrington Middle School
Barrington, IL

Janet Schild
Madison Jr. High School
Naperville, IL

Getting Started

Welcome to *Houghton Mifflin Mathematics*! Before you begin to use this book, take a quick look at some of its special features. That way, you'll be able to get the most out of each lesson!

Using the Lessons

There is something new to learn in each lesson. Here are some things to watch for as you take a quick look at some of the lessons in the book.

- ***Different Way*** boxes point out that sometimes there is more than one way to solve a problem.
- ***Explain Your Thinking*** questions help you check to see whether you understand important ideas in the lesson.
- ***Ask Yourself*** questions guide your thinking about how to do the math.

Learning Math Vocabulary

Math is about more than numbers! To read, write, and talk about math, it helps to know the correct vocabulary to use.

- ***Reading Mathematics*** pages will help remind you of the math vocabulary terms you already know and will prepare you for the new chapter.
- ***Vocabulary*** boxes will list important math words that will be used in the lesson. These words are usually highlighted in the lesson—so you can't miss them!
- ***Using Vocabulary*** feature boxes will remind you of the important math terms in the chapter.

Using Algebra

Algebra is a special kind of math that you will be studying soon. But you actually already have used algebra quite a bit! Here are some examples of ways you use algebra in math.

Different Ways to Use Algebra

Patterns

When you find or continue a pattern, you are using algebra.

Example:

What is the next number likely to be?

2, 4, 6, 8, __

Expressions

When you compare expressions, you are using algebra.

Example:

Write >, <, or = for each ●.

3×4 ● 2×7

Properties

When you use properties to help you find an answer, you are using algebra.

Example:

Find the missing number.

$4 + ■ = 0 + 4$

Equations

When you find a missing number in an equation, you are using algebra.

Example:

Find the missing number.

$8 \times ■ = 24$

Functions

When you complete an input-output table, you are using algebra.

Example:

Follow the rule to complete the table.

Rule: Multiply by 4.

Input	Output
3	12
8	32
6	24

Here are some specific places in your book where you will find these and other kinds of problems that use algebra.

- *n* ***Algebra*** exercises
- ***Using Algebra*** boxes
- ***Show What You Know*** pages and other feature pages

Using Special Features

Show What You Know

Are you ready for a riddle or ready to learn about a whole different number system? These pages let you use the math you have just learned in different ways.

Number Sense

These pages show you that there is more than one way to solve a problem or think about a math idea. Then you can choose the way that makes the most sense to you.

These feature boxes are full of fun facts about things in the world that relate to math.

Have you ever heard the expression "Use your head"? This is the place to do just that!

Look for Internet references. You can use the Web to find brain teasers and other fun and challenging math activities.

Becoming a Better Problem Solver

Problem solving is one of the most important reasons to learn to do mathematics. Here are the four parts of a problem-solving plan that can help you become a better problem solver.

Be sure you really understand the problem.

- Reread the problem carefully.
- Retell the problem in your own words.
- List the information given in the problem.
- Decide what you need to find.

Make a plan to solve the problem.

- Think about the problem and decide how you will try to solve it.
- Choose a strategy to use—see the list on page ix for some choices.
- Choose a method to use, such as estimation, mental math, or paper and pencil.

Find the answer.

- Carry out the plan.
- Adjust your plan or try a different strategy if you need to.
- Check your computations to be sure they are correct.

Look Back

Check that your answer makes sense.

- Did you answer the question that was asked?
- Is your answer labeled correctly?
- Is your answer reasonable?

Problem-Solving Strategies

There are many strategies that can be used to solve problems. As you learn about and practice those strategies, you will be able to choose the best strategy to solve a problem.

Remember, when it comes to problem solving,

- Sometimes you can use several different strategies.
- Sometimes you can use a combination of strategies.
- Sometimes you can use your own strategy.

Here are the strategies you will learn about and use this year.

Problem-Solving Strategies

These strategies can be used for many different kinds of problems.	These strategies are usually used for specific types of problems.
Draw a Diagram	Find a Pattern
Write an Equation	Use Logical Thinking
Make a List	Work Backward
Solve a Simpler Problem	Guess and Check

Now that you know something about the math book you'll be using this year, let's get started! Turn the page to find out what you will be learning in the months to come.

Contents

Remembering Your Facts

CHAPTER 1 Operations With Whole Numbers and Decimals

CHAPTER 2

Data Analysis and Statistics

CHAPTER 3

Fractions and Number Theory

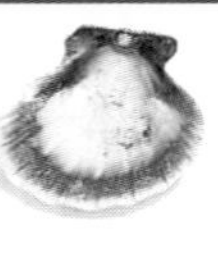

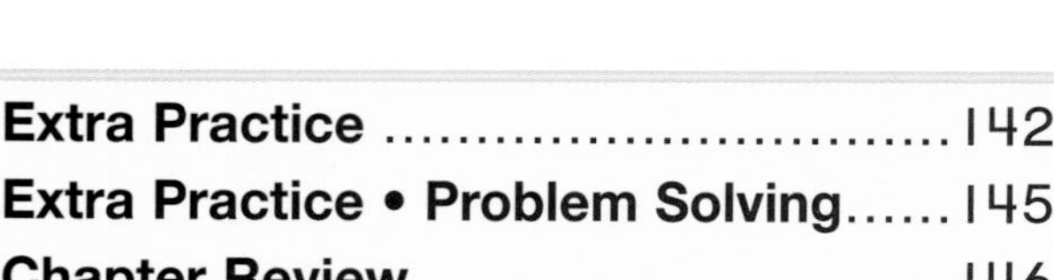

Operations With Fractions

CHAPTER 5 Integers and Rational Numbers

CHAPTER 6

Expressions and Equations

Ratio, Proportion, and Percent

CHAPTER 8

Applications of Percent

CHAPTER 9 Geometry of Plane Figures

Geometry and Measurement

Statistics and Probability

Chapter 12 Coordinate Graphing, Equations, and Integers

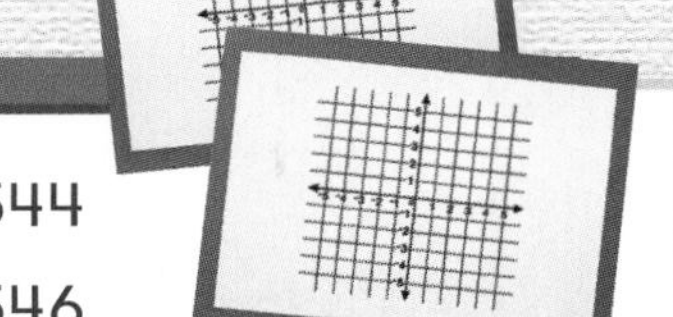

Book Resources

Addition Facts

Add.

1. 4 + 8	**2.** 3 + 5	**3.** 2 + 2	**4.** 2 + 7	**5.** 4 + 4
6. 5 + 9	**7.** 9 + 5	**8.** 3 + 7	**9.** 7 + 7	**10.** 2 + 5
11. 3 + 4	**12.** 9 + 8	**13.** 5 + 5	**14.** 6 + 9	**15.** 2 + 6
16. 2 + 8	**17.** 7 + 8	**18.** 4 + 6	**19.** 5 + 6	**20.** 8 + 8
21. 8 + 9	**22.** 5 + 7	**23.** 3 + 6	**24.** 4 + 5	**25.** 6 + 7
26. 2 + 4	**27.** 2 + 9	**28.** 9 + 9	**29.** 2 + 3	**30.** 3 + 8
31. 4 + 7	**32.** 7 + 9	**33.** 5 + 8	**34.** 6 + 6	**35.** 9 + 6
36. 4 + 8	**37.** 6 + 8	**38.** 3 + 3	**39.** 3 + 9	**40.** 9 + 7

Subtraction Facts

Subtract.

1. 17 − 8	**2.** 17 − 9	**3.** 4 − 2	**4.** 14 − 7	**5.** 16 − 8
6. 14 − 5	**7.** 15 − 7	**8.** 11 − 4	**9.** 13 − 6	**10.** 15 − 6
11. 6 − 2	**12.** 12 − 5	**13.** 10 − 5	**14.** 15 − 9	**15.** 11 − 3
16. 10 − 4	**17.** 11 − 2	**18.** 12 − 4	**19.** 11 − 5	**20.** 9 − 4
21. 14 − 6	**22.** 16 − 7	**23.** 9 − 3	**24.** 5 − 2	**25.** 16 − 9
26. 6 − 3	**27.** 13 − 5	**28.** 12 − 6	**29.** 18 − 9	**30.** 12 − 3
31. 8 − 3	**32.** 10 − 3	**33.** 13 − 4	**34.** 8 − 4	**35.** 7 − 3
36. 10 − 2	**37.** 14 − 9	**38.** 7 − 2	**39.** 9 − 2	**40.** 8 − 2

Multiplication Facts

Multiply.

1. 9 × 8	2. 7 × 6	3. 7 × 5	4. 5 × 4	5. 6 × 3
6. 7 × 3	7. 5 × 2	8. 5 × 9	9. 7 × 7	10. 9 × 5
11. 9 × 4	12. 4 × 4	13. 5 × 3	14. 7 × 2	15. 2 × 2
16. 8 × 2	17. 8 × 8	18. 8 × 7	19. 6 × 5	20. 6 × 4
21. 4 × 2	22. 6 × 9	23. 9 × 7	24. 6 × 6	25. 8 × 5
26. 4 × 3	27. 6 × 2	28. 8 × 9	29. 9 × 6	30. 5 × 5
31. 8 × 4	32. 7 × 9	33. 8 × 6	34. 9 × 3	35. 3 × 3
36. 7 × 4	37. 8 × 3	38. 9 × 2	39. 3 × 2	40. 9 × 9

Division Facts

Divide.

1. $35 \div 5$	**2.** $25 \div 5$	**3.** $8 \div 2$	**4.** $54 \div 9$	**5.** $24 \div 3$
6. $18 \div 2$	**7.** $32 \div 4$	**8.** $24 \div 4$	**9.** $30 \div 5$	**10.** $20 \div 4$
11. $63 \div 7$	**12.** $18 \div 3$	**13.** $48 \div 6$	**14.** $6 \div 2$	**15.** $63 \div 9$
16. $40 \div 5$	**17.** $36 \div 6$	**18.** $9 \div 3$	**19.** $81 \div 9$	**20.** $27 \div 3$
21. $21 \div 3$	**22.** $36 \div 4$	**23.** $10 \div 2$	**24.** $16 \div 4$	**25.** $12 \div 3$
26. $45 \div 9$	**27.** $15 \div 3$	**28.** $16 \div 2$	**29.** $14 \div 2$	**30.** $12 \div 2$
31. $72 \div 9$	**32.** $72 \div 8$	**33.** $4 \div 2$	**34.** $64 \div 8$	**35.** $49 \div 7$
36. $56 \div 7$	**37.** $45 \div 5$	**38.** $28 \div 4$	**39.** $54 \div 6$	**40.** $42 \div 6$

Operations With Whole Numbers and Decimals

Why Learn About Operations With Whole Numbers and Decimals?

We add, subtract, multiply, and divide whole numbers and decimals to solve problems in everyday life.

You can add whole numbers and decimals to find how much money you spend on lunches and snacks in a week. If you multiply the weekly amount by 4, you will have an estimate of what you would spend in a month.

Look at the beautiful, starry sky. There are many billions of stars in the universe. Do you know how many millions are in one billion?

Reviewing Vocabulary

Understanding math language helps you become a successful problem solver. Here are some math vocabulary words you should know.

base (of a power)	the number that is used as a factor when evaluating powers
exponent	the number of times the base is used as a factor
power of 10	a number that can be written as a product of tens
period	a group of three digits in a number set off by commas, such as thousands

2^9 ← exponent
↑
base

Reading Words and Symbols

When you read mathematics, sometimes you read only words, sometimes you read words and symbols, and sometimes you read only symbols.

The location of a digit affects how you read it.

- The number 9,876,292 is read "nine million, eight hundred seventy-six thousand, two hundred ninety-two."
- The number 9^9 is read "nine to the ninth power."

9 = nine
90 = ninety
900 = nine hundred
9,000 = nine thousand

Try These

1. Read each pair of numbers. Then decide whether the value of 8 is the same or different in each pair.

   a. 820 8,439 **b.** 587 24,681 **c.** 228 13.89

2. Identify the number of periods in each of the following numbers.

   a. 487,097 **b.** 635,970,274,167 **c.** 284,592,746

3. Which of the following numbers or expressions contain exponents? How do you read the numbers with exponents?

   a. 58% **b.** 478 **c.** 10^8 **d.** $378 + 23 + 9$ **e.** 2.5×10^3

4. Write *true* or *false* for each statement.

   a. In the number 10^{23}, 10 is the exponent.

   b. The expression 4.6×10^3 is equivalent to $4.6 \times 10 \times 10 \times 10$.

   c. In the expression 128×10^8, 10 is the base.

Upcoming Vocabulary

Write About It **Here are some other vocabulary words** you will use in this chapter. Watch for these words. Write about them in your journal.

ten thousandth

hundred thousandth

millionth

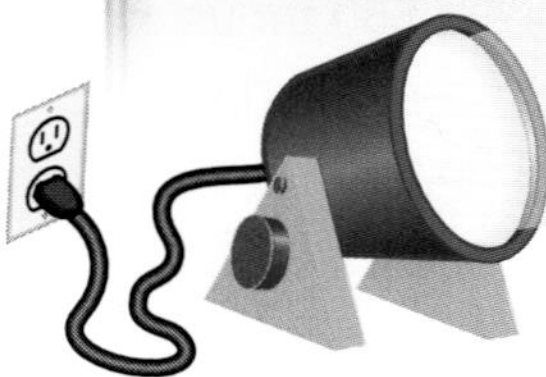

Place Value

You will learn how to read, write, and understand whole numbers and decimals.

New Vocabulary
ten thousandth
hundred thousandth
millionth

Learn About It

You can use the digits 1, 2, 3, 4, 5, 6, 7, 8, 9, and 0 and a decimal point to write any number. The value of each digit in a number depends on its place in the number.

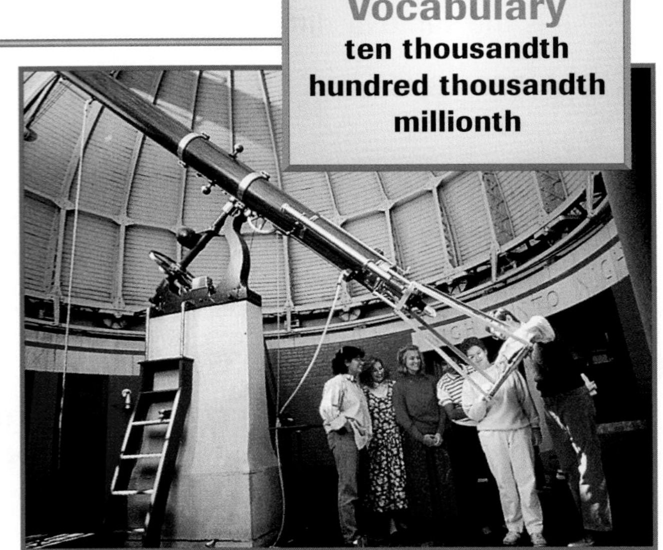

On a visit to an observatory, Carl learned that Pluto has an average distance from the Sun of about 5,913,603,800 km. Twenty times the circumference of Earth is only 0.000136 of the distance from Pluto to the Sun.

Different Ways to Read and Write Numbers

BILLIONS			MILLIONS			THOUSANDS			ONES			DECIMALS					
hundred billions	ten billions	billions	hundred millions	ten millions	millions	hundred thousands	ten thousands	thousands	hundreds	tens	ones	tenths	hundredths	thousandths	ten thousandths	hundred thousandths	millionths
		5,	9	1	3,	6	0	3,	8	0	0.						
		,			,			,			0.	0	0	0	1	3	6

Whole Numbers

Standard form: 5,913,603,800

Word form: five billion, nine hundred thirteen million, six hundred three thousand, eight hundred

Short word form: 5 billion, 913 million, 603 thousand, 800

Expanded form: 5,000,000,000 + 900,000,000 + 10,000,000 + 3,000,000 + 600,000 + 3,000 + 800

Decimals

Standard form: 0.000136

Word form: one hundred thirty-six millionths

Short word form: 136 millionths

Expanded form: 0.0001 + 0.00003 + 0.000006

Another Example Hundred Billions

Standard form: 469,372,580,000

Word form: four hundred sixty-nine billion, three hundred seventy-two million, five hundred eighty thousand

Short word form: 469 billion, 372 million, 580 thousand

Expanded form: 400,000,000,000 + 60,000,000,000 + 9,000,000,000 + 300,000,000 + 70,000,000 + 2,000,000 + 500,000 + 80,000

Explain Your Thinking

- ► How do you know how many zeros to use when you write one hundred billion in standard form?
- ► How is zero used as a placeholder to tell the difference between the numbers 1.607 and 1.67?

Guided Practice

Ask Yourself

- In what place is each digit?

Write each number in word form and in expanded form.

1. 30,528,400 **2.** 2.0516 **3.** 3,000.65

Write the value of each underlined digit.

4. <u>7</u>8,870,043 **5.** 46.504<u>1</u>7 **6.** 4<u>5</u>6,526,000,040 **7.** 7.0000<u>8</u>

Independent Practice

Write each number in word form and in expanded form.

8. 1,462 **9.** 161,062,850 **10.** 6.000015 **11.** 856.093

12. 0.59861 **13.** 45.6107 **14.** 784,310,520,000 **15.** 69.001436

Write each number in standard form.

16. 200,000,000,000 + 10,000,000,000 + 50,000,000 + 40,000 + 3,000 + 90

17. ninety-five and six hundred eighteen ten thousandths

Problem Solving • Reasoning

Use Data Use the table for Problems 18–20.

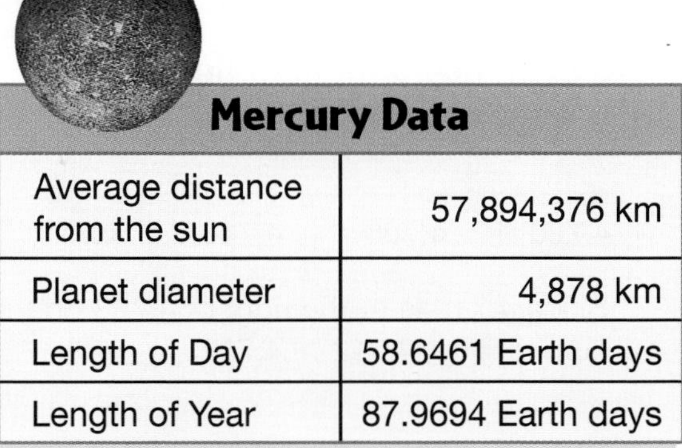

Mercury Data	
Average distance from the sun	57,894,376 km
Planet diameter	4,878 km
Length of Day	58.6461 Earth days
Length of Year	87.9694 Earth days

18. Look at the average distance of the planet Mercury from the sun. Write the value of the digit 9.

19. Write Mercury's length of day and length of year in word form and in expanded form.

20. **Analyze** There are 1,000 meters in 1 kilometer. If you express the diameter of Mercury in meters, what will be the value of the first digit?

Mixed Review • Test Prep

Add or subtract.

21. 1,246 + 987 **22.** 607 − 119 **23.** 5,882 + 4,237 **24.** 10,205 − 9,726

25 What is the remainder when 487 is divided by 7?

A 70 **B** 69 **C** 4 **D** 0

Extra Practice See Set A on page 46.

Compare and Order Numbers

You will learn how to compare and order numbers by using a number line or by comparing digits.

Learn About It

While studying diet and nutrition, Megan learns that milk is an important source of calcium. Which contains more calcium, whole milk or nonfat milk?

Compare **0.276** and **0.285**.

Different Ways to Compare Decimals

You can use a number line.

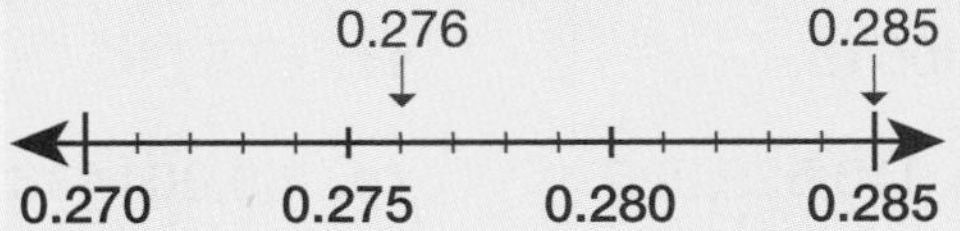

Since 0.285 is to the right of 0.276 on the number line, 0.285 > 0.276.

You can compare digits.

Align the decimal points. Compare digits from left to right until they are different.

0.276
0.285

8 > 7, so the decimal 0.285 > 0.276.

Solution: Since 0.285 > 0.276, nonfat milk contains more calcium.

Different Ways To Compare Whole Numbers

You can use a number line.

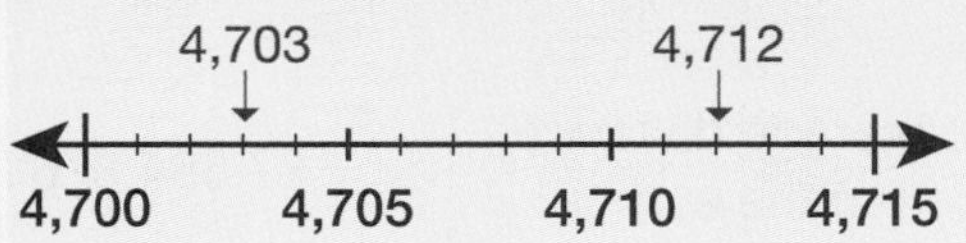

Since 4,712 is to the right of 4,703 on the number line, 4,712 > 4,703.

You can compare digits.

Align the decimal points. Compare digits from left to right until they are different.

4,703
4,712

1 > 0, so 4,712 > 4,703.

Another Example

Order 21.38, 20.30, and 21.88 from least to greatest.

Use a Number Line

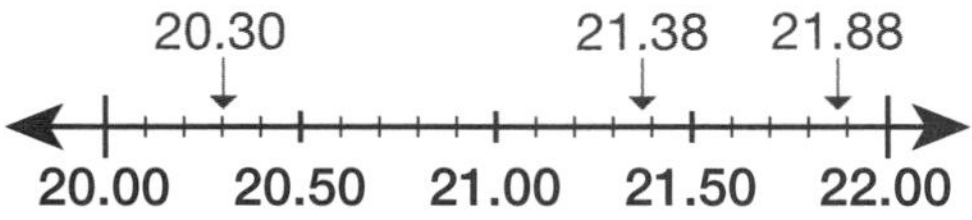

20.30 < 21.38 < 21.88

Compare Digits

First Difference

21.38
20.30
21.88

Second Difference

Explain Your Thinking

- ▶ When comparing 0.338 and 0.388, why can you start by comparing hundredths?
- ▶ Why is it important to align the decimal points when comparing decimals?

Guided Practice

Ask Yourself

- Did I align the decimal points correctly?
- Where do I start comparing digits?

Compare. Write >, <, or = for each ●.

1. 1,463 ● 1,436 **2.** 2,164 ● 2.164 **3.** 0.351 ● 0.3510

Order from greatest to least. Use a number line.

4. 1.53 15.3 1.3 **5.** 0.404 0.440 0.044 0.40 **6.** 258 825 285 852

Independent Practice

Compare. Write >, <, or = for each ●.

7. 8.7 ● 8.70 **8.** 0.55 ● 0.65 **9.** 10.1 ● 1.01 **10.** 216.7 ● 217.6

11. 43.75 ● 47.35 **12.** 99.9 ● 9.99 **13.** 3.203 ● 3.023 **14.** 0.003 ● 0.0030

Order from least to greatest. Use a number line.

15. 5.3 3.6 6.4 **16.** 43.16 43.02 43.5 **17.** 0.11 0.1 0.01

18. 0.0025 0.002 0.027 0.207 **19.** 97.5 9.71 9.07 90.7

Problem Solving • Reasoning

Use Data **Use the table for Problems 20–22.**

20. **Compare** A class compared the sodium content in different kinds of food. Look at the table on the right. Which has less sodium per serving, roast beef or broccoli?

21. Order the foods in the table from greatest to least amount of sodium per serving.

22. **Estimate** Which kind of food has about twice the sodium content per serving as milk has?

Sodium Content

Food	Sodium Per Serving
Cheddar cheese ($\frac{1}{2}$ c)	0.350 g
Roast beef (3 oz)	0.060 g
Broccoli, fresh ($\frac{1}{2}$ c)	0.010 g
Instant oatmeal ($\frac{3}{4}$ c)	0.255 g
Milk, 2% (8 oz)	0.120 g

Mixed Review • Test Prep

Divide.

23. $8\overline{)912}$ **24.** $7\overline{)601}$ **25.** $6\overline{)1,183}$

26 What is the value of the digit 4 in 34,891,760? *(pages 4–5)*

A 40,000 **B** 400,000 **C** 4,000,000 **D** 40,000,000

Extra Practice See Set B on page 46.

Round Numbers

You will learn how to round whole numbers and decimals by using place value.

U.S. dollar

Learn About It

Look at the coins on the right. In September 2000, one Canadian dollar was worth $0.673491 in U.S. currency, and one Mexican peso was worth $0.106769 in U.S. currency. How can these numbers be rounded?

Canadian dollar

Mexican peso

Rounding Rules

- Find the place to which you will round.
- If the digit to its right is 5 or greater, increase the rounding-place digit by one.
- If the digit to its right is less than 5, do not change the rounding-place digit.
- For a whole number, change all digits to the right of the rounded digit to zero.
- For a decimal, drop the digits to the right of the rounded digit.

Round 0.673491 to the nearest hundredth.

Step 1 Find the hundredths place.

0.6**7**3491 The hundredths digit is 7.
↑
hundredths

Step 2 Look at the digit to its right. This digit is in the thousandth place. Round.

0.67**3**491 rounds to 0.67
↑
$3 < 5$, so the 7 does not change.

Solution: The number 0.673491 rounds to 0.67.

Round 0.106769 to the nearest ten thousandth.

Step 1 Find the ten-thousandths place.

0.106**7**69 The ten-thousandths digit is 7.
↑
ten-thousandths

Step 2 Look at the digit to its right. This digit is in the hundred-thousandths place. Round.

0.1067**6**9 rounds to 0.1068
↑
$6 > 5$, so increase 7 to 8.

Solution: The number 0.106769 rounds to 0.1068.

Another Example

Whole Numbers

Round 1,328,940 to the nearest ten thousand.

1,3**2**8,940 $8 > 5$, so increase 2 to 3.

The number 1,328,940 rounds to 1,330,000.

Explain Your Thinking

► Which place do you look at when deciding how to round a number to the nearest whole number? Why?

► If you round to a place in which the digit is zero, what should you do?

Guided Practice

Round each number to the underlined place.

1. 2,564.03 **2.** 0.1282 **3.** 1.95 **4.** 9.6875

5. 100,617.4 **6.** 57,497 **7.** 236 **8.** 52,699

Ask Yourself

- What digit is to the right of the underlined digit?
- Have I used the rounding rules correctly?

Independent Practice

Round each number to the underlined place.

9. 0.236 **10.** 0.45266 **11.** 0.288 **12.** 0.189 **13.** 333.82

14. 0.52417 **15.** 0.562 **16.** 0.18475 **17.** 0.325068 **18.** 436.546

19. 52,417 **20.** 199,756 **21.** 743,268 **22.** 916 **23.** 1,528

24. 457,962 **25.** 836,279 **26.** 348,975 **27.** 82,569,357 **28.** 71,896,256

Problem Solving • Reasoning

Use Data **Use the table for Problems 29–30.**

29. Round each of the amounts in the table to the nearest hundredth.

30. Suppose you exchanged U.S. dollars for British pounds. How many British pounds would you get for $1,000 in U.S. dollars?

31. **Estimate** While on vacation in Europe, Sylvia buys a T-shirt that costs 15.85 euros. Sylvia calculates that the T-shirt costs $13.5993 in U.S. dollars. To the nearest whole dollar, what is the cost of the T-shirt in U.S. dollars?

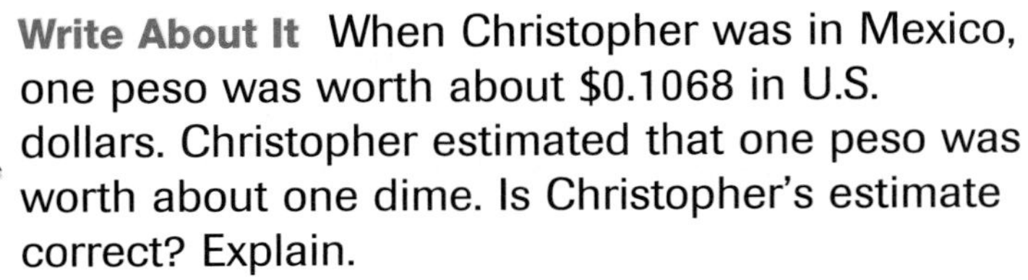

32. **Write About It** When Christopher was in Mexico, one peso was worth about $0.1068 in U.S. dollars. Christopher estimated that one peso was worth about one dime. Is Christopher's estimate correct? Explain.

Currency Equivalents to U.S. $1.00

Currency	Value
Canadian dollar	1.4838
British pound	0.7144
Swedish krona	9.7780
Japanese yen	107.2400
Taiwanese dollar	31.0700
Mexican peso	9.3620
European euro	1.1655

Left: Swedish krona; *Center*: Japanese yen; *Right*: British pound

Mixed Review • Test Prep

Write >, <, or = for each ●. *(pages 6–7)*

33. 2.60 ● 2.06 **34.** 3,303 ● 3,330 **35.** 0.1016 ● 0.1061 **36.** 12.4 ● 12.40

37 What is the product of 92 and 50?

A 142 **B** 460 **C** 4,500 **D** 4,600

Extra Practice See Set C on page 46.

LESSON 4

Place Value and Powers of Ten

You will learn how to relate powers of ten to place value.

Review Vocabulary
product
power of 10
base
factor
exponent

Learn About It

The **product** found by multiplying the number 10 by itself one or more times is a **power of 10**. You use exponents to write very large and very small numbers as powers of 10. Use 10 as the **base** and the number of times that 10 is a **factor** as the **exponent**.

exponent ▼

◀ base

To read 10^4, say "ten to the fourth power."

$10^4 = 10 \times 10 \times 10 \times 10 = 10{,}000$

exponent ▼

◀ base

To read 10^{-4}, say "ten to the negative fourth power."

$10^{-4} = \frac{1}{10 \times 10 \times 10 \times 10} = \frac{1}{10{,}000} = 0.0001$

Study the table below.

Powers of 10			
Power of 10	**Standard Form**	**Fractional Form**	**Place Value**
10^4	10,000	$\frac{10{,}000}{1}$	Ten thousands
10^3	1,000	$\frac{1{,}000}{1}$	Thousands
10^2	100	$\frac{100}{1}$	Hundreds
10^1	10	$\frac{10}{1}$	Tens
10^0	1	$\frac{1}{1}$	Ones
10^{-1}	0.1	$\frac{1}{10}$	Tenths
10^{-2}	0.01	$\frac{1}{100}$	Hundredths
10^{-3}	0.001	$\frac{1}{1{,}000}$	Thousandths
10^{-4}	0.0001	$\frac{1}{10{,}000}$	Ten thousandths

Look at the exponents.
The exponents are positive for numbers greater than 1 and negative for numbers less than 1. The exponent for 1 is zero.

Look at the pattern of zeros.
For numbers greater than 1, the exponent tells the number of zeros in the numerator. For numbers less than 1, the exponent tells the number of zeros in the denominator.

You can write whole numbers and decimals in expanded form, using powers of 10.

$3{,}654 = (3 \times 10^3) + (6 \times 10^2) + (5 \times 10^1) + (4 \times 10^0)$

$0.25 = (2 \times 10^{-1}) + (5 \times 10^{-2})$

Explain Your Thinking

► If the exponent is ^{-}n, how many places will follow the decimal point?

Guided Practice

Write each number in expanded form, using powers of 10.

1. 2,000,000 **2.** 0.0321 **3.** 125,317 **4.** 5.212

Write each number in standard form.

5. $(5 \times 10^5) + (7 \times 10^4) + (2 \times 10^3) + (3 \times 10^2) + (9 \times 10^0)$

6. $(8 \times 10^0) + (4 \times 10^{-1}) + (1 \times 10^{-2})$ **7.** $(5 \times 10^{-1}) + (8 \times 10^{-2}) + (3 \times 10^{-4})$

Ask Yourself

- Should I use a positive exponent or a negative exponent?
- What place value do I start with?

Independent Practice

Write each number in expanded form, using powers of ten.

8. 3,000 **9.** 3.29 **10.** 26,000,000 **11.** 16.5

12. 79 **13.** 3,250,000,000 **14.** 0.0051 **15.** 7.315

Write each number in standard form.

16. $(3 \times 10^4) + (4 \times 10^0)$ **17.** $(6 \times 10^{-1}) + (7 \times 10^{-2})$ **18.** $(8 \times 10^0) + (4 \times 10^{-1})$

19. $(2 \times 10^4) + (3 \times 10^3) + (5 \times 10^1)$ **20.** $(4 \times 10^{-1}) + (9 \times 10^{-2}) + (5 \times 10^{-3})$

Problem Solving • Reasoning

21. A company puts 10 rubber bands in each package, 10 packages in each bundle, and 10 bundles in each box. If one crate holds 10 boxes, how many rubber bands are in each crate?

22. An art teacher buys map pencils for seven fifth-grade classes and three sixth-grade classes. Each class needs 8 boxes of pencils. If there are 2 pencils in a box, how many pencils in all does the teacher buy?

23. **Analyze** On weekends, Derrick works at his father's hardware store. Each Saturday, he opens 10 large crates of different-sized nails. Each crate contains 10 trays, each tray contains 10 boxes, and each box contains 100 nails. What part of one crate does one nail represent? Express your answer as a power of 10.

Using Vocabulary

Write *true* or *false*. Give examples to support your answers.

A All numbers can be expressed by using only powers of ten.

B Any whole number can be used as an exponent.

C The base of a power represents the number of times an exponent is used as a factor.

Mixed Review • Test Prep

Multiply.

24. 572×8 **25.** 66×18 **26.** $4 \times 2,607$ **27.** 331×16

28 What is the sum of 1,095 and 9,982?

A 9,977 **B** 11,077 **C** 12,176 **D** 12,277

Extra Practice See Set D on page 46.

Add and Subtract Whole Numbers and Decimals

You will learn how to add and subtract whole numbers and decimals.

Learn About It

Mary is presenting a report on Mount Everest, the highest mountain in the world. Katrina is presenting a report on Mount McKinley, the highest mountain in the United States. How much taller is Mount Everest than Mount McKinley?

Subtract. **29,035 − 20,320 = *n***

Find 29,035 − 20,320.

Step 1 Align the digits by place value.

```
  29,035
- 20,320
```

Step 2 Subtract. Regroup if necessary.

```
    8 10
  29,035
- 20,320
   8,715
```

Estimate to see if your answer is reasonable.

29,035 rounds to 29,000
20,320 rounds to 20,000
29,000 − 20,000 = 9,000

Since 8,715 is close to 9,000, the answer is reasonable.

Solution: Mount Everest is 8,715 feet taller than Mount McKinley.

Other Examples

A. Add Decimals

0.3517 + 0.483 + 0.1924

```
  1 2 1
  0.3517
  0.4830  ←— Use zero as a placeholder.
+ 0.1924
  1.0271
```

Align the decimal points.

B. Subtract Decimals

2,300.61 − 584.1069

```
  1 12 9 10   0 9 10
  2,300.6100
-   584.1069
  1,716.5031
```

Explain Your Thinking

► Why is it important to align the decimal points when adding and subtracting?

Guided Practice

Find each sum or difference.

1. 1,452 + 7,639 **2.** 545.29 − 82.5 **3.** 13.25 − 8.647

4. 35.26 − 3.6 **5.** 85.36 + 14.2 + 5 **6.** 4,163 − 573.5

Ask Yourself

- Did I align the digits by place value?

Independent Practice

Find each sum or difference. Estimate to see if your answer is reasonable.

7. 53.86 + 7.47 **8.** 941.8 − 7.35 **9.** 5.369 − 2.256 **10.** 7,852.45 + 953.6

11. 325.16 + 76.4 **12.** 4,567 − 558.3 **13.** 14 − 6.8 **14.** 6,987.2 + 3,214.8

15. 8,795.35 − 800 **16.** 0.593 + 0.284 **17.** 3,806 − 3,042 **18.** 14.2 + 0.36 + 1.5

Problem Solving • Reasoning

Solve. Choose a method.

Computation Methods

- Mental Math
- Estimation
- Paper and Pencil
- Calculator

19. **Analyze** Yosemite Falls is divided into three levels. The falls' total height is 2,425 ft tall. The upper level is 1,430 ft tall, and the lower level is 320 ft tall. How tall is the middle level?

20. Kirstin is looking at a map of the Nile River. On the map scale, 1 inch represents 250 miles. If the length of the river on the map is 16.7 inches, about how long is the actual river?

21. **Predict** In the United Kingdom, about 81.1% of the population is English, 9.5% is Scottish, 2.4% is Irish, and 1.9% is Welsh. If the total population is 100%, what percent does not belong to any of these groups?

22. Charles reports these sizes for deserts: Sahara, 3,320,000 mi^2; Gobi, 500,000 mi^2; Chihuahuan, 175,000 mi^2; and Sonoran, 120,000 mi^2. Compare the Sahara's size to the combined size of the other three deserts.

23. The average depth of the Atlantic Ocean is 3,926 m. Its greatest depth is 9,219 m. What is the difference between the average depth and the greatest depth?

24. **Compare** The area of Lake Erie is 9,930 mi^2. The area of Lake Superior is 31,820 mi^2. About how many times as large as Lake Erie is Lake Superior?

Mixed Review • Test Prep

Complete.

25. 2 lb = ■ oz **26.** 12 qt = ■ gal **27.** 3 pt = ■ c **28.** 4 ft = ■ in.

29 Derek ran 200 yards in a football game. How many feet did he run?

A 600 ft **B** 400 ft **C** 100 ft **D** 67 ft

Extra Practice See Set E on page 47.

Problem-Solving Skill: Estimated or Exact Answers

You will learn how to determine whether a problem needs an exact solution or if an estimate is enough.

When you solve a problem, you can sometimes use an estimate. An estimate is often easy to do. At other times you need an exact answer. An exact answer gives you more precise information.

Look at the situations below.

Sometimes you can use an estimate.

Mr. Li is decorating a picture frame with buttons. The buttons cost \$1.85 each. If Mr. Li has \$19.00, does he have enough money to buy 9 buttons?

Since you only need to decide if \$19.00 is equal to or greater than $\$1.85 \times 9$, an estimate is all that is needed.

- Round \$1.85 to \$2.
- Multiply. $\$2 \times 9 = \$18$.

The total cost is less than \$19.00, so Mr. Li has enough money to buy 9 buttons.

Sometimes you need an exact answer.

Renee is making a necklace for her friend Claudia. She buys beads that cost \$3.29 a package. If she has \$10.00, how much money will Renee have left after buying 3 packages of beads?

Because the problem asks for the amount of money left over, an exact answer is needed.

- Find the cost of the beads. $\$3.29 \times 3 = \$9.87$
- Find the amount of money left. $\$10.00 - \$9.87 = \$0.13$

Renee will have \$0.13 left after buying 3 packages of beads.

Look Back When is it better to use an estimate? When is it better to use an exact amount?

Left: Father and daughter building a dollhouse together.

Right: A native Alaskan woman teaches her grandson how to make a fish net.

Guided Practice

Solve. Answer by estimating or calculating.

1. Kathleen wants to buy two red candles and two purple candles. The red candles cost \$5.60 each, and the purple candles cost \$6.19 each. If Kathleen has \$24.50, does she have enough money to buy all four candles?

   Think: Does the problem require an exact answer?

2. Mitch is making a bracelet for Ariel. Beads come in single-color packets only. If each packet costs \$1.15, can Mitch buy at least eight different colors of beads with his \$10.00? How much will eight packets of beads cost?

   Think: Do both questions require that you know the exact cost?

Choose a Strategy

Solve. Use these or other strategies.

Calculator Option

Problem-Solving Strategies

- **Draw a Diagram**
- **Write an Equation**
- **Guess and Check**
- **Find a Pattern**

3. Nancy is weaving a striped rug. She starts with a pink stripe, then weaves a blue stripe, a green stripe, a pink stripe, a blue stripe, a green stripe, and so on. If Nancy continues her pattern, what will be the color of the twentieth stripe?

4. Mary Anne uses seven colors of yarn for a project. She uses 0.75 yard each of three colors, 1.1 yards of one color, and 1.5 yards each of three other colors. How many yards of yarn in all does she use?

5. Mikhala buys 6 large seashells. Each seashell costs \$2.35. If Mikhala gives the cashier \$20.00, how much change should she receive?

6. Caroline buys a sunflower for each of her 8 friends. The flowers cost \$1.98 each. About how much money does Caroline need to buy the flowers?

7. Jenny is making pillowcases for her parents. She has saved \$14.50 to buy fabric. The fabric she wants to buy costs \$3.95 per yard. How many whole yards can Jenny buy?

8. Fred is making a collage of geometric shapes. He has 4 more triangles than circles and twice as many squares as triangles. If Fred has 36 shapes in all, how many of each kind does he have?

Extra Practice See 1–4 on page 49.

Quick Check

Check Your Understanding of Lessons 1–6

Write each number in standard form.

1. 242 million, 65 thousand, 9

2. two hundred forty-three ten thousandths

Order from least to greatest.

3. 250,413.7   250.413   25,062   250.96

Round each number to the underlined place.

4. $4.5\underline{8}7$ **5.** $\underline{1}37.556$

Write each number in expanded form, using powers of 10.

6. 50,000   **7.** 4.0021

Find each sum or difference.

8. 1,070.26 − 338.5   **9.** 29,420.8 + 8,425.31

Solve.

10. Pedro wants to use four colors to paint a chair. Two of the colors cost $2.65 a can. The other two cost $3.22 a can. If Pedro has $9.62, can he buy all the paint? Explain.

How did you do?

If you had difficulty with any items in the Quick Check, you can use the following pages for review and extra practice.

Items	Review These Pages	Do These Extra Practice Items
1–2	pages 4–5	Set A, page 46
3	pages 6–7	Set B, page 46
4–5	pages 8–9	Set C, page 46
6–7	pages 10–11	Set D, page 46
8–9	pages 12–13	Set E, page 47
10	pages 14–15	1–4, page 49

Test Prep • Cumulative Review

Maintaining the Standards

Choose the letter of the correct answer. If a correct answer is not here, choose NH.

1 Which number represents $(5 \times 10^3) + (4 \times 10^2)$?

A 54,000
B 5,400
C 0.0054
D 0.00054

2 Mr. Carr spent $84.50 on groceries this week and $102.75 last week. How much did he spend in all on groceries?

F $18.25
G $102.75
H $187.25
J NH

3 When Alex's pay was calculated, the amount was $18.916. What is this amount rounded to the nearest cent?

A $18 **C** $18.92
B $18.91 **D** $19

4 What is 345,996,111 rounded to the nearest hundred million?

F 400,000,000
G 500,000,000
H 600,000,000
J NH

5 What is the place value of the underlined digit?

45,8<u>9</u>9,331.003

A thousandth
B ten thousandth
C ten thousand
D ten million

6 For the first concert, 1,006 tickets were sold. For tonight's concert only 678 tickets were sold. How many more tickets were sold for the first concert?

F 328 tickets
G 678 tickets
H 1,006 tickets
J 1,684 tickets

7 Which set of numbers is correctly ordered from least to greatest?

A 0.013, 31.03, 3.103, 0.313
B 0.013, 31.03, 3.103, 0.313
C 0.013, 0.313, 3.103, 31.03
D 31.03, 3.103, 0.313, 0.013

8 What is the combined population of Abilene and Austin?

City Populations 1998	
City	**Population**
Abilene	108,257
Plano	219,486
Austin	552,434
El Paso	615,032

Explain How did you use the table to find your answer?

Internet Test Prep
Visit **www.eduplace.com/kids/mhm** for more *Test Prep Practice.*

LESSON 7

Multiply Whole Numbers

You will learn how to multiply whole numbers.

Learn About It

Deanne is training for a swim competition. She starts by jumping rope a little each day. In one week, she jumps for a total of 42 minutes. If she jumps at a rate of 96 jumps per minute, what is the total number of jumps she makes during the week?

Multiply. $42 \times 96 = n$

Find 42 × 96.

Step 1 Multiply by the ones digit. Regroup if necessary.

$$\begin{array}{r} \scriptstyle 1 \\ 42 \\ \times\ 96 \\ \hline 252 \end{array} \longleftarrow 42 \times 6$$

Step 2 Multiply by the tens digit. Regroup if necessary.

$$\begin{array}{r} \scriptstyle 1 \\ \scriptstyle 1 \\ 42 \\ \times\ 96 \\ \hline 252 \\ 3{,}780 \end{array} \longleftarrow 42 \times 90$$

Step 3 Add the partial products.

$$\begin{array}{r} 42 \\ \times\ 96 \\ \hline 252 \\ +\ 3{,}780 \\ \hline 4{,}032 \end{array}$$

Estimate to check your work.

42 rounds to 40
96 rounds to 100

$40 \times 100 = 4{,}000$

4,032 is close to 4,000, so the answer is reasonable.

Solution: Deanne jumps 4,032 times during the week.

Other Examples

A. Multiply by a Three-Digit Number

$$\begin{array}{r} 831 \\ \times\quad 749 \\ \hline 7{,}479 \\ 33{,}240 \\ +\ 581{,}700 \\ \hline 622{,}419 \end{array} \begin{array}{l} \\ \\ \longleftarrow 831 \times 9 \\ \longleftarrow 831 \times 40 \\ \longleftarrow 831 \times 700 \\ \\ \end{array}$$

B. Use the Distributive Property

$$\begin{aligned} 831 \times 749 &= 831 \times (700 + 40 + 9) \\ &= (831 \times 700) + (831 \times 40) + (831 \times 9) \\ &= 581{,}700 + 33{,}240 + 7{,}479 \\ &= 622{,}419 \end{aligned}$$

Explain Your Thinking

- ▶ When a factor has two or more digits, why do you place zeros in the partial products?
- ▶ How can you tell if the product should be greater than or less than the product of the rounded numbers?

Guided Practice

Find each product.

1. 256×7

2. $4{,}902 \times 23$

3. 181×36

4. 22,432 × 8

5. 874 × 24

6. 385 × 521

> **Ask Yourself**
> - Did I estimate to see if the answer is reasonable?
> - Did I use zeros as placeholders in the partial products?

Calculator Option

Independent Practice

Find each product. Estimate to see if your answer is reasonable.

7. 479×7

8. 341×5

9. 147×72

10. $8{,}527 \times 45$

11. 4,693 × 7

12. 247 × 59

13. 22,099 × 6

14. 85,482 × 8

15. 88 × 402

16. 947 × 163

17. 1,637 × 22

18. 3,214 × 12

19. 8,600 × 8

20. 4,621 × 50

21. 5,704 × 82

22. 905 × 604

Problem Solving • Reasoning

Use Data **Use the table for Problems 23–24.**

23. If Joanne jumps for 12 minutes at the rate shown, what will her total number of jumps be?

24. **Compare** In 5 minutes, how many more jumps does Ray complete than Ana?

25. How many inches of rope are needed to make three 84-inch jump ropes, fourteen 96-inch ropes, eleven 108-inch ropes, and two 120-inch ropes?

26. **Write About It** The track coach needs 13 jump ropes. She can buy single ropes for $4.00 each or ropes in packs of 3 for $11.00 per pack. What is the least expensive way to purchase 13 jump ropes? Explain.

Jumping Rates

Jumper	Jumps per minute
Joanne	101
Ray	97
Ana	88

Write the value of the underlined digit. *(pages 4–5)*

27. $0.001\underline{8}9$

28. $1{,}2\underline{3}5{,}679$

29. $99.8\underline{7}01$

30. $1{,}306.97\underline{2}$

31 Which shows $(3 \times 10^2) + (1 \times 10^0) + (5 \times 10^{-2})$ in standard form? *(pages 10–11)*

A 301.5 **B** 301.05 **C** 31.5 **D** 31.05

Extra Practice See Set F on page 47.

Multiply Decimals by Whole Numbers

You will learn how to multiply decimals by whole numbers.

MUSIC POSTERS
Sale
3 for $13.00
Original price $4.69 each

Learn About It

A music store usually sells single posters for $4.69 each. For a limited time, the store has a special offer of three posters for $13.00. How much money will Chuck save if he buys three posters now?

First, find out how much three single posters would cost.

Multiply. **$4.69 × 3 = *n***

Find $4.69 × 3.

Step 1 Multiply the factors as if the decimal point weren't there.

```
  $4.69
×     3
  14 07
```

Step 2 Place the decimal point. The number of decimal places in the product equals the sum of the number of decimal places in the factors.

```
  $4.69  ←    2 decimal places
×     3  ← + 0 decimal places
 $14.07  ←    2 decimal places
```

Solution: Since three posters at $4.69 each would cost $14.07, Chuck will save $14.07 − $13.00, or $1.07, if he buys the posters now.

Estimate to check your work.

$4.69 rounds to $5

$5 × 3 = $15

$14.07 is close to $15, so the answer is reasonable.

Another Example

Zeros in the Product

```
  0.0149  ←    4 decimal places
×      6  ← + 0 decimal places
  0.0894  ←    4 decimal places
```

Explain Your Thinking

► Look at the product in Another Example. What do the zeros to the left of the digit 8 represent?

Guided Practice

Find each product.

1. 2.5 × 2 **2.** 4.1 × 6 **3.** 10.3 × 7 **4.** 1.11 × 58

5. 2.6 × 6 **6.** 5.16 × 15 **7.** 4.04 × 25 **8.** 0.54 × 426

Ask Yourself

- Should the answer be greater than or less than the whole number?
- How many decimal places should the product have?

Independent Practice

Find each product. Estimate to check your work.

9. 2.8 × 3　**10.** 6.5 × 5　**11.** 7.7 × 7　**12.** 4.9 × 8

13. 3.8 × 29　**14.** 4.6 × 12　**15.** 3.2 × 24　**16.** 6.6 × 35

17. 4.3 × 52　**18.** 4.15 × 38　**19.** 8.02 × 59　**20.** 6.23 × 36

21. 7.28 × 14　**22.** 7.01 × 53　**23.** 3.70 × 19　**24.** 12.3 × 29

25. 27.2 × 46　**26.** 19.3 × 22　**27.** 0.406 × 61　**28.** 0.22 × 33

29. 0.52 × 58　**30.** 0.8 × 512　**31.** 4.9 × 163　**32.** 0.34 × 354

Problem Solving • Reasoning

Use Data **Use the picture for Problems 33 and 34.**

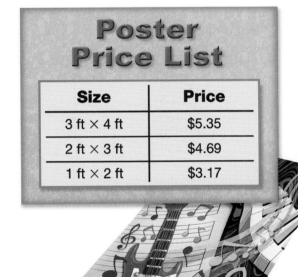

Poster Price List

Size	Price
3 ft × 4 ft	$5.35
2 ft × 3 ft	$4.69
1 ft × 2 ft	$3.17

33. **Analyze** Mai and her three sisters each want to buy three new posters for their bedrooms. Together, they have $40.00. If each buys the same size poster, what is the largest poster each can buy?

34. Jesse has $14.75. He calculates that he can buy one 3 ft × 4 ft poster and three 1 ft × 2 ft posters. Do you agree with his calculation? If not, suggest what posters he could buy in addition to the 3 ft × 4 ft poster.

35. **Estimate** The Glenview Chess Club has designed a poster to advertise its annual tournament. If it costs $2.49 to print one poster, about how much will it cost to print 36 posters?

36. **Write About It** Jack is going to buy two 3-D posters that cost $2.99 each before tax. The tax rate is 8 cents per dollar. Jack calculates that the total cost of the posters will be $11.38. Is this answer reasonable? Explain why or why not.

Mixed Review • Test Prep

Write each number in expanded form, using powers of 10. *(pages 10–11)*

37. 4.76　**38.** 0.0079　**39.** 29,000,000　**40.** 3,280,000,000

41 Which of the following is a prime number?

A 27　**C** 41

B 33　**D** 60

Extra Practice See Set G on page 47.

Multiply Decimals by Decimals

You will learn how to multiply one decimal by another decimal.

Learn About It

Pamela is buying food at the farmers' market. She buys 4.5 pounds of potatoes. If potatoes cost $0.33 per pound, how much will Pamela pay for 4.5 pounds of potatoes?

Multiply. **0.33 × 4.5 = *n***

Find 0.33 × 4.5.

Step 1 Multiply the factors as if the decimal points weren't there.

```
     1
  $0.33
 ×  4.5
    165
 + 1320
   1485
```

Step 2 Place the decimal point in the product.

```
  $0.33  ←  2 decimal places
 ×  4.5  ←  1 decimal place
    165
 + 1 320
 $1.485  ←  3 decimal places
```

Step 3 Since you are working with money, round to the nearest cent.

$1.485 **rounds to** $1.49

Estimate to check your work.

$0.33 **rounds to** $0.30

4.5 **rounds to** 5

$0.30 × 5 = $1.50

$1.49 is close to $1.50, so the answer is reasonable.

Solution: Pamela will pay $1.49 for 4.5 pounds of potatoes.

Another Example

Zeros in the Product

```
   1.839  ←    3 decimal places
 ×  0.05  ←  + 2 decimal places
 0.09195  ←    5 decimal places
```

Explain Your Thinking

► What is the product of 1.525 × 0.004? How do you know where to place the decimal point?

Guided Practice

Find each product.

1. 2.2 × 2.3 **2.** 5.4 × 1.02 **3.** 1.21 × 0.08

4. 12.1 × 2.1 **5.** 5.31 × 6.05 **6.** 0.61 × 0.309

Ask Yourself

- How many decimal places should the product have?

Independent Practice

Find each product. Estimate to see if your answer is reasonable.

7. 4.7×0.2 **8.** 8.9×1.6 **9.** 7.4×4.7 **10.** 3.15×0.22

11. 41.6×4.5 **12.** 31.2×3.33 **13.** 8.51×4.12 **14.** 60.2×4.3

15. 18.3×8.62 **16.** 14.2×34.5 **17.** 41.52×2.6 **18.** 3.482×0.014

19. 561.2×2.15 **20.** 4.215×4.22 **21.** 4.62×3.355 **22.** 8.423×7.64

23. 4.8×4.326 **24.** 125.2×6.54 **25.** 13.7×4.87 **26.** 321.7×46.5

27. 16.3×245.2 **28.** 6.45×84.72 **29.** 4.8×4.326 **30.** 3.751×0.224

Problem Solving • Reasoning

Use Data **Use the prices shown for Problems 31–33.**

Mangoes
$1.49/lb
Oranges
$0.38/lb
Apples
$1.14/lb
Grapes
$1.26/lb
Pineapples
$2.35/each
Bananas
$0.35/lb

31. Janice bought six apples. They weigh 2.38 lb. How much did Janice spend on the apples?

32. Martin plans to make a fruit salad. If he buys a pineapple, 2.53 lb of mangoes, 3.64 lb of oranges, 4.14 lb of bananas, and 2.74 lb of grapes, how much money will Martin spend on fruit?

33. **Write About It** Judy and her father spent $1.89 buying fruit. If they bought 1.5 lb of fruit, what kind of fruit did Judy and her father buy? Explain how you found your answer.

34. **Analyze** At a store's grand opening, every 15th customer gets $10 . Every 50th customer gets a mug. Which customer will be the first to get both $10 and a mug?

Mixed Review • Test Prep

Add or subtract. *(pages 12–13)*

35. $563.4 - 298.3$ **36.** $12{,}768 - 4{,}193$ **37.** $8{,}046.2 + 487.55$ **38.** $0.682 + 1.443$

Choose the letter of the correct answer. *(pages 10–11)*

39 What is 2×10^3 in standard form?

A 2,000 **C** 200
B 1,002 **D** 23

40 What is 5×10^{-2} in standard form?

F 0.005 **H** 0.5
G 0.05 **J** 5.00

Extra Practice See Set H on page 47.

Problem-Solving Strategy: Work Backward

You will learn how to solve a problem by working backward.

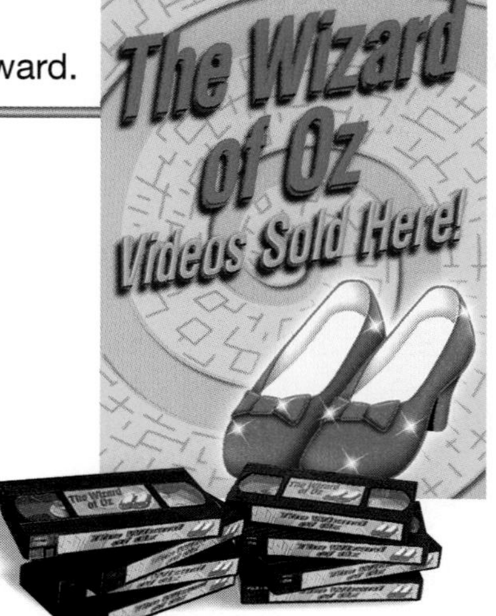

When a problem gives you the result of a sequence of operations, you can work backward to find the amount with which the sequence began.

Problem A school received a shipment of videos of the school play. Half of the videos were sold before lunch. During lunch, 15 were sold. After lunch, three times as many videos were sold as during lunch. Eight videos remained at the end of the day. How many videos were in the shipment?

Understand

What is the question?

How many videos were in the shipment?

What do you know?

- Half were sold before noon.
- 15 were sold during lunch.
- (3×15) were sold after lunch.
- 8 remained at the end of the day.

Plan

How can you find the answer?

Start with what you know and work backward. Because inverse operations "undo" each other, use inverse operations to work backward.

Remember:
Addition and subtraction are inverse operations.
Multiplication and division are inverse operations.

Solve

Start with the number of videos remaining at the end of the day. Then work backward.

- Add the number of videos sold after lunch.
  $8 + (3 \times 15) = 53$
- To that sum, add the number sold during lunch.
  $53 + 15 = 68$
  68 represents the half not sold before lunch.
- To find the total number of videos in the shipment, multiply by 2.
  $68 \times 2 = 136$

There were 136 videos in the shipment.

Look Back

Look back at the problem.

Does your answer make sense? How can you check your answer?

Remember:
- Understand
- Plan
- Solve
- Look Back

Guided Practice

Solve these problems, using the Work Backward strategy.

1. Troy and Amber are learning a scene from a movie for their acting class. The movie is 2 hours 32 minutes long. Their scene begins 44 minutes after the start of the movie. After Troy and Amber's scene is over, 1 hour 36 minutes of the movie remain. How long is Troy and Amber's scene?

   Think: Should you start with the length of the movie or that of the scene?

2. A video store has 50 videos of a popular movie. During the first week, half the videos were rented twice, and half were rented once. During the second week, all were rented once. By the end of the third week, the movie had been rented 167 times. How many times were videos rented during the third week?

   Think: How can the information you know help you find the answer?

Choose a Strategy

Solve. Use these or other strategies.

Problem-Solving Strategies

- **Work Backward**
- **Find a Pattern**
- **Logical Thinking**
- **Write an Equation**

3. Jennifer and Brenda rented three videos: a comedy, a documentary, and a drama. The comedy was 93 minutes long, the documentary was 1 hour 25 minutes, and the drama was 2 hours 8 minutes. If the girls watched two videos that lasted 221 minutes, which ones did they watch?

4. Bruce works in a video store. For a window display, he puts video cases in rows, with one row on top of another. Each row has one case less than the row below it. The top row has 1 case and the bottom row has 6. How many cases does Bruce need for the display?

5. One video costs $14, one costs $18, and the other two cost $9 each. If Trini started with $38 and has $2 left, which videos did she buy?

6. If the following pattern continues, what is the next expression likely to be?

   $0.18 \times 10 \quad 1.8 \times 10 \quad 18.0 \times 10 \quad 180.0 \times 10 \quad 1{,}800 \times 10$

7. Sam is 2 inches shorter than Isobel, who is 3 inches taller than Marlee. Marlee is 6 inches shorter than Noah. Write an equation that you could use to find Noah's height if you knew Sam's height.

8. Sue bought four binders at $4.95 each and a book for $10.95. Gary bought three binders at $7.50 each and a book for $8.95. Did Sue or Gary spend more money? How much more?

Extra Practice See 5–8 on page 49.

Quick Check

Check Your Understanding of Lessons 7–10

Find each product. Estimate to see if your answer is reasonable.

1. 325 × 18

2. 1,540 × 30

3. 234 × 543

4. 854 × 23

5. 3,724 × 7

6. 1,408 × 15

7. 9.7 × 4

8. $8.45 × 16

9. 0.107 × 52

10. $39.99 × 5

11. 1.872 × 22

12. 0.679 × 41

13. 2.9 × 8.4

14. 16.1 × 0.012

15. 6.37 × 1.3

16. 14.5 × 16.88

17. 4.03 × 2.85

18. 0.051 × 0.118

Solve.

19. At the beginning of the year, 27 students signed up to work on the yearbook. During the year, some students left the yearbook staff and other students joined. At the end of the year, there were 35 students on staff. If 20 students joined during the year, how many students left the staff?

How did you do?

If you had difficulty with any items in the Quick Check, you can use the following pages for review and extra practice.

Items	Review These Pages	Do These Extra Practice Items
1–6	pages 18–19	Set F, page 47
7–12	pages 20–21	Set G, page 47
13–18	pages 22–23	Set H, page 47
19	pages 24–25	5–8, page 49

Test Prep • Cumulative Review

Maintaining the Standards

Choose the letter of the correct answer. If a correct answer is not here, choose NH.

1 Eric collected 230 books. Molly collected 151 books. Mark also collected books. Which expression represents the total number of books collected if x = Mark's books?

A $230 + 151 + 2x$

B $230 + 151 + x$

C $230 + 151 - x$

D $230 - 151$

2 Last year, the profit from a business was $100,504. If the profit stays the same for the next five years, how much will the company's total profit be for those five years?

F $100,504 **H** $603,024

G $502,520 **J** $1,005,040

3 Max's family drove 98 miles to attend a birthday party. After the party, they drove to a park. When they arrived at the park they had traveled 110 miles. Which equation represents the distance from the party to the park?

A $98 - m = 110$

B $98 + m = 110$

C $98 + 110 = m$

D $110 + m = 98$

4 Evaluate, given $m = 5$.

$$(m + 6) + 24 + m + (m - 3)$$

F 43

G 42

H 41

J 40

5 The total attendance at a four-day book fair was 2,024 people. If the same number of people attended each day, what was the attendance each day?

A 8,096 people

B 7,590 people

C 605 people

D 506 people

6 Simplify. $(2 \times 12) - (15 \div 3)$

F 3 **H** 21

G 9 **J** NH

7 Which term describes the lines shown in the figure?

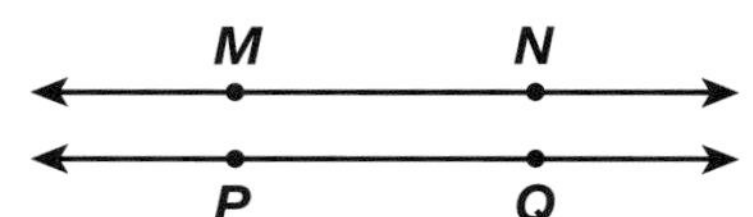

A perpendicular lines

B rays

C parallel lines

D angles

8 Over 6 months, 125,658 people attended events at a civic center. On average, how many people attended events each month?

Explain How did you find your answer?

Safe Site

Internet Test Prep
Visit **www.eduplace.com/kids/mhm** for more *Test Prep Practice.*

Divide Whole Numbers by One-Digit Divisors

You will learn how to divide whole numbers by one-digit divisors.

Learn About It

Felipe calculated that there are 1,483 days remaining until he can get his learning permit to drive. How many whole weeks are there in 1,483 days?

Divide. **1,483 ÷ 7 = ■**

Find 1,483 ÷ 7.

Step 1 There are not enough thousands to divide. Decide where to place the first digit.

```
    2
7)1,483
```

The first digit of the quotient will be in the hundreds place.

Step 2 Divide the hundreds.

```
    2
7)1,483     Multiply. 2 × 7
 −1 4   ←   Subtract. 14 − 14
    0       Compare. 0 < 7
```

Step 3 Bring down the tens digit. Divide the tens.

```
    21
7)1,483
 −1 4↓
    08      Multiply. 1 × 7
    −7  ←   Subtract. 8 − 7
     1      Compare. 1 < 7
```

Step 4 Bring down the ones digit. Divide the ones. Write the remainder.

```
   211 R6
7)1,483
 −1 4
    08
    −7↓
    13      Multiply. 1 × 7 = 7
    −7  ←   Subtract. 13 − 7 = 6
     6      Compare. 6 < 7
```

Check your work. Multiply. Then add.

211 × 7 = 1,477
1,477 + 6 = 1,483

Solution: There are 211 whole weeks in 1,483 days. There are 6 days left over.

Another Example

Zero in the Quotient

```
   5,032 R3
6)30,195
 −30↓↓
    0 19    ←   1 < 6. Write 0 in the quotient.
    −18↓        Bring down the 9. Then
      15        continue to divide.
     −12
       3
```

Explain Your Thinking

► After subtracting, what does it mean if the difference is greater than the divisor?

► When you check your answer, why do you add the remainder?

Guided Practice

Divide. Then check your work.

1. $6\overline{)396}$ **2.** $3\overline{)627}$ **3.** $7\overline{)641}$ **4.** $8\overline{)974}$

5. 505 ÷ 3 **6.** 1,423 ÷ 2 **7.** 2,785 ÷ 9 **8.** 4,876 ÷ 9

Ask Yourself

- Where should I write the first digit in the quotient?

Independent Practice

Divide. Then check your work.

9. $8\overline{)367}$ **10.** $2\overline{)902}$ **11.** $4\overline{)326}$ **12.** $6\overline{)708}$

13. $7\overline{)415}$ **14.** $9\overline{)289}$ **15.** $6\overline{)785}$ **16.** $3\overline{)3,899}$

17. 8,015 ÷ 4 **18.** 1,515 ÷ 5 **19.** 6,954 ÷ 7 **20.** 3,676 ÷ 8

21. 4,432 ÷ 4 **22.** 5,012 ÷ 3 **23.** 8,752 ÷ 6 **24.** 10,800 ÷ 4

Problem Solving • Reasoning

Solve. Whenever you solve problems involving division, the remainder must always be less than the divisor.

25. Ashley's mother drives Ashley between home, school, and swim-team practice each school day of the week. If Ashley's mother drives her a total of 140 miles each week, how many miles does she drive Ashley each day?

26. On Saturday morning, the odometer on Mr. Webb's car read 52,688 miles. On Sunday evening, it read 53,166 miles. If Mr. Webb drove the same distance both days, how far did he drive each day?

27. **Analyze** Felipe and his neighborhood friends held a weekend car wash. They charged $4 to wash cars and $5 to wash vans. Altogether, Felipe and his friends made $97. If they washed 5 vans, how many cars did they wash?

Math Is Everywhere!

SAFETY When the car in front of you passes a fixed point, start counting seconds. To follow at a safe distance, you should pass the same fixed point in no less than 3 seconds.

If the last car in a line passes a fixed point 24 seconds after the first car, and all the drivers in the line are using the 3-second rule, what is the greatest number of cars that could be in the line?

Mixed Review • Test Prep

Round each number to the underlined place. *(pages 8–9)*

28. $3\underline{1}6$ **29.** $4.\underline{2}8$ **30.** $1,8\underline{9}3$ **31.** $0.0\underline{9}7$

32 How many sides does a hexagon have?

A 8 **B** 6 **C** 5 **D** 4

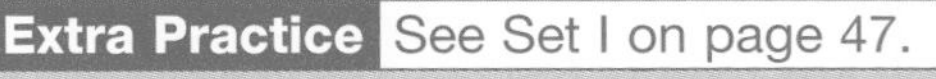

Divide Whole Numbers by Two-Digit Divisors

You will learn how to divide whole numbers by two-digit divisors.

Learn About It

Golf balls often come in packages of three balls. A box contains four packages, or 12 balls. If 4,926 new golf balls were sold at a pro shop, how many boxes were opened?

Divide. **4,926 ÷ 12 = ■**

Find 4,926 ÷ 12.

Step 1 There are not enough thousands to divide. Decide where to place the first digit of the quotient.

$$12\overline{)4{,}926}\quad\text{quotient: }4$$

The first digit of the quotient will be in the hundreds place.

Step 2 Divide the hundreds.

```
      4
 12)4,926
   -4 8
      1
```

Multiply. **4** × **12**
Subtract. **49** − **48**
Compare. **1** < **12**

Step 3 Bring down the tens digit. Divide the tens.

```
     41
 12)4,926
   -4 8
      12
     -12
       0
```

Multiply. **1** × **12**
Subtract. **12** − **12**
Compare. **0** < **12**

Step 4 Bring down the ones digit and divide. Write the remainder.

```
     410 R6
 12)4,926
   -4 8
      12
     -12
       06
       -0
        6
```

6 < **12**, so write **0** in the quotient.

Multiply. **0** × **12**
Subtract. **6** − **0**
Compare. **6** < **12**

Check your work.
Multiply. Then add.
410 × 12 = 4,920
4,920 + 6 = 4,926

Solution: 410 boxes were used completely. Since 6 more balls were sold, 411 boxes were opened.

Another Example

First Estimate of the Quotient Too Large

Find 1,484 ÷ 51.

Think:

```
      3
 50)150
```

```
       3
 51)1,484
   - 1 53
```

153 > 148, so use 2.

Explain Your Thinking

- How do you decide where to place the first digit in the quotient?
- How do you decide whether a digit you try in the quotient is correct or not?

Guided Practice

Divide. Then check your work.

1. $13\overline{)1,562}$ **2.** $54\overline{)2,978}$ **3.** $44\overline{)4,002}$ **4.** $16\overline{)8,608}$

5. 259 ÷ 18 **6.** 358 ÷ 25 **7.** 974 ÷ 64 **8.** 789 ÷ 32

> **Ask Yourself**
> - Where should I place the first digit in the quotient?
> - Do I need to adjust my first estimate?

Independent Practice

Divide. Then check your work.

9. $13\overline{)303}$ **10.** $17\overline{)565}$ **11.** $25\overline{)650}$ **12.** $43\overline{)547}$

13. 862 ÷ 82 **14.** 2,006 ÷ 33 **15.** 8,406 ÷ 63 **16.** 7,106 ÷ 51

17. 674 ÷ 51 **18.** 985 ÷ 75 **19.** 5,216 ÷ 14 **20.** 7,125 ÷ 19

21. 6,523 ÷ 33 **22.** 7,694 ÷ 95 **23.** 11,666 ÷ 11 **24.** 12,500 ÷ 25

Problem Solving • Reasoning

Use Data **Use the table for Problems 26–28.**

Price List

Golf Ball	Dozen	Three-pack
Super Spin	$17.25	$4.32
Distance	$17.45	$4.45
Pro Advantage	$19.76	$4.99
Super Control	$22.35	$5.60

25. The Shady Hill Pro Shop sells used golf balls in packages of one dozen. If the shop has 3,569 used golf balls, how many packages can the shop prepare?

26. **Analyze** Sue likes Pro Advantage golf balls. Jan prefers Super Control golf balls. Sue loses about 10 balls per year, while Jan loses about 5. In one year, what is the least expensive way Sue and Jan can each replace their lost golf balls?

27. Ralph wants to buy Distance golf balls. If he has $30 to spend, how many Distance golf balls can Ralph buy?

28. **Write About It** What would be the least expensive way to buy 37 golf balls of the same type? Explain.

Mixed Review • Test Prep

Find each sum or difference. *(pages 12–13)*

29. 16 − 2.9 **30.** 3,806 − 56.97 **31.** 75.01 + 161 **32.** 16.5 + 13.2 + 0.09

33 Which is the product of 0.34 and 607? *(pages 20–21)*

A 20.638 **B** 187.38 **C** 206.38 **D** 270.56

Extra Practice See Set J on page 48.

Divide Decimals by Whole Numbers

You will learn how to divide decimals by whole numbers.

Learn About It

The tennis team has saved $577.28. Team members want to use the money to buy new uniforms. If there are 8 students on the tennis team, how much money can the team spend per person?

Divide. **$577.28 ÷ 8 = ■**

Find $577.28 ÷ 8.

Step 1 Divide as if the decimal point weren't there.

```
   7216
8)57728
 - 56
    17
  - 16
     12
   -  8
      48
    - 48
       0
```

Step 2 Place the decimal point in the quotient directly above the decimal point in the dividend.

```
   72.16
8)577.28
 - 56
    17
  - 16
     12
   -  8
      48
    - 48
       0
```

Check your work.

72.16 × 8 = 577.28

Solution: The team can spend $72.16 per person.

Other Examples

A. Zeros in the Dividend

Find 16.7 ÷ 4.

```
   4.175
4)16.700  ← Write zeros and bring down to
- 16         find the quotient to more
   0 7       decimal places.
  -  4
     30
   - 28
      20
    - 20
       0
```

B. Divide Whole Numbers

Find 90 ÷ 16.

```
     5.625
16)90.000
 - 80
   10 0
  - 9 6
      40
    - 32
      80
    - 80
       0
```

Explain Your Thinking

- ► When do you need to write zeros in the dividend?
- ► Why don't you write remainders as whole numbers when you divide decimals?

Guided Practice

Divide. Then check your work.

1. $5\overline{)5.5}$ **2.** $4\overline{)30.4}$ **3.** $8\overline{)3.12}$ **4.** $6\overline{)12.24}$

5. $40\overline{)53.5}$ **6.** $16\overline{)5.2}$ **7.** $92\overline{)51.52}$ **8.** $40\overline{)16.24}$

9. 33.201 ÷ 9 **10.** 112.5 ÷ 75 **11.** 8.551 ÷ 17

Ask Yourself

- Where should I place the decimal point in the quotient?
- When should I write a zero in the dividend and continue dividing?

Independent Practice

Divide. Then check your work.

12. $2\overline{)3.6}$ **13.** $7\overline{)0.49}$ **14.** $3\overline{)60.15}$ **15.** $6\overline{)7.2}$

16. $8\overline{)17.92}$ **17.** $8\overline{)8.84}$ **18.** $5\overline{)7.53}$ **19.** $4\overline{)63.04}$

20. 5.125 ÷ 25 **21.** 0.98 ÷ 56 **22.** 52.19 ÷ 17 **23.** 9.186 ÷ 12

24. 12.67 ÷ 14 **25.** 597.54 ÷ 20 **26.** 42.77 ÷ 13 **27.** 475.5 ÷ 15

Problem Solving • Reasoning

28. **Compare** Tennis balls are sold in cans of 3 balls or in cases of 24 cans. Suppose a can of one brand of tennis balls costs $2.58 while a case of the same brand costs $60.48. Which has the lower cost per ball? Explain.

29. **Analyze** The tennis team practices three afternoons a week. Each week, the players use 9 new balls. Over 4 weeks, the team spends $25.92 on practice balls. Balls are sold in cans of 3 balls. What is the cost per can?

30. The tennis team is having 8 tennis rackets restrung. The total cost is $319.60. What is the average cost per racket for restringing?

31. The tennis team went by bus to a tournament. If it took 3 hours to travel 142.8 miles, what was the average number of miles traveled per hour?

32. Study the pattern below. If the pattern continues, what is the eighth set of four balls likely to look like?

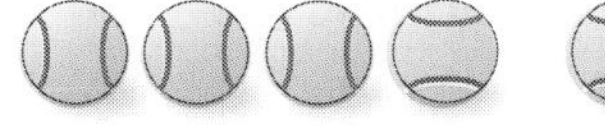
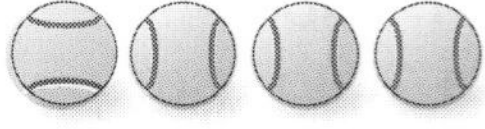
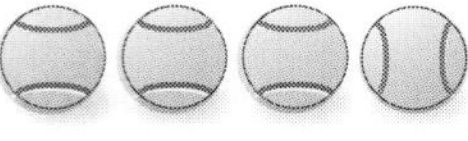

Mixed Review • Test Prep

Order each set of numbers from least to greatest. *(pages 6–7)*

33. 0.45 4.5 4.45 **34.** 1.2 0.01 0.009 **35.** 3.3 4.7 1.9 **36.** 0.08 0.05 0.1

37 What is the product of 23 and 0? *(pages 18–19)*

A 230 **B** 23 **C** 1 **D** 0

Extra Practice See Set K on page 48.

LESSON 14 Divide Decimals by Decimals

You will learn how to divide one decimal by another decimal.

Learn About It

Sometimes you need to divide a decimal by another decimal.

Jana has $4.81 and wants to buy some trading cards. If the trading cards cost $0.74 each, how many cards can Jana buy?

Divide. **$4.81 ÷ $0.74 = ■**

Find 4.81 ÷ 0.74.

Step 1 Change the divisor to a whole number by multiplying both the divisor and the dividend by a power of 10.

$0.74\overline{)4.81}$

Multiply both numbers by 10^2, or 100.

Step 2 Place the decimal point in the quotient. Then divide as you would with whole numbers.

```
    6.   ← decimal point
74)481
  -444
    37
```

Step 3 Place a zero next to the dividend and continue to divide.

```
    6.5
74)481.0
  - 444
     37 0
   - 37 0
        0
```

Check your work.

0.74 × 6.5 = 4.810

Solution: Since Jana cannot buy half a card, drop the decimal part of the quotient. Jana can buy 6 cards.

Another Example

Place Two or More Zeros in the Dividend

Find 34.2 ÷ 2.4.

```
     14.25
2.4)34.200
   - 24
     10.2
    - 9.6
       60
     - 48
       120
      -120
         0
```

Explain Your Thinking

- ► When multiplying to change the divisor to a whole number, how do you know which power of 10 to use?
- ► Why can you write zeros at the end of the dividend to continue dividing?
- ► Why does the answer not change when you multiply both the divisor and the dividend by the same power of ten?

Guided Practice

Divide. Then check your work.

1. $0.44\overline{)4.62}$ **2.** $0.03\overline{)0.24}$ **3.** $3.4\overline{)8.84}$ **4.** $1.6\overline{)8.92}$

5. $6.5 \div 3.2$ **6.** $61.32 \div 1.4$ **7.** $1.222 \div 0.52$

> **Ask Yourself**
> - Should I write zeros in the dividend? If so, how many?
> - Did I multiply by the correct power of 10?

Calculator Option

Independent Practice

Divide. Then check your work.

8. $4.4\overline{)46.2}$ **9.** $0.05\overline{)4.0}$ **10.** $0.7\overline{)21.28}$ **11.** $0.03\overline{)1.215}$

12. $9.5\overline{)2.299}$ **13.** $1.9\overline{)15.447}$ **14.** $0.16\overline{)4.08}$ **15.** $4.2\overline{)8.19}$

16. $5.7\overline{)3.534}$ **17.** $3.3\overline{)66.99}$ **18.** $2.5\overline{)86.5}$ **19.** $3.5\overline{)4.508}$

20. $0.0369 \div 0.9$ **21.** $22.68 \div 6.3$ **22.** $584.61 \div 2.6$ **23.** $2.6 \div 0.32$

24. $7.221 \div 0.08$ **25.** $47.56 \div 3.2$ **26.** $59.04 \div 4.5$ **27.** $6.7204 \div 0.16$

Problem Solving • Reasoning

28. James spent \$12.25 on trading cards. Each card cost \$0.49. How many cards did James buy?

29. **Compare** Tamiko bought 14 cards for \$3.36 and 20 cards for \$5.20. Ricky spent \$6.93 on 11 similar cards. Who got the better deal? Explain.

30. **Analyze** At a card collectors' convention, cards for a total of \$7,843.38 were sold the first day. The second day, cards for a total of \$6,986.94 were sold. If the cost per card was \$3.66, how many cards were sold on each of the two days?

31. **Write Your Own** Write a division word problem that uses only decimals. Give your problem to a classmate to solve.

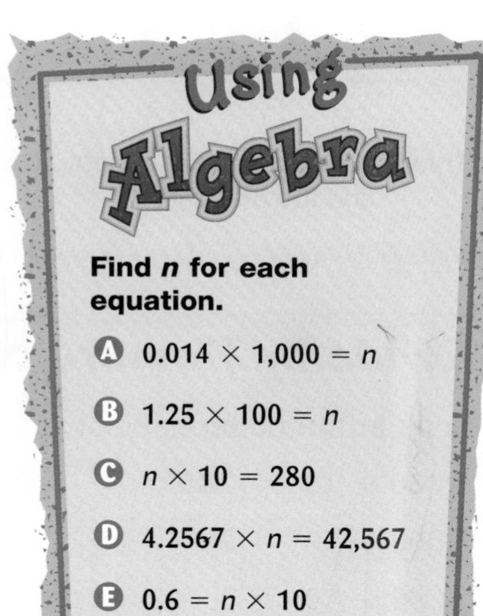

Find n for each equation.

A. $0.014 \times 1{,}000 = n$

B. $1.25 \times 100 = n$

C. $n \times 10 = 280$

D. $4.2567 \times n = 42{,}567$

E. $0.6 = n \times 10$

F. $4.28 = n \times 107$

Mixed Review • Test Prep

Multiply or divide. *(pages 18–19, 28–29)*

32. 6×890 **33.** $644 \div 4$ **34.** 251×73 **35.** $1{,}280 \div 8$

Choose the letter of the correct answer. *(pages 8–9, 12–13)*

36 Evaluate $k + 5.9 + 8.75$, given $k = 17.75$.

A 32.4 **C** 3.1

B 3.24 **D** 0.31

37 Round 6,658,954 to the nearest million.

F 6,000 **H** 6,000,000

G 7,000 **J** 7,000,000

Extra Practice See Set L on page 48.

Mental Math With Powers of 10

You will learn how to use patterns to multiply and divide by powers of 10.

Review Vocabulary
power of 10

Learn About It

Microscopes are used to enlarge images of extremely small objects. Lenses in the microscope can magnify the object by some **power of 10**. Images may appear 10 times, 10^2 times, or even 10^3 times larger than the object itself.

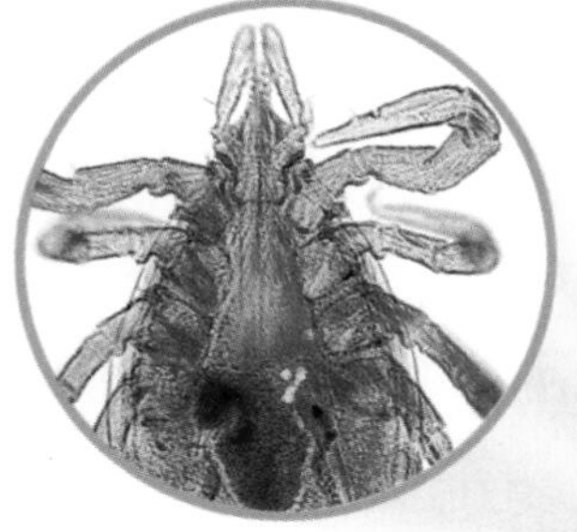

Deer tick magnified 60 times.

Multiply by Powers of 10

Look at the patterns below.

$7 \times 10^1 = 70$	$325 \times 10^1 = 3{,}250$	$4.0813 \times 10^1 = 40.813$
$7 \times 10^2 = 700$	$325 \times 10^2 = 32{,}500$	$4.0813 \times 10^2 = 408.13$
$7 \times 10^3 = 7{,}000$	$325 \times 10^3 = 325{,}000$	$4.0813 \times 10^3 = 4{,}081.3$

Think: How does the exponent help you find the product?

Divide by Powers of 10

Look at the patterns below.

$3{,}000 \div 10^1 = 300$	$607{,}000 \div 10^1 = 60{,}700$	$51.045 \div 10^1 = 5.1045$
$3{,}000 \div 10^2 = 30$	$607{,}000 \div 10^2 = 6{,}070$	$51.045 \div 10^2 = 0.51045$
$3{,}000 \div 10^3 = 3$	$607{,}000 \div 10^3 = 607$	$51.045 \div 10^3 = 0.051045$

Think: How does the exponent help you find the quotient?

Another Example

Patterns With Negative Exponents

$36 \times 10^{-1} = 36 \times \frac{1}{10} = \frac{36}{10} = 3.6$

$36 \times 10^{-2} = 36 \times \frac{1}{100} = \frac{36}{100} = 0.36$

$36 \times 10^{-3} = 36 \times \frac{1}{1{,}000} = \frac{36}{1{,}000} = 0.036$

Explain Your Thinking

- ► When multiplying by a positive power of 10, which way should the decimal point be moved? Why?
- ► When dividing by a positive power of 10, which way should the decimal point be moved? Why?

Guided Practice

Find each product or quotient, using mental math.

1. 34×10^2 **2.** 5.06×10^3 **3.** $57{,}000 \times 10^{-1}$

4. $4{,}800 \div 10^1$ **5.** $6.3 \div 10^3$ **6.** $2{,}640{,}000 \div 10^2$

Ask Yourself

- Which way should the decimal point be moved?
- How many zeros do I need in my answer?

Independent Practice

Find each product or quotient, using mental math.

7. $1{,}500 \div 10^2$ **8.** $13{,}100 \div 10^2$ **9.** $93.1 \div 10^3$ **10.** $95{,}700 \div 10^1$

11. 21×10^1 **12.** 63×10^3 **13.** $32{,}000 \times 10^1$ **14.** 311.05×10^2

15. $6{,}000 \div 10^3$ **16.** $1{,}100 \div 10^1$ **17.** $50.5 \div 10^3$ **18.** $622{,}000 \div 10^3$

19. $4{,}295 \times 10^3$ **20.** $7{,}200 \times 10^{-3}$ **21.** $4{,}002.6 \times 10^3$ **22.** $8{,}000 \times 10^{-2}$

Problem Solving • Reasoning

Use Data **Use the table for Problems 23–24.**

23. **Compare** Under Terry's microscope, the image of an amoeba appears 10 times larger than the amoeba actually is. What is the length of the image?

24. How many millimeters longer is the image of a euglena magnified 100 times than the image of a euglena magnified 10 times?

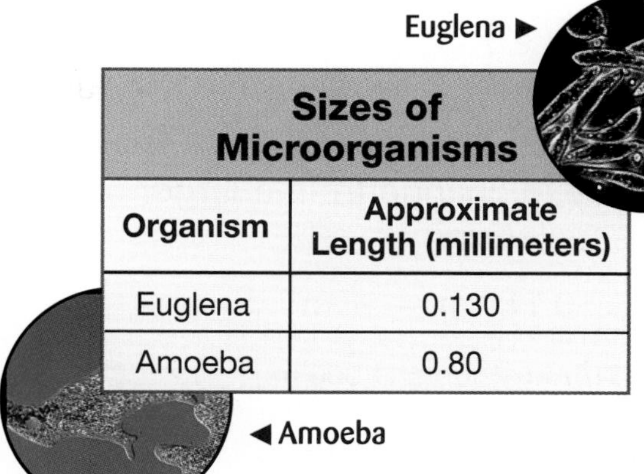

Sizes of Microorganisms

Organism	Approximate Length (millimeters)
Euglena	0.130
Amoeba	0.80

25. The image of the organism that Elaine views through her microscope is enlarged 1,000 times. If the image is 16.5 mm long, what is the size of the organism?

26. **Write About It** The size of an object is 2 mm. An enlarged image of the object is 2,000 mm. Use powers of 10 to explain how the two sizes are related.

Mixed Review • Test Prep

Round to the underlined place. *(pages 8–9)*

27. $1.6\underline{7}3$ **28.** $0.\underline{0}519$ **29.** $4\underline{3}.78$ **30.** $5\underline{1}5.27$

Choose the letter of the correct answer. *(pages 12–13)*

31 What is 54,287 − 1,324?

A 41,047 **B** 52,963 **C** 53,433 **D** 53,163

Extra Practice See Set M on page 48.

Decimals and the Metric System

You will learn how to use powers of 10 to change from one metric unit to another.

Learn About It

The metric system is based on 10 and powers of 10. You can use what you know about multiplying and dividing by powers of 10 to change from one metric unit to another.

Look at the examples below.

Metric Units of Length		
1 kilometer (km)	=	1,000 meters (m)
1 hectometer (hm)	=	100 meters (m)
1 dekameter (dam)	=	10 meters (m)
1 decimeter (dm)	=	0.1 meter (m)
1 centimeter (cm)	=	0.01 meter (m)
1 millimeter (mm)	=	0.001 meter (m)

Changing Metric Units of Length

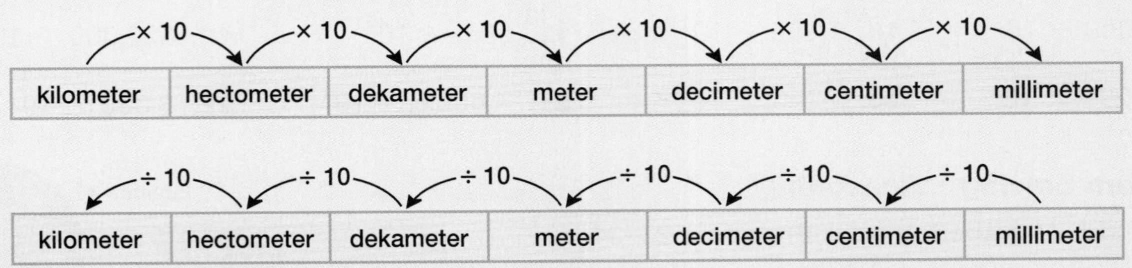

Multiply to change from a larger unit to a smaller unit.

0.11 km = ■ m

Think: 1 km = 1,000 m

$0.11 \times 1{,}000 = 110$

0.11 km = 110 m

Divide to change from a smaller unit to a larger unit.

23 dm = ■ m

Think: 10 dm = 1 m

$23 \div 10 = 2.3$

23 dm = 2.3 m

Changing metric units of mass and capacity follows the same pattern.

Metric Units of Mass		
1,000 milligrams (mg)	=	1 gram (g)
1 dekagram (dag)	=	10 grams (g)
1 hectogram (hg)	=	100 grams (g)
1 kilogram (kg)	=	1,000 grams (g)
1 metric ton (t)	=	1,000 kilograms (kg)

Changing Metric Units of Mass

0.525 t = ■ kg

Think: 1 t = 1,000 kg

$0.525 \times 1{,}000 = 525$

0.525 t = 525 kg

684 mg = ■ g

Think: 1,000 mg = 1 g

$684 \div 1{,}000 = 0.684$

684 mg = 0.684 g

Metric Units of Capacity	
1 liter (L)	= 1,000 milliliters (mL)
1 deciliter (dL)	= 100 milliliters (mL)

Changing Metric Units of Capacity

1.08 dL = ■ mL

Think: 1 dL = 10 mL

1.08 × 100 = 108

1.08 dL = 108 mL

1,630 mL = ■ L

Think: 1,000 mL = 1 L

1,630 ÷ 1,000 = 1.63

1,630 mL = 1.63 L

Explain Your Thinking

► Why do you multiply when changing from a larger to a smaller unit and divide when changing from a smaller to a larger unit?

Guided Practice

Complete.

1. 13 m = ■ cm **2.** 531 cm = ■ dm **3.** 0.03 g = ■ mg

4. 1,500 kg = ■ t **5.** 27 dL = ■ mL **6.** 3.8 L = ■ mL

Ask Yourself

- Am I changing to a smaller unit or a larger unit?
- Which way should the decimal point be moved?

Independent Practice

Complete.

7. If 1 cm = 0.01 m, then 20 cm = ■ m. **8.** If 1 kg = 1,000 g, then 1.5 kg = ■ g.

9. 97 m = ■ cm **10.** 718 dL = ■ mL **11.** 43 mg = ■ g

12. 69.5 kg = ■ g **13.** 0.438 km = ■ cm **14.** 876 mL = ■ L

15. 9.61 t = ■ kg **16.** 622.3 km = ■ m **17.** 0.4 m = ■ mm

Algebra • Functions **Copy and complete each table by following the rule.**

Rule: Multiply by 100

	Input	Output
18.	45	■
19.	■	0.005
20.	8.08	■

Rule: Divide by 1,000

	Input	Output
21.	15,753	■
22.	■	0.022
23.	340	■

Rule: Divide by 100

	Input	Output
24.	■	0.23
25.	45,777	■
26.	■	0.1122

Problem Solving • Reasoning

Use Data Use the blueprint for Problems 27–29.

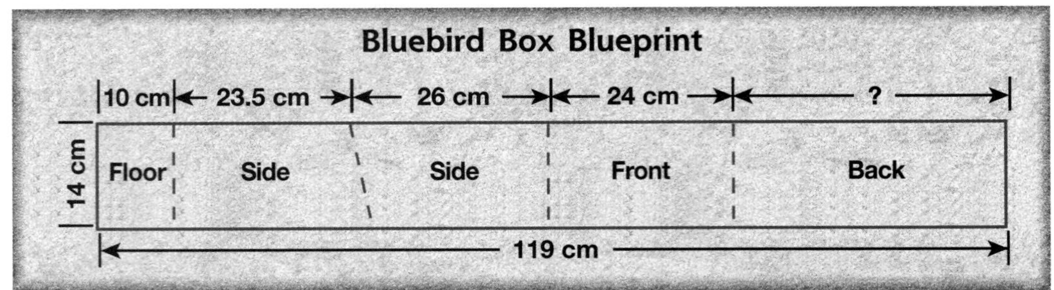

Eastern bluebird

Western bluebird

Mountain bluebird

Bluebird box

27. Compare How many times as great as the width is the length of the board shown on the bluebird-box blueprint?

28. Change all the measures shown on the blueprint to meters and then order them from least to greatest.

29. Analyze Dan is building a bluebird box, using the blueprint shown above. Using millimeters, what will be the length and width of the back piece of the bluebird box?

30. The Nature Club is setting up a trail for the western bluebird. The students space the bluebird boxes about 2,800 decimeters apart. How many kilometers apart are the boxes?

31. The bluebird box needs a round entrance hole. The hole should be 3.8 centimeters across. How many millimeters is 3.8 centimeters?

32. Mrs. Bashkin has a birdbath in her backyard. She uses 4.5 liters of water to fill the birdbath. How many milliliters is 4.5 liters?

Mixed Review • Test Prep

Multiply or divide. *(pages 18–19, 30–31)*

33. 43×85 **34.** $450 \div 11$ **35.** $12 \times 1,226$ **36.** $360 \div 19$

Choose the letter of the correct answer. *(pages 22–23, 36–37)*

37 Estimate the product of 8.61 and 71.09.

A 6,200 **C** 630
B 720 **D** 61

38 What is the quotient of $50.9 \div 10^3$?

F 50,900 **H** 0.0509
G 509 **J** 0.00509

Extra Practice See Set N on page 48.

Practice Game

The Decimal Challenge

Practice operations with decimals by playing this game with a partner. Try to create the largest sum, difference, product, and quotient!

What You'll Need

- *4 sets of number cards, numbered 0–9 (Teaching Tool 1)*
- *a kitchen timer*
- *pencil and paper*

Players
2

2 7 5 1 3

Here's What to Do

The game is played in four rounds: addition, subtraction, multiplication, and division.

1. One player shuffles the number cards. To begin the addition round, each player draws five number cards.
2. The timer is set for 2 minutes. Each player uses all 10 numbers once to create two decimals. The decimals should have at least two digits to the right of the decimal point.
3. When the timer rings, each player adds his or her decimals. The player with the greatest sum wins the round.

Players repeat the steps for the subtraction, multiplication, and division rounds. They try to create, in turn, the greatest difference, product, and quotient. The player who wins the most rounds is the winner.

Share Your Thinking Would you use the same strategy for each operation?

Problem-Solving Application: Use a Bar Graph

You will learn how to use a bar graph to solve a problem.

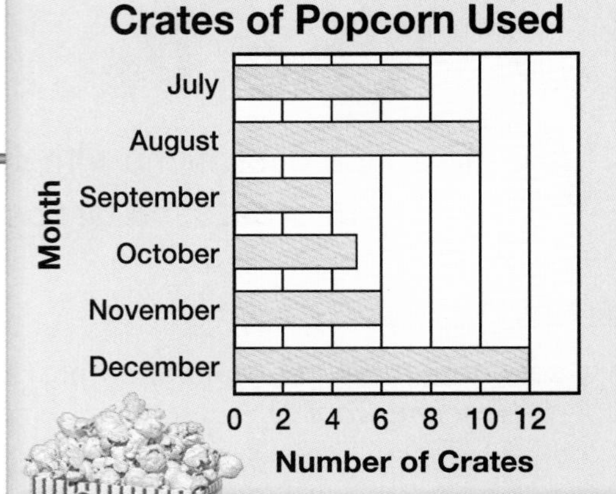

Sometimes you need to use information from a bar graph to solve a problem.

When a theater manager plans how many crates of popcorn to buy, she looks at the average number of crates used in the past. What is the average number of crates of popcorn used in the last six months?

Understand

What is the question?

What is the average number of crates of popcorn used each month?

What do you know?

The bar graph shows the number of crates of popcorn used each month from July through December.

Plan

How can you find the answer?

- Use the bar graph to find the number of crates used each month.
- Add to find the total number of crates.
- Divide that sum by the number of months.

Solve

July	8	
August	10	
September	4	
October	5	
November	6	
December	+ 12	
Total	45	$45 \div 6 = 7.5$

The average number of crates of popcorn used each month is 7.5.

Look Back

Look back at the problem.

How can you decide if your answer is reasonable?

Popcorn is a special variety of corn that pops when exposed to prolonged heat. Most popcorn is grown in the United States.

Remember:
- Understand
- Plan
- Solve
- Look Back

Guided Practice

Solve. Use the bar graph on page 42.

1. What was the average number of crates of popcorn used during the months of September, October, and November?

   Think: Will you use all the bars to answer this question?

2. Did the theater use more crates in October than in September? If so, how many more crates did the theater use?

   Think: How can you use the graph to answer this question?

Choose a Strategy

Solve. Use these or other strategies.

Problem-Solving Strategies

- **Draw a Diagram**
- **Use Logical Thinking**
- **Write an Equation**
- **Find a Pattern**

3. A class made a bar graph of the number of raisins in boxes. The sum of the values for boxes 1, 2, and 3 is 117. Box 1 has 2 raisins fewer than Box 2. Box 2 has 2 raisins fewer than Box 3. How many raisins are in each box?

4. Sandra made a beaded necklace. The pattern she used was 1 white bead, 2 red beads, 3 blue beads. The necklace started and ended with a white bead. She used 15 white beads. How many blue beads did she use?

5. Mark spent half his money on a new CD. Then he spent $3 on food. Finally, he spent half of what he had left at a movie. Then Mark had $5.50 left. How much did Mark start with?

6. Emily has 5 more CDs than Mia. Mia has 12 more CDs than Teri. Teri has twice as many CDs as Paula. Together the four girls have 113 CDs. How many CDs does each girl have?

7. A movie was adapted as a Broadway musical. During one week, the musical had sales of $938,336. If this was an average week, about how much would the yearly sales be?

8. Study the following number pattern. If the pattern continues, what is the next number likely to be?

   2.04   4.08   12.24   48.96   244.80

Extra Practice See 9–11 on page 49.

Quick Check

Check Your Understanding of Lessons 11–17

Divide.

1. $4{,}683 \div 3$ **2.** $5{,}238 \div 9$ **3.** $562 \div 32$ **4.** $1{,}582 \div 16$

5. $0.621 \div 3$ **6.** $5.78 \div 68$ **7.** $45.5 \div 1.25$ **8.** $480.24 \div 0.18$

Find each product or quotient, using mental math.

9. 19×10^4 **10.** 4.6×10^{-2} **11.** $9.7 \div 10^3$ **12.** $871.3 \div 10^4$

Complete.

13. 97 m = ■ cm **14.** 1,118 mL = ■ L **15.** 18.2 hg = ■ kg **16.** 46.3 dam = ■ hm

Solve, using the information in the bar graph.

17. The bar graph shows activities chosen by students at a day camp. Which activities were chosen by an equal number of students? Explain how you know.

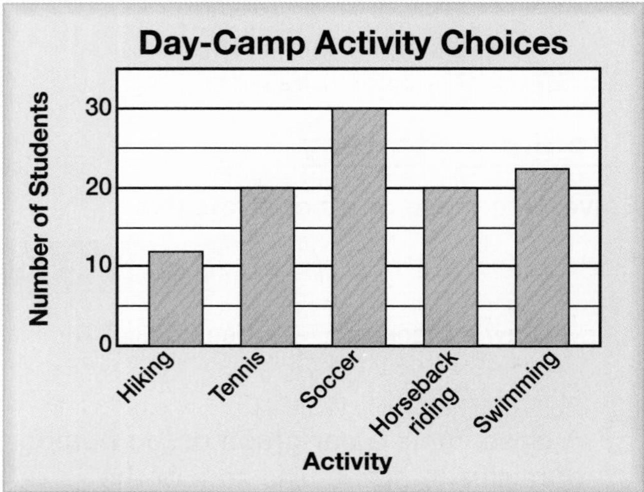

How did you do?

If you had difficulty with any items in the Quick Check, you can use the following pages for review and extra practice.

Items	Review These Pages	Do These Extra Practice Items
1–4	pages 28–31	Set I, page 47; Set J, page 48
5–8	pages 32–35	Set K and Set L, page 48
9–12	pages 36–37	Set M, page 48
13–16	pages 38–40	Set N, page 48
17	pages 42–43	9–11, page 49

Test Prep • Cumulative Review

Maintaining the Standards

Choose the letter of the correct answer.

1. Which shows $1,375.42 rounded to the nearest hundred dollars?

   A $1,400
   B $1,380
   C $1,375
   D $1,000

2. Tony spent 3 hours and 23 minutes on the Internet. He then watched TV for 70 minutes. Altogether, how much time did Tony spend watching TV and using the Internet?

   F 3 hours 92 minutes
   G 4 hours 33 minutes
   H 96 hours
   J 370 hours 23 minutes

3. Which shows 0.2045 in expanded form?

   A $(2 \times 10^1) + (4 \times 10^2) + (5 \times 10^3)$
   B $(2 \times 10^1) + (4 \times 10^3) + (5 \times 10^4)$
   C $(2 \times 10^{-1}) + (4 \times 10^{-3}) + (5 \times 10^{-4})$
   D $(2 \times 10^{-1}) + (4 \times 10^{-2}) + (5 \times 10^{-3})$

4. Sam collected a total of $60.08 for the school fair. If he collected $7.51 per person, how many people contributed?

   F 9 people
   G 8 people
   H 7 people
   J 6 people

5. Which list orders the numbers from least to greatest?

   A 0.55 0.5 0.2 1 0.21
   B 0.55 0.21 0.2 1 0.5
   C 0.2 0.21 0.5 0.55 1
   D 0.5 1 0.2 0.21 0.55

6. Which is the correct word form for the number 45.01?

   F forty-five and one hundredth
   G forty-five and one tenth
   H forty-five hundredths
   J forty-five tenths

7. Which shows $(4 \times 10^8) + (1 \times 10^7)$ in standard form?

   A 2,870
   B 4,100,000
   C 41,000,000
   D 410,000,000

8. Between which two numbers does 0.035 fall on this number line?

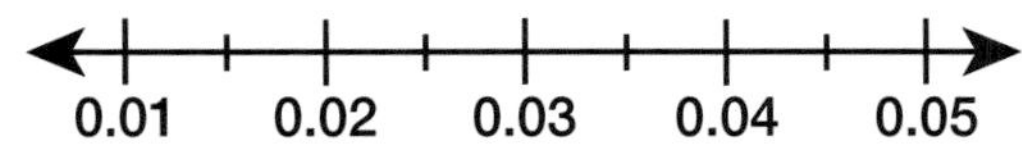

Explain How can you compare decimals on a number line?

Safe Site

Internet Test Prep
Visit **www.eduplace.com/kids/mhm** for more *Test Prep Practice.*

Extra Practice

Set A *(Lesson 1, pages 4–5)*

Write each number in word form and in expanded form.

1. 954,025 **2.** 10.546 **3.** 25,847,633 **4.** 22,006.03

5. 8.03416 **6.** 265.000451 **7.** 77.1414 **8.** 387,426,000,000

Write the value of each underlined digit.

9. $36,\underline{5}00$ **10.** $1\underline{4}1,927,218$ **11.** $1,\underline{2}00,000,000$ **12.** $\underline{2}6,793,654,821$

13. $60.8\underline{7}$ **14.** $227.50\underline{2}1$ **15.** $9.830\underline{4}$ **16.** $0.0041\underline{6}$

Set B *(Lesson 2, pages 6–7)*

Compare. Write >, <, or = for each ●.

1. 360.091 ● 360.019 **2.** 0.001 ● 0.0010 **3.** 11.12 ● 12.12

4. 6,023 ● 6.203 **5.** 59,568 ● 59,569 **6.** 20,202 ● 22,020

Order from greatest to least.

7. 40.6 0.406 4.06 4.60 **8.** 1.8201 182.01 1.8021 18.201

9. 0.385 0.0729 0.461 0.0375 **10.** 5,033 5,303 5,333 5,003

Set C *(Lesson 3, pages 8–9)*

Round each number to the underlined place.

1. $0.\underline{4}7$ **2.** $4.\underline{4}2$ **3.** $3\underline{6}.8$ **4.** $\underline{1}56.7$

5. $3.1\underline{9}2$ **6.** $6\underline{1}9.53$ **7.** $\underline{2},714.6$ **8.** $4,\underline{3}39$

9. $10,\underline{0}67$ **10.** $9.4\underline{6}88$ **11.** $1\underline{0}1,129$ **12.** $\underline{6},870,258$

Set D *(Lesson 4, pages 10–11)*

Write each number in expanded form, using powers of 10.

1. 300,000,000 **2.** 0.0098 **3.** 0.07 **4.** 12,000

5. 0.45 **6.** 250 **7.** 9,200 **8.** 0.03

Write each number in standard form.

9. $(2 \times 10^4) + (5 \times 10^2) + (6 \times 10^0)$ **10.** $(9 \times 10^1) + (7 \times 10^{-1}) + (2 \times 10^{-3})$

Extra Practice

Set E *(Lesson 5, pages 12–13)*

Find each sum or difference.

1. 2,219 + 631 **2.** 7.8 + 1.4 **3.** 81.22 + 0.64

4. 73 + 1.2 **5.** 16.5 + 2.5 **6.** 312 − 287.6

7. 0.472 − 0.083 **8.** 36.42 − 1.44 **9.** 216.75 − 4.12

Set F *(Lesson 7, pages 18–19)*

Find each product.

1. 307 × 4 **2.** 415 × 6 **3.** 850 × 7 **4.** 542 × 81

5. 427 × 22 **6.** 4,804 × 74 **7.** 11,841 × 63 **8.** 6,410 × 39

9. 647 × 142 **10.** 652 × 314 **11.** 421 × 518 **12.** 1,254 × 89

Set G *(Lesson 8, pages 20–21)*

Find each product. Estimate to check your work.

1. 4.5 × 7 **2.** 9.2 × 3 **3.** 6.1 × 6 **4.** 0.84 × 4

5. 20.2 × 13 **6.** 0.092 × 15 **7.** 12.3 × 21 **8.** 3.7 × 27

9. 1.9 × 36 **10.** 62.4 × 41 **11.** 3.6 × 181 **12.** 0.214 × 8

Set H *(Lesson 9, pages 22–23)*

Find each product. Estimate to see if your answer is reasonable.

1. 6.5 × 7.2 **2.** 10.2 × 0.3 **3.** 7.2 × 1.4 **4.** 6.32 × 0.9

5. 12.5 × 2.74 **6.** 6.03 × 2.41 **7.** 62.2 × 4.6 **8.** 3.9 × 21.7

9. 47.1 × 0.254 **10.** 7.82 × 3.21 **11.** 4.42 × 24.7 **12.** 5.3 × 0.82

Set I *(Lesson 11, pages 28–29)*

Divide. Then check your work.

1. $2\overline{)422}$ **2.** $9\overline{)637}$ **3.** $5\overline{)152}$ **4.** $5\overline{)474}$

5. $9\overline{)954}$ **6.** $8\overline{)763}$ **7.** $3\overline{)325}$ **8.** $7\overline{)729}$

9. 2,412 ÷ 2 **10.** 10,541 ÷ 7 **11.** 6,542 ÷ 8 **12.** 42,506 ÷ 8

Extra Practice

Set J *(Lesson 12, pages 30–31)*

Divide. Then check your work.

1. $42\overline{)652}$
2. $13\overline{)913}$
3. $90\overline{)549}$
4. $24\overline{)764}$
5. $34\overline{)878}$
6. $18\overline{)648}$
7. $32\overline{)844}$
8. $19\overline{)978}$
9. $1{,}153 \div 33$
10. $4{,}846 \div 24$
11. $62{,}645 \div 45$
12. $4{,}622 \div 48$

Set K *(Lesson 13, pages 32–33)*

Divide. Then check your work.

1. $6\overline{)2.4}$
2. $8\overline{)3.2}$
3. $3\overline{)21.6}$
4. $7\overline{)9.66}$
5. $33\overline{)215.82}$
6. $4\overline{)0.46}$
7. $8\overline{)32.4}$
8. $9\overline{)492.48}$
9. $6.4 \div 32$
10. $0.48 \div 12$
11. $923.3 \div 25$
12. $1{,}522.5 \div 42$

Set L *(Lesson 14, pages 34–35)*

Divide. Then check your work.

1. $0.5\overline{)2.05}$
2. $1.2\overline{)24.48}$
3. $3.2\overline{)78.4}$
4. $0.9\overline{)806.94}$
5. $9.9\overline{)30.69}$
6. $7.4\overline{)7.844}$
7. $3.7\overline{)19.61}$
8. $1.48 \div 0.08$
9. $4.104 \div 3.8$
10. $1{,}165.8 \div 6.7$
11. $25.688 \div 1.3$
12. $1{,}960.4 \div 0.32$

Set M *(Lesson 15, pages 36–37)*

Find each product or quotient, using mental math.

1. 322×10^1
2. 407×10^2
3. $5{,}217 \times 10^3$
4. $7{,}650 \times 10^{-2}$
5. $619 \div 10^2$
6. $1{,}400 \div 10^1$
7. $2{,}842 \div 10^3$
8. $12{,}580 \div 10^1$
9. 502×10^2
10. $5{,}815 \times 10^{-3}$
11. $6{,}240 \div 10^2$
12. $52{,}000 \div 10^3$

Set N *(Lesson 16, pages 38–40)*

Complete.

1. 425 g = ■ mg
2. 108 cm = ■ m
3. 120 mL = ■ L
4. 4.5 dam = ■ mm
5. 12 g = ■ kg
6. 57 m = ■ km
7. 55 L = ■ dL
8. 3.2 t = ■ kg
9. 0.18 dL = ■ mL

Extra Practice • Problem Solving

Solve. Decide whether an estimate or an exact answer is needed. *(Lesson 6, pages 14–15)*

1. Two CDs cost $24.60 at the local music store. If Jemma and Tom have $55.00, do they have enough money to buy four CDs? Explain.

2. The 162 students at Pine School are going on a field trip. If the students travel in 8 buses, about how many students ride on each bus?

3. Monica's goal this week is to sell 15 tickets to her dance team's spring show. Each ticket costs $6.25. So far, she has collected $81.25. Has Monica met her goal? Explain.

4. Trevor is buying gifts for his family and wants to buy 4 paperback books. Each paperback book costs $5.75. If Trevor has $30.50, how much will he have left after he buys the books?

Solve, using the Work Backward strategy. *(Lesson 10, pages 24–25)*

5. Teresa spent $3\frac{1}{2}$ hours at the library. She spent 1 hour doing research for a paper and 50 minutes reading a novel. She spent $\frac{1}{2}$ of the time remaining doing homework. How much time did Teresa spend on her homework?

6. A bookstore puts 50 copies of a new book on display on Monday. That day, the store sells 8 copies. On Tuesday, 13 copies are sold. On Thursday, there are 19 copies left on display. How many copies did the store sell on Wednesday?

7. Jim's little sister is building a tower with blocks. She adds 5 blocks, and then removes 3 blocks. If she adds 4 more blocks, the tower will have twice as many blocks as when she started. How many blocks did she start with?

8. Arthur goes to a flea market and spends $9.75. He buys a pair of sunglasses, a lemonade, and two books about baseball. If the books are $2.25 each, and the lemonade is $1, how much does the pair of sunglasses cost?

Solve. Use the bar graph. *(Lesson 17, pages 42–43)*

9. During a morning walk, Jill and Ken observed the birds shown in the bar graph. How many birds in all were observed?

10. Hawks, vultures, and owls are birds of prey. How many of the birds observed are birds of prey?

11. Which two kinds of bird show the greatest difference in number counted? Explain how you know.

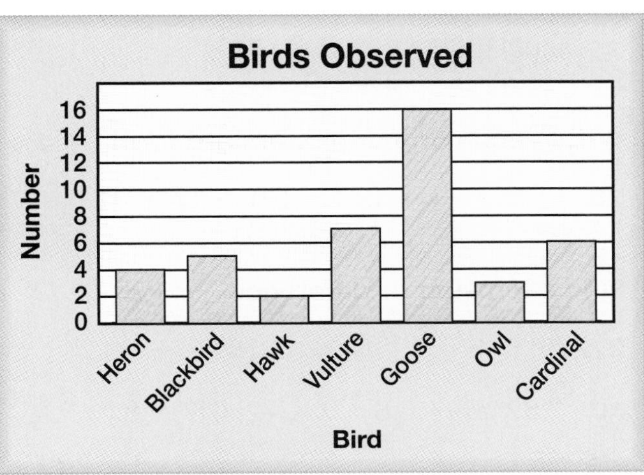

Chapter Review

Reviewing Vocabulary

Write *true* or *false* for each statement.

1. A base is always raised to a power of 10.
2. The exponent in 14^3 indicates that 14 and 3 should be multiplied.
3. One hundred thousand can be written as a power of 10.
4. The decimal 0.045391 rounded to the nearest ten thousandth is 0.0454.

Reviewing Concepts and Skills

Write each number in word form and in expanded form. *(pages 4–5)*

5. 518.60 **6.** 24,254,364 **7.** 25.30075 **8.** 1,118,918.96

Compare. Write >, <, or = for each ●. *(pages 6–7)*

9. 42.6 ● 426 **10.** 2.006 ● 2.06 **11.** 40,876 ● 40.876

12. 1.010 ● 1.0100 **13.** 6.312 ● 6.3012 **14.** 8.55 ● 85.5

Order from least to greatest. *(pages 6–7)*

15. 3.007 31.08 0.994 3.56 **16.** 11.34 0.056 1.54 0.0193

Round each number to the underlined place. *(pages 8–9)*

17. $16.8\underline{5}2$ **18.** $\underline{2}.647$ **19.** $4.62\underline{7}7$ **20.** $3.\underline{9}68$

Write each number in expanded form, using powers of 10. *(pages 10–11)*

21. 9,000,000 **22.** 70 **23.** 0.15 **24.** 0.0002

Write each number in standard form. *(pages 10–11)*

25. $(2 \times 10^5) + (3 \times 10^3) + (7 \times 10^0)$ **26.** $(4 \times 10^4) + (2 \times 10^{-1}) + (9 \times 10^{-2})$

Find each sum or difference. *(pages 12–13)*

27. 42.3 + 8.5 **28.** 18.52 + 63.7 **29.** 4.29 − 2.19

30. 2,564.9 + 8.6 **31.** 2,478 − 6.4 **32.** 150,000,000 − 456,000

Find each product or quotient. *(pages 18–23, 28–37)*

33. $1{,}225 \times 41$ **34.** 25×0.06 **35.** 415.3×4.022 **36.** 5.64×2.003

37. $5{,}478 \div 4$ **38.** $26\overline{)4{,}519}$ **39.** $6\overline{)0.81}$ **40.** $15\overline{)41.7}$

41. $640.22 \div 3.4$ **42.** $0.195 \div 0.15$ **43.** 75×10^3 **44.** $1{,}600 \div 10^2$

Complete. *(pages 38–40)*

45. 629 mL = ■ L **46.** 950 km = ■ m **47.** 3.6 t = ■ g **48.** 7 cm = ■ m

Solve. *(pages 14–15, 24–25, 42–43)*

49. A school needs to buy new classroom chairs to replace broken ones. One new chair costs $40. If 17 new chairs are needed, what will be the total cost to the school?

50. Natasha and her mother are shopping at a farmers' market. They spend $1.50 on squash, $1.92 on eggplant, and $2.70 on tomatoes. If all the vegetables are $1.20 per pound, how many pounds of each vegetable do they buy?

51. The students in a drama club are electing officers for this year. The five students running for office received the votes shown on the bar graph at the right.

a. How many votes were cast in all?

b. How many more votes were received by Katrina than by Laura?

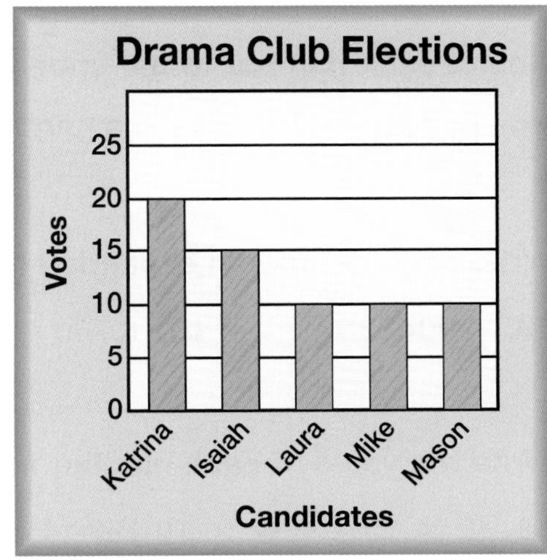

Brain Teasers Math Reasoning

Productive Pairs

Find all the pairs below whose product is 24. Then find sets of three numbers whose product is 24.

8 14 2.4 100 9 3
0.5 2 4 6 10 5 1.2
0.24 0.6 18

What's the Point?

Place the decimal point in the following quotients.

$2.4\overline{)14.28} = 595$

$0.65\overline{)11.96} = 184$

$13\overline{)0.0845} = 00065$

Internet Brain Teasers
Visit **www.eduplace.com/kids/mhm** for more *Brain Teasers.*

Chapter Test

Write each number in word form and in expanded form.

1. 18,575,819 **2.** 0.0134 **3.** 44.86 **4.** 6.08167

Compare. Write >, <, or = for each ●.

5. 320.010 ● 320.10 **6.** 1,540.050 ● 1,540.05 **7.** 0.00054 ● 0.0045

Order from greatest to least.

8. 56.4 7.07 0.692 6.70 **9.** 1,221 192.1 1.291 192.9

Round each number to the underlined place.

10. $14.7\underline{7}4$ **11.** $6\underline{3},588$ **12.** $2.\underline{3}9$ **13.** $101.43\underline{2}5$

Write each number in expanded form, using powers of 10.

14. 0.0045 **15.** 6,700 **16.** 0.97 **17.** 800,000

Write the value of each number in short word form.

18. $(8 \times 10^3) + (7 \times 10^1) + (4 \times 10^0)$ **19.** $(3 \times 10^4) + (2 \times 10^3) + (7 \times 10^{-1})$

Find each sum or difference.

20. 45.7 + 0.06 **21.** 3,596.4 − 18.31 **22.** 54,842 − 1,139

23. 0.0447 + 0.89 **24.** 12,454.67 − 5.998 **25.** 3.0097 + 0.854

Find each product or quotient.

26. 364 × 87 **27.** 4.2 × 1.4 **28.** 224 ÷ 32 **29.** $22.5 \div 10^2$

30. 0.314 × 5 **31.** 146.4 ÷ 12 **32.** 614.88 ÷ 2.4 **33.** $1,642.9 \times 10^3$

Complete.

34. 46.8 km = ■ dam **35.** 6,062 mL = ■ L **36.** 1.8 t = ■ kg **37.** 14.5 mm = ■ m

Solve.

38. Rosa is making piñatas out of newspaper, glue, and colored tissue paper. The supplies she needs to make one piñata cost \$1.79. If Rosa has \$7.00, does she have enough money to make 5 piñatas? Explain.

39. In Gabriel's history class, the students took notes for 15 minutes, watched a video for 8 minutes, and discussed homework for 10 minutes. The time remaining was spent working on research projects. If the class was an hour long, how much time did the students spend on their projects?

40. Kasha and her mother bought 612 g of mangoes, 2,170 g of bananas, and 1,880 g of oranges at the grocery store. How many kilograms of fruit did they buy in all?

Write About It

Solve each problem. Use correct math vocabulary to explain your thinking.

1. The students in Mr. Dorman's science class planted tree seedlings and are monitoring their growth. The bar graph shows the height of each tree in inches. Use the bar graph to answer the questions.

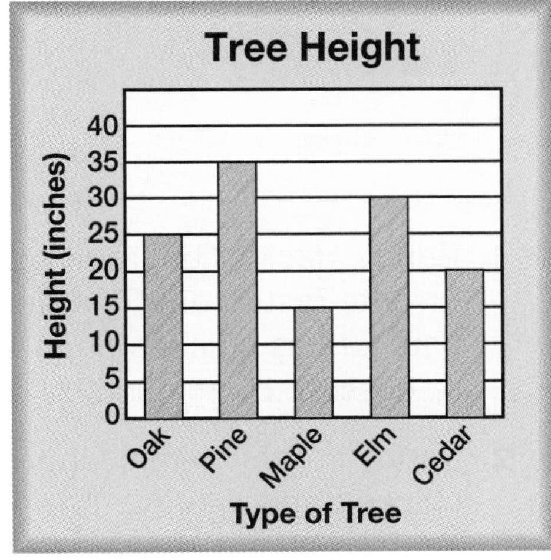

a. Explain how you can use the bar graph to find the difference in height between the tallest tree and the shortest tree.

b. How tall will the maple tree be in six months if it grows 1.75 inches each month? Explain the steps you used to find the answer.

c. Which two trees are closest in height? What is the difference in height between these trees?

2. Tina wants to buy two roses and three carnations as a surprise for her mother. Each rose costs \$1.50, and each carnation costs \$1.20. Tina has \$8.05.

a. If she buys all five flowers, how much money will she have left? Explain the method you used to find the answer.

b. Does she have enough money left to buy more flowers?

Another Look

Use the menu to solve each problem. Show all your work.

Menu
Side Dishes
Taco Salad ... $3.50
Quesadillas .. $2.25
Cheese Nachos $1.50
Baked Potato $1.75
Cole Slaw.... $1.00
Main Dishes
Chicken and Rice $6.95
Beef Fajitas $8.95
Chicken Fingers .. $4.50
Chimichangas $5.95
Beef Burritos $4.95
Desserts
Flan $3.35
Baked Apples $2.45
Fruit Empanadas .. $3.15

1. Randy, Becky, CJ, Lauren, and Ty go to eat dinner at their favorite restaurant. Ty orders quesadillas, beef fajitas, and flan. CJ has chicken fingers and does not order a side dish or dessert. How much do these two meals cost?
2. Randy orders chimichangas. Becky and Lauren each have chicken and rice. All three have quesadillas and baked apples. What is the total cost of these three meals?
3. **Look Back** CJ has a coupon for $10.50 off the total bill. What is the final cost of the five meals?
4. **Analyze** How much will each person pay if Randy, Becky, CJ, Lauren, and Ty divide the bill equally?

Enrichment

Scientific Notation

New Vocabulary
scientific notation

Scientific notation is a way of writing numbers as a product of a number between 1 and 10 and a power of 10.

A number in scientific notation can be written in standard form.

Write 2.9×10^5 in standard form.

- Multiply the first factor by the power of 10.

$10^5 = 100,000$

and $2.9 \times 100,000 = 290,000$

so $2.9 \times 10^5 = 290,000$

Write 4.3×10^{-6} in standard form.

- Multiply the first factor by the power of 10.

$10^{-6} = \frac{1}{1,000,000} = 0.000001$

and $4.3 \times 0.000001 = 0.0000043$

so $4.3 \times 10^{-6} = 0.0000043$

Write 150,000,000 in scientific notation.

Step 1 Move the decimal point to form a number between 1 and 10.

1.50,000,000.

Step 2 Multiply by a power of 10 to get the original number.

$150,000,000 = 1.5 \times 100,000,000$

and $100,000,000 = 10^8$

so $150,000,000 = 1.5 \times 10^8$

Write 0.00097 in scientific notation.

Step 1 Move the decimal point to form a number between 1 and 10.

0.0009.7

Step 2 Multiply by a power of 10 to get the original number.

$0.00097 = 9.7 \times 0.0001$

and $0.0001 = \frac{1}{10,000} = 10^{-4}$

so $0.00097 = 9.7 \times 10^{-4}$

Write each number in scientific notation or standard notation.

1. 4,300,000 **2.** 4.5×10^4 **3.** 8.9×10^3 **4.** 540,000

5. 0.00032 **6.** 1.4×10^{-3} **7.** 5.1×10^{-5} **8.** 0.00092

Explain Your Thinking

► When you are writing a number in scientific notation, how can you use counting to tell what power of ten to use?

CHAPTER 2

Data Analysis and Statistics

Why Learn About Data Analysis and Statistics?

Learning about data analysis and statistics will enable you to collect, organize, and display data in different types of graphs, tables, and diagrams.

If you do research on how the number of computers used in schools has changed over the years, you can plot the data on a graph to show how the number has changed over time.

These two boys are playing soccer. Their coaches might graph the scores of the two teams during the soccer season to compare their performances.

Reviewing Vocabulary

Understanding math vocabulary helps you become a successful problem solver. Here are some math vocabulary words you should know.

mean the quotient of the sum of the data in a set divided by the number of data points in the set

median the middle number in a set of data when the numbers are arranged in order or the average of the two middle numbers

mode the number or numbers that appear most often in a set of data

frequency table a table used to record the number of times an outcome occurs

histogram a type of graph used to display data that have been organized into intervals

Reading Words and Symbols

When you read mathematics, sometimes you read only words, sometimes you read words and symbols, and sometimes you read only symbols.

In this chapter, you will use different kinds of graphs to display and analyze data. Graphs provide information that can be "read" more easily in a picture.

A line plot shows how often something happens.

The line plot on the right shows how many home runs were hit by 15 players in a season.

Each X stands for a player. Two players hit 3 home runs.

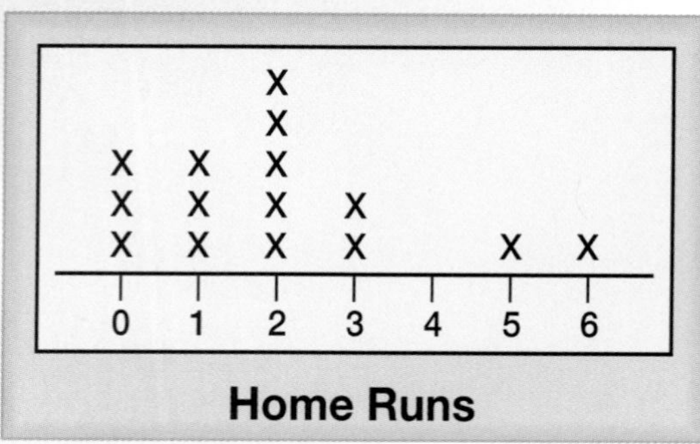

Try These

1. Find the least and greatest numbers in each list.

   a. 23 45 67 54 53 12 45 78 9 b. 4 6 7 2 1 5 12 678 743 2

2. Find the median in each ordered list.

   a. 5, 8, 12 b. 3, 45, 67, 77, 86

   c. 345, 367, 468, 723, 732 d. 897, 899, 907, 986, 1,098

3. Order the numbers from least to greatest.

   a. 34 56 43 21 32 b. 99 67 8 786 567 45 2

4. What is the least number in the list? 34 56 43 21 32

5. What is the greatest number in the list? 99 67 8 786 567 45 2

6. Find the mean of each list of numbers.

   a. 4 and 8 b. 89, 76, 57 c. 56, 32, 7, 5

7. What numbers do these tally marks represent?

   a. 𝍸 III b. 𝍸 𝍸 𝍸 I c. 𝍸 𝍸 IIII

Upcoming Vocabulary

Write About It Here are some other vocabulary words you will learn in this chapter. Watch for these words. Write their definitions in your journal.

data set
measures of central tendency
cluster
gap
outlier
stem-and-leaf plot
stem
leaf
box-and-whisker plot
quartile
extreme

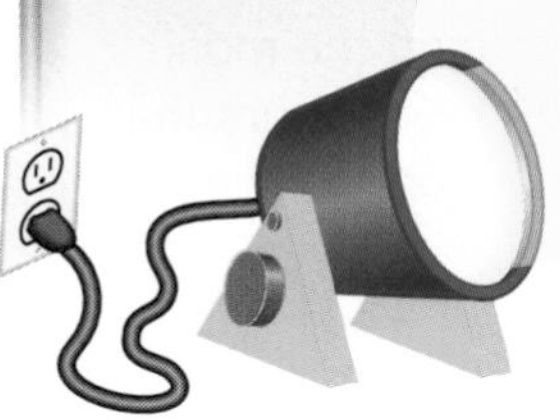

Use Statistics

You will learn how to describe data, using the mean, the median, the mode, and the range.

New Vocabulary
data set

Learn About It

Sometimes you want to use a single number to represent a collection of numbers, or a **data set**. The mean, the median, and the mode can be used to represent a data set. The range represents the spread between the greatest and the least values.

Eleven student volunteers pledged the following number of hours at a senior citizens' center.

1, 5, 5, 5, 7, 8, 10, 10, 15, 17, 60

How can you describe these data?

Different Ways to Describe a Data Set

You can use the mean, or average.

The **mean** of a data set is the quotient of the sum of the data divided by the number of data points in the set.

mean = 143 ÷ 11 = 13

The **mean**, 13, shows that the total amount of time pledged would be the same if each student pledged 13 hours.

You can use the median.

The **median** is the middle number in a set of data when the data are arranged in order. For an even number of data points, the median is the average of the two middle numbers.

median = 8

The **median**, 8, is in the middle. It shows that the number of students pledging less than 8 hours equals the number pledging more than 8 hours.

You can use the mode.

The **mode** is the number or numbers that appear most often in a data set. Sometimes a data set has no mode or has more than one mode.

mode = 5

The **mode,** 5, shows that more students pledged 5 hours than any other amount of time.

You can use the range.

The **range** is the difference between the greatest and the least values in a set of data.

range = 60 − 1 = 59

The **range**, 59, shows that the student who pledged the most time pledged 59 more hours than the student who pledged the least time.

Explain Your Thinking

- ► Can the mean, the median, and the mode ever be the same number? Explain.
- ► When and why do you need to find the mean of two numbers to find the median?

Guided Practice

Find the mean, median, mode, and range for each data set.

1. 7, 10, 3, 2, 5, 7, 1

2. 7, 11, 2, 3, 12, 1

Ask Yourself

- How do I arrange the numbers?
- How many numbers are in the data set?

Independent Practice

Find the mean, median, mode, and range for each data set.

3. 1, 4, 19, 20, 9, 10, 14

4. 54, 72, 12, 90

5. 10, 54, 101, 6

6. 100, 90, 45, 88, 87

7. 94, 350, 20, 20, 106

8. 800, 1,000, 900, 860, 20, 40, 1,000

Problem Solving • Reasoning

9. The Helping Hand shelter serves the following numbers of meals in one week: 22, 25, 31, 25, 30, 32, 45. Find the mean, the median, and the mode.

10. **Logical Thinking** Add one data point to the data set in Problem 9 to create a second mode and to increase the mean of the data set.

11. **Analyze** The mean of four numbers is 20. Three of the numbers are 17, 18, and 23. What is the fourth number?

12. **Write Your Own** Create your own data set that has one mode and a mean that is a whole number. The median should be one of the numbers in your data set.

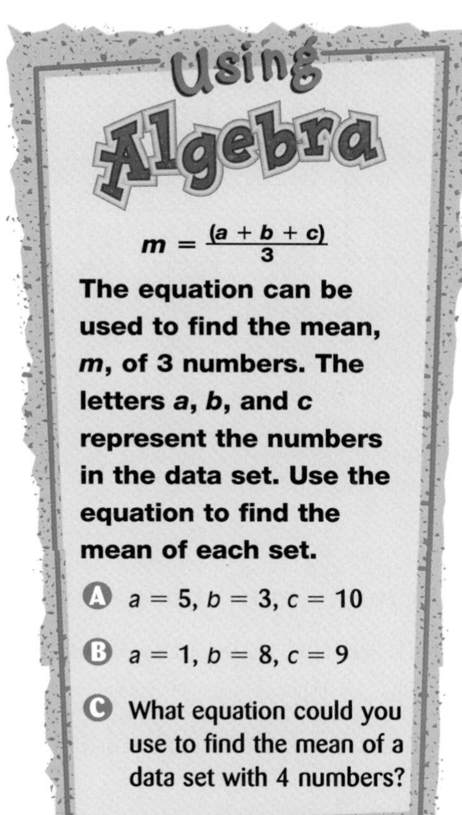

$$m = \frac{(a + b + c)}{3}$$

The equation can be used to find the mean, *m*, of 3 numbers. The letters *a*, *b*, and *c* represent the numbers in the data set. Use the equation to find the mean of each set.

A $a = 5, b = 3, c = 10$

B $a = 1, b = 8, c = 9$

C What equation could you use to find the mean of a data set with 4 numbers?

Mixed Review • Test Prep

Evaluate. *(pages 18–19, 22–23, 28–29, 32–33)*

13. 7.49×0.3

14. $81.27 \div 3$

15. 502×20

16. $3,040 \div 5$

17 Which of these decimals is equivalent to four and eight hundredths? *(pages 4–5)*

A 0.048 **C** 4.08

B 0.48 **D** 4.80

Extra Practice See Set A on page 90.

Read and Make Double Bar Graphs

You will learn how to interpret and make a double bar graph.

Review Vocabulary
double bar graph
scale
interval

Learn About It

Mapleton Middle School is holding student elections. Linda and Amad poll 50 girls and 50 boys to find out which candidates are in the lead in the race for class president. Then they make a **double bar graph** to organize their data.

A double bar graph is useful when you want to compare two data sets.

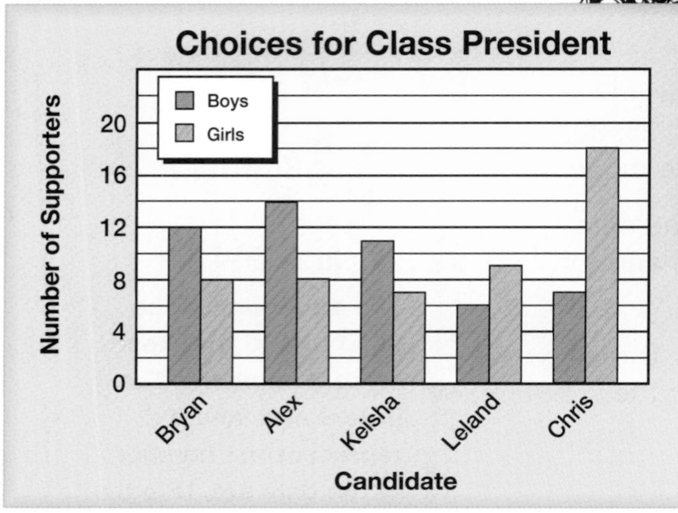
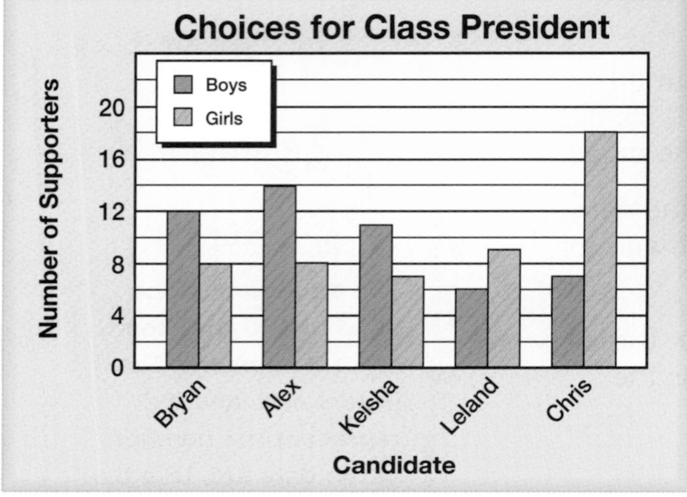

How many more boys than girls plan to vote for Alex?

- Find the difference between the heights of the bars above Alex's name. $14 - 8 = 6$

Six more boys than girls plan to vote for Alex.

Which candidate has the greatest difference between the numbers of boy supporters and girl supporters?

- Find the greatest difference in the heights of the bars above each candidate's name.

Chris has the greatest difference. Eleven more girls than boys plan to vote for Chris.

Linda and Amad are writing an article about the campaign for the student newspaper. In their article they want to compare the number of hours each candidate spent campaigning in school and out of school. They can use a double bar graph to display their data.

Hours Spent Campaigning

Name	In School	Out of School
Bryan	2	$\frac{1}{2}$
Alex	$1\frac{1}{2}$	2
Keisha	$\frac{1}{2}$	3
Leland	3	3
Chris	$\frac{1}{2}$	$\frac{1}{2}$

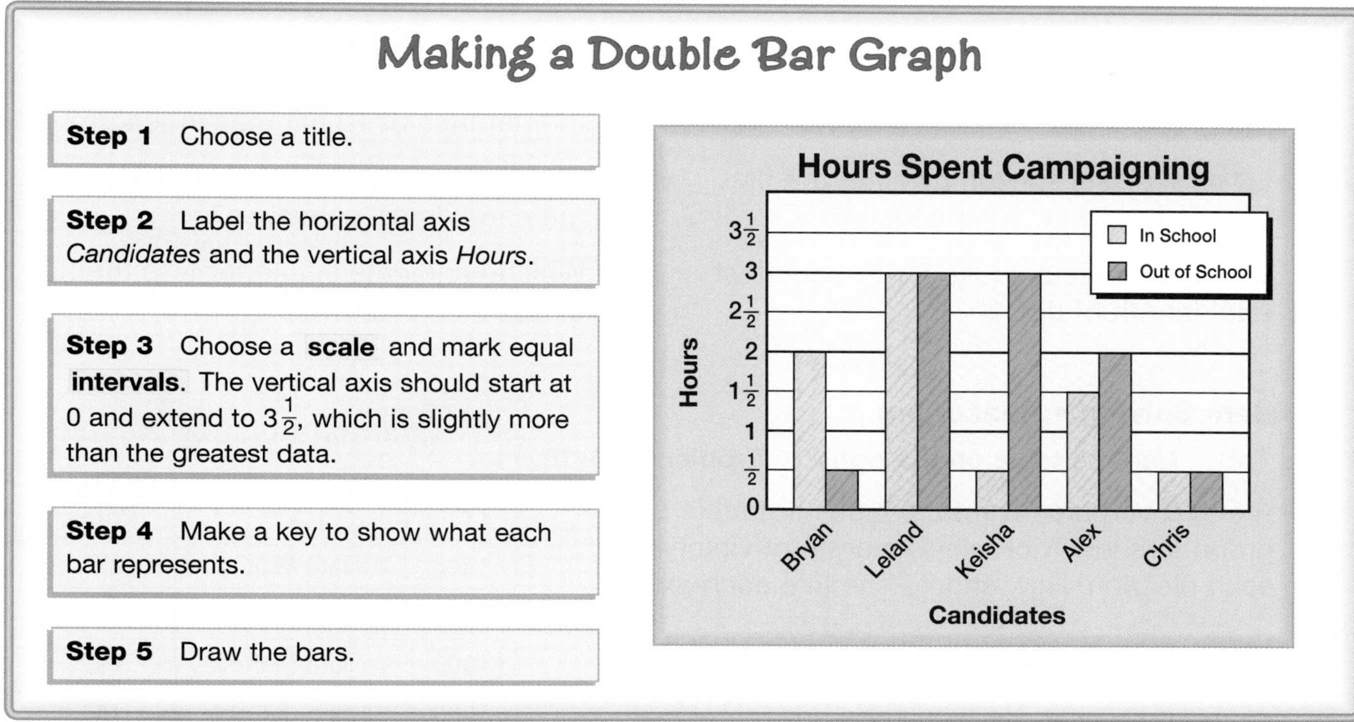

Making a Double Bar Graph

Step 1 Choose a title.

Step 2 Label the horizontal axis *Candidates* and the vertical axis *Hours*.

Step 3 Choose a **scale** and mark equal **intervals**. The vertical axis should start at 0 and extend to $3\frac{1}{2}$, which is slightly more than the greatest data.

Step 4 Make a key to show what each bar represents.

Step 5 Draw the bars.

Explain Your Thinking

- ► Why are all the candidates listed on the same axis?
- ► Are $\frac{1}{2}$-hour intervals a better choice for the vertical axis than 5-hour intervals? Why?

Guided Practice

Use the double bar graph above for Problems 1–4.

1. Which candidate spent the most time campaigning in school?

2. Which candidate had the greatest difference between time spent campaigning in school and time spent campaigning out of school?

3. Which candidate spent the least total time campaigning?

4. The graph displays two data sets. What is the mode or modes of each set?

Ask Yourself

- How do I use the key to determine the category I want?

Independent Practice

Use the table on the right for Problems 5 and 6.

5. To make a double bar graph, what interval would you use on the vertical axis, 1, 2, 5, or 10 minutes? Why?
6. Make a double bar graph to display the data.

Lengths of Speeches (minutes)		
Candidate	**First Speech**	**Second Speech**
Smith	10	15
Jones	5	20
Barrett	20	20
Provost	20	10

Use the double bar graph from Problem 6 for Problems 7–12.

7. Which candidate's two speeches had the greatest difference in length?
8. Which candidate's two speeches had a difference of 10 minutes in length?
9. Is the shortest speech given in the first or the second set of speeches?
10. What is the mean of the lengths of all the candidates' speeches?
11. Which candidate spoke for the greatest total length of time?
12. Which candidate spoke for less total time, Smith or Provost?

Problem Solving • Reasoning

Use Data **Use the table on the right for Problems 13–16.**

13. Predict Veronica wants to make a double bar graph to show McKinley's margin of victory in each election. How should she title each axis?
14. Cedric compares the number of votes each candidate received in 1896 to the number received in 1900. He labels the horizontal axis *Candidate*. What information should Cedric include in the key?
15. Analyze Which interval is the best choice for graphing the votes, 2, 25, or 200? Why?
16. Make a double bar graph to display the data in the table. The key should include different colors to represent McKinley and Bryan.

Presidential Election Results		
Year	**Candidate**	**Electoral Votes**
1896	William McKinley	271
1896	William J. Bryan	176
1900	William McKinley	292
1900	William J. Bryan	155

William J. Bryan

William McKinley

Mixed Review • Test Prep

Evaluate. *(pages 32–37)*

17. 4,000 ÷ 10
18. 3.6 ÷ 5
19. 52.19 ÷ 1.7
20. 12.24 ÷ 0.12

21. Which number is equivalent to 49,621.94 rounded to the hundreds place? *(pages 8–9)*

A 49,600 **B** 49,620 **C** 49,622 **D** 50,000

Extra Practice See Set B on page 90.

Practice Game

Guess the Mode

Practice making graphs by playing this game with your classmates. Check your prediction against your actual data.

What You'll Need

- *two number cubes, labeled 1–6*
- *Teaching Tool 2 or centimeter grid paper*
- *markers or color pencils*

Players
2 or more

Here's What to Do

1. Each player uses Teaching Tool 2 or creates a graph with *Sum Rolled* for the horizontal axis and *Times Rolled* for the vertical axis. The horizontal axis should have 11 columns for the sums 2 through 12. The vertical axis should extend to at least 8.
2. Before starting, each player predicts the mode of the sums and records the prediction. The object of the game is to make a prediction that is close to the mode of the sums after the two number cubes are rolled 24 times.
3. Each player rolls the cubes, finds the sum of the two numbers rolled, and fills in a square on the graph for that sum. Play until each player has rolled and graphed 24 sums.
4. Each player uses his or her graph to find the mode. The player whose prediction is closest to the mode of his or her data is the winner.

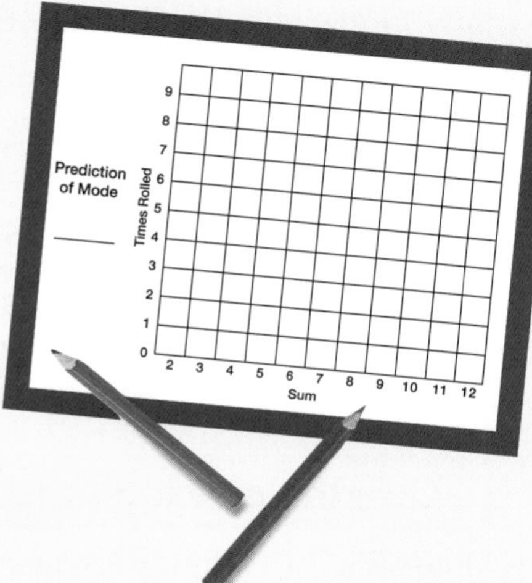

Share Your Thinking How did you predict the mode? Will you change your prediction if you play again? Why?

Frequency Tables and Histograms

You will learn how to read and interpret frequency tables and histograms.

Review Vocabulary
frequency table
histogram

Learn About It

Sometimes you want to find how often data occur in given intervals, or the frequency of events. To do this you need to organize the data in a **frequency table**. You can then display the data in a type of graph called a **histogram**.

Jessica and Nick are staff writers for their school newspaper. For a feature story they asked their classmates how long their latest family vacations lasted.

How many family vacations lasted 5–14 days?

Days on Vacation

1, 2, 2, 2, 3, 3, 5, 5, 7, 7, 7, 7, 7, 10, 10, 10, 12, 12, 14, 14, 14, 15, 18, 21, 21, 21, 24, 24, 60

Different Ways to Display Frequency of Events

You can use a frequency table.

Jessica divides the days into equal intervals. She uses a tally mark to record each response. Then she counts the tally marks and records the frequency.

Lengths of Vacations

Intervals (days)	Tally Marks	Frequency
0–4	~~||||~~ |	6
5–9	~~||||~~ ||	7
10–14	~~||||~~ |||	8
15–19	||	2
20–24	~~||||~~	5
25 and more	|	1

You can use a histogram.

Nick divides the horizontal axis into 5-day intervals. There are no gaps between the intervals in a histogram, so the bars touch each other. The vertical axis shows the frequency in each interval.

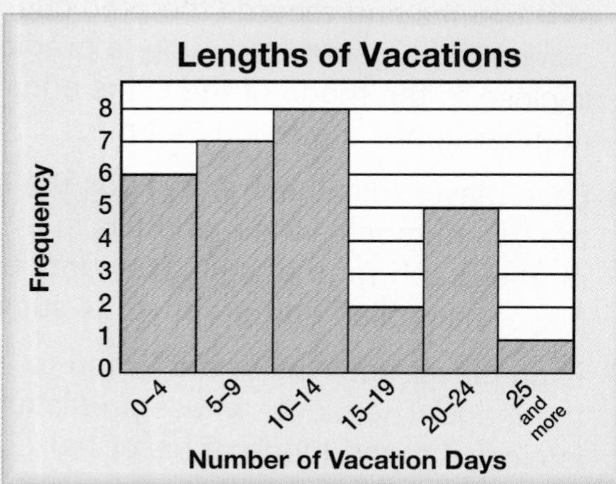

Add the frequency for 5–9 days and the frequency for 10–14 days. $7 + 8 = 15$

Solution: Fifteen family vacations lasted 5–14 days.

Explain Your Thinking

► What are some similarities and differences between the histogram and a bar graph?

Guided Practice

Use the frequency table or the histogram on page 66 for Problems 1–3.

1. How many families spent 0–4 days on vacation?

2. Can you know the length of an individual family's vacation? Why or why not?

3. How many more families spent 5–9 days on vacation than 15–19 days on vacation?

> **Ask Yourself**
> - Which interval should I look at?
> - Do I need to add or subtract?

Independent Practice

Use the histogram on the right for Problems 4–7.

4. How many students exercise less than 20 minutes each day?

5. How many more students exercise 40–49 minutes than 50–59 minutes?

6. What is the maximum possible number of students who don't exercise at all?

7. Do most of the students exercise 30 or more minutes? Explain.

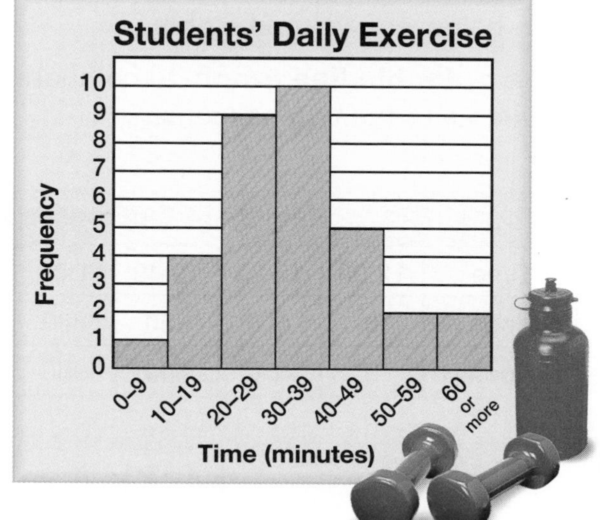

Problem Solving • Reasoning

Use the histogram on the right for Problems 8–11.

8. Look at the histogram. Are most of the skaters less than 15 years old? Explain.

9. **Analyze** Which age group has 6 more skaters than the 20–24 age group? Explain.

10. How many ice skaters are between 10 and 29 years old?

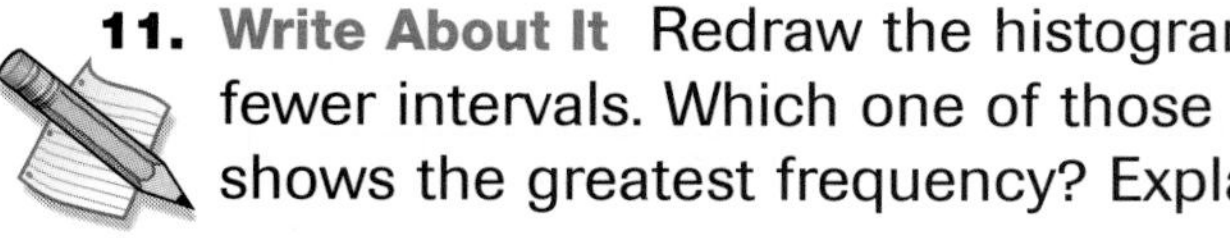

11. **Write About It** Redraw the histogram, using fewer intervals. Which one of those intervals shows the greatest frequency? Explain.

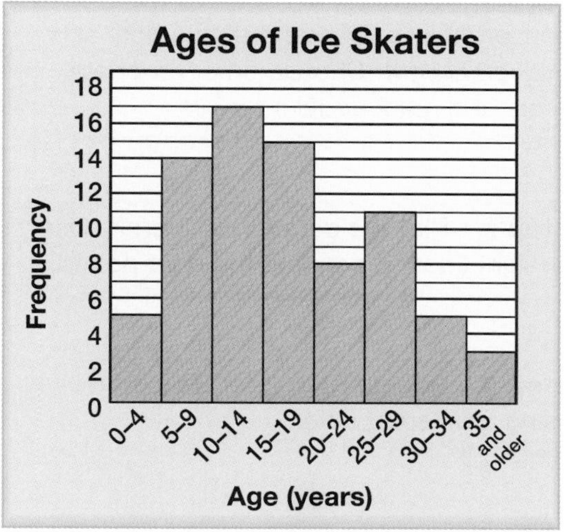

Mixed Review • Test Prep

Complete. *(pages 38–40)*

12. 142.4 g = ■ kg **13.** 0.625 m = ■ mm **14.** 7.6 L = ■ mL

15 What is the product of 423 and 1,000? *(pages 36–37)*

A 4,230 **B** 42,300 **C** 423,000 **D** 4,230,000

Extra Practice See Set C on page 90.

Read and Make Double Line Graphs

You will learn how to interpret and make double line graphs.

Review Vocabulary
double line graph

Learn About It

Two hot-air balloons both lifted off at 12:00 noon. The height above ground was recorded every 20 minutes. The table below shows the heights.

Make a **double line graph** to compare the flights of the two balloons.

Heights of Balloons in feet							
Time	12:00	12:20	12:40	1:00	1:20	1:40	2:00
Balloon A	0	400	650	800	800	600	0
Balloon B	0	450	600	900	900	650	0

Making a Double Line Graph

Step 1 Draw the axes. Label the horizontal axis *Time* and the vertical axis *Balloon Height*. Choose an appropriate scale and mark equal intervals.

Step 2 Plot the data for Balloon *A*. Use straight lines to connect the data points.

Step 3 Repeat Step 2 for Balloon *B*, using a different color.

Step 4 Make a key to show what each line represents. Add a title to the graph.

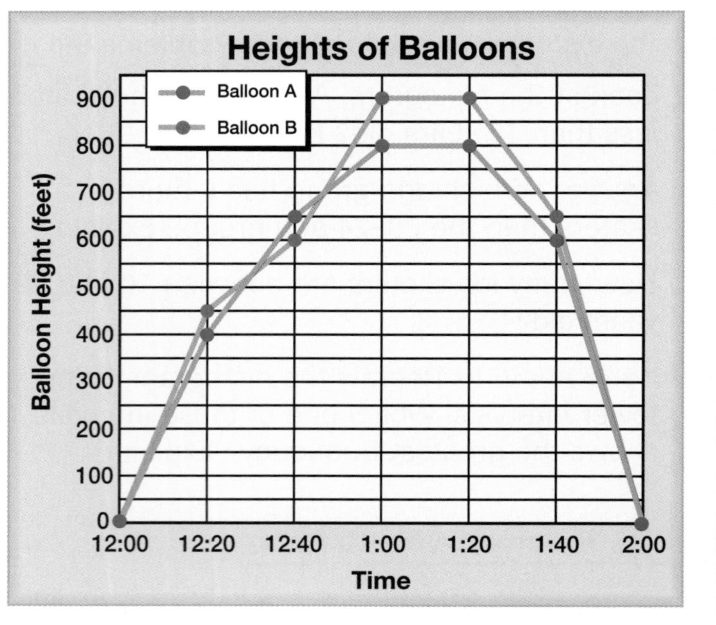

Explain Your Thinking

► How can a double line graph help you compare data?

Guided Practice

Use the graph on page 68 for Problem 1.

1. Which balloon was highest at 12:20? at 12:40? Explain how you know.

2. The table below gives flight data for two balloons. Make a double line graph to compare the heights of the balloons.

Ask Yourself

- Is the information I need to know on the horizontal or the vertical axis?
- What interval should I choose?

Heights of Balloons (feet)							
Time	4:00	4:15	4:30	4:45	5:00	5:15	5:30
Balloon C	0	250	350	500	500	350	300
Balloon D	0	200	400	550	600	500	500

Independent Practice

Use the graph on the right for Problems 3–6.

3. Which model airplane is the first to reach a height of 6 feet?

4. What is the maximum height of *Stealth Stunt?*

5. Estimate the height of *Freedom Flyer* at 17 seconds.

6. At what time is the difference in height between the two planes the greatest? Explain how you found your answer.

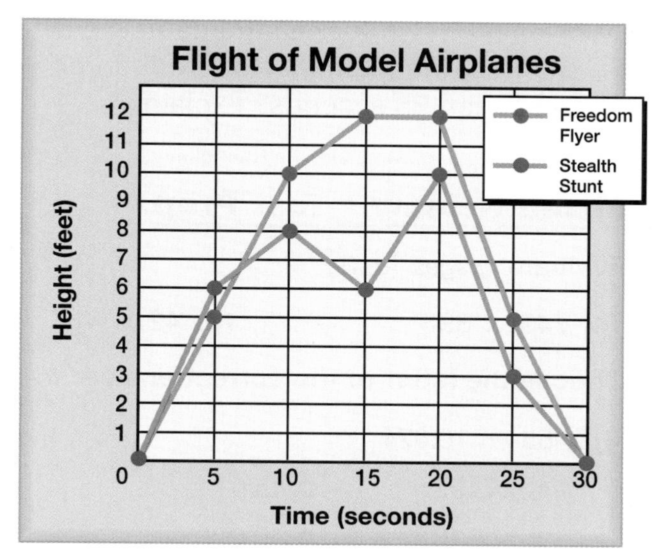

Use the table on the right for Problems 7–9.

7. *Air Acrobat* and *Cloud Climber* started at the same time. The table on the right gives the distance each airplane flew at given times. Display the data in a double line graph.

Distances Flown by Model Airplanes (feet)							
Time (seconds)	0	5	10	15	20	25	30
Air Acrobat	0	10	20	30	35	40	40
Cloud Climber	0	15	25	35	45	45	45

8. Which of the airplanes flew the farthest, *Air Acrobat* or *Cloud Climber*? Explain how you found your answer.

9. Did *Air Acrobat* or *Cloud Climber* land first? Explain how you can use your double line graph to find out.

Problem Solving • Reasoning

Solve. Choose a method.

Computation Methods

• Mental Math • Estimation • Paper and Pencil • Calculator

Use the table for Problems 10–13.

A model-airplane club held two trial flights to find which plane could fly for the longest amount of time. The table on the right shows the flight times in seconds for each plane.

Trial Flight Results (seconds)

Plane	A	B	C	D	E	F	G	H
First Trial	5	22	14	27	31	29	25	31
Second Trial	28	10	52	20	27	20	35	20

10. Find the mean, the median, the mode, and the range for each of the two trial-flight data sets.

11. **Analyze** What would happen to the mean of the first trial if Plane *A* had not flown?

12. **Compare** Look at all the data. Did most of the flights last more than or less than 25 seconds? Explain.

13. **Write About It** What type of graph would you choose to compare the two flight data sets? Explain your choice.

Mixed Review • Test Prep

Evaluate. *(pages 18–19)*

14. 745 × 398 **15.** 42 × 48 **16.** 630 × 6 **17.** 1,507 × 34

Choose the letter of the correct answer. *(pages 12–13, 18–19)*

18 55 − 10.074

A 4.4492 **C** 45.014

B 44.926 **D** 49.926

19 23 × (15 + 14)

F 345 **H** 647

G 359 **J** 667

Model Airplane Display

There are five model airplanes in a row in a display case—a biplane, a glider, a jet, a turboprop, and an ultralight. If the airplanes are arranged following the rules below, what is the order of the models?

1. The biplane cannot be next to the glider or the jet.

2. The turboprop must be next to the jet.

3. The ultralight must be first, and the biplane cannot be last.

Extra Practice See Set D on page 91.

Number Sense

Adding More Data

A survey was sent to 50 families asking how many times anyone in the family went to an amusement park in the past two years. Completed surveys were returned by 18 families, and the results were organized in this line plot.

0	1	2	3	4	5	6	7	8	9	10
	X									
	X									
	X									
X	X	X								
X	X	X	X	X	X					
X	X	X	X	X	X					

1. Find the mean, the median, and the mode of this data set.

Another 10 surveys were returned in the following three weeks. These results were also organized in a line plot.

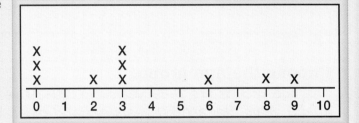

0	1	2	3	4	5	6	7	8	9	10
X			X							
X			X							
X		X	X			X		X	X	

2. Find the mean, the median, and the mode of this data set.

3. How are the two data sets the same? How are they different?

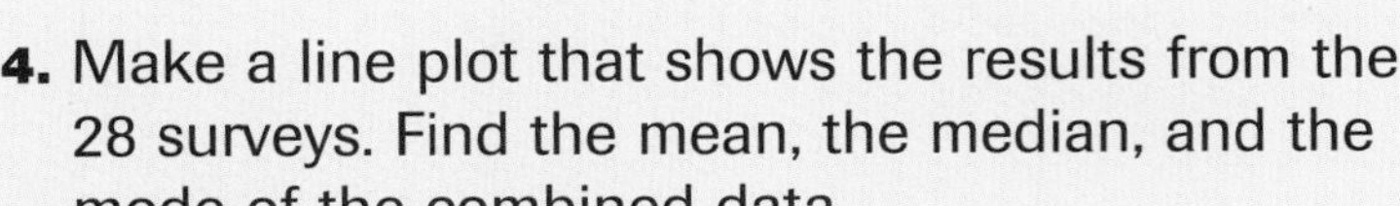

4. Make a line plot that shows the results from the 28 surveys. Find the mean, the median, and the mode of the combined data.

Explain Your Thinking

► How did the mean, the median, and the mode change when the second data set was combined with the first?

Problem-Solving Skill: Use a Graph

You will learn how to solve problems by using a variety of graphs.

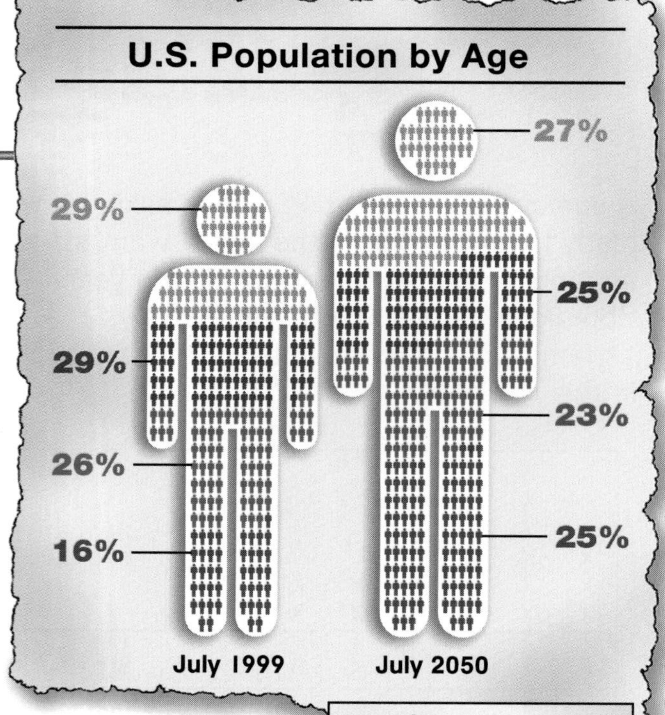

Each (symbol) = 1 million people
Yellow = 0–19 years old
Blue = 20–39 years old
Green = 40–59 years old
Red = 60 years old and older

When you use a graph to solve a problem, you need to know how to interpret the graph.

The pictographs show the U.S. population in July 1999 and the predicted population in July 2050. Each pictograph shows the population divided into age groups. The number of people in each age group is shown by symbols and as a percent of the total population.

Problem Sue will be 62 years old in 2050. How can she find the number of people in the U.S. expected to be her age or older by July 2050?

Choose the pictograph.

Since Sue wants to find information about the U.S. population in July 2050, she should choose the pictograph on the right.

Choose the age group.

The age groups are *0–19 years old*, *20–39 years old*, *40–59 years old*, and *60 years old and older*. Since Sue will be 62 years old, she should choose *60 years old and older*.

Find the information.

Count the number of symbols in the group *60 years old and older*.

There are 99 symbols. Since each symbol represents 1 million people, 99 million people are predicted to be 60 years old and older in July 2050.

Look Back Is there another way to find the number of people 60 years old and older in July 2050?

These people represent different age groups.
Left: 0–9 yr
Left center: 10–19 yr
Right center: 30–39 yr
Right: 50–59 yr

Guided Practice

Use the pictograph on page 72 and the double bar graph on the right to solve.

1. Study both graphs. How is the percent of the population aged 0–19 expected to change between 1999 and 2050?

   Think: Which graph shows the change most clearly, the pictograph or the double bar graph?

2. The number of people aged 40–59 in July 2050 is expected to be 89 million. Is this an increase in number from July 1999?

   Think: How many people were aged 40–59 in July of 1999?

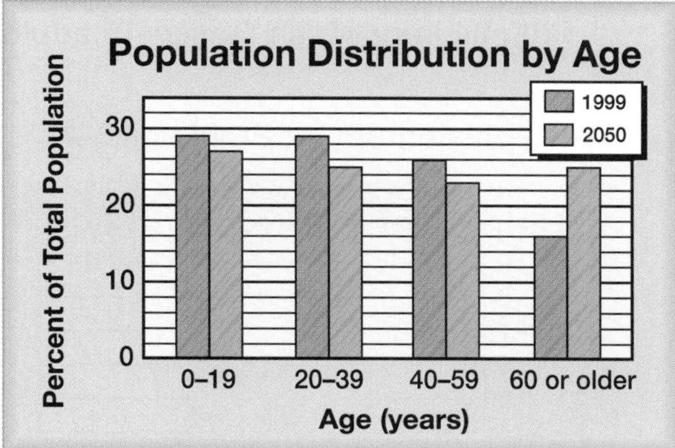

The double bar graph above displays the same information as the pictograph on page 72.

Choose a Strategy

Solve. Use these or other strategies. Use the graphs on pages 72–73 for Problems 3–5.

Problem-Solving Strategies

- **Work Backward**
- **Guess and Check**
- **Write an Equation**
- **Use Logical Thinking**

3. Between July 1999 and July 2050, which age group is predicted to increase the most as a percent of the total population? Explain.

4. In July 1999, what percent of people were aged 40 or older? What percent of people are expected to be aged 40 or older in July 2050?

5. Sue wants to redraw the pictographs, using fewer symbols. Explain how she could do this without making the graphs less accurate.

6. Sally is 2 years older than Mike but 6 years younger than Gina. Vicki is twice as old as Mike. How old is Vicki if Gina is 18 years old?

7. The population of Port Jackson doubled from 1990 to 1997. From 1987 to 1990, it increased by 1,218 people. If the 1997 population was 7,308, what was it in 1987?

8. Jim thinks of a number. If he multiplies the number by 2 and then subtracts 25, he gets the greatest three-digit number possible. What is Jim's number?

Extra Practice See 1–4 on page 93.

Quick Check

Check Your Understanding of Lessons 1–5

1. Find the mean, the median, the mode, and the range for this data set: 49, 52, 57, 45, 49, 48, 51, 45, 45.

2. Use this data to make a double bar graph comparing the number of adults and children at three family reunions: Kirk family—10 adults, 15 children; Wu family—20 adults, 10 children; Walsh family—15 adults, 15 children.

Use the histogram for Problems 3–4.

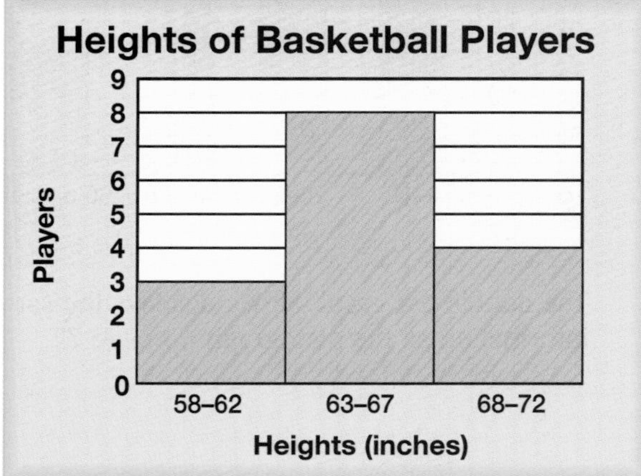

3. How many players are 63–67 in. tall?

4. What is the maximum possible number of players who are 72 in. tall?

Use the line graph for Problems 5–6.

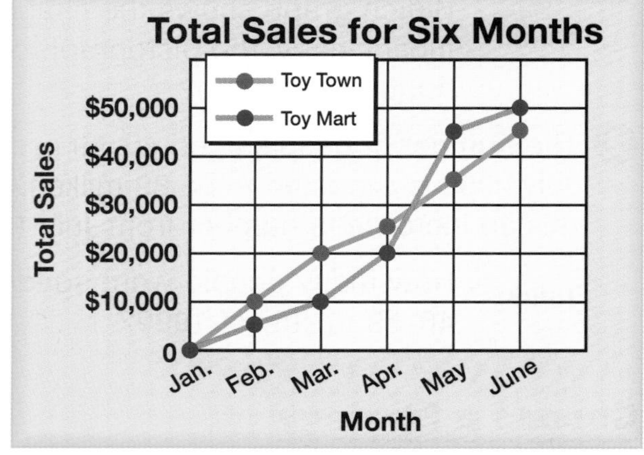

5. What were Toy Mart's sales as of May?

6. How much did Toy Town's sales increase from March to June?

How did you do?

If you had difficulty with any items in the Quick Check, you can use the following pages for review and extra practice.

Items	Review These Pages	Do These Extra Practice Items
1	pages 60–61	Set A, page 90
2	pages 62–64	Set B, page 90
3–4	pages 66–67	Set C, page 90
5–6	pages 68–70	Set D, page 91

Test Prep • Cumulative Review

Maintaining the Standards

Choose the letter of the correct answer.

1. A recycling plant recycled $8\frac{1}{2}$ metric tons of material in the last two weeks. How many kilograms did they recycle?

   A $8\frac{1}{2}$ kilograms
   B 8,000 kilograms
   C 8,500 kilograms
   D 85,000 kilograms

2. Which number is larger than 7,006,900?

   F 7,005,999 **H** 7,006,899
   G 7,006,000 **J** 7,016,000

3. Which is likely to be next if the pattern continues?

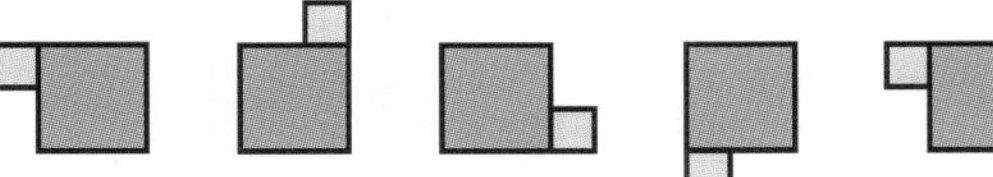

   A 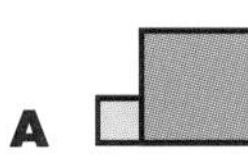
   B 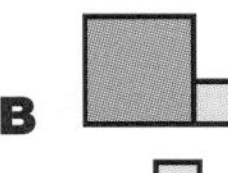
   C 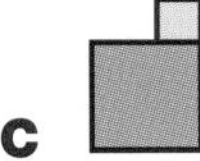
   D 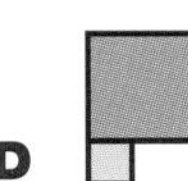

4. The audience for a concert on Friday night was 24,900 people. On Saturday, 29,767 people attended the concert. How many more people attended the concert on Saturday night?

   F 3,867 people **H** 5,767 people
   G 4,867 people **J** 5,867 people

5. Marc has $26. He buys a blank videotape for $2.95 and a new movie for $16.95. Which equation shows how much money Marc has left?

   A $26.00 + $2.95 = $28.95
   B $26.00 − $2.95 = $23.05
   C $26.00 − $19.90 = $6.10
   D $6.10 + $19.90 = $26.00

6. How many sides does a pentagon have?

   F 4
   G 5
   H 6
   J 7

7. Marisa and Marti raised $184.50 for their volleyball team. The team spent the money on 9 volleyballs. How much did they pay for each volleyball?

   A $18.45
   B $20.50
   C $41.00
   D $48.78

8. What is the area of this rectangle?

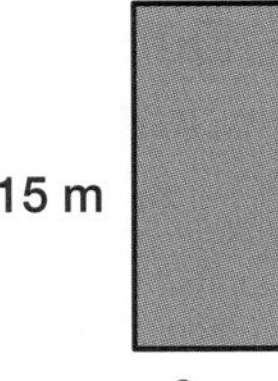

   Explain How did you find your answer?

Safe Site

Internet Test Prep
Visit **www.eduplace.com/kids/mhm** for more *Test Prep Practice.*

Choose the Most Useful Statistical Measure

You will learn how to choose the statistical measure that is most useful for a given situation.

New Vocabulary
measures of central tendency

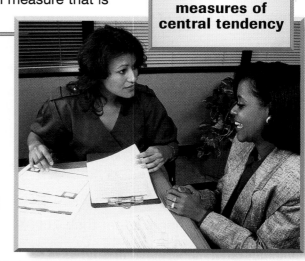

Learn About It

The mean, the median, and the mode are called **measures of central tendency** because they describe the center of a data set. Sometimes one measure may be more useful than another.

Ms. Duncan runs a small company with five employees. While making her plans for the coming year, she determined the mean, the median, and the mode of the current salaries.

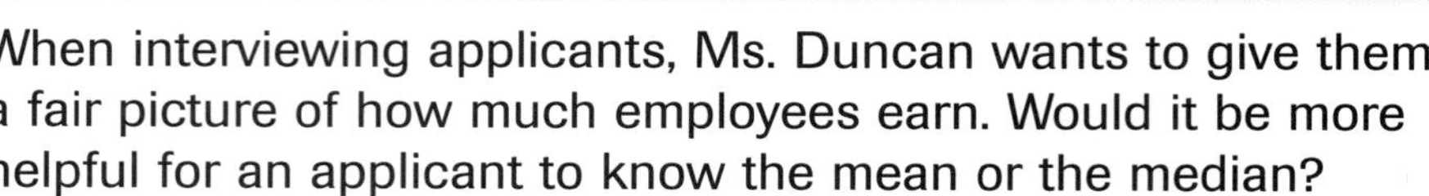

When interviewing applicants, Ms. Duncan wants to give them a fair picture of how much employees earn. Would it be more helpful for an applicant to know the mean or the median?

Since all but one of the salaries are close to the median, the **median** better represents how much a typical worker earns. The one high salary makes the mean higher.

When talking to bankers, Ms. Duncan wants to describe the average salary so they can understand how much is spent on salaries. Would the mean or the median be more helpful?

Since the total amount spent on salaries is the same as if each employee received the mean salary, the **mean** will be more helpful to the bankers.

Salaries
$28,500
$28,500
$31,000
$45,000
$97,000

Mean	$46,000
Median	$31,000
Mode	$28,500

Explain Your Thinking

► Why do you think Ms. Duncan didn't use the mode with the applicants or the bankers?

Guided Practice

Jane's spelling scores on 5 tests were 100, 100, 95, 90, and 5. Find the mean, median, and mode.

1. Which measure gives the most useful information about how well Jane can spell? Explain.
2. Which measure gives the most useful information about what grade Jane will most likely receive? Explain.

Ask Yourself

- Which measure best describes the center of the data?
- Which measure is most useful for the given purpose?

Independent Practice

Bob's spelling scores on 5 tests were 80, 80, 87, 88, and 90. Find the mean, median, and mode.

3. Which measure gives the most useful information about how well Bob can spell? Explain.

4. If Bob studies hard, which measure should he use to predict his next spelling score? Explain.

For each data set, find the mean, median, and mode. Tell which measure is most useful for describing the data. Explain why.

5. The wages paid to 5 substitute teachers last year were \$4,500, \$6,200, \$9,700, \$19,650, and \$19,650. Substitute teachers want to know how much they will earn.

6. Ann spent 5 min, 1 h, 2 h, 6 h, and 6 h using the Internet each day for the last 5 days. She wants to consider how much time she spends on the Internet.

7. Mr. Malone wants to know the average amount of gasoline he uses in a week. In the last 3 weeks, he used 5 gallons, 7 gallons, and 30 gallons.

8. Lou spent 20 min, 20 min, 20 min, 1 h, and 3 h reading each day for the last 5 days. She has an assignment to read an average of an hour every day.

Problem Solving • Reasoning

Use the data set for Problems 9–11. In the data set, *n* represents an unknown age.

14, 46, 19, 10, 39, 22, 24, 77, 19, *n*

9. What value of *n* will result in a mean of 31?

10. What value of *n* will result in a median of 23?

11. What value of *n* will result in a range of 84?

12. **Write About It** Create a set of data and a story in which the mean is the most useful measure. Tell why.

Math Is Everywhere!

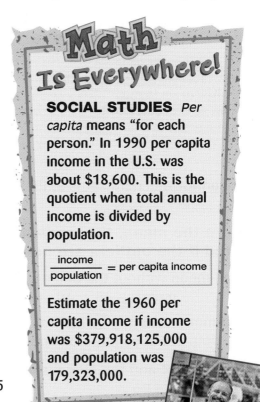

SOCIAL STUDIES *Per capita* means "for each person." In 1990 per capita income in the U.S. was about \$18,600. This is the quotient when total annual income is divided by population.

$$\frac{\text{income}}{\text{population}} = \text{per capita income}$$

Estimate the 1960 per capita income if income was \$379,918,125,000 and population was 179,323,000.

Mixed Review • Test Prep

Evaluate. *(pages 22–23)*

13. 4.82×0.3 14. 0.17×5.1 15. 15.75×2.5

Write the letter of the correct answer. *(pages 6–7)*

16. Order from greatest to least. 0.0321 0.321 0.312

A 0.321 0.0321 0.312
B 0.312 0.0321 0.321
C 0.321 0.312 0.0321
D 0.0321 0.312 0.321

Extra Practice See Set E on page 91.

Clusters, Gaps, and Outliers

You will learn how to use a line plot to show how data are distributed.

New Vocabulary
cluster
gap
outlier

Learn About It

Basketball began in Springfield, Massachusetts, in 1891. Now basketball is played around the world. Last season in Sweden, Olof played 12 basketball games. He scored the point totals below.

0, 2, 4, 2, 12, 4, 28, 10, 0, 10, 4, 32

Use a line plot to organize and describe this data set.

Using a Line Plot

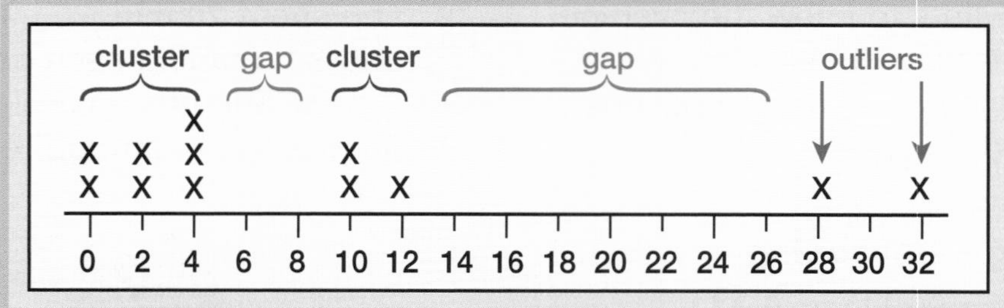

A **cluster** is formed when several data points lie in a small interval.

A **gap** is an interval that contains no data.

An **outlier** is a data point that has a value much greater than or less than other data in the set.

The mean for this data set is 9, the median is 4, and the mode is 4.

How are the mean, the median, and the mode affected if the outliers are not in the data set?

Find the mean without the outliers, 28 and 32.

$$\text{mean} = 48 \div 10 = 4.8$$

- The mean changes by more than 4 points when the data set does not include the outliers.

The median is 4 and the mode is 4.

- The median and mode are unchanged.

The first basketball team at Springfield College in 1891

Explain Your Thinking

► If the outlier 32 is replaced by 46, how will this affect the mean?

► Does a single outlier influence the mode? Explain.

Guided Practice

Use the data set 69, 70, 70, 71, 72, 74, and 92 for Problems 1–4.

1. Make a line plot of the data.

2. Identify any clusters, gaps, and outliers.

3. Find the mean, the median, the mode, and the range.

4. Suppose the outliers are not in the data set. Which statistical measure represents the data best? Explain.

> **Ask Yourself**
>
> • How do I use the line plot to find the median, the mode, and the range?

Independent Practice

Karin played in 14 basketball games last season. Use her game points on the right for Problems 5–10.

5, 6, 21, 22, 23, 23, 24, 25, 25, 26, 26, 26, 27, 29

5. Make a line plot of the data.

6. Identify any clusters, gaps, and outliers.

7. Find the mean, median, mode, and range.

8. How do the outliers affect the mean?

9. Suppose the outliers were were not in the data set. Compare the median and the mode with and without the outliers.

10. What is the least number of games needed to change the mode of the data set?

Problem Solving • Reasoning

Use Data **Use the line plot for Problems 11–13.**

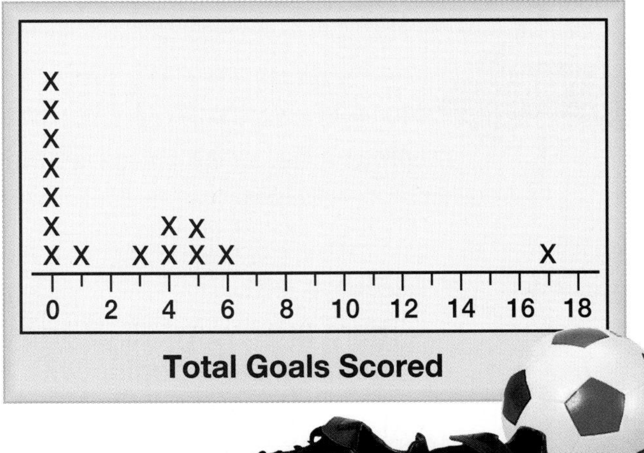

11. The line plot on the right shows the total goals scored over the season by the Taft Middle School soccer team. Identify any clusters, gaps, and outliers. Find the mean, the median, the mode, and the range.

12. **Compare** Suppose the outlier is not in the data set. Then find the mean, the median, the mode, and the range. Compare these results to the results in Problem 11.

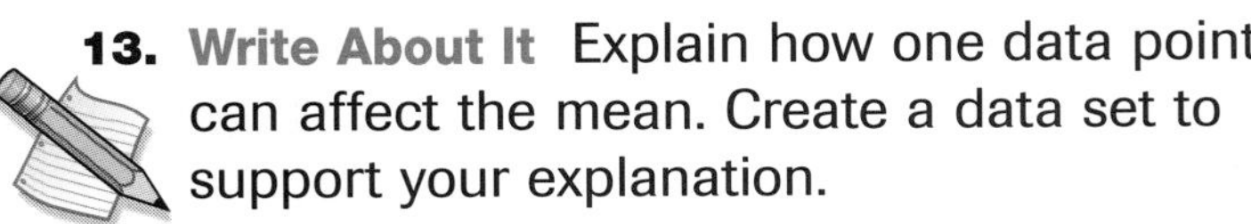

13. **Write About It** Explain how one data point can affect the mean. Create a data set to support your explanation.

Mixed Review • Test Prep

Round to the underlined place. *(pages 8–9)*

14. $48.6\underline{7}6$ **15.** $39.\underline{4}527$ **16.** $4{,}53\underline{7}.31$ **17.** $9.00\underline{5}7$ **18.** $1\underline{8}9.46$

19 How is 0.001 written as a power of ten? *(pages 10–11)*

A 10^{-4} **B** 10^{-3} **C** 10^{3} **D** 10^{4}

Problem-Solving Strategy: Make a List

You will learn how to solve a problem by making a list.

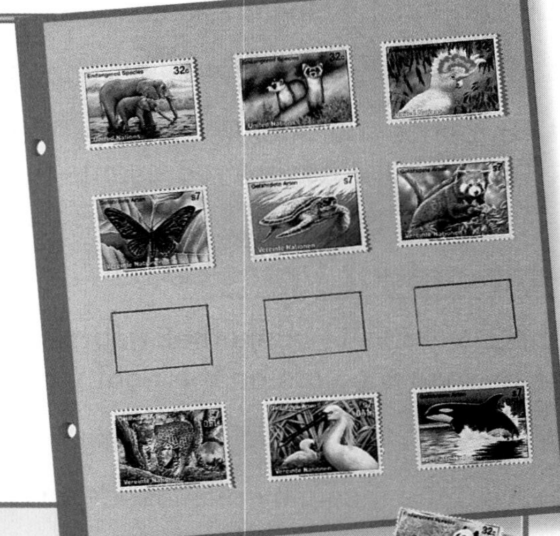

Sometimes you need to find all possible choices to solve a problem. You can make a list to organize the information.

Problem Jake is a stamp collector. Recently, he bought three stamps. His new stamps show an eagle, a panda, and an iguana. Jake wants to arrange his new stamps on a page in his album. How many different ways can he arrange the stamps in a row?

Understand

What is the question?
How many different ways can Jake arrange his three stamps?

What do you know?
There are three different stamps.
Jake wants to arrange them in a row.

Plan

How can you find the answer?
Make a list of all the possible arrangements.

Solve

Make a list.

- There are two ways to arrange the three stamps if Jake begins with the eagle.
- There are two ways to arrange the stamps if he begins with the panda.
- There are two ways if he begins with the iguana.
- There are six possible arrangements for the stamps.

eagle, panda, iguana
eagle, iguana, panda
panda, eagle, iguana,
panda, iguana, eagle
iguana, eagle, panda
iguana, panda, eagle

Look Back

Look back at the problem.
Is your answer reasonable? Explain.

Remember:
- Understand
- Plan
- Solve
- Look Back

Guided Practice

Solve each problem, using the Make a List strategy.

1. Morela has four 33-cent stamps. One has a picture of a flag, one has flowers, one has berries, and one has fish. How many different ways can Morela arrange these four stamps in a row in her album?

After choosing the first stamp, how many choices remain?

2. Ling bought four pennies that were dated 1962, 1966, 1971, and 1976. How many different ways can Ling arrange her four pennies in a row so that the two pennies made in the 1960s are not next to each other?

How can a list be organized to include all the possibilities?

Choose a Strategy

Solve. Use these or other strategies.

Problem-Solving Strategies

- **Make a List**
- **Find a Pattern**
- **Guess and Check**
- **Draw a Diagram**

3. A page in a baseball-card album holds 12 cards. One page has 8 cards on it already. How many ways can the remaining cards be arranged in 2 rows?

4. Margo buys a shirt and a pair of pants for a total of $21. If the shirt costs twice as much as the pants, how much does the shirt cost?

5. Emily collects unusual dolls. She can take two of her four dolls to the doll show. How many ways can Emily choose two dolls?

6. Soo lives 4 houses north of Al. Ty lives 12 houses south of Soo. Ben lives halfway between Al and Ty. How many houses south of Soo does Ben live?

7. At a restaurant, Ian can choose chicken, a hamburger, or fish, each with one vegetable chosen from corn, peas, or beans. How many possible meals are there?

8. Connie has 4 more fish than Jack, who has 6 fewer fish than Nina. Mark has 3 times as many fish as Jack. If Nina has 15 fish, how many does Mark have?

9. Find a pattern in the arrangement of shapes below. If the pattern continues, what is the next likely shape?

Extra Practice See 5–8 on page 93.

Stem-and-Leaf Plots

You will learn how to use stem-and-leaf plots to display large data sets.

New Vocabulary
stem
leaf
stem-and-leaf plot

Learn About It

For their biology project, Adrian and Melanie visited Internet sites for information about redwood trees. In one study, they found the following data set of diameters of redwood tree trunks in inches.

93, 99, 100, 104, 106, 107, 112, 114, 116, 120, 125, 128, 131, 163, 167

How can Adrian and Melanie display their data in a stem-and-leaf plot?

Making a Stem-and-Leaf Plot

Step 1 Write each number as tens and ones.

93 = 9 tens 3 ones
99 = 9 tens 9 ones
100 = 10 tens 0 ones
104 = 10 tens 4 ones
.
.
.
167 = 16 tens 7 ones

Step 2 In the left column, write the number of tens from least to greatest. Each of these tens will be a **stem**.

Step 3 Next to each stem, write the ones digits for all the numbers in the data set that begin with that stem. Order the ones digits from least to greatest. Each of these digits is called a **leaf**.

Step 4 Create a key to show the meaning of each point in the **stem-and-leaf plot**.

Diameters of Redwoods (inches)

Stem	Leaves
9	3 9
10	0 4 6 7
11	2 4 6
12	0 5 8
13	1
14	
15	
16	3 7

Key: 9|3 means 93 inches

Explain Your Thinking

- ► How does a stem-and-leaf plot differ from a line plot?
- ► For what kind of data set would you be most likely to use a stem-and-leaf plot? Why?
- ► How would you use a stem-and-leaf plot to find clusters, outliers, the median, and the mode?

Guided Practice

Use the stem-and-leaf plot on page 82 for Problems 1 and 2.

1. Identify any clusters, gaps, and outliers.
2. Find the mean, the median, the mode, and the range.

Ask Yourself

- What place does the stem represent?
- What place does a leaf represent?

Independent Practice

Use the data set in the chart for Problems 3–6.

12, 11, 19, 17,
34, 12, 23, 16,
13, 23, 12, 24

3. What place value should be used for the stem?
4. Make a stem-and-leaf plot. What place value does a leaf represent?
5. Identify any clusters, gaps, and outliers.
6. Find the mean, the median, the mode, and the range.

Problem Solving • Reasoning

Use the stem-and-leaf plot on the right for Problems 7–10.

7. Find the range, mean, median, and mode for the data.
8. **Compare** Are there any outliers? If so, how do they affect the mean and the median?
9. **Analyze** Suppose you add one data point to the stem-and-leaf plot. The range of the data stays the same, and no new mode is added. The new median is 218. Your data point must be less than what number? Your data point must be greater than what number?
10. **Write About It** Is it easier to use a stem-and-leaf plot or a line plot to identify clusters, gaps, and outliers? Explain.

Heights of Redwoods (feet)

Stem	Leaves
16	3 8
17	
18	
19	9
20	1 5
21	1 3 4 5 8
22	2
23	9 9
24	0 3 6 8 9

Key: 16|3 means 163 feet

Mixed Review • Test Prep

Compare. Write >, <, or = for each ●. *(pages 6–7, 12–13)*

11. 45,234,663 ● 45,324,669
12. 5.043 ● 5.03
13. 4,623 ● 4,632
14. 469.24 ● 12.67 + 266.35

15. What is 398 − 0.23? *(pages 12–13)*
 - **A** 3,977.7
 - **B** 397.77
 - **C** 379.77
 - **D** 39.777

16. What is 41.6 − 32.8? *(pages 12–13)*
 - **F** 7.44
 - **G** 8.08
 - **H** 8.8
 - **J** 74.4

Extra Practice See Set G on page 92.

LESSON 10

Box-and-Whisker Plots

You will learn how to use a box-and-whisker plot to display data.

New Vocabulary

box-and-whisker plot
quartile
extreme

Learn About It

The data set shows the lengths (in meters) of several sauropods, which are among the largest animals that have ever lived.

27, 18, 12, 10, 21, 20, 18, 25, 16

You can use a **box-and-whisker plot**, to show the distribution of these data.

Making a Box-and-Whisker Plot

Step 1 First, order the data from least to greatest. Then find the median.

Next, find the upper and lower **quartiles**, which are the middle values of each half of the data.

The **extremes** are the greatest value and the least value in the data set.

before median: 10, 12, 16, 18 — 18 (median) — after median: 20, 21, 25, 27

10 = lower extreme; 27 = upper extreme

lower quartile: $\frac{(12 + 16)}{2} = 14$

upper quartile: $\frac{(21 + 25)}{2} = 23$

Step 2 Display the five numbers as points above a number line that includes the lower and upper extremes.

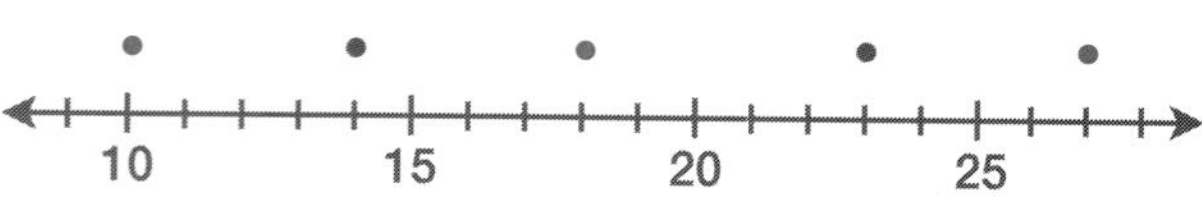

Step 3 Draw a box which ends at the lower and upper quartiles. Draw a vertical line through the box at the median. Draw whiskers from the ends of the box to the least and greatest values.

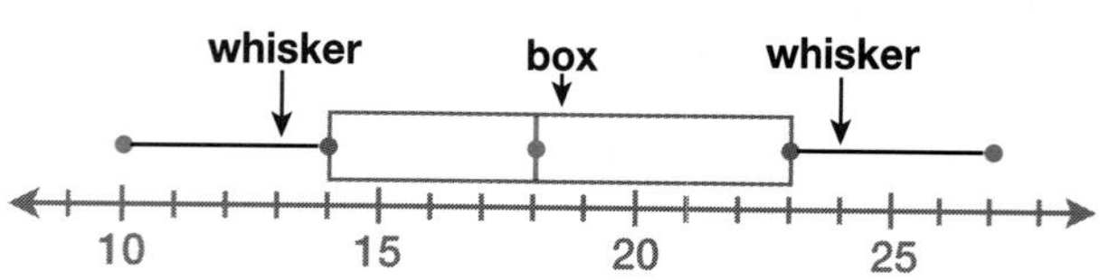

Explain Your Thinking

► About how much of the data are in the box?

Guided Practice

Use the data set below for Problems 1 and 2.

55, 78, 80, 82, 85, 85, 90, 90, 91, 91, 93, 94, 94, 95, 97

1. Find the median, the upper and lower quartiles, and the extremes of the data.

2. Make a box-and-whisker plot to display the data. Write a brief description of the data.

Ask Yourself

- How do I find the quartiles?
- What values do I need to make a box-and-whisker plot?

Independent Practice

The list on the right gives data for the lengths of teeth of several flesh-eating dinosaurs.

Use the data set on the right for Exercises 3 and 4.

3. Find the median, the upper and lower quartiles, and the extremes of the data set.

4. Make a box-and-whisker plot to display the data. Write a description of the data.

Length of Dinosaur Teeth (cm)
15, 18, 5, 8, 12, 10, 14, 18
16, 15, 15, 15, 5, 10, 16

Problem Solving • Reasoning

Use Data **The box-and-whisker plot displays 11 students' scores on a recent math test. Use the plot for Problems 5–8.**

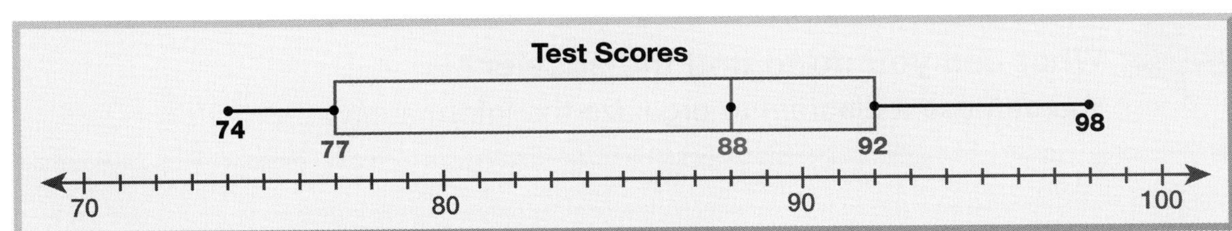

5. Write a set of 11 test scores that this box-and-whisker plot could represent.

6. **Analyze** What would happen to this box if the scores 85 and 87 were added?

7. **Predict** Suppose each score was tripled. How would the shape of this box change?

8. **Write About It** What does each part of the plot represent? Include the points and each part of the box.

Mixed Review • Test Prep

Evaluate. *(pages 32–33, 34–35)*

9. $7\overline{)42.49}$
10. 0.675 ÷ 2.5
11. $5\overline{)35.25}$
12. 32 ÷ 0.5

13. Which choice is a reasonable estimate for 34 × 43? *(pages 18–19)*

A 1,200 **B** 3,400 **C** 4,300 **D** 5,000

Extra Practice See Set H on page 92.

Problem-Solving Application: Use a Diagram

You will learn how to use a diagram to solve a problem.

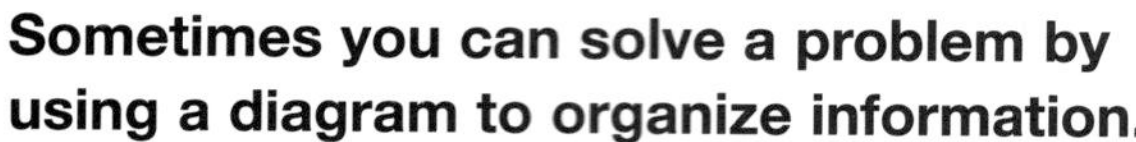

Sometimes you can solve a problem by using a diagram to organize information.

Problem Frederica is having a party. She asks three of her friends to bring their compact discs. Jill brings $\frac{1}{4}$ of the CDs, and Tina brings 6 more than Jill. Nancy brings 24 CDs. How many CDs are brought to the party?

Understand

What is the question?
How many CDs are brought to the party?

What do you know?
Jill brings $\frac{1}{4}$ of the CDs. Tina brings $\frac{1}{4}$ of the CDs plus 6 CDs. Nancy brings 24 CDs.

Plan

What can you do to find the answer?
You can use a diagram to organize the information.

Solve

Use a number strip to represent the number of CDs. Enter the information you have.

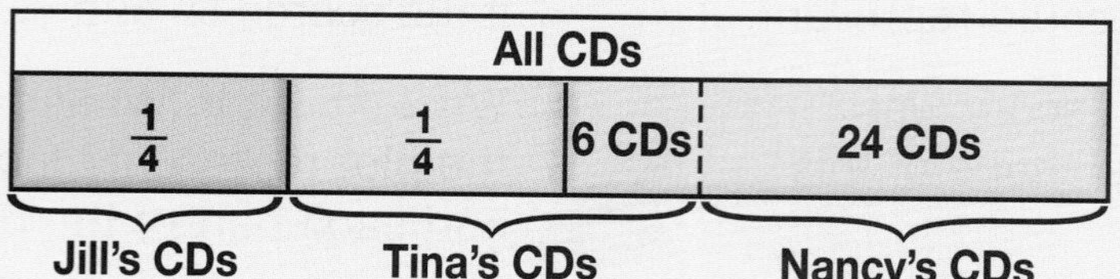

The diagram shows that 6 + 24, or 30, CDs are $\frac{1}{2}$ of the total number of CDs. So there are 60 CDs in all.

Look Back

Look back at the question. Is your answer reasonable?
How many CDs does each person have? Is the total 60?

Guided Practice

Solve.

1. Tina's father has a collection of CDs that includes jazz, country, rock and classical music. Use the diagram below to find how many CDs are in the collection.

   Think: What information should you start with?

2. Felicia spent $36 on refreshments for a party. If the food cost twice as much as the drinks, how much did Felicia spend on food and on drinks?

   Think: How can you use a diagram to help solve this problem?

Country		Jazz $\frac{1}{8}$	Rock		Classical		
						33 CDs	

Choose a Strategy

Solve. Use these or other strategies.

Problem-Solving Strategies

- **Write an Equation**
- **Guess and Check**
- **Find a Pattern**
- **Make a List**

3. One CD has 16 tracks and a playing time of 55 min. The playing time for the first four tracks is twice that of the second four tracks. The playing time for Tracks 9–16 is about 28 minutes. What is the playing time for Tracks 1–4?

4. The average playing time for the 60 CDs at Frederica's party is 48 minutes. The party lasts for 4 hours. About how many complete CDs could be played at the party? (Hint: 4 hours equals how many minutes?)

5. Nancy brought 24 CDs to the party. She brought 2 more country CDs than rock CDs. How many of each kind of CD did she bring?

6. The CD player can mix the order in which the CDs are played. If the CD player can hold 3 CDs, how many ways can the 3 CDs be played?

7. If the pattern continues, what is one possibility for the next two figures?

8. A store sold 15 CD players for a total of $1,477.50 plus tax. The total tax was $88.65. What was the price of each CD player, including tax?

Extra Practice See 9–10 on page 93.

Check Your Understanding of Lessons 6–11

Use the data sets for Problems 1–4.

1. Sam earned \$12, \$19, \$28, \$8, \$11, \$10, and \$10 each week. He wants to determine how much he is likely to earn in the next 5 weeks. Will the mean, the median, or the mode be most useful?

2. Use the data set 46, 42, 44, 33, 43, 47, and 46. Make a line plot. Identify any clusters, gaps, and outliers. Explain how the outlier affects the mean in this data set.

3. Use the data set 23, 4, 37, 20, 5, 34, 8, 4, 41, and 29. Make a stem-and-leaf plot. Find the mean, the median, the mode, and the range of the data.

4. Use the data set 2, 3, 5, 2, 7, 6, 3, 10, 9, 11, 14, 15, and 11. Make a box-and-whisker plot. Find the extremes, the median, and the quartiles.

Solve.

5. In how many different ways can the letters *A*, *B*, *C*, and *D* be arranged in a row if *A* and *D* are never next to each other?

6. In a school cafeteria, one fourth of the sixth graders chose hamburgers and one half chose pizza. The remaining nine sixth graders chose spaghetti. How many students chose pizza?

How did you do?

If you had difficulty with any items in the Quick Check, you can use the following pages for review and extra practice.

Items	Review These Pages	Do These Extra Practice Items
1	pages 76–77	Set E, page 91
2	pages 78–79	Set F, page 91
3	pages 82–83	Set G, page 92
4	pages 84–85	Set H, page 92
5	pages 80–81	5–8, page 93
6	pages 86–87	9–10, page 93

Test Prep • Cumulative Review

Maintaining the Standards

Choose the letter of the correct answer.

1. In which list are the numbers in order from least to greatest?

   A 0.1   0.11   0.01

   B 0.33   0.13   0.013

   C 0.33   0.222   0.211

   D 0.034   0.036   0.038

2. Together, Bill and Sarah bought 5 CDs. Each CD cost $11.50. How much did they spend on the 5 CDs?

   F $11.50

   G $23.00

   H $57.50

   J $575.00

3. Esteban and Beth have $22.88 to buy colored pencils for their art class. Each pencil costs $1.04. How many colored pencils can they buy?

   A 18 colored pencils

   B 20 colored pencils

   C 22 colored pencils

   D 26 colored pencils

4. Round 54.8$\underline{7}$61 to the underlined place.

   F 54.81

   G 54.86

   H 54.87

   J 54.88

5. Which number expresses the product of 32.5 and 3.2?

   A 10,400

   B 104

   C 10.4

   D 10.16

6. Which list shows the correct mean, median, and mode for this data set?

   5, 8, 9, 12, 12, 12, 19

   F mean: 11; median: 12; mode: 12

   G mean: 12; median: 11; mode: 12

   H mean: 11; median: 12; mode: 9

   J mean: 11; median: 14; mode: 12

7. A video store received a shipment of 1,584 videos for its grand opening. There were 36 videos packaged in each box. How many boxes of videos were received in all?

   A 26 boxes

   B 44 boxes

   C 1,584 boxes

   D 57,024 boxes

8. For 10 days in a row, Derek sold 10 cartons of flowers with 100 flowers in each carton. How many flowers did Derek sell in all?

   Explain How did you find your answer?

Internet Test Prep
Visit **www.eduplace.com/kids/mhm** for more *Test Prep Practice.*

Extra Practice

Set A (Lesson 1, pages 60–61)

Find the mean, median, mode, and range for each data set.

1. 3, 5, 6, 7, 2, 7, 5
2. 80, 500, 120, 90, 90, 26
3. 50, 56, 23, 29, 26
4. 33, 27, 29, 33, 42, 58
5. 62, 200, 231, 257, 212, 430
6. 55, 45, 62, 64, 66, 78, 50, 62

Set B (Lesson 2, pages 62–64)

Use the double bar graph for Exercises 1–6.

1. Which group has the fewest adults?
2. Which group has a total of six people?
3. Which group has an equal number of adults and children?
4. How many children are in Group *B*?
5. Which two groups have the same number of people?
6. Are there more adults or children in the groups?

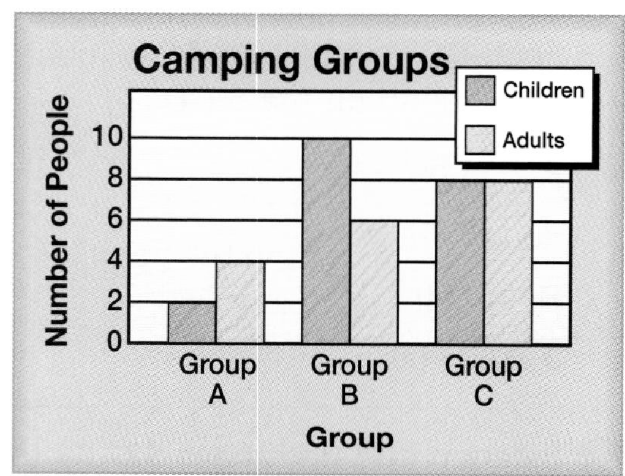

Set C (Lesson 3, pages 66–67)

Use the histogram for Exercises 1–5.

1. How many students study 45–59 minutes a day?
2. How many students study less than 30 minutes a day?
3. How many more students study 45–59 minutes a day than study 60–74 minutes a day?
4. Do most of the students study 45 minutes or more each day? Explain.
5. What is the maximum possible number of students who do not study at all?

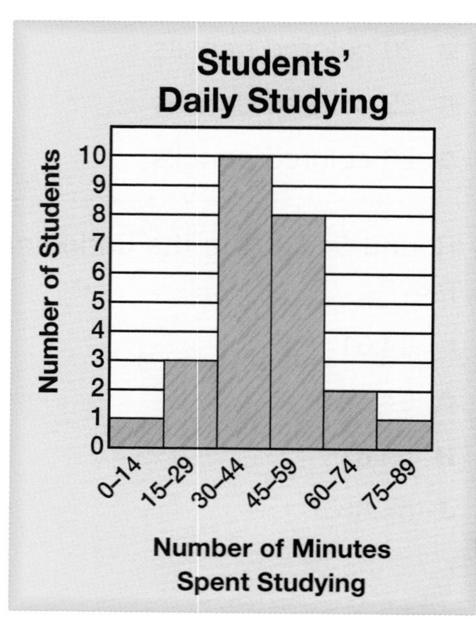

Extra Practice

Set D (Lesson 4, pages 68–70)

Use the double line graph for Exercises 1–4.

1. How long did Elevator 1 wait on the fifth floor?
2. Which elevator went down 5 floors in 1 minute?
3. Which elevator was the first to reach the second floor?
4. At what times were Elevator 1 and Elevator 2 both at the same floor?

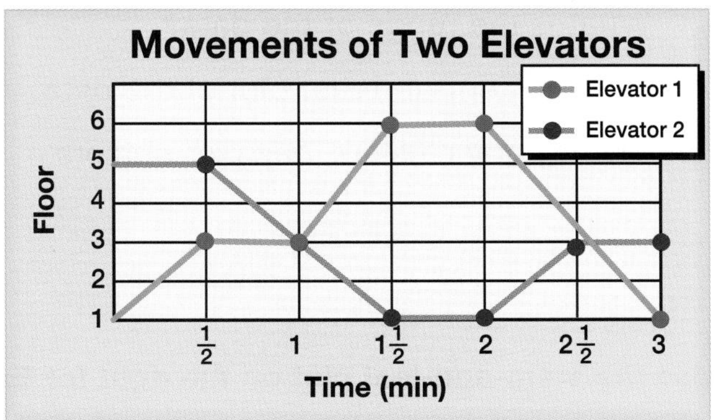

Set E (Lesson 6, pages 76–77)

For each data set, find the mean, the median, and the mode. Tell which measure you find most useful for describing the data. Explain why.

1. Maddie scored 7, 9, 5, 3, 15, and 15 points in 6 basketball games. She wants to show that she is a valuable player.
2. Andy's phone calls lasted 20 min, 7 min, 9 min, 12 min, and 7 min. He wants to show how long a typical phone call is.
3. Mr. and Mrs. Rodriquez collected donations of $50, $125, $10, $210, $50, $24, and $175 for a charity. They want to show that they are good fundraisers.
4. A golf team had scores of 382, 392, 383, 392, and 401 strokes in a tournament. The lowest score wins. The team wants to show that it played well.

Set F (Lesson 7, pages 78–79)

Use the data set 5, 20, 21, 33, 34, 35, 35, 37, 38, and 40 for Exercises 1–6.

1. Make a line plot, using the data.
2. Identify any clusters.
3. Identify any gaps.
4. Identify any outliers.
5. Find the mean, median, mode, and range.
6. Calculate how much the outlier or outliers affect the mean.

Extra Practice

Set G (Lesson 9, pages 82–83)

Use the data set 89, 76, 57, 56, 46, 78, 67, 65 for Exercises 1–3.

1. What is the range of the data?
2. Draw a stem-and-leaf plot of the data.
3. Identify any clusters, gaps, or outliers.

Use the stem-and-leaf plot on the right for Exercises 4–8.

4. How many data points are in this data set?
5. What are the three lowest values in this data set?
6. What are the three highest values in this data set?
7. Find the mean, the median, the mode, and the range.
8. Identify any clusters, gaps, and outliers.

Points Scored	
Stem	**Leaf**
2	0
3	7 9
4	5 5 6
5	
6	3 5
7	2

Key: 2|0 = 20

Set H (Lesson 10, pages 84–85)

Use the data set 2, 4, 3, 5, 10, 8, 2, 6, and 16 for Exercises 1–6.

1. Order the data from least to greatest.
2. Find the median and the extremes.
3. Find the upper and lower quartiles.
4. Draw a box-and-whisker plot.
5. Calculate the mean without the outlier or outliers.
6. How many data points fall inside the box?
7. Look at the box-and-whisker plot below. What are 9 possible numbers in the data set?

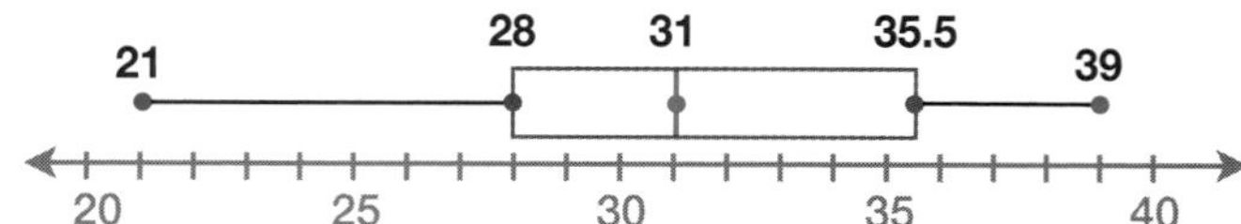

Extra Practice • Problem Solving

Solve. Use the graphs. *(Lesson 5, pages 72–73)*

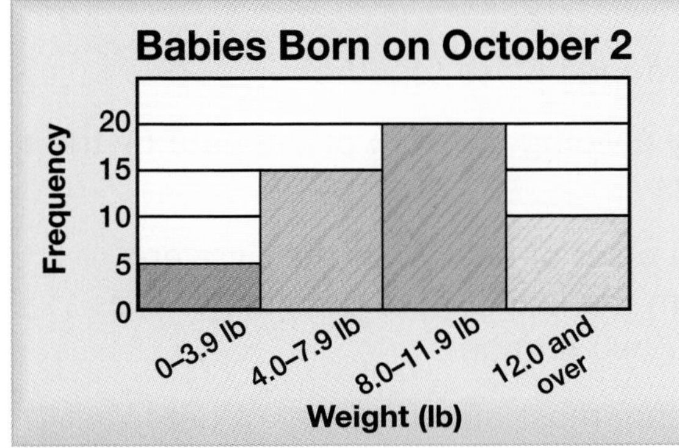

Gallons of Milk Sold

Months	Number of Gallons
January	🐄 🐄
February	🐄
March	🐄 🐄 🐄
April	🐄

Each 🐄 = 50 gallons of milk.

1. In all, how many babies were born on October 2?
2. What is the maximum number of babies that could weigh 12 pounds?
3. How much more milk was sold in March than in February?
4. How many gallons of milk were sold in the months of March and April?

Solve each problem, using the Make a List strategy. *(Lesson 8, pages 80–81)*

5. Margaret does two activities in the afternoon. Her first activity can be pottery, basket weaving, or painting. Her second activity can be soccer or jogging. How many ways can she organize her afternoon?
6. Kendal can choose from 3 salads: Caesar, chef, or garden. He can choose from 3 salad dressings: ranch, French, or Italian. How many different choices of 1 salad and 1 dressing does Kendal have?
7. Leo has 3 pairs of pants and 2 shirts for school. How many different outfits with 1 shirt and 1 pair of pants can Leo make?
8. Josie told Philip he can choose 2 of her 5 favorite baseball cards. How many different pairs can Philip choose?

Solve. *(Lesson 11, pages 86–87)*

9. Suzanne, Matthew, and Cameron are washing cars. Suzanne washes $\frac{1}{4}$ of the cars. Matthew washes 2 more cars than Suzanne, and Cameron washes the other 2 cars. How many cars do Suzanne, Matthew, and Cameron wash altogether?
10. Band students earned $2,500 for new uniforms in three different ways. They earned $\frac{1}{2}$ the total cost with a walkathon. They earned four times as much from car washes as they did from bake sales. How much did they earn washing cars?

Chapter Review

Reviewing Vocabulary

Match each word with a definition.

1. median

2. mode

3. mean

4. cluster

5. outlier

a. several data points grouped close together

b. the quotient found by dividing the sum of the data by the number of data points

c. the middle number in a set of data after the data are arranged in order from the least to the greatest or the average of the middle two numbers

d. the number that appears most often in a set of data

e. a number in a data set that is much larger or much smaller than most of the data

Reviewing Concepts and Skills

Use the line plot for Exercises 6–8. *(pages 60–61, 78–79, 82–83)*

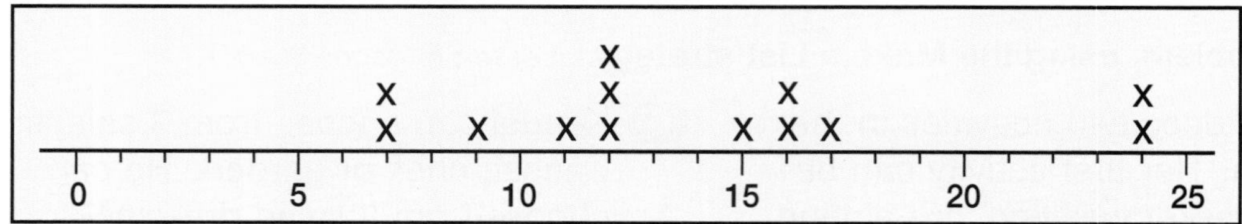

6. What are the mean, the median, the mode, and the range?

7. Identify any clusters, gaps, and outliers.

8. Make a stem-and-leaf plot from the data.

Use the histogram for Exercises 9–11. *(pages 66–67)*

9. How many students have between 4 and 11 cousins?

10. How many more students have 12–15 cousins than 16–19 cousins?

11. What is the greatest number of students that could have no cousins?

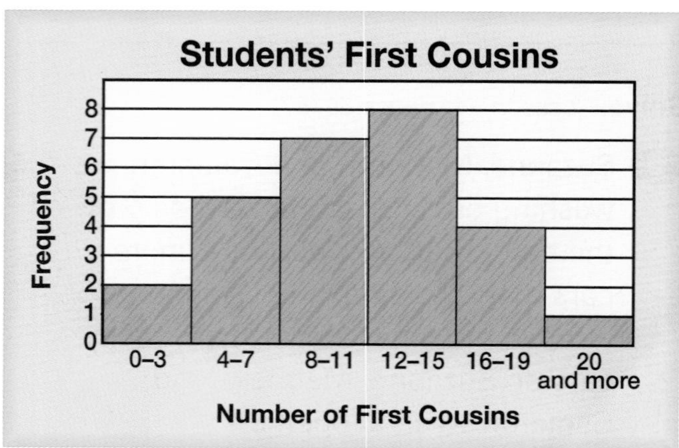

Use the stem-and-leaf plot for Exercises 12–15. *(pages 78–79, 82–83, 84–85)*

Stem	Leaf
2	9
3	3 4 4
4	2
5	4 6
6	1 2

Key: 2 | 9 = 29

12. Find the mean, the mode, and the range.

13. Identify any clusters, gaps, and outliers.

14. Find the median, the extremes, and the quartiles.

15. Use this data to draw a box-and-whisker plot.

Use the graphs for Problems 16–18. *(pages 62–64, 68–70)*

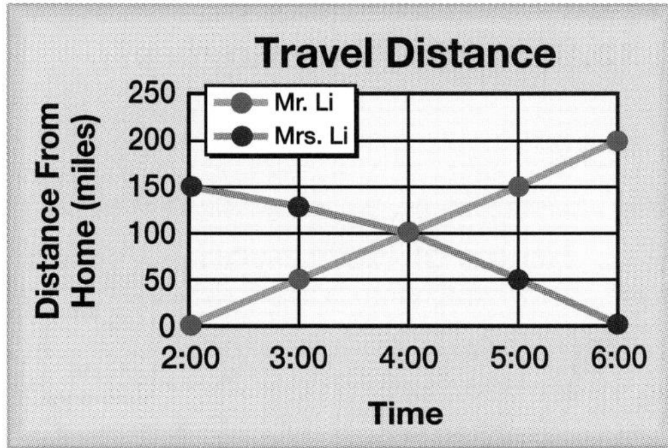

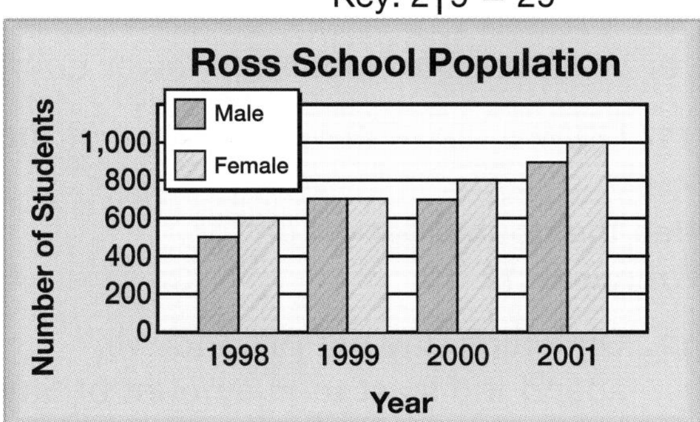

16. Mr. and Mrs. Li meet on their trips. At what time do they meet?

17. At what times is Mr. Li farther away from home than Mrs. Li is?

18. About how many more students were enrolled at Ross School in 2001 than in 1998? Explain how you found your answer.

Solve. *(pages 80–81, 86–87)*

19. Mark can have chicken or beef with corn, beans, or peas for a vegetable. How many choices of one meat and one vegetable does he have?

20. One fourth of Lucy's pets are cats. She has 2 more birds than cats. She has 4 other pets. How many cats does Lu have?

Brain Teaser Math Reasoning

Color Bars

Half as many students like blue as like green. Twice as many like green as like red.

What can you say about how many like red compared with how many like blue?

Draw a bar graph to show these color preferences.

Safe Site

Internet Brain Teasers
Visit **www.eduplace.com/kids/mhm** for more *Brain Teasers.*

Chapter Test

Use the data set 9, 3, 27, 10, 11, 5, 4, 3, 9.

1. Make a line plot of the data.
2. What is the range?
3. What is the mode?
4. What is the mean?
5. Identify any clusters.
6. Identify any gaps.
7. Are there any outliers? Explain.
8. What is the median?
9. What are the upper and lower quartiles?
10. What are the extremes?
11. Draw a box-and-whisker plot of the data.

Use the double bar graph for Exercises 12–13.

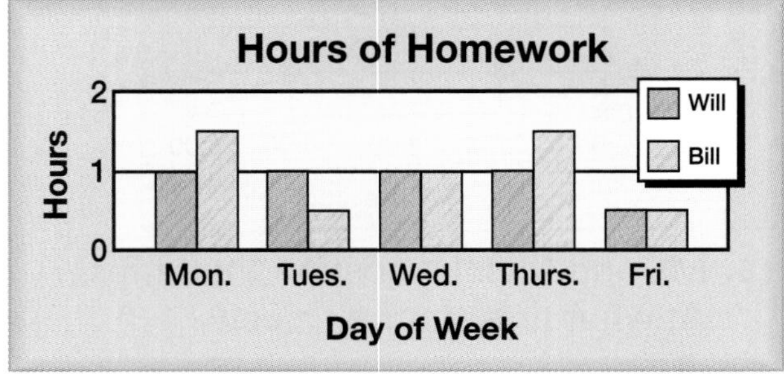

12. On which day did Bill and Will spend the least total amount of time doing homework?
13. On which day or days did Will spend more time doing homework than Bill did?

Use the histogram for Exercises 14–15.

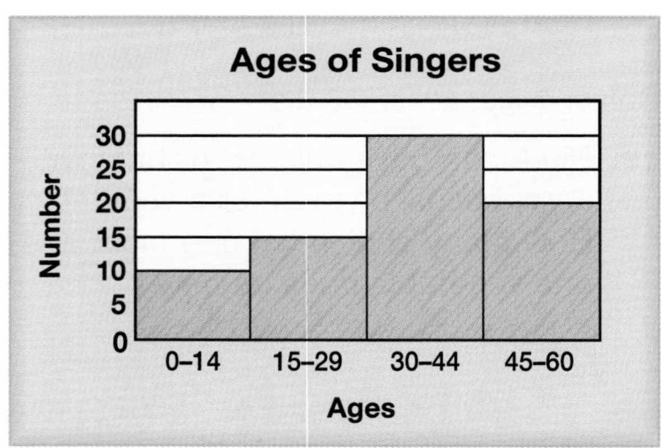

14. What is the greatest number of singers that can be 15 years old?
15. How many singers are 30 years old or older?

Solve. Use the double line graph for Exercises 16–18.

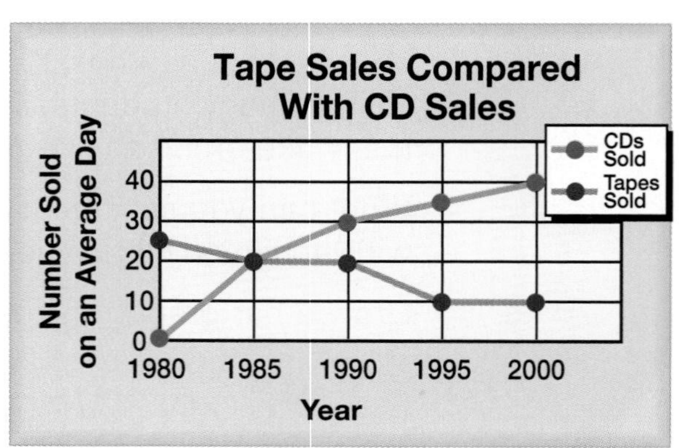

16. Explain how you can tell in what years more CDs were sold than were tapes.
17. How can you tell when the same numbers of tapes and CDs were sold?
18. Based on the graph, could you reasonably expect more tapes to be sold in 2005 than in 2000? Explain your answer.

Solve.

19. Annika has four magazines sitting on a table. How many different ways can she arrange them in a row?

20. Elizabeth, Irene, and Oscar go to the library. In all, they check out 32 books. If Irene checks out 2 less books than Elizabeth, and Oscar checks out 10 books, how many books does Elizabeth check out?

Write About It

Solve each problem. Use correct math vocabulary to explain your thinking.

1. Dominique looked at the stem-and-leaf plot that Fred created. She then said to Fred, "I didn't know your family included a 2-year-old and an 8-year-old."

   a. Explain why the statement Dominique made was incorrect.

   b. Write the correct ages of Fred's family members.

Ages of Fred's Family Members

Stem	Leaf
1	2 8
2	2
3	
4	6 8
5	

Key: 1 | 2 = 12

2. Emily has 1 red shirt, 2 blue shirts, 1 pair of jeans, and 1 pair of slacks. How many different combinations of a shirt and pants can she make?

   a. Represent the problem with a drawing, with numbers, or in some other way.

   b. Show your work to find the answer.

   c. Explain how you know that your answer is correct.

Another Look

For science class, Valerie made a table that included the average daily temperatures for a two-week period in October in two years.

Average Daily Temperatures (°F)		
Date	**1999**	**2000**
October 1	72°	75°
October 2	71°	73°
October 3	65°	75°
October 4	66°	70°
October 5	70°	70°
October 6	73°	75°
October 7	77°	73°
October 8	75°	69°
October 9	70°	68°
October 10	73°	70°
October 11	67°	68°
October 12	60°	70°
October 13	65°	74°
October 14	69°	71°

1. Use Valerie's table to make a double line graph.
2. Find the mean, the median, the mode, and the range for the two-week period for each year.
3. **Look Back** Which day or days were closest to the mean temperature in each year?
4. **Analyze** Study Valerie's data from both years and predict the temperature for October 15 of each year. Justify your prediction. Which statistic was most helpful in making your prediction? Explain.

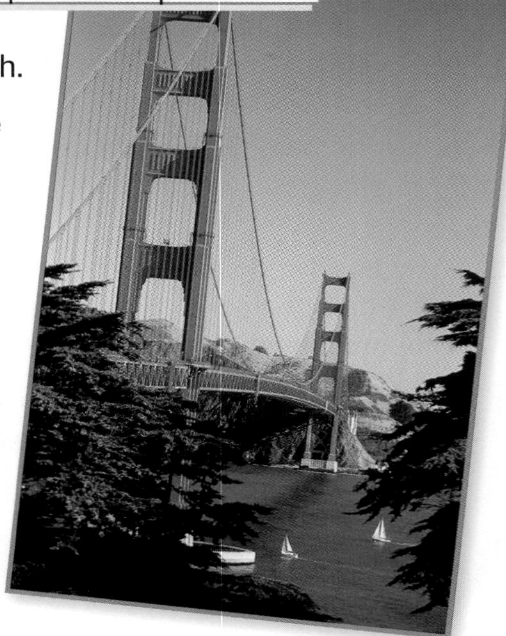

Enrichment

Different Graph Scales

People who make graphs sometimes use special techniques to make a graph easy to use. Look at the table of states with the greatest population on July 1, 1999. Then look at the way the data are displayed in the graph below.

State Population: July 1, 1999	
State	**Population**
California	33,145,121
Florida	15,111,244
Illinois	12,128,370
New York	18,196,601
Pennsylvania	11,994,016
Texas	20,044,141

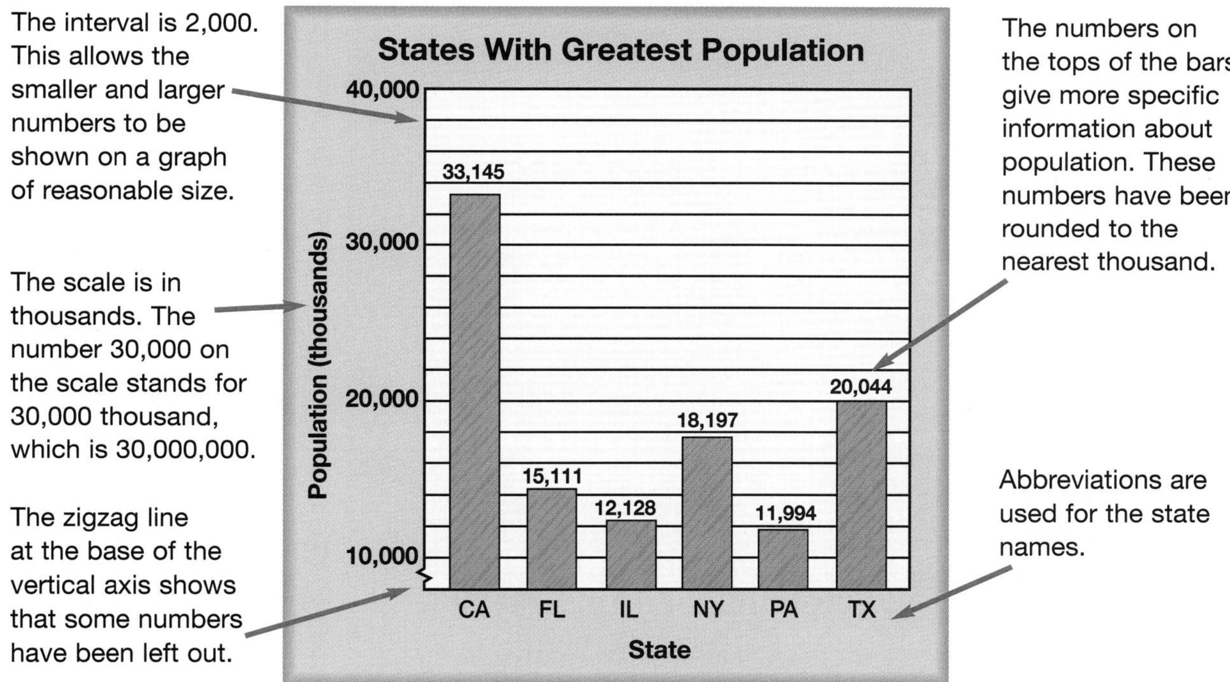

The interval is 2,000. This allows the smaller and larger numbers to be shown on a graph of reasonable size.
The scale is in thousands. The number 30,000 on the scale stands for 30,000 thousand, which is 30,000,000.
The zigzag line at the base of the vertical axis shows that some numbers have been left out.
States With Greatest Population
40,000
30,000
20,000
10,000
Population (thousands)
33,145
15,111
12,128
18,197
11,994
20,044
CA
FL
IL
NY
PA
TX
State
The numbers on the tops of the bars give more specific information about population. These numbers have been rounded to the nearest thousand.
Abbreviations are used for the state names.

Use the graph to answer the questions.

1. How would you use the graph to write the population of Florida in standard form?
2. If the scale showed population in millions, how would you write the numbers on the scale?
3. The population of Connecticut on July 1, 1999, was 3,285,031. How would you change the scale to add Connecticut?

Explain Your Thinking

► What do you need to consider when you are choosing a scale?

CHAPTER 3

Fractions and Number Theory

Why Learn About Fractions and Number Theory?

Learning about fractions will help you to compare them and to understand the relationship between fractions and decimals. Learning number theory will extend your understanding of the meaning of numbers.

Fractions are used often in everyday life. When you use money, the name of some coins show what fraction of a dollar they are. When you cook, you use measuring spoons and cups that are labeled with fractions.

These students are in a woodworking class. They use fractions to help them make the necessary calculations to measure and cut the wood.

FIR
DRILL PR

Reviewing Vocabulary

Understanding math language helps you become a successful problem solver. Here are some math vocabulary words you should know.

base	the factor used repeatedly in an expression involving exponents; in the expression 10^3 the base is 10
composite number	a number that has more than two factors
exponent	the number that shows how many times a base is used as a factor; the exponent in 10^3 is 3
factor	a number being multiplied to obtain a product
improper fraction	a fraction with a numerator that is greater than or equal to the denominator
multiple	the product of a given number and any whole number
prime number	a number with exactly two factors, 1 and itself

Reading Words and Symbols

When you read mathematics, sometimes you read only words, sometimes you read words and symbols, and sometimes you read only symbols. Which of these symbols have you seen before?

$>$	is greater than
$<$	is less than
$=$	equals, or is equal or equivalent to
$\div$	is divided by
$0.\overline{3}$	a repeating decimal

16 ounces = 1 pound

Try These

1. Compare. Write $>$, $<$, or $=$ for each ●.

   a. 12 ● 10 b. 0.5 ● 0.05 c. $\frac{1}{2}$ ● $\frac{1}{3}$

2. Write *true* or *false* for each statement. Rewrite each false statement to make it true.

   a. A factor of a number is always greater than the number itself.
   b. One multiple of a number is the number itself.
   c. A composite number has exactly two factors.
   d. All whole numbers have a factor of 1.
   e. The number $2\frac{1}{2}$ is an example of a proper fraction.
   f. An improper fraction has a numerator that is greater than its denominator.

3. Rewrite each expression, using words.

   a. $\frac{1}{5} < \frac{2}{5}$ b. $\frac{9}{10} > \frac{1}{2}$ c. $0.5 = \frac{1}{2}$

Upcoming Vocabulary

Write About It Here are some other vocabulary words you will learn in this chapter. Watch for these words. Write their definitions in your journal.

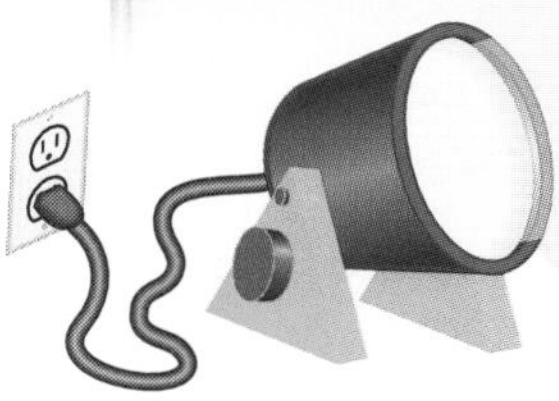

prime factorization

greatest common factor (GCF)

greatest common divisor (GCD)

least common multiple (LCM)

equivalent fractions

simplest form

common denominator

least common denominator (LCD)

repeating decimal

terminating decimal

Factors and Prime Numbers

You will learn that prime numbers are whole numbers that have only two factors.

Review Vocabulary
prime number
composite number

Learn About It

A **prime number** is a whole number with exactly two factors, 1 and the number itself. The first five prime numbers are 2, 3, 5, 7, and 11. A **composite number** is a whole number that has more than two factors. The number 1 is neither prime nor composite.

A museum has 100 coins from ancient Greece. How many ways could the coins be displayed in equal rows? Knowing whether 100 is a prime number or a composite number can help you answer this question.

You can use division to find the factors of 100.

Begin by trying to divide 100 by each number, starting with 1. List the results that show pairs of factors. When a factor is repeated, you can stop. Then use that list to show the ways the coins can be displayed.

$100 \div 1 = 100$, so 1 and 100 are factors. → Show 1 row of 100 or 100 rows of 1.
$100 \div 2 = 50$, so 2 and 50 are factors. → Show 2 rows of 50 or 50 rows of 2.
$100 \div 4 = 25$, so 4 and 25 are factors. → Show 4 rows of 25 or 25 rows of 4.
$100 \div 5 = 20$, so 5 and 20 are factors. → Show 5 rows of 20 or 20 rows of 5.
$100 \div 10 = 10$, so 10 is a factor. → Show 10 rows of 10.

Note: $100 \div 3 = 33$ R1, so 3 is not a factor and is not included in the list. The same is true for 6, 7, 8, and 9.

Solution: Because 100 is a composite number, there are many ways to display the coins. There are 9 ways to display the coins in equal rows.

Explain Your Thinking

- Why is the number 1 neither prime nor composite?
- How many ways could a prime number of coins be displayed in equal rows?

Guided Practice

List all factor pairs for each number. Then identify each number as *prime* or *composite*.

1. 12 **2.** 21 **3.** 32 **4.** 50

5. 11 **6.** 36 **7.** 48 **8.** 51

Ask Yourself

- Did I list 1 and the number as factors?
- Did I divide and then use the divisor and quotient as factors?

Independent Practice

List all factor pairs for each number. Then identify each number as *prime* or *composite*.

9. 18 **10.** 30 **11.** 31 **12.** 25 **13.** 86 **14.** 105 **15.** 17

Problem Solving • Reasoning

Use Data **Use the table for Problems 16–18.**

16. In ancient Greece, a mathematician named Eratosthenes became interested in prime and composite numbers. He developed a method, known as the Sieve of Eratosthenes, for finding primes. Follow his steps to decide whether 53 is a prime number.

- Copy the table at the right.
- Cross out 1, since 1 is not a prime.
- Circle 2 because 2 is a prime. Cross out all of the multiples of 2.
- Go to the next number that is not crossed out. Circle it. Then cross out its multiples.
- Repeat the previous step until all the numbers are either circled or crossed out. The circled numbers are prime numbers.

The Sieve of Eratosthenes

1	2	3	4	5	6	7	8	9	10
11	12	13	14	15	16	17	18	19	20
21	22	23	24	25	26	27	28	29	30
31	32	33	34	35	36	37	38	39	40
41	42	43	44	45	46	47	48	49	50
51	52	53	54	55	56	57	58	59	60
61	62	63	64	65	66	67	68	69	70
71	72	73	74	75	76	77	78	79	80
81	82	83	84	85	86	87	88	89	90
91	92	93	94	95	96	97	98	99	100

17. Using your copy of the Sieve of Eratosthenes, write an ordered list of all the prime numbers between 1 and 100.

18. **Logical Thinking** Could you extend the Sieve to find prime numbers greater than 100? Demonstrate that this can or cannot be done.

19. **Analyze** Multiply any two primes. Show the product as the product of two factors. How many groups of two factors can you list? Explain why.

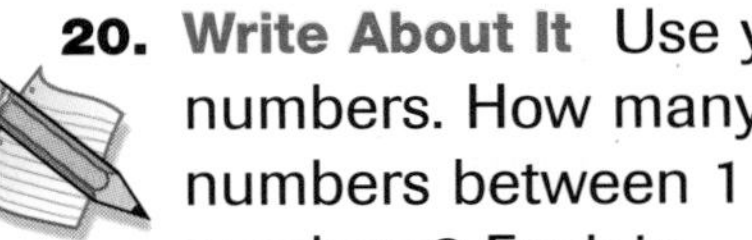

20. **Write About It** Use your list of prime numbers. How many of the prime numbers between 1 and 100 are even numbers? Explain.

Mixed Review • Test Prep

Write each number in word form. *(pages 4–5)*

21. 624,682 **22.** 200 + 6 + 0.7 + 0.02 **23.** 5,000 + 400 + 30 + 9

24 What is the mean of this data: 2, 9, 10, 11, 12? *(pages 60–61)*

A 6.8 **B** 7.7 **C** 8.8 **D** 10.2

Extra Practice See Set A on page 142.

Exponents

You will learn how to use exponents to write expressions involving repeated multiplication.

Review Vocabulary
exponent
base

Learn About It

Many numbers can be written as the product of repeated factors. For example,

$16 = 2 \times 2 \times 2 \times 2.$

When a factor is repeated, the product can be written using an exponent.

$16 = 2^4$ $\quad 2^4$ is read as "two to the fourth."

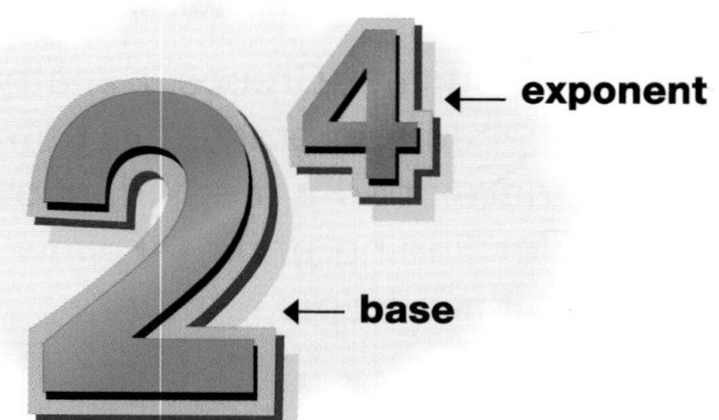

The **exponent** (4) tells how many times the **base** (2) is used as a factor.

Use exponents to write the expression $2 \times 2 \times 2 \times 3 \times 3$.

Write $2 \times 2 \times 2 \times 3 \times 3$, using exponents.

Step 1 Count the number of times each number (base) is used as a factor.

$2 \times 2 \times 2$
used three times

3×3
used two times

Step 2 Write the exponent for each base.

$2 \times 2 \times 2 \times 3 \times 3 = 2^3 \times 3^2$

Solution: Another way to write $2 \times 2 \times 2 \times 3 \times 3$ is $2^3 \times 3^2$.

Other Examples

A. Write as a Product of Factors

$2^4 \times 3 \times 5^2 = ■$

$2 \times 2 \times 2 \times 2 \times 3 \times 5 \times 5$

B. Evaluate an Expression

$2^3 \times 5 = ■$

$2 \times 2 \times 2 \times 5 = 8 \times 5 = 40$

Explain Your Thinking

► The number 25 can be written as 5^2. If you wrote $3 = 3^{■}$, what exponent would you use? Explain.

Guided Practice

Write each using exponents.

1. $2 \times 2 \times 5 \times 5$ **2.** $2 \times 2 \times 3 \times 5 \times 5$

Write each as a product of factors. Then evaluate.

3. 2^3 **4.** 3^5 **5.** $3^2 \times 7^2$ **6.** $2^3 \times 3 \times 5^2$

Ask Yourself

- Did I write the factors with no exponents only once?
- Did I count the number of times a factor was used?

Independent Practice

Write each using exponents.

7. $3 \times 3 \times 7$ **8.** $4 \times 4 \times 9$ **9.** $5 \times 5 \times 8 \times 8$ **10.** $6 \times 6 \times 6 \times 7$

Write each as a product of factors.

11. $4^3 \times 5$ **12.** $2^2 \times 7^2$ **13.** 5^3 **14.** $3^2 \times 10^2$ **15.** $2^5 \times 3 \times 7$

Evaluate each expression.

16. 2×3^4 **17.** $2^2 \times 3$ **18.** $2^5 \times 3^2$ **19.** $5^2 \times 7$ **20.** 9^3

21. $7^2 \times 8$ **22.** 2^6 **23.** 3^7 **24.** 7^4 **25.** $8^2 \times 10^4$

Problem Solving • Reasoning

26. Predict Write each number in this list, using an exponent of 2. If this pattern continues, what is the tenth number likely to be?

4 9 16 25 36 49

27. The number 625 is the product of 25 and 25. Express the number 625 as a product of 5s. Write 625, using an exponent with 5 as a base.

28. Compare Compare the expression $2^3 \times 3$ with $2^4 \times 3$. How many times greater is the value of the second expression than the first?

29. Write About It Describe how the following expression can be simplified, without eliminating all of the exponents.

$1^4 \times 2^3 \times 2 \times 5$

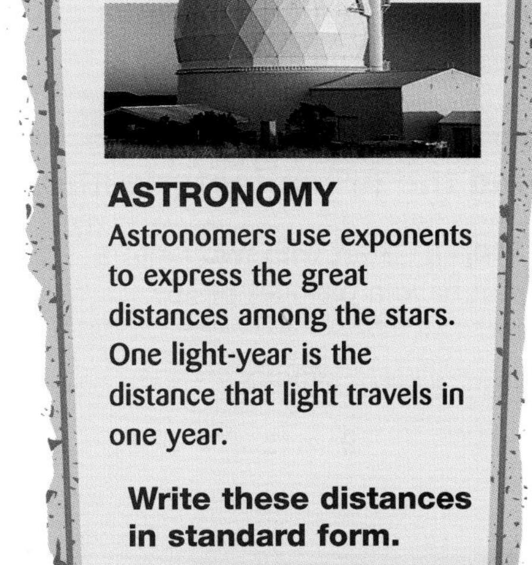

ASTRONOMY
Astronomers use exponents to express the great distances among the stars. One light-year is the distance that light travels in one year.

Write these distances in standard form.

Star	Distance in Light-Years
Hadar	4.9×10^2
Betelgeuse	5.2×10^2
Rigel	9.0×10^2
Deneb	1.6×10^3

Mixed Review • Test Prep

Divide. *(pages 32–35)*

30. $9.78 \div 4$ **31.** $25.74 \div 2.2$

32. $45.36 \div 2.7$ **33.** $34.83 \div 3$

Choose the letter of the correct answer. *(pages 4–7)*

34 Choose the list that is ordered from least to greatest.

A 0.18, 0.65, 0.05 **C** 0.05, 0.18, 0.65

B 0.65, 0.18, 0.05 **D** 0.18, 0.05, 0.65

35 Which of the following shows 14 and 21 thousandths?

F 14.0021 **H** 14.21

G 21.14 **J** 14.021

Extra Practice See Set B on page 142.

Prime Factorization

You will learn how to express composite numbers as products of prime numbers.

New Vocabulary
prime factorization

Learn About It

A **prime factorization** expresses a composite number as a product of prime factors.

Example: The prime factorization of 12 is $2 \times 2 \times 3$.

The factors in a prime factorization often are written in order from least to greatest.

Look at the T-shirts to the right. The T-shirts come in 3 different colors, 3 different styles, and 5 different sizes. There are $3 \times 3 \times 5$, or 45, different types of T-shirts.

You can use a factor tree to find the prime factorization of a number. A factor tree is complete when each branch ends with a prime.

Find the prime factorization of 45.

Step 1 Start with two factors that have a product of 45.

45
9 × 5

Step 2 Factor 9 and 5.

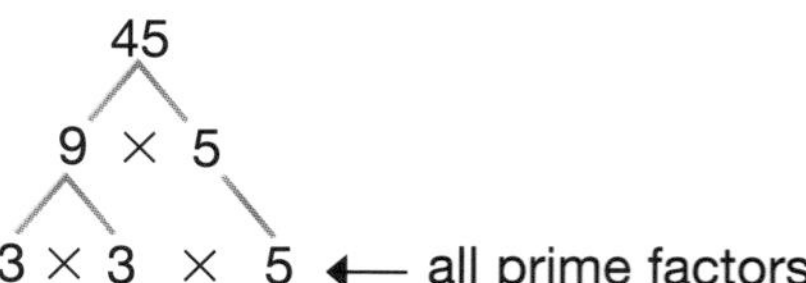

Step 3 Rewrite the prime factorization using exponents.

$3 \times 3 \times 5 = 3^2 \times 5$

Solution: The prime factorization of 45 is $3 \times 3 \times 5$ or $3^2 \times 5$.

Check your work.
Check that all factors are prime numbers.
Multiply. $3 \times 3 \times 5 = 45$

Another Example

More Than 3 Factors

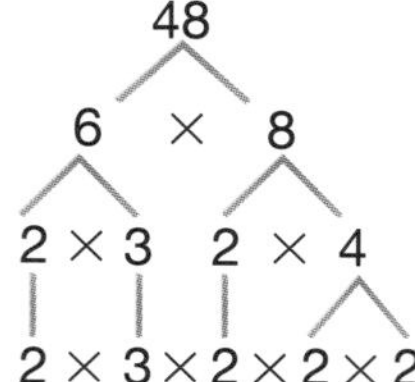

The prime factorization of 48 is $2 \times 2 \times 2 \times 2 \times 3$, or $2^4 \times 3$.

Explain Your Thinking

- Why can you choose either 9×5 or 15×3 to start a factor tree for 45?
- Why is it helpful to know the prime numbers less than 20 when finding a prime factorization?

Guided Practice

Draw a factor tree to show the prime factorization of each. Then rewrite, using exponents.

1. 16 **2.** 15 **3.** 30 **4.** 28

5. 25 **6.** 39 **7.** 625 **8.** 2,500

Ask Yourself

- Are all the factors prime numbers?
- Did I use exponents correctly to show the number of times each factor occurs?

Independent Practice

Draw a factor tree to show the prime factorization of each. Then rewrite, using exponents. If the number is prime, write *prime*.

9. 14 **10.** 22 **11.** 26 **12.** 48 **13.** 37

14. 42 **15.** 91 **16.** 97 **17.** 108 **18.** 1,440

Complete each factor tree for the number 24.

19.

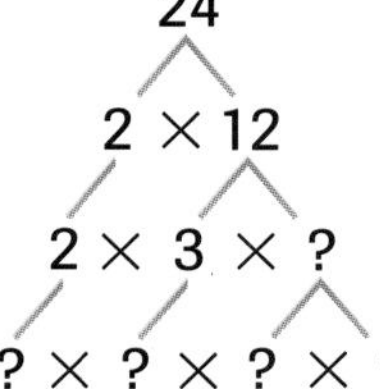

24
2 × 12
2 × 3 × ?
? × ? × ? × ?

20.

24
3 × 8
? × ? × ?
? × ? × ? × ?

21.

24
? × 6
? × ? × ? × ?

Problem Solving • Reasoning

Use Data **Use the diagram for Problems 24 and 25.**

22. Name the common prime factors for 24 and 48.

23. **Patterns** Find the prime factorization of 9, 27, 81, and 243. Find a pattern. If this pattern continues, what would be the prime factorizations of the next two numbers?

24. Name the number represented by the factor tree shown at the right.

25. **Write About It** Could this be the factor tree for any other number? Explain why or why not.

Mixed Review • Test Prep

Calculate the following values for this data set:
12, 14, 18, 23, 24, 24, 25. *(pages 60–61)*

26. mean **27.** median **28.** mode **29.** range

30 Which fraction is equivalent to $\frac{2}{3}$?

A $\frac{3}{4}$ **B** $\frac{5}{6}$ **C** $\frac{6}{9}$ **D** $\frac{10}{8}$

Extra Practice See Set C on page 142.

Divisibility Rules

You will learn how to test a number to see if it is divisible by 2, 3, 4, 5, 6, 9, or 10.

Learn About It

The 196 campers at Camp Lakeway play games that require equal groups. For the groups to be equal, 196 must be divisible by the number of campers in each group. Knowing the divisibility rules can help the counselors decide the size of the groups possible for the games. The counselors have different games that require 2, 3, 4, 5, 6, 9, or 10 campers on each team. Which games can they plan to play?

Use the chart of divisibility rules to decide which games the counselors can use.

Campers on a Team	Works with 196 Campers?	How do you know?
2	Yes	196 is even.
3	No	$1 + 9 + 6 = 16$; $16 \div 3 = 5$ R1
4	Yes	Last two digits of 196 are 96; $96 \div 4 = 24$
5	No	Last digit is 6, not 5 or 0.
6	No	196 is divisible by 2, but it is not divisible by 3.
9	No	$1 + 9 + 6 = 16$; $16 \div 9 = 1$ R7
10	No	Last digit is 6, not 0.

Divisibility Rules

Rule	Examples
2: Last digit is even.	**Yes:** 2, 186, 330 **No:** 7, 141, 881
3: Sum of the digits is divisible be 3.	**Yes:** 18, 96, 432 **No:** 26, 193, 637
4: Number made up of last two digits is divisible by 4.	**Yes:** 88, 680, 772 **No:** 74, 702, 998
5: Last digit is 5 or 0.	**Yes:** 85, 685, 770 **No:** 52, 629, 804
6: It is divisible by 2 and by 3.	**Yes:** 96, 528, 996 **No:** 86, 513, 994
9: Sum of the digits is divisible by 9.	**Yes:** 99, 198, 612 **No:** 91, 173, 802
10: Last digit is 0.	**Yes:** 80, 770, 800 **No:** 94, 649, 905

Solution: The counselors can use only games that require 2 or 4 players on a team.

Explain Your Thinking

- Why does the divisibility test for 6 include testing for divisibility by both 2 and 3?
- Can you think of another way to test for divisibility by 4? Explain.

Guided Practice

Determine whether the first number listed is divisible by the second number.

1. 124 2 **2.** 97 2 **3.** 135 5 **4.** 250 5

5. 24 2 **6.** 32 6 **7.** 15 6 **8.** 36 6

Ask Yourself

- Did I check the last digit to test for divisibility?
- Did I add digits to test for divisibility?

Independent Practice

Copy and complete this table. Place a check mark to show divisibility.

		126	1,410	835	5,461	2,205
9.	Divisible by 2					
10.	Divisible by 5					

Determine whether the first number listed is divisible by the second number.

11. 256 4 **12.** 426 6 **13.** 2,745 5 **14.** 916 6 **15.** 603 10

16. 4,389 9 **17.** 5,624 4 **18.** 596 3 **19.** 143 9 **20.** 8,346 2

21. 9,231 3 **22.** 2,001 3 **23.** 991 9 **24.** 734 4 **25.** 9,801 9

26. 2,560 5 **27.** 850 10 **28.** 432 6 **29.** 4,381 6 **30.** 78,929 9

Problem Solving • Reasoning

31. Test 48 and 68 for divisibility by 2, 3, 4, 6, and 9. Present your answer in a table.

32. Starting with 1,000, list the first five numbers that are divisible by 9.

33. **Analyze** For next year, the counselors have planned activities requiring groups of 2, 3, 4, and 6. What is the smallest number of campers that can form groups of 2, 3, 4, and 6?

34. **Write About It** A counselor invented this divisibility test for 8: If a number is divisible by both 2 and 4, it is divisible by 8. Explain the error in this test. Support your answer with examples.

Mixed Review • Test Prep

Multiply. *(pages 20–23)*

35. 4.55×6 **36.** 8.50×7.1 **37.** 0.43×9 **38.** 0.22×8.3

39 Which type of graph best shows the growth of a plant over time? *(pages 68–69)*

A bar **C** stem-and-leaf plot
B line **D** histogram

Extra Practice See Set D on page 142.

LESSON 5

Greatest Common Factor

You will learn how to find the greatest common factor of two or more numbers.

New Vocabulary

greatest common factor (GCF)

greatest common divisor (GCD)

Learn About It

Eighteen sixth-graders and 24 seventh-graders will march in rows in the Veterans Day parade. Each row requires the same number of students. If the sixth- and seventh-graders are in separate rows, what is the greatest number of students that can be in a row?

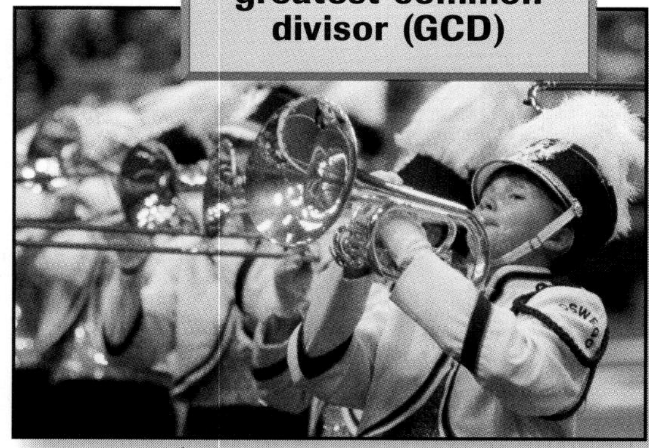

To determine this number, you must find the greatest factor that is common to 18 and 24. This number is called the **greatest common factor (GCF).** The greatest common factor is sometimes called the **greatest common divisor (GCD).**

Different Ways to Find the Greatest Common Factor

You can make a list.

Step 1 List the factors of both numbers.

18: 1, 2, 3, 6, 9, 18

24: 1, 2, 3, 4, 6, 8, 12, 24

Step 2 Circle the common factors of 18 and 24. The greatest factor circled is the GCF.

18: (1), (2), (3), (6), 9, 18

24: (1), (2), (3), 4, (6), 8, 12, 24 The GCF is 6.

You can use prime factorization.

Step 1 Write the prime factorization of both numbers. Circle the factors common to both.

18 = (2) × 3 × (3)

24 = (2) × 2 × 2 × (3)

Step 2 Find the product of the common factors.

$GCF = 2^1 \times 3^1$

$= 2 \times 3 = 6$

Solution: The GCF of 18 and 24 is 6.

Other Examples

A. GCF Is One of the Numbers

12 = (2) × (2) × (3)

24 = (2) × (2) × 2 × (3)

108 = (2) × (2) × 3 × 3 × (3)

GCF: 2 × 2 × 3 = 12

B. Use Exponents

54 = (2) × 3 × (3) × (3)

36 = (2) × 2 × (3) × (3)

GCF: $2 \times 3^2 = 18$

Explain Your Thinking

► Why can the greatest common factor also be called the greatest common divisor?

► In the prime factorization method above, why do you multiply 2 × 3 rather than 2 × 2 × 3 × 3?

Guided Practice

Find the GCF of each pair of numbers by listing the factors of each.

1. 6, 15 **2.** 8, 12 **3.** 20, 30 **4.** 25, 35

5. 24, 72 **6.** 32, 48 **7.** 15, 36 **8.** 36, 56

Ask Yourself

- Did I use only prime numbers as factors?
- Did I multiply all the common prime factors?

List all primes under 20. Then find the GCF for each pair of numbers, using prime factorization.

9. 9, 16 **10.** 18, 20 **11.** 11, 22 **12.** 12, 18

13. 24, 60 **14.** 14, 18 **15.** 15, 36 **16.** 18, 24

Independent Practice

Find the GCF of each pair of numbers by listing the factors of each.

17. 22, 33 **18.** 14, 35 **19.** 24, 36 **20.** 40, 50

21. 64, 72 **22.** 90, 96 **23.** 13, 52 **24.** 72, 96

List all primes under 20. Then find the GCF of each pair of numbers, using prime factorization.

25. 49, 56 **26.** 41, 82 **27.** 99, 121

28. 36, 57 **29.** 15, 18 **30.** 36, 39

31. 48, 60 **32.** 24, 40 **33.** 25, 45

34. 5, 16 **35.** 52, 117 **36.** 26, 91

Find the GCF of each group of numbers. Use either method.

37. 36, 48 **38.** 45, 63 **39.** 32, 80

40. 300, 144 **41.** 84, 120 **42.** 45, 54

43. 144, 24 **44.** 60, 80 **45.** 64, 100

46. 9, 12, 18 **47.** 24, 28, 36 **48.** 8, 28, 52

49. 12, 18, 42 **50.** 44, 66, 88 **51.** 20, 30, 45

52. 24, 36, 52 **53.** 28, 42, 63 **54.** 35, 50, 75

55. 36, 60, 72 **56.** 32, 64, 96 **57.** 32, 36, 45

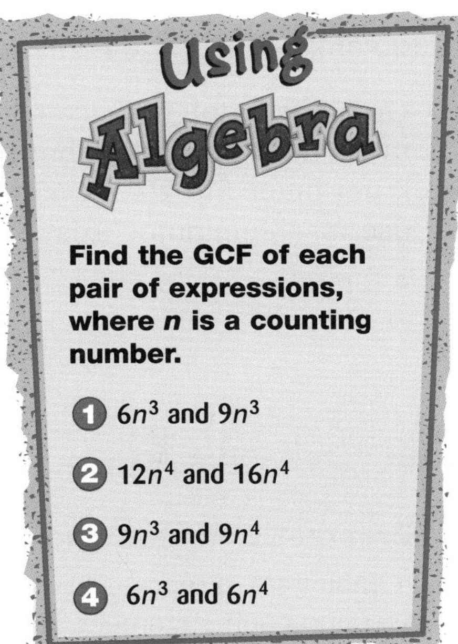

Find the GCF of each pair of expressions, where n is a counting number.

1. $6n^3$ and $9n^3$
2. $12n^4$ and $16n^4$
3. $9n^3$ and $9n^4$
4. $6n^3$ and $6n^4$

Problem Solving • Reasoning

Use Data Use the table to solve Problems 58 and 59.

Balloons for Float	
Color	**Number**
Red	150
Blue	54

58. Jan decorates a parade float with groups of blue or red balloons. Each group has the same number of balloons. If Jan uses all of the balloons, what is the greatest number of balloons in each group?

59. **Analyze** Thirty red balloons and 18 blue balloons break. Jan rearranges those that remain. What is the greatest number of balloons that can be in each new group if each group has the same number of balloons?

60. The GCF of two numbers is 22. One of the numbers is 198. What is the least possible value of the other number?

61. **Write About It** What is the GCF of any two prime numbers? What is the GCF of any composite number and any prime number?

Mixed Review • Test Prep

Complete. *(pages 38–41)*

62. 120 cm = ■ m **63.** 2.9 mm = ■ dm **64.** 320 m = ■ mm **65.** 312 dL = ■ L

66 On a bar graph Mei-Lin shows the number of minutes it takes her to complete her homework each day for 5 days. If her times are 25, 25, 45, 8, 55, what interval should she use for the minutes axis? *(pages 62–63)*

A 5 min **B** 50 min **C** 60 min **D** 100 min

Logical Thinking

Greatest Common Factor

In each item, *n* represents a counting number. Write *true* or *false* to describe each statement. Use examples to explain your answers.

1. The GCF of the expressions $4n$ and $6n$ is $2n$.

2. The GCF of the expressions n and n^2 is n.

3. The GCF of the expressions n and $n + 5$ is n.

4. The GCF of the expressions $2n$ and $2n + 1$ is $2n$.

Extra Practice See Set E on page 143.

Number Sense

Finding the GCF

Here are two ways to find the greatest common factor of large numbers. Find the greatest common factor (GCF) of 294 and 378.

You can find the GCF of 294 and 378 by dividing by common prime factors.

Step 1 Divide both numbers by the smallest common prime divisor.

$2\overline{)294} = 147 \qquad 2\overline{)378} = 189$

Step 2 Divide both quotients by the smallest common prime divisor.

$3\overline{)147} = 49 \qquad 3\overline{)189} = 63$

Step 3 49 and 63 are not both divisible by 2, 3, or 5, but they are both divisible by 7.

$7\overline{)49} = 7 \qquad 7\overline{)63} = 9$

Step 4 No prime number divides both 7 and 9. The GCF is the product of all the common prime divisors.

$2 \times 3 \times 7$

Solution: The GCF of 294 and 378 $= 2 \times 3 \times 7 = 42$

You can also find the GCF without finding common factors.

Step 1 Divide the larger number by the smaller number.

$294\overline{)378}$

$294\overline{)378}$ = 1 R84; 378 − 294 = 84

Step 2 Note the remainder. Divide the previous divisor by the remainder.

$84\overline{)294}$ = 3 R42; 294 − 252 = 42

Step 3 Note the remainder. Divide the previous divisor by the remainder. When the remainder is 0, the divisor is the GCF.

$42\overline{)84}$ = 2; 84 − 84 = 0

When the remainder is 0, the divisor is the GCF.

Solution: The largest number that divides both 294 and 378 is 42.

Explain Your Thinking

- How do these methods differ from the ways you have been finding the GCF? How are they similar?

LESSON 6

Least Common Multiple

You will learn how to find the least common multiple of two or more numbers.

New Vocabulary
least common multiple (LCM)

Learn About It

Mark's boat can travel around the lake in 60 minutes. His cousin's boat can travel around the same lake in 45 minutes. If both boats leave the dock at the same time, traveling around the lake in opposite directions, how many minutes will pass before the two boats pass the dock at the same time?

Finding the least common multiple of 60 and 45 will help you find the answer. The **least common multiple (LCM)** is the least number that is a multiple of two or more numbers.

Different Ways to Find the LCM

You can make a list.

Step 1 List some multiples of 60 and 45. Circle all of the common multiples.

60: 60, 120, (180), 240, 300, (360), 420, 480

45: 45, 90, 135, (180), 225, 270, 315, (360)

Step 2 Identify the least common multiple.

180

The LCM of 60 and 45 is 180.

You can use prime factorization.

Step 1 Write the prime factorization of 60 and 45, using exponents.

$60 = 2^2 \times 3 \times 5$

$45 = 3^2 \times 5$

Step 2 For each of the three different prime factors, circle the greatest power.

$(2^2) \times 3 \times (5)$

$(3^2) \times 5$

Step 3 The product of the greatest powers of the prime factors is the LCM.

$\text{LCM} = 2^2 \times 3^2 \times 5 =$

$2 \times 2 \times 3 \times 3 \times 5 = 180$

Solution: In 180 minutes, the two boats will pass the dock at the same time.

Explain Your Thinking

- If the LCM of two numbers is equal to the product of the two numbers, what must be true about their common factors?
- When is the LCM of two numbers the same as one of the numbers? Use an example to explain your answer.

Guided Practice

Use a list or prime factorization to find the LCM of each pair of numbers.

1. 4, 5 **2.** 16, 36 **3.** 5, 17 **4.** 4, 42

5. 12, 18 **6.** 20, 25 **7.** 12, 24 **8.** 9, 14

> **Ask Yourself**
>
> - Did I circle the greatest power of each different prime factor?

Independent Practice

Find the prime factorization of each number. If the number is prime, write *prime number*.

9. 9 **10.** 13 **11.** 45 **12.** 63 **13.** 107

14. 21 **15.** 81 **16.** 105 **17.** 100 **18.** 288

Use a list or prime factorization to find the LCM of each group of numbers.

19. 6, 14 **20.** 16, 6 **21.** 9, 12 **22.** 11, 13 **23.** 17, 51

24. 12, 20 **25.** 11, 4 **26.** 28, 42 **27.** 5, 6, 10 **28.** 12, 16, 24

Problem Solving • Reasoning

Use Data **Use the illustration for Problem 29.**

29. **Analyze** Zelda and Tom are placing two rows of tiles on the kitchen wall. The first row has tiles that are 4 in. by 4 in. The next row has tiles that are 3 in. by 3 in.

a. How many of each tile will Zelda and Tom need to buy for a 9-ft span?

b. In a 9-ft span of tiles, how many times will the tiles line up?

30. A commuter train to Town *A* leaves the station every 30 min. A train to Town *B* leaves every 45 min. If both trains leave the station at 6:00 A.M., when will a train to Town *A* and a train to Town *B* next leave the station at the same time?

31. **Write About It** The LCM of two numbers is $2^3 \times 3^3 \times 5$. Find two pairs of numbers that fit this description. Write a paragraph to explain how you found your answer.

Mixed Review • Test Prep

Multiply. *(pages 22–23)*

32. 0.68×0.023 **33.** 4.5×0.96 **34.** 0.19×0.381 **35.** 9.9×0.01

36 Chad needs to round 175.054 to the nearest whole number. What should he write?

A 200 **B** 176 **C** 175.1 **D** 175

Extra Practice See Set F on page 143.

Problem-Solving Strategy: Use Logical Thinking

You will learn how to use logical thinking to solve a problem.

You can use a Venn diagram to help you solve a problem.

Problem The local video store is keeping track of how many people rent comedy and science-fiction videos. How many different people rented one or both kinds of videos in the past month if 7 people rented both kinds of videos?

Rentals Last Month

Comedy	22
Science Fiction	14

Understand

What is the question?

How many people rented one or both kinds of videos in the past month?

What do you know?

- Twenty-two people rented comedy videos.
- Fourteen people rented science-fiction videos.
- Seven of these people rented both kinds.

Plan

How can you find the answer?

Draw a Venn diagram and include the information you know.

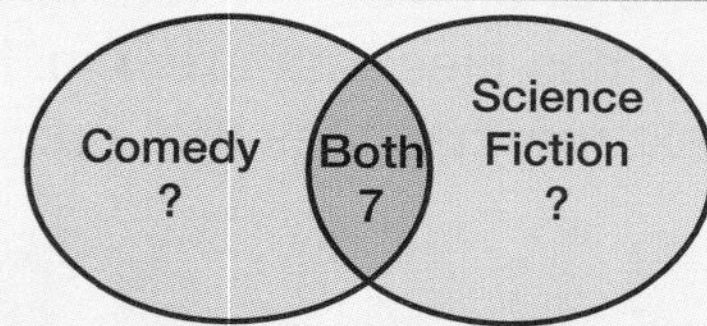

Solve

Use a Venn diagram.

Subtract 7 from 22 and 7 from 14.

Add the numbers of each section in the Venn diagram.

Comedy $22 - 7 = 15$ | Both 7 | Science Fiction $14 - 7 = 7$

$15 + 7 + 7 = 29$

Twenty-nine people rented one or both kinds of videos.

Look Back

Look back at the question.

Is your answer reasonable? Tell why.
Explain how you can check your answer.

Remember:
- Understand
- Plan
- Solve
- Look Back

Guided Practice

Solve these problems, using the Logical Thinking strategy.

1. In Ms. Francon's class, 14 students saw the latest action movie and 18 saw the latest animated movie. Eight students saw both. If all the students saw one or both movies, how many students are in Ms. Francon's class?

   Think: Can you use a Venn diagram to solve this problem?

2. Thirty students went to an adventure movie. Each student bought something at the refreshment stand. Twelve bought bottled water and 23 bought popcorn. Some students bought both. How many students bought both bottled water and popcorn?

   Think: Can you use a Venn diagram to check your answer?

Choose a Strategy

Solve. Use these or other strategies.

Problem-Solving Strategies

- **Use Logical Thinking**
- **Write an Equation**
- **Draw a Diagram**
- **Make a List**

3. A survey asks if students are over 12 years old, are male or female, or play a sport. How many different categories of students exist?

4. Jodi has four styles of T-shirts, two styles of shorts, and three styles of caps. How many different combinations of shirt, shorts, and cap can she wear?

5. Jan asked some of her classmates what type of music they like. Nine replied "country" and 7 replied "rock." Two of the people she asked replied both "country" and "rock." How many classmates did Jan ask about music?

6. The cafeteria has a soup bar and a salad bar. One day, 91 students bought lunch at the food bars. If 64 students bought soup and 42 students bought salad, how many students bought both soup and salad?

7. Hamburger buns are sold in packages of 8. Hamburger patties are sold by the dozen. Mia bought the same number of buns and patties. What is the least number of each she could have bought?

8. Each brick in one row is 6 inches long. Each brick in the next row is 10 inches long. Both rows align at the left. How long is each row the first time the ends of the bricks align at the right?

Extra Practice See 1–4 on page 145.

Quick Check

Check Your Understanding of Lessons 1–7

Identify each number as *prime* or *composite*.

1. 18 **2.** 37 **3.** 106

Write each using exponents.

4. $3 \times 3 \times 3 \times 7$ **5.** $6 \times 6 \times 7$ **6.** $5 \times 5 \times 7 \times 7$

Draw a factor tree to show each prime factorization. Then rewrite, using exponents.

7. 35 **8.** 54 **9.** 120

Determine whether the first number listed is divisible by the second number.

10. 111 3 **11.** 654 6 **12.** 430 4

Find the GCF of each pair of numbers, then find their LCM.

13. 8, 12 **14.** 21, 35 **15.** 24, 20

Solve.

16. Lindsey has 14 pictures of her family and 8 pictures of her pets. Five of the pictures show both her family and her pets. How many pictures does she have in all?

How did you do?

If you had difficulty with any items in the Quick Check, you can use the following pages for review and extra practice.

Items	Review These Pages	Do These Extra Practice Items
1–3	pages 104–105	Set A, page 142
4–6	pages 106–107	Set B, page 142
7–9	pages 108–109	Set C, page 142
10–12	pages 110–111	Set D, page 142
13–15	pages 112–114, pages 116–117	Sets E and F, page 143
16	pages 118–119	1–4, page 145

Test Prep • Cumulative Review

Maintaining the Standards

Choose the letter of the correct answer.

1. Which is the expanded form of 4,786,067?

   A 4,000,000 + 700,000 + 80,000 + 6,000 + 60 + 7

   B 4,000,000 + 786,000 + 67

   C 4,000,000 + 700,000 + 80,000 + 6,000 + 67

   D 4,700,000 + 80,000 + 6,067

2. On the first day of their vacation, Carmen's family drove 124.6 miles. The next day they traveled 67.8 miles. Then they drove another 111.2 miles. How far had the family traveled?

   F 303.8 miles

   G 303.6 miles

   H 235.6 miles

   J 192.4 miles

3. Use the graph to determine how many students were absent on Tuesday and Wednesday.

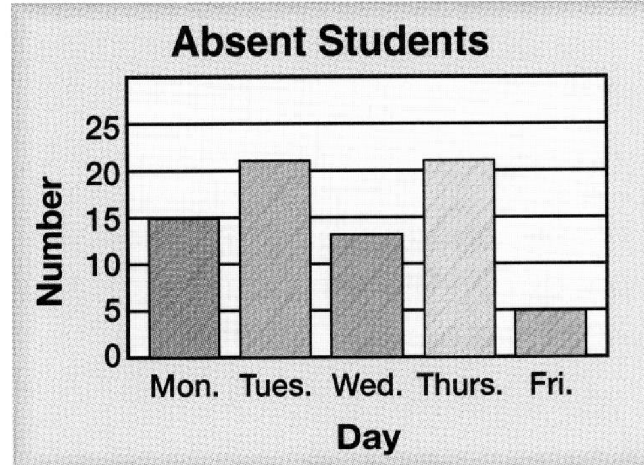

   A 31 students   **C** 42 students

   B 34 students   **D** 75 students

4. The school store sells notebook binders for $2.36. If the store sold 26 binders on Tuesday, what was the income from binder sales on that day?

   F $61.36   **H** $61.16

   G $61.26   **J** $0.09

5. Choose the decimal that is read "8 and 24 ten thousandths."

   A 8.24   **C** 8.0024

   B 8.024   **D** 8.00024

6. Which number represents the product of 89 and 76?

   F 1.17   **H** 6,763

   G 13   **J** 6,764

7. Carie bought a box of greeting cards for her mother. The price marked on the box was $8.28. If there are 12 cards in the box, what is the price per card?

   A $0.99   **C** $0.79

   B $0.89   **D** $0.69

8. Find the mean of the data given below.

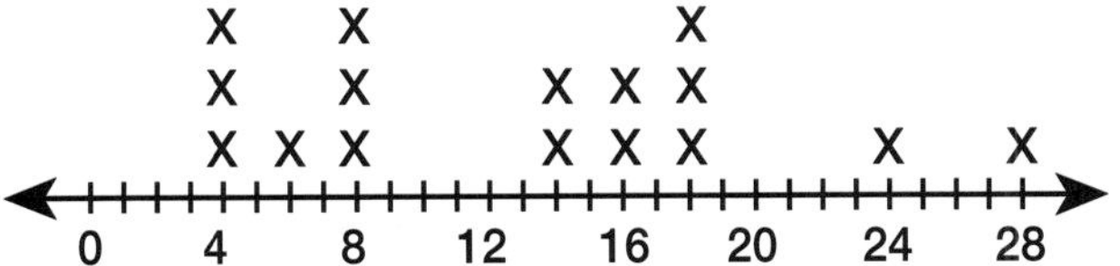

   Explain How did you find your answer?

Safe Site

Internet Test Prep
Visit **www.eduplace.com/kids/mhm** for more *Test Prep Practice.*

LESSON 8

Write Equivalent Fractions

You will learn how to find equivalent fractions.

New Vocabulary
equivalent fractions

Learn About It

Equivalent fractions represent the same number. The fractions $\frac{1}{1}$, $\frac{2}{2}$, $\frac{3}{3}$, and $\frac{4}{4}$ are equivalent to the number 1. One way to find an equivalent fraction is to multiply or divide the numerator and denominator by the same counting number.

Ben, Akiko, and some friends brought 16 small bags of sunflower seeds to the school baseball game. They ate the seeds from 12 of the bags.

The fraction $\frac{12}{16}$ represents the amount of seeds they ate. What is another way to write $\frac{12}{16}$ as a fraction?

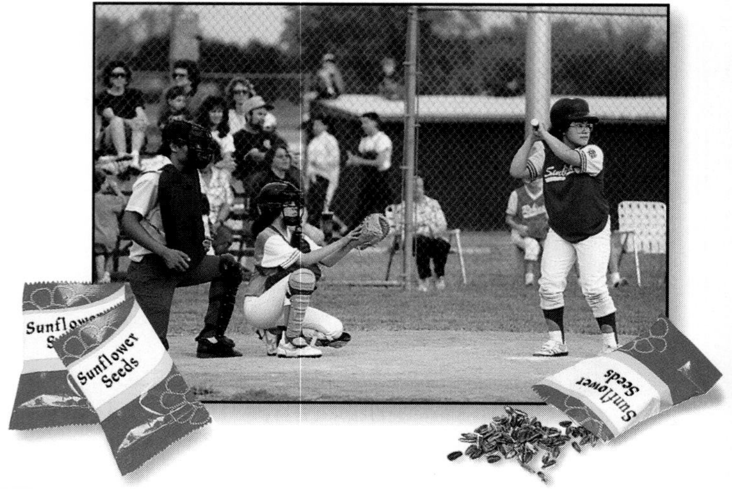

Different Ways to Find Equivalent Fractions

You can multiply.

Multiply numerator and denominator by the same counting number.

$\frac{12}{16} = \frac{12 \times 2}{16 \times 2} = \frac{24}{32}$ **Think:** $\frac{12}{16} = \frac{12}{16} \times \frac{2}{2} = \frac{24}{32}$

You can divide.

Divide numerator and denominator by the same counting number.

$\frac{12}{16} = \frac{12 \div 4}{16 \div 4} = \frac{3}{4}$ **Think:** $\frac{12}{16} = \frac{3 \times 4}{4 \times 4} = \frac{3}{4} \times \frac{4}{4} = \frac{3}{4}$

Solution: $\frac{24}{32}$ and $\frac{3}{4}$ are equivalent fractions for $\frac{12}{16}$.

Another Example

Given a Specific Denominator

$\frac{9}{21} = \frac{■}{7}$ **Think:** $21 \div 3 = 7$

$\frac{9 \div 3}{21 \div 3} = \frac{3}{7}$ $\frac{3}{7}$ is equivalent to $\frac{9}{21}$.

Explain Your Thinking

- ► Why do you get an equivalent fraction when you multiply or divide both numerator and denominator by the same number?
- ► How can you tell if two fractions are equivalent?

Guided Practice

Write two equivalent fractions. Use multiplication to write one and division to write the other.

1. $\frac{4}{6}$ **2.** $\frac{6}{8}$ **3.** $\frac{6}{14}$ **4.** $\frac{10}{16}$ **5.** $\frac{6}{24}$

Ask Yourself

- Did I multiply or divide the numerator and denominator by the same number?

Independent Practice

Write two equivalent fractions. Use multiplication to write one and division to write the other.

6. $\frac{8}{14}$ **7.** $\frac{8}{10}$ **8.** $\frac{15}{33}$ **9.** $\frac{6}{9}$ **10.** $\frac{5}{15}$

11. $\frac{6}{26}$ **12.** $\frac{8}{12}$ **13.** $\frac{21}{24}$ **14.** $\frac{12}{16}$ **15.** $\frac{14}{28}$

Write an equivalent fraction with the given denominator.

16. $\frac{8}{20} = \frac{■}{5}$ **17.** $\frac{10}{15} = \frac{■}{3}$ **18.** $\frac{7}{42} = \frac{■}{6}$ **19.** $\frac{16}{28} = \frac{■}{7}$

20. $\frac{6}{21} = \frac{■}{7}$ **21.** $\frac{15}{20} = \frac{■}{4}$ **22.** $\frac{16}{32} = \frac{■}{8}$ **23.** $\frac{30}{100} = \frac{■}{10}$

Problem Solving • Reasoning

Solve. Choose a method.

• Mental Math • Estimation • Paper and Pencil • Calculator

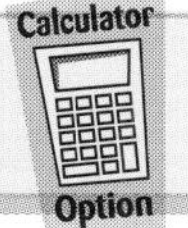

24. Leon flipped a penny 100 times for a math experiment. The penny came up "heads" 52 times. Express the results of his experiment as a fraction. Then write two equivalent fractions.

25. **Predict** Amy is putting her baseball cards in her new album. The album has 48 pages, and each page holds 4 baseball cards. Will Amy's album hold all 175 of her baseball cards? Explain.

26. **Analyze** During the regular season, a baseball team plays 56 games. If the team wins 5 out of every 7 games, the players will make it to the playoffs. How many games must the team win to make the playoffs? Find an equivalent fraction to solve the problem.

27. **Estimate** Kathy is reading a book that has 176 pages. Casey is reading a book that has 208 pages. They each have read $\frac{3}{8}$ of their books. Which of them has read more pages in their book? Tell how many pages each person has read.

Mixed Review • Test Prep

Multiply. *(pages 18–19, 36–37)*

28. 3,345 × 4 **29.** 68,078 × 100 **30.** 107 × 94 **31.** 1,209 × 1,000

Choose the letter of the correct answer. *(pages 106–109)*

32 Which is the prime factorization of 36?

A 2×3 **C** 2×3^2

B $2^2 \times 3$ **D** $2^2 \times 3^2$

33 What is 6^3?

F 18 **H** 729

G 216 **J** 1,824

Extra Practice See Set G on page 143.

LESSON 9

Simplest Form

You will learn how to use the GCF to write fractions in simplest form.

New Vocabulary
simplest form

Learn About It

A fraction is in **simplest form** when the only common factor of the numerator and denominator is 1.

Louis and Berta are going to a cabin that is 64 miles from their home. They have traveled 48 miles.

What fraction, in simplest form, represents the part of the distance they have traveled so far? You need to find the simplest form of $\frac{48}{64}$.

Different Ways to Find Simplest Form

You can use the GCF.

Step 1 Use prime factorization to find the GCF of the numerator and denominator.

$48 = (2) \times (2) \times (2) \times (2) \times 3$

$64 = (2) \times (2) \times (2) \times (2) \times 2 \times 2$

GCF of 48 and 64 $= 2 \times 2 \times 2 \times 2 = 2^4 = 16$

Step 2 Divide the numerator and denominator by their GCF.

$$\frac{48 \div 16}{64 \div 16} = \frac{3}{4}$$

You can cancel common factors.

Step 1 Use prime factorization to factor the numerator and denominator.

$$\frac{48}{64} = \frac{2 \times 2 \times 2 \times 2 \times 3}{2 \times 2 \times 2 \times 2 \times 2 \times 2}$$

Step 2 Cancel pairs of common factors.

Remember: $\frac{2}{2} = 1$

$$\frac{\overset{1}{\cancel{2}} \times \overset{1}{\cancel{2}} \times \overset{1}{\cancel{2}} \times \overset{1}{\cancel{2}} \times 3}{\underset{1}{\cancel{2}} \times \underset{1}{\cancel{2}} \times \underset{1}{\cancel{2}} \times \underset{1}{\cancel{2}} \times 2 \times 2} = \frac{3}{2 \times 2} = \frac{3}{4}$$

Solution: Louis and Berta have completed $\frac{3}{4}$ of their trip.

Other Examples

A. Improper Fraction

$\frac{6}{4}$

Simplify the fraction.

$$\frac{6}{4} = \frac{\overset{1}{\cancel{2}} \times 3}{\underset{1}{\cancel{2}} \times 2} = \frac{3}{2}$$

So, $\frac{6}{4} = \frac{3}{2}$

B. Mixed Number

$3\frac{6}{8}$

Simplify the fraction.

$$\frac{6 \div 2}{8 \div 2} = \frac{3}{4}$$

So, $3\frac{6}{8} = 3\frac{3}{4}$

Explain Your Thinking

- Which method of simplifying $\frac{48}{64}$ do you find easier? Why?
- Why do you need to divide both the numerator and the denominator by the same number?

Guided Practice

Write each fraction in its simplest form.

1. $\frac{6}{8}$ **2.** $\frac{12}{14}$ **3.** $5\frac{15}{42}$ **4.** $1\frac{44}{64}$

Write the missing numerator or denominator.

5. $\frac{4}{5} = \frac{48}{■}$ **6.** $\frac{10}{50} = \frac{■}{300}$ **7.** $\frac{9}{24} = \frac{■}{8}$ **8.** $\frac{10}{32} = \frac{5}{■}$

Ask Yourself

- Did I find the prime factorization for both the numerator and denominator?
- Did I write each mixed number in simplest form?

Independent Practice

Write each fraction in its simplest form.

9. $\frac{12}{24}$ **10.** $\frac{22}{48}$ **11.** $\frac{16}{36}$ **12.** $\frac{55}{121}$ **13.** $\frac{61}{63}$ **14.** $\frac{42}{45}$

15. $\frac{195}{39}$ **16.** $\frac{84}{77}$ **17.** $1\frac{14}{20}$ **18.** $3\frac{15}{4}$ **19.** $\frac{115}{10}$ **20.** $7\frac{14}{35}$

Write the missing numerator or denominator.

21. $\frac{18}{30} = \frac{3}{■}$ **22.** $\frac{14}{18} = \frac{■}{72}$ **23.** $\frac{66}{99} = \frac{2}{■}$ **24.** $\frac{49}{63} = \frac{147}{■}$

Problem Solving • Reasoning

25. Jessica and Adrian's family are on a trip to the Baseball Hall of Fame 450 miles away. They travel for 132 miles and stop to ask directions. Then they travel for 100 miles and stop to eat. They travel 118 more miles and stop to fill the car with gas. In simplest form, what fraction of the trip have they completed?

26. **Analyze** A school year has 180 days. If today is the 100th day, what fraction of the school year has been completed? Write your answer in simplest form.

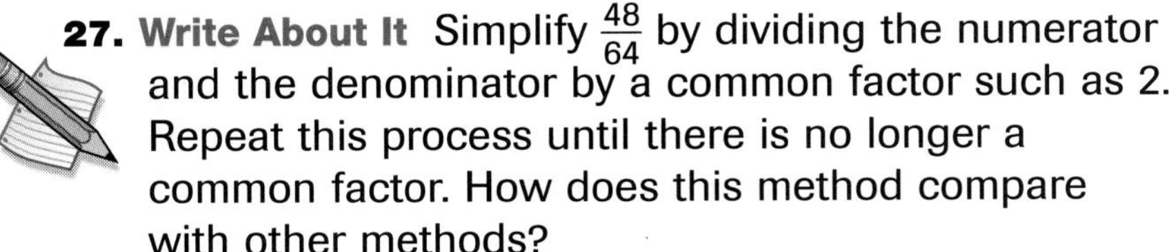

27. **Write About It** Simplify $\frac{48}{64}$ by dividing the numerator and the denominator by a common factor such as 2. Repeat this process until there is no longer a common factor. How does this method compare with other methods?

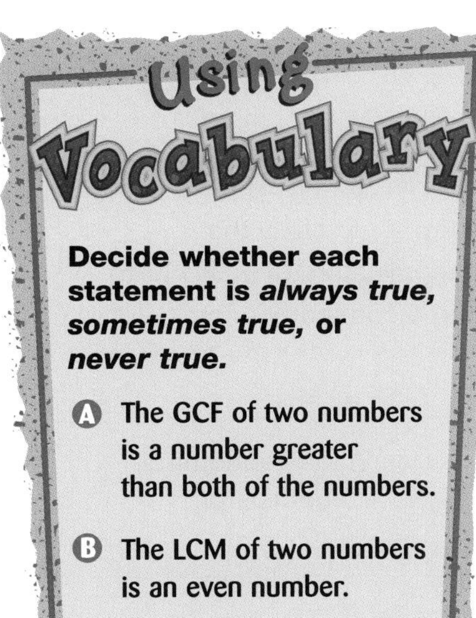

Using
Vocabulary
Decide whether each statement is *always true*, *sometimes true*, or *never true*.
A The GCF of two numbers is a number greater than both of the numbers.
B The LCM of two numbers is an even number.
C Equivalent fractions have the same value.

Mixed Review • Test Prep

Divide. *(pages 30–31, 32–33)*

28. 3,624 ÷ 12 **29.** 128.64 ÷ 32 **30.** 81,906 ÷ 11 **31.** 8,897.2 ÷ 29

32 What is the sum of 1,216 and 907? *(pages 12–13)*

A 2,123 **C** 1,124

B 2,113 **D** 995

Extra Practice See Set H on page 143.

Compare and Order Fractions

You will learn how to compare and order fractions.

New Vocabulary
common denominator
least common denominator (LCD)

Learn About It

Two fractions have a **common denominator** if their denominators are the same. For example, the fractions $\frac{2}{4}$ and $\frac{3}{4}$ have a common denominator. The **least common denominator (LCD)** of two fractions is the least common multiple of their denominators.

The school Environmental Club has decided to record rainfall data for each month. Members found that in April, $\frac{5}{8}$ inch of rain fell. In May, $\frac{7}{12}$ inch fell. In which month was there more rain? You need to compare $\frac{5}{8}$ and $\frac{7}{12}$.

Different Ways to Compare Fractions

You can use any common denominator.

Step 1 Multiply the denominators of $\frac{5}{8}$ and $\frac{7}{12}$ to find a common denominator.

$8 \times 12 = 96$

Use 96 as the common denominator.

Step 2 Write equivalent fractions with the common denominator of 96.

$\frac{5}{8} = \frac{5}{8} \times \frac{12}{12} = \frac{60}{96}$

$\frac{7}{12} = \frac{7}{12} \times \frac{8}{8} = \frac{56}{96}$

Step 3 Compare. Sixty unit fractions of $\frac{1}{96}$ is greater than 56 unit fractions of $\frac{1}{96}$.

$\frac{60}{96} > \frac{56}{96}$, so $\frac{5}{8} > \frac{7}{12}$

You can use the least common multiple of the denominators as the LCD.

Step 1 Use the prime factorization to find the LCM of the denominators of $\frac{5}{8}$ and $\frac{7}{12}$.

$8 = 2^3 \qquad 12 = 2^2 \times 3$

The LCM is $2^3 \times 3$, or 24.

Step 2 Write equivalent fractions with the LCM as the common denominator.

$\frac{5}{8} = \frac{5}{8} \times \frac{3}{3} = \frac{15}{24}$

$\frac{7}{12} = \frac{7}{12} \times \frac{2}{2} = \frac{14}{24}$

Step 3 Compare. 15 unit fractions of $\frac{1}{24}$ is greater than 14 unit fractions of $\frac{1}{24}$.

$\frac{15}{24} > \frac{14}{24}$, so $\frac{5}{8} > \frac{7}{12}$

Solution: Since $\frac{5}{8} > \frac{7}{12}$, more rain fell in April.

Other Examples

A. Use Number Lines to Order

Order $\frac{2}{5}$, $\frac{3}{4}$, and $\frac{2}{3}$ from greatest to least.

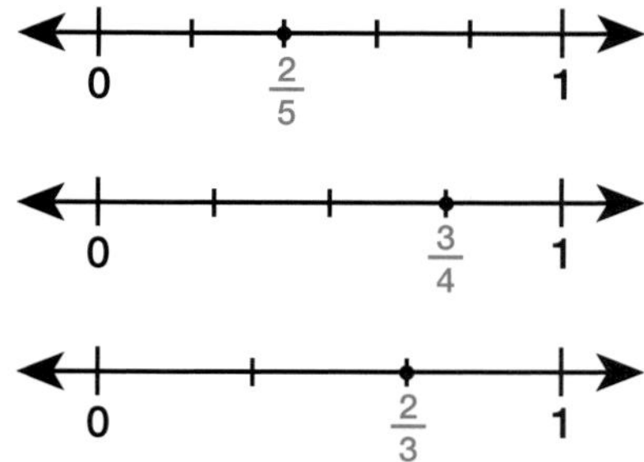

$\frac{2}{5}$ is farthest to the left and $\frac{3}{4}$ is farthest to the right, so $\frac{3}{4} > \frac{2}{3} > \frac{2}{5}$.

B. Use Equivalent Fractions to Order

Order $\frac{3}{5}$, $\frac{9}{10}$, and $\frac{4}{7}$ from least to greatest.

$\frac{3}{5} \times \frac{14}{14} = \frac{42}{70}$

$\frac{9}{10} \times \frac{7}{7} = \frac{63}{70}$

$\frac{4}{7} \times \frac{10}{10} = \frac{40}{70}$

A common denominator of 5, 10, and 7 is 70.

$\frac{40}{70} < \frac{42}{70} < \frac{63}{70}$, so $\frac{4}{7} < \frac{3}{5} < \frac{9}{10}$.

Explain Your Thinking

- What is the difference between an LCM and an LCD?
- Why is it often easier to compare fractions by finding the LCD?

Guided Practice

Compare. Write >, <, or = for each ⬬.

1. $\frac{3}{4}$ ⬬ $\frac{1}{6}$
2. $\frac{7}{8}$ ⬬ $\frac{8}{10}$
3. $2\frac{3}{4}$ ⬬ $5\frac{2}{3}$
4. $3\frac{4}{5}$ ⬬ $3\frac{3}{7}$

Order from greatest to least. Use a number line.

5. $\frac{1}{3}$ $\frac{7}{12}$ $\frac{5}{6}$
6. $\frac{3}{4}$ $\frac{7}{8}$ $\frac{13}{16}$
7. $\frac{3}{4}$ $\frac{5}{7}$ $\frac{9}{14}$

Ask Yourself

- Did I remember to find the LCD?
- Did I remember to compare the numerators after finding the LCD?

Independent Practice

Compare. Write >, <, or = for each ⬬.

8. $\frac{3}{6}$ ⬬ $\frac{4}{8}$
9. $\frac{4}{5}$ ⬬ $\frac{10}{15}$
10. $\frac{4}{6}$ ⬬ $\frac{1}{3}$
11. $\frac{3}{5}$ ⬬ $\frac{1}{2}$
12. $4\frac{1}{8}$ ⬬ $4\frac{1}{12}$
13. $\frac{2}{3}$ ⬬ $\frac{5}{8}$
14. $\frac{1}{3}$ ⬬ $\frac{2}{5}$
15. $\frac{1}{8}$ ⬬ $\frac{1}{16}$
16. $\frac{5}{9}$ ⬬ $\frac{4}{8}$
17. $5\frac{1}{2}$ ⬬ $6\frac{3}{8}$
18. $\frac{3}{5}$ ⬬ $\frac{2}{3}$
19. $\frac{1}{4}$ ⬬ $\frac{2}{3}$
20. $\frac{5}{8}$ ⬬ $\frac{10}{16}$
21. $\frac{2}{9}$ ⬬ $\frac{1}{3}$
22. $7\frac{5}{6}$ ⬬ $7\frac{9}{10}$

Order from greatest to least. Use a number line.

23. $\frac{5}{6}$ $\frac{3}{4}$ $\frac{1}{2}$
24. $\frac{3}{7}$ $\frac{3}{5}$ $\frac{3}{8}$
25. $\frac{2}{9}$ $\frac{1}{6}$ $\frac{2}{3}$
26. $\frac{5}{9}$ $\frac{1}{4}$ $\frac{11}{18}$
27. $\frac{4}{5}$ $\frac{17}{20}$ $\frac{3}{4}$

Algebra • Expressions **Compare. Write >, <, or = for each ⬬.**

28. $\frac{x}{8}$ ⬬ $\frac{4}{6}$, given $x = 3$
29. $\frac{3}{5}$ ⬬ $\frac{x}{5}$, given $x = 7$
30. $\frac{x}{7}$ ⬬ $\frac{3}{y}$, given $x = 3$, $y = 7$

Problem Solving • Reasoning

Use Data Use the rain gauges to solve Problems 31–32.

31. Which month had more rain—January or February?

32. The rainfall for which month could be expressed as $2\frac{27}{36}$?

33. **Analyze** It rained 10 days in March and 10 days in April. A reporter said that a greater part of April had rain than did March. Explain how this is possible.

34. **Patterns** Find a pattern. How do you know the numbers in this pattern are decreasing?

$\frac{1}{2}$ $\frac{1}{3}$ $\frac{1}{4}$ $\frac{1}{5}$ $\frac{1}{6}$

35. **Patterns** Find a pattern. How do you know the numbers in this pattern are increasing?

$\frac{1}{2}$ $\frac{2}{3}$ $\frac{3}{4}$ $\frac{4}{5}$ $\frac{5}{6}$

Mixed Review • Test Prep

Round to the underlined place. *(pages 8–9)*

36. $34.9\underline{6}5$ **37.** $1\underline{5}6.89$ **38.** $1.0\underline{0}34$ **39.** $\underline{2},544.8$

40. $8.90\underline{5}5$ **41.** $27\underline{5}.49$ **42.** $3.\underline{1}057$ **43.** $9.9\underline{9}75$

Choose the letter of the correct answer. *(pages 122–123)*

44 Which fraction is not equivalent to $\frac{2}{3}$?

A $\frac{20}{30}$ **B** $\frac{4}{9}$ **C** $\frac{8}{12}$ **D** $\frac{4}{6}$

45 What is the value of x in $\frac{x}{4} = \frac{12}{16}$?

F 1 **G** 2 **H** 3 **J** 4

Logical Thinking

Mystery Fraction

- Its numerator and denominator are both prime numbers.
- Its numerator is less than its denominator.
- Its numerator and denominator differ by 2.
- The sum of its numerator and denominator is 21, 22, 23, or 24.

Name this fraction in its simplest form.

Practice Game

Ordering Fractions

Practice ordering fractions by playing this game with a partner.

What You'll Need

- *a spinner with the numbers 1, 3, 4, 6, 8, 9*
- *paper and pencil*

Players 2–4

Here's What to Do

1. Each player makes a fraction by spinning the spinner two times. The smaller number is the numerator, and the greater number is the denominator. If a player spins the same number twice, the player should spin the spinner again.
2. The players write both fractions on a sheet of paper.
3. The players decide mentally which fraction is greater, using $>$ or $<$ to record their prediction.
4. The players check their predictions. Each player with the correct answer scores 10 points.

Repeat the steps until one player has 50 points. For a longer game, repeat until one player has 100 points.

Share Your Thinking When estimating which fraction is greater, what strategies do you use? Why is it important to look at both the numerator and the denominator when comparing fractions?

Problem-Solving Skill: Interpret Remainders

You will learn how to use remainders when solving problems.

When you solve a problem that has a remainder, you need to decide how to interpret the remainder.

Look at the situations below.

Sometimes you ignore the remainder.

Gladys collects shells. On one vacation, she gathered many small shells at the beach. Gladys collected 100 shells to give to 7 friends. How many shells does each friend receive if Gladys gives each friend the same number of shells?

$$100 \div 7 = 14 \text{ R2}$$

Each friend receives 14 shells. The remainder, 2, is not part of the solution, since 2 shells cannot be divided among 7 people.

Sometimes the remainder is the solution.

Gladys will add the shells that she doesn't give to her friends to her collection. How many shells will Gladys have left for her collection after she gives her friends their shells?

$$100 \div 7 = 14 \text{ R2}$$

After Gladys gives her friends the same number of shells, she will have 2 shells left for her collection.

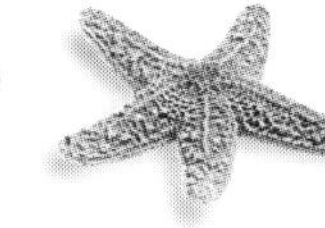

Sometimes the remainder affects the solution.

Gladys wants to buy some boxes to hold the 66 shells in her collection. Each box will hold 9 shells. How many boxes does she need?

$$66 \div 9 = 7 \text{ R3}$$

Since 7 boxes will hold all but 3 shells, Gladys needs to buy 8 boxes for all her shells.

Look Back Why does thinking about the question in each situation help you decide what to do with the remainder?

Fishing flies are made to resemble real flies and bugs like the ones swarming around this fisherman.

Guided Practice

Solve.

1. Felix and two friends bought a box of 40 fishing flies and divided them equally. How many flies did each person get?

   Think: Is $\frac{1}{3}$ of a fishing fly reasonable?

2. Each school bus can hold 44 students. How many school buses are needed to take 120 students to the beach?

   Think: Is the remainder a necessary part of the solution?

Choose a Strategy

Solve. Use these or other strategies.

Calculator Option

Problem-Solving Strategies

- **Write an Equation**
- **Make a List**
- **Use Logical Thinking**
- **Work Backward**

3. During the latest beach cleanup, 140 pieces of trash were collected. Susan picked up $\frac{1}{4}$ of this trash. How many pieces of trash did Susan pick up during the trash cleanup?

4. Sarah sells necklaces made from shells. At the end of one day, she sold 12 necklaces and collected $54. If each necklace sold for the same price, what was the selling price of each necklace?

5. Alexa and her friends built 9 sandcastles one weekend. They worked on the 9 sandcastles for 6 hours. On average, how many sandcastles did Alexa and her friends build in 1 hour?

6. Mr. Franzell is building shelves for his cabin. Each shelf is 4 feet long. He has 2 pieces of lumber, each 9 feet long. How many 4-foot boards can he cut from the lumber?

7. For a fall fundraiser, the band members sold 720 raffle tickets. It took 24 days for the band members to sell all of the raffle tickets. There are 45 members in the band. What was the average number of raffle tickets sold by each band member?

8. Look at the table below. Predict how many decimal places will be required to represent $\frac{1}{32}$ as a decimal.

$\frac{1}{2}$	$\frac{1}{4}$	$\frac{1}{8}$	$\frac{1}{16}$	$\frac{1}{32}$
0.5	0.25	0.125	0.0625	■

Extra Practice See 5–6 on page 145.

Quick Check

Check Your Understanding of Lessons 8–11

Write two equivalent fractions. Use multiplication to write one and division to write the other.

1. $\frac{9}{12}$ **2.** $\frac{8}{18}$ **3.** $\frac{7}{28}$

Write each fraction in its simplest form.

4. $\frac{15}{30}$ **5.** $\frac{24}{36}$ **6.** $\frac{15}{25}$

Use common denominators, number lines, or equivalent fractions to compare. Write >, <, or = for each ⬮.

7. $\frac{3}{8}$ ⬮ $\frac{2}{3}$ **8.** $\frac{3}{4}$ ⬮ $\frac{2}{3}$ **9.** $\frac{5}{6}$ ⬮ $\frac{10}{15}$

Solve.

10. Joe has 50 baseball cards he wants to divide equally among 6 friends. How many baseball cards can he give to each of his friends? How many will he have left for himself?

How did you do?

If you had difficulty with any items in the Quick Check, you can use the following pages for review and extra practice.

Items	Review These Pages	Do These Extra Practice Items
1–3	pages 122–123	Set G, page 143
4–6	pages 124–125	Set H, page 143
7–9	pages 126–128	Set I, page 144
10	pages 130–131	5–6, page 145

Test Prep • Cumulative Review

Maintaining the Standards

Choose the letter of the correct answer.

1. Ryan needs to display some data for his science project. His data show what percent of a budget is spent on electricity, water, food, transportation, and clothing. Which of the following would best display these data?

   A number line
   B coordinate grid
   C circle graph
   D line plot

2. There are 25 marbles in a jar. Five are red, 10 are blue, and 10 are green. What is the probability of drawing a red marble?

   F $\frac{4}{5}$
   G $\frac{3}{5}$
   H $\frac{2}{5}$
   J $\frac{1}{5}$

3. Which number is the product of 0.0129×5?

   A 0.645
   B 0.0645
   C 0.00645
   D 0.000645

4. Which number represents the quotient of 10,000 divided by 10?

   F 10
   G 100
   H 1,000
   J 10,000

5. Nicholas gained the following number of yards playing football in the last game: 2, 5, 3, 8, 2, 9, 6. Find the mean of the number of yards Nicholas gained.

   A 7 yards
   B 5 yards
   C 4 yards
   D 2 yards

6. Evaluate $4x - 3$, given $x = 2$.

   F 7
   G 6
   H 5
   J 4

7. Jennifer bought a hamburger for $2.13 and french fries for $1.09. Becky bought a chicken sandwich for $3.99 and onion rings for $2.45. Compare the cost of Jennifer's purchase to Becky's.

   A Jennifer spent more than Becky.
   B Jennifer spent one third as much as Becky.
   C Jennifer spent one half as much as Becky.
   D Jennifer spent twice as much as Becky.

8. Mrs. Reed has finished grading her mathematics tests. Find the median score on Mrs. Reed's math tests.

Stem	Leaf
7	1 3 3 6 7
8	3 4 6 6 7 8
9	4 5 6 8 8 9

Explain How did you find your answer?

Internet Test Prep
Visit **www.eduplace.com/kids/mhm** for more *Test Prep Practice.*

LESSON 12

Fractions, Mixed Numbers, and Decimals

You will learn how to compare and order fractions, mixed numbers, and decimals.

Average Daily Internet Use	
Name	**Hours**
Fred	1.6
Liliana	$\frac{3}{4}$
Tina	$1\frac{4}{5}$
Jason	$\frac{3}{2}$
Jessica	0.6

Learn About It

To compare decimals, fractions, and mixed numbers, express the numbers in the same form.

Mr. Klein asked a group of students to record the amount of time they spend on the Internet on school nights. How can Mr. Klein compare the amounts of time spent by Fred and Tina?

Compare 1.6 and $1\frac{4}{5}$.

Step 1 Write 1.6 as a fraction with 10 as the denominator.

$1.6 = 1\frac{6}{10} = \frac{16}{10}$

Step 2 Change $1\frac{4}{5}$ to an equivalent fraction with 10 as the denominator.

$1\frac{4}{5} = \frac{9}{5} = \frac{18}{10}$

Step 3 Compare the fractions.

$\frac{16}{10} < \frac{18}{10}$, so $1.6 < 1\frac{4}{5}$

Solution: 1.6 hours $< 1\frac{4}{5}$ hours

Remember:

$1.6 = 1 + 0.6$

$1\frac{4}{5} = 1 + \frac{4}{5}$

$\frac{3}{2} = \frac{2}{2} + \frac{1}{2}$

Mr. Klein wants to put the amounts of time for Fred, Tina, and Jason in order. You can use number lines to order fractions, mixed numbers, and decimals.

Order 1.6, $1\frac{4}{5}$, and $\frac{3}{2}$ from least to greatest.

Step 1 Draw three number lines of equal length. Write each as a mixed number. Mark the locations of the three mixed numbers.

$1.6 = 1\frac{6}{10}$

$\frac{3}{2} = 1\frac{1}{2}$

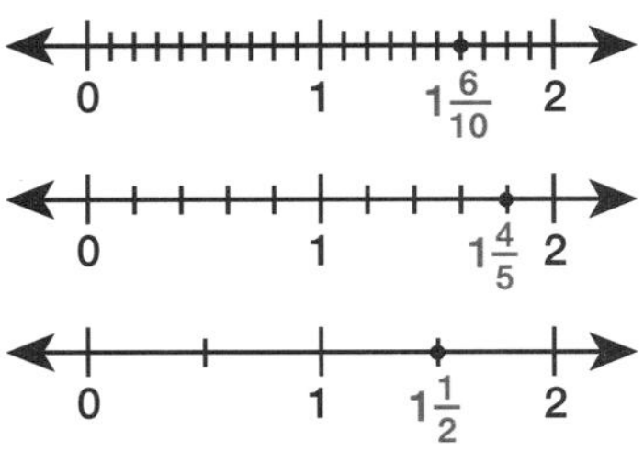

Step 2 Compare. The number farthest to the left is the least. The number farthest to the right is the greatest.

$1\frac{1}{2} < 1\frac{6}{10} < 1\frac{4}{5}$

Solution: $\frac{3}{2} < 1.6 < 1\frac{4}{5}$

Explain Your Thinking

▶ Why do you write an equivalent fraction with a power of 10 in the denominator in order to compare a fraction and a decimal?

Guided Practice

Compare. Write in order from least to greatest.

1. $\frac{5}{10}$ 0.6 0.55 **2.** $1\frac{4}{5}$ $1\frac{1}{2}$ 1.7 **3.** 0.65 0.85 $\frac{15}{20}$

4. 0.75 2.45 $1\frac{1}{5}$ **5.** $\frac{9}{25}$ $\frac{3}{10}$ 0.8 **6.** $4\frac{3}{4}$ 4.3 $4\frac{7}{10}$

Ask Yourself

- Did I find an equivalent fraction with 10 or 100 in the denominator?

Independent Practice

Compare. Write in order from least to greatest.

7. 0.3 1.4 $\frac{9}{10}$ **8.** 2.5 2.15 $2\frac{4}{5}$ **9.** $\frac{25}{20}$ $1\frac{3}{4}$ 1.5 **10.** 0.42 $\frac{24}{100}$ $\frac{18}{50}$

11. $\frac{1}{3}$ 0.35 $\frac{2}{5}$ **12.** 0.08 $\frac{24}{100}$ $\frac{6}{10}$ **13.** $\frac{7}{10}$ 0.65 $\frac{1}{2}$ **14.** $\frac{9}{10}$ 0.85 $\frac{4}{5}$

15. $2\frac{4}{5}$ 2.3 $2\frac{3}{4}$ **16.** 9.2 $9\frac{6}{10}$ $9\frac{8}{20}$ **17.** $1\frac{1}{3}$ 1.5 $1\frac{6}{10}$ **18.** $\frac{3}{4}$ 0.70 $\frac{2}{3}$

Problem Solving • Reasoning

19. **Compare** Jill watches TV an average of 1.6 hours each day. John watches $1\frac{3}{5}$ hours each day. Who watches more television?

20. Jeremy surfed the Internet for $\frac{7}{10}$ of an hour last night before he did his homework. Mike surfed the Internet $\frac{5}{8}$ of an hour before supper. Express both fractions as decimals. Who spent more time on the Internet?

21. Don listens to the radio 1.2 hours each day. Pat listens 1 hour 15 minutes. Carl listens $1\frac{5}{15}$ hours. Order the times from least to greatest.

22. **Write About It** Choose two fractions and two decimals and order them. Tell what method you used and explain why you chose that method.

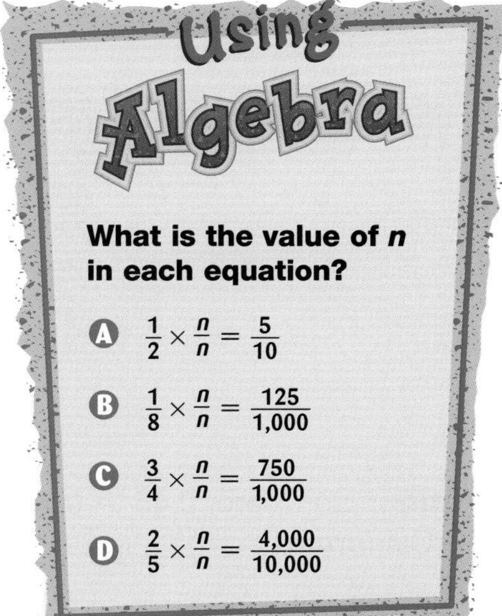

What is the value of *n* in each equation?

A $\frac{1}{2} \times \frac{n}{n} = \frac{5}{10}$

B $\frac{1}{8} \times \frac{n}{n} = \frac{125}{1,000}$

C $\frac{3}{4} \times \frac{n}{n} = \frac{750}{1,000}$

D $\frac{2}{5} \times \frac{n}{n} = \frac{4,000}{10,000}$

Mixed Review • Test Prep

Write each number in standard form. *(pages 4–5)*

23. 600 + 5 + 0.07 + 0.006 **24.** one hundred five million **25.** 16 million

26 What is the quotient of 75.6 ÷ 0.42? *(pages 34–35)*

A 18 **B** 1.80 **C** 180 **D** 18.0

Extra Practice See Set J on page 144.

Terminating and Repeating Decimals

You will learn how to express fractions as either terminating or repeating decimals.

New Vocabulary
terminating decimal
repeating decimal

Learn About It

Alaska is the largest state in the United States. Texas is about $\frac{9}{20}$ the size of Alaska. California is about $\frac{3}{11}$ the size of Alaska. Which state is larger, California or Texas?

To solve the problem, you can compare fractions by changing each fraction to a decimal. To change a fraction to a decimal, divide the numerator by the denominator.

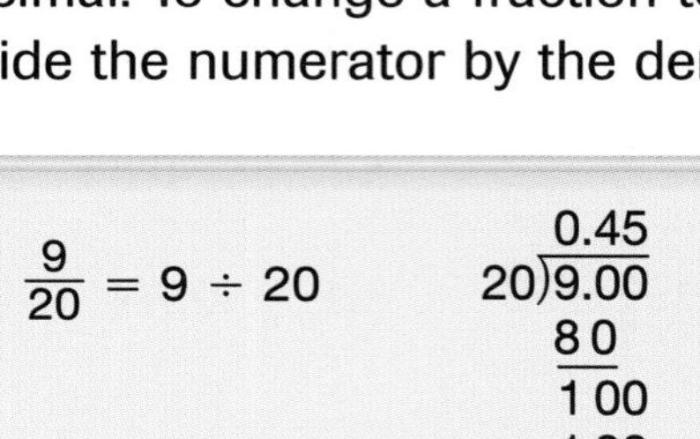

$\frac{9}{20} = 9 \div 20$

```
   0.45
20)9.00
   8 0
   1 00
   1 00
      0
```

In the first example, you can end the division when there is a remainder of zero. This decimal is called a **terminating decimal.** If the division is continued, it will only produce additional zeros. This does not change the value of the quotient.

$\frac{3}{11} = 3 \div 11$

```
   0.2727...
11)3.0000...
   2 2
     80
     77
      30
      22
       80
       77
        3
```

In the second example, the digits 2 and 7 repeat in the quotient. A decimal is called a **repeating decimal** when a pattern of numbers repeats continuously somewhere after the decimal point, and they are not all zeros.

A bar is usually placed above the repeating digits. $0.\overline{27}$

Solution: Compare. $0.45 > 0.\overline{27}$, so $\frac{9}{20} > \frac{3}{11}$. Texas is larger than California.

Another Example

One Repeating Digit

Find the decimal equivalent of $\frac{5}{6}$.

```
  0.83̅
6)5.00
  4.8
    20
    18
     2   Remainder of 2 repeats.
```

$\frac{5}{6} = 0.8\overline{3}$

Explain Your Thinking

- Sometimes a repeating decimal is written as 0.27272727... to show that the pattern continues. How would you write the decimal for $\frac{5}{6}$ in this way?
- How would you write 0.263888... with a bar?

Guided Practice

Write each fraction as a decimal. Use a bar to show repeating decimals.

1. $\frac{5}{12}$ **2.** $\frac{2}{9}$ **3.** $\frac{4}{5}$ **4.** $\frac{4}{6}$

5. $\frac{1}{11}$ **6.** $\frac{3}{4}$ **7.** $\frac{45}{54}$ **8.** $\frac{10}{90}$

> **Ask Yourself**
> - Did I stop dividing too soon?
> - Did I place a bar over all the repeating digits?

Independent Practice

Write each fraction as a decimal. Use a bar as needed.

9. $\frac{18}{20}$ **10.** $\frac{3}{5}$ **11.** $\frac{5}{9}$ **12.** $\frac{9}{11}$ **13.** $\frac{3}{10}$ **14.** $\frac{1}{2}$

15. $\frac{5}{6}$ **16.** $\frac{6}{8}$ **17.** $\frac{1}{3}$ **18.** $\frac{11}{12}$ **19.** $\frac{3}{8}$ **20.** $\frac{7}{11}$

21. $\frac{1}{6}$ **22.** $\frac{5}{11}$ **23.** $\frac{1}{4}$ **24.** $\frac{2}{3}$ **25.** $\frac{7}{8}$ **26.** $\frac{1}{12}$

27. $\frac{1}{8}$ **28.** $\frac{4}{11}$ **29.** $\frac{3}{6}$ **30.** $\frac{5}{8}$ **31.** $\frac{7}{9}$ **32.** $\frac{20}{36}$

Problem Solving • Reasoning

Use Data **Use the table for Problems 33 and 34.**

33. What fraction of the 50 states were admitted between 1951 and 2000? Write this fraction as a decimal.

34. Of the states admitted before 1901, what fraction were admitted between 1751 and 1800? Write this fraction as a decimal.

35. Analyze Fran has a collection of 22 state pennants. She displays 4 pennants on a shelf and hangs the others on a wall. What fraction of her pennants are displayed on the wall? Express your answer as a decimal.

36. Write About It Make a prediction regarding which denominators between 1 and 20 will result in a terminating decimal. Explain your prediction.

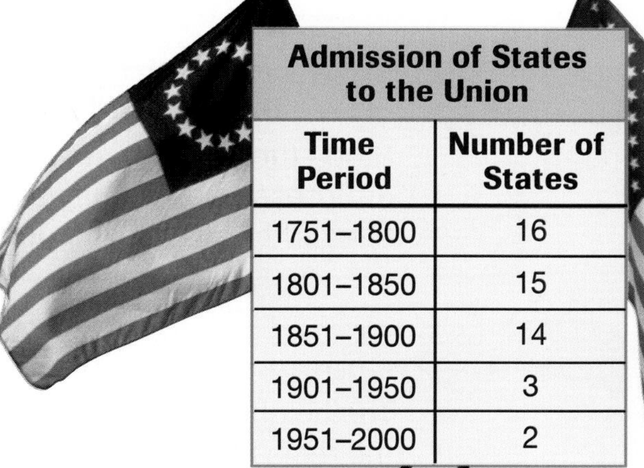

Admission of States to the Union

Time Period	Number of States
1751–1800	16
1801–1850	15
1851–1900	14
1901–1950	3
1951–2000	2

Mixed Review • Test Prep

Find the GCF of each pair of numbers. *(pages 112–115)*

37. 12, 16 **38.** 20, 24 **39.** 16, 17 **40.** 24, 36 **41.** 10, 20

42 What is 36.7886 rounded to the nearest thousandth? *(pages 8–9)*

A 36.80 **B** 36.789 **C** 36.79 **D** 36.788

Problem-Solving Application: Using Fractions in a Bar Graph

You will learn how to use fractions in a bar graph.

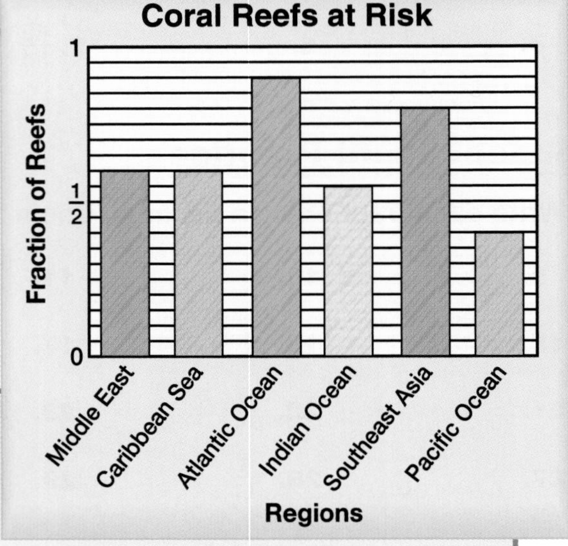

Sometimes you need to show data in different forms. A bar graph is one way to display data.

Problem The graph shows the fraction of coral reefs considered to be at risk for damage in different regions. Use the graph to identify the reefs at least and greatest risk.

Understand

What is the question?

Which reefs are at least and greatest risk?

What do you know?

The risk for each region is given on the graph.

Plan

How can you find the answer?

Study the graph to determine how the data are presented. Identify the information needed to answer the questions.

Compare the heights of the bars.

The heights of the bars show the fraction of the reefs at risk in a particular region of the world. Look at the tallest bar and identify the region it represents. Look at the shortest bar and identify the region it represents.

The region with the greatest risk is the Atlantic Ocean. The region with the least risk is the Pacific Ocean.

Look Back

Look back at the question.

Are your answers reasonable? How would comparing the fractions represented by the bars validate your answers?

Left: A biologist ties a live piece of coral onto a dead piece. In time, new coral growth will be seen on the reef. *Below:* Brain coral grows on a reef.

Remember:
- ▶ Understand
- ▶ Plan
- ▶ Solve
- ▶ Look Back

Guided Practice

Solve. Use the graph on page 138.

1. Which regions have a fraction of reefs at risk that is greater than the risk in the Indian Ocean?

   Think: To which bar should you compare the other bars?

2. If $\frac{3}{5}$ is the fraction of reefs at risk worldwide, which areas shown have a lower than worldwide risk?

   Think: What denominator should you use when you compare the data?

Choose a Strategy

Solve. Use these or other strategies. For Exercises 3, 4, and 7, use the graph on page 138.

Problem-Solving Strategies

- **Find a Pattern**
- **Work Backward**
- **Make a List**
- **Use Logical Thinking**

3. What fractions of reefs in each region are *not* threatened? *Hint*: How can you use the information on the bar graph to find the answer without subtracting?

4. If $\frac{4}{5}$ represents the fraction of reefs at risk in Southeast Asia, which region has only half the reefs at risk that Southeast Asia has?

5. At the aquarium, Andy watched whales for 45 min. He spent half of his time there watching sharks. The rest of the time he watched a film. The film was 10 minutes long. How long was he at the aquarium?

6. Find a pattern in the number sequence. Use your pattern to predict the next likely number. Explain your thinking.

   $\frac{1}{2}$ $\frac{3}{5}$ $\frac{5}{8}$ $\frac{7}{11}$

7. In which regions of the world are more than $\frac{1}{2}$ of the reefs threatened? In which regions are less than $\frac{1}{2}$ of the reefs threatened? Explain the method you used to find the answers.

8. Find a pattern in the figures. Use your pattern to predict the number of dots that likely will be in the next two figures.

Extra Practice See 7–9 on page 145.

Quick Check

Check Your Understanding of Lessons 12–14

Compare. Order from least to greatest.

1. $\frac{6}{10}$ 0.8 $\frac{3}{4}$

2. $1\frac{3}{5}$ 1.8 $1\frac{2}{3}$

3. $4\frac{1}{5}$ 4.3 $4\frac{1}{4}$

4. $2\frac{1}{3}$ 2.35 2.13

Write each fraction as a decimal. Use a bar as needed.

5. $\frac{4}{9}$

6. $\frac{5}{12}$

7. $\frac{17}{22}$

8. $\frac{16}{15}$

9. $\frac{2}{3}$

10. $\frac{2}{4}$

11. $\frac{4}{5}$

12. $\frac{5}{11}$

Solve.

13. What fraction of the students at Henderson Elementary walk to school? What fraction of the students at Scott Elementary do not walk to school?

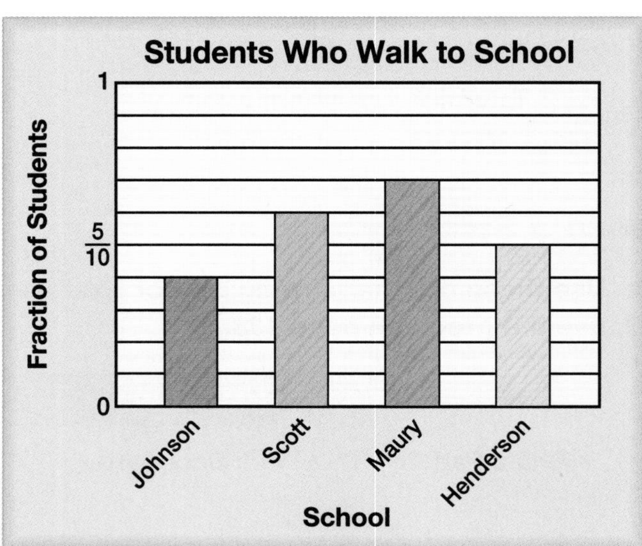

How did you do?

If you had difficulty with any items in the Quick Check, you can use the following pages for review and extra practice.

Items	Review These Pages	Do These Extra Practice Items
1–4	pages 134–135	Set J, page 144
5–12	pages 136–137	Set K, page 144
13	pages 138–139	7–9, page 145

Test Prep • Cumulative Review

Maintaining the Standards

Write the letter of the correct answer.

1 How many meters are equal to 0.25 kilometer?

A 2.5 m

B 25 m

C 250 m

D 2,000 m

2 Jake's family bought 8.5 pounds of tomatoes at a farmer's market. If tomatoes are $1.59 a pound, how much did they pay for the tomatoes?

F $0.19

G $13.51

H $13.52

J $13.55

3 Each softball team in the city league has 16 team members. There are 14 softball teams. In all, how many players are on the city teams?

A 214

B 215

C 224

D 234

4 Which of the following numbers is a prime number?

F 1

G 4

H 15

J 17

5 Australia had a population of 18,783,551 in 1999. What is the correct short word form for 18,783,551?

A 18,000,000 + 783,000 + 551

B 18 million, 783 thousand, 551

C 18 million, 700 thousand, 83 ten thousandths, 551

D 18 million, 783 thousand, 5 hundreds, 51

6 Nancy worked 13.5 hours last week and was paid $6.50 an hour. How much money did Nancy earn?

F $87.75

G $87.50

H $84.50

J $78.00

7 Student Council members volunteered the following hours to help beautify the school: 2, 4, 3, 6, 4, 3, 4, 5. What is the mode of the number of hours worked?

A 31 **C** 3.9

B 4 **D** 3

8 Identify an outlier in the given data.

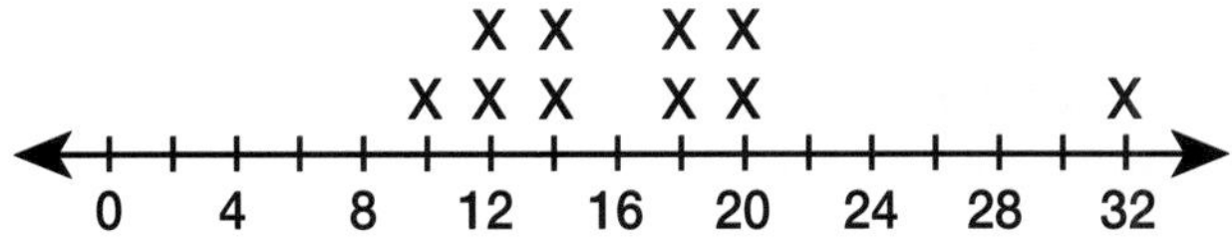

Explain How did you make your choice?

Internet Test Prep
Visit **www.eduplace.com/kids/mhm** for more *Test Prep Practice.*

Extra Practice

Set A *(Lesson 1, pages 104–105)*

List all factor pairs for each number. Then identify each number as *prime* or *composite*.

1. 14 **2.** 22 **3.** 27 **4.** 40 **5.** 50 **6.** 44

7. 17 **8.** 16 **9.** 35 **10.** 25 **11.** 13 **12.** 101

13. 24 **14.** 64 **15.** 61 **16.** 81 **17.** 90 **18.** 102

Set B *(Lesson 2, pages 106–107)*

Write each using exponents.

1. $3 \times 3 \times 5$ **2.** $2 \times 2 \times 7 \times 7$ **3.** $5 \times 5 \times 5 \times 7 \times 11$

4. $2 \times 2 \times 2$ **5.** $2 \times 3 \times 3 \times 3$ **6.** $2 \times 2 \times 3 \times 3 \times 3 \times 5$

Evaluate each expression.

7. $2^2 \times 3^2$ **8.** 3^4 **9.** $2^3 \times 3$ **10.** $2^2 \times 3^3$ **11.** $5^3 \times 7$

12. $7^2 \times 3^2$ **13.** 2^5 **14.** 5×11^2 **15.** $3^3 \times 5$ **16.** $2^2 \times 5^3$

Set C *(Lesson 3, pages 108–109)*

Draw a factor tree to show each prime factorization. Then rewrite, using exponents. If the number is prime, write *prime*.

1. 8 **2.** 12 **3.** 22 **4.** 16 **5.** 25 **6.** 26

7. 27 **8.** 28 **9.** 29 **10.** 30 **11.** 31 **12.** 32

13. 33 **14.** 34 **15.** 35 **16.** 36 **17.** 37 **18.** 38

Set D *(Lesson 4, pages 110–111)*

Determine if the first number listed is divisible by the second number.

1. 128 2 **2.** 67 2 **3.** 105 5 **4.** 187 5

5. 1,077 3 **6.** 142 9 **7.** 364 4 **8.** 1,122 6

9. 256 4 **10.** 1,560 4 **11.** 816 6 **12.** 303 6

13. 516 6 **14.** 1,224 4 **15.** 999 3 **16.** 1,000 8

Extra Practice

Set E *(Lesson 5, pages 112–114)*

Find the GCF for each group of numbers by using prime factorization or listing the factors of each.

1. 44, 33 **2.** 28, 35 **3.** 48, 36 **4.** 20, 50

5. 20, 18 **6.** 26, 39 **7.** 48, 64 **8.** 24, 44

9. 18, 48 **10.** 45, 60 **11.** 16, 80 **12.** 200, 144

13. 144, 24 **14.** 45, 54 **15.** 24, 28, 36 **16.** 12, 18, 42

Set F *(Lesson 6, pages 116–117)*

Find the LCM of each group of numbers by using prime factorization or listing the factors of each.

1. 10, 20 **2.** 18, 36 **3.** 12, 18 **4.** 3, 5

5. 8, 12 **6.** 12, 20 **7.** 10, 4 **8.** 14, 42

9. 24, 18 **10.** 30, 25 **11.** 8, 14 **12.** 18, 6

13. 15, 12 **14.** 7, 13 **15.** 5, 6, 10 **16.** 12, 18, 24

Set G *(Lesson 8, pages 122–123)*

Write two equivalent fractions. Use multiplication to write one and division to write the other.

1. $\frac{3}{9}$ **2.** $\frac{18}{64}$ **3.** $\frac{16}{26}$ **4.** $\frac{14}{30}$ **5.** $\frac{14}{18}$

6. $\frac{52}{200}$ **7.** $\frac{18}{64}$ **8.** $\frac{21}{63}$ **9.** $\frac{26}{100}$ **10.** $\frac{14}{21}$

11. $\frac{12}{48}$ **12.** $\frac{9}{42}$ **13.** $\frac{7}{21}$ **14.** $\frac{15}{20}$ **15.** $\frac{16}{32}$

Set H *(Lesson 9, pages 124–125)*

Write each fraction in its simplest form.

1. $\frac{8}{24}$ **2.** $\frac{22}{46}$ **3.** $\frac{16}{38}$ **4.** $\frac{44}{121}$ **5.** $\frac{18}{63}$

6. $\frac{34}{35}$ **7.** $\frac{105}{35}$ **8.** $\frac{74}{111}$ **9.** $\frac{35}{35}$ **10.** $\frac{30}{36}$

11. $\frac{25}{10}$ **12.** $\frac{21}{35}$ **13.** $\frac{18}{15}$ **14.** $\frac{12}{18}$ **15.** $\frac{66}{72}$

Extra Practice

Set I (Lesson 10, pages 126–128)

Use a common denominator to compare. Write >, <, or = for each ⬬.

1. $\frac{1}{8}$ ⬬ $\frac{1}{9}$ **2.** $\frac{3}{4}$ ⬬ $\frac{3}{6}$ **3.** $\frac{1}{4}$ ⬬ $\frac{2}{3}$ **4.** $\frac{5}{6}$ ⬬ $\frac{2}{10}$

Use number lines to compare. Write >, <, or = for each ⬬.

5. $\frac{2}{5}$ ⬬ $\frac{2}{3}$ **6.** $\frac{2}{5}$ ⬬ $\frac{1}{3}$ **7.** $\frac{5}{8}$ ⬬ $\frac{9}{16}$

8. $\frac{2}{9}$ ⬬ $\frac{1}{3}$ **9.** $\frac{3}{7}$ ⬬ $\frac{4}{9}$ **10.** $\frac{5}{12}$ ⬬ $\frac{3}{8}$

11. $\frac{2}{3}$ ⬬ $\frac{5}{9}$ **12.** $\frac{3}{8}$ ⬬ $\frac{1}{3}$ **13.** $\frac{4}{6}$ ⬬ $\frac{6}{10}$

Write in order from least to greatest.

14. $\frac{1}{5}$ $\frac{3}{5}$ $\frac{5}{6}$ **15.** $\frac{2}{3}$ $\frac{1}{2}$ $\frac{3}{4}$ **16.** $\frac{3}{5}$ $\frac{5}{7}$ $\frac{7}{11}$ **17.** $\frac{5}{12}$ $\frac{3}{8}$ $\frac{3}{10}$

Set J (Lesson 12, pages 134–135)

Compare. Write in order from least to greatest.

1. 0.45 $\frac{33}{100}$ 0.09 **2.** $\frac{5}{8}$ 1.05 $1\frac{1}{5}$ **3.** $1\frac{3}{4}$ $2\frac{1}{5}$ 1.5

4. $\frac{2}{3}$ 0.6 $\frac{3}{4}$ **5.** 2.5 $2\frac{4}{9}$ $2\frac{3}{5}$ **6.** 1.3 1.03 $1\frac{33}{100}$

7. $3\frac{4}{5}$ 3.4 3.51 **8.** $\frac{6}{7}$ $\frac{7}{8}$ 0.9 **9.** 2.1 3.06 $3\frac{1}{50}$

10. $\frac{17}{25}$ 1.6 $1\frac{15}{32}$ **11.** $9\frac{81}{100}$ 9.82 $9\frac{4}{5}$ **12.** $6\frac{3}{8}$ 6.12 6.02

Set K (Lesson 13, pages 136–137)

Write each fraction as a decimal. Use a bar to show repeating decimals.

1. $\frac{1}{8}$ **2.** $\frac{2}{9}$ **3.** $\frac{5}{2}$ **4.** $\frac{1}{12}$

5. $\frac{8}{9}$ **6.** $\frac{23}{20}$ **7.** $\frac{4}{3}$ **8.** $\frac{18}{25}$

9. $\frac{3}{4}$ **10.** $\frac{1}{3}$ **11.** $\frac{2}{5}$ **12.** $\frac{4}{9}$

13. $\frac{7}{11}$ **14.** $\frac{3}{10}$ **15.** $\frac{3}{16}$ **16.** $\frac{1}{6}$

Extra Practice • Problem Solving

Solve. Use the Logical Thinking strategy or another strategy. *(Lesson 7, pages 118–119)*

1. Mr. Lin asked how many students go bowling and 19 raised their hands. When he asked how many play soccer, 17 raised their hands. All students raised their hands at least once, and 8 raised their hands twice. How many students are in Mr. Meyers' class?

2. The cash register in the Blue Heron School cafeteria showed that 123 students bought spaghetti and 56 bought vegetable soup. The total number of students who bought lunch was 146. How many students had both spaghetti and vegetable soup?

3. Leo is choosing classes for next year. Three drama classes, 2 art classes, and 3 music classes are offered. Leo can choose one class from each category. How many different choices of classes are possible?

4. Twenty students in Ms. Taylor's class live near a park. Thirteen students live near a grocery store. If there are 25 students in Ms. Taylor's class, how many live near both a park and a grocery store?

Solve. Decide how to interpret each remainder. *(Lesson 11, pages 130–131)*

5. Bill won 10 passes to the movies. He and two friends went to the movies together until there were not enough tickets left for all three of them. Bill then used the leftover tickets himself. How many movies did Bill get to see?

6. The students in the sixth-grade class are baking loaves of bread to sell at a bake sale. They have 20 cups of flour. The recipe they are using calls for 3 cups of flour for each loaf. How many loaves of bread can they make?

Solve. Use a bar graph. *(Lesson 14, pages 138–139)*

The students in one county found that river pollution is becoming less frequent. They graphed the results.

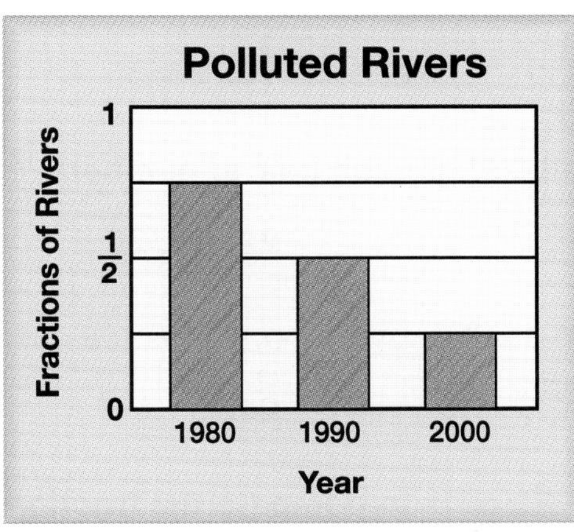

7. In which year were twice as many rivers polluted as in 2000?

8. In which year were $\frac{1}{3}$ as many rivers polluted as in 1980?

9. According to the data in the graph, would you predict that a greater number of rivers or a lesser number of rivers would be polluted in 2010 than in 2000?

Chapter Review

Reviewing Vocabulary

Write *always, sometimes,* or *never* for each statement. Give an example to support your answer.

1. A composite number is one that has more than two factors.

2. The LCM of two numbers is smaller than either of the two numbers.

3. The simplest form of a fraction has a prime number in the denominator.

4. The GCF of two numbers is smaller than both of the numbers.

5. Odd numbers are prime numbers.

Write a definition of the term and give an example.

6. equivalent fractions **7.** exponent **8.** terminating decimal

Reviewing Concepts and Skills

Draw a factor tree to show each prime factorization. Then rewrite, using exponents. If the number is prime, write *prime*. *(pages 104–105, 108–109)*

9. 21 **10.** 33 **11.** 27 **12.** 18

13. 12 **14.** 30 **15.** 48 **16.** 61

Find the GCF for each pair of numbers. *(pages 112–114)*

17. 24, 30 **18.** 20, 50 **19.** 30, 75 **20.** 45, 105

Find the LCM of each pair of numbers. *(pages 116–117)*

21. 3, 8 **22.** 15, 20 **23.** 8, 12 **24.** 36, 72

Evaluate each expression. *(pages 106–107)*

25. $2^2 \times 3 \times 5$ **26.** $5^2 \times 7$ **27.** $2^3 \times 3 \times 5$

Write >, <, or = to compare the fractions in each pair. *(pages 126–128)*

28. $\frac{1}{2}$ ● $\frac{16}{30}$ **29.** $\frac{3}{5}$ ● $\frac{12}{20}$ **30.** $\frac{25}{125}$ ● $\frac{2}{5}$

Write each fraction in its simplest form. *(pages 122–123, 124–125)*

31. $\frac{6}{18}$ **32.** $\frac{22}{34}$ **33.** $\frac{8}{12}$ **34.** $\frac{5}{25}$ **35.** $\frac{18}{3}$ **36.** $\frac{33}{44}$

Write each decimal as a fraction or mixed number. Write each fraction or mixed number as a decimal. If needed, use a bar for repeating decimals. *(pages 136–137)*

37. 0.25 **38.** $2\frac{1}{2}$ **39.** 4.30 **40.** 0.7 **41.** $1\frac{2}{3}$ **42.** $\frac{9}{20}$

Determine whether the following numbers are divisible by 2, 3, 4, 5, 6, 9, or 10. *(pages 110–111)*

43. 87 **44.** 105 **45.** 135

46. Order from least to greatest on a number line. $\frac{1}{4}$ $\frac{8}{10}$ $\frac{2}{5}$ $\frac{3}{10}$ *(pages 134–135)*

Solve. *(pages 118–119, 130–131, 138–139)*

47. A relay race has a distance of 3.2 miles. There are 4 runners on each team. If each runner runs exactly $\frac{1}{4}$ of the course, how many miles will each run?

48. In Mr. Gray's history class, 14 students have computers at home and 18 have televisions. Twelve students have both. Two students have neither. How many students are in Mr. Gray's class?

49. Three tenths of the students take music lessons, $\frac{6}{10}$ play sports, and $\frac{1}{5}$ are in the chess club. Make a bar graph to compare the fractions of students who take music lessons, play sports, or are in chess club.

Brain Teasers Math Reasoning

Sums and Products

Find two numbers whose sum is 14 and whose product is 48.

Find two numbers whose sum is 19 and whose product is 34.

A Question of Age

Elsa is 22 years younger than her father. Today, Elsa is half as old as her father was four years ago. How old are Elsa and her father?

Internet Brain Teasers
Visit **www.eduplace.com/kids/mhm** for more *Brain Teasers.*

Chapter Test

Find the prime factorization for each of the following numbers. Express in exponent form. If the number is prime, write *prime*.

1. 15 **2.** 22 **3.** 103 **4.** 42

Find the GCF for each pair of numbers.

5. 26, 30 **6.** 35, 75 **7.** 100, 75 **8.** 27, 72

Find the LCM of each pair of numbers.

9. 8, 36 **10.** 15, 25 **11.** 32, 12 **12.** 16, 64

Evaluate each expression.

13. $2^4 \times 5$ **14.** 5×7^2 **15.** $2^4 \times 3^2 \times 5$ **16.** $3^3 \times 4 \times 2^2$

Write >, <, or = to compare the fractions in each pair.

17. $\frac{10}{20}$ ● $\frac{15}{30}$ **18.** $\frac{3}{5}$ ● $\frac{12}{24}$ **19.** $\frac{70}{175}$ ● $\frac{2}{5}$ **20.** $\frac{13}{24}$ ● $\frac{3}{8}$

21. $\frac{3}{7}$ ● $\frac{5}{12}$ **22.** $\frac{5}{9}$ ● $\frac{7}{12}$ **23.** $\frac{1}{11}$ ● $\frac{6}{33}$ **24.** $\frac{1}{3}$ ● $\frac{12}{36}$

Write each fraction in its simplest form.

25. $\frac{10}{25}$ **26.** $\frac{18}{4}$ **27.** $\frac{9}{24}$ **28.** $\frac{13}{3}$

29. $\frac{6}{18}$ **30.** $\frac{13}{26}$ **31.** $\frac{24}{39}$ **32.** $\frac{14}{28}$

Write each decimal as a fraction or mixed number in simplest form. Write each fraction or mixed number as a decimal. Use a bar for repeating decimals.

33. $6\frac{3}{5}$ **34.** 0.8 **35.** $\frac{9}{50}$ **36.** $4\frac{2}{3}$

37. 0.36 **38.** $\frac{7}{11}$ **39.** 3.08 **40.** 3.75

Determine if the following numbers are divisible by 2, 3, 4, 5, 6, 9, or 10.

41. 51 **42.** 92 **43.** 138 **44.** 60

Order from least to greatest on a number line.

45. $\frac{7}{10}$ $\frac{3}{5}$ $\frac{5}{10}$ **46.** $\frac{5}{12}$ $\frac{1}{6}$ $\frac{3}{8}$ **47.** 1.8 $1\frac{1}{2}$ $\frac{17}{10}$

Solve.

48. In a class of 26 students, 12 ride their bicycle to school at least once each week. Twenty come to school by car at least once each week. Two students use neither a bicycle nor a car to get to school. How many students use both a bicycle and a car each week to get to school?

49. Clint has $14 to spend on books at the bookstore. If each book costs $3, how many books can Clint buy? How much money will he have left?

50. Three fifths of the students in Amelia's grade have a mammal as a pet. One fifth have birds as pets. Three tenths have fish, reptiles, or amphibians for pets. Make a bar graph to compare the popularity of the different kinds of pets.

Write About It

Solve each problem. Use correct math vocabulary to explain your thinking.

1. On a test, Daniel was asked whether 114 is divisible by 2, 3, 4, 5, 6, 9, or 10. He responded that 114 is divisible by 2, 3, 4 and 9.

   a. Explain why Daniel's answer is incorrect.

   b. Show how to find the correct answer.

2. Sixty-four musicians and 32 singers will be sitting in the auditorium to audition for the school play. The musicians and singers will be sitting in separate sections. Each row will have the same number of students.

   a. What is the greatest number of students that can sit in each row?

   b. Explain the method you used to find the answer.

Another Look

Liliana, Casey, and Shang want to make a large batch of trail mix that is similar to a small bag that they bought. To discover the ingredients and proportions in the small bag, they counted every item in the bag. The bag contained the following:

Trail Mix Ingredients
10 sunflower seeds
30 raisins
15 fruit chews
45 oat cereal pieces
45 corn cereal pieces
Trail Mix
Fruit & Nut Mix

1. Liliana wants to make certain that the large batch has the same fractional parts as the small bag. What fraction of each ingredient makes up the whole? Show your answers in simplest form.
2. If they have a supply of 200 sunflower seeds, how much of each other ingredient will they need if they use all of the sunflower seeds?
3. **Look Back** Check your answer by verifying the fractional parts of the large batch. Are they identical to those of the small bag?
4. **Analyze** If they decide to add 15 apricot pieces, how will it change the fractional parts of the trail mix?

Enrichment

New Vocabulary
perfect
deficient
abundant

Perfect Numbers

A number is **perfect** if the sum of its divisors equals the number. All divisors are included in the sum except the number itself.

Example: Divisors of 6: 1, 2, 3
Sum of divisors: $1 + 2 + 3 = 6$.
Compare the sum and number: $6 = 6$
6 is a perfect number.

A number is **deficient** if the sum of its divisors is less than the number.

Example: Divisors of 8: 1, 2, 4
Sum of divisors: $1 + 2 + 4 = 7$
Compare the sum and number: $7 < 8$.
8 is a deficient number.

A number is **abundant** if the sum of its divisors is greater than the number.

Example: Divisors of 18: 1, 2, 3, 6, 9
Sum of divisors: $1 + 2 + 3 + 6 + 9 = 21$
Compare the sum and number: $21 > 18$.
18 is an abundant number.

Classify each number as perfect, deficient, or abundant.

1. 10 **2.** 12 **3.** 13 **4.** 28

5. 16 **6.** 30 **7.** 42 **8.** 50

Explain Your Thinking

- Maureen says all whole numbers are either perfect, deficient, or abundant. Is she correct? Explain.
- Collin says that if the sum of all factors of a number is twice the number, it is a perfect number. Is he correct? Explain.

CHAPTER 4

Operations With Fractions

Why Learn About Operations With Fractions?

There are many situations in daily life when you add, subtract, multiply, and divide fractions.

When you read an ad that says all clothing is on sale at $\frac{1}{4}$ off the original price, you multiply the price by the fraction to find out how much money you will save.

This girl and her grandfather are making cookies with a favorite recipe. If they want to make half as many cookies as the original recipe makes, they will use fractions to find the amounts of some ingredients.

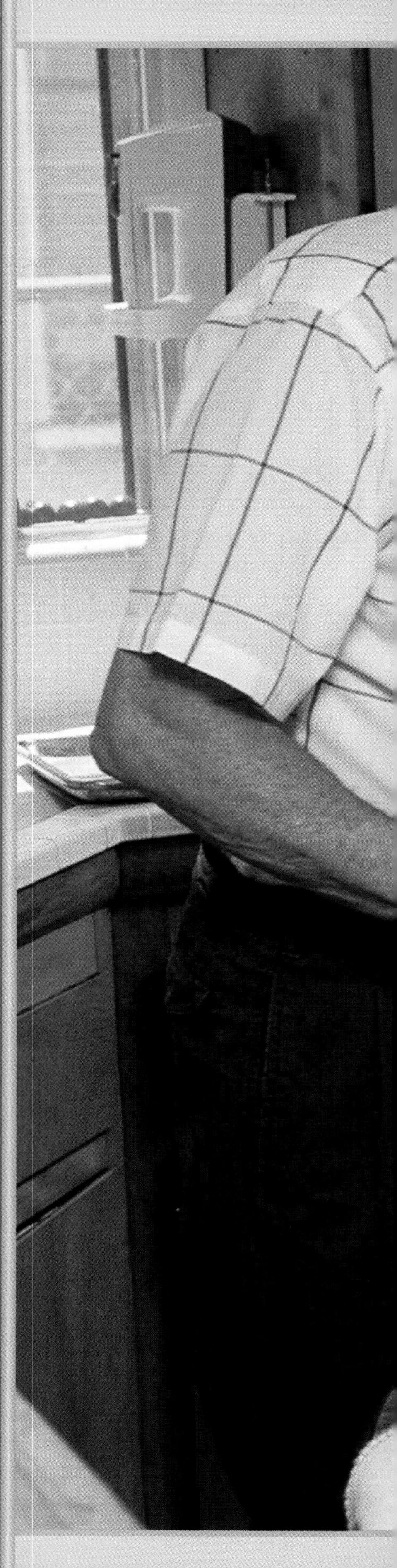

Reviewing Vocabulary

Understanding math language helps you become a successful problem solver. Here are some math vocabulary words you should know.

denominator	the number below the bar in a fraction
dividend	the number being divided in division
divisor	the number that divides the dividend in division
improper fraction	a fraction in which the numerator is greater than or equal to the denominator
mixed number	a number that is the sum of a whole number and a fraction
numerator	the number above the bar in a fraction
quotient	the answer in division

divisor → $4\overline{)3}$ ← dividend, **0.75** ← quotient

$\frac{3}{4}$ — 3 ← numerator, 4 ← denominator

Reading Words and Symbols

When you read mathematics, sometimes you read only words, sometimes you read words and symbols, and sometimes you read only symbols.

All of these statements are different ways to say the same thing.

- ► three fourths
- ► $\frac{3}{4}$
- ► 3 divided by 4
- ► $3 \div 4$
- ► the quotient of 3 divided by 4
- ► $4\overline{)3}$
- ► 0.75

Try These

Choose the letter of the best answer.

1. Which fraction has 5 as the denominator?

   a. $\frac{5}{4}$ **b.** $\frac{4}{5}$ **c.** $5\frac{1}{4}$ **d.** $\frac{5}{6}$

2. Which is the same as $3 + \frac{1}{2}$?

   a. $\frac{4}{3}$ **b.** $\frac{3}{4}$ **c.** $3\frac{1}{2}$ **d.** $\frac{2}{3}$

3. Which fraction shows 6 divided by 7?

   a. $\frac{6}{7}$ **b.** $\frac{7}{6}$ **c.** $1\frac{1}{6}$ **d.** $\frac{1}{6}$

4. Which fraction is an improper fraction?

   a. $\frac{3}{4}$ **b.** $\frac{4}{3}$ **c.** $\frac{4}{5}$ **d.** $\frac{7}{8}$

Write the word that belongs in each blank to make each sentence true.

5. The ____ is the number that divides the dividend in division.
6. The ____ is the answer in division.
7. The ____ is the least number that is a common multiple of two or more numbers.
8. An improper fraction is a fraction in which the ____ is greater than or equal to the ____.

Upcoming Vocabulary

Write About It **Here are some other vocabulary words** you will learn in this chapter. Watch for these words. Write their definitions in your journal.

greatest common factor
least common multiple
least common denominator
reciprocal
invert

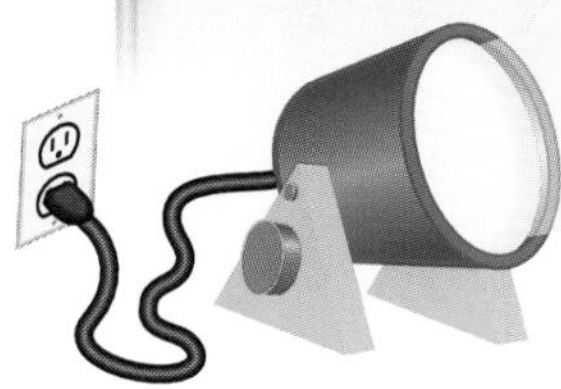

Add and Subtract Fractions With Like Denominators

You will learn how to add and subtract both fractions and mixed numbers with like denominators.

Learn About It

On a tour of Washington, D.C., Emilia walked $\frac{5}{10}$ mile in the morning and $\frac{4}{10}$ mile in the afternoon. How far did she walk in all?

Add. $\frac{5}{10} + \frac{4}{10} = n$

How much farther did she walk in the morning than in the afternoon?

Subtract. $\frac{5}{10} - \frac{4}{10} = d$

Find $\frac{5}{10} + \frac{4}{10}$.

To add fractions with like denominators, add the numerators. Keep the same denominator.

$$\frac{5}{10} + \frac{4}{10} = \frac{5+4}{10} = \frac{9}{10}$$

Find $\frac{5}{10} - \frac{4}{10}$.

To subtract fractions with like denominators, subtract the second numerator from the first numerator. Keep the same denominator.

$$\frac{5}{10} - \frac{4}{10} = \frac{5-4}{10} = \frac{1}{10}$$

Solution: That day Emilia walked $\frac{9}{10}$ mile in all.

Solution: She walked $\frac{1}{10}$ mile farther in the morning.

Other Examples

A. Adding Mixed Numbers

$$\begin{array}{r} 2\frac{5}{9} \\ +\ 3\frac{7}{9} \\ \hline 5\frac{12}{9} \end{array}$$

- Add the fractions.
- Add the whole numbers.
- Simplify the answer.

$$5\frac{12}{9} = 5 + \boxed{\frac{9}{9}} + \frac{3}{9} = 6\frac{3}{9} = 6\frac{1}{3}$$

B. Subtracting Mixed Numbers

$$\begin{array}{r} 5\frac{1}{3} \\ -\ 1\frac{2}{3} \\ \hline \end{array}$$

1 < 2, so rename.

$$4 + \boxed{\frac{3}{3}} + \frac{1}{3} \quad = \quad 4\frac{4}{3}$$
$$= \ -\ 1\frac{2}{3}$$
$$3\frac{2}{3}$$

Check:

$$\begin{array}{r} 3\frac{2}{3} \\ +\ 1\frac{2}{3} \\ \hline 4\frac{4}{3} \end{array} = 4 + \boxed{\frac{3}{3}} + \frac{1}{3} = 5\frac{1}{3}$$

Explain Your Thinking

- ► When is it necessary to rename fractions?
- ► Look at Examples *A* and *B*. When is a mixed number in simplest form?

Guided Practice

Find each sum or difference. Write each answer in simplest form.

1. $\frac{2}{9} + \frac{5}{9}$ **2.** $4\frac{2}{5} + 7\frac{3}{5}$ **3.** $\frac{3}{8} + \frac{1}{8}$ **4.** $2\frac{7}{8} + \frac{7}{8}$

5. $4\frac{5}{7} - 1\frac{3}{7}$ **6.** $5\frac{3}{10} - 3\frac{9}{10}$ **7.** $\frac{5}{6} - \frac{1}{6}$ **8.** $8\frac{3}{4} - \frac{1}{4}$

Ask Yourself

- Do the fractions have like denominators?
- Can I simplify the sum or difference?

Independent Practice

Find each sum or difference. Write each answer in simplest form.

9. $\frac{1}{5} + \frac{2}{5}$ **10.** $6\frac{4}{9} + 3\frac{8}{9}$ **11.** $\frac{4}{5} + 7\frac{3}{5}$ **12.** $\frac{3}{10} + \frac{2}{10}$ **13.** $3\frac{3}{8} + 2\frac{5}{8}$

14. $\frac{6}{7} - \frac{3}{7}$ **15.** $5\frac{1}{4} - 2\frac{3}{4}$ **16.** $\frac{7}{10} - \frac{3}{10}$ **17.** $3\frac{1}{5} - \frac{1}{5}$ **18.** $4\frac{7}{9} - 3\frac{1}{9}$

Problem Solving • Reasoning

Use Data **Use the map for Problems 19, 20, and 22.**

19. On a tour of Washington, D.C., Mr. Saguchi's class walks $\frac{3}{4}$ mile to the Lincoln Memorial. Then they walk to the Museum of Natural History. How far do they walk in all?

20. **Analyze** Sue walked from the Lincoln Memorial to the Air and Space Museum. Sam walked from the Capitol to the Museum of Natural History. How much farther did Sue walk than Sam?

21. **Predict** Melissa walks $\frac{9}{10}$ mile on Tuesday and $\frac{3}{10}$ mile on Wednesday. How much farther will she need to walk to complete 2 miles?

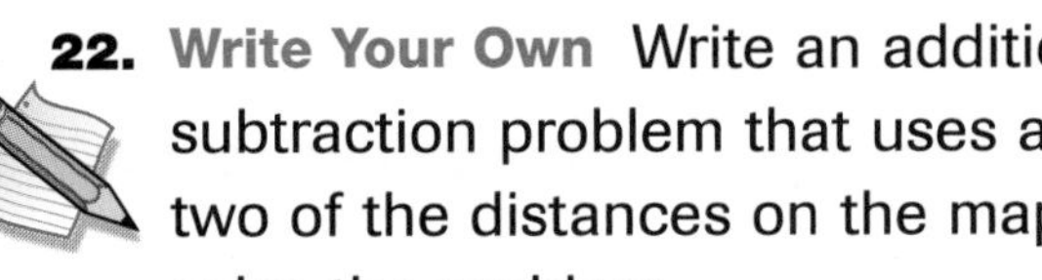

22. **Write Your Own** Write an addition or subtraction problem that uses at least two of the distances on the map. Then solve the problem.

Mixed Review • Test Prep

Express each number, using exponents. *(pages 108–109)*

23. 27 **24.** 16 **25.** 25 **26.** 8

27 Solve. $68{,}544 \div 63 = n$ *(pages 30–31)*

A 1,068 **B** 1,072 **C** 1,088 **D** 1,099

Add Fractions and Mixed Numbers

You will learn how to add mixed numbers and add fractions that have unlike denominators.

Review Vocabulary
least common multiple (LCM)

Learn About It

Jean made a chef's hat and apron for her father. How much fabric did Jean use?

Add. $\frac{1}{2} + 1\frac{1}{3} = n$

Chef's Hat
$\frac{1}{2}$ yard of fabric

Chef's Apron
$1\frac{1}{3}$ yards of fabric

Different Ways to Add Fractions and Mixed Numbers

You can use fraction strips.

Step 1 Use fraction strips to model the numbers.

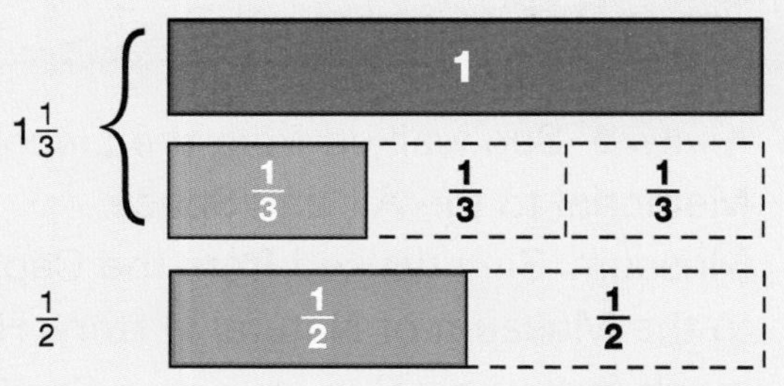

Step 2 Unit-fraction lengths are not the same, so use equivalent strips. Then count shaded parts.

1 | 1
$\frac{1}{3} = \frac{2}{6}$ | $\frac{1}{6}$ $\frac{1}{6}$ $\frac{1}{6}$ $\frac{1}{6}$ $\frac{1}{6}$ $\frac{1}{6}$
$\frac{1}{2} = \frac{3}{6}$ | $\frac{1}{6}$ $\frac{1}{6}$ $\frac{1}{6}$ $\frac{1}{6}$ $\frac{1}{6}$ $\frac{1}{6}$

$1\frac{2}{6} + \frac{3}{6} = 1\frac{5}{6}$

You can use any common denominator.

Step 1 Write equivalent fractions. Multiply the denominators to find a common denominator.

$2 \times 3 = 6$ ← common denominator

$\frac{1}{3} = \frac{1}{3} \times \frac{2}{2} = \frac{2}{6}$

$\frac{1}{2} = \frac{1}{2} \times \frac{3}{3} = \frac{3}{6}$

Step 2 Add the numerators. Place the sum over the common denominator.

$$\begin{array}{rcr} 1\frac{1}{3} & = & 1\frac{2}{6} \\ +\frac{1}{2} & = & +\frac{3}{6} \\ \hline & & 1\frac{5}{6} \end{array}$$

Think:
$\frac{2+3}{6} = \frac{5}{6}$

Solution: Jean used $1\frac{5}{6}$ yards of fabric.

You can also use the **least common multiple (LCM)** of the denominators to add fractions with unlike denominators. Often the LCM is less than the product of the denominators. The smaller number may make calculations easier.

Find $\frac{5}{6} + \frac{3}{4}$.

Step 1 Find the least common multiple (LCM) of the denominators.

Multiples of 6: 6, (12), 18, 24, ...

Multiples of 4: 4, 8, (12), 16, ...

The LCM is 12.

Step 2 Write equivalent fractions, using the LCM.

$$\frac{5}{6} = \frac{5}{6} \times \frac{2}{2} = \frac{10}{12}$$

$$\frac{3}{4} = \frac{3}{4} \times \frac{3}{3} = \frac{9}{12}$$

Step 3 Add the numerators. Simplify the sum.

$$\frac{10}{12} + \frac{9}{12} = \frac{19}{12}$$

$$= \frac{12}{12} + \frac{7}{12}$$

$$= 1\frac{7}{12}$$

Other Examples

A. Two Fractions

$$\frac{1}{3} = \frac{7}{21}$$

$$+\frac{2}{7} = +\frac{6}{21}$$

$$\frac{13}{21}$$

B. More Than Two Addends

$$4\frac{3}{4} \quad 2\frac{3}{5} \quad +1\frac{1}{6}$$

LCM of 4, 5, 6 is 2 × 2 × 3 × 5, or 60.

$$4\frac{3}{4} = 4\frac{45}{60}$$

$$2\frac{3}{5} = 2\frac{36}{60}$$

$$+1\frac{1}{6} = +1\frac{10}{60}$$

$$7\frac{91}{60} = 8\frac{31}{60}$$

Explain Your Thinking

► Find $\frac{5}{6} + \frac{3}{4}$, using 24 (the product of the denominators) as the common denominator. Explain how this is different from using the LCM as the common denominator. Which way did you find easier? Why?

Guided Practice

Find each sum. Write each answer in simplest form.

1. $\frac{3}{5} + \frac{4}{15}$

2. $\frac{5}{6} + \frac{1}{4}$

3. $\frac{11}{14} + \frac{3}{4} + \frac{1}{2}$

4. $1\frac{2}{3} + \frac{1}{3}$

5. $6\frac{3}{5} + 4\frac{2}{3}$

6. $\frac{1}{6} + \frac{2}{5} + \frac{1}{3}$

7. $5\frac{7}{10} + \frac{4}{5}$

8. $17\frac{3}{4} + 4\frac{2}{3}$

9. $3\frac{1}{9} + \frac{3}{18}$

Ask Yourself

- What is the LCM of the denominators?
- Can I simplify the sum?

Independent Practice

Find each sum. Express each answer in simplest form.

10. $\frac{1}{3}+\frac{1}{2}$ **11.** $3\frac{2}{5}+1\frac{2}{3}$ **12.** $\frac{11}{15}+\frac{2}{3}$ **13.** $\frac{1}{6}+2\frac{3}{4}$

14. $\frac{1}{2}+\frac{6}{7}$ **15.** $\frac{2}{9}+6\frac{11}{12}$ **16.** $9\frac{3}{7}+\frac{5}{21}$ **17.** $2\frac{7}{12}+5\frac{1}{8}$

18. $2\frac{1}{3}+\frac{1}{6}$ **19.** $4\frac{4}{5}+\frac{7}{20}$ **20.** $6\frac{2}{3}+5\frac{1}{2}$ **21.** $8\frac{3}{8}+2\frac{3}{4}$

22. $5\frac{3}{5}+4\frac{2}{5}$ **23.** $9+5\frac{7}{8}$ **24.** $6\frac{3}{10}+3\frac{5}{8}$ **25.** $\frac{9}{10}+\frac{5}{6}+\frac{2}{3}$

26. $\frac{8}{15}+\frac{1}{6}+\frac{1}{2}$ **27.** $6\frac{7}{8}+2\frac{3}{4}$ **28.** $\frac{5}{6}+\frac{5}{9}+\frac{5}{12}$ **29.** $\frac{2}{5}+\frac{3}{4}+\frac{7}{10}$

30. $2\frac{1}{2} + \frac{3}{4}$ **31.** $3\frac{2}{3} + 2\frac{5}{8}$ **32.** $7\frac{1}{10} + 3\frac{1}{4}$ **33.** $4\frac{1}{3} + 2\frac{3}{4}$

Problem Solving • Reasoning

Use Data **Use the list for Problems 34 and 35.**

34. **Analyze** Jenna, Stefan, and Luke are in the class play. How much fabric is needed to make all three costumes?

35. Stefan's costume requires $1\frac{1}{8}$ yd of gold fabric for the pants and $\frac{3}{4}$ yd gold fabric for the top. The rest of his costume is a red cape. How many yards of fabric are needed for the cape?

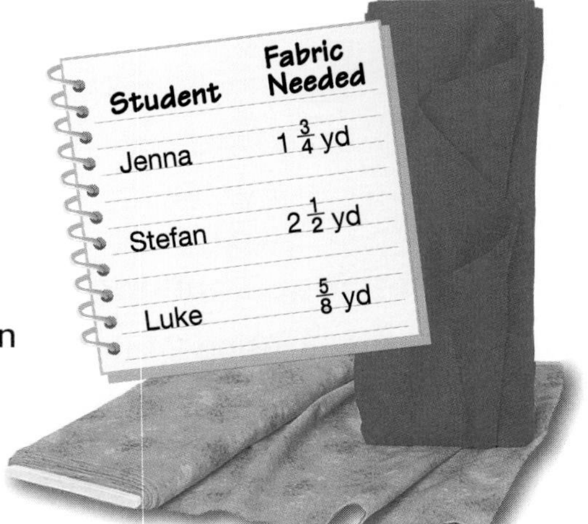

36. **Predict** Mia is designing the programs for the play. Printed information takes up $\frac{7}{8}$ of a page. The art Mia created takes up $\frac{1}{6}$ of a page. Will the printed information and the artwork fit on one page? Show your work.

37. **Write About It** The first act of the class play lasts $\frac{1}{2}$ h. The next two acts each last $\frac{1}{4}$ h, and the time between acts is 5 min. If a person in the audience has to leave after 1 h, will the person get to see the whole play? Explain your answer.

Mixed Review • Test Prep

Solve. *(pages 12–13)*

38. 8,292 + 1,463 **39.** 6,785.24 − 2,970.65 **40.** 3,706.2 + 2,436.9 **41.** 30 − 12.017

42 What is the value of n in the equation $n \div 3 = 51$? *(pages 28–29)*

A 17 **B** 54 **C** 153 **D** 217

Extra Practice See Set B on page 192.

Practice Game

Spin for the Sum

Practice finding the sum of fractions by playing this game with a partner. Try to be the first person to get 10 points!

What You'll Need

- *a spinner with four equal parts, labeled 1, 2, 3, and 4*

Players
2

Here's What To Do

1. The first player spins the spinner twice. The number from the first spin is the numerator of a fraction, and the number from the second spin is the denominator.
2. The second player repeats Step 1 to obtain another fraction.
3. Both players add the two fractions and compare their answers. Each correct sum earns one point for the player.

Players continue repeating Steps 1–3. The first player to reach a total of 10 points wins.

Share Your Thinking Other than adding quickly and correctly, is there another strategy for winning the game? Explain your answer.

Subtract Fractions and Mixed Numbers

You will learn how to subtract fractions and mixed numbers that have different denominators.

Learn About It

On Wednesday, Dana placed $3\frac{1}{2}$ cups of seed in her bird feeder. On Thursday, she sees that the feeder has only $1\frac{2}{3}$ cups of seed left. How many cups of seed did the birds eat?

Subtract. $\mathbf{3\frac{1}{2} - 1\frac{2}{3} = n}$

Find $3\frac{1}{2} - 1\frac{2}{3}$.

Step 1 Find any common denominator. Write the equivalent fractions.

$$\frac{1}{2} = \frac{1}{2} \times \frac{3}{3} = \frac{3}{6}$$

$$\frac{2}{3} = \frac{2}{3} \times \frac{2}{2} = \frac{4}{6}$$

Step 2 Rename fractions. Then rename $3\frac{3}{6}$ as $2\frac{9}{6}$ so that you can subtract easily.

$$3\frac{3}{6} = 2 + \frac{6}{6} + \frac{3}{6} = 2\frac{9}{6}$$

$$-1\frac{4}{6} \qquad -1\frac{4}{6}$$

Step 3 Subtract the fractions and then the whole numbers.

$$2\frac{9}{6} - 1\frac{4}{6} = 1\frac{5}{6}$$

Solution: The birds ate $1\frac{5}{6}$ cups of seed.

Another Example

Use the LCM

$$4\frac{2}{3} = 4\frac{4}{6}$$

$$-1\frac{1}{6} = -1\frac{1}{6}$$

$$3\frac{3}{6} = 3\frac{1}{2}$$

Explain Your Thinking

- ► In the example above, why was $3\frac{1}{2}$ renamed as $2\frac{9}{6}$?
- ► Do you always need to rename both fractions when you are subtracting with unlike denominators?

Guided Practice

Find each difference. Express each answer in simplest form.

1. $\frac{3}{5} - \frac{4}{15}$ **2.** $\frac{2}{3} - \frac{1}{2}$ **3.** $4\frac{7}{8} - 2\frac{3}{4}$ **4.** $4\frac{1}{3} - 1\frac{2}{3}$

5. $\frac{4}{9} - \frac{5}{12}$ **6.** $\frac{5}{6} - \frac{1}{3}$ **7.** $5\frac{1}{3} - 3\frac{3}{4}$ **8.** $6\frac{2}{9} - 4\frac{2}{3}$

Ask Yourself

- Do I have to rename the mixed number?
- Do I have to simplify the answer?

Independent Practice

Find each difference. Express each answer in simplest form.

9. $9\frac{5}{6} - \frac{1}{6}$ **10.** $4\frac{1}{2} - \frac{3}{4}$ **11.** $7\frac{1}{3} - \frac{5}{6}$ **12.** $\frac{3}{8} - \frac{1}{6}$ **13.** $\frac{3}{4} - \frac{3}{8}$

14. $2\frac{1}{2} - 1\frac{2}{5}$ **15.** $\frac{5}{6} - \frac{1}{2}$ **16.** $2\frac{1}{3} - \frac{2}{3}$ **17.** $2\frac{5}{9} - \frac{2}{3}$ **18.** $3\frac{5}{7} - \frac{1}{2}$

19. $10 - 3\frac{2}{5}$ **20.** $5\frac{5}{6} - 3\frac{1}{4}$ **21.** $6\frac{1}{2} - 2\frac{1}{2}$ **22.** $8\frac{4}{9} - 4\frac{2}{3}$ **23.** $3\frac{5}{7} - 1\frac{3}{4}$

24. $5\frac{5}{12} - 1\frac{7}{8}$ **25.** $4\frac{3}{7} - \frac{3}{7}$ **26.** $7\frac{9}{10} - 2\frac{5}{6}$ **27.** $6\frac{7}{9} - 3\frac{3}{4}$ **28.** $6\frac{2}{5} - \frac{3}{10}$

Problem Solving • Reasoning

Use Data **Use the package labels for Problems 30–32.**

29. **Analyze** Viola's bird feeder holds $4\frac{1}{2}$ cups of seed. If the birds eat $2\frac{3}{4}$ cups of seed, how many cups of seed are left in the feeder?

30. Benito made one cup of birdseed mix with $\frac{5}{8}$ part oil sunflower seeds and $\frac{3}{8}$ part striped sunflower seeds. Find the difference between the amount of oil sunflower seeds in Benito's mix and the amount of oil sunflower seeds in one cup of the Special Bird Seed. Then find the difference between the two striped sunflower seed amounts.

31. **Predict** For a large feeder, Keiko fills a 10-cup pitcher with Special Bird Seed. How many cups of sunflower seeds will probably be in her feeder?

32. **Write About It** Chickadees prefer sunflower chips, while other birds prefer oil sunflower seeds. Which mix of birdseed is more likely to attract chickadees? Explain your answer.

Mixed Review • Test Prep

Find the mean of the following data sets. *(pages 60–61)*

33. 25, 26, 27, 30 **34.** 2, 2, 7, 9, 13, 15 **35.** 45, 45, 46, 47, 50

36 What is the GCF of 18 and 22? *(pages 112–114)*

A 2 **C** 9

B 4 **D** 11

Problem-Solving Skill: Multistep Problems

You will learn how to solve problems that have more than one step.

When you solve a problem that has more than one step, you need to think about several things before you can find the solution.

Xavier is making two shelves to hold his books. Each shelf will be $3\frac{1}{2}$ feet long. He cuts the shelves from a board that is 8 feet long. After he cuts the shelves, will he have enough wood left to place a 16-inch board under his rock collection?

Think about what information you are given in the problem.

Xavier is cutting two $3\frac{1}{2}$-foot shelves from an 8-foot board.

Think about what information you need to find out.

You need to find the total length of the two shelves and the length of the remaining piece of board.

Think about what operations you will use to solve the problem.

Add to find the total length of the two shelves.

$3\frac{1}{2}$ ft + $3\frac{1}{2}$ ft = 7 ft

Subtract to find the length of the remaining piece of board.

8 ft − 7 ft = 1 ft

Compare the remaining length with the length Xavier needs to place under his rock collection.

Since 1 foot is less than 16 inches, Xavier does not have the length of board he wants for his rock collection.

Look Back Why is it helpful to ask yourself what information you need to solve the problem? How does separating the problem into clear steps make it easier to solve?

Left: A young volunteer for Habitat for Humanity checks a building foundation to make sure it is level.

Right: Schoolchildren help to build a neighborhood playscape.

Guided Practice

Use more than one step to solve each problem.

1. Karyn needs two shelves to display a collection of ceramic horses. One shelf should be $2\frac{2}{3}$ feet long, and the other should be $3\frac{1}{4}$ feet long. Karyn has a board that is 6 feet long. Is this board long enough to make both shelves?

   Think: What is the first information you must find?

2. The picture frame that Sivan plans to make has two sides that are each $1\frac{2}{5}$ feet long. The other two sides are each $\frac{4}{5}$ foot long. What is the total length of framing material that Sivan needs to make the picture frame?

   Think: What is the length of the two long sides? the two short sides?

Choose a Strategy

Solve. Use these or other strategies.

Problem-Solving Strategies

- Draw a Diagram
- Work Backward
- Write an Equation
- Use Logical Thinking

3. Nancy is making five shelves. Each shelf is $2\frac{1}{2}$ inches longer than the one above it. Her top shelf is 10 inches long. How long is the bottom shelf?

4. Gary is putting molding around three sides of his door frame. Two sides are $8\frac{1}{4}$ feet long, and one side is $3\frac{1}{16}$ feet long. How much molding must he buy?

5. Jeff had $\frac{1}{2}$ ft of rope. Mark had 9 in. of rope. Peg had more rope than Mark. Cal had twice as much rope as Peg. Who had the most rope?

6. Kaspar used $3\frac{5}{8}$ feet of a longer piece of wood to build his neighbor's birdhouse. He had $\frac{11}{16}$ foot of wood left. How much wood did Kaspar have to start with?

7. A carpenter is making a window frame. Two sides are $2\frac{1}{2}$ feet long, and two sides are $1\frac{1}{8}$ feet long. What is the total length of wood the carpenter needs to make the frame?

8. Brooke is making a magazine rack. Two sides will be $1\frac{1}{4}$ feet long, and two sides will be $\frac{7}{8}$ foot long. How much wood will Brooke have left if she uses a board that is 5 feet long?

Extra Practice See 1–2 on page 195.

Quick Check

Check Your Understanding of Lessons 1–4

Find each sum or difference. Write each answer in simplest form.

1. $\frac{1}{5} + \frac{3}{5}$

2. $\frac{2}{3} + \frac{2}{3}$

3. $\frac{6}{7} - \frac{2}{7}$

4. $\frac{3}{4} - \frac{1}{4}$

5. $\frac{1}{3} + \frac{1}{4}$

6. $2\frac{1}{3} + \frac{5}{8}$

7. $\frac{2}{15} + \frac{3}{10} + \frac{1}{2}$

8. $4\frac{1}{4} + 3\frac{15}{16}$

9. $\frac{3}{4} - \frac{3}{8}$

10. $\frac{5}{6} - \frac{2}{9}$

11. $2\frac{5}{6} - 2\frac{4}{5}$

12. $7\frac{2}{15} - 4\frac{3}{5}$

Solve.

13. Bill reads $10\frac{3}{4}$ pages in his library book before he goes to sleep. While waiting for the bus the next morning, he reads another $6\frac{1}{2}$ pages. He still has $4\frac{3}{4}$ pages to read to finish the story. How many pages long is the story?

14. Each night Vicki reads $12\frac{1}{2}$ pages in her book. On Wednesday night, she started reading at the top of page 50. On what page did she start reading on the previous Monday night? Did she start at the top, bottom, or middle of the page? How do you know?

How did you do?

If you had difficulty with any items in the Quick Check, you can use the following pages for review and extra practice.

Items	Review These Pages	Do These Extra Practice Items
1–4	pages 156–157	Set A, page 192
5–8	pages 158–160	Set B, page 192
9–12	pages 162–163	Set C, page 192
13–14	pages 164–165	1–2, page 195

Test Prep • Cumulative Review

Maintaining the Standards

Choose the letter of the correct answer.

1. What is the standard form for the number sixty-four and two thousand, three hundred fifty-five ten thousandths?

   A 64.2355
   B 642.355
   C 6,423.55
   D 642,355

2. Which number makes the number sentence true?

   5,372.908 − 4,607.139 = ■

   F 764.769
   G 765.769
   H 765.770
   J 765.771

3. Which number is an outlier in the following set of data?

   17, 21, 13, 20, 32, 15

   A 32
   B 21
   C 17
   D 13

4. Antonio read 4 books in May, 5 books in June, 3 books in July, and 4 books in August. What is the mean for the data set of the number of books he read in 4 months?

   F 2
   G 3
   H 4
   J 5

5. What is the mode for the following set of data?

   43, 46, 48, 51, 48, 45

   A 45 **C** 48
   B 47 **D** 51

6. What is the correct standard form for the expression $2^2 \times 3^2 \times 4^2$?

   F 24 **H** 288
   G 144 **J** 576

7. What is the LCM of 16 and 20?

   A 2 **C** 320
   B 80 **D** 7,040

8. Look at the graph. What fraction of the newsletter budget does the club spend on printing and paper?

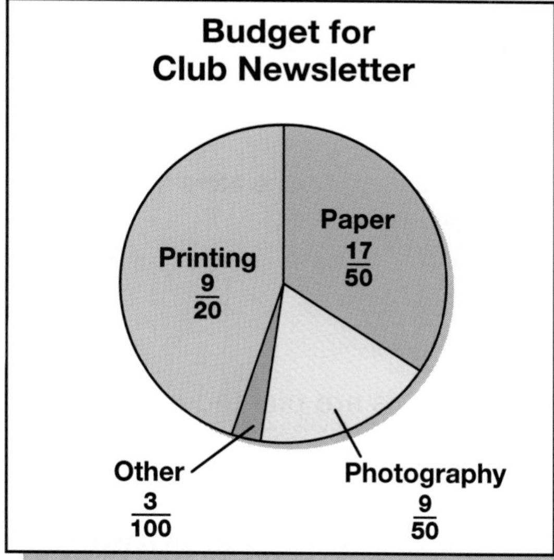

Explain How did you find your answer?

Internet Test Prep
Visit **www.eduplace.com/kids/mhm** for more *Test Prep Practice.*

LESSON 5

Multiply Fractions

You will learn how to multiply fractions.

Review Vocabulary
prime factorization

Learn About It

Maria plants $\frac{2}{3}$ of her garden with vegetables. Five sevenths of that area is planted with beans. What part of Maria's whole garden is planted with beans?

Multiply. $\frac{2}{3} \times \frac{5}{7}$

Different Ways to Multiply Fractions

You can draw a diagram.

Step 1 Separate one square into three equal parts. Shade two parts to show $\frac{2}{3}$.

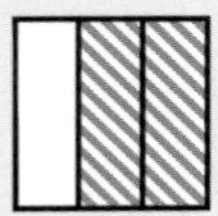

$\frac{2}{3}$

Step 2 Separate the square into seven equal parts.

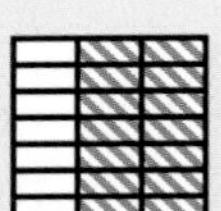

The number of congruent rectangles is 21, the product of the denominators.

Step 3 Shade five of the seven equal parts to show $\frac{5}{7}$.

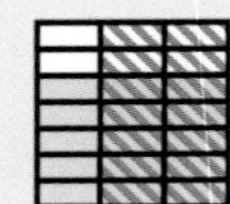

$\frac{2}{3} \times \frac{5}{7} = \frac{10}{21}$

The number of rectangles that are shaded twice is 10, the product of the numerators.

You can find the product.

Step 1 Multiply the numerators to find the numerator of the product.

$$\frac{2}{3} \times \frac{5}{7} = \frac{2 \times 5}{\blacksquare} = \frac{10}{\blacksquare}$$

Step 2 Multiply the denominators to find the denominator of the product. Simplify the product.

$$\frac{2}{3} \times \frac{5}{7} = \frac{10}{3 \times 7} = \frac{10}{21}$$

When both fractions are less than 1, the product is less than 1.

Solution: Beans are planted in $\frac{10}{21}$ of Maria's garden.

You can also use **prime factorization** to multiply fractions.

- Write the prime factorization of each numerator and denominator.

$$\frac{5}{6} \times \frac{2}{7} = \frac{5 \times 2}{3 \times 2 \times 7}$$

- Simplify, using the prime factorization. Cancel common factors and then multiply.

$$\frac{5 \times \overset{1}{\cancel{2}}}{3 \times \underset{1}{\cancel{2}} \times 7} = \frac{5}{3 \times 7} \times \boxed{1} = \frac{5}{21}$$

Another Example

Fraction of a Whole Number

$\frac{4}{5} \times 2 = \frac{4}{5} \times \frac{2}{1}$

$\frac{4 \times 2}{5 \times 1} = \frac{8}{5} = 1\frac{3}{5}$

Explain Your Thinking

► Why is it helpful to rewrite the numerator and denominator as products of prime factors?

Guided Practice

Ask Yourself

- How can I rewrite a whole number as a fraction?
- Is my answer reasonable?

Multiply. Write each product in simplest form.

1. $\frac{1}{3} \times \frac{1}{4}$ **2.** $3 \times \frac{4}{7}$ **3.** $\frac{5}{6} \times \frac{1}{3}$ **4.** $5 \times \frac{3}{5}$

5. $\frac{1}{2} \times \frac{2}{5}$ **6.** $\frac{1}{2} \times \frac{1}{3}$ **7.** $\frac{7}{8} \times 7$ **8.** $2 \times \frac{4}{7}$

Independent Practice

Multiply. Write each product in simplest form.

9. $\frac{2}{5} \times \frac{1}{6}$ **10.** $4 \times \frac{2}{3}$ **11.** $\frac{2}{3} \times \frac{4}{7}$ **12.** $\frac{3}{7} \times \frac{3}{7}$ **13.** $\frac{5}{8} \times 16$

14. $5 \times \frac{4}{5}$ **15.** $\frac{9}{10} \times 3$ **16.** $7 \times \frac{1}{2}$ **17.** $6 \times \frac{2}{3}$ **18.** $\frac{7}{8} \times \frac{7}{12}$

19. $\frac{3}{11} \times 2$ **20.** $\frac{5}{12} \times \frac{3}{16}$ **21.** $\frac{3}{16} \times \frac{4}{5}$ **22.** $\frac{3}{8} \times \frac{5}{8}$ **23.** $5 \times \frac{7}{10}$

Problem Solving • Reasoning

24. Luis plans to use 3 plots for his garden that are each 1 yd^2. He is going to plant tomatoes in $\frac{2}{3}$ of his garden. How many square yards of Luis's garden will be planted with tomatoes?

25. **Logical Thinking** Donny's garden is 20 ft by 20 ft. The garden is divided into 16 equal square plots. Draw a diagram of the garden. Then find the length and width of a rectangle that is $\frac{3}{8}$ of a square plot.

26. **Predict** Maggie's garden is one square yard. She plants $\frac{5}{9}$ of this area with marigolds. How many square feet are planted in the marigolds?

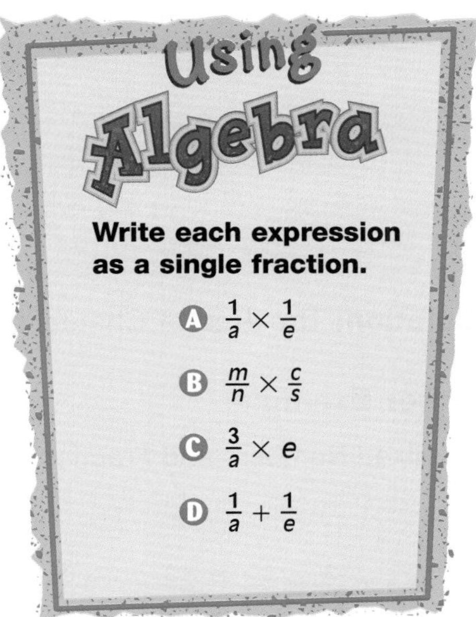

Write each expression as a single fraction.

A $\frac{1}{a} \times \frac{1}{e}$

B $\frac{m}{n} \times \frac{c}{s}$

C $\frac{3}{a} \times e$

D $\frac{1}{a} + \frac{1}{e}$

Mixed Review • Test Prep

Write each number in word form. *(pages 4–5)*

27. 12,703 **28.** 5,383,429 **29.** 7,084.01

30 What is the mode for the data set 7, 7, 3, 4, 4, 6, 5, 5, 4? *(pages 60–61)*

A 7 **B** 6 **C** 5 **D** 4

Extra Practice See Set D on page 192.

LESSON 6 Multiply Mixed Numbers

You will learn how to multiply mixed numbers.

Learn About It

Chantel is staying with her grandparents for the summer. Her grandmother is making a family quilt and Chantel wants to help. Her grandmother gives Chantel one square patch to sew. For part of her square, Chantel cuts a piece of red cloth to make a rectangle that measures $2\frac{3}{4}$ inches by $3\frac{1}{3}$ inches. What is the area of Chantel's rectangle?

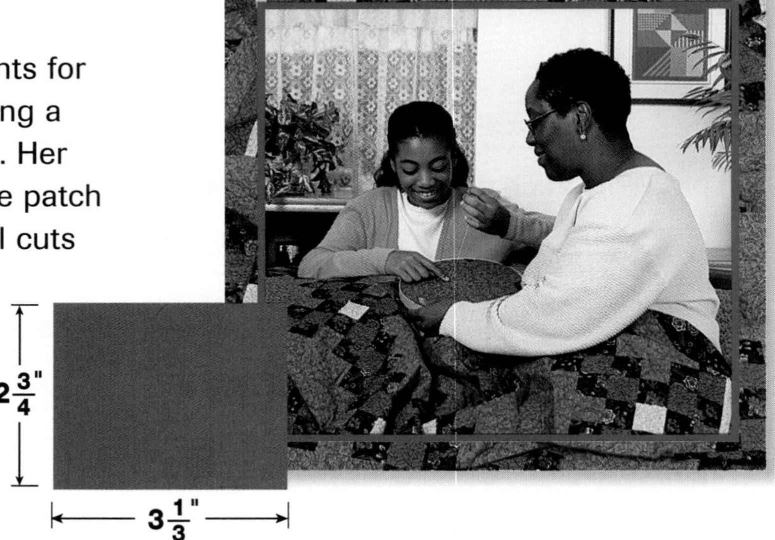

To find the area, use the formula $A = l \times w$.

Multiply. $\boldsymbol{A = 2\frac{3}{4} \times 3\frac{1}{3}}$

Find $2\frac{3}{4} \times 3\frac{1}{3}$.

Step 1 Rename $2\frac{3}{4}$ and $3\frac{1}{3}$ as improper fractions. Write the whole numbers as fractions.

$$2\frac{3}{4} = \left(\frac{2}{1} \times \frac{4}{4}\right) + \frac{3}{4} = \frac{8}{4} + \frac{3}{4} = \frac{11}{4}$$

$$3\frac{1}{3} = \left(\frac{3}{1} \times \frac{3}{3}\right) + \frac{1}{3} = \frac{9}{3} + \frac{1}{3} = \frac{10}{3}$$

Step 2 Simplify by using prime factorization. Cancel common factors and then multiply.

$$\frac{11}{4} \times \frac{10}{3} = \frac{11 \times \overset{1}{\cancel{2}} \times 5}{\underset{1}{\cancel{2}} \times 2 \times 3} =$$

$$\frac{11 \times 5}{2 \times 3} = \frac{55}{6} = 9\frac{1}{6}$$

Solution: The area of Chantel's rectangle is $9\frac{1}{6}$ square inches.

Other Examples

A. Mixed Numbers and Fractions

$$4\frac{2}{5} \times \frac{3}{11} =$$

$$\frac{22}{5} \times \frac{3}{11} = \frac{2 \times \overset{1}{\cancel{11}} \times 3}{5 \times \underset{1}{\cancel{11}}} = \frac{2 \times 3}{5}$$

$$= \frac{6}{5} = 1\frac{1}{5}$$

B. Mixed Numbers and Whole Numbers

$$2\frac{1}{3} \times 6 =$$

$$\frac{7}{3} \times \frac{6}{1} = \frac{7 \times 2 \times \overset{1}{\cancel{3}}}{\underset{1}{\cancel{3}}} = \frac{7 \times 2}{1}$$

$$= \frac{14}{1} = 14$$

Explain Your Thinking

- Is $2\frac{3}{4}$ the same as $2 + \frac{3}{4}$, or is it the same as $2 \times \frac{3}{4}$?
- Explain why you can't find $2\frac{3}{4} \times 3\frac{1}{3}$ by finding $(2 \times 3) + (\frac{3}{4} \times \frac{1}{3})$.

Guided Practice

Multiply. Write each product in simplest form.

1. $\frac{1}{2} \times 2\frac{3}{4}$ **2.** $5\frac{4}{7} \times 1\frac{2}{3}$ **3.** $6 \times 2\frac{1}{2}$ **4.** $4\frac{5}{6} \times 2\frac{1}{4}$

5. $3 \times 2\frac{2}{5}$ **6.** $2\frac{3}{5} \times 2$ **7.** $2\frac{2}{3} \times 4\frac{1}{2}$ **8.** $4\frac{3}{8} \times 2\frac{4}{5}$

Ask Yourself

- Can I simplify the product, using prime factorization?
- Did I cancel all common factors?

Independent Practice

Multiply. Write each product in simplest form.

9. $5\frac{1}{3} \times 2\frac{1}{4}$ **10.** $\frac{3}{11} \times \frac{4}{9}$ **11.** $\frac{7}{10} \times 5$ **12.** $\frac{2}{5} \times 3\frac{1}{3}$

13. $\frac{3}{7} \times 2\frac{5}{8}$ **14.** $1\frac{1}{8} \times 2\frac{2}{3}$ **15.** $\frac{3}{4} \times \frac{8}{12}$ **16.** $4\frac{1}{2} \times \frac{3}{4}$

17. $5 \times 3\frac{1}{5}$ **18.** $\frac{2}{7} \times 2\frac{5}{8}$ **19.** $2\frac{2}{5} \times 6\frac{2}{3}$ **20.** $9\frac{3}{5} \times 3\frac{3}{4}$

Problem Solving • Reasoning

21. **Predict** Henri cuts a piece of purple cloth into a rectangle that measures $2\frac{1}{2}$ inches by $5\frac{1}{3}$ inches. What is the area of Henri's rectangle?

22. **Logical Thinking** One patch of a quilt is a 1-foot square. Draw a diagram dividing this square into inches. How many square inches are in 1 square foot?

23. **Analyze** Last year the club made a quilt with an area of $16\frac{1}{2}$ square feet. If $\frac{2}{3}$ of the quilt was red, how many square feet were red?

24. A finished quilt measures $4\frac{2}{3}$ feet by 6 feet. What is the area of the finished quilt?

ART Quilts are an important part of many cultures. Some quilts tell a story. This quilt is called *Hoop Dreams*. It is $48\frac{1}{2}$ in. long.

What length of fabric would be needed to add backing to three quilts this size?

Mixed Review • Test Prep

Find the value of *n* in each equation. *(pages 122–123)*

25. $\frac{6}{8} = \frac{n}{32}$ **26.** $\frac{12}{15} = \frac{4}{n}$ **27.** $\frac{24}{64} = \frac{3}{n}$ **28.** $\frac{54}{72} = \frac{n}{4}$

29 Which is another form of $2 \times 2 \times 3 \times 5$? *(pages 108–109)*

A $2 \times 3^2 \times 5$ **C** $2 \times 3 \times 5^2$

B $2^2 \times 3 \times 5$ **D** $2^2 \times 3^2 \times 5^2$

Extra Practice See Set E on page 193.

Reciprocals

You will learn how to find the reciprocal of a number.

New Vocabulary
reciprocal
invert

Learn About It

Find the products.

$3 \times \frac{1}{3} = \blacksquare$ $\frac{5}{4} \times \frac{4}{5} = \blacksquare$ $2\frac{1}{2} \times \frac{2}{5} = \blacksquare$

What pattern do you see?

Each of the products above is equal to 1. Any two numbers whose product is 1 are **reciprocals** of each other. Each pair of numbers above are reciprocals.

The reciprocal of a fraction is the fraction inverted. **Invert** means to reverse the numerator and denominator.

Find the reciprocal of $\frac{1}{8}$.

The reciprocal of $\frac{1}{8}$ is $\frac{8}{1}$, or 8.

Other Examples

A. Reciprocals of Positive Whole Numbers

Find the reciprocal of 14.

- First write 14 as a fraction. $14 = \frac{14}{1}$
- Then invert the fraction. $\frac{1}{14}$

Check: $\frac{14}{1} \times \frac{1}{14} = 1$

B. Reciprocals of Mixed Numbers

Find the reciprocal of $3\frac{1}{2}$.

- First write $3\frac{1}{2}$ as an improper fraction. $3\frac{1}{2} = \frac{7}{2}$
- Then invert the fraction. $\frac{2}{7}$

Check: $\frac{7}{2} \times \frac{2}{7} = 1$

Explain Your Thinking

► What can you say about the reciprocal of a proper fraction?

► Is there a number that gives a product of 1 when it is multiplied by 0? Why or why not? Then can 0 have a reciprocal?

Guided Practice

Find the reciprocal of each number.

1. $\frac{11}{5}$ **2.** $2\frac{1}{4}$ **3.** 9 **4.** $\frac{3}{10}$

5. $8\frac{2}{3}$ **6.** $\frac{1}{7}$ **7.** $4\frac{5}{8}$ **8.** $\frac{15}{11}$

Ask Yourself

- What is this number renamed as a fraction?
- Do the two numbers have a product of 1?

Independent Practice

Find the reciprocal of each number.

9. $\frac{1}{6}$ **10.** $4\frac{1}{2}$ **11.** $\frac{3}{4}$ **12.** 3 **13.** $\frac{9}{4}$ **14.** $7\frac{5}{8}$

15. 1 **16.** $5\frac{2}{3}$ **17.** $\frac{7}{9}$ **18.** 27 **19.** $\frac{2}{5}$ **20.** $3\frac{2}{5}$

21. $\frac{1}{3}$ **22.** 22 **23.** $\frac{10}{7}$ **24.** $\frac{5}{23}$ **25.** 12 **26.** $9\frac{7}{8}$

Problem Solving • Reasoning

Solve. Choose a method.

Computation Methods

- Mental Math
- Estimation
- Paper and Pencil
- Calculator

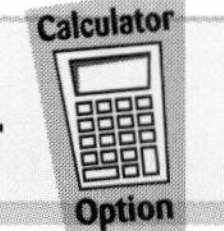

27. Ann, Heather, and Jacob each ate one piece of a pie that was cut into seven pieces. What is the reciprocal of the fractional part of pie they ate?

28. Roland is making lemonade. His recipe calls for 3 lemons for every 2 cups of water. How many lemons does Roland need to make 30 cups of lemonade?

29. **Analyze** Carolina is wrapping 3 gifts. She needs $\frac{5}{6}$ foot of wrapping paper to cover each gift box. She has a piece of wrapping paper that is $2\frac{3}{4}$ feet long. Does she have enough paper? Explain.

30. Nine musicians in the school orchestra play a stringed instrument, and $\frac{2}{3}$ of those play the violin. If the string section makes up $\frac{1}{2}$ the orchestra, how many musicians are in the orchestra?

31. Dan made the graph at the right to show how he spent his allowance. He needs to make a new graph because the one shown is no longer correct. Now he spends twice as much on entertainment and half as much on food as he did before. Now what fraction of his allowance will appear on the graph as "Other"?

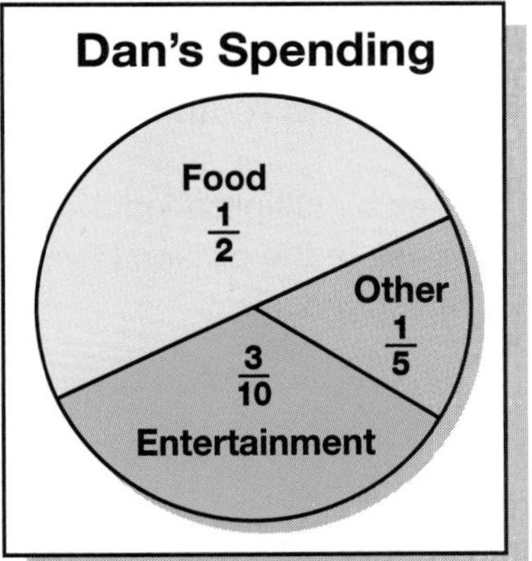

Mixed Review • Test Prep

Determine if the first number is divisible by the second number. *(pages 110–111)*

32. 234 2 **33.** 736 9 **34.** 1,038 3 **35.** 511 7

Choose the letter of the correct answer. *(pages 28–31)*

36 75 ÷ 4

A 18 **C** 18 R2

B 18 R1 **D** 18 R3

37 136 ÷ 20

F 6 R6 **H** 6 R16

G 6 R14 **J** 6 R18

Extra Practice See Set F on page 193.

Divide by a Fraction

You will learn to divide one fraction by another fraction.

Review Vocabulary
reciprocal
invert

Learn About It

Giorgio is preparing dinner for his grandfather's visit. He has $\frac{3}{4}$ cup of salsa to divide among several tacos. Each taco needs $\frac{3}{16}$ cup of salsa. How many tacos can Giorgio top with salsa?

Divide. $\mathbf{\frac{3}{4} \div \frac{3}{16} = n}$

Different Ways to Divide by a Fraction

You can use unit fractions.

Step 1 Convert $\frac{3}{4}$ to unit fractions of $\frac{1}{16}$.

$\frac{3}{4}$: $\frac{1}{4}$ $\frac{1}{4}$ $\frac{1}{4}$ | $\frac{1}{4}$

$\frac{12}{16}$: $\frac{1}{16}$ $\frac{1}{16}$ $\frac{1}{16}$ $\frac{1}{16}$ $\frac{1}{16}$ $\frac{1}{16}$ $\frac{1}{16}$ $\frac{1}{16}$ $\frac{1}{16}$ $\frac{1}{16}$ $\frac{1}{16}$ $\frac{1}{16}$ | $\frac{1}{16}$ $\frac{1}{16}$ $\frac{1}{16}$ $\frac{1}{16}$

Step 2 Rewrite the problem using 16ths.

$$\frac{3}{4} \div \frac{3}{16} = \frac{12}{16} \div \frac{3}{16}$$
$$= \frac{12 \div 3}{16 \div 16}$$

Step 3 Divide 12 unit fractions of $\frac{1}{16}$ each by 3 unit fractions of $\frac{1}{16}$.

$$12 \div 3 = 4$$

So $\frac{12}{16} \div \frac{3}{16} = 4$.

You can multiply by the reciprocal.

Step 1 Rewrite as a multiplication problem, using the **reciprocal** of the divisor. Remember to **invert** to find the reciprocal.

$$\frac{3}{4} \div \frac{3}{16}$$
$$= \frac{3}{4} \times \frac{16}{3}$$

Step 2 Simplify by using prime factorization. Cancel common factors. Then multiply.

$$\frac{3}{4} \times \frac{16}{3}$$
$$= \frac{\overset{1}{\cancel{3}} \times \overset{1}{\cancel{2}} \times \overset{1}{\cancel{2}} \times 2 \times 2}{\underset{1}{\cancel{2}} \times \underset{1}{\cancel{2}} \times \underset{1}{\cancel{3}}}$$
$$= \frac{4}{1} = 4$$

Solution: Giorgio can top 4 tacos with salsa.

Why this works: $\frac{3}{4} \div \frac{3}{16} = \frac{3 \times 16}{4 \times 16} \div \frac{4 \times 3}{4 \times 16}$

$= \frac{3 \times 16}{4 \times 3} = \frac{3}{4} \times \frac{16}{3}$

Once you have a common denominator of 4 × 16, you can divide the numerators.

Another Example

Improper Fraction as a Divisor

$\frac{2}{3} \div \frac{5}{4} = \frac{2}{3} \times \frac{4}{5} = \frac{8}{15}$

Explain Your Thinking

▶ Why does $\frac{8}{3} \div \frac{2}{3} = 8 \div 2$?

▶ How can you use multiplication to check a division problem?

Guided Practice

Ask Yourself

- Did I use the reciprocal of the divisor?
- Did I multiply by the reciprocal?

Find each quotient. Write each quotient in simplest form.

1. $\frac{2}{3} \div \frac{3}{4}$ **2.** $\frac{7}{3} \div \frac{5}{6}$ **3.** $\frac{1}{5} \div \frac{2}{3}$ **4.** $\frac{3}{2} \div \frac{7}{8}$

5. $\frac{3}{5} \div \frac{3}{10}$ **6.** $\frac{4}{5} \div \frac{2}{9}$ **7.** $\frac{5}{9} \div \frac{7}{3}$ **8.** $\frac{5}{6} \div \frac{11}{10}$

Independent Practice

Find each quotient. Write each quotient in simplest form.

9. $\frac{3}{11} \div \frac{6}{7}$ **10.** $\frac{8}{9} \div \frac{4}{3}$ **11.** $\frac{4}{5} \div \frac{5}{6}$ **12.** $\frac{2}{7} \div \frac{3}{2}$ **13.** $\frac{3}{10} \div \frac{6}{25}$

14. $\frac{11}{6} \div \frac{5}{2}$ **15.** $\frac{3}{14} \div \frac{6}{7}$ **16.** $\frac{7}{6} \div \frac{7}{8}$ **17.** $\frac{2}{3} \div \frac{3}{7}$ **18.** $\frac{7}{10} \div \frac{3}{5}$

19. $\frac{14}{3} \div \frac{4}{21}$ **20.** $\frac{9}{10} \div \frac{1}{5}$ **21.** $\frac{7}{8} \div \frac{21}{40}$ **22.** $\frac{4}{3} \div \frac{2}{5}$ **23.** $\frac{9}{10} \div \frac{6}{5}$

Problem Solving • Reasoning

24. Giorgio's father makes $\frac{2}{3}$ quart of juice for dinner. Giorgio pours the juice into glasses that hold $\frac{1}{6}$ quart each. How many glasses does Giorgio fill?

25. Explain Joyce mixed $1\frac{3}{4}$ pounds of nuts with $2\frac{1}{2}$ pounds of raisins. She put the mixture into $\frac{1}{4}$-pound bags. How many bags did Joyce fill? Explain how you found your answer.

26. At dinner, $\frac{5}{6}$ of a pie is eaten. Each piece of pie is $\frac{1}{12}$ of the whole pie. How many pieces of pie are left?

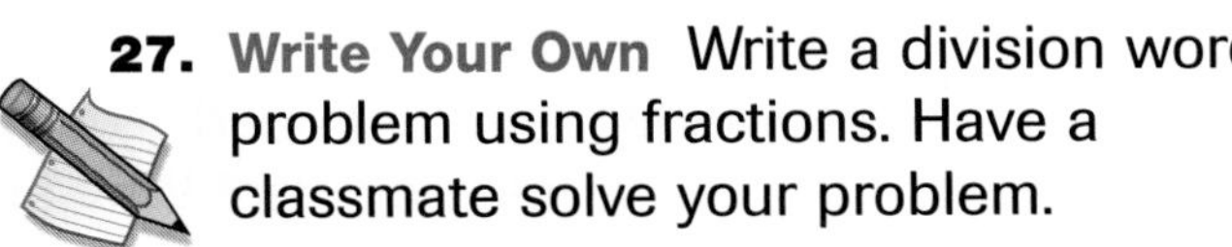

27. Write Your Own Write a division word problem using fractions. Have a classmate solve your problem.

Mixed Review • Test Prep

Compare. Write >, <, or = for each ●. *(pages 6–7, 126–128)*

28. 309 ● 407 **29.** 7,086 ● 6,999 **30.** $\frac{1}{2}$ ● $\frac{34}{68}$ **31.** $\frac{7}{8}$ ● $\frac{3}{4}$

32 $1.04 \div 5.2 = n$ *(pages 34–35)*

A 0.02 **B** 0.2 **C** 2.0 **D** 20.0

Extra Practice See Set G on page 193.

Divide Fractions and Whole Numbers

You will learn how to divide a fraction by a whole number and a whole number by a fraction.

Learn About It

Derika is making cards to send her friends. She has $\frac{2}{3}$ of a sheet of handmade paper. She wants to make 4 cards. How much of the sheet of paper can she use for each card?

Divide. $\frac{2}{3} \div 4 = n$

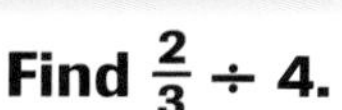

Find $\frac{2}{3} \div 4$.

Step 1 Rename the whole number as a fraction with a denominator of 1.

$\frac{2}{3} \div \frac{4}{1}$

Step 2 Rewrite as a multiplication problem using the reciprocal of the divisor.

$\frac{2}{3} \times \frac{1}{4}$

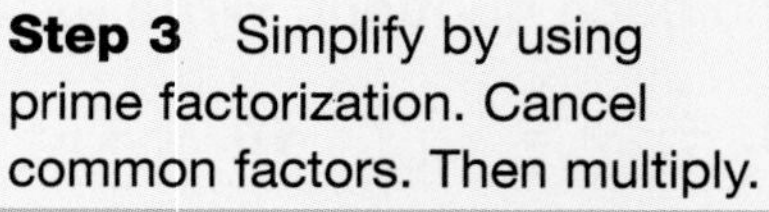

Step 3 Simplify by using prime factorization. Cancel common factors. Then multiply.

$\frac{2}{3} \times \frac{1}{4} = \frac{\cancel{2}^{1} \times 1}{3 \times 2 \times \cancel{2}_{1}} = \frac{1}{3 \times 2} = \frac{1}{6}$

Solution: Derika can use $\frac{1}{6}$ of a sheet for each card.

Another Example

Whole Number Dividend

$3 \div \frac{3}{5} = \frac{3}{1} \div \frac{3}{5} = \frac{\cancel{3}^{1}}{1} \times \frac{5}{\cancel{3}_{1}} = \frac{1}{1} \times \frac{5}{1} = \frac{5}{1} = 5$

Explain Your Thinking

- ► Is the quotient of a whole number divided by a proper fraction always greater than the whole number? Why or why not?
- ► Why does it make sense to simplify before you multiply?

Guided Practice

Find each quotient. Write each quotient in simplest form.

1. $6 \div \frac{3}{4}$ **2.** $\frac{2}{3} \div 8$ **3.** $4 \div \frac{7}{5}$ **4.** $\frac{11}{10} \div 3$

5. $\frac{7}{9} \div 14$ **6.** $5 \div \frac{1}{5}$ **7.** $8 \div \frac{4}{5}$ **8.** $\frac{2}{3} \div 10$

Ask Yourself

- Did I use the reciprocal of the divisor?
- Did I multiply by the reciprocal?

Independent Practice

Find each quotient. Write each quotient in simplest form.

9. $5 \div \frac{1}{7}$ **10.** $\frac{4}{7} \div 8$ **11.** $6 \div \frac{4}{9}$ **12.** $\frac{6}{5} \div 2$ **13.** $3 \div \frac{3}{4}$

14. $\frac{5}{3} \div 6$ **15.** $4 \div \frac{9}{5}$ **16.** $\frac{8}{5} \div 8$ **17.** $2 \div \frac{2}{5}$ **18.** $\frac{7}{4} \div 5$

19. $10 \div \frac{5}{6}$ **20.** $\frac{5}{4} \div 9$ **21.** $\frac{8}{9} \div 4$ **22.** $7 \div \frac{3}{2}$ **23.** $\frac{5}{8} \div 3$

n **Algebra • Equations** **Solve for *n*.**

24. $\frac{3}{4} \times 12 = n$ **25.** $20 \div \frac{4}{5} = n$ **26.** $\frac{15}{16} \div \frac{3}{4} = n$ **27.** $7\frac{3}{8} \times \frac{2}{3} = n$

Problem Solving • Reasoning

Use Data **Use the recipe to answer Problems 30–32.**

Recipe for Homemade Paper

1. Fill blender with $\frac{4}{5}$ cup of water.
2. Add $\frac{1}{5}$ cup of recycled paper scraps.
3. Cover blender. Blend on medium high for a few seconds.
4. Roll into sheets and dry.

28. Jan is making party bags. She has 3 pounds of peanuts and puts $\frac{1}{3}$ pound in each bag. How many bags can she fill?

29. **Predict** Vanessa has 3 feet of wrapping paper. She wants to wrap 4 gifts that require $\frac{3}{4}$ foot of paper each. Does she have enough wrapping paper?

30. Benicio has 7 cups of recycled paper scraps. How many batches of homemade paper can he make?

31. **Analyze** If Jana wants to make three batches of homemade paper, how much water will she need? How many cups of paper scraps?

32. **Write About It** Another way to state the paper-making instructions is to say, "Use 4 parts water to 1 part paper scraps." Why is this true?

Mixed Review • Test Prep

Write each number as a power of 10. *(pages 10–11)*

33. 100,000 **34.** 10 million **35.** 0.01 **36.** one thousandth

Choose the letter of the correct answer. *(pages 116–117)*

37 Find the LCM for 10 and 26.

A 10 **C** 130
B 12 **D** 260

38 Find the LCM for 12 and 32.

F 4 **H** 16
G 8 **J** 96

Divide Mixed Numbers

You will learn how to divide one mixed number by another mixed number.

Learn About It

Mr. Washington is setting up his new beehives. His shipment of bees weighs $7\frac{1}{2}$ pounds. Each hive holds $2\frac{1}{2}$ pounds of bees. How many new hives can Mr. Washington set up with this shipment of bees?

Divide. $7\frac{1}{2} \div 2\frac{1}{2} = n$

Find $7\frac{1}{2} \div 2\frac{1}{2}$.

Step 1 Rename the mixed numbers as improper fractions.

$$7\frac{1}{2} \div 2\frac{1}{2} = \frac{15}{2} \div \frac{5}{2}$$

Step 2 Rewrite as a multiplication problem, using the reciprocal of the divisor.

$$\frac{15}{2} \times \frac{2}{5}$$

Step 3 Simplify by using prime factorization. Cancel common factors. Then multiply.

$$\frac{15}{2} \times \frac{2}{5} = \frac{3 \times \overset{1}{\cancel{5}} \times \overset{1}{\cancel{2}}}{\underset{1}{\cancel{2}} \times \underset{1}{\cancel{5}}} = 3$$

Solution: Mr. Washington can set up 3 new hives.

Other Examples

A. Mixed Numbers and Fractions

$$4\frac{3}{8} \div \frac{5}{6} = \frac{35}{8} \div \frac{5}{6} = \frac{35}{8} \times \frac{6}{5}$$

$$= \frac{\overset{1}{\cancel{5}} \times 7 \times \overset{1}{\cancel{2}} \times 3}{2 \times 2 \times \underset{1}{\cancel{2}} \times \underset{1}{\cancel{5}}} = \frac{21}{4}$$

$$= 5\frac{1}{4}$$

B. Mixed and Whole Numbers

$$3 \div 6\frac{3}{5} = \frac{3}{1} \div \frac{33}{5} = \frac{3}{1} \times \frac{5}{33}$$

$$= \frac{\overset{1}{\cancel{3}} \times 5}{1 \times \underset{1}{\cancel{3}} \times 11}$$

$$= \frac{5}{11}$$

Explain Your Thinking

► How is multiplying by a proper fraction related to dividing by a mixed number?

Guided Practice

Divide. Express each quotient in simplest form.

1. $4\frac{2}{3} \div 6$

2. $1\frac{1}{2} \div \frac{5}{6}$

3. $2\frac{3}{5} \div 1\frac{7}{10}$

4. $4\frac{8}{9} \div 2\frac{2}{3}$

5. $3\frac{1}{3} \div 6\frac{2}{3}$

6. $2\frac{5}{12} \div 3\frac{1}{3}$

Ask Yourself

- Did I change the mixed numbers to improper fractions?
- Did I invert the divisor?

Independent Practice

Divide. Express each quotient in simplest form.

7. $2\frac{1}{2} \div 3$ **8.** $10 \div 2\frac{3}{4}$ **9.** $3 \div 2\frac{3}{8}$ **10.** $4\frac{5}{7} \div 3\frac{2}{3}$

11. $\frac{1}{2} \div 3\frac{4}{5}$ **12.** $3\frac{3}{4} \div 2$ **13.** $2\frac{4}{5} \div \frac{7}{8}$ **14.** $2\frac{1}{3} \div 1\frac{2}{5}$

15. $3\frac{2}{3} \div 2\frac{1}{2}$ **16.** $\frac{2}{3} \div 4\frac{1}{6}$ **17.** $\frac{3}{4} \div 2\frac{1}{3}$ **18.** $6\frac{3}{4} \div 2\frac{1}{4}$

Problem Solving • Reasoning

19. Nick is making a sieve to strain the honey he collects. He cuts a board that is 9 feet long into pieces that are $1\frac{1}{2}$ feet long. How many pieces does he have when he is finished?

20. **Estimate** Ian is helping Nick make the sieve. He cuts a screen that is 7 feet long into $1\frac{3}{4}$-foot pieces. How many pieces of screen does he have?

21. **Logical Thinking** Tamara has collected 10 pounds of honey. She packs the jars of honey into boxes. How many boxes will she need if $1\frac{2}{3}$ pounds of honey fits into each box? Tamara's brother needs $3\frac{1}{3}$ pounds of honey to send to one of his customers. How many boxes of honey does he need?

22. **Analyze** Jeremy can wash one car in $\frac{1}{2}$ hour. At that rate, how many cars can he wash in $2\frac{3}{4}$ hours? Solve this problem using three different methods: divide, use a diagram, and change the times to minutes before dividing.

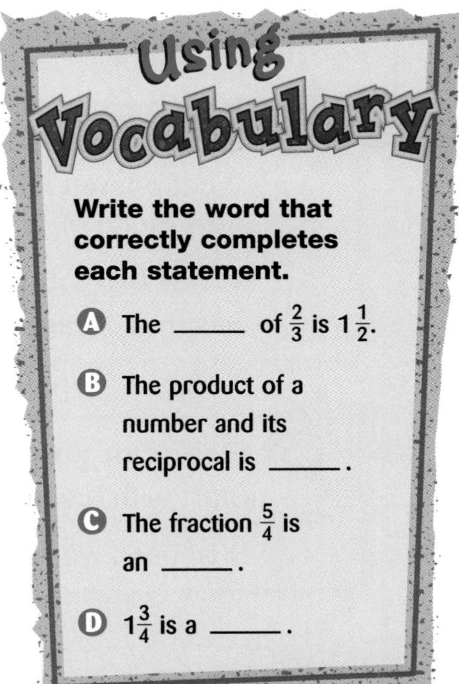

Using
Vocabulary
Write the word that correctly completes each statement.
A The ______ of $\frac{2}{3}$ is $1\frac{1}{2}$.
B The product of a number and its reciprocal is ______.
C The fraction $\frac{5}{4}$ is an ______.
D $1\frac{3}{4}$ is a ______.

Mixed Review • Test Prep

Determine if each number is a prime number. *(pages 104–105)*

23. 29 **24.** 47 **25.** 53 **26.** 39 **27.** 77 **28.** 41

Choose the letter of the correct prime factorization. *(pages 108–109)*

29 12

A 3×4 **C** 2×3^2

B 3×4^2 **D** $2^2 \times 3$

30 100

F 2×5^2 **H** 2×50

G $2^2 \times 5^2$ **J** $2^2 \times 25$

Extra Practice See Set I on page 194.

Problem-Solving Strategy: Solve a Simpler Problem

You will learn how to solve a problem by first solving a simpler problem.

If a problem seems difficult, try solving a similar, simpler problem first.

Problem Susi has $\frac{5}{8}$ yard of chain for making jewelry. She wants to give $\frac{2}{3}$ of the chain to someone else. Should Susi add, subtract, multiply, or divide to find out how much to give away?

Understand

What is the question?

What operation should Susi use to find out how much of the chain she will give away?

What do you know?

Susi has $\frac{5}{8}$ yard of chain. She will give $\frac{2}{3}$ of it away.

Plan

How can you find the answer?

Start with a simpler problem.

Susi has 2 yards of chain. She wants to give $\frac{1}{2}$ of it away.

Solve

Solve the simpler problem.

What is $\frac{1}{2}$ of 2 yards? $\frac{1}{2}$ of $2 = \frac{1}{2} \times \frac{2}{1} = \frac{2}{2}$ or 1

Susi would give away 1 yard of chain.

Solve the original problem.

What is $\frac{2}{3}$ of $\frac{5}{8}$ yard? $\frac{2}{3} \times \frac{5}{8} = \frac{\overset{1}{\cancel{2}} \times 5}{3 \times \underset{1}{\cancel{2}} \times 2 \times 2} = \frac{5}{12}$

Susi would give away $\frac{5}{12}$ yard of chain.

Look Back

Look back at the problem.

Is your answer reasonable? Explain.

Remember:
- Understand
- Plan
- Solve
- Look Back

Guided Practice

Use the Solve a Simpler Problem strategy to solve each problem.

1. Mark made a 45-inch paper-clip chain. If each paper clip is $1\frac{1}{4}$ inches long, how many paper clips did Mark use to make the chain?

   Think: If the chain was 10 inches long, and the paper clips were 2 inches long, how would you solve the problem?

2. Darla has 150 packages of ribbon. Each package has $24\frac{1}{2}$ inches of ribbon. How much ribbon does Darla have?

   Think: If Darla had two packages, and each package contained 10 inches of ribbon, how would you solve the problem?

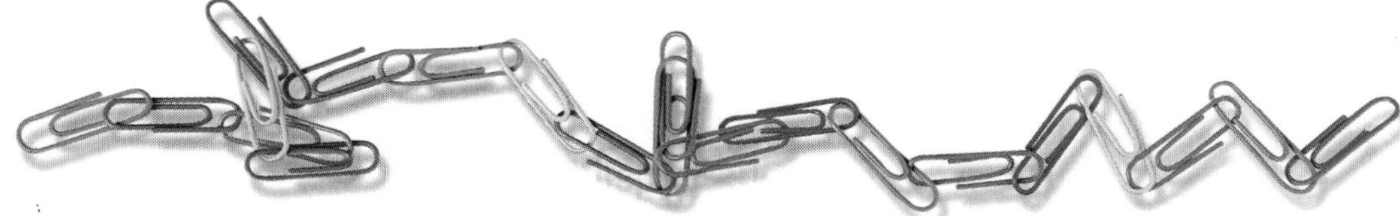

Choose a Strategy

Solve. Use these or other strategies.

Problem-Solving Strategies

- **Solve a Simpler Problem**
- **Make a List**
- **Use Logical Thinking**
- **Work Backward**

3. Susi has orders for 5 bracelets. Three need $6\frac{1}{2}$ inches of chain, and two need $8\frac{1}{4}$ inches of chain. With $36\frac{1}{4}$ inches of chain, does Susi have enough?

4. Short necklaces are about 15 inches long. How many short necklaces can Susi make from a piece of chain $68\frac{3}{4}$ inches long?

5. Fancy ribbon costs $6 a yard. Plain ribbon costs $4 a yard. Sid and Derika need $3\frac{1}{6}$ yards of fancy ribbon and $2\frac{1}{4}$ yards of plain ribbon. How much will the ribbon cost?

6. The sixth-graders are decorating the classroom for a party. They need four $5\frac{2}{3}$-foot streamers and six $10\frac{3}{4}$-foot streamers. How many feet of streamers do they need?

7. Julie and Gayle sell half of their paperback books at a yard sale. They donate one fifth of the remaining books to the library and keep 60 books. How many books did they have to start with?

8. The shop class is making wind chimes. Each wind chime needs five $12\frac{3}{8}$-inch pieces of cord and one $42\frac{1}{4}$-inch piece of cord. How much cord is needed for 30 wind chimes?

Extra Practice See 3–5 on page 195.

Quick Check

Check Your Understanding of Lessons 5–11

Multiply. Write each product in simplest form.

1. $\frac{1}{2} \times \frac{2}{3}$

2. $\frac{3}{5} \times 4\frac{5}{6}$

3. $5\frac{4}{9} \times 1\frac{2}{7}$

Write the reciprocal.

4. $\frac{4}{11}$

5. 21

6. $4\frac{7}{10}$

Divide. Write each quotient in simplest form.

7. $\frac{2}{3} \div \frac{1}{2}$

8. $\frac{9}{10} \div \frac{2}{5}$

9. $12 \div \frac{3}{4}$

10. $\frac{1}{2} \div 3$

11. $5\frac{5}{7} \div \frac{4}{21}$

12. $1\frac{3}{4} \div 1\frac{15}{16}$

Solve.

13. Brendon must paint a 48-foot fence. If he can paint $5\frac{1}{3}$ feet in 1 hour, how long will it take Brendon to paint the fence?

14. Amy wants to wrap 6 presents. Each present requires $2\frac{7}{8}$ feet of ribbon. How much ribbon does Amy need to wrap all of the presents?

How did you do?

If you had difficulty with any items in the Quick Check, you can use the following pages for review and extra practice.

ITEMS	REVIEW THESE PAGES	DO THESE EXTRA PRACTICE ITEMS
1–3	pages 168–171	Sets D–E, pages 192–193
4–6	pages 172–173	Set F, page 193
7–8	pages 174–175	Set G, page 193
9–10	pages 176–177	Set H, page 193
11–12	pages 178–179	Set I, page 194
13–14	pages 180–181	3–5, page 195

Test Prep • Cumulative Review

Maintaining the Standards

Choose the letter of the correct answer.

1. Which number is divisible by 3?

   A 7,345

   B 7,245

   C 7,145

   D 7,045

2. Which number makes the number sentence true?

   $$\frac{18}{42} = \frac{3}{\blacksquare}$$

   F 4

   G 5

   H 6

   J 7

3. Which decimal represents the fraction $\frac{12}{18}$?

   A $0.\overline{5}$

   B $0.\overline{6}$

   C $0.\overline{7}$

   D $0.\overline{8}$

4. What is the correct word form for the number 7.349?

   F seven and three hundred forty-nine thousandths

   G seven and three hundred forty-nine

   H seven and three hundred forty-nine hundredths

   J seven and three hundred forty-nine millionths

5. What is the correct standard form for the expression 5×10^{-2}?

   A 500

   B 5.00

   C 0.50

   D 0.05

6. Lou practiced the guitar for $\frac{1}{2}$ hour on Monday, $\frac{3}{4}$ hour on Wednesday, and $\frac{2}{3}$ hour on Friday. How many hours did Lou practice the guitar this week?

   F $\frac{11}{12}$ hour

   G $1\frac{5}{6}$ hours

   H $1\frac{11}{12}$ hours

   J 2 hours

7. Chantal has $\frac{5}{8}$ yard of cloth. She wants to give $\frac{1}{2}$ of her cloth to a friend. How many yards of cloth will she give to her friend?

   A $\frac{5}{16}$ yard

   B $\frac{5}{10}$ yard

   C $\frac{1}{2}$ yard

   D $\frac{5}{8}$ yard

8. Look for a pattern in the shapes below. Draw the next two likely shapes in the pattern.

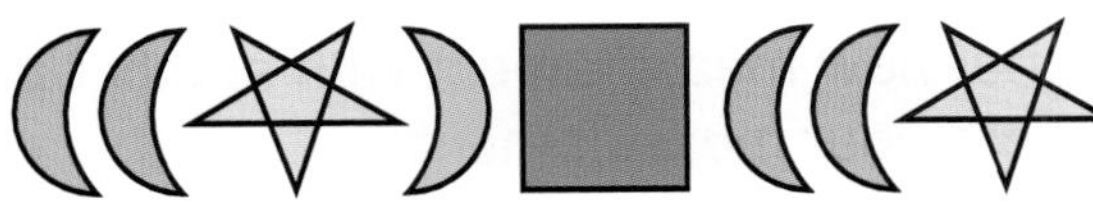

Explain How did you find your answer?

Customary Units of Length

You will learn how to change between units of length in the customary system.

Learn About It

Work in groups to measure the length of your classroom. As you do this, you will learn how customary units of length are related.

How long is your classroom? You will use three different units to find this measurement.

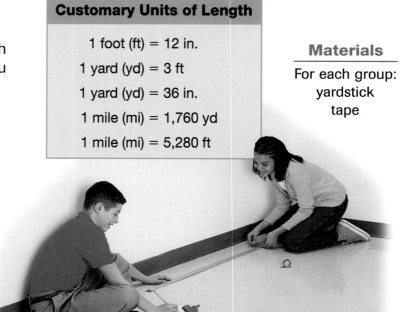

Customary Units of Length
1 foot (ft) = 12 in.
1 yard (yd) = 3 ft
1 yard (yd) = 36 in.
1 mile (mi) = 1,760 yd
1 mile (mi) = 5,280 ft

Materials

For each group:
yardstick
tape

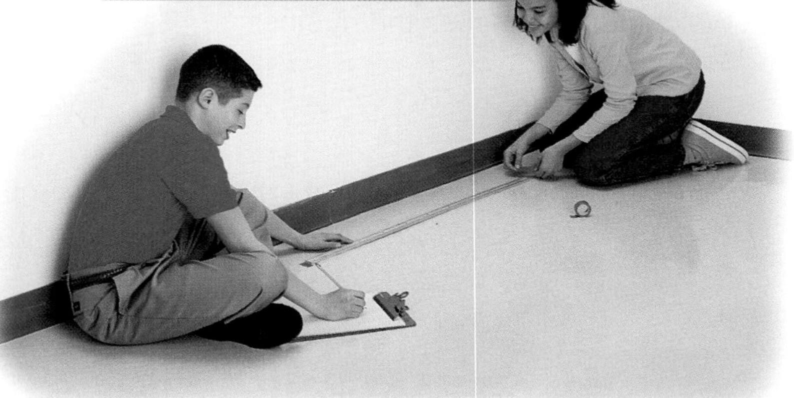

Complete the steps below.
Record your answers like this Length: ___ yards ___ feet ___ inches

Step 1 Use the yardstick to find out how many whole yards there are in the length of your classroom. Mark the end of your measurement with a piece of tape. Record your measurement.

Step 2 Measure the number of whole feet between the tape mark and the classroom wall. Mark the end of your new measurement with another piece of tape. Record your measurement.

Step 3 Measure the remaining portion in inches and record your measurement.

- How can you express the length of your classroom only in inches? First, look at the table of customary units and the two examples at the right. Then use items *A–D* on page 185.

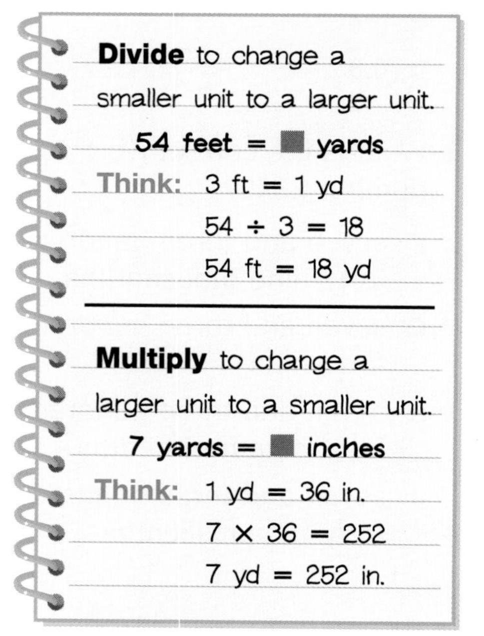

Divide to change a smaller unit to a larger unit.
54 feet = ■ yards
Think: 3 ft = 1 yd
54 ÷ 3 = 18
54 ft = 18 yd
Multiply to change a larger unit to a smaller unit.
7 yards = ■ inches
Think: 1 yd = 36 in.
7 × 36 = 252
7 yd = 252 in.

Change your yard and feet measurements to inches. Then add the three values to find the length of your classroom in inches.

A. number of yards measured = ■ inches

B. number of feet measured = ■ inches

C. number of inches measured = ■ inches

D. total classroom length = ■ inches

Try It Out

Copy and complete the tables below.

	Inches	Feet	Yards
1.	■	■	2
2.	■	$4\frac{1}{2}$	■
3.	36	■	■
4.	■	■	$18\frac{1}{3}$

	Yards	Miles
5.	3,520	■
6.	■	$3\frac{1}{2}$
7.	■	$5\frac{1}{4}$
8.	10,560	■

Complete.

9. If 3 ft = 1 yd, then 2 ft = ■ yd.

10. If 12 in. = 1 ft, then 3 in. = ■ ft.

11. If 1 yd = 36 in., then $\frac{1}{2}$ yd = ■ in.

12. If 1 mi = 1,760 yd, then 3 mi = ■ yd.

13. If 5,280 ft = 1 mi, then 1,760 ft = ■ mi.

14. If 12 in. = 1 ft, then 17 in. = ■ ft.

15. If 36 in. = 1 yd, then 81 in. = ■ yd.

16. If 1,760 yd = 1 mi, then 880 yd = ■ mi.

Answer these questions.

17. Think about things you measure. Why might you choose one unit over another when measuring length?

18. **Explain** How would you find the number of miles that are in one million inches?

Write about it! Talk about it!

Use what you have learned to answer each question.

19. What kinds of things might you measure in inches? in feet? in yards? in miles?

20. Decide which unit of length would be best to measure each of the following: a pencil, a desk, a soccer field, the distance from your house to your school, your textbook. Justify each decision.

Extra Practice See Set J on page 194.

Customary Units of Capacity and Weight

You will learn how to change capacity and weight measures in the customary system.

Learn About It

The Bicycle Club is planning a mountain-bike ride. The students will be riding for almost $2\frac{1}{2}$ hours. Mr. Schulman, the club's adviser, recommends that each student carry 48 fluid ounces of water on the ride. How many quarts of water does each student need?

Calculate. **48 fl oz = ■ qt**

Find how many quarts equal 48 fluid ounces.

Step 1 Write the equality that relates fluid ounces and quarts.
1 qt = 32 fl oz

Step 2 To change from a smaller unit to a larger unit, divide.
$48 \div 32 = 1\frac{1}{2}$
48 fl oz = $1\frac{1}{2}$ qt

Customary Units of Measure

1 pound (lb) = 16 ounces (oz)
1 ton (T) = 2,000 lb

1 cup (c) = 8 fluid ounces (fl oz)
1 pint (pt) = 2 c = 16 fl oz
1 quart (qt) = 2 pt = 4 c
1 gallon (gal) = 4 qt = 8 pt

Another Example

Change Weights

$1\frac{3}{4}$ tons = n pounds

1 T = 2,000 lb

$1\frac{3}{4} \times 2{,}000 = 3{,}500$

$1\frac{3}{4}$ T = 3,500 lb

Explain Your Thinking

► How do you know whether to multiply or divide when changing from one unit to another?

Guided Practice

Complete.

1. 40 oz = ■ lb **2.** 5 c = ■ fl oz **3.** 3 pt = ■ qt

4. 5 qt = ■ pt **5.** 2 qt = ■ gal **6.** $2\frac{1}{2}$ T = ■ lb

Ask Yourself

- Which equality should I use?
- Am I changing to a larger unit or a smaller unit?

Independent Practice

Complete.

7. 8 c = ■ pt **8.** 8 lb = ■ oz **9.** $\frac{3}{4}$ qt = ■ pt **10.** 5,500 lb = ■ T

11. $\frac{1}{4}$ T = ■ lb **12.** 52 oz = ■ lb **13.** 1 qt = ■ gal **14.** $\frac{3}{4}$ c = ■ fl oz

15. If 1 c = 8 fl oz, then 28 fl oz = ■ c. **16.** If 1 pt = 2 c, then 9 pt = ■ c.

Choose the most reasonable unit of measure for each. Write *oz, lb, T, fl oz, c, pt, qt,* or *gal*.

17. a glass of milk **18.** your body weight **19.** a handful of flour

20. a truckload of bricks **21.** the water in a fish tank **22.** a pitcher of juice

Problem Solving • Reasoning

23. Before the ride, Geoff drank two 8-fluid-ounce glasses of water. After the ride, he drank two more glasses of water. If Geoff drank 48 fluid ounces during the ride, how many cups of water did he drink the day of the ride?

24. Analyze At the end of the ride, everyone drank 16 fluid ounces of a sports drink. If 12 students and 2 adults rode bikes, how many gallons of sports drink did the riders drink?

25. Estimate Angelina made $5\frac{7}{8}$ pounds of potato salad for a picnic. She divided the salad into 6-ounce servings. Approximately how many servings of potato salad did Angelina make?

26. Write Your Own Write a word problem that includes weight or capacity measures. Your word problem should require at least two steps to be solved. Exchange problems and have a classmate solve your problem.

Solve for *n*.

A $7.5 \times n = 90$

B $40 \div n = 2.5$

C $2\frac{1}{4} \times n = 36$

D $144 \div n = 4$

E $72 \div n = 4.5$

F $3.1 \times n = 16{,}368$

Mixed Review • Test Prep

Write as decimals. Round each answer to the nearest tenth. *(pages 134–135)*

27. $\frac{25}{42}$ **28.** $\frac{38}{76}$ **29.** $\frac{44}{15}$ **30.** $\frac{193}{278}$

31 What is 1,000,000 as a power of ten? *(pages 36–37)*

A 10^7 **B** 10^6 **C** 10^5 **D** 10^4

Extra Practice See Set K on page 194.

Problem-Solving Application: Use Measurement

You will learn how to solve problems involving measurement.

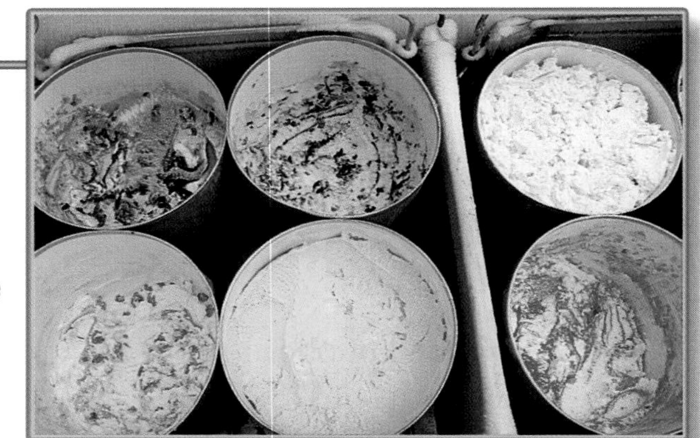

To solve problems, you must use measurements accurately.

Problem Ms. Chang wants to add an insulation strip to the top edges of her ice cream case. The top of the case is a rectangle $1\frac{3}{4}$ ft wide and $2\frac{1}{2}$ ft long. The insulation is sold in strips that are 1 foot long. How many strips of insulation does she need to buy?

Understand

What is the question?

How many strips of insulation are needed?

What do you know?

- The top of the case is a rectangle $1\frac{3}{4}$ feet by $2\frac{1}{2}$ feet.
- The insulation comes in 1-foot strips.

Plan

How can you find the answer?

Find the perimeter of the top. Since each strip of insulation is 1 foot long, the number of feet in the perimeter will equal the number of strips needed.

Solve

Find the perimeter.

$P = 2l + 2w$

$= (2 \times 1\frac{3}{4} \text{ ft}) + (2 \times 2\frac{1}{2} \text{ ft})$

$= 3\frac{1}{2} \text{ ft} + 5 \text{ ft} = 8\frac{1}{2} \text{ ft}$

Round $8\frac{1}{2}$ ft to 9 ft to find the number of strips of insulation.
Ms. Chang needs to buy 9 strips of insulation.

Look Back

Look back at the problem.

Is your answer reasonable? Explain.

Left: These two friends can't wait to sample their homemade ice cream.

Right: "Peter the Alchemist" is the nickname of this man who is a taster for an ice-cream company.

Remember:
- ▶ Understand
- ▶ Plan
- ▶ Solve
- ▶ Look Back

Guided Practice

Solve.

1. Ms. Chang ordered a sign $2\frac{1}{3}$ yards wide to put in the shop window. The window is $7\frac{1}{2}$ feet wide. Will the sign fit in the window?

   Think: How can you compare yards with feet?

2. Ms. Chang sells ice cream by the scoop and by the container. She sells a quart of ice cream for $1.50. How much would $1\frac{1}{2}$ gallons of ice cream cost?

   Think: How many quarts are in $1\frac{1}{2}$ gallons?

Choose a Strategy

Solve. Use these or other strategies.

Calculator Option

Problem-Solving Strategies

- **Write an Equation**
- **Work Backward**
- **Use Logical Thinking**
- **Guess and Check**

3. The shop's dining area needs to be tiled. Each square tile has an area of 144 in.^{2} and a thickness of $\frac{1}{4}$ in. If the dining area is 15 ft wide and 24 ft long, how many tiles are needed to cover the floor? (Hint: Area = length × width)

4. On Friday, Ms. Chang used $5\frac{1}{4}$ lb of strawberries. The day before, she used 2 lb less than this, and on Wednesday, she used $\frac{1}{2}$ lb less than on Thursday. How many ounces of strawberries did she use in these three days?

5. One day, Ms. Chang spent 9 hours 45 minutes at the shop. One third of this time was spent helping customers. How much time did she spend helping customers? Estimate to check if your answer is reasonable.

6. The world's biggest ice cream sundae was made in Anaheim, California, in 1985. The sundae was 12 feet high. It was made with 4,667 gallons of ice cream. How many quarts of ice cream were used in the sundae?

7. As part of her supplies, Ms. Chang ordered $11\frac{1}{2}$ lb of nuts. Half of her order was for peanuts. How many pounds of peanuts did she order?

8. Ounces and tons are units of weight. How many ounces are in $1\frac{1}{2}$ tons? Show your calculation and explain your reasoning at each step.

Extra Practice See 6–9 on page 195.

Quick Check

Check Your Understanding of Lessons 12–14

Complete.

1. If 12 in. = 1 ft, then 5 in. = ■ ft.
2. If 1 yd = 36 in., then $10\frac{1}{4}$ yd = ■ in.
3. If 1 mi = 5,280 ft, then $5\frac{2}{5}$ mi = ■ ft.
4. If 3 ft = 1 yd, then $9\frac{3}{8}$ ft = ■ yd.

Complete.

5. If 8 fl oz = 1 c, then 23 fl oz = ■ c.
6. If 1 lb = 16 oz, then $4\frac{1}{2}$ lb = ■ oz.
7. If 1 gal = 4 qt, then 6 qt = ■ gal.
8. If 2,000 lb = 1 T, then 125 lb = ■ T.

Solve.

9. Mr. Pride sells 2 scoops of ice cream on a cone for $1.95. Two scoops of his ice cream are equal to 1 cup. How much money will customers have paid when Mr. Pride has sold 1 gallon of ice cream?
10. A machine knits scarves that are 1 yard long. The machine produces $4\frac{1}{2}$ inches of scarf material per minute. How long does it take the machine to knit one scarf?

How did you do?

If you had difficulty with any items in the Quick Check, you can use the following pages for review and extra practice.

Items	Review These Pages	Do These Extra Practice Items
1–4	pages 184–185	Set J, page 194
5–8	pages 186–187	Set K, page 194
9–10	pages 188–189	6–9, page 195

Test Prep • Cumulative Review

Maintaining the Standards

Choose the letter of the correct answer.

1. Michael weighs the rocks in his collection. One rock weighs $\frac{1}{8}$ lb, another weighs $\frac{3}{8}$ lb, and a third weighs $\frac{5}{8}$ lb. How much does his collection weigh altogether?

   A $\frac{6}{8}$ lb **C** 1 lb
   B $\frac{7}{8}$ lb **D** $1\frac{1}{8}$ lb

2. Jackie uses the computer for $\frac{5}{8}$ hour. Jorge uses it for 0.7 hour, and Phil uses the computer for 40 minutes. Who uses the computer for the greatest amount of time?

   F Jackie
   G Phil
   H Jorge
   J Jackie and Jorge

3. Which is the standard form of the number six hundred thirty million, five hundred thousand, nine hundred twenty?

   A 630,592
   B 635,920
   C 630,500,920
   D 630,500,920,000

4. Which amount makes the sentence true?

   If 1 yd = 36 in., then $\frac{1}{4}$ yd = ■ in.

   F 4 **H** 8
   G 6 **J** 9

5. Mrs. Yu pays $6.60 for four identical pairs of exercise socks. How much does 1 pair of socks cost?

   A $1.50
   B $1.55
   C $1.60
   D $1.65

6. Jill has a ribbon that is $24\frac{1}{2}$ inches long. She cuts the ribbon into pieces that are $6\frac{1}{8}$ inches long. How many pieces of ribbon does she have now?

   F 4
   G $4\frac{1}{4}$
   H $5\frac{1}{2}$
   J 6

7. The stem-and-leaf plot shows the high temperatures for one January in Niagara Falls, New York. What are the highest and lowest temperatures listed?

Niagara Falls, New York January Temperatures (°F)

Stem	Leaf
0	5 6 8 8 9
1	0 1 1 1 3 4 5 6 7 7 8 9 9
2	0 1 3 3 4 5 5 6
3	1 1 2 4 6

Explain How did you find your answer?

Internet Test Prep
Visit **www.eduplace.com/kids/mhm** for more *Test Prep Practice.*

Extra Practice

Set A (Lesson 1, pages 156–157)

Find each sum or difference. Write each answer in simplest form.

1. $\frac{1}{2} + 2\frac{1}{2}$ **2.** $1\frac{2}{3} + \frac{2}{3}$ **3.** $\frac{3}{7} - \frac{2}{7}$ **4.** $1\frac{3}{4} - \frac{1}{4}$

5. $\frac{1}{8} + \frac{3}{8}$ **6.** $3\frac{2}{3} + \frac{1}{3}$ **7.** $\frac{2}{9} + \frac{4}{9}$ **8.** $3\frac{1}{4} + 1\frac{3}{4}$

9. $\frac{5}{8} - \frac{3}{8}$ **10.** $4\frac{3}{7} - 1\frac{2}{7}$ **11.** $\frac{5}{6} - \frac{1}{6}$ **12.** $5\frac{1}{4} - 2\frac{3}{4}$

13. $\frac{11}{21} - \frac{4}{21}$ **14.** $6\frac{1}{15} - 3\frac{8}{15}$ **15.** $9\frac{7}{20} + \frac{13}{20}$ **16.** $\frac{14}{33} + \frac{25}{33}$

Set B (Lesson 2, pages 158–160)

Find each sum. Write each answer in simplest form.

1. $\frac{1}{3} + 4\frac{1}{2}$ **2.** $9\frac{2}{3} + \frac{2}{5}$ **3.** $4\frac{3}{8} + \frac{2}{5}$ **4.** $1\frac{3}{4} + \frac{5}{12}$

5. $\frac{1}{4} + \frac{3}{5}$ **6.** $4\frac{2}{7} + \frac{1}{14}$ **7.** $3\frac{2}{9} + \frac{2}{3}$ **8.** $\frac{1}{4} + \frac{3}{5} + \frac{1}{8}$

9. $\frac{5}{6} + \frac{3}{8}$ **10.** $7\frac{1}{3} + \frac{5}{6}$ **11.** $4\frac{3}{5} + 1\frac{3}{10}$ **12.** $\frac{5}{6} + \frac{1}{2} + \frac{2}{3}$

13. $\frac{1}{2} + \frac{3}{7}$ **14.** $8\frac{3}{10} + \frac{2}{15}$ **15.** $\frac{3}{4} + 2\frac{2}{5}$ **16.** $\frac{7}{9} + \frac{7}{10} + \frac{3}{5}$

Set C (Lesson 3, pages 162–163)

Find each difference. Write each answer in simplest form.

1. $7\frac{1}{2} - \frac{2}{3}$ **2.** $12\frac{5}{8} - \frac{2}{3}$ **3.** $2\frac{3}{7} - \frac{1}{2}$ **4.** $5\frac{2}{3} - \frac{2}{5}$

5. $4\frac{1}{8} - \frac{5}{6}$ **6.** $\frac{2}{3} - \frac{1}{4}$ **7.** $6\frac{2}{9} - \frac{5}{6}$ **8.** $\frac{5}{8} - \frac{1}{4}$

9. $\frac{3}{4} - \frac{1}{6}$ **10.** $5\frac{5}{6} - \frac{5}{8}$ **11.** $2\frac{9}{10} - 1\frac{2}{5}$ **12.** $3\frac{1}{4} - 2\frac{2}{5}$

13. $1\frac{2}{3} - \frac{3}{4}$ **14.** $\frac{17}{20} - \frac{4}{5}$ **15.** $8\frac{5}{12} - \frac{2}{9}$ **16.** $10\frac{4}{7} - 2\frac{9}{10}$

Set D (Lesson 5, pages 168–169)

Multiply. Write each product in simplest form.

1. $\frac{5}{8} \times \frac{1}{2}$ **2.** $\frac{7}{10} \times \frac{4}{5}$ **3.** $\frac{5}{9} \times \frac{12}{13}$ **4.** $\frac{3}{7} \times \frac{8}{9}$

5. $\frac{2}{3} \times 9$ **6.** $\frac{4}{5} \times \frac{1}{8}$ **7.** $\frac{6}{11} \times \frac{1}{6}$ **8.** $\frac{2}{5} \times \frac{1}{3}$

9. $\frac{3}{10} \times \frac{4}{5}$ **10.** $\frac{2}{13} \times \frac{5}{8}$ **11.** $\frac{7}{15} \times 3$ **12.** $\frac{20}{21} \times \frac{7}{10}$

Extra Practice

Set E (Lesson 6, pages 170–171)

Multiply. Write each product in simplest form.

1. $2\frac{3}{8} \times 1\frac{1}{2}$ **2.** $7\frac{7}{8} \times 2\frac{4}{7}$ **3.** $3\frac{3}{4} \times 5\frac{1}{3}$ **4.** $9\frac{7}{9} \times 2\frac{5}{11}$

5. $9\frac{9}{10} \times 1\frac{2}{3}$ **6.** $4\frac{4}{5} \times 2\frac{1}{8}$ **7.** $7\frac{1}{3} \times 2\frac{3}{4}$ **8.** $5\frac{1}{5} \times 2\frac{9}{13}$

9. $5\frac{5}{12} \times 2\frac{4}{5}$ **10.** $5\frac{4}{9} \times 6\frac{3}{7}$ **11.** $14\frac{2}{5} \times \frac{2}{3}$ **12.** $23\frac{2}{5} \times 5\frac{5}{6}$

13. $3\frac{5}{9} \times 1\frac{1}{8}$ **14.** $\frac{8}{11} \times 10\frac{3}{4}$ **15.** $\frac{17}{20} \times 3\frac{1}{3}$ **16.** $8\frac{5}{8} \times 1\frac{2}{3}$

Set F (Lesson 7, pages 172–173)

Find the reciprocal of each number.

1. $2\frac{1}{2}$ **2.** $1\frac{2}{3}$ **3.** $\frac{14}{23}$ **4.** $9\frac{2}{17}$

5. $4\frac{3}{8}$ **6.** $\frac{6}{11}$ **7.** $\frac{4}{9}$ **8.** $3\frac{1}{4}$

9. $\frac{1}{50}$ **10.** $\frac{7}{30}$ **11.** $8\frac{5}{22}$ **12.** 25

13. $7\frac{3}{10}$ **14.** $2\frac{9}{13}$ **15.** $\frac{34}{49}$ **16.** 100

Set G (Lesson 8, pages 174–175)

Find each quotient. Write each quotient in simplest form.

1. $\frac{1}{2} \div \frac{3}{5}$ **2.** $\frac{4}{9} \div \frac{2}{3}$ **3.** $\frac{7}{15} \div \frac{3}{10}$ **4.** $\frac{2}{11} \div \frac{4}{13}$

5. $\frac{3}{16} \div \frac{1}{8}$ **6.** $\frac{5}{6} \div \frac{15}{16}$ **7.** $\frac{6}{7} \div \frac{21}{25}$ **8.** $\frac{12}{13} \div \frac{5}{26}$

9. $\frac{5}{7} \div \frac{5}{49}$ **10.** $\frac{3}{14} \div \frac{3}{4}$ **11.** $\frac{7}{9} \div \frac{5}{18}$ **12.** $\frac{3}{10} \div \frac{9}{10}$

13. $\frac{11}{12} \div \frac{5}{6}$ **14.** $\frac{1}{20} \div \frac{4}{5}$ **15.** $\frac{2}{3} \div \frac{16}{27}$ **16.** $\frac{8}{21} \div \frac{1}{18}$

Set H (Lesson 9, pages 176–177)

Find each quotient. Write each quotient in simplest form.

1. $\frac{1}{2} \div 5$ **2.** $14 \div \frac{2}{3}$ **3.** $10 \div \frac{5}{9}$ **4.** $\frac{5}{7} \div 3$

5. $16 \div \frac{7}{12}$ **6.** $20 \div \frac{10}{11}$ **7.** $24 \div \frac{9}{10}$ **8.** $6 \div \frac{7}{8}$

9. $7 \div \frac{5}{7}$ **10.** $12 \div \frac{6}{15}$ **11.** $\frac{20}{21} \div 8$ **12.** $30 \div \frac{7}{10}$

Extra Practice

Set I *(Lesson 10, pages 178–179)*

Divide. Express each quotient in simplest form.

1. $1\frac{1}{2} \div 4$ **2.** $8\frac{7}{8} \div \frac{1}{16}$ **3.** $11\frac{2}{5} \div \frac{4}{5}$ **4.** $2\frac{4}{7} \div 7\frac{1}{5}$

5. $22 \div 3\frac{2}{3}$ **6.** $3\frac{5}{9} \div 16$ **7.** $4\frac{2}{7} \div \frac{20}{21}$ **8.** $4\frac{3}{8} \div 15$

9. $10\frac{1}{2} \div \frac{5}{7}$ **10.** $12\frac{2}{5} \div 5\frac{1}{6}$ **11.** $5\frac{1}{4} \div 5\frac{5}{6}$ **12.** $30 \div \frac{3}{10}$

13. $2\frac{14}{15} \div 1$ **14.** $6\frac{9}{10} \div \frac{4}{15}$ **15.** $13 \div 2\frac{4}{11}$ **16.** $3\frac{1}{4} \div 7\frac{3}{7}$

Set J *(Lesson 12, pages 184–185)*

Copy and complete the tables below.

	Inches	Feet	Yards
1.	48	■	■
2.	■	$6\frac{1}{3}$	■
3.	■	■	$3\frac{1}{2}$

	Yards	Miles
4.	440	■
5.	■	$6\frac{1}{5}$
6.	5,280	■

Complete.

7. If 1 yd = 36 in., then $\frac{1}{4}$ yd = ■ in.

8. If 1 mi = 5,280 ft, then $5\frac{1}{2}$ mi = ■ ft.

9. If 12 in. = 1 ft, then 23 in. = ■ ft.

10. If 3 ft = 1 yd, then 1 ft = ■ yd.

Set K *(Lesson 13, pages 186–187)*

Complete.

1. $\frac{1}{2}$ T = ■ lb **2.** 13 fl oz = ■ c **3.** 7 pt = ■ qt **4.** 15 qt = ■ pt

5. 8 qt = ■ gal **6.** 3 T = ■ lb **7.** 9 c = ■ pt **8.** 540 lb = ■ T

9. 15 fl oz = ■ c **10.** 25 oz = ■ lb **11.** $2\frac{1}{4}$ T = ■ lb **12.** 12 qt = ■ gal

13. $1\frac{1}{2}$ gal = ■ qt **14.** 3 pt = ■ c **15.** 18 fl oz = ■ c **16.** 7 qt = ■ pt

17. 5 c = ■ pt **18.** $\frac{1}{4}$ c = ■ fl oz **19.** 13 lb = ■ oz **20.** $2\frac{3}{4}$ qt = ■ pt

Extra Practice • Problem Solving

Solve. Use multiple steps. *(Lesson 4, pages 164–165)*

1. Joel needs two shelves to display his coin collection. One shelf should be $2\frac{2}{3}$ feet long, and the other shelf should be $4\frac{3}{5}$ feet long. Joel has a board that is 7 feet long. Is this board long enough to make both shelves?

2. Amy bought 10 feet of wood to build a cage for her pet snake. She used $8\frac{3}{5}$ feet of the wood. Her brother needs $1\frac{5}{8}$ feet of wood for a toy car he is building. Will there be enough wood left over to build the car?

Solve. Use the Solve a Simpler Problem strategy or another strategy. *(Lesson 11, pages 180–181)*

3. Kate's mom is planning a party for her. She wants to tape eight $8\frac{1}{2}$-foot pink streamers and four $11\frac{1}{3}$-foot green streamers on the ceiling. How many feet of streamers will she use in all?

4. Eli has 12 paper strips. He wants to connect the strips to see if they will reach across the room. If each strip is $\frac{3}{4}$ foot long, and the room is $8\frac{1}{2}$ feet wide, will the strips reach across the room?

5. Glenna is making a picture frame for her arts-and-crafts class. The picture frame she plans to make has two sides that are each $1\frac{1}{3}$ feet long. The other two sides are each $2\frac{5}{8}$ feet long. What is the total length of framing material that Glenna needs to make the picture frame?

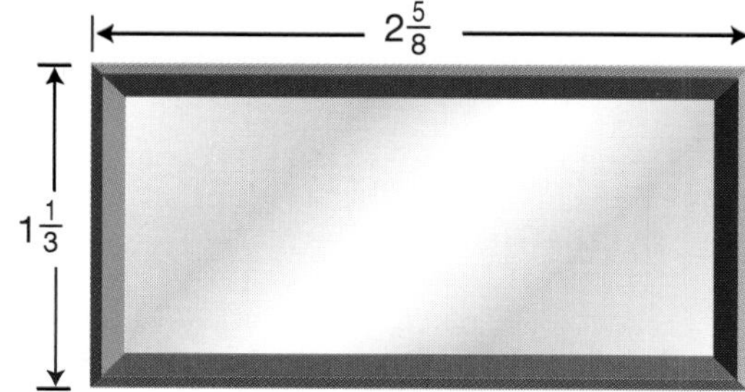

Solve. Use measurement. *(Lesson 14, pages 188–189)*

6. Dana is making bracelets for 5 friends. Each bracelet will be $6\frac{3}{5}$ inches long. The material she bought costs \$1.40 per foot. How much did it cost Dana to buy the material needed to make all of the bracelets?

7. Ryan ate 12 oz of vegetables on Friday. The day before, he ate 18 oz of vegetables. On Wednesday, he ate 18 oz of vegetables. How many pounds of vegetables did Ryan eat on these three days?

8. Mr. Conway sells a pint of fresh-squeezed orange juice for \$1.25. At that rate, how much would $1\frac{1}{2}$ gallons of orange juice cost?

9. The instructions on the label of a liquid fertilizer say to use 5 fluid ounces for each gallon of water. How much fertilizer should be used in 1 quart of water?

Chapter Review

Reviewing Vocabulary

Write *always, sometimes,* or *never* for each question. Give an example to support your answer.

1. The denominator of a proper fraction is less than the numerator.
2. The least common multiple of two numbers is their product.
3. When two proper fractions have the same denominator, the one with the greater numerator is the greater fraction.
4. When a fraction is in simplest form, the numerator and denominator have no common factor other than 1.

Match each term with its definition.

5. **improper fraction**
6. **reciprocals**
7. **invert**
8. **numerator**

A two numbers whose product is 1

B the number over the bar in a fraction

C a fraction in which the numerator is greater than or equal to the denominator

D to reverse the numerator and denominator

Reviewing Concepts and Skills

Solve. Write each answer in simplest form. *(pages 156–157, 158–160, 162–163, 168–169, 170–171)*

9. $\frac{7}{8} + \frac{5}{8}$ **10.** $\frac{11}{12} + \frac{2}{3}$ **11.** $1\frac{3}{8} + 2\frac{1}{2}$ **12.** $\frac{3}{4} + \frac{1}{3} + \frac{7}{8}$

13. $\frac{9}{10} - \frac{3}{10}$ **14.** $\frac{15}{16} - \frac{3}{4}$ **15.** $2\frac{5}{6} - 1\frac{2}{3}$ **16.** $7\frac{1}{10} - 6\frac{4}{5}$

17. $\frac{3}{7} \times \frac{5}{6}$ **18.** $18 \times \frac{7}{8}$ **19.** $4\frac{1}{2} \times \frac{2}{3}$ **20.** $1\frac{5}{8} \times 3\frac{1}{5}$

Find the reciprocal of each number. *(pages 172–174)*

21. $\frac{3}{8}$ **22.** 5 **23.** $25\frac{3}{5}$ **24.** $13\frac{7}{8}$

Solve. Write each answer in simplest form. *(pages 174–175, 176–177, 178–179)*

25. $\frac{6}{11} \div \frac{2}{3}$ **26.** $1\frac{7}{9} \div 8$ **27.** $1\frac{1}{2} \div 2\frac{1}{3}$ **28.** $12\frac{3}{5} \div 3\frac{3}{10}$

Copy and complete the tables below. *(pages 184–185)*

	Inches	Feet	Yards
29.	■	$2\frac{1}{2}$	■
30.	60	■	■
31.	■	■	$3\frac{1}{3}$
32.	■	$7\frac{3}{4}$	■

	Yards	Miles
33.	■	$1\frac{1}{2}$
34.	6,160	■
35.	■	$3\frac{2}{5}$
36.	2,200	■

Complete. *(pages 184–185, 186–187)*

37. If 12 in. = 1 ft, then 8 in. = ■ ft.

38. If 5,280 ft = 1 mi, then 1,760 ft = ■ mi.

39. If 1 T = 2,000 lb, then $3\frac{1}{2}$ T = ■ lb.

40. If 8 fl oz = 1 c, then 20 fl oz = ■ c.

41. If 4 c = 1 qt, then 9 c = ■ qt.

42. If 1 gal = 8 pt, then $2\frac{1}{4}$ gal = ■ pt.

Solve. *(pages 164–165, 180–181, 188–189)*

43. Jerri's garden has an area of 35 square yards and a length of $4\frac{2}{3}$ yards. How wide is her garden?

44. Five students each bring $2\frac{1}{4}$ packages of construction paper to school. How many packages of construction paper do they have in all?

45. Brenda's car goes 319 miles on $14\frac{1}{2}$ gallons of gas. How far will her car go on 5 gallons of gas?

46. Kristy is building a picture frame. The length is $1\frac{3}{4}$ feet. The width is $\frac{1}{3}$ foot greater than the length. How much material does she need for the frame?

Brain Teaser Math Reasoning

FUNNY FRACTIONS

Gene wrote a number on a piece of paper. He then told Sue that the reciprocal of his number was an improper fraction greater than 1. Sue says that Gene's number could be a mixed number. Jerry says that it could be a proper fraction. Which statement is correct? Explain and give examples to show your thinking.

Safe Site

Internet Brain Teasers
Visit **www.eduplace.com/kids/mhm** for more *Brain Teasers.*

Chapter Test

Solve. Write each answer in simplest form.

1. $\frac{3}{4} - \frac{1}{4}$ **2.** $\frac{5}{8} + \frac{3}{8}$ **3.** $2\frac{3}{10} + \frac{9}{10}$ **4.** $4\frac{7}{9} - 1\frac{5}{9}$

5. $\frac{2}{5} + \frac{1}{3}$ **6.** $1\frac{5}{8} + \frac{1}{4}$ **7.** $2\frac{3}{8} + 8\frac{11}{12}$ **8.** $\frac{3}{4} + \frac{5}{6} + \frac{2}{3}$

9. $\frac{1}{4} - \frac{1}{12}$ **10.** $3\frac{7}{8} - 2\frac{1}{2}$ **11.** $4\frac{5}{8} - \frac{5}{6}$ **12.** $5\frac{9}{20} - 3\frac{9}{10}$

13. $\frac{2}{3} \times \frac{9}{11}$ **14.** $\frac{3}{4} \times \frac{8}{9}$ **15.** $15 \times \frac{1}{3}$ **16.** $\frac{5}{8} \times 36$

17. $1\frac{3}{5} \times \frac{1}{2}$ **18.** $\frac{2}{3} \times 4\frac{1}{2}$ **19.** $1\frac{4}{7} \times 2\frac{4}{5}$ **20.** $5\frac{1}{4} \times 3\frac{1}{7}$

Find the reciprocal of each number.

21. $\frac{5}{7}$ **22.** $7\frac{1}{3}$ **23.** 99 **24.** $\frac{14}{17}$ **25.** $6\frac{7}{10}$

Solve. Write each answer in simplest form.

26. $\frac{5}{8} \div \frac{5}{6}$ **27.** $\frac{9}{10} \div \frac{2}{3}$ **28.** $\frac{7}{12} \div \frac{3}{4}$ **29.** $\frac{17}{18} \div \frac{5}{9}$

30. $3 \div \frac{3}{4}$ **31.** $\frac{8}{9} \div 6$ **32.** $\frac{4}{5} \div 10$ **33.** $12 \div \frac{2}{3}$

34. $5\frac{3}{4} \div \frac{3}{4}$ **35.** $7\frac{1}{3} \div 1\frac{1}{3}$ **36.** $\frac{5}{6} \div 2\frac{7}{9}$ **37.** $5\frac{7}{10} \div 5\frac{1}{4}$

Copy and complete the tables below.

	Inches	Feet	Yards
38.	18	■	■
39.	■	■	$2\frac{1}{2}$

	Yards	Miles
40.	■	3
41.	2,640	■

Complete.

42. $3\frac{1}{2}$ yd = ■ in. **43.** 1,320 ft = ■ mi **44.** 32 fl oz = ■ c

45. 4 T = ■ lb **46.** 1 pt = ■ gal **47.** 7 c = ■ pt

Solve.

48. Felicia cuts 3 pieces, each $2\frac{2}{3}$ feet long, from a 10-foot board. How long is the piece that is left?

49. As part of an exercise program, Sean walked $2\frac{3}{4}$ miles each day for one week. How many miles did he walk in all?

50. John has 1 quart of milk. He uses 10 fluid ounces to make hot chocolate. His father needs $2\frac{1}{2}$ cups of milk to make custard. Will there be enough milk left for John's father to make the custard? Explain.

Write About It

Solve each problem. Use correct math vocabulary to explain your thinking.

1. Mike is going on a bike ride with five of his friends. Each of the boys will drink 2 pints of water during the ride. Mike's mom asks how many quarts of water they will need in total for the ride. Mike quickly calculates 6×2 and says they will need 12 quarts of water.

- **a.** Explain what he did wrong.
- **b.** Show how to find the correct answer.

2. Maria is putting trim around three sides of the door frames in her dollhouse. There are 3 door frames in all. Each frame has two sides that are $5\frac{1}{8}$ inches long and one side that is $2\frac{11}{16}$ inches wide. How many feet of trim must she buy?

- **a.** Represent the problem with numbers.
- **b.** Show your work to find the answer.
- **c.** Explain how you know that your answer is correct.

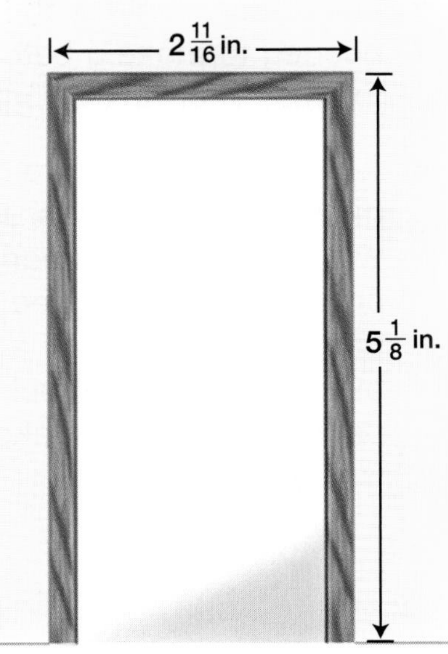

Another Look

Use the table of units and the list of ingredients to solve Problems 1–4. Add, multiply, and divide mixed numbers and fractions as needed to solve each problem. Show your work.

Customary Units of Volume
1 teaspoon (tsp) = $\frac{1}{3}$ tablespoon
1 tablespoon (tbsp) = $\frac{1}{2}$ ounce
1 ounce (oz) = $\frac{1}{8}$ cup
3 teaspoons = 1 tablespoon
1 ounce = 2 tablespoons
1 cup (c) = 8 ounces

Buttermilk Pancakes (Makes 10 four-inch pancakes)

Dry Ingredients	Liquid Ingredients
$1\frac{1}{2}$ c cake flour	$1\frac{1}{4}$ c buttermilk
$2\frac{1}{2}$ tbsp sugar	$\frac{1}{4}$ c water
$\frac{1}{2}$ tsp salt	2 tbsp melted butter
$\frac{3}{4}$ tsp baking soda	$\frac{1}{4}$ c egg whites
$1\frac{3}{4}$ tsp baking powder	

1. How many teaspoons equal 1 ounce? How many ounces is $\frac{1}{2}$ teaspoon of salt equal to? Express your answer as a fraction.

2. The ingredients are for a recipe to make 10 four-inch buttermilk pancakes. Jon wants to make only half that many pancakes. How much baking powder will Jon need? Express your answer as a fraction.

3. **Look Back** What is the total amount of dry ingredients needed to make a batch of 10 buttermilk pancakes? Express your answer in ounces.

4. **Analyze** Jon wants to make buttermilk pancakes for himself and 4 friends. Jon estimates that each person will eat 4 four-inch pancakes. Jon needs to know the amount of each ingredient needed to make four pancakes for himself and each friend with no leftover batter. Rewrite the recipe so that there is enough pancake batter to make 4 pancakes for each of 5 people.

Enrichment

Central Angles

An angle that has its vertex at the center of a circle is called a central angle. Central angles show parts of a circle and are measured in degrees (°).

You can use the measures of central angles to show parts of a circle as fractions.

- Since there are 360° in a circle, $\frac{90}{360}$ is the fraction that shows this part of the circle.

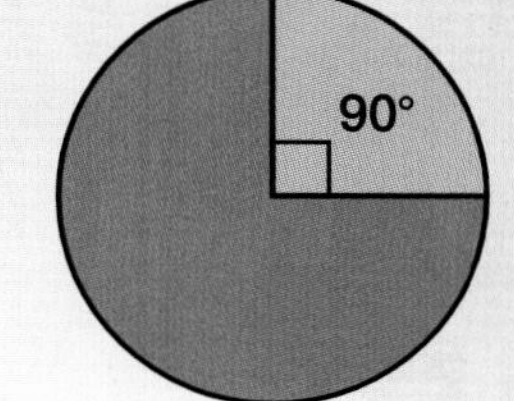

- When $\frac{90}{360}$ is simplified, the result is $\frac{1}{4}$.

So 90° is $\frac{1}{4}$ of a circle.

Show each central angle as a fraction of a circle.

1. 180° **2.** 45° **3.** 270° **4.** $22\frac{1}{2}$°

5. 4° **6.** 24° **7.** 10° **8.** 30°

Now determine the central angle measure in degrees for each part of a circle.

9. $\frac{1}{5}$ **10.** $\frac{1}{10}$ **11.** $\frac{3}{8}$ **12.** $\frac{2}{3}$

13. $\frac{1}{40}$ **14.** $\frac{1}{6}$ **15.** $\frac{3}{4}$ **16.** $\frac{5}{12}$

Explain Your Thinking

Each degree of an angle can be divided further into 60 minutes. Based on what you have already learned, how many minutes would be represented by $\frac{1}{2}$ degree? Explain your thinking.

CHAPTER 5

Integers and Rational Numbers

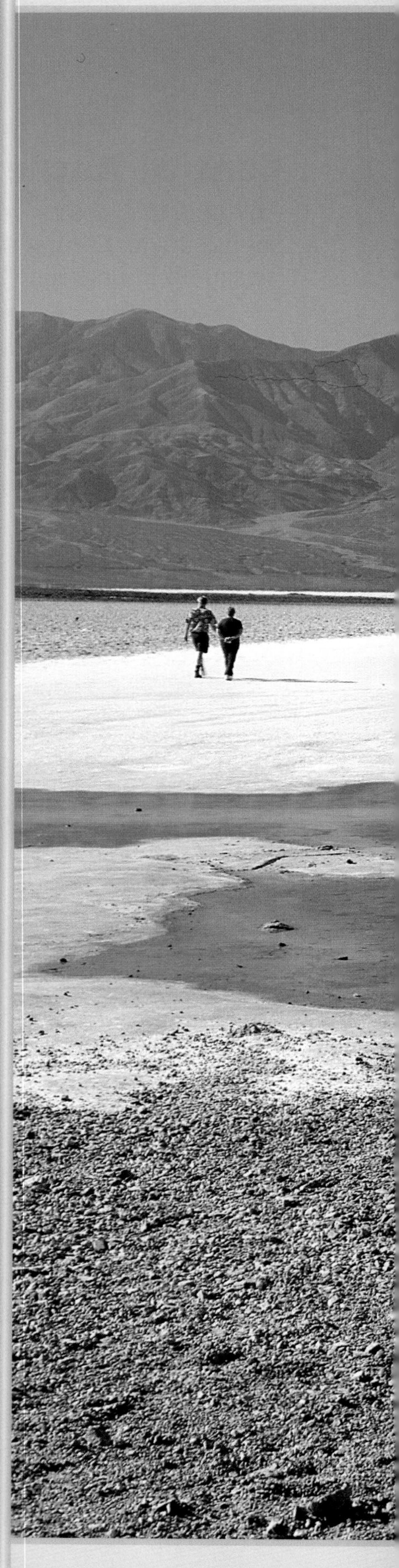

Why Learn About Integers and Rational Numbers?

Learning about integers and rational numbers will help you better understand the meaning of numbers and the relationships that exist among them.

When you compare the temperatures of different places around the world, you may need to use positive and negative integers and to convert between different temperature units.

This sign describes the elevation of a town in Death Valley called Badwater. Elevation is the distance above or below sea level.

Badwater
ELEV. - 282 ft.

Reading Mathematics

Reviewing Vocabulary

Understanding math language helps you become a successful problem solver. Here are some math vocabulary words you should know.

absolute value the distance of a number from zero on a number line

integers the collection of numbers consisting of counting numbers, their opposites, and zero

negative integer an integer less than zero

opposite numbers two numbers that are the same distance from zero, but on opposite sides of zero on a number line

positive integer an integer greater than zero

Reading Words and Symbols

When you read mathematics, sometimes you read only words, sometimes you read words and symbols, and sometimes you read only symbols.

All of these statements represent the same number.

- positive seven
- $^{+}7$
- 7

Try These

1. Write whether each of the following is a *positive integer,* a *negative integer,* or *neither.*

   a. 23 **b.** $^-5$ **c.** 0 **d.** $^-\frac{3}{4}$

   e. $^-140$ **f.** 1 **g.** $^-7.8$ **h.** $^+62$

2. Write an integer that describes each situation. Then write the absolute value of that integer.

   a. a loss of $12 **b.** 30°C above zero

3. Write *true* or *false* for each statement.

   a. The opposite of a number is always positive.

   b. The set of integers includes zero.

   c. The absolute value of a number is always greater than the number itself.

4. Write the opposite of each number.

   a. $^-6$ **b.** 14 **c.** $^-18$ **d.** $^-1$

5. Fill in the blanks with numbers that make the sentence true.

   If ____ is the negative integer, then ____ is its opposite,

   and ____ is its absolute value.

Upcoming Vocabulary

Write About It **Here are some other vocabulary words** you will learn in this chapter. Watch for these words. Write their definitions in your journal.

rational number

additive inverse

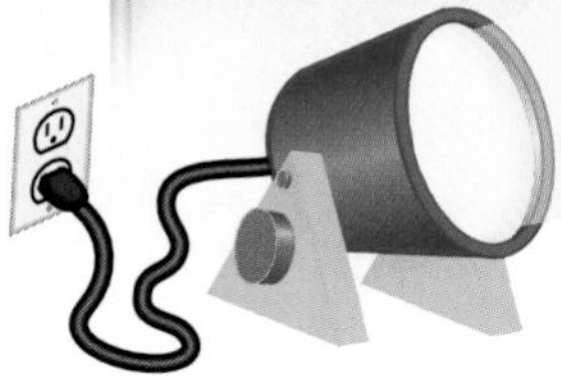

Integers

You will learn about the set of numbers called integers.

Review Vocabulary
integers
positive integers
negative integers
opposite numbers
absolute value

Learn About It

You can use a number line to display numbers called **integers**. The set of integers consists of the counting numbers, their opposites, and zero.

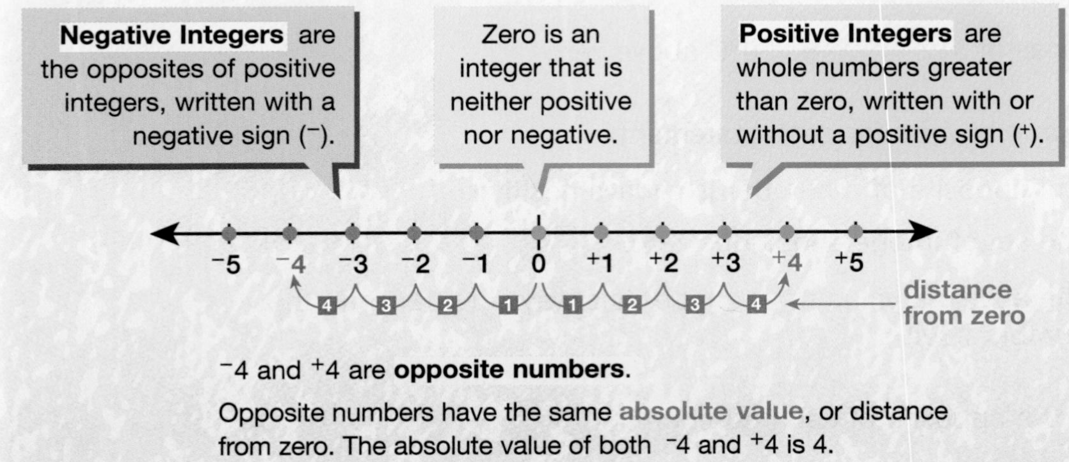

Negative Integers are the opposites of positive integers, written with a negative sign (⁻).
Zero is an integer that is neither positive nor negative.
Positive Integers are whole numbers greater than zero, written with or without a positive sign (⁺).
⁻5 ⁻4 ⁻3 ⁻2 ⁻1 0 ⁺1 ⁺2 ⁺3 ⁺4 ⁺5
4 3 2 1 1 2 3 4
distance from zero

⁻4 and ⁺4 are **opposite numbers**.

Opposite numbers have the same **absolute value**, or distance from zero. The absolute value of both ⁻4 and ⁺4 is 4.

Olivia's mother tries to buy shares of stock when the price is low and sell shares when the price is high. The table shows a daily change in the price per share of companies in which she owns stock.

Which stocks have increased in price? Which stocks have decreased in price?

Changes in Share Price

Company	Change (in $)
A	⁻1
B	⁺2
C	⁻6
D	⁺5

Use a number line to analyze the change in share prices.

Step 1 Plot the price changes per share on a number line.

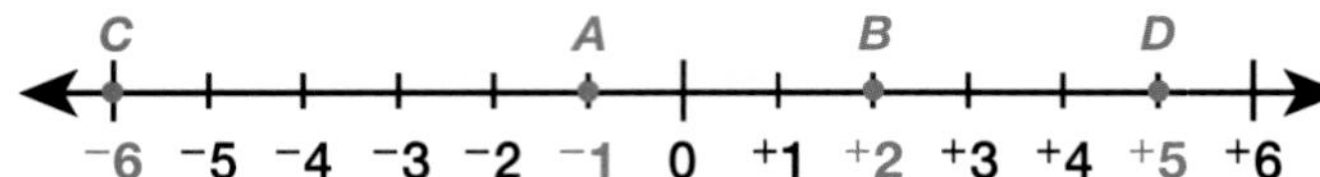

Step 2 Identify the stocks that have increased in price.

The price changes for Companies *B* and *D* are **positive** integers. The price per share of their stock has increased.

Step 3 Identify the stocks that have decreased in price.

The price changes for Companies *A* and *C* are **negative** integers. The price per share of their stock has decreased.

Solution: The share price has increased for Companies *B* and *D* and decreased for Companies *A* and *C*.

Explain Your Thinking

- What number has the same absolute value as $^{-}8$? Explain why.
- What number is its own opposite?

Guided Practice

If the number is an integer, write its opposite. If it is not, write *no*.

1. $^{+}48$ **2.** $^{+}2.6$ **3.** $^{-}325$ **4.** $\frac{7}{10}$

Ask Yourself

- When is a number an integer?
- Is the integer negative or positive?

Independent Practice

If the number is an integer, write its opposite. If it is not, write *no*.

5. $^{-}0.4$ **6.** $^{+}71$ **7.** $^{-}1,320$ **8.** $^{-}6\frac{1}{8}$ **9.** $^{+}2$

10. $^{-}29$ **11.** $^{-}4.65$ **12.** $^{-}625$ **13.** $^{+}11$ **14.** 0

15. $\frac{2}{3}$ **16.** $^{+}870$ **17.** $^{-}78$ **18.** $^{+}2\frac{1}{6}$ **19.** $^{+}31$

Problem Solving • Reasoning

Use the number line for Problems 20 and 21.

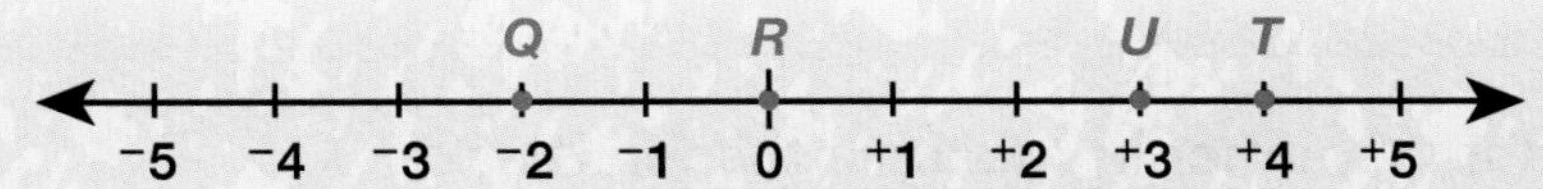

Q, *R*, *U*, and *T* represent daily changes in per-share prices of several companies.

20. Which company's price per share did not change?

21. **Compare** Which company had a greater change in share price, *Q* or *U*?

22. **Analyze** A stock is priced at \$27 on Monday. It shows a change of $^{+}5$ on Tuesday and a change of $^{-}1$ on Wednesday. What is its price then?

23. **Write About It** Think about absolute value. When is the absolute value of an integer the same as the opposite of that integer? Explain.

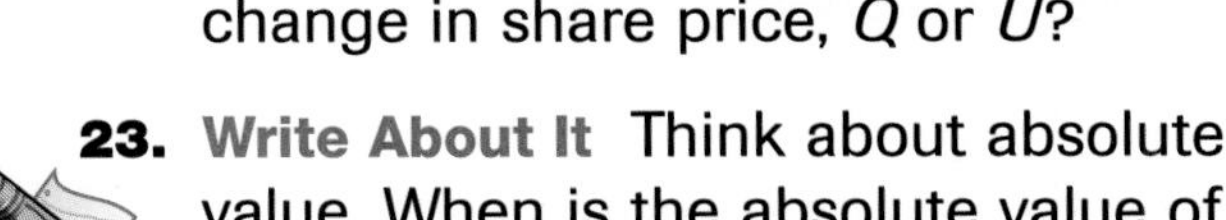

Mixed Review • Test Prep

Subtract. Express each answer in simplest form. *(pages 162–163)*

24. $\frac{7}{9} - \frac{1}{2}$ **25.** $2\frac{1}{4} - 1\frac{1}{6}$ **26.** $\frac{3}{4} - \frac{1}{3}$ **27.** $1\frac{5}{6} - \frac{2}{3}$

28 2 quarts = ■ *(pages 186–187)*

A 6 c **B** $\frac{1}{2}$ gal **C** 20 oz **D** 2 pt

Extra Practice See Set A on page 238.

LESSON 2 Compare and Order Integers

You will learn how to compare and order integers.

Learn About It

When it is winter in the Northern Hemisphere, it is summer in the Southern Hemisphere. Likewise, when it is summer in the Northern Hemisphere, it is winter in the Southern Hemisphere.

The table shows January temperatures in different places around the world. Which is warmer in January—Alaska or Australia?

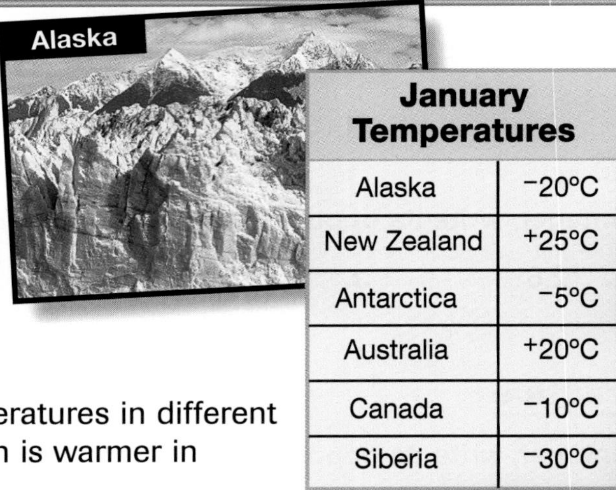

January Temperatures	
Alaska	$^{-}20$°C
New Zealand	$^{+}25$°C
Antarctica	$^{-}5$°C
Australia	$^{+}20$°C
Canada	$^{-}10$°C
Siberia	$^{-}30$°C

Australia

Use a number line to compare the two temperatures.

Step 1 Locate the two temperatures on a number line.

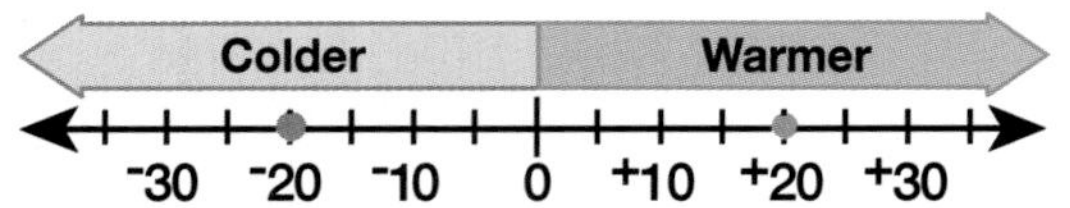

Step 2 Compare. On a number line, integers increase in value from left to right.

$^{+}20$°C > $^{-}20$°C
$^{+}20$°C is to the right of $^{-}20$°C, so it is warmer in Australia than it is in Alaska.

Solution: In January, it is warmer in Australia than in Alaska.

Another Example

Order Integers
Order the temperatures in the table from lowest to highest.

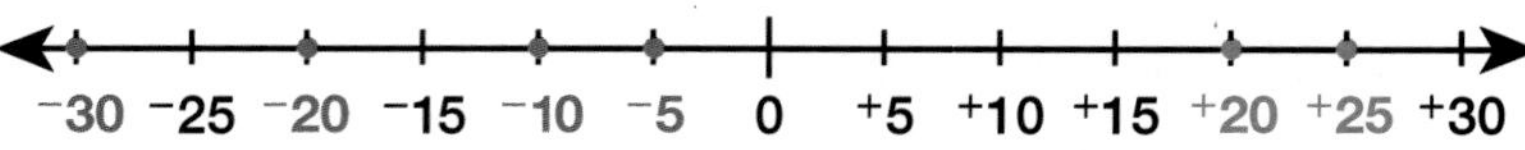

From lowest to highest: $^{-}30$°C, $^{-}20$°C, $^{-}10$°C, $^{-}5$°C, $^{+}20$°C, $^{+}25$°C

Explain Your Thinking

- ▶ How can you use a number line to decide if $^{-}20$°C is colder than $^{-}30$°C?
- ▶ Which of the January temperatures is closest to 0°C? How can you decide?

Guided Practice

Compare. Write > or < for each ●.

1. $^{-}5$ ● $^{-}4$　**2.** $^{+}33$ ● $^{-}33$　**3.** $^{+}19$ ● $^{+}18$

Ask Yourself

- Did I look at the sign of the integers?

Order from least to greatest.

4. $^{+}8$　$^{-}3$　$^{+}11$　$^{-}7$　**5.** $^{-}2$　$^{-}14$　$^{+}14$　**6.** $^{+}9$　0　$^{+}17$　$^{-}6$

Independent Practice

Compare. Write > or < for each ●.

7. $^{-}6$ ● $^{-}7$ **8.** $^{-}4$ ● $^{+}5$ **9.** $^{+}44$ ● $^{+}80$ **10.** $^{-}41$ ● 0

11. $^{-}38$ ● $^{-}16$ **12.** $^{+}11$ ● $^{-}12$ **13.** $^{-}7$ ● $^{-}20$ **14.** $^{-}1$ ● $^{+}1$

Order from least to greatest.

15. $^{-}6$ $^{+}5$ $^{-}1$ $^{-}4$

16. 0 $^{-}4$ $^{-}3$ $^{-}7$ $^{+}7$

17. $^{+}15$ 0 $^{-}21$ $^{-}18$

18. $^{+}16$ $^{+}13$ $^{-}5$ $^{-}6$

19. $^{+}10$ $^{-}10$ $^{-}20$ $^{+}30$

20. $^{-}30$ $^{-}1$ $^{+}40$ $^{-}8$ $^{+}12$

21. $^{-}9$ 0 $^{+}11$ $^{+}23$

22. $^{+}5$ $^{-}4$ $^{+}1$ $^{-}5$ $^{-}2$

23. $^{-}11$ $^{+}6$ $^{-}9$ $^{-}10$

Algebra • Expressions Translate each of the following into an expression. Then use a number line to graph the integer described.

24. Point *A*: the integer 3 more than $^{-}9$

25. Point *B*: the integer 4 less than $^{-}5$

26. Point *C*: the integer 6 more than $^{-}6$

27. Point *D*: the integer 7 less than $^{+}3$

Problem Solving • Reasoning

Use the table for Problems 28–29.

July Temperatures	
Alaska	$^{+}15$°C
Antarctica	$^{-}70$°C
Argentina	$^{-}3$°C
Australia	$^{+}5$°C
Kenya	$^{+}35$°C
New Zealand	$^{-}1$°C

28. **Compare** The table shows the July temperature in different places around the world. In July, is it warmer in Argentina or New Zealand?

29. Order the places from lowest to highest temperature. Which place is the coldest? Which is the warmest?

30. **Logical Thinking** On a number line, integer *A* is to the left of integer *B* and to the right of integer *C*. Integer *D* is to the right of integer *B*. Order the integers from greatest to least.

31. **Write About It** Describe in your own words how you would use a number line to compare and order the integers $^{-}5$, $^{+}3$, and $^{-}14$. Explain each step. Use drawings if you need.

Mixed Review • Test Prep

Divide. *(pages 34–35)*

32. 6.4 ÷ 0.16 **33.** 48.6 ÷ 2.43 **34.** 0.045 ÷ 0.9 **35.** 1.25 ÷ 0.025

36 Which is the prime factorization of 48? *(pages 108–109)*

A $2^3 \times 6$ **B** $2^4 \times 3$ **C** $2^2 \times 3 \times 4$ **D** 4×12

Extra Practice See Set B on page 238.

Problem-Solving Strategy: Draw a Diagram

You will learn how to solve a problem by drawing a diagram.

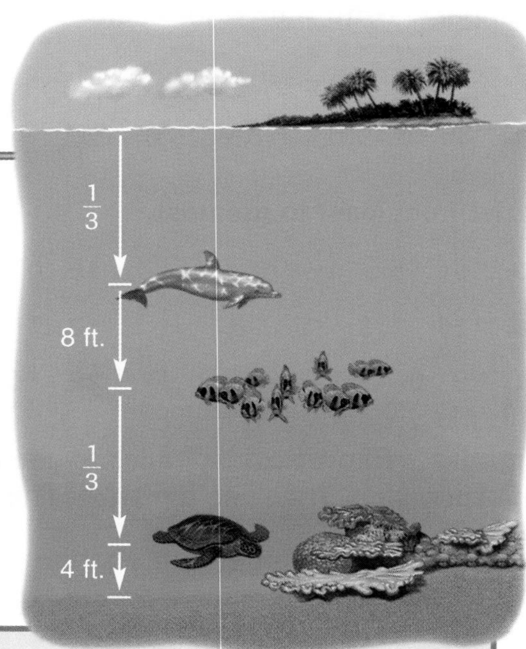

Sometimes drawing a diagram can help you solve a problem.

Problem While scuba diving, Emily dives to view a coral reef. From the surface, she dives $\frac{1}{3}$ of the distance to the reef before seeing a dolphin. She continues down another 8 feet and pauses to watch a school of fish. She dives another $\frac{1}{3}$ of the distance where she sees a turtle and then 4 more feet to get to the reef. How far below the surface is the reef?

Understand

What is the question?

How far below the surface of the water is the coral reef?

What do you know?

Emily dove $\frac{1}{3}$ of the distance to the reef. Then she dove another 8 feet. Then, she dove another $\frac{1}{3}$ of the distance to the reef and finally another 4 feet to reach the reef.

Plan

How can you find the answer?

You can draw a diagram to organize the information.

Solve

Let a number strip represent the number of feet to the coral reef. Mark it in thirds. Enter the given information.

First part of dive	Third part of dive	Second part (8 ft) Last part (4 ft)

0 — $\frac{1}{3}$ — $\frac{2}{3}$ — 1

Since each third of the distance is 12 ft (8 ft + 4 ft), the coral reef is 36 feet below the surface.

Remember: Write information on the number strip about thirds first.

Look Back

Look back at the problem.

How far from the surface was Emily after each dive?

Scuba divers look at coral.

Remember:
- ▶ Understand
- ▶ Plan
- ▶ Solve
- ▶ Look Back

Guided Practice

Solve each problem, using the Draw a Diagram strategy.

1. Lyle dove 12 feet below the surface, which was $\frac{1}{4}$ the distance of his deepest dive. How far below the surface was his deepest dive?

   Think: Into how many equal parts should the diagram be divided?

2. A submarine dives 15 meters below sea level. Then it dives 20 meters deeper. What integer expresses the position of the submarine compared to sea level?

   Think: What integer should be used to represent sea level?

Choose a Strategy

Solve. Use these or other strategies.

Problem-Solving Strategies

- **Work Backward**
- **Make a List**
- **Use Logical Thinking**
- **Draw a Diagram**

3. Ty began scuba diving 7 years ago when he was 16 years old. Pat began 13 years ago. When she began, Pat was 4 years younger than Ty was when he began. How much older than Ty is Pat?

4. The temperature on Sunday was 87°F. On Saturday the temperature was 4° higher. On Friday the temperature was 7° lower than on Saturday. Use integers to express each temperature.

5. Dan is on a 3-day hike. The first day, he hikes $\frac{1}{3}$ of the trail. The next day, he hikes $\frac{1}{3}$ of the trail plus $1\frac{1}{2}$ miles. The last day, he hikes $3\frac{1}{2}$ miles to the end of the trail. How long is the trail?

6. Jana pays $15 toward a boat rental. Marc pays $\frac{1}{4}$ of the rental fee. Barry pays $3 more than Jana pays, and Kendra pays $5 more than Marc. How much is the boat rental?

7. The high temperature for a day was $^{+}3$°C. What was the low temperature that day if the range of temperatures for that day was 7°C?

8. Kara borrows $57 from her mother to buy a wet suit. If Kara decreases her debt by $4 each week, how many weeks will it take to pay her mother back?

Extra Practice See 1–3 on page 241.

Quick Check

Check Your Understanding of Lessons 1–3

If the number is an integer, write its opposite. If it is not, write *no*.

1. 19 **2.** $^-4.5$ **3.** $+\frac{1}{5}$

Compare. Write > or < for each ●.

4. $^+28$ ● $^+21$ **5.** $^-6$ ● $^+1$ **6.** $^-13$ ● $^-19$

Order from greatest to least.

7. $^+6$ $^-2$ $^-1$ $^+3$ **8.** $^-10$ $^+12$ $^+9$ $^-5$ **9.** $^+54$ $^-49$ $^-60$ $^-55$

Solve.

10. A hiking trail ends at a greater elevation than it begins. An increase of 42 feet represents $\frac{3}{8}$ of the total elevation change. What integer represents the change in elevation from the beginning of the trail to its end?

11. Suppose a temperature of $^+4$°F decreases by 5°F for each of two consecutive hours. What is the temperature after two hours?

How did you do?

If you had difficulty with any items in the Quick Check, you can use the following pages for review and extra practice.

Items	Review These Pages	Do These Extra Practice Items
1–3	pages 206–207	Set A, page 238
4–9	pages 208–209	Set B, page 238
10–11	pages 210–211	1–3, page 241

Test Prep • Cumulative Review

Maintaining the Standards

Choose the letter of the correct answer.

1 The values in which pattern are decreasing?

A $\frac{1}{2}, \frac{2}{3}, \frac{3}{4}, \frac{4}{5}$

B $\frac{1}{2}, \frac{2}{4}, \frac{3}{6}, \frac{4}{8}$

C $\frac{1}{6}, \frac{1}{7}, \frac{1}{8}, \frac{1}{9}$

D $\frac{1}{4}, \frac{1}{3}, \frac{1}{2}, 1$

2 What is the greatest place value of the data in the following stem-and-leaf plot?

Stem-and-Leaf Plot

Stem	Leaf
24	1 3 6
25	
26	5 4
27	2 2
28	3 6 8

F tenths
G ones
H tens
J hundreds

3 Suppose water is to be poured from a 250 mL container into a 5 L container. What is the least number of times the smaller container would need to be filled and emptied in order to fill the larger container?

A 2 times
B 5 times
C 20 times
D 50 times

4 The school cafeteria sells 4 kinds of sandwiches and 5 kinds of drinks. How many different choices of lunches are possible if every lunch consists of a sandwich and a drink?

F 45 choices
G 20 choices
H 18 choices
J 9 choices

5 For a school project, Lucy made a box-and-whisker plot to record the number of points scored in her school's basketball games. What value represents the upper quartile?

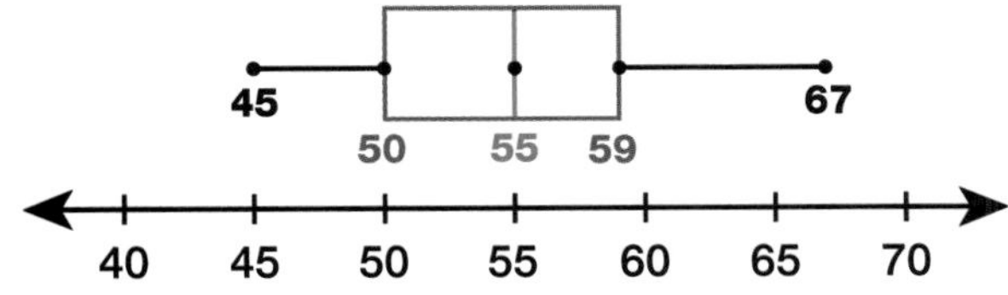

A 55 points
B 59 points
C 62 points
D 67 points

6 Maurice's family drove 420.4 miles to visit their state's capital at an average speed of 64.3 miles per hour. To the nearest whole hour, how many hours did they drive?

Explain Show how you found your answer.

Safe Site

Internet Test Prep
Visit **www.eduplace.com/kids/mhm** for more *Test Prep Practice.*

LESSON 4

Add Integers

You will learn how to add integers.

Learn About It

Two dolphins jump 10 feet above the water, then turn and dive 30 feet below that height. How many feet below the surface did their dives take them?

Add. $^{+}10 + ^{-}30 = n$

Different Ways to Add Integers

You can use a number line.

Step 1 Begin at 0. Move right 10 units to show $^{+}10$.

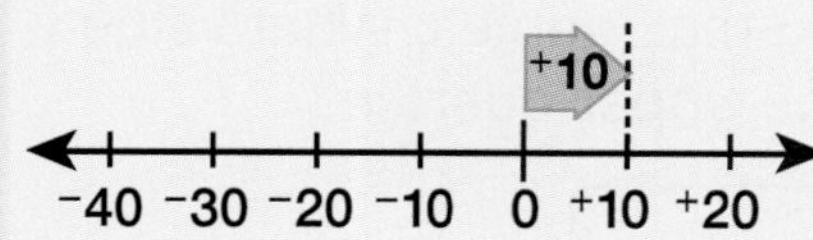

Step 2 Then, starting at $^{+}10$, move left 30 units to show $^{-}30$.

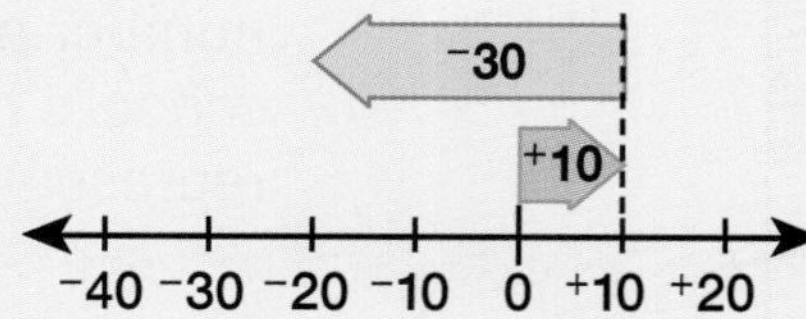

Step 3 The point at which you stop is the sum.

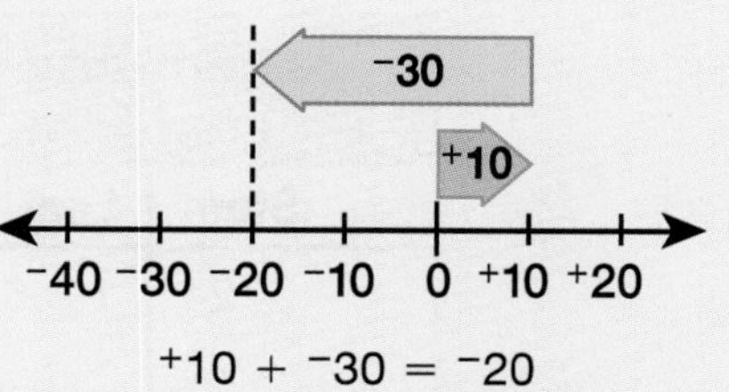

$^{+}10 + ^{-}30 = ^{-}20$

If the integers have different signs, you can subtract absolute values and use a rule to decide on the sign.

Step 1 Subtract the lesser absolute value from the greater.

$^{+}10 + ^{-}30 = n$

The absolute value of $^{+}10$ is 10.
The absolute value of $^{-}30$ is 30.

$30 - 10 = 20$

Step 2 Use the rule to decide if the answer will be positive or negative.

Since $^{-}30$ has a greater absolute value than $^{+}10$, the answer will be negative.

$^{+}10 + ^{-}30 = ^{-}20$

Rule: The sum of a positive integer and a negative integer will have the same sign as the integer with the greater absolute value.

Solution: The dolphins are 20 feet below the surface. Their location is $^{-}20$ feet.

Explain Your Thinking

- ► How can you use absolute value to find the sum of two integers that have the same sign?
- ► When is the sum of a positive and a negative integer positive? When is the sum negative?

Guided Practice

Add. Use a number line to help.

1. $^{-}8 + ^{+}7$ **2.** $^{-}11 + ^{-}3$ **3.** $^{-}9 + ^{+}9$

4. $^{+}5 + ^{+}8$ **5.** $^{+}9 + ^{-}4$ **6.** $^{+}6 + ^{-}7$

> **Ask Yourself**
> - In which direction do I count on the number line?
> - Did I use the correct sign for the sum?

Write the missing addend.

7. $^{+}9 + ■ = ^{-}4$ **8.** $^{-}5 + ■ = ^{-}11$ **9.** $^{-}2 + ■ = ^{+}6$

10. $■ + ^{-}3 = ^{+}7$ **11.** $■ + ^{+}6 = 0$ **12.** $■ + ^{-}5 = ^{-}9$

Independent Practice

Add. Use a number line to help.

13. $^{-}7 + ^{+}6$ **14.** $^{-}1 + ^{-}2$ **15.** $^{+}8 + ^{-}10$ **16.** $^{+}8 + ^{-}5$

17. $^{-}3 + ^{-}2$ **18.** $^{+}7 + ^{-}4$ **19.** $^{-}7 + ^{+}11$ **20.** $^{+}2 + ^{+}6$

21. $^{-}5 + ^{+}9$ **22.** $^{-}16 + 0$ **23.** $^{+}4 + ^{-}3$ **24.** $^{-}13 + ^{-}1$

Add.

25. $^{+}10 + ^{-}11$ **26.** $^{+}11 + ^{+}10$ **27.** $^{-}17 + ^{+}4$ **28.** $^{-}21 + ^{+}22$

29. $^{+}19 + ^{-}1$ **30.** $^{+}17 + ^{-}17$ **31.** $^{-}11 + 0$ **32.** $^{-}3 + ^{-}5$

33. $^{-}1 + ^{-}4$ **34.** $^{-}14 + ^{+}29$ **35.** $^{+}16 + ^{-}9$ **36.** $^{+}7 + ^{-}10$

Write the missing addend.

37. $^{-}10 + ■ = ^{+}2$ **38.** $^{+}7 + ■ = ^{-}11$ **39.** $^{-}2 + ■ = ^{-}2$ **40.** $^{-}8 + ■ = ^{-}10$

41. $^{+}13 + ■ = ^{+}6$ **42.** $^{-}1 + ■ = ^{+}8$ **43.** $^{+}5 + ■ = ^{-}5$ **44.** $0 + ■ = ^{-}3$

45. $^{-}6 + ■ = ^{+}21$ **46.** $^{+}10 + ■ = ^{+}14$ **47.** $^{-}3 + ■ = ^{+}4$ **48.** $^{-}5 + ■ = ^{-}18$

Algebra • Functions **Complete each table by following the rule. If the rule is not given, write a rule.**

49. Rule: Add $^{+}8$

Input	Output
−6	■
+9	■
−13	■
−8	■

50. Rule: Add $^{-}7$

Input	Output
+15	■
−6	■
+3	■
−7	■

51. Rule: ______________

Input	Output
+10	+6
+2	−2
−1	−5
−7	−11

Problem Solving • Reasoning

Solve. Choose a method.

Computation Methods

• Mental Math • Estimation • Paper and Pencil • Calculator

52. Analyze Lynn measures Tuffy the dolphin's performance on a point system. Tuffy gains 5 points for diving through a ring, loses 2 points for missing her cue, then gains 4 points for a jump. How many points did Tuffy earn during this routine?

53. Tuffy's first dive takes her 21 feet below the surface of the water. Her next three dives take her 17 feet, 9 feet, and 12 feet below the surface. Her last dive takes her 31 feet below the surface. Use an integer to describe the mean depth of Tuffy's dives.

54. A cave is 485 feet deep. The entrance to the cave is 1,833 feet above sea level. Is the bottom of the cave above or below sea level? How far above or below sea level is the bottom?

55. Explain In 1999 a company's sales were \$82 million. In 2000 its sales changed by $^{-}$\$24 million. In 2001 the sales changed by $^{+}$\$2 million. What were the company's sales in 2001? Explain.

Mixed Review • Test Prep

Multiply. Express each answer in simplest form. *(pages 168–171)*

56. $\frac{1}{3} \times \frac{3}{4}$ **57.** $6 \times \frac{1}{8}$ **58.** $\frac{1}{5} \times 5\frac{2}{15}$ **59.** $\frac{5}{6} \times 3\frac{2}{3}$

Choose the letter of the correct answer. *(pages 124–125)*

60 Which fraction is in simplest form?

A $\frac{4}{6}$ **B** $\frac{3}{15}$ **C** $\frac{5}{7}$ **D** $\frac{2}{8}$

61 What is the simplest form of $\frac{4}{16}$?

F $\frac{2}{8}$ **G** $\frac{1}{16}$ **H** $\frac{4}{16}$ **J** $\frac{1}{4}$

Visual Thinking

Hidden Face

The faces of a cube are numbered $^{-}1$, $^{-}2$, $^{-}3$, $^{-}4$, $^{-}5$, and $^{-}6$. Three views of the cube are shown.

In View *C*, what integer is on the top of the cube?

View A

View B

View C

Extra Practice See Set C on page 238.

Number Sense

Adding Integers

Counters can help you understand how to add integers. Use yellow counters to represent positive integers. Use red counters to represent negative integers.

Use counters to find the sum of $^{+}4$ and $^{-}6$.

Find $^{+}4 + {}^{-}6$.

You need 4 yellow counters to represent $^{+}4$.

You need 6 red counters to represent $^{-}6$.

Pair a yellow counter with a red counter until you have only one color left. Each yellow-red pair represents $^{-}1 + {}^{+}1$, or 0.

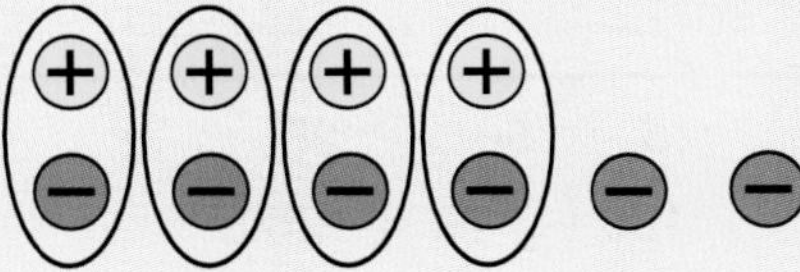

The number of unpaired counters is the sum.

- If the counters are yellow, the sum is positive.
- If the counters are red, the sum is negative.

Two red counters are left.

Solution: $^{+}4 + {}^{-}6 = {}^{-}2$

Explain Your Thinking

► How is using counters to add like using a number line to add?

LESSON 5

Subtract Integers

You will learn how to subtract integers.

Review Vocabulary
integers

Learn About It

Just as you can use a number line or a rule to add **integers**, you can use a number line or a rule to subtract integers.

Subtract. **⁻100 − ⁻75 = ■**

Different Ways to Subtract Integers

You can use a number line.

Step 1 Begin at 0. Move left 100 units to show ⁻100.

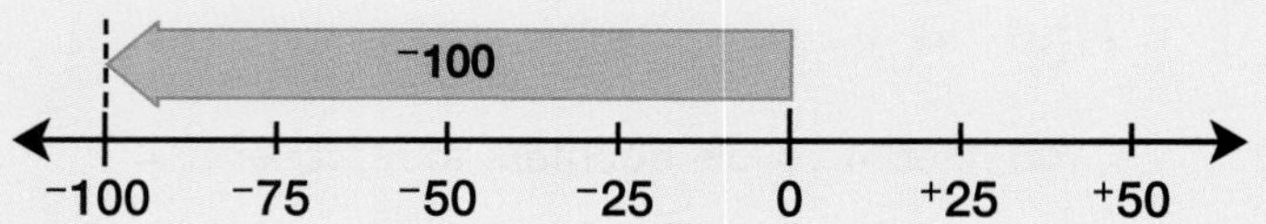

Step 2 To add ⁻75, you would move left 75 units. So to subtract ⁻75, move right 75 units.

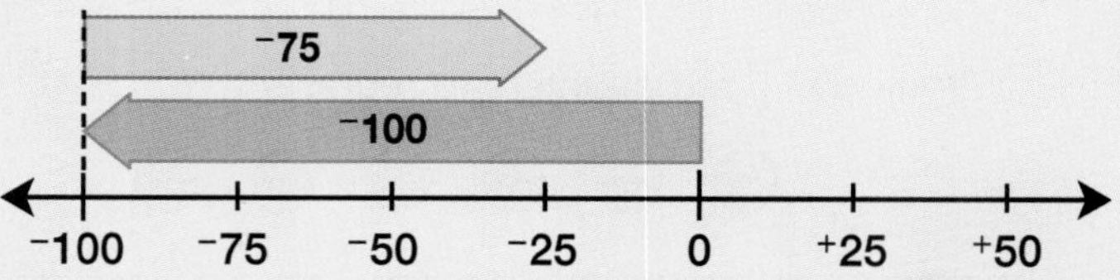

Step 3 The point at which you stop is the difference.

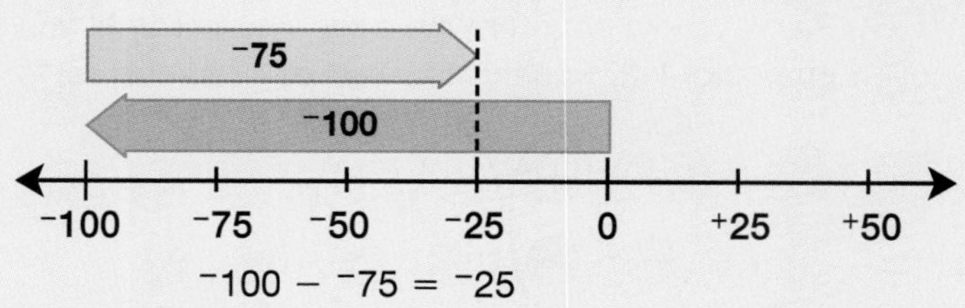

⁻100 − ⁻75 = ⁻25

You can use a rule.

Rule: Subtracting an integer is the same as adding its opposite.

⁻100 − ⁻75
⁻100 + ⁺75 = ⁻25

Solution: ⁻100 − ⁻75 = ⁻25.

Other Examples

A. Negative Difference

Find ⁻9 − ⁺5.

⁻9 − ⁺5 = ⁻9 + ⁻5
= ⁻14

B. Positive Difference

Find ⁺8 − ⁻7.

⁺8 − ⁻7 = ⁺8 + ⁺7
= ⁺15

C. Difference of Two Positive Integers

Find ⁺6 − ⁺10.

⁺6 − ⁺10 = ⁺6 + ⁻10
= ⁻4

Explain Your Thinking

► How are adding and subtracting integers related?

Guided Practice

Complete each statement.

1. Subtracting $^{+}6$ is the same as adding ■.
2. Subtracting $^{-}2$ is the same as adding ■.

> **Ask Yourself**
> - Did I change the sign of the second integer and add?

Subtract.

3. $^{-}10 - {}^{+}7$
4. $^{+}8 - {}^{-}3$
5. $^{-}3 - {}^{-}2$
6. $^{+}5 - {}^{+}10$
7. $^{-}4 - 0$
8. $0 - {}^{+}7$
9. $^{-}7 - {}^{-}2$
10. $^{-}4 - {}^{+}8$

Independent Practice

Complete each statement.

11. Subtracting $^{-}1$ is the same as adding ■.
12. Subtracting $^{-}3$ is the same as adding ■.
13. Subtracting 0 is the same as adding ■.
14. Subtracting $^{+}3$ is the same as adding ■.

Complete each related equation.

15. $^{+}9 - {}^{+}2 =$ ■
    $^{+}9 + {}^{-}2 =$ ■
16. $^{-}9 - {}^{+}10 =$ ■
    $^{-}9 + {}^{-}10 =$ ■
17. $^{-}5 - {}^{-}4 =$ ■
    $^{-}5 + {}^{+}4 =$ ■
18. $^{+}6 - {}^{-}1 =$ ■
    $^{+}6 + {}^{+}1 =$ ■
19. $^{-}7 - {}^{-}12 =$ ■
    $^{-}7 + {}^{+}12 =$ ■
20. $^{+}3 - {}^{+}5 =$ ■
    $^{+}3 + {}^{-}5 =$ ■
21. $^{-}15 - {}^{+}20 =$ ■
    $^{-}15 + {}^{-}20 =$ ■
22. $^{+}18 - {}^{+}9 =$ ■
    $^{+}18 + {}^{-}9 =$ ■
23. $^{-}25 - {}^{-}11 =$ ■
    $^{-}25 + {}^{+}11 =$ ■
24. $^{-}21 - {}^{-}8 =$ ■
    $^{-}21 + {}^{+}8 =$ ■

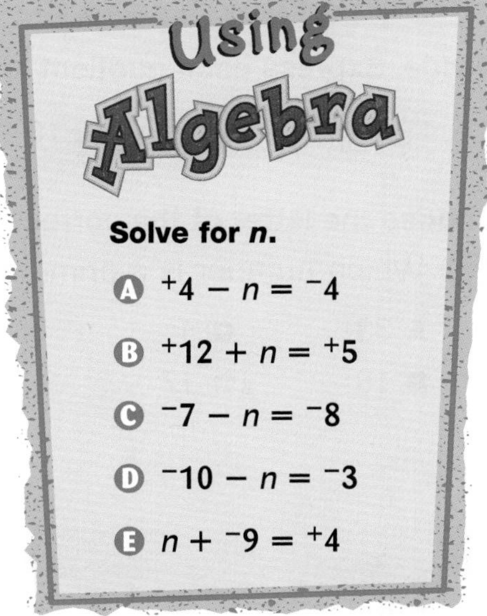

Subtract.

25. $^{+}11 - {}^{-}4$
26. $^{+}3 - {}^{+}10$
27. $0 - {}^{+}2$
28. $0 - {}^{-}13$
29. $^{-}4 - {}^{+}8$
30. $^{-}5 - {}^{-}5$
31. $^{+}4 - {}^{+}1$
32. $^{-}4 - {}^{+}1$
33. $^{-}11 - {}^{+}14$
34. $^{-}17 - {}^{-}9$
35. $^{-}9 - {}^{+}5$
36. $^{-}7 - {}^{-}8$
37. $^{+}3 - {}^{-}3$
38. $^{+}7 - {}^{+}6$
39. $^{-}5 - {}^{+}10$
40. $^{-}2 - 0$

Problem Solving • Reasoning

41. Danielle travels from Frankfurt north to Hamburg. Colin travels from Frankfurt south to the Black Forest. Their trains leave at the same time and travel at the same speed. After one hour, the distance between them is 300 km. Where is Danielle? Where is Colin?

42. **Analyze** Kayla and Travis started at the same place on an east-west road. Kayla began traveling east. After one hour, the midpoint between Kayla's and Travis's positions was west of the starting point. In which direction did Travis travel? Who traveled faster?

43. In a game, a player's scores on five successive turns were $^{+}8$, $^{-}11$, $^{+}7$, $^{-}7$, $^{+}6$. After which two turns was the player's total score the same? How many points were scored altogether during those five turns?

44. Suppose the temperature of liquid nitrogen inside a container was $^{-}197$°C before it decreased 3°C during each of three consecutive hours. What was the temperature of the liquid nitrogen at the end of the three hours?

45. **Logical Thinking** Two integers have a sum of $^{-}2$. The difference of the greater integer subtracted from the lesser integer is $^{-}2$. The sum of the absolute values of the integers is 2. What are the integers?

46. **Write Your Own** Choose a positive integer greater than 100. Choose an integer less than $^{-}10$. Write a situation that can be represented by the positive integer subtracted from the negative integer.

Mixed Review • Test Prep

Divide. Express each quotient in simplest form. *(pages 176–179)*

47. $4\frac{1}{8} \div \frac{3}{6}$ **48.** $10 \div 3\frac{1}{2}$ **49.** $\frac{3}{4} \div 1\frac{1}{5}$ **50.** $3\frac{1}{4} \div 1\frac{1}{3}$

Choose the letter of the correct answer. *(pages 104–105)*

51 Which number is a prime number?

A 33 **C** 4
B 18 **D** 17

52 Which numbers are factors of 18?

F 1 and 18 **H** 9 and 2
G 6 and 3 **J** all of the above

Write *true* or *false*.
Give examples to support your answer.

53. All integers have an opposite.

54. The sum of a positive integer and a negative integer is always a negative integer.

55. Zero is a positive integer.

Extra Practice See Set D on page 239.

Practice Game

Zero In on Zero

Practice adding and subtracting integers by playing this game with a partner. Try to get as close to zero as you can!

What You'll Need

- *a spinner with 10 sections labeled 0–9 (Teaching Tool 5)*
- *paper and a pencil for each player*

Players
2

Here's What to Do

1. Each player starts with 5 points.
2. The first player spins. If the spinner lands on a line, spin again.
3. He or she chooses to add or subtract the number on the spinner from his or her point total.

Players take turns until each player has had five turns. The player whose point total after five turns is closest to zero wins.

Share Your Thinking Is subtraction the best strategy when a player has a negative point total? Explain why or why not.

LESSON 6

Multiply Integers

You will learn how to multiply integers.

Learn About It

Anne and her family rent a paddleboat for three days during their vacation. If they return the boat by 4:00 P.M., there is a $2.00 credit. If they return the boat after 4:00 P.M., there is a $2.00 penalty. Think about what might happen when they return the boat.

Before 4:00 p.m.		After 4:00 p.m.	
Receiving 3 $2.00 credits is the same as receiving $6.00. $^{+}3 \times {}^{+}2 = {}^{+}6$	If they lose their 3 $2.00 credits, it is the same as losing $6.00. $^{-}3 \times {}^{+}2 = {}^{-}6$	Receiving 3 $2.00 penalties is the same as being charged $6.00. $^{+}3 \times {}^{-}2 = {}^{-}6$	If the clerk loses 3 $2.00 penalties, it is the same as receiving $6.00. $^{-}3 \times {}^{-}2 = {}^{+}6$

Different Ways to Multiply Integers

You can use repeated addition.

Find $^{+}3 \times {}^{+}2$.
$^{+}3 \times {}^{+}2 = {}^{+}2 + {}^{+}2 + {}^{+}2 = {}^{+}6$

Find $^{+}3 \times {}^{-}2$.
$^{+}3 \times {}^{-}2 = {}^{-}2 + {}^{-}2 + {}^{-}2 = {}^{-}6$

You can use rules.

Find $^{-}3 \times {}^{+}2$.

- First find the product of the absolute values of the integers. $3 \times 2 = 6$
- Then use rules to decide if the product will be positive or negative. $^{-}3 \times {}^{+}2 = {}^{-}6$

Rules:

- The product of two integers with different signs is always negative.
- The product of two integers with the same sign is always positive.
- If one factor is zero, the product is zero.

Explain Your Thinking

► How could you use a number line to multiply integers?

Guided Practice

Write each expression as a multiplication problem. Then simplify.

1. $^{+}8 + {}^{+}8 + {}^{+}8 + {}^{+}8$

2. $^{-}2 + {}^{-}2 + {}^{-}2 + {}^{-}2 + {}^{-}2$

Find each product.

3. $^{+}7 \times {}^{-}4$

4. $^{+}3 \times {}^{+}12$

5. $^{-}2 \times {}^{-}6$

Ask Yourself

- What is the product of the absolute values?
- What sign should I use?

Independent Practice

Write each expression as a multiplication problem. Then simplify.

6. $^{-}7 + {}^{-}7 + {}^{-}7$

7. $^{+}8 + {}^{+}8 + {}^{+}8 + {}^{+}8 + {}^{+}8$

8. $^{+}3 + {}^{+}3 + {}^{+}3 + {}^{+}3 + {}^{+}3$

9. $^{-}5 + {}^{-}5 + {}^{-}5 + {}^{-}5$

Find each product.

10. $^{-}4 \times {}^{-}7$

11. $^{-}8 \times {}^{+}9$

12. $^{+}5 \times {}^{+}6$

13. $^{-}6 \times {}^{-}6$

14. $^{+}7 \times {}^{-}8$

15. $^{-}1 \times {}^{+}4$

16. $^{+}11 \times {}^{-}4$

17. $^{+}9 \times 0$

18. $^{-}9 \times {}^{+}9$

19. $^{-}13 \times {}^{-}3$

20. $^{+}9 \times {}^{-}7$

21. $^{-}6 \times {}^{+}8$

22. $^{+}10 \times {}^{-}10$

23. $0 \times {}^{-}43$

24. $^{-}5 \times {}^{-}19$

25. $^{-}4 \times {}^{+}12$

Problem Solving • Reasoning

26. **Compare** If Max returns a video he rented within 24 hours, he is given a $1 credit toward his next rental. If he returns a movie after it is due, he is charged a $3 penalty. In one month, Max returns two videos late and three within 24 hours. How much of a credit or a penalty does he have at the video store?

27. **Analyze** Julia and Ana are playing a board game. Each time one girl's playing piece lands on a square owned by the other, she must pay the owner a $13 penalty. Ana begins the game with $225. How much money does she have after landing on 4 squares owned by Julia?

28. **Logical Thinking** The product of two integers is $^{-}48$. The difference when the lesser integer is subtracted from the greater integer is $^{+}16$. What are the integers?

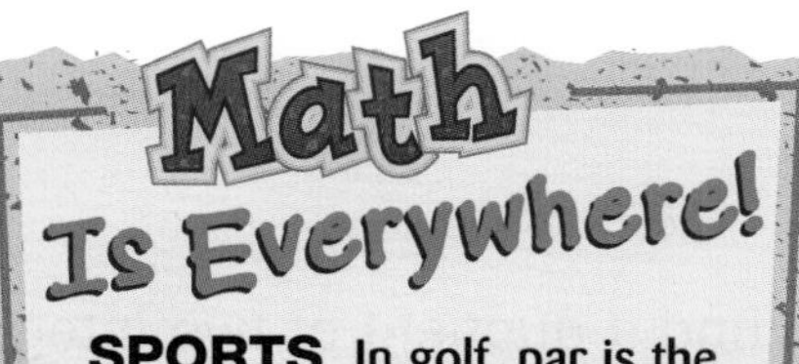

SPORTS In golf, par is the number of strokes considered necessary to hit the ball into each hole. Suppose players could say that they hit $^{-}1$ on a hole, meaning they had used 1 stroke less than par for that hole.

- What would $^{+}1$ mean?
- What would 0 mean?

Mixed Review • Test Prep

Find each sum or difference. *(pages 12–13)*

29. 94.75 + 6.02

30. 446.7 − 51.02

31. 16 − 7.35

Choose the letter of the correct answer. *(pages 122–123)*

32 What is an equivalent fraction for $\frac{2}{6}$?

A $\frac{8}{24}$

B $\frac{1}{4}$

C $\frac{8}{36}$

D $\frac{2}{12}$

33 Which fractions are equivalent?

F $\frac{2}{10}, \frac{5}{20}$

G $\frac{1}{3}, \frac{3}{15}$

H $\frac{2}{9}, \frac{1}{18}$

J $\frac{2}{3}, \frac{10}{15}$

Extra Practice See Set E on page 239.

LESSON 7

Divide Integers

You will learn how to divide integers.

Learn About It

Just as rules can help you add, subtract, and multiply integers, rules can also help you divide integers.

Rules for Dividing Integers

Integers With the Same Sign

The quotient of two integers with the same sign is always positive.

$^{+}45 \div {}^{+}9 = {}^{+}5$

$^{-}45 \div {}^{-}9 = {}^{+}5$

Integers With Different Signs

The quotient of two integers with different signs is always negative.

$^{+}45 \div {}^{-}9 = {}^{-}5$

$^{-}45 \div {}^{+}9 = {}^{-}5$

To find a quotient of two integers, use absolute values and the rules.

Divide. $\mathbf{^{-}32 \div {}^{-}4 = \blacksquare}$

Find $^{-}32 \div {}^{-}4$.

Step 1 Find the quotient of the absolute values of the integers.

$32 \div 4 = 8$

Step 2 Use the rules.

The two integers have the same sign, so the quotient is positive.

Step 3 Write the quotient with the correct sign.

$^{-}32 \div {}^{-}4 = {}^{+}8$

Check your work. Multiply.

$^{+}8 \times {}^{-}4 = {}^{-}32$

Solution: $^{-}32 \div {}^{-}4 = {}^{+}8$

Another Example

Integers with Different Signs

$^{-}18 \div {}^{+}3 = \blacksquare$

$^{-}18 \div {}^{+}3 = {}^{-}6$

Think: The absolute value of $^{-}18$ is 18 and of $^{+}3$ is 3. The signs are different.

Explain Your Thinking

- How can you tell if a quotient of two integers will be negative? positive?
- How do the rules for the sign of the product of two integers explain the rules for the sign of the quotient of two integers?

Guided Practice

Find each quotient. Check your work.

1. $^{+}9 \div {}^{+}3$
2. $^{-}9 \div {}^{-}3$
3. $^{+}14 \div {}^{+}7$
4. $^{-}4 \div {}^{+}2$
5. $^{-}28 \div {}^{-}4$
6. $^{+}36 \div {}^{-}3$
7. $^{+}48 \div {}^{-}8$
8. $^{-}15 \div {}^{+}3$

Ask Yourself

- Are the signs the same or different?
- Which sign do I use for the quotient?

Independent Practice

Find each quotient. Check your work.

9. $^{+}21 \div {}^{+}3$
10. $^{+}20 \div {}^{-}2$
11. $^{-}16 \div {}^{+}4$
12. $^{-}15 \div {}^{-}3$
13. $^{-}30 \div {}^{-}10$
14. $^{+}28 \div {}^{-}7$
15. $^{+}25 \div {}^{-}5$
16. $^{+}36 \div {}^{+}6$
17. $^{-}100 \div {}^{-}20$
18. $^{-}49 \div {}^{+}7$
19. $^{-}14 \div {}^{-}2$
20. $^{-}60 \div {}^{-}15$
21. $^{+}64 \div {}^{-}32$
22. $^{-}36 \div {}^{-}9$
23. $^{+}72 \div {}^{-}8$
24. $^{-}54 \div {}^{+}6$

Problem Solving • Reasoning

25. A pilot has 1,700 feet of altitude to perform loops. With every loop, her altitude decreases by 400 feet. How many loops can she safely perform?

26. A plane, approaching a runway for landing, loses 10,000 feet of altitude in 20 minutes. At that rate, how many feet does the plane lose in one minute?

27. **Compare** Which has the greatest quotient?
$^{-}14 \div 7$ $\quad$ $14 \div {}^{-}7$ $\quad$ $^{-}14 \div {}^{-}7$

28. Rose watches her younger brother as he plays a game. For each two steps forward he walks, he walks backward three steps. If he takes a total of 27 steps, how many steps forward did he take? How many steps behind his starting point will he be?

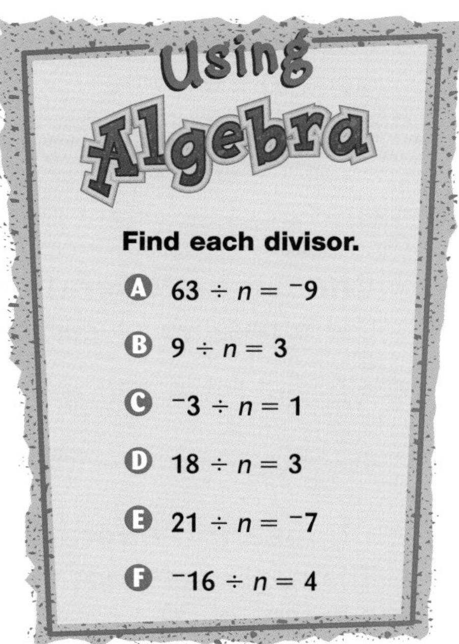

Find each divisor.

A. $63 \div n = {}^{-}9$

B. $9 \div n = 3$

C. $^{-}3 \div n = 1$

D. $18 \div n = 3$

E. $21 \div n = {}^{-}7$

F. $^{-}16 \div n = 4$

Mixed Review • Test Prep

Find each sum. Express each answer in simplest form. *(pages 158–160)*

29. $2\frac{3}{5} + \frac{2}{3}$
30. $\frac{1}{3} + \frac{2}{7}$
31. $9 + 2\frac{3}{8}$
32. $6\frac{1}{4} + 1\frac{2}{5}$

Choose the letter of the correct answer. *(pages 110–111, 116–117)*

33. What is the least common multiple of 18 and 24?

A 24 **C** 72
B 36 **D** 432

34. Which number is divisible by 1, 2, 3, 4, and 6?

F 105 **H** 45
G 94 **J** 132

Extra Practice See Set F on page 239.

Problem-Solving Skill: Choose the Operation

You will learn how to choose the operations necessary to solve problems involving integers.

Treasure Hunt
Start by the Big Oak Tree.
1 Walk 15 steps North.
2 Walk 30 steps South.
3 Walk South a third of the steps you just walked South.
Start digging!
X

When you solve a multistep problem, you need to decide which operations to use.

Look at the situation below.

Terry is helping Eric understand a note that describes the location of a buried treasure. What operations do they need to use to find the treasure?

Choose the operation for 1.

The position of the big oak tree is zero. Use a positive integer to represent steps to the north.

Addition: $0 + {}^{+}15 = {}^{+}15$

Choose the operation for 2.

Use a negative integer to represent steps to the south.

Addition: ${}^{+}15 + {}^{-}30 = {}^{-}15$

Choose the operations for 3.

The number of steps to the south is one third of 30.

Division: $30 \div 3 = 10$

Since these 10 steps are south, use ${}^{-}10$.

Addition: ${}^{-}15 + ({}^{-}10) = {}^{-}25$

The treasure is located at ${}^{-}25$, or 25 steps south of the big oak tree.

Look Back How do you decide what operation to choose?

In 1622 the Spanish galleon *Nuestra Señora de Atocha* sank off the coast of Florida. The coins and bowl are part of the Atocha's treasure found in the late 20th century.

Guided Practice

Solve.

1. Eric and Terry cannot find the treasure. Eric looks at the note again. He notices a smudge on the "3" in the directions in 2. Eric thinks that 2 reads, "Walk 90 steps south." Where is the treasure if Eric is correct?

Think: Which operations are necessary to solve this problem?

2. Mario dives 33 meters to the bottom of the ocean to investigate a shipwreck. The deck of the wrecked ship is 7 meters above the ocean floor. How far below the surface of the water is the deck of the wrecked ship?

Think: Would a diagram help me solve this problem?

Choose a Strategy

Solve. Use these or other strategies.

Problem-Solving Strategies

- **Make a List**
- **Draw a Diagram**
- **Find a Pattern**
- **Write an Equation**

3. Suppose a group of divers begin at the surface and dive 15 feet every 30 seconds. How many seconds does it take the divers to reach a depth of 150 feet?

4. To find a treasure, Yoko walks 50 steps to the east, 45 steps to the west, and then 20 steps to the east. Where is the treasure located compared to the place where Yoko started?

5. Help Peter and Elizabeth locate a hidden treasure by finding the likely missing number in the following pattern: $^{-}81$, $^{-}27$, $^{-}9$, ?, $^{-}1$. Explain your answer.

6. One-half the number of minutes in one day less three times the number of minutes in one hour is what number? Show your work.

7. Manuela finds a treasure note in the attic of her grandmother's house. The note reads "Find the sum of all the integers greater than $^{-}3$ and less than $^{+}4$. Then walk that number of steps to the west." How many steps west does Manuela need to walk?

8. For each math question Margo and Claudia answer correctly, they receive $^{+}1$ point. For each incorrect answer, they receive $^{-}1$ point. Margo has 27 points. Claudia answers 32 questions correctly and 4 incorrectly. Who has the most points?

Extra Practice See 4–7 on page 241.

Quick Check

Check Your Understanding of Lessons 4–8

Add.

1. $^{+}5 + {}^{-}9$ **2.** $^{-}4 + {}^{-}17$ **3.** $^{-}6 + {}^{+}12$

Subtract.

4. $^{-}11 - {}^{-}3$ **5.** $^{+}8 - {}^{-}9$ **6.** $^{-}4 - {}^{+}3$

Find each product.

7. $^{-}6 \times {}^{+}6$ **8.** $^{-}4 \times {}^{-}12$ **9.** $^{+}7 \times {}^{-}20$

Find each quotient.

10. $^{-}56 \div {}^{-}7$ **11.** $^{+}75 \div {}^{-}15$ **12.** $^{-}81 \div {}^{+}9$

Solve.

13. In a recent tournament, Trevor played 4 rounds of golf. The scores for his rounds were 2 under par ($^{-}2$), 1 over par ($^{+}1$), par (0), and 3 over par ($^{+}3$). For the tournament, was Trevor under par, over par, or at par? Explain.

How did you do?

If you had difficulty with any items in the Quick Check, you can use the following pages for review and extra practice.

Items	Review These Pages	Do These Extra Practice Items
1–3	pages 214–217	Set C, page 238
4–6	pages 218–220	Set D, page 239
7–9	pages 222–223	Set E, page 239
10–12	pages 224–225	Set F, page 239
13	pages 226–227	4–7, page 241

Test Prep • Cumulative Review

Maintaining the Standards

Choose the letter of the correct answer.

1 Use exponents to write the prime factorization of 900.

A $2 \times 3 \times 5$

B $2^2 \times 3^2 \times 5^2$

C $2^2 \times 3^3 \times 5^2$

D $5^2 \times 6$

2 If a cyclist drinks eight 8-ounce bottles of water during a trip, how many pints of water is the cyclist drinking?

F 2 pints

G 4 pints

H 6 pints

J 8 pints

3 A school collected donations for a new flagpole. The donations were \$5, \$3, \$2, \$1, \$5, \$5, \$4, \$2, \$1, \$5, \$3, \$3, \$1, and \$10. What was the range of the donations?

A \$9

B \$5

C \$3

D \$1

4 What is the simplest form of the fraction $\frac{66}{121}$?

F $\frac{6}{11}$

G $\frac{6}{121}$

H 0.54

J $\frac{66}{121}$

5 A team is selling T-shirts with 4 different designs and 4 sizes. How many different choices include one of each design and size?

A 4 choices

B 8 choices

C 12 choices

D 16 choices

6 What fraction is represented by the fraction strips?

F $\frac{7}{11}$

G $\frac{4}{8}$

H $\frac{7}{8}$

J $\frac{3}{8}$

7 Juan's mother is making hamburgers for a family gathering. She bought 3 pounds of hamburger meat. How many hamburgers will she make if she wants each hamburger to have about $\frac{1}{4}$ pound of meat?

Explain Show how you found your answer.

Safe Site

Internet Test Prep
Visit **www.eduplace.com/kids/mhm** for more *Test Prep Practice.*

LESSON 9

Rational Numbers

You will learn how to identify, compare, and order rational numbers.

New Vocabulary
rational number

Learn About It

A **rational number** is a number that can be expressed in the form $\frac{a}{b}$, where *a* and *b* are integers and *b* is not zero. Rational numbers include whole numbers such as 1 and 2 (since $1 = \frac{1}{1}$ and $2 = \frac{2}{1}$), integers such as 0 and $^-1$ (since $0 = \frac{0}{1}$ and $^-1 = \frac{^-1}{1}$), and fractions such as $\frac{1}{3}$ and $-\frac{7}{8}$.

Use the definition of rational numbers to show that each number is rational.

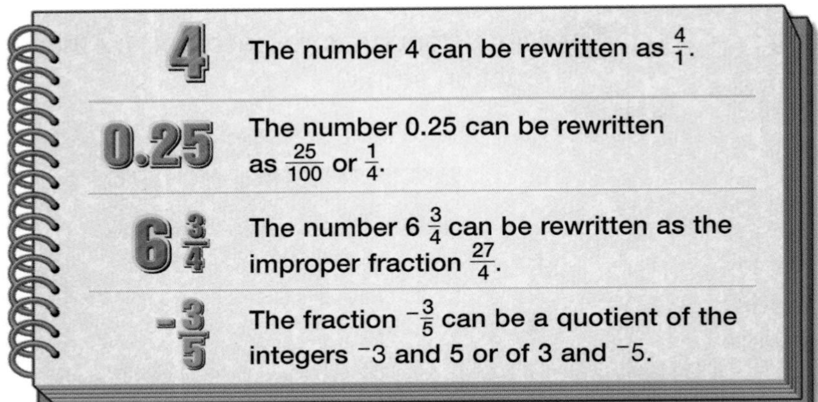

4	The number 4 can be rewritten as $\frac{4}{1}$.
0.25	The number 0.25 can be rewritten as $\frac{25}{100}$ or $\frac{1}{4}$.
$6\frac{3}{4}$	The number $6\frac{3}{4}$ can be rewritten as the improper fraction $\frac{27}{4}$.
$-\frac{3}{5}$	The fraction $-\frac{3}{5}$ can be a quotient of the integers $^-3$ and 5 or of 3 and $^-5$.

Use a number line to order rational numbers.

Locate each rational number.
Approximate a value when necessary.

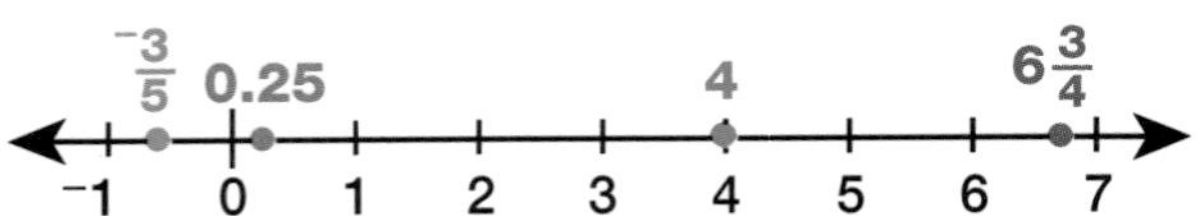

Explain Your Thinking

► When you write an integer or a whole number using the form $\frac{a}{b}$, what do you use as the denominator?

► How can you tell when one rational number is greater than, less than, or equal to another rational number?

Guided Practice

Rewrite each number in the form $\frac{a}{b}$ and locate it on a number line. Then write the numbers in order from greatest to least.

1. $-\frac{5}{5}$ $\frac{1}{4}$ 0.2

2. $^-3\frac{1}{2}$ 2.6 $^-4$

Ask Yourself

- Did I recognize the number farthest right as the greatest number and the number farthest left as the least number?

Independent Practice

Rewrite each number in the form $\frac{a}{b}$ and locate it on a number line. Then order the numbers in Exercises 3–10 from greatest to least.

3. 0.25 **4.** 5 **5.** $^{-}13$ **6.** $^{-}0.5$

7. $3\frac{1}{3}$ **8.** $\frac{3}{2}$ **9.** $^{-}2\frac{3}{4}$ **10.** $-\frac{19}{4}$

Compare. Write >, <, or = for each ⬤. If necessary, use a number line.

11. $\frac{1}{3}$ ⬤ 0.3 **12.** $^{-}1.8$ ⬤ $\frac{-8}{5}$ **13.** $\frac{-7}{4}$ ⬤ $^{-}1\frac{2}{3}$ **14.** $1\frac{2}{5}$ ⬤ 1.4

Order from least to greatest.

15. $\frac{27}{21}$ $1\frac{1}{3}$ 1.4 **16.** $\frac{13}{25}$ 0.6 $\frac{7}{8}$

17. $^{-}1\frac{7}{12}$ $^{-}1.85$ $-\frac{9}{5}$ **18.** $^{-}2.45$ $-\frac{32}{15}$ $-\frac{57}{19}$

Problem Solving • Reasoning

19. **Predict** Consider the numbers

$3\frac{1}{2}$, $1\frac{1}{2}$ $-\frac{1}{2}$, $^{-}2\frac{1}{2}$, ...

Find a pattern. If the pattern continues, what are the most likely next three numbers?

20. **Analyze** In order to win an attendance prize, at least $\frac{85}{100}$ of the 32 students in Mr. Ash's mathematics class must be present each day for a week. The attendance records for the week show 1, 3, 3, 2, and 5 students absent. Did the class win the prize? Explain.

21. **Write About It** Suppose your friend was absent the day your mathematics class learned about rational numbers. Write a few sentences explaining how your friend can identify a rational number.

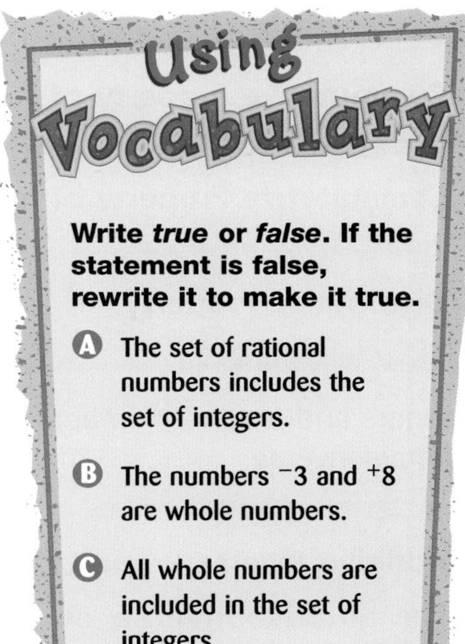

Write *true* or *false*. If the statement is false, rewrite it to make it true.

A The set of rational numbers includes the set of integers.

B The numbers $^{-}3$ and $^{+}8$ are whole numbers.

C All whole numbers are included in the set of integers.

Mixed Review • Test Prep

Write the reciprocal of each number. *(pages 172–173)*

22. $\frac{3}{25}$ **23.** $2\frac{1}{6}$ **24.** $\frac{1}{8}$ **25.** $3\frac{3}{5}$

Choose the letter of the correct answer. *(pages 4–7)*

26 What is the standard form for 6 and 23 thousandths?

A 23,006 **C** 6.023
B 6.23 **D** 6.0023

27 Which statement is true?

F $0.566 < 0.07$ **H** $0.34 < 0.022$
G $4.05 > 40.5$ **J** $8.09 > 8.01929$

Extra Practice See Set G on page 240.

LESSON 10

Rational Numbers and Their Properties

You will learn how to solve problems by using the properties of rational numbers.

New Vocabulary
additive inverse

Learn About It

The table below summarizes the properties of whole numbers and integers that you have learned earlier. These same properties are also true for all rational numbers.

Properties of Rational Numbers

Property	Example
Associative Property of Addition	$(\frac{1}{2} + \frac{3}{5}) + \frac{3}{4} = \frac{1}{2} + (\frac{3}{5} + \frac{3}{4})$
Associative Property of Multiplication	$(\frac{2}{3} \times \frac{4}{7}) \times \frac{1}{6} = \frac{2}{3} \times (\frac{4}{7} \times \frac{1}{6})$
Commutative Property of Addition	$\frac{3}{4} + \frac{5}{6} = \frac{5}{6} + \frac{3}{4}$
Commutative Property of Multiplication	$\frac{2}{5} \times \frac{1}{3} = \frac{1}{3} \times \frac{2}{5}$
Distributive Property	$4(\frac{1}{4} + \frac{2}{3}) = (4 \times \frac{1}{4}) + (4 \times \frac{2}{3})$

Integers and rational numbers share another property. Each has an additive inverse.

Additive Inverse Property

The **additive inverse** of any number is the opposite of that number. The sum of a number and its additive inverse is zero.

$^{+}11 + (^{-}11) = 0$

Another Example

Use the Additive Inverse Property to Solve an Equation

$$n + \frac{3}{4} = 8$$
$$n + (\frac{3}{4} + {}^{-}\frac{3}{4}) = 8 + {}^{-}\frac{3}{4}$$
$$n = 7\frac{1}{4}$$

Think: $\frac{3}{4}$ and $^{-}\frac{3}{4}$ are additive inverses.

Explain Your Thinking

- ▶ Why is the sum of any number and its additive inverse zero?
- ▶ Why does the Additive Inverse Property not apply to the set of whole numbers?

Guided Practice

Complete each equation. Tell which property you used.

1. $\frac{5}{6} + {}^-\frac{3}{4} = \blacksquare + \frac{5}{6}$
2. $(\frac{1}{2} \times \frac{2}{3}) \times \blacksquare = \blacksquare \times (\blacksquare \times \frac{6}{7})$
3. $\blacksquare + 16 = 0$
4. $3(\frac{1}{4} + \blacksquare) = (3 \times \blacksquare) + (3 \times \frac{5}{7})$

Ask Yourself

- Does each side of the equation have the same value?

Independent Practice

Complete each equation. Tell which property you used.

5. $\frac{3}{7} + {}^-\frac{2}{3} = \blacksquare + \frac{3}{7}$
6. $({}^-4 \times \frac{1}{3}) \times \blacksquare = \blacksquare \times (\blacksquare \times \frac{6}{7})$
7. $\blacksquare + 8 = 0$
8. $\frac{4}{3} \times \frac{5}{7} = \frac{5}{7} \times \blacksquare$
9. $\frac{4}{5} + \blacksquare = 0$
10. $\frac{2}{3} + (\frac{1}{4} + \blacksquare) = (\blacksquare + \frac{1}{4}) + \frac{6}{7}$
11. $\blacksquare \times (\frac{1}{5} \times \frac{2}{3}) = (\frac{2}{7} \times \blacksquare) \times \blacksquare$
12. ${}^-\frac{6}{7} + \blacksquare = 0$

n **Algebra • Equations** **Use an additive inverse to solve for *n*. Show your work.**

13. $n + \frac{7}{8} = 15$
14. $n + 0.59 = 4.25$
15. $n - \frac{3}{11} = 6\frac{1}{2}$
16. $n - 2.01 = 100$
17. $n + 3\frac{4}{5} = 4$
18. $n + \frac{17}{20} = 9\frac{2}{3}$
19. $n - 0.66 = 1$
20. $n - \frac{13}{9} = 12\frac{5}{6}$
21. $n + 87 = 50$

Problem Solving • Reasoning

Use the chart for Problems 22 and 23.

Yards Gained or Lost

$^+2$	$^-1$	$^+5$	0
$^-4$	$^+9$	$^-3$	$^-3$
$^+6$	$^-12$	0	$^+1$

22. **Explain** A running back carried a football 12 times. Did those carries result in a total gain or total loss of yards?
23. How many yards would the running back need to gain on one additional carry to have a mean of $^+4$ yards per carry?

Mixed Review • Test Prep

Find each sum or difference. Write the answer in simplest form. *(pages 156–160)*

24. $\frac{5}{8} + \frac{1}{8}$
25. $\frac{7}{5} - \frac{2}{5}$
26. $1\frac{3}{4} + \frac{1}{3}$
27. $3\frac{2}{4} - \frac{1}{4}$

28. What is the greatest common factor of 45 and 54? *(pages 112–114)*

A 1 **B** 9 **C** 27 **D** 540

Problem-Solving Application: Use Integers

You will learn how to solve problems using integers.

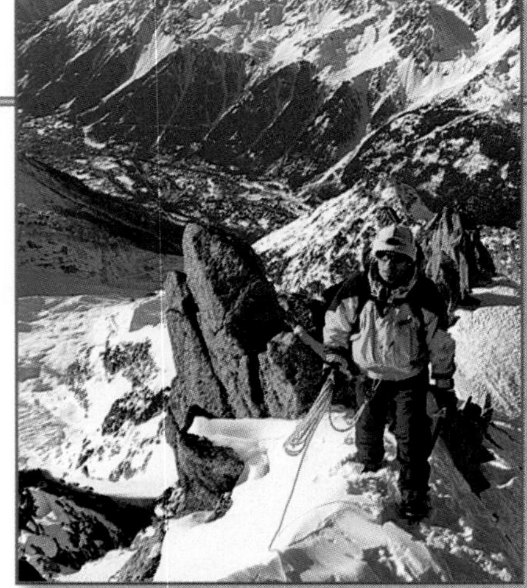

Sometimes you can solve problems by representing values as integers.

Problem Eiko and Karyn are mountain climbing. When they begin their climb at the base of the mountain, the temperature is 10°F. Suppose that for every increase in elevation of 1,000 feet, the temperature decreases about 5°F. About what is the temperature after they climb 4,000 feet?

Understand

What is the question?

What is the temperature after Eiko and Karyn climb 4,000 feet?

What do you know?

When they begin, the temperature is 10°F. The temperature decreases about 5°F with every increase of 1,000 feet of elevation.

Plan

What can you do to find the answer?

Divide the distance climbed by 1,000 feet. Multiply the quotient by $^{-}5$°F. Add the product, or change in temperature, to the starting temperature of 10°F.

$^{+}4{,}000 \div {}^{+}1{,}000 = {}^{+}4$ ⟵ This represents units of 1,000 feet.

Think: For every increase of 1,000 feet ($^{+}1{,}000$ ft), the temperature decreases about 5 degrees ($^{-}5$°F).

$^{+}4 \times {}^{-}5° = {}^{-}20°$

$^{+}10° + {}^{-}20° = {}^{-}10°$

The temperature is about $^{-}10$°F at 4,000 feet.

Look Back

Look back at the question. Is your answer reasonable?

Would you expect the temperature to be warmer or colder as elevation increases?

Tents and supplies are at the base camp of an expedition to Mt. Everest.

Remember:
- ► Understand
- ► Plan
- ► Solve
- ► Look Back

Guided Practice

Solve. Use the information on page 234 for Problem 2.

1. After six hours, the temperature at the camp has decreased from 10°F to $^-14$°F. If the temperature decreased by the same amount each hour, by how many degrees did the temperature decrease each hour?

   Think: What values can you represent as integers? What operations are needed to solve the problem?

2. Karl and Monica ski down a mountain slope from an elevation of 3,000 feet. At 3,000 feet, the temperature is $^-7$°F. What would you estimate the temperature to be when they reach the bottom of the mountain slope?

   Think: Will the temperature become warmer or colder as they ski down the slope?

Choose a Strategy

Solve. Use these or other strategies.

Problem-Solving Strategies

- **Write an Equation**
- **Choose the Operation**
- **Find a Pattern**
- **Draw a Diagram**

3. A climate lab has a Temperature-Altitude (TA) Chamber. The TA Chamber uses refrigeration to lower the temperature from $^+70$°F to $^-60$°F in 10 hours. If the rate of decrease is constant, how many degrees does the temperature decrease each hour?

4. Julius bought 23 shares of stock in Company *A*. Two weeks later he bought 35 more shares of Company *A*. A month later, he sold 19 shares of Company *A* and 27 shares of Company *B*. How many shares of Company A stock does Julius have left?

5. The wind is blowing at 40 mi/h, so the air feels 83°F colder than the actual temperature. If the air feels $^-128$°F, what is the actual air temperature?

6. With pre-cooling, the temperature in the TA Chamber drops 10°F per minute. At that rate, how long will it take the TA Chamber to cool from $^+70$°F to $^-50$°F?

7. Jodi is thinking of a whole number. If she multiplies the number by 2 and adds 8, the result will be 4 times as great as her original number. What is Jodi's original number?

8. Luka is three years older than Mario. Six years ago, Luka was twice as old as Mario was at that time. How old were Luka and Mario six years ago? How old are Luka and Mario now?

Extra Practice See 8–9 on page 241.

Quick Check

Check Your Understanding of Lessons 9–11

Rewrite each number in the form $\frac{a}{b}$ and locate it on a number line. Then order the numbers in Exercises 1–3 from greatest to least.

1. $^{-}0.7$ **2.** $^{+}3\frac{1}{3}$ **3.** $^{-}14$

Compare. Write >, <, or = for each ●. If necessary, use a number line.

4. $\frac{5}{6}$ ● 0.85 **5.** $^{-}2\frac{1}{2}$ ● $^{-}2.5$ **6.** 1.6 ● $^{-}\frac{8}{5}$

Order from least to greatest.

7. $\frac{13}{10}$ $1\frac{1}{2}$ 1.4 **8.** $^{-}5\frac{1}{4}$ 6 $^{-}5.1$ **9.** $^{-}2$ $^{-}1.9$ $^{-}\frac{5}{2}$

Complete each equation. Tell which property you used.

10. $\frac{1}{2} + \frac{3}{4} = ■ + \frac{1}{2}$

11. $(\frac{7}{8} \times \frac{1}{3}) \times ■ = ■ \times (■ \times \frac{6}{7})$

12. $■ + 26 = 0$

13. $\frac{1}{10} \times ■ = \frac{3}{7} \times \frac{1}{10}$

Solve.

14. The temperature at 6:00 A.M. was $^{+}4$°F. By noon the temperature had decreased by 2 degrees. If the low temperature of the day was $^{-}11$°F and was recorded at 11:30 P.M., by how many degrees did the temperature decrease from 6:00 A.M. to 11:30 P.M.?

How did you do?

If you had difficulty with any items in the Quick Check, you can use the following pages for review and extra practice.

Items	Review These Pages	Do These Extra Practice Items
1–9	pages 230–231	Set G, page 240
10–13	pages 232–233	Set H, page 240
14	pages 234–235	8–9, page 241

Test Prep • Cumulative Review

Maintaining the Standards

Choose the letter of the correct answer. If a correct answer is not here, choose NH.

1 Which decimal represents $\frac{2}{11}$?

A $0.\overline{18}$

B $0.\overline{1}8$

C $0.1\overline{8}$

D $0.1\overline{88}$

---

2 1, 2, 3, and 6 represent all the factors of which composite number?

F 12

G 6

H 1

J NH

---

3 Lance walks for exercise. Saturday he walked $1\frac{5}{8}$ miles and Sunday he walked $\frac{3}{8}$ mile. How much farther did Lance walk on Saturday?

A $1\frac{4}{8}$ miles

B 2 miles

C $2\frac{5}{8}$ miles

D NH

---

4 There were 345,710 recorded births in Canada from 1997–1998. There were 340,891 recorded births from 1998–1999. How many fewer recorded births were there from 1998–1999 than from 1997–1998?

F 4,820

G 4,819

H 4,918

J 686,601

---

5 Waymon ordered $\frac{3}{4}$ pound of deli ham at the grocery store. Which fraction is an equivalent fraction for $\frac{3}{4}$?

A $\frac{3}{8}$

B $\frac{6}{8}$

C $\frac{6}{4}$

D $\frac{4}{3}$

---

6 Identify the lower extreme on the box-and-whisker plot.

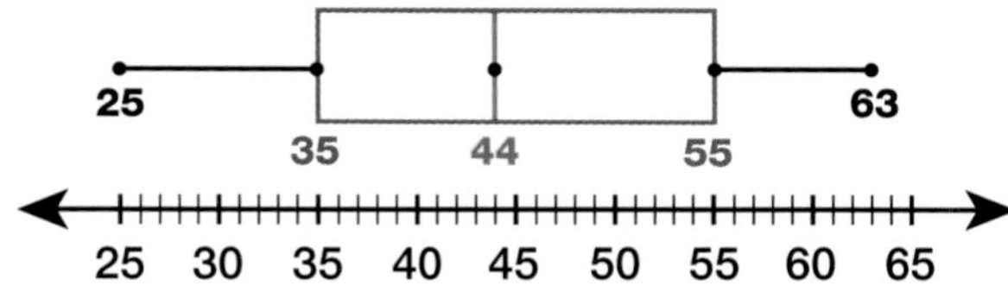

F 63

G 55

H 35

J 25

---

7 Kim has a length of ribbon $10\frac{1}{2}$ feet long. She needs to cut pieces that are each $1\frac{3}{4}$ feet long for an art project. How many pieces of ribbon can she cut that are each $1\frac{3}{4}$ feet long?

Explain Show how you found your answer.

Safe Site

Internet Test Prep
Visit **www.eduplace.com/kids/mhm** for more *Test Prep Practice.*

Extra Practice

Set A (Lesson 1, pages 206–207)

If the number is an integer, write its opposite. If it is not, write *no*.

1. $^{-}86\frac{1}{2}$
2. $^{+}6$
3. $^{+}0.58$
4. $^{-}1$
5. $^{-}744$
6. $^{+}9\frac{3}{4}$
7. 0
8. $^{-}4.37$
9. $^{+}323$
10. $^{-}\frac{1}{3}$
11. $^{+}45.3$
12. $^{+}77$

Set B (Lesson 2, pages 208–209)

Compare. Write > or < for each ●.

1. $^{-}14$ ● $^{-}15$
2. $^{+}3$ ● $^{-}3$
3. $^{-}8$ ● 0
4. $^{+}14$ ● $^{-}18$
5. $^{-}2$ ● $^{+}1$
6. $^{-}56$ ● $^{-}60$
7. $^{+}17$ ● $^{+}16$
8. 0 ● $^{-}1$
9. $^{-}6$ ● $^{+}5$
10. $^{-}44$ ● $^{-}45$
11. $^{+}13$ ● $^{-}15$
12. $^{+}24$ ● $^{+}42$

Order from least to greatest.

13. $^{-}12$ $^{+}6$ $^{-}18$ $^{-}2$
14. $^{-}4$ $^{+}4$ 0 $^{-}3$ $^{+}5$
15. $^{+}17$ $^{-}20$ $^{+}18$ $^{-}19$
16. $^{+}1$ $^{-}7$ $^{-}1$ 0 $^{+}8$
17. $^{+}50$ $^{+}15$ $^{-}5$ $^{-}15$
18. $^{-}6$ $^{-}8$ $^{-}7$ $^{+}4$ $^{+}5$
19. $^{+}14$ $^{-}41$ $^{-}1$ $^{+}11$
20. $^{-}2$ $^{-}6$ $^{+}2$ 0 $^{+}6$
21. $^{+}35$ $^{-}31$ $^{-}26$ $^{+}40$

Set C (Lesson 4, pages 214–216)

Add. Use a number line if necessary.

1. $^{-}12 + ^{-}6$
2. $^{+}3 + ^{-}8$
3. $^{+}7 + ^{-}7$
4. $^{+}5 + ^{+}3$
5. $^{-}5 + ^{+}9$
6. $^{-}11 + ^{-}4$
7. $^{+}8 + ^{-}9$
8. $^{-}4 + ^{-}4$
9. $^{+}1 + ^{-}7$
10. $^{-}6 + ^{+}6$
11. $^{-}12 + ^{+}13$
12. $^{-}19 + 0$

Write the missing addend.

13. $^{+}8 + ■ = ^{+}2$
14. $^{-}4 + ■ = ^{-}13$
15. $^{-}5 + ■ = ^{+}7$
16. $^{+}10 + ■ = 0$
17. $^{-}12 + ■ = ^{+}3$
18. $^{+}5 + ■ = ^{-}1$
19. $^{-}6 + ■ = ^{+}6$
20. $^{-}17 + ■ = ^{-}4$

Extra Practice

Set D (*Lesson 5, pages 218–220*)

Subtract.

1. $^{-}4 - {}^{+}3$ **2.** $^{-}18 - 0$ **3.** $^{+}10 - {}^{-}6$ **4.** $^{+}5 - {}^{+}7$

5. $^{-}9 - {}^{-}8$ **6.** $^{-}7 - {}^{+}8$ **7.** $^{+}4 - {}^{+}3$ **8.** $^{-}6 - {}^{-}6$

9. $^{-}13 - {}^{+}2$ **10.** $^{-}6 - {}^{-}9$ **11.** $^{+}11 - {}^{-}11$ **12.** $^{-}2 - {}^{+}9$

13. $^{-}15 - {}^{-}15$ **14.** $^{+}10 - {}^{+}10$ **15.** $^{+}7 - {}^{-}6$ **16.** $^{-}16 - {}^{+}4$

Complete each pair of related equations.

17. $^{+}7 + {}^{-}3 = ■$
$^{+}7 - {}^{+}3 = ■$

18. $^{-}6 - {}^{-}4 = ■$
$^{-}6 + {}^{+}4 = ■$

19. $^{-}11 - {}^{+}8 = ■$
$^{-}11 + {}^{-}8 = ■$

Set E (*Lesson 6, pages 222–223*)

Find each product.

1. $^{-}1 \times {}^{+}5$ **2.** $^{-}6 \times {}^{-}7$ **3.** $^{+}4 \times {}^{-}3$ **4.** $^{+}5 \times {}^{+}6$

5. $^{-}9 \times {}^{-}2$ **6.** $^{-}8 \times {}^{+}8$ **7.** $^{+}20 \times 0$ **8.** $^{-}14 \times {}^{-}2$

9. $^{+}3 \times {}^{-}1$ **10.** $^{+}4 \times {}^{+}12$ **11.** $^{-}7 \times {}^{+}5$ **12.** $^{-}9 \times {}^{-}8$

13. $0 \times {}^{-}15$ **14.** $^{-}10 \times {}^{-}8$ **15.** $^{+}16 \times {}^{-}3$ **16.** $^{-}7 \times {}^{+}4$

17. $^{+}11 \times {}^{+}4$ **18.** $^{-}13 \times {}^{+}2$ **19.** $^{-}15 \times {}^{-}3$ **20.** $^{+}6 \times {}^{+}9$

Set F (*Lesson 7, pages 224–225*)

Find each quotient.

1. $^{-}45 \div {}^{-}9$ **2.** $^{+}21 \div {}^{-}7$ **3.** $^{+}42 \div {}^{+}21$ **4.** $^{-}48 \div {}^{+}8$

5. $^{+}36 \div {}^{-}6$ **6.** $^{-}100 \div {}^{+}10$ **7.** $^{-}30 \div {}^{-}5$ **8.** $^{+}20 \div {}^{+}2$

9. $^{-}14 \div {}^{-}7$ **10.** $^{+}50 \div {}^{-}2$ **11.** $^{-}17 \div {}^{+}1$ **12.** $^{-}18 \div {}^{-}9$

13. $^{+}66 \div {}^{-}11$ **14.** $^{-}64 \div {}^{-}8$ **15.** $^{+}81 \div {}^{-}9$ **16.** $^{-}35 \div {}^{+}5$

17. $^{-}90 \div {}^{-}3$ **18.** $^{+}200 \div {}^{+}20$ **19.** $^{-}40 \div {}^{+}4$ **20.** $^{+}16 \div {}^{-}1$

Extra Practice

Set G (Lesson 9, pages 230–231)

Rewrite each as a rational number of the form $\frac{a}{b}$ and locate it on a number line. Then order the numbers in Exercises 1–8 from greatest to least.

1. $^{-}0.36$ **2.** 54 **3.** $^{-}0.1$ **4.** $7\frac{1}{2}$

5. 0.91 **6.** $-3\frac{2}{3}$ **7.** 2.7 **8.** $^{-}9$

Compare. Write >, <, or = for each ●. If necessary, use a number line.

9. $\frac{2}{3}$ ● $\frac{3}{4}$ **10.** 4.5 ● $4\frac{1}{2}$ **11.** $^{-}1$ ● $-\frac{5}{4}$

12. 0.5 ● $\frac{1}{2}$ **13.** $^{-}2.6$ ● $-\frac{5}{2}$ **14.** $\frac{6}{5}$ ● 1.4

15. $^{-}1.85$ ● $-1\frac{3}{4}$ **16.** $1\frac{1}{2}$ ● $\frac{3}{2}$ **17.** $^{-}5.25$ ● $-\frac{1}{2}$

18. $^{-}0.5$ ● $\frac{1}{10}$ **19.** $2\frac{4}{5}$ ● $\frac{11}{4}$ **20.** 0 ● $-\frac{3}{4}$

21. $\frac{7}{10}$ ● $^{-}1.7$ **22.** 7.3 ● 6.7 **23.** $-3\frac{1}{5}$ ● $-\frac{11}{4}$

24. $^{-}0.125$ ● $-\frac{1}{8}$ **25.** $\frac{1}{9}$ ● $-\frac{2}{3}$ **26.** $9\frac{1}{6}$ ● $9\frac{5}{12}$

27. $+\frac{3}{11}$ ● $+\frac{7}{5}$ **28.** 0 ● $^{-}0.1$ **29.** $^{-}0.45$ ● $-\frac{9}{20}$

Set H (Lesson 10, pages 232–233)

Complete each equation. Tell which property you used.

1. $-\frac{2}{3} \times$ ■ $= \frac{1}{6} \times -\frac{2}{3}$

2. ■ $+ 9 = 0$

3. ■ $\times (\frac{1}{7} \times \frac{3}{2}) = (\frac{1}{3} \times \frac{1}{7}) \times$ ■

4. $3 + -\frac{3}{4} = -\frac{3}{4} +$ ■

5. $\frac{1}{5} + (\frac{2}{3} +$ ■$) = ($■ $+ \frac{2}{3}) + \frac{7}{8}$

6. $-\frac{3}{5} +$ ■ $= 0$

7. $^{-}15 + 15 =$ ■

8. ■ $+ 1\frac{1}{4} = 1\frac{1}{4} + {}^{-}6$

9. $(\frac{5}{4} \times \frac{1}{8}) \times \frac{2}{5} =$ ■ $\times$ (■ $\times \frac{2}{5})$

10. $8(3 + \frac{1}{2}) = (8 \times$ ■$) + (8 \times \frac{1}{2})$

11. $(\frac{1}{9} + \frac{2}{3}) +$ ■ $=$ ■ $+ (\frac{2}{3} + \frac{2}{6})$

12. ■$(\frac{1}{4} + \frac{1}{2}) = (6 \times \frac{1}{4}) + (6 \times \frac{1}{2})$

13. $^{-}11 +$ ■ $= 0$

14. $\frac{7}{10} \times \frac{3}{10} =$ ■ $\times \frac{7}{10}$

15. $\frac{7}{8} + (\frac{1}{5} + \frac{3}{8}) =$ (■ + ■) $+ \frac{3}{8}$

16. $3(\frac{1}{5} + \frac{1}{10}) =$ (■ × ■) $+ (3 \times \frac{1}{10})$

Extra Practice • Problem Solving

Solve. Use the Draw a Diagram strategy or another strategy. *(Lesson 3, pages 210–211)*

1. Phoebe, Enrique, Tina, and Stuart are running a relay race. Phoebe runs $\frac{1}{2}$ mile. Enrique runs $\frac{1}{4}$ of the race. Tina runs $\frac{1}{4}$ mile more than Phoebe, or the same distance as Enrique. Stuart runs the rest of the race. How long is the race?

2. Kyra is knitting a scarf for a charity auction. On Sunday she knits $\frac{1}{3}$ of the scarf. On Tuesday she knits $\frac{1}{3}$ of the scarf and an additional 10 rows. On Friday she knits the remaining 60 rows. How many rows does Kyra knit altogether?

3. Jon and Anne had an equal amount of money. Jon spent $10. Anne spent $30. Now Jon has twice as much money as Anne. How much did they each have at first?

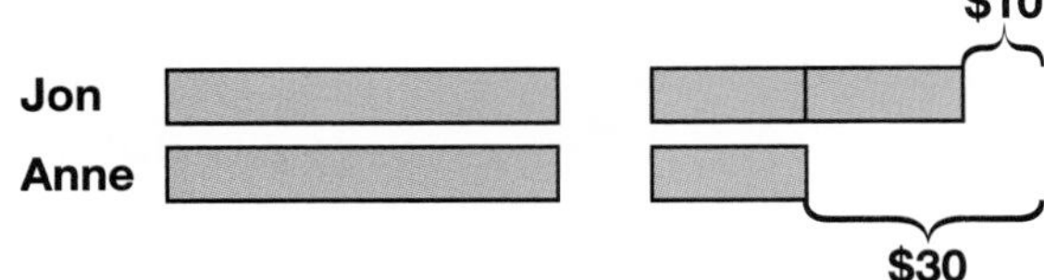

Solve. Choose the necessary operations. *(Lesson 8, pages 226–227)*

4. Suzanne found the following note on her birthday: "In order to find your present, walk 20 steps to the east. Then walk twice as far to the west. Finally, walk 10 steps to the east." Where is Suzanne's gift located compared to where she started?

5. Rama is planting seeds in his garden. First, he walks 16 steps north to plant tomato seeds. Then he walks 20 steps south to plant pepper seeds. Next, he walks 2 steps north to plant squash seeds. Where are the squash seeds compared to where Rama started?

6. A diver was seeking sunken treasure. She dove 90 feet below the surface before encountering a school of fish. She then swam 10 feet up before diving $\frac{2}{3}$ times as far as she had originally. How many feet below the surface was she at that time?

7. At 11:00 P.M., the temperature was 76°F. By 7:00 A.M., the temperature had dropped to 60°F. What integer represents the change in temperature between 11:00 P.M. and 7:00 A.M.? If the decrease was constant, what was the temperature at midnight?

Solve. Use integers. *(Lesson 11, pages 234–235)*

8. Some problems on Dana's 100-point mathematics test are worth 4 points and others are worth 2 points. If she misses 2 problems worth 4 points and 2 problems worth 2 points, what score did she earn?

9. A cold front in Carson caused the temperature to drop from 15°F to $^-9$°F in 12 hours. If the temperature decreased by the same amount each hour, how many degrees did the temperature drop per hour?

Chapter Review

Reviewing Vocabulary

Write *always, sometimes,* or *never* for each question. Give an example to support your answer.

1. Every integer is a fraction.
2. Negative integers are rational numbers.
3. The absolute value of a number is the number itself.

Match each word with a definition.

4. additive inverse	**A** the distance a number is from 0 on the number line
5. rational number	**B** any number that can be expressed in the form $\frac{a}{b}$ where $b \neq 0$
6. absolute value	**C** that number which gives a sum of 0 when added to a given number

Reviewing Concepts and Skills

If the number is an integer, write its opposite. If it is not, write *no*. *(pages 206–207)*

7. $^{+}14$ **8.** $^{-}6\frac{1}{3}$ **9.** $^{+}8.4$ **10.** $^{-}9$

Compare. Write >, <, or = for each ⬤. *(pages 208–209)*

11. $^{+}4$ ⬤ $^{-}4$ **12.** 0 ⬤ $^{-}5$ **13.** $^{-}16$ ⬤ $^{-}17$ **14.** $^{-}9$ ⬤ $^{+}8$

Order from least to greatest. *(pages 208–209, 230–231)*

15. $^{+}3$ $^{-}3$ 0 $^{+}6$ $^{-}8$ **16.** $^{-}12$ $^{-}20$ $^{+}18$ $^{+}7$ **17.** $^{-}9$ $^{+}6$ $^{-}7$ $^{-}11$ $^{+}10$

18. $^{+}2\frac{1}{2}$ $^{-}3$ $^{-}0.5$ $^{+}5$ **19.** $-\frac{16}{5}$ $^{+}3.5$ $+\frac{3}{4}$ $^{-}2$ **20.** $^{+}1.6$ $^{-}1\frac{5}{8}$ 0 $^{+}2$ $^{-}2$

Add or subtract. *(pages 214–220)*

21. $^{-}14 + {}^{+}6$ **22.** $^{+}11 - {}^{+}12$ **23.** $^{-}8 - {}^{-}3$ **24.** $^{+}10 + {}^{-}9$

25. $^{-}7 - {}^{+}5$ **26.** $^{-}4 + {}^{+}15$ **27.** $^{+}12 - {}^{-}12$ **28.** $^{-}6 + {}^{-}5$

Find each product or quotient. *(pages 222–225)*

29. $^{+}5 \times {}^{+}10$ **30.** $^{-}60 \div {}^{-}6$ **31.** $^{-}11 \times {}^{-}2$ **32.** $^{+}45 \div {}^{-}5$

33. $^{-}48 \div {}^{+}4$ **34.** $^{-}7 \times {}^{+}5$ **35.** $^{+}18 \div {}^{+}6$ **36.** $^{+}12 \times {}^{-}2$

Rewrite each in the form $\frac{a}{b}$, where $b \neq 0$, and locate the number on a number line. Then order the numbers in Exercises 37–40 from greatest to least. *(pages 230–231)*

37. $^{-}7\frac{1}{2}$ **38.** 2 **39.** 0.35 **40.** $^{-}6$

Compare. Write >, <, or = for each ●. If necessary, use a number line. *(pages 230–231)*

41. $-\frac{5}{2}$ ● 2.5 **42.** $1\frac{3}{4}$ ● $\frac{7}{4}$ **43.** $^{-}5\frac{1}{5}$ ● $^{-}5.3$

Complete each equation. Tell which property you used. *(pages 232–233)*

44. $■ \times \frac{4}{5} = \frac{4}{5} \times -\frac{1}{7}$

45. $\frac{3}{5} + (■ + \frac{1}{2}) = (\frac{3}{5} + \frac{1}{6}) + ■$

46. $(^{-}3 \times \frac{1}{4}) \times ■ = {}^{-}3 \times (■ \times \frac{5}{6})$

47. $\frac{4}{3} + ■ = 0$

48. $6(\frac{1}{6} \times \frac{1}{3}) = (6 \times ■) + (■ \times \frac{1}{3})$

49. $\frac{3}{8} + \frac{5}{8} = ■ + \frac{3}{8}$

Solve. *(pages 210–211, 226–227, 234–235)*

50. The quotient of a greater integer divided by a lesser integer is $^{-}1$. The sum of the integers is 0. The product of the integers is the same as the difference of the lesser integer and the greater integer. What are the integers?

51. On Monday, $\frac{1}{4}$ of the students in Chip's grade were absent. On Wednesday, twice as many students were absent as on Monday. If there are 40 students in Chip's grade, how many of them were absent on Wednesday?

Brain Teasers Math Reasoning

Absolute Inverse?

When will a given integer have an absolute value that is the same as its additive inverse? Give an example.

Rational Reality

Can you think of some real-life situations that use rational numbers? Do your examples have anything in common with each other?

Safe Site

Internet Brain Teasers
Visit **www.eduplace.com/kids/mhm** for more *Brain Teasers.*

Chapter Test

Compare. Write >, <, or = for each ●.

1. $^{+}12$ ● $^{-}13$ **2.** $^{-}9$ ● 0 **3.** $^{-}8$ ● $^{-}14$ **4.** $-\frac{9}{4}$ ● $-\frac{4}{9}$

Order from greatest to least.

5. $^{+}11$ $^{+}14$ $^{-}7$ $^{-}12$ **6.** $^{+}1$ $^{-}8\frac{1}{3}$ $^{-}6.3$ 0 $^{-}1$ **7.** $^{+}\frac{28}{5}$ $^{-}6$ $^{+}9$ $^{-}\frac{2}{5}$ $^{+}4.96$

Solve.

8. Which of the numbers $^{+}3$, $^{-}\frac{1}{2}$, $^{+}0.76$, $^{-}9$, $^{+}\frac{3}{4}$ are integers? Explain.

9. What number is the additive inverse of 8?

10. Which has a greater absolute value, $^{-}12$ or $^{-}13$? Explain how you know.

Add or subtract.

11. $^{-}9 + ^{-}8$ **12.** $^{+}13 - ^{-}6$ **13.** $^{+}20 + ^{-}2$ **14.** $^{-}4 - ^{-}5$

15. $^{+}12 - ^{+}7$ **16.** $^{-}9 + ^{+}5$ **17.** $^{-}14 - ^{+}8$ **18.** $^{+}6 + ^{+}7$

Find each product or quotient.

19. $^{-}77 \div ^{-}11$ **20.** $^{+}4 \times ^{-}6$ **21.** $^{+}42 \div ^{-}7$ **22.** $^{-}72 \div ^{+}9$

23. $^{-}9 \times ^{+}1$ **24.** $^{+}36 \div ^{+}12$ **25.** $^{-}4 \times ^{-}5$ **26.** $^{+}6 \times ^{+}8$

Write each as a rational number of the form $\frac{a}{b}$ where $b \neq 0$.

27. $^{-}6\frac{2}{5}$ **28.** 0.9 **29.** $^{-}0.75$ **30.** $1\frac{1}{2}$

Write >, <, or = for each ●.

31. $1\frac{3}{4}$ ● $\frac{3}{2}$ **32.** $-\frac{7}{2}$ ● $^{-}4.8$ **33.** $-\frac{1}{4}$ ● 0.25

34. 0.6 ● $\frac{3}{5}$ **35.** $-3\frac{1}{3}$ ● $^{-}3.3$ **36.** 5 ● $^{-}5.5$

Complete each equation. Tell what property you used.

37. $(\frac{1}{8} \times \frac{2}{3}) \times ■ = \frac{1}{8} \times (■ \times \frac{1}{5})$

38. $^{-}4(\frac{3}{4} + ■) = (^{-}4 \times ■) + (^{-}4 \times \frac{1}{2})$

Solve.

39. While playing a game, Sylvia takes 4 paces left, 7 paces right, then 15 paces back to the left. What is her final position compared to where she started?

40. The temperature was 10°F at noon. By midnight the temperature had dropped to $^{-}2$°F. If the decrease was constant, by how many degrees did the temperature decrease each hour?

Write About It

1. Juliana is swimming laps using 4 different strokes for swim practice. She swims 12 laps of freestyle. Next, she swims butterfly for $\frac{1}{4}$ of the total number of laps. Then she swims breaststroke for 6 more laps than she swam butterfly. Finally, she swims backstroke for 8 laps.

a. Draw a diagram to represent the information given.

b. Use your diagram to determine how many laps Juliana swam in all. Explain your method.

2. Suppose Liza and Chung hiked up to the top of a hill which is 450 feet above sea level. From the top, they return to a trailhead that is 150 feet below sea level. It takes them 15 minutes to descend 150 feet.

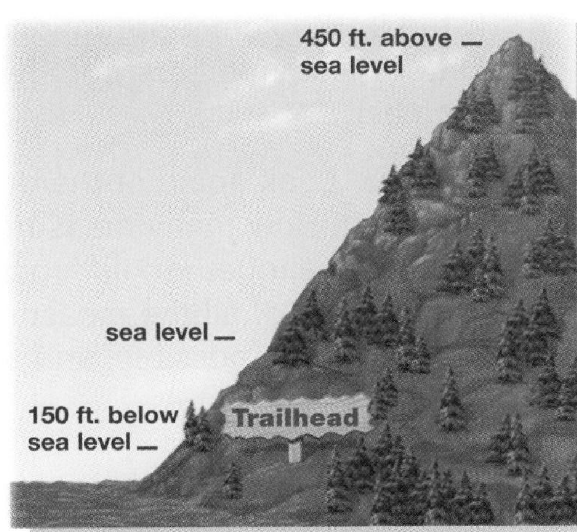

a. What operation(s) will you choose to find out how long it takes them to reach the trailhead? Why?

b. How long does it take Liza and Chung to reach the trailhead from the top of the hill?

c. Is the distance from the top of the hill to the trailhead a positive or negative integer? Explain your reasoning.

Another Look

Hope is a scientist who is studying beach erosion. As part of her research, Hope is using an instrument that measures height above or below sea level to measure the height of sand dunes. For different dunes, she measures the number of feet from the top of the dune to sea level. Her results are shown below.

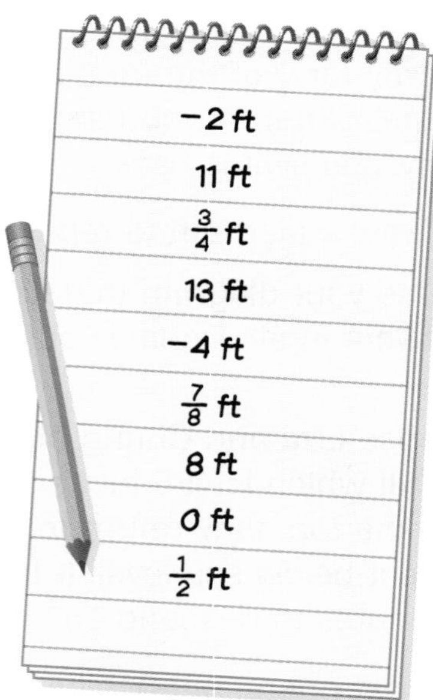

1. Of the data Hope collected, which are integers? Order the integers from least to greatest. What is the product of the integers?

2. Hope is walking from the highest elevation she measured to the lowest. When she completes her walk, by how many feet will her elevation have changed?

3. **Look Back** Which numbers that were not listed in Problem 1 are rational numbers? Order these numbers from least to greatest.

4. **Analyze** Look again at the data Hope collected. How many measurements did she make altogether? Is it possible to find the average of all the measurements? Explain. If it is possible, find the average.

Enrichment

Spinner Games

You may be familiar with spinners, such as those used in various board games. Spinners are also used in the study of probability. Although spinner outcomes are typically colors or positive whole numbers, integers can also be used for spinner outcomes.

Consider these spinners. Suppose the spinners were used to play the games that are described below.

Spinner A

$^{+}1$ $^{-}2$ $^{-}4$ $^{+}3$

Spinner B

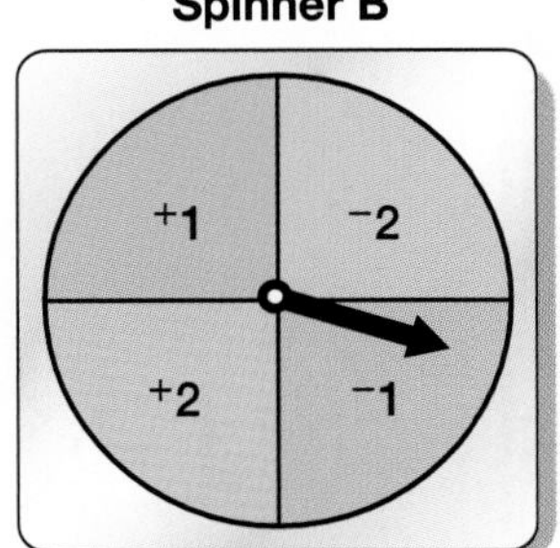

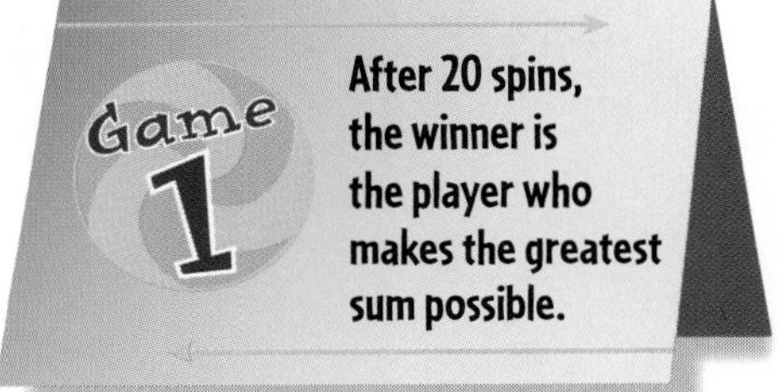

Game
1
After 20 spins, the winner is the player who makes the greatest sum possible.

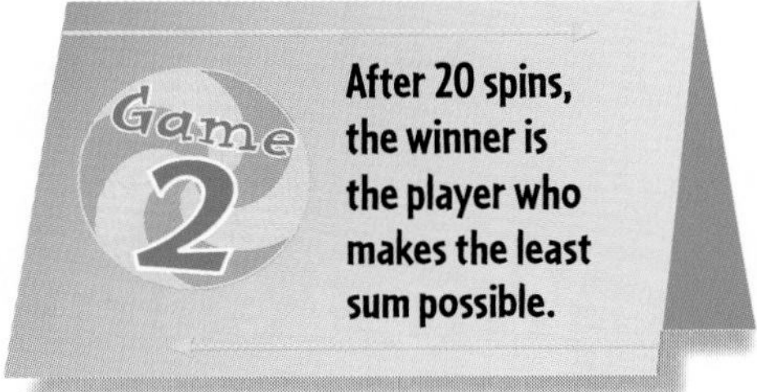

Game
2
After 20 spins, the winner is the player who makes the least sum possible.

Use the spinners and the game descriptions to answer the questions that follow.

1. Suppose you and a friend want to play Game 1, and your friend offers you the opportunity to choose the spinner you would like to use. Your friend will use the other spinner. Which spinner offers you the best chance of winning Game 1? Explain.
2. Suppose you and a friend want to play Game 2, and your friend chooses the spinner he or she would like to play with. You must play with the other spinner. Which spinner would you like your friend to choose so you would have the best chance of winning Game 2? Explain.
3. Work with a partner to construct the spinners. Then play each game to test your predictions.

CHAPTER 6

Expressions and Equations

Why Learn About Expressions and Equations?

Learning how to use expressions and equations can help you solve a variety of problems.

If you ran two more miles this week than last week, you can write an expression to represent the number of miles you ran this week.

This research scientist uses a model of a DNA molecule along with various equations to learn more about how DNA works in the human body.

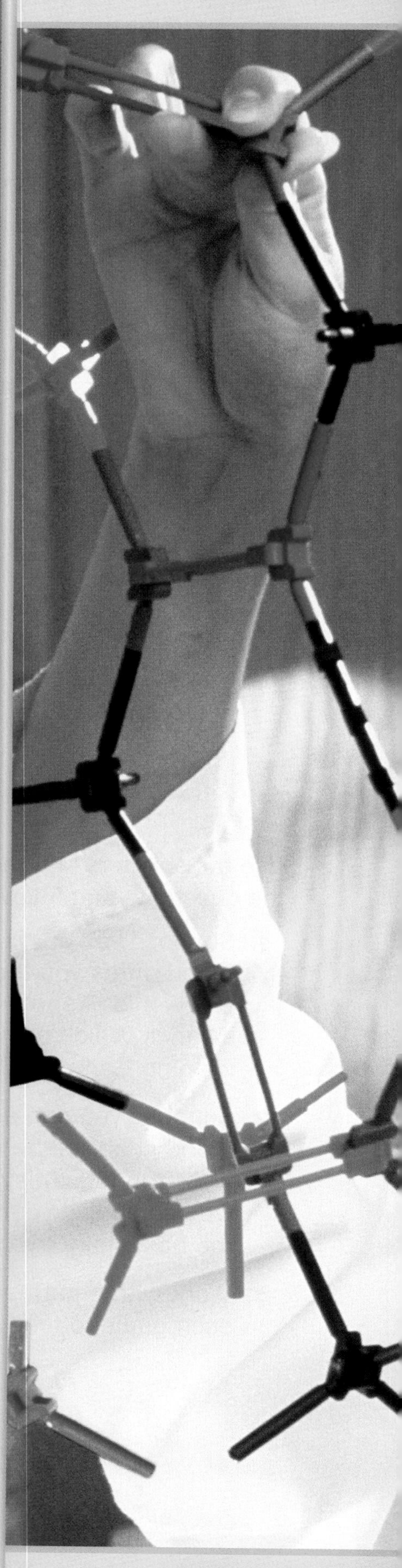

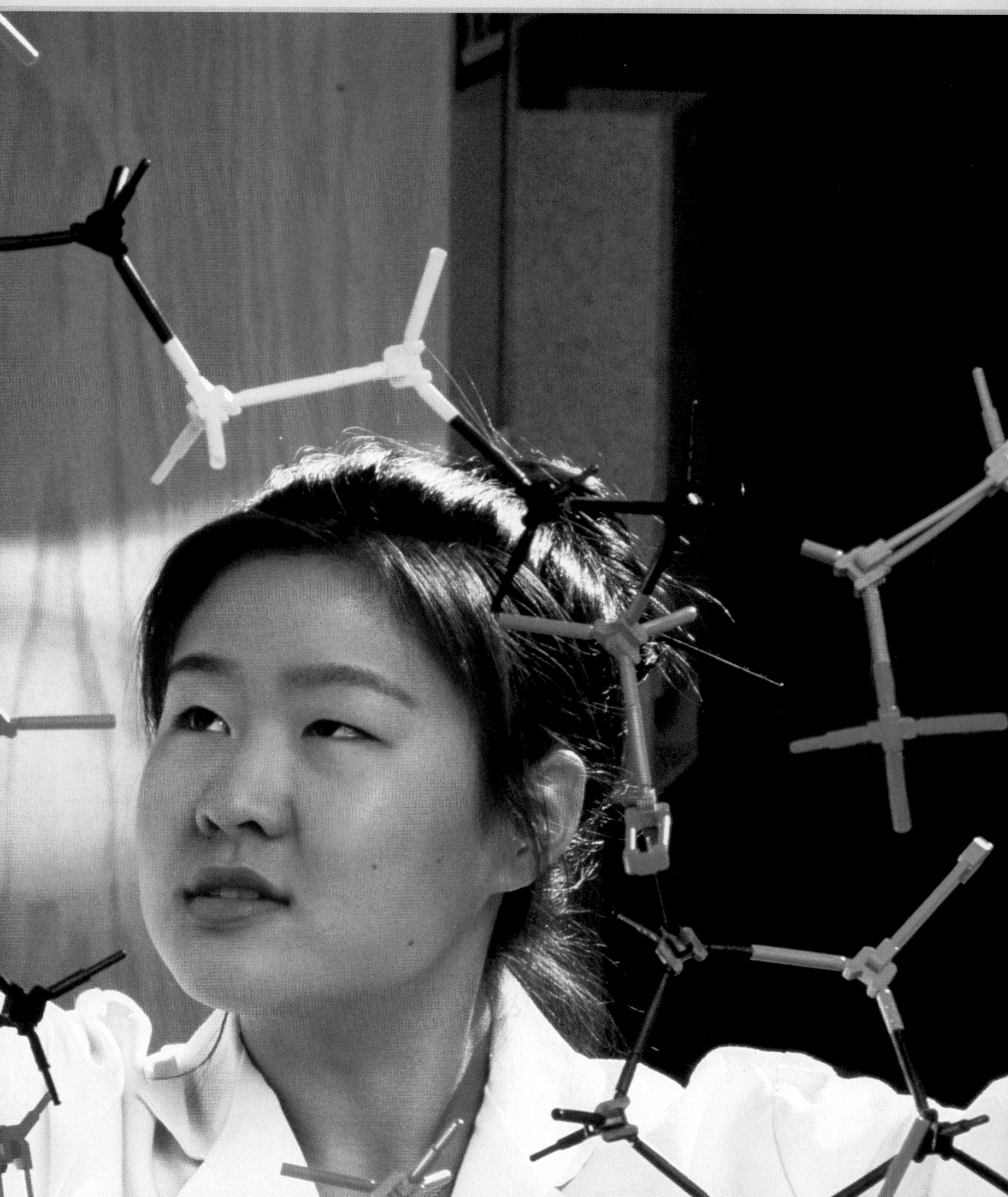

Reviewing Vocabulary

Understanding math language helps you become a successful problem solver. Here are some math vocabulary words you should know.

Associative Property	changing the grouping of numbers does not change their sum or product
Commutative Property	changing the order of numbers does not change their sum or product
Distributive Property	the product of a number a and a sum $(b + c)$ is equal to the sum of $a \times b$ and $a \times c$
Identity Property	the sum of any number and zero is that number; the product of a number and 1 is that number
reciprocal	any of two numbers whose product is 1; 2 and $\frac{1}{2}$ are reciprocals: $2 \times \frac{1}{2} = 1$
Zero Property	the product of a number and zero is zero

Reading Words and Symbols

When you read mathematics, sometimes you read only words, sometimes you read words and symbols, and sometimes you read only symbols.

All of these represent the same equation.

- four times a number, increased by seven, equals fifteen
- 4 times n plus 7 equals 15
- $(4 \times n) + 7 = 15$
- $4 \times n + 7 = 15$

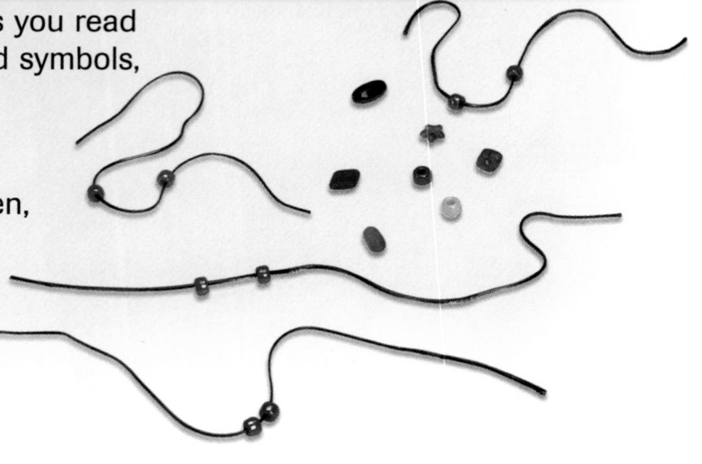

Try These

1. Write the reciprocal of each number.

   a. $\frac{3}{4}$ b. 6 c. $\frac{7}{8}$

   d. 100 e. $\frac{9}{9}$ f. 32

2. Find the number or numbers that make the expressions equal.

   a. $(3 + 4) + 6 = (6 + ■) + 3$ b. $45 \times ■ = 0$

   c. $5 \times 7 \times 3 = ■ \times 5 \times 3$ d. $(4 \times 1) + (4 \times 2) = 4 \times (■ + ■)$

   e. $1{,}221 \times ■ = 1{,}221$ f. $883 + ■ = 883$

3. Write a mathematical expression for each.

   a. a number minus 7 b. the product of 7 and a number

   c. 7 increased by a number d. a number divided by 7

4. Write *true* or *false* for each statement. Rewrite each false statement to make it true.

   a. The product of any number and its reciprocal is 1.

   b. The product of zero and a number is that number.

   c. Another way of writing "40 plus a number" is $40 + n$.

   d. Changing the grouping of numbers changes their product.

Upcoming Vocabulary

Write About It **Here are some other vocabulary words** you will learn in this chapter. Watch for these words. Write their definitions in your journal.

evaluate

algebraic expression

inverse operations

variable

Use Addition Properties to Evaluate Expressions

You will learn how to use properties of addition to help you evaluate expressions.

New Vocabulary
evaluate
algebraic expression
variable

Learn About It

A knowledge of the addition properties can help you **evaluate** mathematical expressions.

Properties of Addition

Commutative Property

The order in which numbers are added does not affect their sum.
$3 + 8 = 8 + 3$

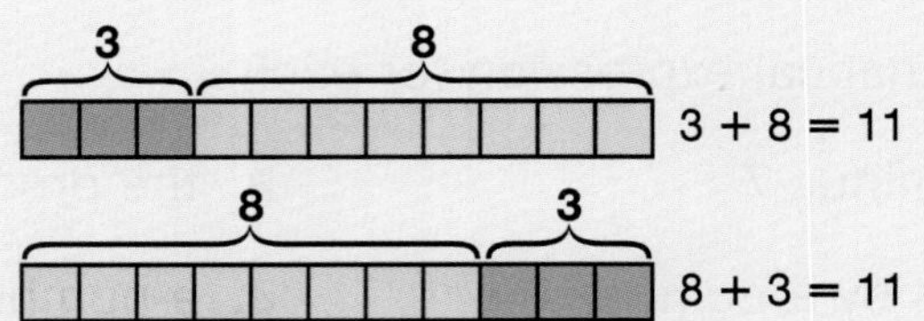

The Commutative Property allows you to add two or more numbers in any order.

All these sums are the same.

$2 + 3 + 5$ $3 + 2 + 5$ $5 + 2 + 3$
$2 + 5 + 3$ $3 + 5 + 2$ $5 + 3 + 2$

Associative Property

The way in which numbers are grouped does not affect their sum.
$(2 + 6) + 4 = 2 + (6 + 4)$

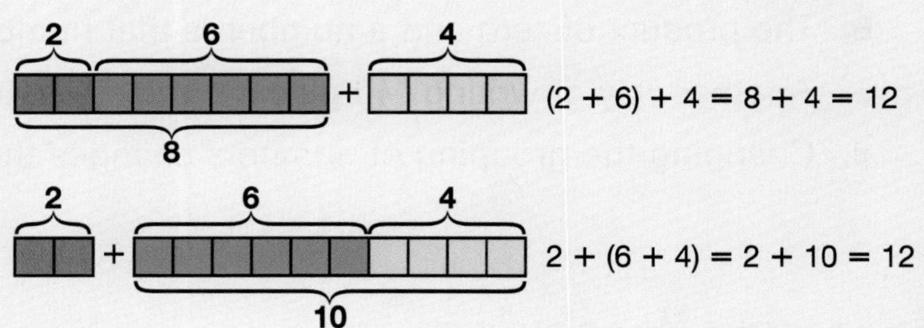

The Associative Property allows you to group three or more numbers in any way to add them.

All these sums are the same.

$[(2 + 3) + 4] + 5$ $2 + [3 + (4 + 5)]$
$2 + [(3 + 4) + 5]$ $[2 + (3 + 4)] + 5$

Identity Property

The sum of any number and zero is that number.
$5 + 0 = 5$

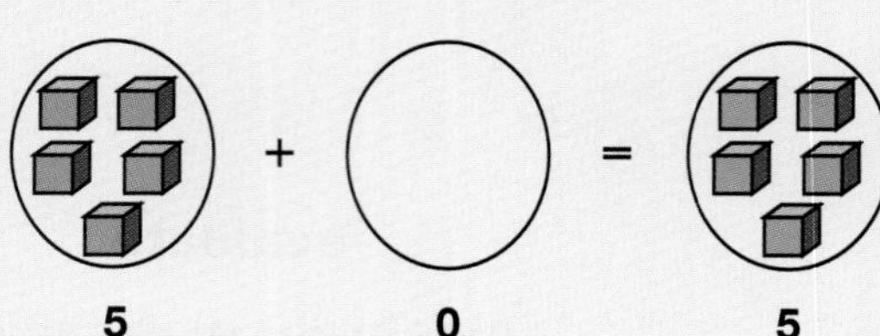

Algebraic expressions are expressions that contain one or more variables. A **variable** is a letter that represents a number.

The properties of addition can be shown by using algebraic expressions.

Commutative Property	Associative Property	Identity Property
$a + b = b + a$	$(a + b) + c = a + (b + c)$	$a + 0 = a$

Another Example

Evaluate Expressions

Evaluate, given $p = 10$ and $r = 35$.

$97 + p + 3 + 25 + r$

$97 + 10 + 3 + 25 + 35$ ⟵ Substitute for p and r.

$97 + 3 + 25 + 35 + 10$ ⟵ Commutative Property

$(97 + 3) + (25 + 35) + 10$ ⟵ Associative Property

$100 + 60 + 10$

170

Explain Your Thinking

- ► Why can there not be a Commutative Property of Subtraction?
- ► How can using the Associative Property help you add numbers mentally?

Guided Practice

Evaluate. Tell what property or properties you used.

1. $47 + (89 + 13)$

2. $43 + 0$

3. $(9 + 13) + 17$

4. $p + 0$

5. $r + (r + 8)$, given $r = 5$

6. $4 + m + 6$, given $m = 5$

Ask Yourself

- Did I group numbers so they were easy to add?
- Did I tell which properties I used?

Use >, <, or = to make each statement true.

7. $(94 + 22) + 12$ ● $(22 + 12) + 94$

8. $(5 + 29) + 18$ ● $29 + 18$

9. $26 - (15 + 2)$ ● $(26 + 15) - 2$

10. $232 + t + 73$ ● $73 + t + 232$

11. $(s + 0) + 4$ ● $4 + (1 + s)$

12. $(m + n) + (r + q)$ ● $(r + n) + (m + q)$

Independent Practice

Evaluate. Tell what property or properties you used.

13. $3 + 65 + 12$

14. $78 + 10 + 12$

15. $39 + 0 + 9$

16. $57 + 89 + 43$

17. $13 + 32 + a$, given $a = 7$

18. $85 + (b + 6)$, given $b = 20$

Use >, <, or = to make each statement true.

19. $18.4 + 0$ ● 18.4

20. $178 + a + 17$ ● $178 + a + 16$

21. $12.5 + (55 + 23)$ ● $(12.5 + 23) + 45$

22. $10 + 6$ ● $10 + 15$

23. $(b + c) + (d + e)$ ● $(b + d) + (c + e)$

24. $67 + c$ ● $60 + 7 + c$

Algebra • Properties **Use addition properties to show that the expressions are equal. At each step, indicate what property you used.**

25. $(s + 63) + 19$ and $(63 + 19) + s$

26. $p + (18 + 0)$ and $18 + p$

Problem Solving • Reasoning

Use Data **Use the graph for Problems 27–28.**

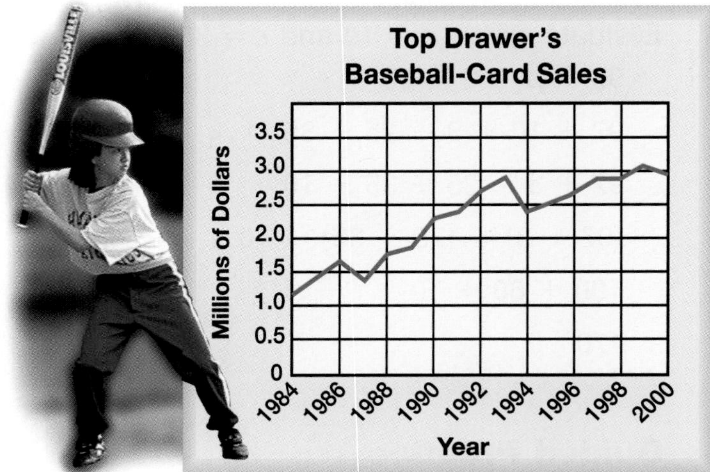

27. Top Drawer has been selling baseball cards since 1984. What is the greatest number of consecutive years that sales increased?

28. **Logical Thinking** Sometime after 1984, two other baseball-card companies began selling baseball cards. Tell which years these two companies likely began selling cards. Support your answer with data from the graph.

29. **Compare** Kelly paid \$14.95 for a box of baseball cards. Then she bought 2 packs of cards at \$2.50 per pack. Finally, she sold some of her cards for \$28.50. Compare what Kelly has spent on baseball cards to what she has earned selling them.

30. **Write About It** Imagine that you have discovered an ancient form of mathematics. While interpreting a scroll, you come across this notation.

9↑7 ∥ 2   5↑4 ∥ 1   8↑6 ∥ 2   1↑1 ∥ 0

Explain what you think the symbols ↑ and ∥ mean.

Mixed Review • Test Prep

Compare. Write >, <, or = for each ●. *(pages 208–209, 214–220)*

31. $^{-}3 - {}^{+}5$ ● $^{+}3 + {}^{-}5$

32. $^{+}16 - {}^{+}7$ ● $^{-}27 + {}^{+}31$

33. $^{+}2 - {}^{-}7$ ● $^{+}7 - {}^{-}2$

34. $^{-}27 - {}^{+}6$ ● $^{+}2 + {}^{-}30$

35 Which is the mode of 16, 71, 25, 16, 54, 27? *(pages 60–61)*

A 16 **B** 71 **C** 35 **D** 55

Extra Practice See Set A on page 290.

Practice Game

250 Sums

Play this game with a partner to practice evaluating expressions by using mental math.

What You'll Need

- *paper and pencil*

Players
2

Here's What to Do

1. Player 1 chooses a number from 1 to 50, writes it on a sheet of paper, and passes the paper to Player 2.
2. Player 2 chooses a number from 1 to 50, writes it on the sheet of paper, and mentally adds it to Player 1's number.
3. Player 1 chooses a number from 1 to 50, writes it down, and mentally adds this number to the sum found in Step 2.
4. Players continue in this manner. The player who chooses the number that adds exactly to 250 is the winner. If a player chooses a number that results in a sum of more than 250, he or she loses the game.

Take turns starting and see who can win 3 out of 5 games.

What can I add to make the sum 199?

Share Your Thinking What strategy can you use to guarantee that you will always be the player who reaches the sum of 250?

LESSON 2

Use Multiplication Properties to Evaluate Expressions

You will learn how to use properties of multiplication to evaluate expressions.

Learn About It

You can use multiplication properties to help you evaluate mathematical expressions.

Properties of Multiplication

Commutative Property

Changing the order of factors does not change their product.

$a \times b = b \times a$

Example: $3 \times 20 = 20 \times 3$

Associative Property

Changing the grouping of factors does not change their product.

$a \times (b \times c) = (a \times b) \times c$

Example: $9 \times (4 \times 3) = (9 \times 4) \times 3$

Identity Property

The product of a number and 1 is that number.

$f \times 1 = f$

Example: $45 \times 1 = 45$

Zero Property

The product of a number and 0 is 0.

$g \times 0 = 0$

Example: $15 \times 0 = 0$

Another Example

Evaluate $30 \times n \times 4$, given $n = 5$.

$30 \times 5 \times 4$ ⟵ Substitute.
$30 \times (5 \times 4)$ ⟵ Associative Property
30×20 ⟵ Multiply.
600

Explain Your Thinking

- ▶ Compare the Identity Property of Multiplication with the Identity Property of Addition. How are they similar? How are they different?
- ▶ How can you evaluate the expression $a \times b \times c \times 0$ without substituting or multiplying?

Guided Practice

Evaluate each expression and tell what property you used.

1. $3 \times 15 \times 60$

2. $250 \times 2 \times 1$

3. $4 \times (5 \times 70)$

4. $1{,}256 \times 0 \times 5$

Ask Yourself

- Did I use multiplication properties to help me do mental math?

Name the property or properties shown in each.

5. $n \times 5 \times 0 = 0$ **6.** $3 \times 57 = 57 \times 3$ **7.** $45 \times (5 \times 3) = (45 \times 5) \times 3$

8. $6 \times t = t \times 6$ **9.** $4 \times 3.5 = 1 \times 4 \times 3.5$ **10.** $(18 \times 33) \times 10 = (33 \times 10) \times 18$

Independent Practice

Evaluate each expression and tell what property you used.

11. $1 \times (65 \times 4)$ **12.** $1.2 \times 18 \times 10$ **13.** $(4.2 \times 2) \times (5 \times 0.2)$

14. $8.8 \times 12 \times 10$ **15.** $6.7 \times 0 \times 5$ **16.** $(6 \times 4) \times (12 \times 0) \times (18 \times 2)$

17. $21 \times b \times 4$, given $b = 2$ **18.** $(23.5 \times m) \times 2$, given $m = 5$

19. $4.8 \times c \times 1.0$, given $c = 25$ **20.** $4 \times (s \times 4) \times s$, given $s = 5$

Evaluate each expression, given $p = 3.5$, $q = 0.24$, and $s = 10$.

21. $p \times 4.5 \times s$ **22.** $q \times 2 \times 5$ **23.** $(s \times 8) \times 1$ **24.** $(0 \times q) \times p \times s$

25. $(q \times s) \times 2$ **26.** $10 \times 10 \times p$ **27.** $24.5 \times p$ **28.** $(s \times p) \times (3 \times s) \times (0.1 \times s)$

Problem Solving • Reasoning

Use Data **Use the table for Problems 29 and 30.**

Wheel Prices for In-line Skates	
Brand Name	**Cost per Wheel**
Rad Wheels	\$4.95
Competition	\$5.50
Power Rollers	\$7.25

29. Sam bought 8 wheels for his in-line skates. Write and evaluate an expression that shows how much he spent if he bought Competition wheels.

30. **Analyze** Amy bought a set of 8 of the most expensive wheels and a set of 8 of the least expensive wheels. Write and evaluate an expression that compares the costs of the two sets.

31. **Logical Thinking** A number is twice the product of 10 and 3. Write an expression to show this number. Then evaluate the expression.

32. **Write About It** Study the two rectangles. What property can you use to show that there are the same number of squares in each rectangle? Explain.

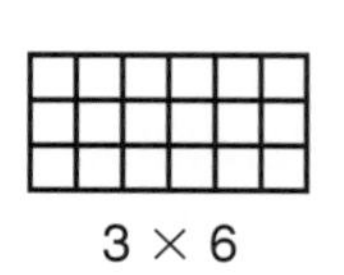

3×6

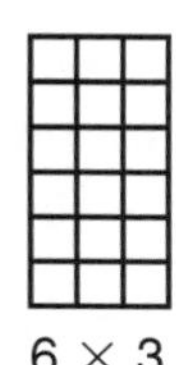

6×3

Mixed Review • Test Prep

Solve. *(pages 12–13, 18–19, 34–35, 136–137)*

33. $10{,}005 - 999$ **34.** 507×23 **35.** $3 \div 11$ **36.** $64.7 \div 0.5$

37 Which decimal is the same as $3\frac{4}{5}$? *(pages 134–135)*

A 3.45 **B** 4.35 **C** 3.80 **D** 3.25

LESSON 3 Order of Operations

You will learn how to complete operations in the correct order.

Learn About It

When evaluating expressions, it is important to complete all operations in the correct order.

Order of Operations

1. Always do operations in parentheses first.
2. Rewrite any exponents.
3. Multiply and divide from left to right.
4. Add and subtract from left to right.

Dennis, Susan, and Sid simplified the expression $3 + 8 \times 6 - 4$, but they each got a different result.

Which student applied the correct order of operations and got the correct result?

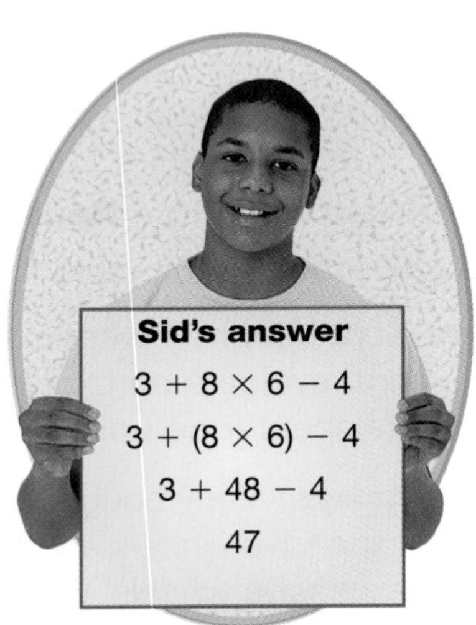

Solution: Sid solved the problem correctly. First he multiplied. Then he added and subtracted from left to right.

Other Examples

A. Two Operations in Parentheses

Simplify $4 + (6 + 12 \div 3)$.

$4 + (6 + 12 \div 3)$ ← Divide within parentheses.

$4 + (6 + 4)$ ← Add within parentheses.

$4 + 10$ ← Add.

14

B. Exponents and Parentheses

Simplify $(4 \times 3^2) \times 6 \div 2^2$.

$(4 \times 3^2) \times 6 \div 2^2$ ← Rewrite exponent in parentheses.

$(4 \times 9) \times 6 \div 2^2$ ← Multiply within parentheses.

$36 \times 6 \div 2^2$ ← Rewrite exponent.

$36 \times 6 \div 4$ ← Multiply.

$216 \div 4$ ← Divide.

54

Explain Your Thinking

- ▶ When evaluating expressions, why is it important to have rules for the order of operations?
- ▶ In expanded form, the number 540 is written $5 \times 100 + 4 \times 10$. How does the order of operations help you read this number?

Guided Practice

Simplify each expression. At each step, indicate what operation you performed.

1. $7 + 3 \times 6$
2. $6 - 3 \times 2 + 4$
3. $(10 - 6) \div 2$
4. $3^2 + (4 + 4^2) \div 2$
5. $(18 + 7) \times (11 - 7)$
6. $3^2 + (4 - 1)^2 \times 5$
7. $(4 \times 8) \div 16 + 8$
8. $2 + 3 \times 4 + 5 \times 6$

Ask Yourself

- Did I use the order of operations correctly?
- Did I indicate the operation I used at each step?

Simplify each expression, given $a = 2$, $b = 3$, and $c = 5$.

9. $36 - (a + b \times c)$
10. $a^2 + b^2 \times c^2$
11. $c - a \times 2 \div (b + 1)$
12. $60 \times a^2 \div 2 \times b \times c$
13. $(14 \times b) - c \times a$
14. $(b + 3)^2 \times 4 + c - a$

Independent Practice

Simplify each expression. At each step, indicate what operation you performed.

15. $7 + 20 \times 4$
16. $4 - (28 + 9)$
17. $92 \times (3 + 5)$
18. $17 \times 20 - (17 + 20)$
19. $7 \times (8 - 3)$
20. $4^2 \div 8 - 4$
21. $(1{,}000 \div 100) \div 10$
22. $1000 \div (100 \div 10)$
23. $(32 - 27)^2 \times 2$
24. $90 - 5 \times 5 \times 2$
25. $3 \times 8 + 5 \times 8$
26. $3 \times (2 + 8)^2 - 5 \times (4 - 3)$

Evaluate each expression, given $m = 1$, $s = 4$, and $t = 10$.

27. $t \div (s + m) \times t^2$
28. $t \times s - m \times t$
29. $23 + m \times s - t$
30. $m \times s \times t - s \times t$
31. $(s^2 - m \times t)^2 + 41$
32. $40 \times t - (s \div m + 11 \times 6)$

Evaluate each expression, given $n = 5$.

33. $4 + 5 \times 6 \div n$
34. $39 \times 8 - (n + 4)^2$
35. $(4 \times 12) + (n \div 5)$
36. $10 \div n + 7^2$
37. $15 \div (n \times 2 - 7) + 1$
38. $2 \times n - 3 + n \times 4$
39. $(30 \times n^2 + 20) \div 7$
40. $(5 \times 10) \times (2 \times n - 10)$
41. $(20 \div 2 \times n)^2 + 39$

Problem Solving • Reasoning

Use Data **Use the picture for Problems 42 and 43.**

42. When Jasmine went to the skateboard store, she bought 4 wheels, 2 helmets, and 2 decals. Write an expression that shows how much Jasmine spent. Evaluate your expression, using the correct order of operations.

43. How much would you need if you wanted to buy 1 board, 2 trucks, 4 wheels, and one kneepad?

44. **Logical Thinking** John is 26 years younger than his father. John's father is 6 years older than John's mother. Write an expression that shows how old John is. Evaluate your expression, given that John's mother is 33 years old.

45. **Write Your Own** Write an expression that contains parentheses, exponents, and at least two operations. Challenge a friend to evaluate the expression.

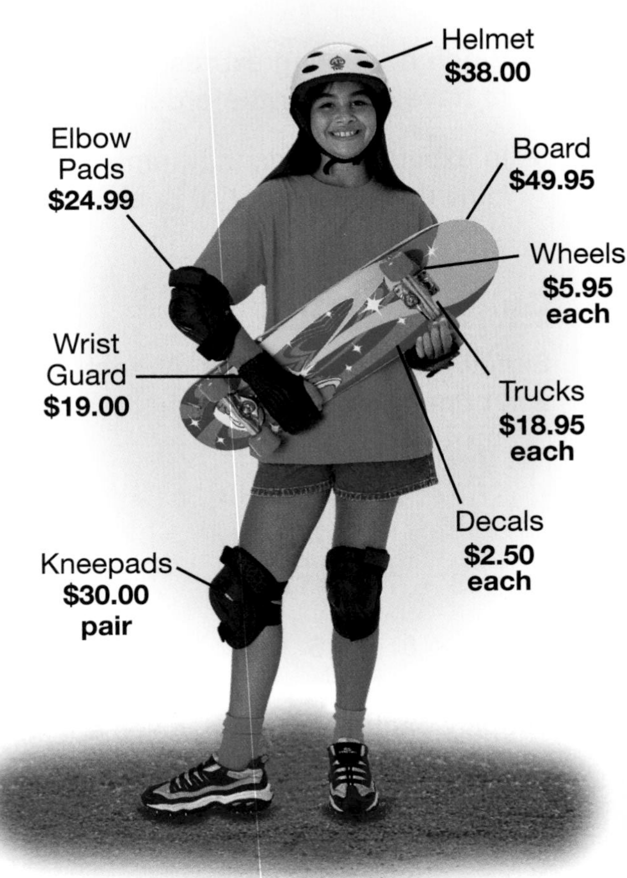

Mixed Review • Test Prep

Solve. *(pages 156–163, 178–179)*

46. $3\frac{1}{2} \div \frac{2}{3}$ **47.** $8\frac{2}{5} + 9\frac{4}{5}$ **48.** $1\frac{1}{3} + 2\frac{2}{5}$ **49.** $8 - 6\frac{1}{5}$

Choose the letter of the correct answers. *(pages 206–207)*

50 Which number is an integer?

A $^{-}5.3$ **C** $^{+}0.6$

B $\frac{5}{7}$ **D** $^{-}61$

51 Which integer is the opposite of $^{+}56$?

F $^{+}56$ **H** $^{-}56$

G $^{-}5.6$ **J** $^{+}65$

Logical Thinking

Eight Digits

Each letter in this puzzle represents a different digit. What digits do each of the letters represent? Hint: S = 5, N = 6.

```
  S E V E N
−   N I N E
  E I G H T
```


Extra Practice See Set C on page 290.

Show What You Know

Using Vocabulary

Use the property given to rewrite each expression. The new expression should have the same value as the one shown.

1. $10 + 3 \times 5$ Commutative Property of Multiplication

2. $9 \times (8.9 + 4.6)$ Commutative Property of Addition

3. $(10 \times 34) \times 2.6$ Associative Property of Multiplication

4. $4 \times (2 + 0)$ Identity Property of Addition

5. $9.8 + (14 \times 1) - 36$ Identity Property of Multiplication

6. $50 + (45 - 13 \times 0)$ Zero Property of Multiplication

Unwind It

Evaluate each expression, given $n = 15$. Use the correct order of operations.

1. $3 \times 5 + n$

2. $4 \times n + 5$

3. $4 \times (2 + n^2) + 3$

4. $n \div 3 \div 5$

5. $7 \times n + 68$

6. $n + 3 \times n$

Parentheses Plan

Put parentheses in each of the following to make the expressions equal.

1. $3 + 4 \times 6 = 42$

2. $2 + 3^2 = 25$

3. $4 \div 4 \times 4 \times 4 = 1$

4. $4 + 4 \div 4 + 4 = 1$

5. $4 + 4 \div 4 + 4 = 4.5$

6. $3 \times 8 + 6^2 - 8 \div 2 = 26$

LESSON 4

Use the Distributive Property to Evaluate Expressions

You will learn how to use the Distributive Property to evaluate expressions and solve problems mentally.

Learn About It

The Distributive Property gives you another way to evaluate a number multiplied by a sum or a difference.

Distributive Property

The product of a number a and a sum $(b + c)$ is equal to the sum of $a \times b$ and $a \times c$.

With a Sum

$3 \times (4 + 5) = 3 \times 4 + 3 \times 5$

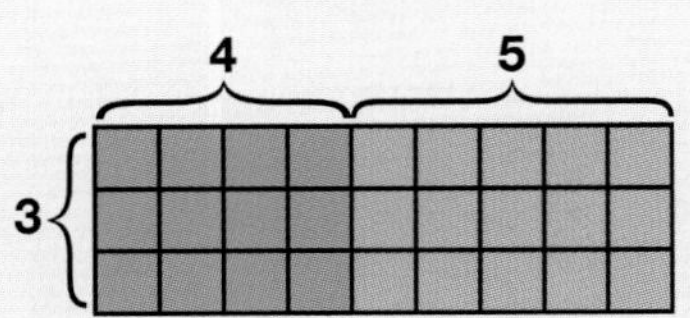

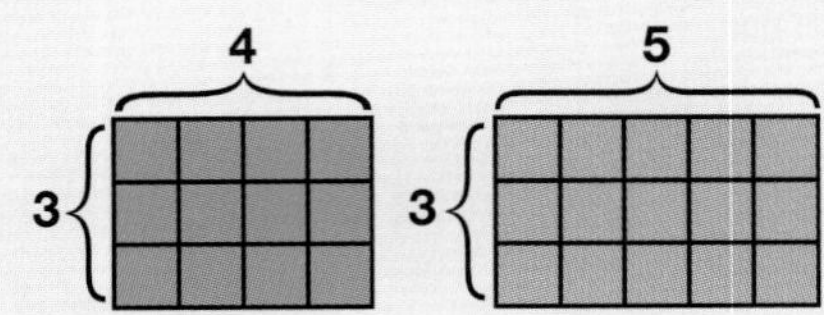

$3 \times (4 + 5) = 3 \times 9 = 27$

$3 \times 4 + 3 \times 5 = 12 + 15 = 27$

With a Difference

$3 \times (5 - 4) = 3 \times 5 - 3 \times 4$

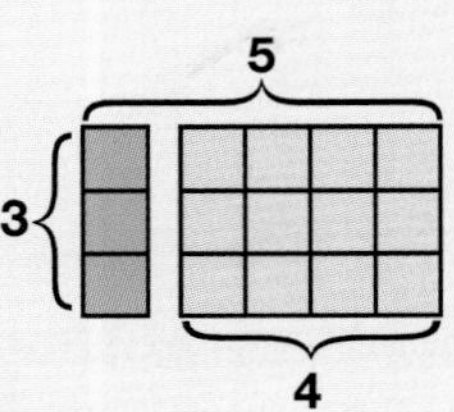

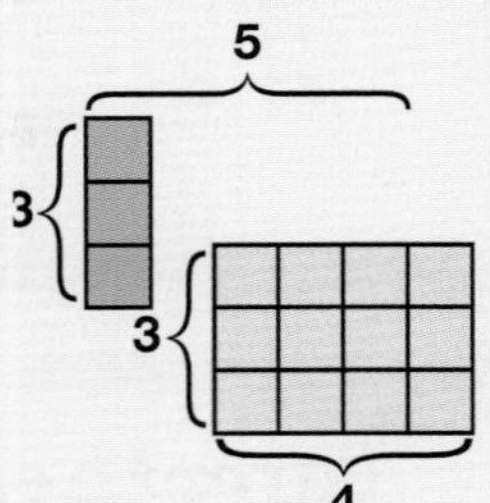

$3 \times (5 - 4) = 3 \times 1 = 3$

$3 \times 5 - 3 \times 4 = 15 - 12 = 3$

Another Example

Numbers as Sums

$$\begin{aligned} 4 \times 18 &= 4 \times (10 + 8) \\ &= 4 \times 10 + 4 \times 8 \\ &= 40 + 32 \\ &= 72 \end{aligned}$$

Explain Your Thinking

- ► How can you use the Distributive Property to help you solve problems mentally?
- ► In the example, why is it helpful to show 18 as the sum of 10 and 8?

Guided Practice

Rewrite each, using the Distributive Property. Then simplify. Use mental math whenever possible.

1. $5 \times (50 + 6)$ **2.** $4 \times (40 - 7)$

3. $(4 \times 37) + (6 \times 37)$ **4.** 124×70

5. $(12 \times 18) - (2 \times 18)$ **6.** $(2 \times 35) + (2 \times 35)$

Ask Yourself

- Did I use the Distributive Property to make mental math easier?

Independent Practice

Rewrite each, using the Distributive Property. Then simplify. Use mental math whenever possible.

7. $8 \times (2 + 15)$ **8.** $15 \times (80 + 60)$ **9.** 6×135 **10.** $4.5 \times (10 - 2)$

11. $4.2 \times (27 + 78)$ **12.** $1.52 \times (58 + 19)$ **13.** $6 \times (1.5 + 3.7)$ **14.** $(10 + 5) \times 43$

15. $(10 + 6) \times 1.5$ **16.** $25 \times (4 + 3)$ **17.** $3.1 \times 16 + 3.1 \times 79 + 3.1 \times 5$

Problem Solving • Reasoning

Use Data **Use the graph for Problems 19–21.**

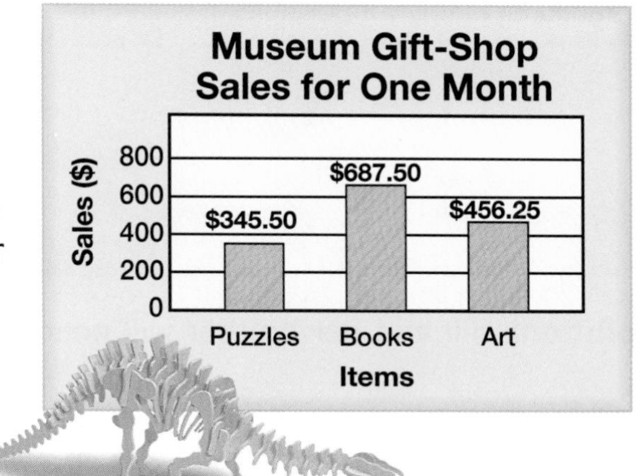

18. In a gift shop, puzzles sell for $14.95. On three days, there were 14, 21, and 13 puzzles sold. How much money did the gift shop make from selling puzzles on these three days? Write your answer as the product of a number and a sum and as the sum of products.

19. Predict The graph shows the sales of puzzles, books, and art in a typical month. Write an expression that shows the total sales likely in a 12-month period.

20. Analyze In addition to gift-shop sales, the museum makes $450 a month on concerts and $625 on special events. What is the total monthly revenue for these three types of income?

21. Estimate The gift-shop is adding a line of T-shirts that will sell for $14.95 each. How many T-shirts will the gift shop have to sell to increase monthly sales to at least $2,000?

Mixed Review • Test Prep

Complete. *(pages 38–39, 184–187)*

22. ____mL = 5.6 L **23.** $3\frac{1}{2}$ gal = ____qt **24.** 54 in. = ____yd **25.** ____lb = 56 oz

26 What is $(x + 25) - y$, if $x = 16.4$ and $y = 10.25$? *(pages 252–254)*

A 18.35 **B** 18.37 **C** 19.65 **D** 31.15

LESSON 5 Evaluate Expressions With Fractions

You will learn how to evaluate expressions containing fractions.

Learn About It

Jill and her brother volunteered to make cookies and muffins for a school hiking trip. They want to make $1\frac{1}{2}$ times the amount of each recipe. How much flour will they need?

Muffin Recipe
2 c flour
$\frac{1}{4}$ c sugar
$\frac{1}{4}$ c brown
Cookie Recipe
$1\frac{1}{4}$ c flour
$\frac{1}{4}$ c sugar
wn sugar

Evaluate. $\mathbf{1\frac{1}{4} \times 1\frac{1}{2} + 2 \times 1\frac{1}{2}}$

Find $1\frac{1}{4} \times 1\frac{1}{2} + 2 \times 1\frac{1}{2}$.

Step 1 Rewrite mixed numbers as improper fractions. Simplify if possible.

$$1\frac{1}{4} \times 1\frac{1}{2} + 2 \times 1\frac{1}{2}$$
$$\frac{5}{4} \times \frac{3}{2} + 2 \times \frac{3}{2}$$

Step 2 Evaluate, using the correct order of operations.

$$\frac{5}{4} \times \frac{3}{2} + 2 \times \frac{3}{2}$$
$$\frac{15}{8} + \frac{6}{2}$$

Step 3 Simplify the expression.

$$\frac{15}{8} + \frac{6}{2} = \frac{15}{8} + \frac{24}{8}$$
$$= \frac{39}{8}$$
$$= 4\frac{7}{8}$$

Solution: Jill and her brother will need $4\frac{7}{8}$ cups of flour.

Another Example

Use Properties

Evaluate $\frac{2}{3} \times a + \frac{1}{3} \times a$, when $a = \frac{4}{5}$.

$(\frac{2}{3} \times \frac{4}{5}) + (\frac{1}{3} \times \frac{4}{5})$ ⟵ Substitute $\frac{4}{5}$ for *a*.

$(\frac{2}{3} + \frac{1}{3}) \times \frac{4}{5}$ ⟵ Distributive Property

$1 \times \frac{4}{5}$

$\frac{4}{5}$ ⟵ Identity Property

Explain Your Thinking

► How could you have used the Distributive Property to solve the problem above? Show your work.

Guided Practice

Evaluate each expression, given $a = \frac{1}{2}$. Name the property you used.

1. $(\frac{3}{8} + a \div 6) \times 0$
2. $(a + {}^{-}a) + 2\frac{1}{2} \times 6$
3. $(a + a + a) + 0 + 8\frac{2}{3}$
4. $6\frac{2}{3} \times a + \frac{1}{3} \times a$

Ask Yourself

- Did I use properties to simplify expressions?
- Did I perform the operations in the correct order?

Independent Practice

Evaluate each expression, given $a = \frac{2}{3}$. Name the property you used.

5. $\frac{11}{12} + a + \frac{1}{12}$ **6.** $2\frac{4}{5} - (1 \times a)$ **7.** $a \times (2 + 18 + 10)$ **8.** $\frac{4}{7} \times a - \frac{2}{7} \times a$

9. $(\frac{7}{10} + \frac{4}{3}) + a$ **10.** $(a + \frac{4}{10}) + \frac{3}{5}$ **11.** $a \times \frac{19}{6} - a \times \frac{7}{6}$ **12.** $4\frac{2}{3} + (a + 2\frac{7}{8})$

13. $(\frac{7}{11} - \frac{7}{11}) \times \frac{2}{5}$ **14.** $(10 \times a) + (2 \times a)$ **15.** $\frac{1}{5} - \frac{1}{5} + \frac{5}{6} \times a$ **16.** $a \times (\frac{1}{9} + \frac{8}{9})$

17. $3 \times \frac{1}{4} \times a$ **18.** $a \times (2\frac{2}{3} - 2\frac{4}{6})$ **19.** $(a + \frac{3}{5}) + 3\frac{1}{5}$ **20.** $a \times (\frac{1}{2} \times \frac{1}{2}) \times a$

Problem Solving • Reasoning

21. The expression $1\frac{1}{2} + \frac{5}{6} + 1\frac{3}{8}$ describes the number of miles a hiker would have to walk from the parking area, around a lake, and back. Simplify the expression.

22. Alan wants to make 15 batches of cookies and 12 batches of biscuits. For each batch, cookies take $\frac{1}{2}$ cup of butter and biscuits take $\frac{1}{3}$ cup of butter. Write and evaluate an expression that shows how much butter Alan will need.

23. Estimate The hikers drove $6\frac{2}{5}$ miles from the school to the camp entrance. Then they drove half that distance from the entrance to their campsite. About how many miles did they drive from the school to the campsite?

24. Analyze Brian has a collection of 40 nature pictures. Two fifths of the pictures are of deer, one fourth are of birds, and the rest are of flowers. How many flower pictures does Brian have in his collection?

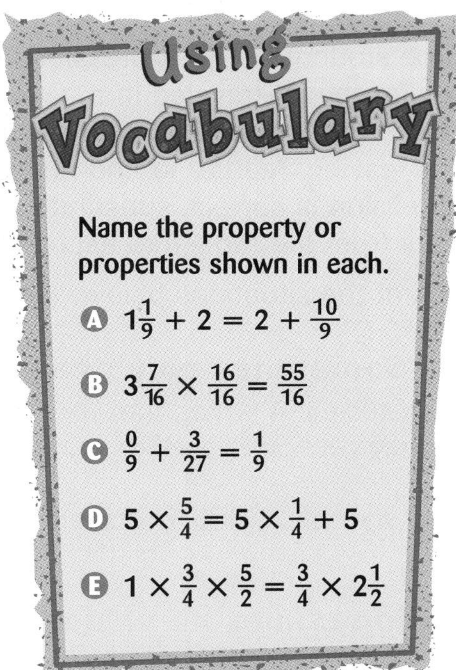

Name the property or properties shown in each.

A $1\frac{1}{9} + 2 = 2 + \frac{10}{9}$

B $3\frac{7}{16} \times \frac{16}{16} = \frac{55}{16}$

C $\frac{0}{9} + \frac{3}{27} = \frac{1}{9}$

D $5 \times \frac{5}{4} = 5 \times \frac{1}{4} + 5$

E $1 \times \frac{3}{4} \times \frac{5}{2} = \frac{3}{4} \times 2\frac{1}{2}$

Mixed Review • Test Prep

Simplify each expression. *(pages 258–260)*

25. $5 + 3 \times 4 + 6$ **26.** $(6 + 1)^2 - 6 \times 2$

27. $26 - 6 \times 3 + 2 \times 2$ **28.** $8 + 2 \times 4^2 - 6$

Choose the letter of the correct answer. *(pages 82–83)*

29 A stem-and-leaf plot contains the data 16, 18, 25, 28, 14, 17, 29. Which digit is a stem?

A 8 **B** 6 **C** 3 **D** 2

Extra Practice See Set E on page 291.

Problem-Solving Skill: Choose the Expression

You will learn how to choose the expression that correctly represents a given situation.

When trying to solve some kinds of problems, you need to decide what expression correctly represents the situation.

A jet traveled nonstop from Seattle to Detroit. The table shows how many miles the plane had traveled after each hour.

Three students write expressions to describe how far the jet traveled in a given number of hours, where h represents the number of hours after leaving Seattle. To find out which student's expression is correct, substitute the number of hours from the table into each expression.

Look at the situations below.

Miles Traveled From Seattle to Detroit

Time (hours)	1	2	3	4
Distance (miles)	485	970	1,455	1,940

Sometimes only one value is correct.

Student A writes the expression $h + 484$.

$1 + 484 = 485$
$2 + 484 = 486$
$3 + 484 = 487$
$4 + 484 = 488$

One value, 485, is correct.

Sometimes no values are correct.

Student B writes the expression $h \div 2 \times 485$.

$1 \div 2 \times 485 = 242.5$
$2 \div 2 \times 485 = 485$
$3 \div 2 \times 485 = 727.5$
$4 \div 2 \times 485 = 970$

All the values are incorrect.

Sometimes all the values are correct.

Student C writes the expression $h \times 485$.

$1 \times 485 = 485$
$2 \times 485 = 970$
$3 \times 485 = 1{,}455$
$4 \times 485 = 1{,}940$

All the values are correct. The expression $h \times 485$ is the correct expression.

Look Back When testing an expression, why is it important to try several numbers?

The *Gossamer Albatross* was the first human-powered aircraft to cross the English Channel.

Guided Practice

Choose the expression that correctly represents each situation.

1. As a jet leaves Seattle, it gains 745 feet in elevation every 10 minutes. Which expression represents the elevation of the jet after t minutes?

   a. $(\frac{t}{10}) \times 745$ **b.** $(t \times 10) \times 74.5$
   c. $t \times 745$ **d.** $745 + 10t$

    What happens to the elevation when t increases by 1 minute?

2. On one toll road, the cost for the first mile is $1.80. Each additional mile costs $0.30. Which expression describes the toll paid based on the number of miles (m) driven?

   a. $1.80 + m \times 0.30$ **b.** $1.80 \times m$
   c. $1.80\,m \times 0.30$ **d.** $1.80 + (m - 1) \times 0.30$

    Is the cost for every mile the same?

Choose a Strategy

Solve. Use these or other strategies.

Problem-Solving Strategies

- **Work Backward**
- **Write an Equation**
- **Solve a Simpler Problem**
- **Use Logical Thinking**

3. When Gary arrived at the airport, it was 10:25 A.M. He drove 69 miles to the airport at an average speed of 46 mi/h. What time did he leave his house?

4. Taxi fares include a flat-rate drop charge plus a mileage charge of $2.50 per mile. Write an expression that represents the total cost of any taxi ride.

5. The train from Seattle to Vancouver travels at 48 miles per hour. How far does the train travel in 30 minutes?

6. Bill traveled 380 miles in 7.5 hours. Gina traveled 980 miles in 18.25 hours. Who traveled faster?

7. The table shows how much Zach earned and how much he saved for each of five months. Choose the expression that represents the amount of money Zach saves from what he earns (e).

Amount Earned	$220	$450	$300	$630	$510
Amount Saved	$47	$70	$55	$88	$76

   a. $e - 183$ **b.** $e \div 6 + 1$ **c.** $e \div 10 + 25$ **d.** $5 \times e$

Extra Practice See 1–4 on page 293.

Quick Check

Check Your Understanding of Lessons 1–6

Evaluate. Tell what property or properties you used.

1. $(1\frac{1}{5} + 12) + \frac{3}{5}$

2. $\frac{7}{8} \times 1$

3. $c \times (10 + 8)$, given $c = 11$

4. $3 \times 6 \times 6 \times 0$

5. $b + 0$

6. $(12 \times n) \times r$, given $n = 3$, $r = \frac{1}{6}$

Evaluate each expression. At each step, indicate what operation you performed.

7. $(22 + 19) + 12 \div 3$

8. $(30 \times w) - (2\frac{1}{3} + w)$, given $w = 20$

9. $75 + 6 \times \frac{3}{4} \times 2$

10. $6 + g \times (g + 5)^2 \div 4$, given $g = 2$

Rewrite each, using the Distributive Property. Then simplify.

11. $(6 \times 10) + (10 \times 25) + (10 \times 25)$

12. $12 \times (4 + 0.5 + 2)$

13. $(9 \times 3) - (3 \times 5) - (3 \times 3)$

Solve.

14. Jason's family drives 45 mi/h while on vacation. What expression describes the number of miles Jason's family travels after h hours?

a. $45 \times h$ **b.** $45 + h$ **c.** $h - 45$ **d.** $h \div 45$

How did you do?

If you had difficulty with any items in the Quick Check, you can use the following pages for review and extra practice.

Items	Review These Pages	Do These Extra Practice Items
1–6	pages 252–254, 256–257, 264–265	Set A, page 290 Set B, page 290 Set E, page 291
7–10	pages 258–260	Set C, page 290
11–13	pages 262–263	Set D, page 291
14	pages 266–267	1–4, page 293

Test Prep • Cumulative Review

Maintaining the Standards

Choose the letter of the correct answer.

1 Which decimal is equivalent to $\frac{3}{8}$?

A 0.038
B 0.375
C 0.38
D 2.67

2 Which number is the reciprocal of $2\frac{3}{4}$?

F $\frac{6}{4}$
H $\frac{4}{3}$
G $\frac{4}{11}$
J $\frac{11}{4}$

3 Darin recorded the following temperatures: $^{-}1$, 3, $^{-}4$, $^{-}2$, and 4 degrees. What is the order of the temperatures from least to greatest?

A 4, 3, $^{-}1$, $^{-}2$, $^{-}4$
B $^{-}1$, $^{-}2$, $^{-}4$, 3, 4
C $^{-}4$, 3, $^{-}2$, $^{-}1$, 4
D $^{-}4$, $^{-}2$, $^{-}1$, 3, 4

4 When Marcie went rock climbing, she climbed up 11 feet and then slid back 4 feet. Then she slid back 2 feet more. At what height was Marcie after she slid back twice?

F 17 feet
G 13 feet
H 5 feet
J 2 feet

5 Which decimal is equivalent to $\frac{1}{9}$?

A 0.1
C $0.\overline{1}$
B 0.11
D 0.91

6 Layla bought 23 balloons for $0.37 each. How much did she spend on balloons?

F $62.16
G $22.63
H $8.51
J $8.50

7 Gary's new bedroom measures $9\frac{1}{2}$ feet × $10\frac{1}{4}$ feet. What is the area of the room?

A $97\frac{3}{8}$ feet
B $97\frac{3}{8}$ square feet
C 39.5 square feet
D 19.75 square feet

8 Luke wants to give a one-cup serving of orange juice to each of 4 guests. If 2 cups equals 16 fl oz, what is the least expensive way to buy the juice?

Fresh Juice	
8 oz	$1.28
12 oz	$1.80
16 oz	$2.24

Explain How did you find your answer?

Safe Site

Internet Test Prep
Visit **www.eduplace.com/kids/mhm** for more *Test Prep Practice.*

Write Addition and Subtraction Expressions

You will learn how to write mathematical expressions that include addition and subtraction.

Review Vocabulary
algebraic expression
variable

Learn About It

The theater club members rented a hall to present their play. They used money from ticket sales to cover the $125 per night rental fee. Write an **algebraic expression** that shows how much money the club had left of their ticket sales on any given night after paying the rent.

Step 1 Identify the variable.

The amount of money from ticket sales is unknown, so it is the variable.

Use t to represent ticket sales.

Step 2 Write the expression.

The amount of money from ticket sales minus the amount of rent:

$t - 125$

Solution: The expression $t - 125$ describes how much money the drama club had left each night after paying the rent.

Another Example

Expressions With Multiple Operations

87 more than a number n, decreased by the sum of 7 and $^-8$.

$(n + 87) - (7 + {}^-8)$

$(n + 87) - {}^-1$

$n + 88$

Explain Your Thinking

- Why is the term **variable** used to name the quantity that you don't know?
- What words or phrases in the example indicate addition? subtraction?

Guided Practice

Write an algebraic expression for each. Then evaluate, given $n = 5$.

1. a number n increased by 12
2. the sum of a number n and 36.5
3. 87 decreased by a number n
4. a number n decreased by 48
5. 36.78 more than a number n, decreased by 22.76

Ask Yourself

- Did I substitute the correct mathematical symbols for words and phrases?
- Did I substitute the correct quantity for the variable?

Independent Practice

Write an algebraic expression for each. Then evaluate, given $x = 8$ and $y = 16.55$.

6. x decreased by 1.5

7. 16 increased by y decreased by 38

8. x plus y decreased by 18

9. x increased by 48

10. 16 less than the sum of x and 34

11. x plus 43 decreased by 18

12. the sum of x and y and 10

13. the sum of x and y decreased by 48

n **Algebra • Equations** **Write each equation, using mathematical symbols. Then solve for p.**

14. The sum of p and 45 is 56.

15. A number p decreased by 65 is 10.

16. The sum of 15 and p is 54.

17. The sum of p and 8 minus 4 is 16.

Problem Solving • Reasoning

Use Data **Use the graph for Problems 19 and 20.**

18. On its opening night, *Our Town* had $385 in ticket sales. Write an expression that shows the club's profit after paying the rent (r) and receiving the concession money (c).

19. Tickets sold for $5 each for *Annie* and *Little Shop of Horrors*. How much more money did the theater club make on *Annie* than on *Little Shop of Horrors*?

20. **Compare** *Hamlet* ran for four nights and *Our Town* ran for six nights. Both plays sold the same number of tickets each night. If tickets for each play were $6.50, how much more money in ticket sales did the club make on *Hamlet* each night?

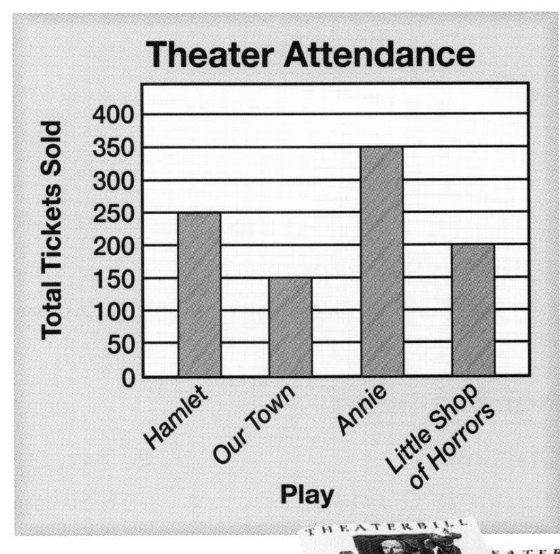

Mixed Review • Test Prep

Write the factors of each number. Then tell if it is prime or composite. *(pages 104–105)*

21. 16 **22.** 5 **23.** 27 **24.** 62 **25.** 72 **26.** 51

27 Which has the same value as 402,009? *(pages 10–11)*

A $4 \times 10^5 + 2 \times 10^3 + 9 \times 10^1$

B $4 \times 10^6 + 2 \times 10^4 + 9 \times 10^0$

C $4 \times 10^5 + 2 \times 10^3 + 9 \times 10^0$

D $4 \times 10^4 + 2 \times 10^3 + 9 \times 10^1$

Extra Practice See Set F on page 291.

Write Multiplication and Division Expressions

You will learn how to write mathematical expressions that include multiplication and division.

Learn About It

Mike and Josh want to cover their rectangular driveway with gravel. They need to purchase 2 cubic feet of gravel per square yard of driveway. Write an expression that shows how many cubic feet of gravel they need to purchase. Remember, to find the area of a rectangle, multiply the length (l) by the width (w).

Step 1 Use words to represent the situation.	**Step 2** Identify the variables.	**Step 3** Write a mathematical expression.
two times length times width	$l \leftarrow$ length in yards $w \leftarrow$ width in yards	$2 \times l \times w$ or $2 \cdot l \cdot w$ or $2lw$ Multiplication can be shown in these ways.

Solution: The expression $2 \times l \times w$ shows how many cubic feet of gravel Mike and Josh need to purchase.

Other Examples

A. Division
56 cards divided into *n* stacks

$56 \div n$

B. Two Operations
86 times the quantity 34 minus 8

$86 \times (34 - 8)$

Explain Your Thinking

- ► In Example *A*, what does the variable *n* represent?
- ► In Example *B*, what does the word *quantity* indicate?

Guided Practice

Write an algebraic expression for each phrase. Then evaluate, given $n = 0.5$.

1. the product of 3 and a number *n*
2. the product of a number *n* and the sum of 8 and 11
3. a number *n* divided by 2
4. the quantity 45 minus 22, times the quantity 86 times a number *n*
5. the quantity 123 minus 41, divided by the sum of 1.5 and some number *n*

Ask Yourself

- Did I substitute the correct quantity for the variable?
- Did I use the correct order of operations?

Independent Practice

Write an algebraic expression for each. Then evaluate, given $l = 10$ and $w = 12$.

6. a number w divided by 6
7. the sum of l and twice w
8. the length of a room l times the width of a room w, which is then multiplied by 48
9. the number 144 divided by the quantity w minus l
10. a number w times 4.65, which is then increased by 98
11. the quantity l plus w, times the product of l and w
12. the sum of 6 and 14.8, which is then divided by l
13. the quantity w times 3, minus the quantity l times 3
14. the product of l and w which is then divided by the quantity 23 minus 3
15. 21 times the quantity w decreased by 5, which is then increased by l

Problem Solving • Reasoning

16. Josh and Mike are purchasing an irrigation system to water three 10-foot rows and four 8-foot rows in a garden. Brand *A* costs $0.35 per foot. Write an expression that shows the cost of Brand *A*.
17. **Compare** Brand *B* irrigation system costs $0.38 per foot. Write an expression that shows how much more Josh and Mike would spend on Brand *B* than on Brand *A*.
18. **Analyze** Lily bulbs are planted two per foot and produce $5 worth of flowers per bulb. Tulip bulbs are planted eight per foot and produce $3 worth of flowers per bulb. If you pay the same price for each type of bulb, which bulb is more profitable?
19. **Write Your Own** Describe in words a mathematical situation that involves multiplication and division. Then write and evaluate an expression that represents the situation.

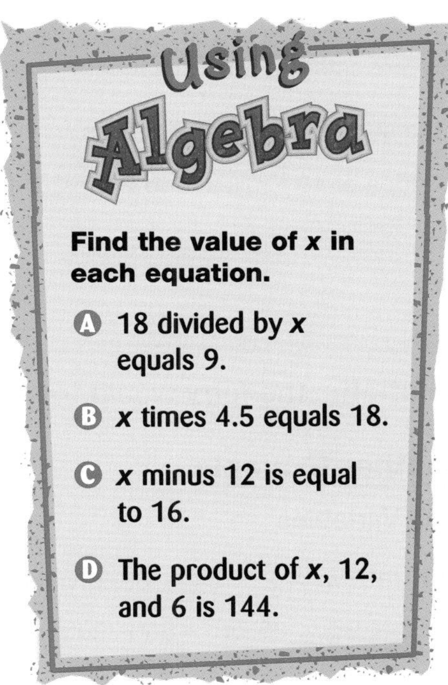

Find the value of x in each equation.

A 18 divided by x equals 9.

B x times 4.5 equals 18.

C x minus 12 is equal to 16.

D The product of x, 12, and 6 is 144.

Mixed Review • Test Prep

Write three equivalent fractions for each. *(pages 122–123)*

20. $\frac{1}{3}$ 21. $\frac{2}{5}$ 22. $\frac{25}{30}$ 23. $\frac{12}{16}$ 24. $\frac{5}{8}$ 25. $\frac{10}{20}$

26. Which group shows numbers ordered from least to greatest? *(pages 126–128)*

A $\frac{2}{3}$ $\frac{1}{3}$ $\frac{6}{10}$ $\frac{7}{8}$

B $\frac{7}{8}$ $\frac{2}{3}$ $\frac{6}{10}$ $\frac{1}{3}$

C $\frac{7}{8}$ $\frac{6}{10}$ $\frac{1}{3}$ $\frac{2}{3}$

D $\frac{1}{3}$ $\frac{6}{10}$ $\frac{2}{3}$ $\frac{7}{8}$

Extra Practice See Set G on page 291.

Write Expressions With Fractions

You will learn how to write mathematical expressions with fractions.

Learn About It

Safe Shuttle Ferry Service carries passengers to towns located on small islands along the coast. The ferry map is posted by the dock.

Write and evaluate an expression that describes the total distance a ferry would travel if it made one round trip to each island every day.

Step 1 Write a word expression that represents the total distance.

the sum of 2 trips of $9\frac{3}{5}$ miles,

2 trips of $19\frac{1}{4}$ miles, and 2 trips of $12\frac{1}{2}$ miles

Step 2 Convert the word expression to a mathematical expression. Then evaluate.

$$2 \times 9\frac{3}{5} + 2 \times 19\frac{1}{4} + 2 \times 12\frac{1}{2}$$

$$2 \times (9\frac{3}{5} + 19\frac{1}{4} + 12\frac{1}{2})$$

$$2 \times (9\frac{12}{20} + 19\frac{5}{20} + 12\frac{10}{20})$$

$$2 \times 40\frac{27}{20} = 2 \times 41\frac{7}{20} = 82\frac{7}{10}$$

Solution: The ferry would travel $82\frac{7}{10}$ miles every day.

Another Example

With Variables

Evaluate $m \times 2 \times 9\frac{3}{5} \times 85$, given $m = 4$.

$4 \times 2 \times 9\frac{3}{5} \times 85$ ⟵ Substitute.

$(4 \times 2 \times 85) \times 9\frac{3}{5}$ ⟵ Commutative and Associative properties

$680 \times 9\frac{3}{5}$

$680 \times \frac{48}{5} = 6{,}528$ ⟵ Rewrite $9\frac{3}{5}$ as an improper fraction.

Explain Your Thinking

- ► Why might it be helpful to write a word expression before a mathematical one?
- ► How does using variables help you to solve more than one particular problem?

Guided Practice

Rewrite each word expression as an algebraic expression. Then evaluate, given $n = 1\frac{1}{2}$.

1. the quantity $3\frac{1}{2}$ plus n, times $\frac{4}{5}$

2. $\frac{3}{8}$ less than n, times $\frac{4}{5}$

3. $4\frac{1}{2}$ per hour for n hours, plus $12\frac{1}{2}$

4. n divided by $2\frac{1}{4}$

Ask Yourself

- Did I rewrite mixed numbers as improper fractions?
- Did I use the correct order of operations to simplify expressions?

Independent Practice

Rewrite each word expression as an algebraic expression. Use *n* as a variable where needed. Then evaluate, given $n = \frac{2}{3}$.

5. $1\frac{1}{2}$ times a number, plus $20\frac{4}{5}$
6. $7\frac{3}{8}$ doubled plus a number
7. $5\frac{1}{2}$ times a number divided by 22
8. $\frac{1}{2}$ times $\frac{1}{2}$ times $\frac{1}{2}$ of a number
9. a number divided by $\frac{2}{5}$, plus that number
10. the quantity $4\frac{1}{2}$ plus $3\frac{1}{6}$ divided by a number
11. a number is tripled and then the product is increased by 13
12. $\frac{3}{4}$ divided by the sum of a number and $\frac{7}{8}$

Algebra • Properties **Rewrite each word expression as an algebraic expression. Simplify if possible. State what property you used to simplify.**

13. the sum of the product of $3\frac{1}{2}$ and n and the product of $6\frac{1}{2}$ and n
14. 5 minus the sum of $\frac{1}{2}n$, $\frac{1}{4}n$, and $\frac{3}{8}n$

Problem Solving • Reasoning

Solve. Use the map on page 274 for Problems 15 and 16.

15. The ferry's operating costs are $31.00 per mile. Write an expression for the cost of n round trips from Monroe to Lincoln. Then evaluate the expression, given $n = 6$.
16. **Analyze** A one-way ferry ticket for the Monroe-Lincoln route costs $8.50. There is no round-trip discount. Write an expression that shows how much Safe Shuttle makes if n passengers make one round trip.

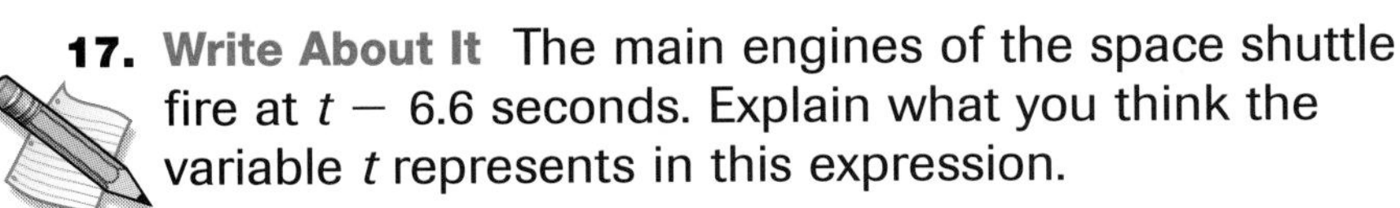

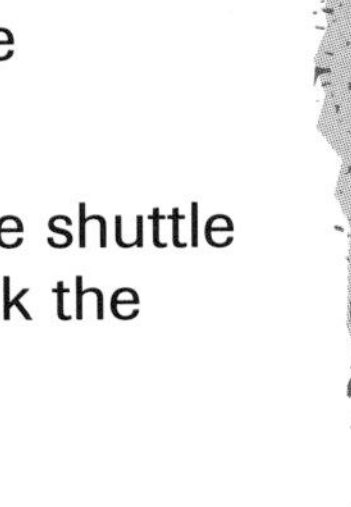

17. **Write About It** The main engines of the space shuttle fire at $t - 6.6$ seconds. Explain what you think the variable t represents in this expression.

Math Is Everywhere!

SOCIAL STUDIES
People once used knots tied in a rope to find a ship's speed. The rope was attached to a log, which was thrown into the water behind the ship. As the ship moved away, the pilot counted the knots that passed in a certain amount of time. The number counted was the ship's speed. Today, a ship traveling at 20 knots is going about 23 mi/h. How could you convert mi/h to knots?

Mixed Review • Test Prep

Solve. *(pages 158–163, 178–179, 222–225)*

18. $^-5 \times 7$
19. $\frac{1}{2} + 2\frac{5}{8}$
20. $16 - 10\frac{5}{6}$
21. $^+25 \div {}^-5$
22. $\frac{2}{3} \div 2\frac{1}{2}$
23. $10 \times {}^-40$

24. Which is equal to 36 pints? *(pages 186–187)*

A $6\frac{1}{2}$ gal **B** $4\frac{1}{2}$ gal **C** 6 gal **D** 4 gal

Problem-Solving Strategy: Write an Expression

You will learn how to write expressions to help you solve problems.

Problem Glenda had two part-time jobs last summer. In June she worked at Fran's Fast Food and earned $6 per hour. In July she did yard work for $5 per hour plus a fee of $10 for each yard. If Glenda worked a total of 60 hours at each job and worked on 15 yards, how much did she earn at each job that summer?

Understand

What is the question?
How much did Glenda earn at each of her part-time jobs?

What do you know?
- At Fran's Fast Food, she earned $6 per hour.
- Doing yard work, she earned $5 per hour plus a fee of $10 for each yard.
- She worked 60 hours at each job and worked on 15 yards.

Plan

How can you find the answer?
Write expressions to show how much Glenda earned at each job, where n is the number of hours worked, and y is the number of yards she worked on. Then evaluate each expression.

Solve

Fran's Fast Food: $6n$ — When $n = 60$, $6n = 6 \times 60 = 360$.

Yard work: $5n + 10y$ — When $y = 15$, $n = 60$, $10y + 5n = 10 \times 15 + 5 \times 60 = 450$.

During the summer, Glenda earned $360 at Fran's Fast Food and $450 doing yard work.

Look Back

Look back at the problem.
Do the amounts earned seem reasonable, based on the rate of pay for each job?

Remember:
- ▶ Understand
- ▶ Plan
- ▶ Solve
- ▶ Look Back

Guided Practice

Write an expression and then evaluate.

1. A cross-country trainer gets paid $25 for each practice. She also receives $50 for each meet. If the cross-country team has 4 practices and one meet each week, how much will she earn in 4 weeks?

   Think: What variables will I use in the expression?

2. Cal cleans houses for a fee of $15 plus $8 per hour. Write an algebraic expression that shows how much Cal earns per job. Then evaluate, given that he works 2.5 hours on one job.

   Think: How many variables will there be in this expression?

Choose a Strategy

Solve. Use these or other strategies.

- Use Logical Thinking
- Write an Expression
- Work Backward
- Make a List

3. Raymond earns $3.25 per hour plus $1.25 for each pizza he delivers. Write an algebraic expression that shows how much Raymond earns. Then evaluate the expression, given that Raymond works 4 hours and delivers 16 pizzas.

4. Bob earns $8 per hour. Karen earns $10 plus $6 per hour. Susan earns $20 plus $4 per hour. Kevin earns $25 plus $2 per hour. If each person works 7 hours, who will earn the most? Who will earn the least?

5. Sarah, Bethany, Lucas, and Michael are the new sixth-grade class officers. They are to sit on four chairs in a row and have a group picture taken. In how many different ways can the four officers sit in the four chairs?

6. A mechanic charges $25 per hour plus the cost of parts. Write an algebraic expression for that situation. Then evaluate the expression, given that the mechanic works 3 hours and the cost of parts is $52.

7. Patricia earns $7.50 per hour at her job. Write an algebraic expression that shows how much Patricia earns. Then evaluate the expression, given that Patricia works 22 hours in one week.

8. Paul gave one friend half of the apples he had, plus one more. He gave a second friend half of what was left, plus one more. He gave a third friend his last apple. How many did Paul start with?

Extra Practice See 5–6 on page 293.

Quick Check

Check Your Understanding of Lessons 7–10

Write an algebraic expression for each. Then evaluate, given $k = 3$ and $m = 7.75$.

1. the sum of *k* and *m* increased by 9
2. the quantity *m* plus 4, decreased by *k*
3. 26 decreased by *m*, plus 2.5
4. 8 plus the product of 12 and 3
5. 35 minus *m*, divided by 2
6. the quantity 3 times *m*, minus *k*
7. $\frac{1}{2}$ plus $\frac{1}{3}$ divided by $\frac{1}{4}$
8. the sum of $14\frac{1}{2}$ and *k*, times $\frac{2}{5}$
9. $4\frac{1}{8}$ times *k* plus $12\frac{1}{6}$
10. 2 times *m* doubled plus $\frac{5}{8}$

Solve.

11. On Saturday the cinema sold 58 tickets for the matinee at $4.00 per ticket and 126 tickets in the evening at $6.50 per ticket. Write and evaluate an expression that represents the total amount of money the cinema made on Saturday.
12. Claire solves 40 math problems in 30 minutes. She spends an equal amount of time on each problem. Write and evaluate an expression that represents how long it takes Claire to solve each problem.

How did you do?

If you had difficulty with any items in the Quick Check, you can use the following pages for review and extra practice.

Items	Review These Pages	Do These Extra Practice Items
1–3	pages 270–271	Set F, page 291
4–6	pages 272–273	Set G, page 291
7–10	pages 274–275	Set H, page 292
11 and 12	pages 276–277	5–6, page 293

Test Prep • Cumulative Review

Maintaining the Standards

Choose the letter of the correct answer.

1 Wind and rain are eroding the soil on a riverbank. Three inches of soil are eroded every year for 6 years. Which problem represents the expression

$^-3 + {}^-3 + {}^-3 + {}^-3 + {}^-3 + {}^-3$?

A $^-3 \times {}^-3$

B $^-3 \times {}^-6$

C $^-3 \times 6$

D $^-6 \times 3$

2 There are 8 pints in a gallon, and there are 4 cups in 2 pints. Which expression shows how to find the number of cups in a gallon?

F $8 \div 4 \times 2$

G $8 \div 2 \times 4$

H 4×2

J $4 + 2$

3 Find the quotient $977{,}000 \div 1{,}000$.

A 997,700

B 97,700

C 9,770

D 977

4 William withdrew $18 from his savings account every month for a year. Which product shows the amount of money William withdrew?

F $18 \times {}^-18$

G $18 \times \frac{1}{12}$

H 18×12

J 18×1

5 Ricardo's rain gauge showed $2\frac{1}{2}$ inches of rain on Thursday and $\frac{35}{100}$ inch of rain on Friday. How much more rain fell on Thursday?

A $\frac{7}{8}$ inch

B $2\frac{10}{100}$ inches

C $2\frac{3}{20}$ inches

D $2\frac{17}{20}$ inches

6 LeAnn traveled 1,176 miles on her first vacation. On her second vacation she traveled 1,225 miles. How many more miles did LeAnn travel on her second vacation?

F 49 miles

G 50 miles

H 51 miles

J 2,401 miles

7 Find the difference: $3\frac{5}{7} - \frac{1}{5}$.

A $3\frac{18}{35}$

B $3\frac{17}{35}$

C $3\frac{16}{35}$

D $3\frac{15}{35}$

8 Mary's brother recorded her basketball scores for 14 games. Which number represents the mode of the data?

Mary's Scores						
5	7	22	22	23	24	24
25	25	26	26	26	27	29

Explain Tell how you found your answer.

Safe Site

Internet Test Prep
Visit **www.eduplace.com/kids/mhm** for more *Test Prep Practice.*

Equations With Addition and Subtraction

You will learn how to use addition and subtraction to solve equations.

New Vocabulary
inverse operations

Learn About It

To solve some equations, you need to use inverse operations. **Inverse operations** are two operations that have opposite effects. Addition and subtraction are inverse operations.

To train for a bicycle trip, Emma rides every day. At the end of each week, she records the odometer reading in her riding journal. On Monday morning, Emma's odometer read 456 miles. On Sunday evening, it read 534 miles. To find out how far she rode that week, Emma wrote this equation.

$$456 + n = 534$$

How many miles did Emma ride that week?

To solve this equation, use inverse operations to get the variable, n, by itself on one side of the equals sign. This is called "isolating the variable."

Solve $456 + n = 534$.

Step 1 Use inverse operations to isolate the variable. Since n is added to a number, use subtraction.

$$n + 456 = 534$$
$$n + 456 - 456$$

inverse operations

Step 2 Perform the same operation on both sides of the equals sign.

$$n + 456 - 456 = 534 - 456$$

Isolate the variable. ⟶ $n = 534 - 456$

$$n = 78$$

Check your work.

$$456 + n = 534$$
$$456 + 78 = 534$$
$$534 = 534$$

So $n = 78$ is correct.

Solution: Emma rode 78 miles that week.

Another Example

Two Operations

$45.85 = z + 56.75 - 38.15$

$45.85 = z + 18.60$

$45.85 - 18.60 = z + 18.60 - 18.60$

$45.85 - 18.60 = z$ ⟵ Isolate the variable.

$27.25 = z$

Explain Your Thinking

- When you use inverse operations to solve an equation, why must you complete the same operation on both sides of the equals sign?
- Why is it helpful to isolate the variable when solving an equation?

Guided Practice

Solve. State the inverse operation you used.

1. $4.56 + c = 184.72$ **2.** $a + 5 - 4 = 23$

3. $8 + n = 18$ **4.** $m + 6 + 12 = 38$

Ask Yourself

- Did I use inverse operations to isolate the variable?

Independent Practice

Solve. State the inverse operation you used.

5. $y + 5 = 14$ **6.** $a - 8 = 12$ **7.** $s + 98 - 27 = 138$

8. $c + 45.6 - 38.25 = 112.76$ **9.** $12 + d = 45$ **10.** $3 + f - 17 = 43$

11. $q + 45 = 98 + 36 \times 2$ **12.** $19 + g + 45 = 118$ **13.** $56 + e = 19 - 67$

14. $t + 23 - 36 + 23 = 59$ **15.** $j + 38 = 4 + 5 \times 3$ **16.** $35 - 56 = 47 + h$

17. $12 + 28 \div 4 = p - 3$ **18.** $2 \times 3 \div 4 = 5 + s$ **19.** $2 + x = 2 \times 2 - 2 \div 2$

Problem Solving • Reasoning

Solve. Choose a method.

Computation Methods

- Mental Math
- Estimation
- Paper and Pencil
- Calculator

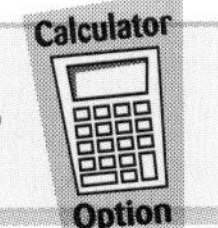

20. This year, Ashton is going to ride in a 55-mile bike race. The greatest number of miles she has ridden in one day is 22 miles. How many more miles must she be able to ride to complete the race in one day?

21. A local bicycle shop sponsors a fundraising bicycle ride. George was able to get a total of $9 in pledges for every mile he rides. If he rides the entire 65-mile course, how much money will he raise?

22. **Logical Thinking** Annie has decided to make the 55-mile bike trip in 2 days. If Annie can ride 18 miles per day now, how many more miles will she need to be able to ride in one day to cover half the trip each day?

23. **Analyze** Ian completed a 6-day bicycle trip. He averaged 43 miles each day. On the first 5 days he rode 40 miles, 46 miles, 42 miles, 42 miles, and 44 miles. How many miles did he ride on the sixth day?

Mixed Review • Test Prep

Evaluate. *(pages 36–37)*

24. 24×10^2 **25.** 5.52×10^6 **26.** $1,258 \div 10^3$ **27.** $40.02 \div 10^6$

28 What is 2,432.651 rounded to the nearest hundredth? *(pages 8–9)*

A 2,400 **B** 2,433 **C** 2,432.66 **D** 2,432.65

Extra Practice See Set I on page 292.

Equations With Multiplication and Division

You will learn how to use multiplication and division to solve equations.

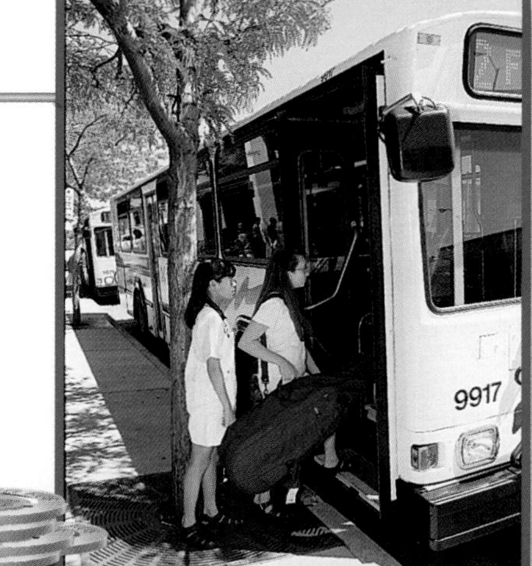

Learn About It

Winona pays \$38.50 a month for bus fare to and from her music lessons. If each bus ride costs \$1.75, how many bus rides does she take each month? To answer this question, use the following equation.

$1.75 \times n = 38.50$

You can use inverse operations to solve this equation.

METRO BUS 1.75 TOKEN

Solve $1.75 \times n = 38.50$.

Step 1 Use inverse operations to isolate the variable. Since n is being multiplied by a number, use division.

$$n \times 1.75 = 38.50$$

$$n \times 1.75 \div 1.75$$

Step 2 Perform the same operation on both sides of the equals sign.

$$n \times 1.75 \div 1.75 = 38.50 \div 1.75$$

$$n = 38.50 \div 1.75$$

$$n = 22$$

Check your work.

$1.75 \times n = 38.50$
$1.75 \times 22 = 38.50$
$38.50 = 38.50$
So $n = 22$ is correct.

Solution: Winona takes 22 bus rides each month.

Another Example

Use Multiplication to Solve

$\frac{a}{8} = 12$

$\frac{a}{8} \times 8 = 12 \times 8$ ← Multiply both sides by 8.

$a = 12 \times 8$ ← Isolate the variable.

$a = 96$

Check: $\frac{a}{8} = 12$

$\frac{96}{8} = 12$

$12 = 12$

So $a = 96$ is correct.

Explain Your Thinking

► How can you easily check your work when solving equations?

Guided Practice

Solve. State the inverse operation you used.

1. $4.5 \times c = 18$

2. $a \times 4 = 24$

3. $n \div 7 = 8$

4. $m \div 12 = 30$

Ask Yourself

- Did I perform the same operation on both sides of the equals sign?

Independent Practice

Solve. State the inverse operation you used.

5. $d \div 9 = 2$ **6.** $c \div 3 = 9$ **7.** $2 \times e = 14$ **8.** $f \div 5 = 3$

9. $y \times 8 = 64$ **10.** $j \div 7 = 49$ **11.** $k \times 4 = 36$ **12.** $m \div 45 = 3$

13. $120 \times u = 240$ **14.** $m \div 12 = 36$ **15.** $p \times 18 = 18$ **16.** $t \div 15 = 10$

Algebra • Functions **Write an equation to show how the input (*m*) is changed to the output (*n*).**

17.

Input (*m*)	Output (*n*)
12	24
1	2
51	102
12.6	25.2

18.

Input (*m*)	Output (*n*)
120	30
100	25
60	15
16	4

19.

Input (*m*)	Output (*n*)
60	30
55	25
50	20
40	10

Problem Solving • Reasoning

Use Data **Use the advertisement for Problems 21–23.**

20. Mr. Cruz pays Jill \$4.50 to shovel his driveway when it snows. How many times would Jill have to shovel his driveway to earn \$90?

21. Mike bought a season pass and paid a total of \$180 to ski. How many days did he ski?

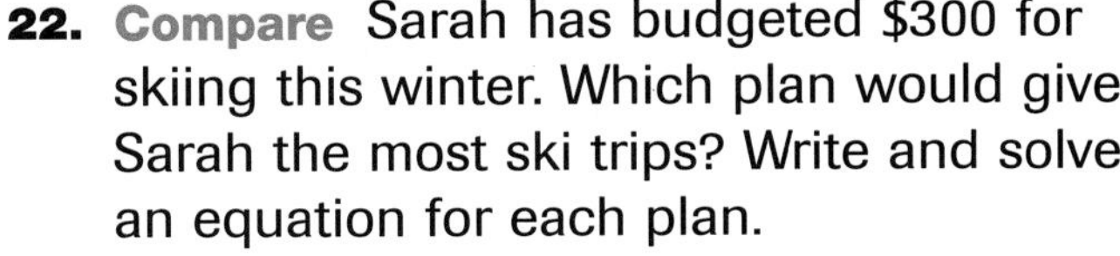

22. **Compare** Sarah has budgeted \$300 for skiing this winter. Which plan would give Sarah the most ski trips? Write and solve an equation for each plan.

23. **Analyze** How many days would a person need to ski to make the value of Plan 1 equal to the value of Plan 2?

Mixed Review • Test Prep

Write the fraction in simplest form that is equivalent to each decimal. *(pages 134–135)*

24. 0.244 **25.** 12.56 **26.** 0.05 **27.** 0.007 **28.** 25.204

29 Which is the reciprocal of $\frac{10}{20}$? *(pages 172–173)*

A $\frac{20}{10}$ **B** $\frac{1}{2}$ **C** $2\frac{1}{2}$ **D** $\frac{4}{3}$

LESSON 13

Equations With Fractions

You will learn how to use inverse operations to solve equations with fractions.

Review Vocabulary
reciprocal

Learn About It

Cheryl's Saint Bernard had puppies. The vet told her that the puppies will gain about $1\frac{1}{2}$ pounds each week. Cheryl wants to know how many weeks it will be before the puppies gain 20 pounds. She wrote the equation $n \times 1\frac{1}{2} = 20$, where n represents the number of weeks.

Solve $n \times 1\frac{1}{2} = 20$.

Step 1 Rewrite $1\frac{1}{2}$ as an improper fraction.

$$n \times 1\frac{1}{2} = 20$$
$$n \times \frac{3}{2} = 20$$

Step 2 Multiply both sides of the equation by the **reciprocal** of $\frac{3}{2}$, which is $\frac{2}{3}$.

$$n \times \frac{3}{2} \times \frac{2}{3} = 20 \times \frac{2}{3}$$
$$n \times 1 = \frac{40}{3}$$

Step 3 Simplify.

$$n = 13\frac{1}{3}$$

Check your work.

$$20 = 13\frac{1}{3} \times 1\frac{1}{2}$$
$$20 = \frac{40}{3} \times \frac{3}{2}$$
$$20 = \frac{120}{6}$$
$$20 = 20$$

Solution: It will be $13\frac{1}{3}$ weeks before the puppies gain 20 pounds.

Another Example

Use Addition

$$8\frac{1}{5} = x - 4\frac{1}{2}$$

$\frac{41}{5} = x - \frac{9}{2}$ ⟵ Use improper fractions.

$\frac{41}{5} + \frac{9}{2} = x - \frac{9}{2} + \frac{9}{2}$ ⟵ Use the inverse operation.

$\frac{82}{10} + \frac{45}{10} = x$ ⟵ Isolate the variable.

$$\frac{127}{10} = x$$

$$12\frac{7}{10} = x$$

Explain Your Thinking

- ► How was an inverse operation used to solve the equation in the problem above?
- ► What property of multiplication was used to isolate the variable in the problem above? Explain.

Guided Practice

Solve. Simplify first. State the inverse operation you used.

1. $x \div \frac{1}{3} = 1\frac{1}{4}$

2. $s - \frac{5}{6} = 10\frac{1}{3}$

3. $q + 4\frac{1}{3} - \frac{1}{8} = 6\frac{7}{8}$

4. $\frac{1}{2} \times v = 3\frac{1}{2}$

> **Ask Yourself**
> - Did I rewrite mixed numbers as improper fractions?
> - Did I state the inverse operation used?

Independent Practice

Solve. Simplify first. State the inverse operation you used.

5. $18 \times d = \frac{2}{3}$

6. $\frac{2}{3} \times e = 14$

7. $\frac{y}{12} = \frac{1}{2}$

8. $v + \frac{3}{7} \times 3 = 2\frac{1}{7}$

9. $y \times 7 = 5\frac{1}{4}$

10. $j + \frac{5}{7} = 25$

11. $k \times \frac{4}{5} = 20$

12. $\frac{3}{4} \div 9 \times m = 3\frac{1}{2}$

13. $m \div \frac{3}{8} = \frac{1}{2}$

14. $t - 4 \div 6 = 1\frac{1}{3}$

15. $3 + \frac{1}{5} + n = 23$

16. $c \div (1\frac{1}{4} + 1) = 5\frac{1}{2}$

Problem Solving • Reasoning

Use Data **Use the table for Problems 17 and 18.**

17. Before the puppies were born, Cheryl checked on what the expenses would be. What will Cheryl's expenses be if her dog has 6 puppies?

18. If the puppies are healthy at 8 weeks old, Cheryl will sell them for \$550 each. If her dog gives birth to 6 puppies, and Cheryl sells all of them, how much money will she receive?

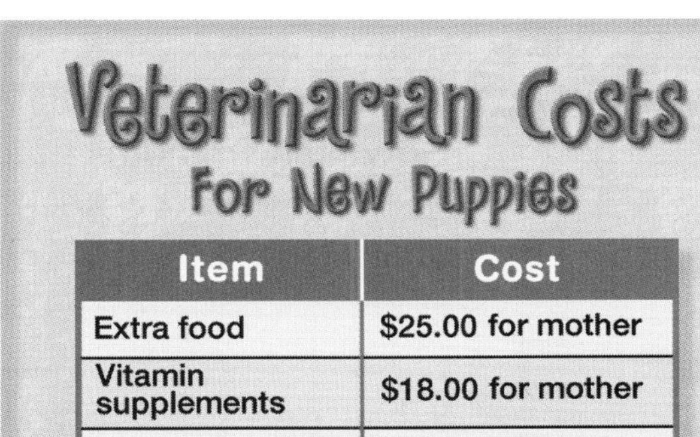

Veterinarian Costs For New Puppies

Item	Cost
Extra food	\$25.00 for mother
Vitamin supplements	\$18.00 for mother
Veterinary exams	\$75.00 for mother
Puppy shots	\$16.00 per puppy
Puppy exams	\$20.00 per puppy
Puppy collars	\$3.00 per puppy

19. The vet told Cheryl that her 120-lb dog would gain about $2\frac{1}{2}$ pounds per week before she has her puppies. Write an expression that shows about how much her dog will weigh at any given week *n*.

20. After the puppies are born, Cheryl's dog will eat $3\frac{1}{2}$ pounds of food each day. Cheryl has 60 pounds of dog food. At this rate, about how many days will 60 pounds of dog food last?

Mixed Review • Test Prep

Solve. Tell the properties you used. *(pages 232–233)*

21. ${}^+\frac{1}{2} + 0 = x$

22. ${}^-0.56 + {}^-16.2 = {}^-16.2 + x$

23. $({}^-0.05 \times {}^-\frac{1}{3}) \times {}^+\frac{5}{6} = {}^-0.05 \times (n \times {}^+\frac{5}{6})$

24 What is $3^2 + 5 \times 3 - 10$? *(pages 258–260)*

A 32 **B** 18 **C** 14 **D** 8

Extra Practice See Set K on page 292.

Problem-Solving Application: Use an Equation

You will learn how to use equations to solve problems.

Sometimes you need to use equations to help you solve problems.

Problem A phone company offers two long-distance plans. For each plan you pay a monthly service charge and a reduced per-minute rate during the days and hours the plan is in effect.

Bill's parents subscribe to Plan *A*. They make all their calls during the effective hours. How many minutes of long-distance calls can they make each month and still keep their charges less than $20?

Telephone Calling Plans

	Plan A Weekdays	Plan B Weekends
Effective Hours	7 AM - 9 PM	7 AM Sat. to 7 AM Mon.
Monthly Service Charge	$4.95	$6.95
Plan Rate	$0.10 / min	$0.07 / min
Off-Hours Rate	$0.15 / min	$0.15 / min

Understand

What is the question?
How many minutes of long-distance calls will keep their charges less than $20.00?

What do you know?
- monthly service charge = $4.95
- per-minute charge = $0.10
- maximum amount to spend = $20.00

Plan

What can you do to find the answer?
Write an equation and solve it.

Solve

Solve.
Write the equation. Then solve it.
Let m = the number of minutes of calls.

$$4.95 + 0.10m = 20.00$$
$$4.95 - 4.95 + 0.10m = 20.00 - 4.95$$
$$0.10m = 15.05$$
$$\frac{0.10m}{0.10} = \frac{15.05}{0.10}$$
$$m = 150.50$$

Bill's parents can make 150 minutes of phone calls each month.

Look Back

Look back at the question. Is your answer reasonable?
Why didn't you round your answer to 151 minutes?

Remember:
- ▶ Understand
- ▶ Plan
- ▶ Solve
- ▶ Look Back

(Left) Alexander Graham Bell and his invention, the first telephone. *(Right)* The AT&T Global Network Operations Center in Bedminster, New Jersey, manages local and long-distance telephone services.

Guided Practice

Solve.

1. Mandy's family subscribes to Plan *B*. How many minutes in phone calls can Mandy's family make during plan hours each month and keep their bill under $30.00 dollars?

   Think: What equation can be used to describe Plan *B*?

2. When Benjamin uses his phone card, he is charged $1.50 for the first 2 minutes. Each additional minute costs him $0.40. If one of his calls cost him $4.70, how long was the call?

   Think: Do you want to know how much he paid or how many minutes he talked?

Choose a Strategy

Solve. Use these or other strategies.

Calculator Option

Problem-Solving Strategies

- **Write an Equation**
- **Work Backward**
- **Make a List**
- **Use Logical Thinking**

3. Richard's family subscribes to both plans. In May they made 34 minutes of phone calls on Plan *A* and 72 minutes of phone calls on Plan *B*. How much was their long-distance phone bill for May?

4. Teleprise charges $0.22 per minute at all times with no monthly fee. If Mandy's family makes only 60 minutes of weekend phone calls each month, which is a better deal, Plan *B* or Teleprise's offer?

5. CellPhone's monthly service charge is $29.95. Their plan provides 60 minutes of free calls. Each additional minute costs $0.42. If Julianne's bill was $45.91, how many minutes did she use her cell phone that month?

6. Study the numbers listed below. What are the numbers that would come before $^{-}11$ and after 22? Describe, in words, the pattern.

   $^{-}11$ $^{-}8$ $^{-}4$ 1 7 14 22

7. One month, Cynthia made 75 minutes of long-distance phone calls at $0.10 per minute and 35 minutes of long-distance calls at a higher rate. Her bill was only $25.00. If she paid $10.50 in service charges that month, how much was the higher rate?

8. Amy has three rocks, each of which weighs less than 12 lb. Her scale accurately weighs only 12 lb or more. She puts the rocks on the scale two at a time and comes up with the following weights: 13 lb, 16 lb, and 15 lb. What is the weight of each rock?

Extra Practice See 7–9 on page 293.

Quick Check

Check Your Understanding of Lessons 11–14

Solve. State the inverse operation you used.

1. $16 + d = 235$

2. $54 + e = 17 - 11$

3. $g - 48 + 15 = 118$

4. $(36 - 65) + k = 31$

5. $j \div 7 = 23$

6. $3 \times n \times 2 = 24$

7. $p - 42 \times 2 \times 3 = 36$

8. $t + 6 \div 9 = 3$

9. $s \div \frac{5}{7} = 35$

10. $m \times \frac{3}{8} = \frac{1}{2}$

11. $v + \frac{1}{2} \times 6 = 4\frac{1}{5}$

12. $7 \times n \times \frac{1}{4} = 21$

Solve.

13. Nick is saving money to buy a new mountain bike. He needs \$110. Nick earns \$20 for mowing lawns in his neighborhood. He has also saved \$30 from his allowance. Write and solve an equation describing how many lawns Nick has to mow in order to have enough money to buy the bike.

14. Sophie has \$8.00 to spend at a bead shop. She is buying a clasp that costs \$2, and the beads she wants to buy cost \$0.40 each. Write and solve an equation describing how many beads Sophie can buy.

How did you do?

If you had difficulty with any items in the Quick Check, you can use the following pages for review and extra practice.

Items	Review These Pages	Do These Extra Practice Items
1–4	pages 280–281	Set I, page 292
5–8	pages 282–283	Set J, page 292
9–12	pages 284–285	Set K, page 292
13 and 14	pages 286–287	7–9, page 293

Test Prep • Cumulative Review

Maintaining the Standards

Choose the letter of the correct answer.

1 Liz needs $2\frac{1}{4}$ cups sugar for a pie recipe and $1\frac{2}{3}$ cups sugar for a cake recipe. How much sugar does Liz need to bake the pie and the cake?

A $3\frac{11}{12}$ cups
C $3\frac{1}{4}$ cups
B $3\frac{3}{4}$ cups
D $\frac{7}{12}$ cup

2 Find the difference $^{-}18 - (^{-}13)$.

F 5
H $^{-}21$
G $^{-}5$
J $^{-}18$

3 Donna spent $2.50, $3, $4, $3.50, $3, and $2 for snacks last week. What is the median of the amounts that Donna spent on snacks last week?

A $2
B $3
C $3.50
D $4

4 Which number is a prime number?

F 0
G 1
H 16
J 17

5 Sean lives $\frac{3}{4}$ mile from his school. James lives $\frac{1}{2}$ as far from school. How far from school does James live?

A $\frac{3}{8}$ mile
C $\frac{1}{8}$ mile
B $\frac{1}{4}$ mile
D $1\frac{1}{4}$ miles

6 Round 12,456,008 to the nearest hundred thousand.

F 12,456,000
G 12,450,000
H 12,400,000
J 12,500,000

7 Which number is the additive inverse of $^{-}9\frac{1}{5}$?

A $\frac{-46}{5}$
B $\frac{5}{46}$
C $\frac{46}{5}$
D $9\frac{46}{5}$

8 Renee works at a video store. She sold 2 A-type videos and 3 C-type videos. What expression represents the total cost of the 5 videos she sold?

Video Prices	
A	$15.95
B	19.95
C	25.95

Explain Is there more than one expression that can be used?

Safe Site

Internet Test Prep
Visit **www.eduplace.com/kids/mhm** for more *Test Prep Practice.*

Extra Practice

Set A (Lesson 1, pages 252–254)

Evaluate. Tell what property or properties you used.

1. $15 + (34 + 15)$
2. $16.3 + 0$
3. $m + (m + 12)$, given $m = 7$
4. $19 + 12 + 4$
5. $t + 0$
6. $f + 6 + 12$, given $f = 8$

Use >, <, or = to make each statement true.

7. $4 + 6 + 3$ ⬬ $7 + 6$
8. $(r + s) + (t + u)$ ⬬ $(u + r) + (t + s)$
9. $35 + (11 + 8)$ ⬬ $(8 + 30) + 11$
10. $6 + h + 20$ ⬬ $21 + 6 + h$

Set B (Lesson 2, pages 256–257)

Evaluate. Tell what property or properties you used.

1. $12 \times 2 \times 5$
2. $(5 \times 5) \times (4 \times 4)$
3. $5 \times 3 \times 8 \times 2 \times 10$
4. $3.3 \times 0 \times 8$
5. 75×1
6. $2.4 \times 5 \times 20$

Evaluate each expression, given $p = 3$, $s = 5$, and $w = 1.3$.

7. $10 \times (p \times w)$
8. $(7.5 + 5) \times p$
9. $(7 \times s) + (s \times 3)$
10. $(6.1 \times p) + w$
11. $w \times 0$
12. $(s \times p) + (w \times p)$

Set C (Lesson 3, pages 258–260)

Simplify each expression. At each step, indicate what operation you performed.

1. $4 \times 7 + 2$
2. $(5 \times 7) - (5 + 7)$
3. $100 - 3 \times 4 \times 2$
4. $(44 - 12) \div 2$
5. $11 \times (9 - 6)$
6. $2 \times 5 + 2 + 5$
7. $16 + 4 \times 5$
8. $(400 \div 10) \div 4$
9. $2 \times (1 + 3)^2 + (3 \times 3) - 10$

Evaluate each expression, given $b = 3$ and $m = 6$.

10. $20 - (b \times 6)$
11. $57 - (b \times m)$
12. $4 \times (3 + 5)^2 - 3 \times (2 + 4)$
13. $1 + b \times m + 2$
14. $36 \div m + (b + 4)^2$
15. $b - (m \times 42 - 10^2)$

Extra Practice

Set D *(Lesson 4, pages 262–263)*

Rewrite each, using the Distributive Property. Then simplify.

1. $(13 \times 3) - (13 \times 2)$
2. $2.5 \times (4 + 10)$
3. $4 \times (10 + 12 + 5)$
4. $5 \times (9 - 3.5)$
5. $14 \times (6 + 0.05)$
6. $(8 \times 2) + (2 \times 3) + (2 \times 6)$
7. $(7 \times 7) + (7 \times 8)$
8. $30 \times (2 - 4)$
9. $6 \times (9.8 + 7 + 4)$

Set E *(Lesson 5, pages 264–265)*

Evaluate each expression, given $c = \frac{1}{4}$. Name the property you used.

1. $(c + \frac{7}{8}) + 1\frac{1}{8} + 5$
2. $1\frac{1}{4} + c + 7 \times \frac{1}{4}$
3. $(c \times \frac{3}{4}) + (c \times \frac{1}{8}) \times 2$
4. $4\frac{2}{5} + (1\frac{1}{5} + c)$
5. $(c - \frac{1}{16}) \times 3 + 0$
6. $c \times \frac{1}{8} \times \frac{1}{2} \times 8$
7. $c \times 5 + 1\frac{1}{2} \times 5$
8. $(\frac{3}{4} - c) \times 0 - 3$
9. $\frac{2}{4} \times c + \frac{1}{2} \times 4$
10. $4 \times c \times 2 \times 12$
11. $c \times (4 + 8)$
12. $c \times 11 \times \frac{1}{8} \times 0$

Set F *(Lesson 7, pages 270–271)*

Write an algebraic expression for each. Then evaluate, given $g = 4$ and $h = 8.25$.

1. g increased by 2.6
2. the sum of g and h increased by 1.5
3. $\frac{1}{2}$ the quantity g plus 17.5
4. the quantity h plus 5 decreased by 13
5. h decreased by 5
6. h minus the quantity g plus 6.2
7. 64 increased by g plus h
8. h plus g decreased by 12
9. h decreased by 7
10. 41 decreased by g plus 3.4

Set G *(Lesson 8, pages 272–273)*

Write an algebraic expression for each. Then evaluate, given $n = 5$.

1. the product of 6 plus n and 3
2. the sum of 17 and n, divided by 2.2
3. 8 divided by 10 plus n
4. the quantity 8.4 times 2 minus n
5. the sum of n and 9, times 3
6. n plus the product of 14 and 9
7. 21 plus n, divided by 1.30
8. n feet of fabric times $1.25 per foot

Extra Practice

Set H (Lesson 9, pages 274–275)

Rewrite each word expression as an algebraic expression. Use n as a variable. Then evaluate, given $n = \frac{3}{4}$. Write the answers in simplest form.

1. a number times 3, plus $\frac{1}{2}$
2. a number times 12, minus $\frac{1}{8}$
3. a number divided by $\frac{1}{4}$
4. 6 plus $\frac{1}{12}$, decreased by a number
5. $\frac{1}{3}$ less than a number, times 4
6. 6 divided by a number, plus $2\frac{1}{8}$
7. $\frac{1}{6}$ multiplied by n, minus $\frac{1}{8}$
8. $\frac{2}{5}$ times $\frac{1}{2}$ divided by 3
9. $\frac{1}{4}$ is doubled then increased by a number
10. the quantity $\frac{1}{4}$ plus $\frac{3}{12}$, times the sum of a number and $\frac{1}{2}$

Set I (Lesson 11, pages 280–281)

Solve. State the inverse operation you used.

1. $p + 12 = 15$
2. $s - 9 = 5$
3. $d - 5 + 45 = 48$
4. $w + 2 + 6 = 12$
5. $18 - 20 = f - 10$
6. $q + 16 = 7 + 5 \times 2$
7. $e - 13 = 33$
8. $3.4 + v = 6.1$
9. $15 + k + 4 = 55 - 32$
10. $54 + r + 3 = 46$
11. $z - 18 = 9 + 9$
12. $c + 22.7 + 14.5 = 49.5$

Set J (Lesson 12, pages 282–283)

Solve. State the inverse operation you used.

1. $t \times 4 = 48$
2. $d \div 100 = 4$
3. $2 \times m = 34$
4. $f \times 8 \div 2 = 12$
5. $b \div (8 - 6) = 1$
6. $q \times 14 \times 3 = 42$
7. $a \div 5 \times 6 = 29$
8. $u \div (62 - 44) = 6$
9. $12 \times n \times 4 = 384$
10. $j - 36 \times 14 = 19$
11. $z \div 64 = 4$
12. $c \times 3 \times 6 \times 2 = 180$

Set K (Lesson 13, pages 284–285)

Solve. Simplify first. State the inverse operations you used.

1. $6 \div 2 \times e = 9$
2. $z - 5 = 1\frac{2}{3}$
3. $u \div 8 = \frac{1}{2}$
4. $7 \times s = 4\frac{2}{3}$
5. $j \div \frac{3}{4} = 13\frac{1}{3}$
6. $4 \times \frac{1}{8} + r = 4\frac{3}{4}$
7. $12 \times \frac{1}{5} + p = 7$
8. $a \div (8 + \frac{1}{4}) = \frac{1}{2}$
9. $6 \times v \times 3 = 2\frac{1}{4}$
10. $m + (2 \times 3) = 8$
11. $4 \times k \times 2 = \frac{2}{5}$
12. $\frac{1}{12} \times w = \frac{2}{3}$

Extra Practice • Problem Solving

Solve. Write an expression that correctly represents each situation. *(Lesson 6, pages 266–267)*

1. Terry's car goes 34 miles for every gallon of gas in the gas tank. How far can Terry travel if his car has *g* gallons of gas in the tank?

2. Chandri's family has a car that gets 40 miles per gallon. If each gallon costs $1.35, how much will it cost Chandri's family to go *n* miles?

3. Sara sells bracelets for $3.50 each. If a person buys 3 or more, she charges $3.00 for each one. How much did Sara earn if she sold less than 3 to one customer and more than 3 to another?

4. For a bike-a-thon, Andrew rode his bicycle at a constant speed for 20 miles. What expression shows how many miles per hour he was traveling if he was traveling for *t* hours?

Write an expression and evaluate. *(Lesson 10, 276–277)*

5. Sam's science class studies the growth of 50 bacterial cells in a petri dish. Every 40 minutes, the cells reproduce and there are 50 more cells in the petri dish. How many bacteria are there after 120 minutes?

6. Damon's class is studying another type of bacteria in order to compare the growth rates of the two types. The 50 cells Damon's class is studying have doubled twice in 120 minutes. How often do they double?

Write an equation. Then solve. *(Lesson 14, pages 286–287)*

7. Ethan has $20.00 to spend on art supplies. He wants to buy brushes, one set of paints, and 2 packets of paper. If the paper costs $2.50 per packet, the paints cost $12.00, and the brushes cost $1.50 each, how many brushes can Ethan buy?

8. Ethan decides not to buy the set of paints. Instead, he chooses to buy two $3.50 sets of colored pencils for his brother and himself. If his other purchases remain the same, how much money will Ethan have left?

9. Three students played a quiz game. Each player scored 2 points for a right answer and 3 points for each bonus question he or she answered correctly. If each person had 4 right answers, how many bonus questions did each person answer correctly?

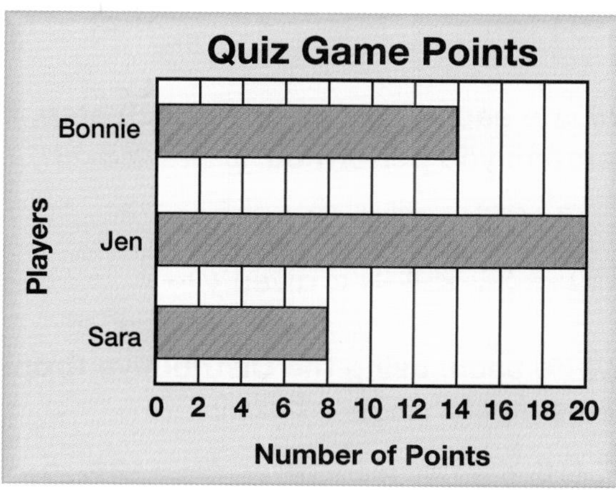

Chapter Review

Reviewing Vocabulary

Write *always, sometimes,* or *never* for each statement. Give an example to support your answer.

1. Addition and subtraction are used to evaluate expressions.
2. An algebraic expression contains at least one variable.
3. The inverse operation of division is subtraction.
4. The reciprocal of a fraction is equal to the denominator of the fraction.

Match each example with the appropriate property.

5. $12 \times 3 = 3 \times 12$
6. $(2 + 9) + 4 = 2 + (9 + 4)$
7. $24 \times 1 = 24$
8. $6 \times (5 + 2) = (6 \times 2) + (6 \times 5)$

a. Associative Property of Addition
b. Identity Property of Multiplication
c. Commutative Property of Multiplication
d. Distributive Property

Reviewing Concepts and Skills

Use >, <, or = to make each statement true. *(pages 252–257)*

9. $11 + 0$ ● 0×11
10. $6.5 + 4$ ● $4 + 6.5$
11. $(4 + 8) + g$ ● $(g + 8) + 4$
12. 16×16 ● $16 \times 10 + 16 \times 7$
13. $10 \times 5 \times 2$ ● 50×4
14. $(p + q) + (r + s)$ ● $(p + r) + (q + s)$

Evaluate each expression. Tell what property you used. *(pages 264–265)*

15. $2 \times 14 \times 5$
16. $15 \times 0 \times \frac{1}{5}$
17. $5.5 \times (n + 3.5)$, given $n = 10$
18. 34×1
19. $(\frac{1}{3} \times 4) \times (\frac{1}{3} \times 5)$
20. $(7 \times a) \times 4$, given $a = \frac{2}{4}$

Evaluate each expression. At each step, indicate what operation you performed. *(pages 258–261)*

21. $(7 \times 6) - (7 + 3)$
22. $3 \times (4 \times \frac{1}{6}) + (11 + 2) - 9$
23. $9 + 2\frac{1}{3} \times 4 \div y$, given $y = \frac{1}{2}$
24. $(2 \times 4)^2 + 15 - s$, given $s = 12$

Rewrite each, using the Distributive Property. Then simplify. *(pages 262–265)*

25. $(18 \times 4) + (4 \times 3)$
26. $5 \times (7\frac{3}{4} + 3)$
27. $2 \times (11 + 8 + 4)$

Write an algebraic expression for each. Then evaluate, given $j = 6$ and $k = \frac{1}{4}$. *(pages 270–275)*

28. $\frac{1}{2}$ the quantity j increased by 12

29. j divided by 3 then multiplied by k

30. the product of j and k doubled

31. 19 decreased by j plus 4

32. $\frac{4}{5}$ divided by k, minus $\frac{1}{5}$

33. the sum of j and k, times $\frac{1}{2}$ of j

Solve. State the inverse operation you used. *(pages 280–285)*

34. $z - 11 + 25 = 24$

35. $a \div 250 = \frac{1}{2}$

36. $(7 + 8) \times c = 45$

37. $m + 3.5 + 9.6 = 17.8$

38. $\frac{1}{9} \times v = \frac{1}{6}$

39. $y + 11 \div 3 = 7$

40. $k \times 4 \times 9 \times 3 = 216$

41. $t - 14 = 20 - 18$

42. $r - 5 \times 3 = \frac{1}{3}$

Solve. *(pages 266–267, 276–277, 286–287)*

43. Tina types 70 words per minute and has been typing for $1\frac{1}{2}$ hours. What expression can you use to find how many words has she typed?

44. At Gregor's sister's wedding, each person who is invited may bring someone with them. 120 people accepted the invitation. One third of those who accepted are bringing someone along. Write and evaluate an expression describing how many guests will attend the wedding.

45. Liz is shopping at a bookstore where some books are regular price and some are half off. The regular price of each book is \$7.00. Liz spends a total of \$35.00. Write an equation that can be used to find how many books Liz bought. Then solve the equation, given that she bought 2 books at half price.

Brain Teasers Math Reasoning

How Many Hundreds?

Use order of operations to solve this problem with mental math.

$100 \times 100 \times (100 - 100) + (100 + 100) - 100$

Equal Halves

Write and solve an equation for this word expression. One half times a number times $\frac{1}{2}$ equals $\frac{1}{2}$.

Internet Brain Teasers
Visit **www.eduplace.com/kids/mhm** for more *Brain Teasers.*

Chapter Test

Use >, <, or = to make each statement true.

1. $(3 + 2) + (6 + 8)$ ⬬ $(6 + 2) + (3 + 8)$
2. $14 + 0$ ⬬ 0
3. $(m + 5) + 12$ ⬬ $(m + 12) + 5$
4. $15 + 11$ ⬬ $7 + 20$
5. $16 + 7 + 4$ ⬬ $7 + 16 + 4$
6. 13 ⬬ 13×0

Evaluate each expression. Tell what property you used.

7. 19×0
8. $(\frac{1}{2} \times \frac{1}{3}) + (\frac{3}{4} \times \frac{1}{3})$
9. $(9 \times 6) \times h$, given $h = \frac{1}{3}$
10. $\frac{4}{5} \times 1$
11. $q \times (q + 7)$, given $q = \frac{1}{2}$
12. $2 \times 3.5 \times 5$
13. $1 \times 8 \times 9$
14. $(4 + d) \times (7 + d)$, given $d = 6$
15. $12 \times 0 \times 14$

Evaluate each expression. At each step, indicate what operation you performed.

16. $(1 + 3) \times (2 + 5)^2 \div 4$
17. $48 - (\frac{1}{3} \times w)$, given $w = 12$
18. $(47 + 4) - (3 \times d)$, given $d = 6$
19. $(300 \div 5) \div 10$

Rewrite each, using the Distributive Property. Then simplify.

20. $r \times (3 + 6 + 2)$
21. $4 \times (11 + 5)$
22. $(12 \times 2) + (9 \times 2)$

Write an algebraic expression for each. Then evaluate, given $y = \frac{2}{3}$ and $z = 8$.

23. the sum of y and z, decreased by $5\frac{1}{2}$
24. the product of z plus 3 and 10
25. 7 increased by the product of z and 12
26. $\frac{1}{3}$ the quantity 12 divided by y
27. the quantity z plus 3, minus y
28. the quantity y times z divided by 2

Solve. State the inverse operation you used.

29. $f + 1\frac{1}{2} = 1\frac{1}{3} + 4$
30. $9 \times 11 + e = 20$
31. $q - 6 \div 9 = 2$
32. $22 - 7 = c + 8$
33. $g \times \frac{3}{4} = \frac{5}{8}$
34. $6 \times r \times 7 = 126$
35. $a \div 100 = 4 \times 5$
36. $b + 3 \times 20 = \frac{3}{4}$
37. $(7 + 5) \times u = 64$

38. What is the reciprocal of $\frac{4}{3}$? What is the product of any number and its reciprocal?

39. Lauren is baking muffins for a school fair. For every 2 cups of flour, she makes 12 muffins. If she uses 8 cups of flour, how many muffins is she making? Write and evaluate an expression to describe the total number of muffins.

40. Tyler and Cate are working on a group project that has a total of 45 questions to answer. They have completed $\frac{2}{5}$ of the questions. Write and solve an equation for how many questions they have left to solve.

Write About It

Solve each problem. Use correct math vocabulary to explain your thinking.

1. At a local café, a bowl of soup costs $2.50 and a large salad costs $3.75. If you order both soup and salad, it is a combination and the cost is reduced. Lena, Mark, and Reggie went to the café and ordered a meal that cost $13.50.

a. Write an equation to represent the situation.

b. Explain why you chose the operation(s) you did to describe the situation.

c. Solve the equation, given that the meal consisted of 1 bowl of soup and 2 combinations. As you solve the equation, explain each step, including any inverse operations.

2. Indra's father is building a fence that requires the use of 4 boards for every 8 feet of fence he builds. The fence has one side that measures 24 feet and two sides that measure 12 feet each.

a. Write an expression describing how many boards Indra's father will need for the entire fence.

b. Explain the order of operations for the expression you have written. Then evaluate the expression.

Another Look

Cheryl is delivering 4 packages of calculators to Dr. Divisor's office building in Mathville. Each of the offices in the building has a number from 1 to 25, but instead of numbers, the office directory shows only algebraic expressions!

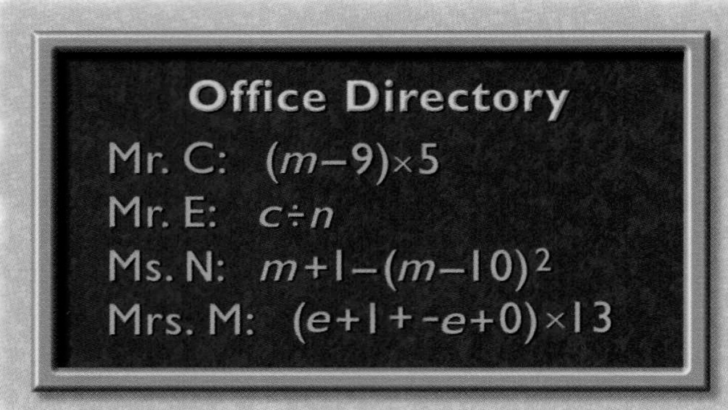

1. Use the information in the directory to help Cheryl find:

a. Mrs. M's office (m)

b. Mr. C's office (c)

c. Ms. N's office (n)

d. Mr. E's office (e)

2. Mrs. G's office number is one half the product of Mr. E's and Ms. N's office numbers. Write an equation that shows how to find Mrs. G's office number. Then solve the equation.

3. **Look Back** What properties of addition and multiplication did you use to find Mrs. M's office number?

4. **Analyze** The offices on the first floor are numbered 1 to 5. Those on the second floor are numbered 6 to 10, and so on. The elevator on each floor is numbered 0. Which expression shows any office number if you know the floor number, f, and how far from the elevator it is, e?

a. $f \times e$ **b.** $f \times e + (f - 1) \times (5 - e)$

c. $f + e$ **d.** $f - (1 \times 5) + e$

Enrichment

Time Zones

A time zone is an area in which all clocks are set to the same time. The system of time zones, which is used all over the world, is called Standard Time. As you travel west through the time zones in the continental U.S., the time changes to one hour earlier than the previous time zone. As you travel east through each time zone, the time changes to one hour later.

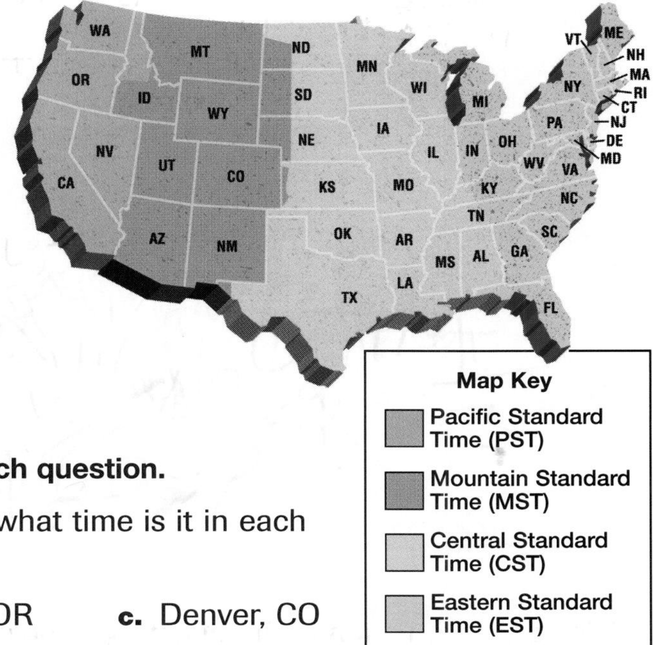

Map Key

- Pacific Standard Time (PST)
- Mountain Standard Time (MST)
- Central Standard Time (CST)
- Eastern Standard Time (EST)

Use the map of time zones to answer each question.

1. If it is 3:30 P.M. in New Orleans, LA, what time is it in each of these cities?

   a. Indianapolis, IN **b.** Eugene, OR **c.** Denver, CO

Suppose you are in St. Paul, MN, in the CST zone, and you want to call your aunt in Seattle, WA. What algebraic equation would help you find the correct time in the PST zone? The PST zone is two time zones west of the CST zone, and therefore the time is 2 hours earlier than the time in the CST zone.

$$PST = CST - 2\text{ h}$$

Use what you know about time zones to solve each problem.

2. Use an equation to find the time in each city, if it is 7:00 A.M. in Tulsa, OK.

   a. Miami, FL **b.** Reno, NV **c.** Kansas City, KS

3. Janine's family takes a train from Alabama to North Carolina. The train ride lasts 12 hours. If they leave Alabama at 6:30 A.M., at what time will they arrive in North Carolina?

4. Write an algebraic equation that shows how to convert MST to CST.

Explain Your Thinking

What is the greatest time difference possible between any two cities in the continental United States? Explain your thinking.

Ratio, Proportion, and Percent

Why Learn About Ratio, Proportion, and Percent?

Learning about ratio, proportion, and percent can help you compare quantities and understand the relationship between them.

When you read a map and use the scale to figure out the distance between two places, you are using proportion.

This group has just finished lunch, and the woman is looking at the check. She is using mental math to find a percent of the total so that she can leave a tip.

Reviewing Vocabulary

Understanding math language helps you become a successful problem solver. Here are some math vocabulary words you should know.

decimal a number with one or more digits to the right of a decimal point

denominator the number under the bar in a fraction

equation a statement that uses an equals sign to show that two expressions are equal

fraction a number that names a part of a whole or a part of a set

mixed number a number written with a whole number and a fraction

numerator the number above the bar in a fraction

percent a ratio that compares a number with 100

Reading Words and Symbols

When you read mathematics, sometimes you read only words, sometimes you read words and symbols, and sometimes you read only symbols.

All of these symbols represent the same part of a whole.

Symbol	Read as
$\frac{1}{2}$	one half, or one divided by two
50%	fifty percent
$\frac{50}{100}$	fifty hundredths
0.5	five tenths

Try These

1. Identify each ■ below as a numerator or a denominator.

   a. $\frac{2}{■}$ (3) b. $5\frac{7}{■}$ (8) c. $6\frac{■}{12}$ (11) d. $\frac{■}{16}$ (23)

2. Replace each ■ with one of the following choices so the numbers in **a–d** are equivalent.

   3, 4, 75, 100

   a. $\frac{3}{■}$ b. 0.■ c. $\frac{75}{■}$ d. $\frac{■}{4}$

3. Write each ratio as a percent.

   a. $\frac{2}{100}$ b. $\frac{50}{100}$ c. $\frac{5}{100}$ d. $\frac{90}{100}$

   e. $\frac{200}{100}$ f. $\frac{150}{100}$ g. $\frac{525}{100}$ h. $\frac{100}{100}$

4. Which of the following is an equation?

   a. $(4 \times 6) + 11 - m$ b. $5 \times d \times 7 = 105$ c. $9 + 6 - 15$

5. Identify each number as a whole number, a fraction, or a mixed number.

   a. $\frac{126}{42}$ b. $3\frac{5}{12}$ c. $\frac{7}{8}$ d. 5,449

Upcoming Vocabulary

Write About It **Here are some other vocabulary words** you will learn in this chapter. Watch for these words. Write their definitions in your journal.

ratio
rate
equivalent ratios
proportion
scale
scale drawing

Ratios

You will learn how to use a ratio to compare two numbers.

New Vocabulary
ratio

Learn About It

A **ratio** compares two numbers. The two numbers being compared are called the terms. Ratios can be expressed in three forms. Each form is read as "the ratio of *a* to *b*."

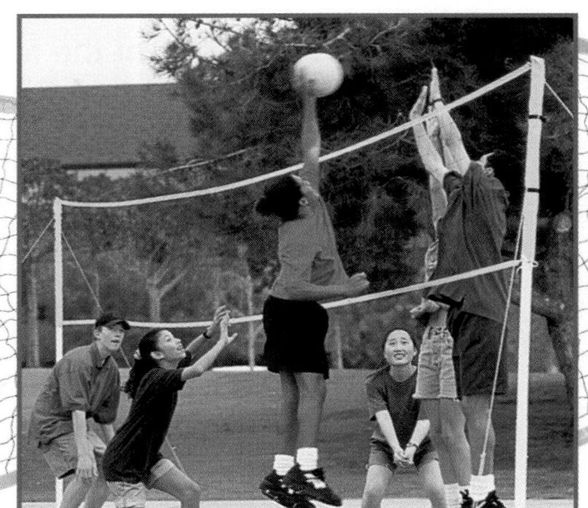

Fraction form	$\frac{a}{b}$
Word form	*a* to *b*
Ratio form	$a:b$

There are 22 students in coach Aldan's gym class. On Friday, 10 students played basketball and 12 students played volleyball. You can use a ratio to compare the number of students who played basketball with the number of students who played volleyball.

Step 1 Write a ratio in fraction form to compare the number of basketball players with the number of volleyball players.

$$\frac{\text{number of basketball players}}{\text{number of volleyball players}} = \frac{10}{12} \begin{matrix} \leftarrow \text{first term} \\ \leftarrow \text{second term} \end{matrix}$$

The ratio of basketball players to volleyball players is 10 to 12.

Step 2 Simplify the ratio by canceling common factors of both terms.

$$\frac{10}{12} = \frac{5 \times \overset{1}{\cancel{2}}}{6 \times \underset{1}{\cancel{2}}} = \frac{5}{6}$$

The ratio of basketball players to volleyball players is 5 to 6.

Solution: The ratio $\frac{5}{6}$ compares the number of students who played basketball with the number of students who played volleyball.

Another Example

Batting Averages as Ratios

A baseball player is at bat 500 times and gets 126 hits.

The ratio of hits to at-bats is 126 to 500, or 126:500, or $\frac{126}{500}$. As a batting average, the ratio is written 0.252.

Explain Your Thinking

- ► How could you show the ratio of volleyball players to basketball players?
- ► Ratios are often written in fraction form. Explain why the ratio $\frac{10}{12}$ in the problem above is *not* a fraction.

Guided Practice

Simplify each ratio if possible. Then express each in two other forms.

1. 5 kg to 30 kg **2.** 6:25 **3.** 9 in. to 1 ft **4.** $\frac{30}{2}$

Ask Yourself

- Do I need to change the unit of either measure?
- Which number do I write first in the ratio?

Independent Practice

Simplify each ratio if possible. Then express each in two other forms.

5. 5 miles to 2 miles **6.** $\frac{20}{45}$ **7.** 75:25 **8.** 50:13

9. 2 days to 3 hours **10.** 2 to 1 **11.** $\frac{17}{2}$ **12.** 5 to 8

Write each ratio in fraction form. Simplify if possible.

13. 8 boys:16 girls **14.** 8 to 3 **15.** 120:90 **16.** 150:7

17. 24 nails to 3 hammers **18.** 4:7 **19.** 2:6 **20.** 15 to 5

Problem Solving • Reasoning

Use Data **Use the table for Problems 21–23.**

21. Express the number of students to the number of teachers at Wilson Middle School as a ratio. Then simplify the ratio.

22. Find the ratio of the total number of students to the total number of classrooms. Then simplify the ratio.

23. **Compare** Which school has the lowest student-to-teacher ratio? How do you know?

Students, Teachers, and Classrooms at Three Different Middle Schools

School	Parkview	Scenic	Wilson
Students	144	180	108
Teachers	12	20	9
Classrooms	11	18	9

Mixed Review • Test Prep

Evaluate each expression, given $x = 5$ and $y = 3$. *(pages 252–254, 264–265)*

24. $(x - 3.2) + y$ **25.** $5 + (x - y)$ **26.** $(x + \frac{3}{4}) - y$ **27.** $19 - x + (y + 1)$

Choose the letter of the correct answer. *(pages 270–271)*

Jenny is 2 years older than Tim. Bob is 5 years younger than Tim.

28 Tim's age = t. Jenny's age = ■

A $7 - t$ **C** $t + 2$

B $t - 2$ **D** $t + 5$

29 Bob's age = b. Tim's age = ■

F $b + 5$ **H** $b - 5$

G $2 + 5 + t$ **J** $2 + 5 - t$

Extra Practice See Set A on page 336.

Rates

You will learn how to use a special type of ratio to compare quantities with different units.

New Vocabulary
rate

Learn About It

A **rate** is a ratio that compares two quantities with different units of measure. A rate in which the second term is 1 is called a unit rate.

Before leaving on a trip to a family reunion, Mr. Garcia filled the car's gas tank. After driving 250 miles, he bought 10 gallons of gas to refill the tank. How many miles did the car travel on 1 gallon of gas?

Step 1 Identify the quantities to be compared. Then write a rate.

$\frac{250}{10}$ ⟵ miles, ⟵ gallons

Step 2 Simplify the rate to find the unit rate.

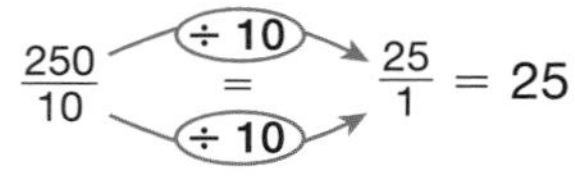

$$\frac{250}{10} \xrightarrow{\div 10} \frac{25}{1} = 25$$

MILEAGE LOG

DATE	NOTES	ODOMETER READING
8/22	Started out gas tank full	35,768
	10 gallons needed to fill tank	36,018

Solution: The car traveled 25 miles on 1 gallon of gas. So the unit rate, or gasoline mileage, was 25 miles per gallon.

Another Example

Second Term Less Than One

Express "30 miles in $\frac{1}{2}$ hour" as a unit rate.

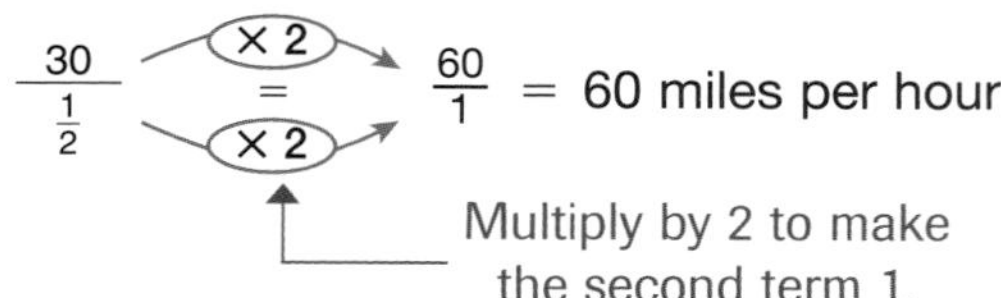

$$\frac{30}{\frac{1}{2}} \xrightarrow{\times 2} \frac{60}{1} = 60 \text{ miles per hour}$$

Multiply by 2 to make the second term 1.

Explain Your Thinking

- ▶ When writing a rate, why does it matter which number is the first term and which is the second term?
- ▶ What do you know about the second term in the rate "7 dollars *per* hour"? Explain.

Guided Practice

Write each as a unit rate.

1. 40 miles in 2 hours

2. 50 miles in $\frac{1}{2}$ hour

3. 1 inch in 2 months

4. 4 miles in 2 hours

5. 450 miles on 15 gallons

6. $1.56 for 12

Ask Yourself

- Have I written the right second term?
- What do I do if the second term is less than 1?

Independent Practice

Write each as a unit rate.

7. 36 for \$12

8. \$6 for 3 lb of grapes

9. 24 puppies in 3 days

10. 30 mi on 1.5 gal

11. 7 commercials in $\frac{1}{2}$ h

12. 25 yd in 30 s

13. \$192 for 24 h

14. 350 mi in 5 h

15. 20 pillows for \$5

16. \$16 for 32 photos

17. 300 mi on 20 gal

18. \$12 for 12 containers

19. 200 mi in 4 h

20. 8 tests in 2 weeks

21. \$84 grocery bill for 7 days

Problem Solving • Reasoning

22. Magda travels to the family reunion on a motorcycle. She rides 126 miles on 3 gallons of gas. How many miles per gallon does the motorcycle get?

23. **Compare** Louis and Franco are making the family breakfast. Louis paid \$0.84 for half a dozen eggs. Franco paid \$1.20 for 8 eggs. Who paid the lower cost per egg?

24. **Estimate** Terrance averages 7 yards a pass during the football game. Estimate how many passes he needs to throw to total at least 100 yards. Then check your estimate.

25. **Write Your Own** Write a problem that uses a rate of bags of dog food per dog. Then solve the problem.

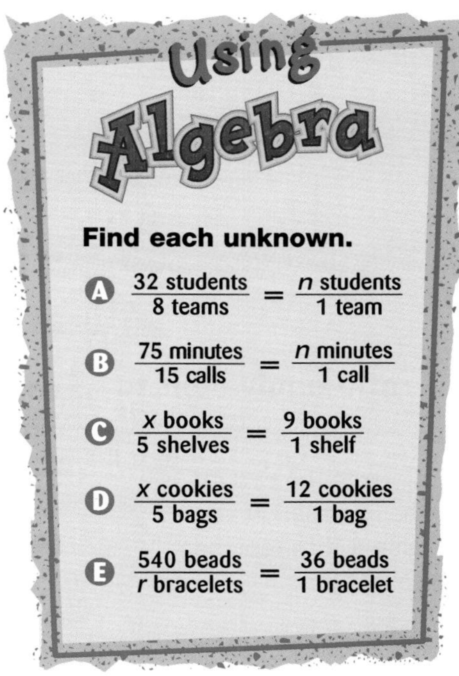

Using
Algebra
Find each unknown.
A $\frac{32 \text{ students}}{8 \text{ teams}} = \frac{n \text{ students}}{1 \text{ team}}$
B $\frac{75 \text{ minutes}}{15 \text{ calls}} = \frac{n \text{ minutes}}{1 \text{ call}}$
C $\frac{x \text{ books}}{5 \text{ shelves}} = \frac{9 \text{ books}}{1 \text{ shelf}}$
D $\frac{x \text{ cookies}}{5 \text{ bags}} = \frac{12 \text{ cookies}}{1 \text{ bag}}$
E $\frac{540 \text{ beads}}{r \text{ bracelets}} = \frac{36 \text{ beads}}{1 \text{ bracelet}}$

Mixed Review • Test Prep

Solve. *(pages 280–281)*

26. $9 + a = 20$

27. $n - 6 = 4$

28. $m - 15 = 0$

29. $14 + t = 17$

Choose the letter of the correct answer. *(pages 258–260)*

30 Simplify $28 \div (7 + 7)$.

A 2 **B** 7 **C** 11 **D** 14

31 Simplify $(14 - 4) \times 3 - 2$.

F 0 **G** 4 **H** 10 **J** 28

Extra Practice See Set B on page 336.

Equivalent Ratios

You will learn how to use an equivalent ratio to find a missing term.

New Vocabulary
equivalent ratios

Learn About It

When you multiply or divide both terms of a ratio by a number other than 0, the resulting terms make up an **equivalent ratio**.

$$\frac{1}{2} = \frac{1 \times 2}{2 \times 2} = \frac{2}{4} \qquad \frac{2}{4} = \frac{2 \div 2}{4 \div 2} = \frac{1}{2}$$

The ratios $\frac{1}{2}$ and $\frac{2}{4}$ are equivalent ratios.

During the summer, Bill mowed the same lawns every week. In 4 weeks he made $160. How much money did he make in 12 weeks?

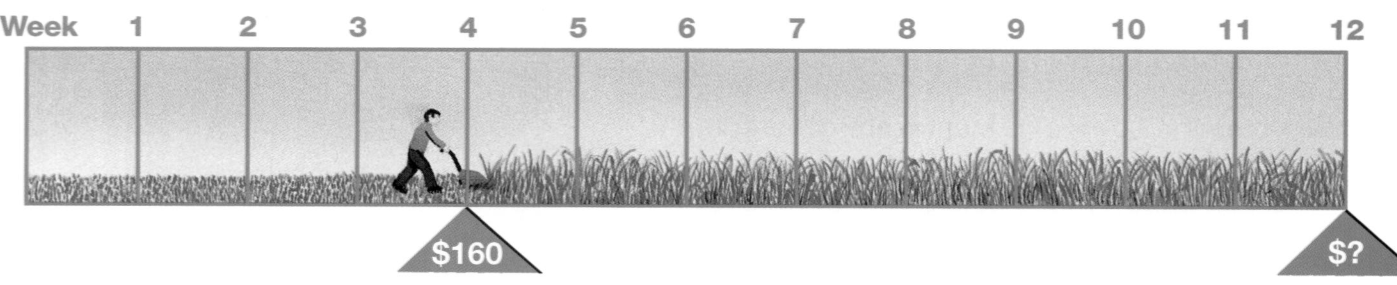

Find a ratio equivalent to $\frac{4}{160}$ whose first term is 12.

Step 1 Write the two ratios, using the information you know. Use a ■ to represent the missing term.

weeks → $\frac{4}{160} = \frac{12}{■}$ ← dollars

Step 2 Find the number that, when multiplied by 4, will give the product 12.

$\frac{4}{160} = \frac{12}{■}$ (× 3 on top, × ? on bottom)

Step 3 Use this factor to find the missing term.

$\frac{4}{160} = \frac{12}{480}$ (× 3 on top, × 3 on bottom)

Solution: Bill made $480 in 12 weeks.

Other Examples

A. Missing First Term

$$\frac{4 \text{ weeks}}{28 \text{ dollars}} = \frac{■ \text{ weeks}}{168 \text{ dollars}}$$

$\frac{4}{28} = \frac{24}{168}$ (× 6 on top, × 6 on bottom)

24 weeks

B. Find a Unit Rate

$$\frac{28 \text{ dollars}}{4 \text{ weeks}} = \frac{■ \text{ dollars}}{1 \text{ week}}$$

$\frac{28}{4} = \frac{7}{1}$ (÷ 4 on top, ÷ 4 on bottom)

7 dollars per week

Explain Your Thinking

► To find an equivalent ratio, why do you need to multiply or divide both terms by the same number?

Guided Practice

Find the missing term in each.

1. $\frac{3}{4} = \frac{n}{12}$ **2.** $\frac{72}{144} = \frac{n}{16}$ **3.** $\frac{21}{n} = \frac{147}{196}$ **4.** $\frac{5}{16} = \frac{25}{n}$

Ask Yourself

- Have I multiplied or divided both terms by the same number?
- Did I solve for the missing term?

Independent Practice

Find the missing term in each.

5. $\frac{5}{8} = \frac{10}{k}$ **6.** $\frac{4}{6} = \frac{y}{30}$ **7.** $\frac{12}{3} = \frac{m}{1}$ **8.** $\frac{15}{9} = \frac{5}{p}$ **9.** $\frac{7}{14} = \frac{t}{2}$

10. $\frac{2}{5} = \frac{p}{25}$ **11.** $\frac{18}{6} = \frac{6}{d}$ **12.** $\frac{12}{3} = \frac{4}{q}$ **13.** $\frac{56}{8} = \frac{y}{2}$ **14.** $\frac{14}{2} = \frac{7}{n}$

15. $\frac{33}{11} = \frac{k}{1}$ **16.** $\frac{25}{5} = \frac{5}{y}$ **17.** $\frac{8}{24} = \frac{16}{h}$ **18.** $\frac{24}{6} = \frac{4}{p}$ **19.** $\frac{56}{64} = \frac{p}{8}$

Compare. Write = or ≠ for each ⬬.

20. $\frac{3}{5}$ ⬬ $\frac{9}{15}$ **21.** $\frac{12}{4}$ ⬬ $\frac{4}{1}$ **22.** 4:3 ⬬ 8:6 **23.** 5 to 20 ⬬ 10 to 40

Problem Solving • Reasoning

Use Data **Use the bar graph for Problems 24–26.**

24. During the first week of summer, Ben bathed 5 dogs. How many dogs will he need to bathe to earn $125?

25. **Estimate** Daisy wants to earn at least $150 during the summer. During the first week, she weeded 3 gardens. How many more gardens will she need to weed to meet her goal?

26. **Analyze** Kendra washed 4 cars during the first week. The next week, she lowered her price per car by $2 and washed twice as many cars. How much did she earn that week?

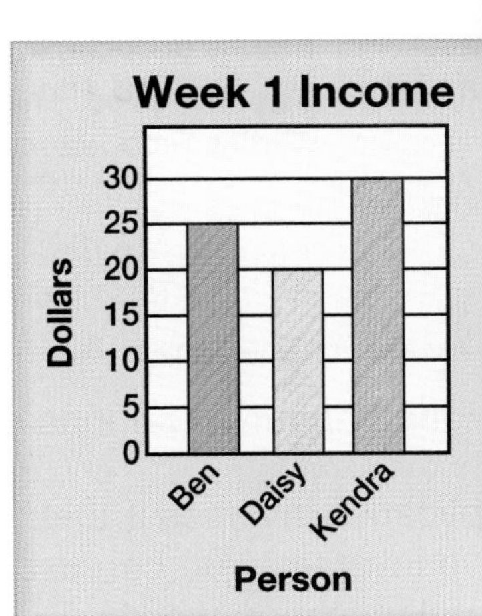

Mixed Review • Test Prep

Compare. Write > or < for each ⬬. *(pages 6–7, 208–209)*

27. $^-5$ ⬬ $^-3$ **28.** 69 ⬬ 81 **29.** $^-4$ ⬬ $^-10$ **30.** 2 ⬬ $^-43$

31 Isabel's test scores are 80, 80, 85, 90, and 95. What is the lowest score she can make on the next test to raise her average? *(pages 60–61)*

A 80 **B** 82 **C** 86 **D** 87

Extra Practice See Set C on page 336.

LESSON 4 Solve Proportions

You will learn how to write and solve proportions.

New Vocabulary
proportion

Learn About It

The ratio of Mars' gravity to Earth's gravity is about $\frac{2}{5}$. This means that an object that weighs 2 pounds on Mars would weigh about 5 pounds on Earth. In 1996, NASA sent a rover weighing about 25 pounds on Earth to study Mars. About how much did the rover weigh on Mars?

Weight on Earth	Weight on Mars
25 lb	?

To find out, write a proportion by using two ratios. A **proportion** is a statement which shows that two ratios are equivalent.

weight on Mars → $\frac{2}{5} = \frac{m}{25}$ ← rover's weight on Mars
weight on Earth → ← rover's weight on Earth

You can use cross multiplication to find a missing term in a proportion.

Solve for *m*. $\frac{2}{5} = \frac{m}{25}$

Step 1 Write the proportion.

$\frac{2}{5} = \frac{m}{25}$

Step 2 Identify the terms to be multiplied. These are the cross products.

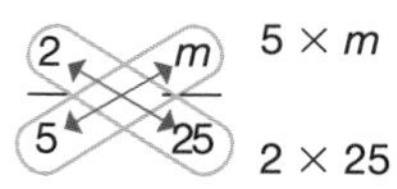

$5 \times m$

2×25

Step 3 Set the cross products equal to each other. Solve for *m*.

$2 \times 25 = 5 \times m$
$50 = 5 \times m$
$10 = m$

Solution: The rover weighed about 10 pounds on Mars.

Two numbers are multiplicative inverses if their product is 1. For example, 3 and $\frac{1}{3}$ are multiplicative inverses. You can use multiplicative inverses to understand why cross multiplication works.

$\frac{a}{b} = \frac{c}{d}$	*a, b, c,* and *d* form any proportion, where $b \neq 0$ and $d \neq 0$.
$\frac{a}{b} \times \frac{b}{a} = \frac{c}{d} \times \frac{b}{a}$	If you multiply both sides of the equation by the multiplicative inverse of $\frac{a}{b}$, which is $\frac{b}{a}$, the products are equal.
$1 = \frac{c \times b}{d \times a}$	Because $\frac{c \times b}{d \times a}$ is equal to 1, the numerator and denominator must be equal.
$c \times b = d \times a$ $a \times d = b \times c$	The cross products are equal.

You can use cross multiplication to find out if two ratios form a proportion.

Do $\frac{14}{35}$ and $\frac{2}{5}$ form a proportion?

Step 1 Write the two ratios.	**Step 2** Write the cross products.	**Step 3** If the cross products are equal, the ratios are equivalent.
$\frac{14}{35}$ $\frac{2}{5}$	$\frac{14}{35} \times \frac{2}{5}$ 14×5 ■ 35×2	$70 = 70$ The cross products are equal.

Solution: Since the cross products are equal, the ratios are equivalent and, therefore, form a proportion.

Another Example

Missing Second Term

$\frac{3}{4} = \frac{9}{s}$ Cross multiply. $\frac{3}{4} \times \frac{9}{s}$ $3 \times s = 36$

Solve the equation. $3 \times s \div 3 = 36 \div 3$

$s = 12$

Explain Your Thinking

► Why can you multiply or divide both sides of an equation by the same number and still have the equation be true?

Guided Practice

Use cross products to find the missing term in each proportion.

1. $\frac{t}{12} = \frac{3}{4}$ **2.** $\frac{18}{f} = \frac{3}{1}$ **3.** $\frac{8}{16} = \frac{5}{h}$ **4.** $\frac{2}{5} = \frac{p}{25}$

Write the cross products for each pair of ratios. Do the two ratios form a proportion? Write *yes* or *no*.

5. $\frac{5}{15}$ $\frac{10}{30}$ **6.** $\frac{2}{3}$ $\frac{4}{9}$ **7.** $\frac{12}{3}$ $\frac{6}{2}$ **8.** $\frac{3}{8}$ $\frac{12}{32}$

Ask Yourself

- Did I write the cross products correctly?
- Are the cross products equal?

Independent Practice

Use cross products to find the missing term in each proportion.

9. $\frac{5}{2} = \frac{10}{a}$ **10.** $\frac{3}{h} = \frac{9}{3}$ **11.** $\frac{12}{c} = \frac{3}{1}$ **12.** $\frac{7}{m} = \frac{2}{4}$ **13.** $\frac{e}{15} = \frac{6}{5}$

14. $\frac{3}{21} = \frac{k}{14}$ **15.** $\frac{120}{30} = \frac{s}{5}$ **16.** $\frac{h}{18} = \frac{3}{6}$ **17.** $\frac{100}{20} = \frac{5}{x}$ **18.** $\frac{24}{j} = \frac{8}{12}$

19. $\frac{f}{15} = \frac{8}{5}$ **20.** $\frac{5}{5} = \frac{7}{p}$ **21.** $\frac{12}{5} = \frac{24}{d}$ **22.** $\frac{27}{18} = \frac{6}{n}$ **23.** $\frac{30}{25} = \frac{u}{10}$

24. $\frac{q}{21} = \frac{2}{14}$ **25.** $\frac{7}{8} = \frac{21}{r}$ **26.** $\frac{12}{5} = \frac{36}{g}$ **27.** $\frac{100}{t} = \frac{10}{12}$ **28.** $\frac{3}{8} = \frac{n}{16}$

Problem Solving • Reasoning

Use Data Use the table to solve Problems 29–32.

Table of Relative Weights		
Weight of Object on Planet (pounds)	Weight on Earth (pounds)	Approximate Ratio of Weights
Mercury—about 40	100	$\frac{2}{5}$
Venus—about 90	100	$\frac{9}{10}$
Jupiter—about 240	100	$\frac{12}{5}$
Saturn—about 90	100	$\frac{9}{10}$
Neptune—about 110	100	$\frac{11}{10}$

29. If Leo weighs 80 pounds on Earth, about how much would he weigh on Mercury?

30. **Compare** Scientists want to send a probe first to Saturn and then to Neptune. The probe will weigh 27 pounds on Saturn. About how much will the probe weigh on Neptune?

31. **Analyze** Jan says that 480 pounds on Jupiter is the same as 80 pounds on Mercury. Is Jan right? Explain.

32. **Write About It** On which planet could you jump higher, Mercury or Venus? Explain your reasoning.

Mixed Review • Test Prep

Solve for *n*. *(pages 280–283)*

33. $n \times 12 = 36$

34. $1 + 2 \times n = 13$

35. $27 \div n = 3$

36. $3 \times (7 - n) = 9$

Choose the letter of the correct answer. *(pages 252–254, 262–263)*

37 Which expression shows the Distributive Property correctly applied to 8×15?

A $8 + 3 \times 8 + 5$

B $8 \times 3 + 8 \times 5$

C $8 + 6 \times 8 + 9$

D $8 \times 6 + 8 \times 9$

38 What is the value of p in $52 + (36 + 5) = (52 + p) + 5$?

F 46

G 21

H 11

J 36

Logical Thinking

Relationships

A planet's escape velocity (in meters per second) is the lowest speed at which an object must travel to escape the planet's gravity. Compare the data on escape velocity with the data in the table above. Describe any connection you see between the planets' escape velocities and the ratios of weights shown in the third column above.

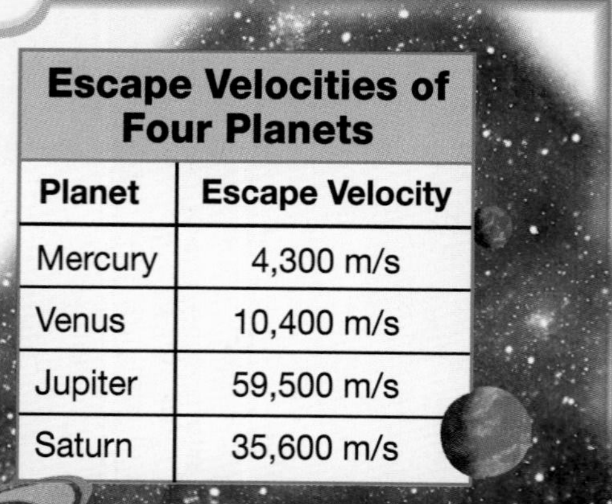

Escape Velocities of Four Planets	
Planet	Escape Velocity
Mercury	4,300 m/s
Venus	10,400 m/s
Jupiter	59,500 m/s
Saturn	35,600 m/s

Extra Practice See Set D on page 337.

Practice Game

Bargain Hunting

Practice using estimation and rates by playing this game with a partner. Try to spend the least money!

Players
2

What You'll Need

- *copy of a shopping list for each player (Teaching Tool 6)*

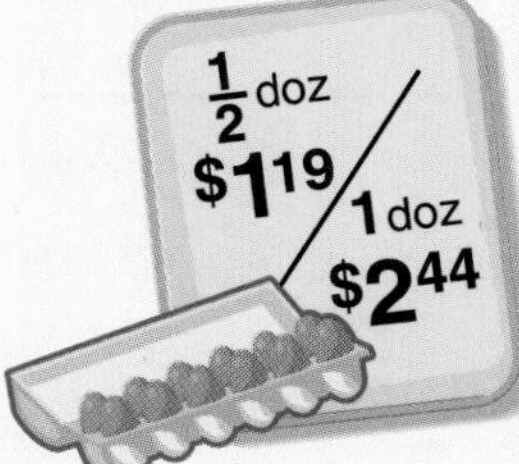

Shopping List

4 gal milk
48 oz jam
16 oranges
3 dozen eggs
10 lb potatoes

Here's What to Do

1. Each player estimates the least expensive way to buy the items on the grocery list.
2. One player acts as cashier and determines how much the other player's groceries cost.
3. Players then trade roles.
4. The player who spends the least amount of money during his or her shopping trip wins the game.

Variation: Players create their own versions of the shopping list. Then they follow Steps 1–4.

Share Your Thinking Does a smaller amount of a product always have a less expensive unit price? Explain why or why not.

Problem-Solving Strategy: Write an Equation

You will learn how to solve a problem by writing an equation.

Sometimes writing an equation is the easiest way to solve a problem. Before you write an equation, you need to understand the problem.

Problem Ryan's mom buys a box of his favorite cereal. Each serving in the box has 210 calories, and 20 of the calories in each serving are from fat. If the box has a total of 1,890 calories, how many calories from fat are in the box of cereal?

Understand

What is the question?

How many calories from fat are in the box of cereal?

What do you know?

Each serving has 210 calories.
Each serving has 20 calories from fat.
The box has a total of 1,890 calories.

Plan

How can you find the answer?

Write an equation that will help you find the number of calories from fat in the box of cereal.

Solve

Write the equation and solve.

fat calories per serving → 20; total calories per serving → 210; fat calories in one box → c; total calories in one box → 1,890

$$\frac{20}{210} = \frac{c}{1{,}890}$$

$20 \times 1{,}890 = 210 \times c$ ← Use cross products.

$37{,}800 = 210 \times c$

$180 = c$

There are 180 calories from fat in the box of cereal.

Look Back

Look back at the problem.

Do you know how many servings are in the box? Explain.

Remember:
- ► Understand
- ► Plan
- ► Solve
- ► Look Back

Guided Practice

Write an equation to solve each problem.

1. There are 605 grams in a box of Corinne's favorite cereal. Each day she eats 2 servings for breakfast. If there are 10 servings of cereal in one box, how many grams does Corinne eat each day?

   Think: What will the variable in your equation represent?

2. A package of pretzels has 4,950 calories and 450 milligrams of sodium. If each pretzel has 33 calories, how many milligrams of sodium does each pretzel have?

   Think: Can you use cross multiplication to help you solve the problem?

Choose a Strategy

Solve. Use these or other strategies.

Problem-Solving Strategies

- **Write an Equation**
- **Use Logical Thinking**
- **Work Backward**
- **Guess and Check**

3. A jar of dried fruit contains 10 servings and 100 calories. If there are 5 pieces of fruit in one serving, how many calories are in one piece?

4. Eddy and Cecilia each buy a drink. Eddy drinks 16 fl oz in 20 minutes. Cecilia drinks 20 fl oz in 24 minutes. Who drinks at a faster rate?

5. One serving of peanuts contains 14 grams of fat. If an entire jar of peanuts contains 532 grams of fat and 190 grams of protein, how many grams of protein are in one serving of peanuts?

6. Wayne bought 2 boxes of raisins and 3 packages of sunflower seeds to make trail mix. He spent $5.38. If one package of sunflower seeds cost $1.00, how much did each box of raisins cost?

7. Ray plays a dart-throw game 3 times and pops 1 balloon. Frank tries 6 times and pops 5 balloons. Gary pops one more balloon than Ray pops. Together, the three boys must pop 12 balloons to win a prize. How many more balloons must they pop?

8. Anna spent $7.08 on 2 different types of onions—red and yellow. She bought 4 lb of each type of onion. The red onions were $0.05 more per pound than the yellow onions. How much did she spend on each pound of red onions? on each pound of yellow onions?

Extra Practice See 1–4 on page 339.

Quick Check

Check Your Understanding of Lessons 1–5

Simplify each ratio if possible. Then express each in two other forms.

1. 60 pens to 4 pencils **2.** 6:30 **3.** $\frac{15}{3}$

Write each as a unit rate.

4. 100 mi on 4 gal

5. \$2.40 for 16 minutes

6. 78 questions in 3 hours

7. 20 for 10 dollars

Find the missing term in each.

8. $\frac{2}{5} = \frac{8}{y}$ **9.** $\frac{10}{15} = \frac{q}{45}$ **10.** $\frac{18}{m} = \frac{6}{9}$ **11.** $\frac{1{,}200}{20} = \frac{x}{1}$

Compare. Write = or ≠ for each ⬬.

12. $\frac{1}{2}$ ⬬ $\frac{10}{20}$ **13.** 5:2 ⬬ 15:5 **14.** 6 to 10 ⬬ 12 to 20 **15.** $\frac{8}{3}$ ⬬ $\frac{32}{9}$

Solve.

16. As a waitress, Peg worked for \$6 an hour. In addition, she received \$10 in tips. How many hours did she work if she earned \$34 in all?

How did you do?

If you had difficulty with any items in the Quick Check, you can use the following pages for review and extra practice.

Items	Review These Pages	Do These Extra Practice Items
1–3	pages 304–305	Set A, page 336
4–7	pages 306–307	Set B, page 336
8–15	pages 308–309	Set C, page 336
8–11	pages 310–312	Set D, page 337
16	pages 314–315	1–4, page 339

Test Prep • Cumulative Review

Maintaining the Standards

Choose the letter of the correct answer.

1 Which integer correctly completes the number sentence?

$$^{-}12 + \blacksquare = {}^{+}5$$

A $^{-}17$

B $^{-}7$

C $^{+}7$

D $^{+}17$

2 In a football game, Allen is at the 30-yard line. He gains 5 yards, loses 3 yards, then gains 7 yards. What is Allen's final position?

F 33-yard line

G 35-yard line

H 39-yard line

J 45-yard line

3 Marge has $6.55. After she lends some money to Sarah, she has $4.70 left. How much money did Marge lend to Sarah?

A $1.85

B $2.25

C $4.70

D $11.25

4 Fiona bought 15 apples for a pie and 18 peaches for a cobbler. What is the ratio of apples to peaches?

F $\frac{18}{15}$

G $\frac{6}{5}$

H 5:6

J 2:3

5 Which shows rational numbers ordered from least to greatest?

A $-\frac{3}{4}$ $\;-1\frac{2}{3}$ $\;+\frac{5}{6}$ $\;+1\frac{1}{6}$

B $-1\frac{2}{3}$ $\;-\frac{3}{4}$ $\;+1\frac{1}{6}$ $\;+\frac{5}{6}$

C $-\frac{3}{4}$ $\;-1\frac{2}{3}$ $\;+1\frac{1}{6}$ $\;+\frac{5}{6}$

D $-1\frac{2}{3}$ $\;-\frac{3}{4}$ $\;+\frac{5}{6}$ $\;+1\frac{1}{6}$

6 Derek is going to a theme park for three days. How much money does Derek save if he buys the three-day pass under Plan 2?

Theme Park	
Plan 1	Plan 2
$21.50 all-day pass	$55 for 3-day pass

F $9.50

G $21.50

H $33.50

J $12.50

7 On a test, Leonard is asked to find the missing term in the proportion $\frac{12}{3} = \frac{k}{6}$. He answers that the missing term k is 15. Is Leonard's answer correct?

Explain Use words or equations to support your answer.

Safe Site

Internet Test Prep
Visit **www.eduplace.com/kids/mhm** for more *Test Prep Practice.*

Distance, Speed, and Time

You will learn that speed is a rate that compares distance with time.

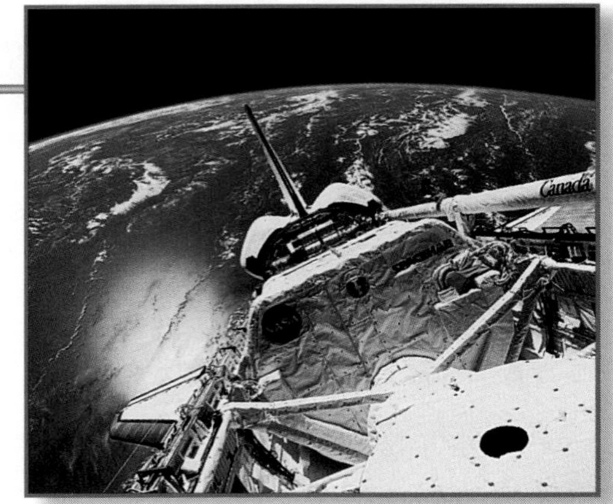

Learn About It

Did you ever wonder how fast the space shuttle travels? As it orbits Earth, the space shuttle travels approximately 420,000 miles in a day. Speed is a rate—a ratio of distance to time. About how many miles does the shuttle travel per hour in orbit?

Find the speed.

Step 1 Write the formula relating speed, distance, and time.

$$\text{speed} = \frac{\text{distance}}{\text{time}}$$

$$s = \frac{d}{t}$$

Step 2 Substitute the information you know in the formula. Then simplify to find the unit rate.

$$s = \frac{420{,}000 \text{ mi}}{24 \text{ h}}$$

$$s = \frac{17{,}500 \text{ mi}}{1 \text{ h}} = 17{,}500 \text{ mi/h}$$

Solution: The space shuttle travels about 17,500 mi/h in orbit.

A slash, /, is often used for the word *per*.

Explain Your Thinking

► What is the difference between distance and distance per hour?

► How are these equations related?

$d = s \times t \qquad s = \frac{d}{t}$

Other Examples

A. Find Distance

Find the distance traveled in 5 hours at 30 mi/h.

$s = \frac{d}{t}$

$30 = \frac{d}{5}$

$30 \times 5 = \frac{d}{5} \times 5$

$d = 150$ mi

B. Find Average Speed

If you walk 10 blocks in 20 minutes, what is your average speed in blocks per minute?

$s = \frac{d}{t}$

$s = \frac{10}{20} = \frac{1}{2}$

$s = \frac{1}{2}$ block per minute

Your average speed is $\frac{1}{2}$ block per minute.

Guided Practice

Find the speed (s) or the distance (d).

1. $s = ■$
$d = 225$ mi
$t = 5$ h

2. $s = 300$ mi/h
$d = ■$
$t = 6$ h

3. $s = 20$ mi/h
$d = ■$
$t = 6$ min

Ask Yourself

- Do I need to change the unit of a measure?
- How do I label my answer?

Independent Practice

Find the speed (*s*) or the distance (*d*).

4. $s = \blacksquare$ $d = 25$ ft $t = 1$ h

5. $s = \blacksquare$ $d = 60$ mi $t = 2.5$ h

6. $s = 250$ mi/h $d = \blacksquare$ $t = 2$ h

7. $s = \blacksquare$ $d = 42$ in. $t = 7$ min

8. $s = 45$ mi/h $d = \blacksquare$ $t = \frac{1}{3}$ h

Use the formula relating speed, distance, and time to find out if the speeds in each pair are equivalent. Write *yes* or *no*.

9. $\frac{150 \text{ mi}}{3 \text{ h}}$ $\frac{50 \text{ mi}}{1 \text{ h}}$

10. $\frac{28 \text{ mi}}{4 \text{ h}}$ $\frac{4 \text{ mi}}{1 \text{ h}}$

11. $\frac{100 \text{ ft}}{10 \text{ s}}$ $\frac{10 \text{ ft}}{1 \text{ s}}$

12. $\frac{250 \text{ yd}}{50 \text{ s}}$ $\frac{5 \text{ yd}}{5 \text{ s}}$

13. $\frac{25 \text{ mi}}{2 \text{ h}}$ $\frac{100 \text{ mi}}{4 \text{ h}}$

14. $\frac{300 \text{ mi}}{12 \text{ h}}$ $\frac{50 \text{ mi}}{6 \text{ h}}$

Problem Solving • Reasoning

Use the table for Problems 16 and 17.

Skylab 1	
Minutes per orbit	93
Distance per orbit	approximately 26,600 miles
Total distance traveled	11.5 million miles
Length of mission	approximately 28 days

15. Analyze Astronauts use a chair-shaped craft called a Manned Maneuvering Unit (MMU) to move around in space. *Skylab 1* is about 120 feet long. If it takes 2 seconds for an MMU to travel the length of *Skylab 1*, how fast does the MMU travel in ft/s?

16. Compare *Skylab 3*'s mission lasted approximately three times longer than *Skylab 1*'s did. Calculate the following for *Skylab 3*.

a. approximate length of mission

b. approximate distance traveled

17. At about what speed does *Skylab 1* orbit Earth? Express your answer in mi/h.

18. Write About It Use reference books or the Internet to find more information about space vehicles. Write a problem about distance, speed, and time that can be solved by using rates.

The *Skylab* space station in orbit around Earth.

Mixed Review • Test Prep

Evaluate each expression, given $b = 3$. *(pages 252–254, 256–260)*

19. $(5.2 \times b) \times 2$

20. $(b - 1) \times 0$

21. $(6 + 7) \times b$

22. $27 \times (b + 2)$

23 What is $\frac{8}{5} \div 6$? *(pages 176–177)*

A $9\frac{2}{3}$ **B** $\frac{4}{15}$ **C** $\frac{5}{48}$ **D** $3\frac{3}{4}$

Extra Practice See Set E on page 337.

Scale Drawings

You will learn how scale drawings represent larger or smaller objects.

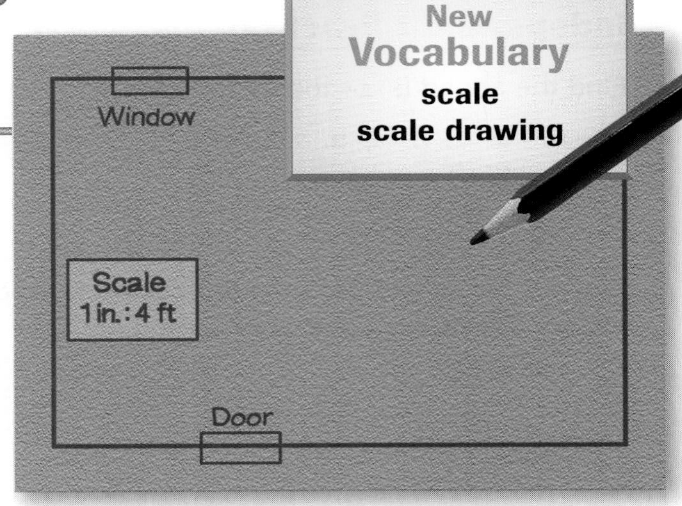

Learn About It

A **scale** is a ratio of the measurements in a drawing of an object to the corresponding measurements of the actual object. When a drawing is created using a scale, it is called a **scale drawing**. Use the scale on the right to find the actual length and width of the room shown.

Step 1 Write a ratio of the length of the room in the drawing to the actual length of the room (l).

length in drawing → $\frac{3 \text{ in.}}{l \text{ ft}}$ ← actual length

Step 2 Write a proportion that shows this ratio is equivalent to the scale. Use cross multiplication to find l.

length in drawing, actual length → $\frac{3 \text{ in.}}{l \text{ ft}} = \frac{1 \text{ in.}}{4 \text{ ft}}$ ← length in drawing, actual length

$\frac{3}{l} \times \frac{1}{4}$

$l = 12$ ft

Step 3 Repeat these steps to find the actual width of the room (w).

$\frac{2 \text{ in.}}{w \text{ ft}} = \frac{1 \text{ in.}}{4 \text{ ft}}$

$\frac{2}{w} \times \frac{1}{4}$

$w = 8$ ft

Solution: The actual room is 8 feet wide and 12 feet long.

Another Example

Drawing Is Larger Than Object

Width of object in drawing: 30 in.
Scale: 3 in. : 1 in.

Find the actual width, w, of the object.

$\frac{30}{w} = \frac{3}{1}$

$30 \times 1 = w \times 3$ ← Cross multiply.

$30 = w \times 3$

$10 = w$

The actual width is 10 in.

Explain Your Thinking

- ► Why is order important in proportions?
- ► If the scale 1 in. : 1 in. is used to make a scale drawing, what do you know about the object(s) in the drawing?

Guided Practice

Use the scale 1 in. : 3 ft to solve Problems 1–3.

1. length in drawing: 3 in. actual length: ■
2. width in drawing: $\frac{1}{2}$ in. actual width: ■
3. height in drawing: ■ actual height: 30 ft

Ask Yourself

- Did I use the correct units (inches or feet) in my answers?

Independent Practice

Use the scales below to find the actual measure(s) of each object.

1 in. : 2 ft **4.** room is $7\frac{1}{2}$ in. by 8 in. **5.** chair is 1 in. wide **6.** rug is 5 in. by 6 in.

$\frac{1}{2}$ in. : 1 ft **7.** model dresser is 3 in. by 1.5 in. **8.** diameter of model table is 4 in.

Use the scale 1 in. : 75 mi to find each missing measure.

9. ■ in. to 150 mi **10.** 3 in. to ■ mi **11.** ■ in. to 300 mi **12.** $\frac{1}{3}$ in. to ■ mi

13. $7\frac{1}{2}$ in. to ■ mi **14.** ■ in. to 75 mi **15.** ■ in. to 25 mi **16.** $\frac{1}{5}$ in. to ■ mi

Problem Solving • Reasoning

17. The wingspan of an airplane measures 90 ft. A model of the airplane has a wingspan of $4\frac{1}{2}$ inches. What scale was used to build the model?

18. An architect's drawing of a room has a scale of 1 in. : 1 ft. What are the measurements of the actual room if it is 30 in. by 16 in. in the drawing?

19. **Compare** You are comparing two scale drawings of your neighborhood. The scale of the first drawing is 1 in. : 12 ft. The scale of the second drawing is 1 in. : 1 ft. Each drawing is on an $8\frac{1}{2}$ in. by 11 in. piece of paper. Which drawing shows more of the neighborhood?

20. **Analyze** Both Anna and Ralf are making a scale drawing of their classroom. Anna uses a scale of 2 in. : 6 ft. Ralf uses a scale of 3 in. : 6 ft. What is the ratio of the measures on Anna's drawing to the corresponding measures on Ralf's?

SOCIAL STUDIES In 1912, President William H. Taft approved regulations for the shape of the United States flag. An official U.S. flag must have a width-to-length ratio of 1:1.9 ($\frac{1}{1.9}$). If you want to make an official U.S. flag that is 9.5 m wide, what will its length be?

Mixed Review • Test Prep

Solve. *(pages 12–13, 214–216, 218–220)*

21. $^{-}3 + 9$ **22.** $^{-}2 - (^{-}5)$ **23.** $5 - (^{-}4)$ **24.** $206 + 918$

Choose the letter that shows the correct value of *f*. *(pages 284–285)*

25 $22\frac{5}{8} + f = 25$

A $2\frac{1}{8}$ **C** $3\frac{1}{4}$

B $2\frac{3}{8}$ **D** $3\frac{1}{2}$

26 $f - \frac{2}{3} = 3\frac{1}{2}$

F $2\frac{1}{6}$ **H** $4\frac{1}{6}$

G $2\frac{2}{3}$ **J** $3\frac{1}{3}$

Extra Practice See Set F on page 337.

LESSON 8

Problem-Solving Skill: Is the Answer Reasonable?

You will learn how to decide whether or not an answer to a problem is reasonable.

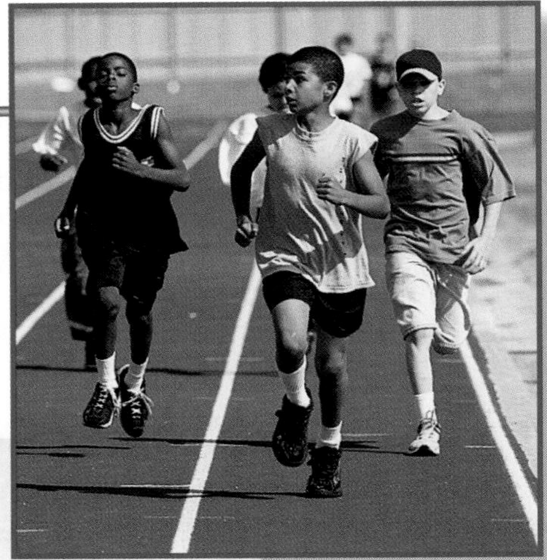

After you have solved a problem, look back at the information in the problem and decide whether or not the answer is reasonable.

Look at the situations below.

Sometimes the calculations are incorrect.

Jay and Roberto exercise together every day after school. They spend 24 minutes stretching and 30 minutes running. Jay calculated how much time they spend exercising each week.

$24 + 30 = 54$ min each day

$54 \times 5 = 270$ min each week

$270 \div 6 = 45$ hours each week

Jay's answer is unreasonable. They exercised for a little less than an hour each day. So his answer should be just under 5 hours.

Sometimes the problem is misinterpreted.

On a map, the scale is 2 cm:4 km. Kay needs to know the distance in kilometers between two cities that are 8 cm apart on the map. She used a proportion to solve the problem.

$\frac{2}{4} = \frac{d}{8}$ $4d = 2 \times 8$ $d = 4$ The cities are 4 km apart.

Kay's answer is unreasonable. The scale shows that 2 cm on the map represents 4 km. The cities are more than 2 cm apart on the map, therefore they must actually be more than 4 km apart.

Look Back When checking for a reasonable answer, why is it important to look back at the information given in the problem?

Left: An athlete competes in the Girl's Long Jump event at the National Junior Olympics.
Right: A gymnast practices her routine.

Guided Practice

Determine whether each answer is reasonable. Explain why or why not.

1. Kim practices her gymnastics routines for 20 minutes on Monday. She practices twice as long on Tuesday. When Kim compares Monday's time with Tuesday's time, she writes the ratio 2:1. Is her ratio reasonable?

Which number should appear first in the ratio?

2. At a track and field meet, Paula jumped 8 feet, $11\frac{3}{4}$ feet, 9 feet, and $10\frac{1}{2}$ feet in the long jump. She said that her average jump was 12 feet. Is this a reasonable average?

Think: Is her solution too large or too small?

Choose a Strategy

Solve. Use these or other strategies.

Problem-Solving Strategies

- **Use Logical Thinking**
- **Write an Equation**
- **Draw a Diagram**
- **Find a Pattern**

3. After she writes her essay, Martha will pay Mario \$2 per page to type it and \$4 to type her reference pages. Her paper will be 3 pages long and have 1 reference page. Mario says he will earn \$6. Is this reasonable? Why or why not?

4. Clara is 12 years old. At present, the ratio of Clara's age to her brother's age is 2:1. When Clara was 10, was the ratio of her age to her brother's age equivalent to the present ratio? Explain your reasoning.

5. In a right triangle, three line segments are drawn connecting the midpoints of the sides of the right triangle. What shape is formed by these new line segments?

6. Gina and Victoria must each find the ratio of the lengths of their arm spans to their heights. Gina calculates 5:1, and Victoria calculates 12:1. Are their results reasonable? Why or why not?

7. Look at the pattern below. What number is likely to come next?

$$\frac{1}{8} \quad \frac{1}{4} \quad \frac{1}{2} \quad \frac{1}{1} \quad \frac{2}{1} \quad \frac{4}{1}$$

8. Trinh and Marisol share an amount of money in a ratio of 4:5. If Marisol has \$10 more than Trinh, how much money does each person have?

Extra Practice See 5–7 on page 339.

Quick Check

Check Your Understanding of Lessons 6–8

Find the speed (s) or the distance (d).

1. $s = ■$, $d = 300$ mi, $t = 2$ h
2. $s = ■$, $d = 15$ mi, $t = \frac{1}{4}$ h
3. $s = 20$ mi/h, $d = ■$, $t = 30$ min

Use the scale 1 in.:$\frac{1}{2}$ ft to find the measure(s) of each image in a scale drawing.

4. actual classroom is 20 ft by 28 ft
5. actual bookshelf is 6 ft high

Use the scale 1 in.:2 ft to find the actual measure(s) of each object.

6. model bed is 3 in. long
7. drawing of bedroom is 5 in. by 7 in.

Write an equation to solve each problem.

8. In the restaurant where David works, entrees cost \$6, and soft drinks cost \$1.50. David invites his 4 family members to eat at the restaurant. Each person will order one entree and one soft drink. David thinks that \$40 is enough to pay for everyone's meal, including his own. Is this reasonable? Explain your answer.

How did you do?

If you had difficulty with any items in the Quick Check, you can use the following pages for review and extra practice.

Items	Review These Pages	Do These Extra Practice Items
1–3	pages 318–319	Set E, page 337
4–7	pages 320–321	Set F, page 337
8	pages 322–323	5–7, page 339

Test Prep • Cumulative Review

Maintaining the Standards

Choose the letter of the correct answer.

1 At a local pet store, the ratio of canaries to parakeets is 11 to 15. How can this ratio be written in a different way?

A 15 to 11 **C** $\frac{11}{15}$

B $\frac{15}{11}$ **D** 11 out of 15

2 What is the value of c in the equation $c \div 3 = 12$?

F 3 **H** 4

G 15 **J** 36

3 Evaluate the expression $(4 - \frac{2}{3}) \times 2 \div \frac{1}{3}$.

A $1\frac{1}{3}$ **C** 12

B $1\frac{1}{9}$ **D** 20

4 Kieran can run six laps around the track in 30 minutes. At this rate, how long will it take him to run 10 laps?

F 34 minutes **H** 50 minutes

G 18 minutes **J** 60 minutes

5 A map uses a scale of 1 in.:400 mi. If a distance on the map measures $4\frac{1}{2}$ in., how many miles is the actual distance?

A 88 miles

B 100 miles

C 1,600 miles

D 1,800 miles

6 Which shows numbers ordered from least to greatest?

F $^-1.8$ $^-0.6$ $^+\frac{1}{3}$ $^+\frac{4}{5}$

G $^-0.6$ $^-1.8$ $^+\frac{1}{3}$ $^+\frac{4}{5}$

H $^-0.6$ $^-1.8$ $^+\frac{4}{5}$ $^+\frac{1}{3}$

J $^-1.8$ $^-0.6$ $^+\frac{4}{5}$ $^+\frac{1}{3}$

7 What fraction does point A represent on the number line?

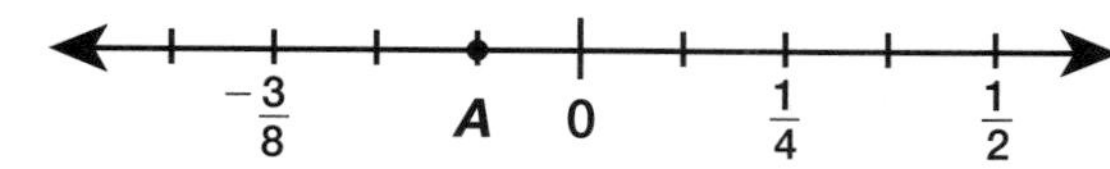

A $^-1$

B $-\frac{1}{4}$

C $-\frac{1}{2}$

D $-\frac{1}{8}$

8 Write and solve algebraic equations for each.

a. The product of 8 and a number is 72.

b. The quantity 72 plus a number, decreased by 72, is 8.

Explain Show how you solved each equation.

Safe Site

Internet Test Prep
Visit **www.eduplace.com/kids/mhm** for more *Test Prep Practice.*

Decimals and Percents

You will learn how to compare numbers by writing equivalent decimals and percents.

Learn About It

Some students visited a local recycling plant. They discovered that only a small percent of all discarded glass, aluminum, and paper is recycled. They wanted to compare the percents of these three materials that are recycled. Order the amounts of the materials recycled from least to greatest.

Materials Recycled	
glass	0.12
aluminum	0.38
paper	26%

Compare 0.12, 0.38, and 26%.

Step 1 Write equivalent percents for 0.12 and 0.38.

$0.12 = \frac{12}{100} = 12\%$

$0.38 = \frac{38}{100} = 38\%$

Step 2 Order the three percents from least to greatest.

$12\% < 26\% < 38\%$

Solution: glass (12%) < paper (26%) < aluminum (38%)

Other Examples

A. Write an Equivalent Decimal

18.5% = 0.18.5 = 0.185

158% = 1.58. = 1.58

Move the decimal point two places to the left and remove the percent sign.

B. Percents Over 100

1.56 = 1.56.% = 156%

Move the decimal point two places to the right and write a percent sign.

Explain Your Thinking

► Why is it helpful to write numbers in the same form before you compare them?

► Is it easier for you to compare decimals or percents? Explain why.

Guided Practice

Express each decimal as a percent. Then order from least to greatest.

1. 17% 0.56 0.18

2. 250% 2.49 200%

Write an equivalent percent or decimal for each.

3. 48% **4.** 2.38 **5.** 77% **6.** 6.01

7. 37.5% **8.** 6.8 **9.** 0.125 **10.** 404%

Ask Yourself

- Is the decimal or percent greater than or less than 1?
- Did I move the decimal point in the proper direction?

Independent Practice

Express each decimal as a percent. Then order from least to greatest.

11. 18% 0.15 99%
12. 0.22 0.01 0.83
13. 78% 48% 0.50
14. 75% 1.01 0.40
15. 115% 91% 0.90
16. 0.01 0.02 5%

Write an equivalent percent or decimal for each.

17. 15%
18. 3%
19. 0.99
20. 1.58
21. 140%
22. 15.9%
23. 0.015
24. 0.01
25. 0.5%
26. 10.1

n **Algebra • Equations** **Solve for *n*.**

27. $0.45 = n\%$
28. $1.6 = n\%$
29. $n\% = 0.01$
30. $n = 15\%$
31. $n = 149\%$
32. $38.5\% = n$

Problem Solving • Reasoning

Solve. Choose a method.

Computation Methods

• **Mental Math** • **Estimation** • **Paper and Pencil** • **Calculator**

33. The class found that, on average, a local landfill contains about twice as much construction waste as industrial waste. If these wastes together account for 9% of total landfill waste, about what percent of total landfill waste is made up of construction waste?

34. Compare The students find that 52% of all their neighbors recycle newspapers and aluminum cans. The other people in the neighborhood do not recycle at all. Which group is larger, newspaper and can recyclers or people who do not recycle at all?

35. Analyze Ms. Simmons's students find that, on average, 0.72 of every pound of material in a local landfill is household waste. Approximately what percent of the material in that landfill is not household waste?

36. Patterns The class discovers that one city landfill was filled as follows during a 6-year period: 1995, 40% full; 1997, 0.45 full; 1999, 0.55 full; and 2001, 70% full. If the pattern continues, by 2003, what percent will likely be filled?

Mixed Review • Test Prep

Identify the property shown. *(pages 256–257, 262–263)*

37. $1 \times h = h \times 1$
38. $7 \times 0 = 0$
39. $3 \times 94 = (3 \times 90) + (3 \times 4)$

40 What value of g makes the equation $1{,}328 + g = 1{,}783$ true? *(pages 280–281)*

A 400 **B** 455 **C** 3,111 **D** 2,083

Extra Practice See Set G on page 338.

Fractions and Percents

You will learn how to express fractions as percents.

Learn About It

Students at Lake View Elementary School are choosing their events for field day. Three out of every four students signed up for the three-legged race. What percent of the students signed up for this event?

Convert. $\frac{3}{4} = \blacksquare\%$

Different Ways to Change Fractions to Percents

You can use equivalent fractions.

Step 1 Write an equivalent fraction with a denominator of 100.

$\frac{3}{4} \xrightarrow{\times 20} = \frac{75}{100}$ (multiply numerator and denominator by 20)

Step 2 Write the fraction as a percent.

$\frac{75}{100} = 75\%$

You can divide the numerator by the denominator to obtain a decimal.

Step 1 Divide.

$$\begin{array}{r} 0.75 \\ 4\overline{)3.00} \\ -\,28 \\ \hline 20 \\ -\,20 \\ \hline 0 \end{array}$$

Step 2 Write the decimal as a percent.

$0.75 = 75\%$

Solution: Seventy-five percent of the students signed up for the three-legged race.

Other Examples

A. Percents to Fractions

$20\% = \frac{20}{100}$

$= \frac{1}{5}$ ⟵ Simplify.

B. Numerator Greater Than Denominator

$\frac{5}{4} = \frac{125}{100} = 125\%$ (× 25 numerator and denominator)

Explain Your Thinking

► How could you write $\frac{a}{20}$ as a percent?

► Explain why 100% is equal to 1.

Guided Practice

Write an equivalent percent or fraction in simplest form.

1. $\frac{1}{4}$ **2.** $\frac{2}{5}$ **3.** 75% **4.** $\frac{17}{20}$ **5.** 160%

6. 80% **7.** $\frac{9}{10}$ **8.** $\frac{50}{200}$ **9.** 145% **10.** 2%

Ask Yourself

- Can I write an equivalent fraction?
- Can I divide the numerator by the denominator?

Independent Practice

Write an equivalent percent or fraction in simplest form.

11. $\frac{3}{4}$ **12.** $\frac{4}{5}$ **13.** $\frac{10}{4}$ **14.** $\frac{3}{10}$ **15.** 16%

16. 40% **17.** 85% **18.** 205% **19.** 120% **20.** $\frac{3}{50}$

21. $\frac{49}{20}$ **22.** $\frac{1}{2}$ **23.** 14% **24.** $\frac{100}{25}$ **25.** $\frac{3}{1}$

26. $\frac{1}{10}$ **27.** 38% **28.** 95% **29.** $\frac{9}{5}$ **30.** 10%

Problem Solving • Reasoning

Use Data **Use the circle graph for Problems 33 and 34.**

31. Two out of every five students plan to enter the sack race. What percent of students will enter?

32. Analyze The entire sixth-grade class will be divided equally into four teams. What percent of the students will be on each team?

33. What fraction of the students in the wheelbarrow race are sixth-graders? What percent are fourth-graders?

34. Write About It Do the fifth-grade students represent $\frac{7}{20}$ or $\frac{9}{20}$ of the students in the wheelbarrow race? Explain.

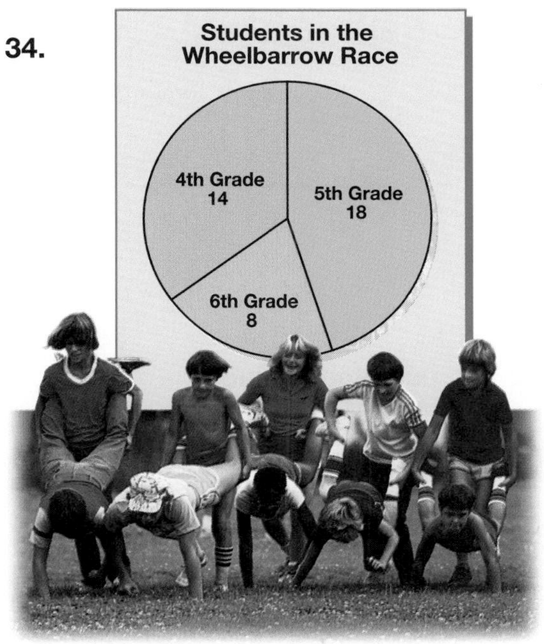

Mixed Review • Test Prep

Write an expression for each phrase. Evaluate each expression, given $z = 2.4$. *(pages 258–260, 270–275)*

35. z times 19 **36.** one third of z **37.** the sum of 8.7 and z times 4.6

38 What is the value of b in the equation $5 \times b - 10 = 5$? *(pages 280–283)*

A 2 **B** 15 **C** 5 **D** 3

Extra Practice See Set H on page 338.

LESSON 11

Fractions, Decimals, and Percents

You will learn how to compare fractions, decimals, and percents.

Learn About It

Veronica, Sam, and Jamie are competing in a pie-eating contest at the county fair. Whoever can eat the most pie in one minute will win. So far, Veronica has eaten 0.8 of her pie. Sam has eaten $\frac{3}{10}$, and Jamie has eaten 40% of her pie. Who has eaten the most pie so far? Who has eaten the least?

Compare 0.8, $\frac{3}{10}$, and 40% of one pie.

Different Ways to Compare Fractions, Decimals, and Percents

You can use a number line to show parts of a unit.

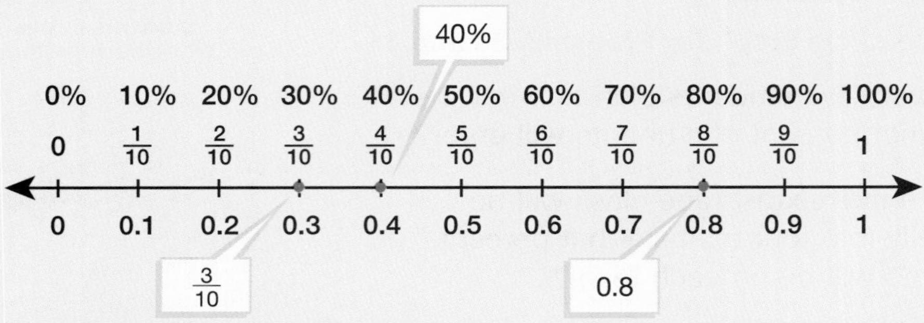

You can use place value.

- Change all of the numbers to decimals in hundredths.
- Compare.

	ones	.	tenths	hundredths
0.8	0	.	8	0
$\frac{3}{10}$	0	.	3	0
40%	0	.	4	0

Solution: So far, Veronica has eaten the most pie. Sam has eaten the least.

Another Example

With Mixed Numbers

Compare 20%, 1.10, and $1\frac{1}{2}$.

20% = 0.20

$1\frac{1}{2}$ = 1.50

1.10 = 1.10

$1\frac{1}{2} > 1.10 > 20\%$

Explain Your Thinking

► In the problem above, could you change all of the numbers to fractions in order to compare them? Why or why not?

Guided Practice

Order each set from the least to the greatest part of a unit.

1. 0.65 $\frac{3}{5}$ 3.0 $\frac{1}{2}$

2. $\frac{5}{6}$ $\frac{80}{100}$ 1.2 1.9

3. 0.12 $\frac{1}{10}$ 11% 0.20

4. $\frac{6}{5}$ 125% 0.95

5. $\frac{3}{5}$ $\frac{1}{2}$ 0.61 65%

6. $\frac{7}{5}$ 43% 1.95

> **Ask Yourself**
> - Can I use a number line to compare the numbers?
> - Can I use place value to compare numbers?

Independent Practice

Order each set from the least to the greatest part of a unit.

7. 1.1 $\frac{7}{10}$ 99%

8. 4% 0.05 $\frac{2}{20}$

9. $\frac{1}{2}$ 63% 0.6

10. $\frac{14}{5}$ 3.0 250%

11. 0.13 0.31 3.1%

12. $\frac{80}{200}$ 51% $\frac{1}{2}$

Order each set from the greatest to the least part of a unit.

13. 65% $\frac{4}{5}$ 0.9

14. 3.2 $\frac{3}{2}$ 0.8 $\frac{3}{4}$

15. $\frac{1}{10}$ 0.15 13% 1.0

16. 10% $\frac{1}{5}$ 0.65

17. $\frac{3}{4}$ $\frac{4}{5}$ 28%

18. $\frac{9}{4}$ 2.26 2.6 230%

Problem Solving • Reasoning

19. Matthew has a roll of tickets that he can use for any ride at the fair. He uses 15% of his roll to ride the roller coaster and 0.05 of the roll to ride the merry-go-round. For which ride did he use more tickets?

20. Stacy entered her birdhouse in the arts-and-crafts competition at the fair. Thirty-two percent of the entries won blue ribbons, $\frac{2}{5}$ were awarded red ribbons, and 0.28 won green ribbons. Which color ribbon was awarded most?

21. Logical Thinking John and Mary each played ring toss 8 times. Mary won $\frac{1}{4}$ of her games. John lost 25% of his games. Who won more games?

22. Write Your Own Write a problem that involves comparing fractions, decimals, and percents. Challenge a classmate to solve your problem.

Mixed Review • Test Prep

Round each number to the place of the underlined digit. *(pages 8–9)*

23. $5\underline{0}3.21$ **24.** $\underline{2}51.6$ **25.** $0.0\underline{0}9$ **26.** $0.9\underline{9}9$ **27.** $99\underline{7}.96$

Choose the letter of the correct answer. *(pages 20–21, 34–35)*

28 3.6 × 54

A 1.944 **C** 194.4

B 19.44 **D** 1,944

29 363.4 ÷ 2.3

F 1,580 **H** 158

G 171 **J** 68.5

Extra Practice See Set I on page 338.

Problem-Solving Application: Use Proportions

You will learn how to use proportions to solve problems.

When you write a proportion, you need to know what information to use.

Richard is taking a typing class so that he can type faster on his computer. During his typing test, he typed 100 words correctly in 5 minutes. At that rate, how long will it take him to type a 600-word paper?

Understand

What is the question?

If Richard types 100 words in 5 minutes, how long will it take him to type a 600-word paper?

What do you know?

- Typing rate: 100 words in 5 minutes
- Paper length: 600 words

Plan

How can you find the answer?

Write a proportion.

$$\frac{100}{5} = \frac{600}{m}$$

number of words → 100; time taken to type 100 words → 5; number of words in paper → 600; time taken to type 600 words → m

Solve

Use cross multiplication to solve.

$$\frac{100}{5} \times \frac{600}{m}$$

$$100 \times m = 600 \times 5$$

$$m = 30$$

Think: $\frac{100 \times m}{100} = \frac{600 \times 5}{100}$

It will take him 30 minutes to type a 600-word paper.

Look Back

Look back at the question. Is your answer reasonable?

How many words can Richard type per minute?

Left: A picture of women working in a typing pool. *Right*: An old-fashioned typewriter.

Remember:
- Understand
- Plan
- Solve
- Look Back

Guided Practice

Solve.

1. Fern types 12 words per minute on a pretest. At this rate, how many words can Fern type in an hour?

   Think: How many minutes are in an hour?

2. Caddie can type 2,700 words in 2.5 hours. How does this rate compare with Fern's typing rate on the test? Explain.

   Think: How many words per minute can Caddie type?

Choose a Strategy

Solve. Use these or other strategies.

Problem-Solving Strategies

- **Write an Equation**
- **Work Backward**
- **Use Logical Thinking**
- **Draw a Diagram**

3. If Richard can increase his typing speed by two words per minute each week, what will his typing speed be at the end of 6 weeks? What will it be at the end of 9 weeks?

4. Four of the typing students receive awards for having the fastest typing rates. The four students account for $\frac{1}{7}$ of the students in the typing class. How many students are in the class?

5. One fifth of the people at Ali's family reunion live out of town. Forty percent of these people drove more than 100 miles to get there. If there are 50 people at Ali's family reunion, how many of them live more than 100 miles away?

6. Fern's English class has 26 students. The classroom has 10 rows of four seats each. If the students fill all the seats in a row before starting a new row, what is the ratio of rows with no students to rows with at least 1 student?

7. A job requires someone who can type 40 words per minute. Glen can type 1,300 words in $\frac{1}{2}$ hour. Does Glen type fast enough to get the job?

8. Bill and Mari both start typing a 2,000-word report at the same time. Bill types 800 words in 30 min. Mari types 1,000 words in 45 min. Who will finish first?

9. The ratio of boys to girls in English class is 2 to 7. What percent of the students are girls? What percent of the students are boys? Round your answers to the nearest tenth.

10. Is it possible for a student to increase his reading rate by 130%? Is it possible for 130% of the students in a literature class to increase their reading rates? Explain why or why not.

Extra Practice See 8–11 on page 339.

Quick Check

Check Your Understanding of Lessons 9–12

Express each decimal as a percent. Then order from least to greatest.

1. 50% 0.48 30%

2. 0.04 1.4 40%

Write an equivalent percent or decimal for each.

3. 38%

4. 0.05

5. 1.45

6. 10.5%

Write an equivalent percent or fraction in simplest form.

7. $\frac{3}{5}$

8. 68%

9. $\frac{7}{5}$

10. 120%

11. 4.09%

12. $\frac{9}{10}$

Order the numbers in each group from greatest to least.

13. 0.67 $\frac{2}{3}$ 84%

14. 0.3 0.03 $\frac{1}{3}$

15. $\frac{7}{5}$ 66% 1.59

16. $\frac{1}{2}$ $\frac{70}{200}$ 65%

Solve.

17. Thomas can type twice as fast as Willie. If Willie can type 20 words per minute, how many words can Thomas type in half an hour?

How did you do?

If you had difficulty with any items in the Quick Check, you can use the following pages for review and extra practice.

Items	Review These Pages	Do These Extra Practice Items
1–6	pages 326–327	Set G, page 338
7–12	pages 328–329	Set H, page 338
13–16	pages 330–331	Set I, page 338
17	pages 332–333	8–11, page 339

Test Prep • Cumulative Review

Maintaining the Standards

Choose the letter of the correct answer.

1 Ali bought a new book and read $\frac{1}{5}$ of the book that day. That evening, he read $\frac{1}{6}$ of the book. During the next day, he read $\frac{1}{3}$ of it. How much of the book does Ali have left to read?

A $\frac{1}{3}$

B $\frac{21}{30}$

C $\frac{3}{10}$

D $\frac{2}{5}$

2 What is the product $^{-}7 \times {}^{+}8 \times {}^{-}2$?

F $^{+}112$

G $^{-}112$

H $^{+}28$

J $^{-}28$

3 Mona drives 150 miles in $2\frac{1}{2}$ hours. At this rate, how far can she drive in 4 hours?

A 240 miles

B 250 miles

C 350 miles

D 400 miles

4 What is the value of m in the equation $m - 54 = 68$?

F 14

G 100

H 122

J 367

5 The table shows average monthly temperatures from December to May. What was the average temperature for those six months?

Average Monthly Temperatures	
Month	**Temperature**
Dec.	$^{-}6$°C
Jan.	$^{-}2$°C
Feb.	1°C
Mar.	5°C
Apr.	10°C
May	16°C

A 5°C

B 6.7°C

C 4°C

D 3.2°C

6 Which of the following is correct?

F $55\% < 0.24$

G $0.015 > 8\%$

H $67\% < 0.65$

J $0.93 > 38\%$

7 Use a number line to order the numbers from least to greatest.

1.5 6% $\frac{4}{5}$ 0.82

Explain How did you decide where to place each number on the number line?

Safe Site

Internet Test Prep
Visit **www.eduplace.com/kids/mhm** for more *Test Prep Practice.*

Extra Practice

Set A (Lesson 1, pages 304–305)

Simplify each ratio if possible. Then express each in two other forms.

1. 12 ft to 10 ft
2. 8:13
3. $\frac{15}{5}$
4. 15 miles to 6 miles
5. 110 to 2
6. $\frac{25}{60}$
7. 16 roses to 3 daisies
8. 16 shoes to 4 sandals
9. 12 to 24
10. 10:12
11. 4 dogs to 10 cats
12. 5:101
13. 6 books to 3 shelves
14. 50 students to 5 teachers
15. $\frac{60}{2}$

Set B (Lesson 2, pages 306–307)

Write each as a unit rate.

1. 60 mi in 3 h
2. $550 for 11 tickets
3. 48 concerts in 4 years
4. $18 for 3 dinners
5. 150 mi in 3 h
6. 9 feet in 3 minutes
7. 75 books for $3
8. $15 in 3 h
9. 8 commercials in 20 min
10. 36 pages in 3 hours
11. 115 mi on 5 gal
12. 12 pounds in 3 boxes
13. $10 for 40 students
14. 150 miles in 3 hours
15. 6 ft in 1 s

Set C (Lesson 3, pages 308–309)

Find the missing term in each.

1. $\frac{2}{8} = \frac{4}{a}$
2. $\frac{3}{9} = \frac{m}{18}$
3. $\frac{s}{5} = \frac{3}{15}$
4. $\frac{4}{d} = \frac{2}{14}$
5. $\frac{12}{e} = \frac{3}{1}$
6. $\frac{c}{150} = \frac{12}{15}$
7. $\frac{12}{5} = \frac{n}{100}$
8. $\frac{75}{100} = \frac{3}{h}$
9. $\frac{10}{7} = \frac{x}{14}$
10. $\frac{3}{8} = \frac{12}{k}$
11. $\frac{z}{3} = \frac{4}{6}$
12. $\frac{13}{15} = \frac{52}{y}$
13. $\frac{1}{2} = \frac{m}{10}$
14. $\frac{16}{4} = \frac{4}{x}$
15. $\frac{6}{a} = \frac{18}{15}$
16. $\frac{b}{1} = \frac{20}{5}$
17. $\frac{24}{72} = \frac{d}{144}$
18. $\frac{1}{5} = \frac{e}{45}$
19. $\frac{t}{80} = \frac{56}{20}$
20. $\frac{11}{x} = \frac{55}{10}$

Extra Practice

Set D (Lesson 4, pages 310–312)

Write the cross products for each pair of ratios. Do the two ratios form a proportion? Write *yes* or *no*.

1. $\frac{2}{9}$ $\frac{6}{27}$
2. $\frac{4}{8}$ $\frac{1}{2}$
3. $\frac{20}{3}$ $\frac{80}{12}$
4. $\frac{7}{5}$ $\frac{1}{15}$
5. $\frac{11}{5}$ $\frac{11}{5}$
6. $\frac{14}{4}$ $\frac{40}{14}$
7. $\frac{21}{27}$ $\frac{7}{9}$
8. $\frac{1}{3}$ $\frac{6}{48}$

Use cross products to find the missing term in each proportion.

9. $\frac{240}{6} = \frac{40}{a}$
10. $\frac{212}{8} = \frac{b}{2}$
11. $\frac{78}{c} = \frac{26}{3}$
12. $\frac{3}{7} = \frac{21}{d}$
13. $\frac{x}{17} = \frac{8}{1}$
14. $\frac{16}{b} = \frac{128}{40}$
15. $\frac{30}{25} = \frac{u}{30}$
16. $\frac{15}{c} = \frac{10}{20}$

Set E (Lesson 6, pages 318–319)

Find the speed (*s*) or the distance (*d*).

1. $s = ■$, $d = 165$ mi, $t = 3$ h
2. $s = ■$, $d = 90$ miles, $t = 5$ h
3. $s = 600$ mi/h, $d = ■$, $t = 20$ h
4. $s = 15$ mi/h, $d = ■$, $t = \frac{2}{3}$ h
5. $s = ■$, $d = 2$ mi, $t = 4$ h
6. $s = 30$ mi/h, $d = ■$, $t = 30$ min

Use the formula relating speed, distance, and time to find out if the speeds in each pair are equivalent. Write *yes* or *no*.

7. $\frac{75 \text{ mi}}{3 \text{ h}}$ $\frac{100 \text{ mi}}{4 \text{ h}}$
8. $\frac{27 \text{ ft}}{3 \text{ s}}$ $\frac{39 \text{ ft}}{9 \text{ s}}$
9. $\frac{50 \text{ yd}}{8 \text{ s}}$ $\frac{25 \text{ yd}}{2 \text{ s}}$
10. $\frac{3 \text{ mi}}{15 \text{ min}}$ $\frac{24 \text{ mi}}{120 \text{ min}}$

Set F (Lesson 7, pages 320–321)

Use the scale 1 in.: 2 ft to find the measure(s) of each image in a scale drawing.

1. actual room is 12 ft by 14 ft
2. actual tabletop is 6 ft long
3. actual window is 4 ft by 5 ft
4. actual dresser is 4 ft high

Use the scale $\frac{1}{4}$ in.: 1 ft to find the actual measure(s) of each object.

5. model car is 4 in. long
6. model bicycle is $\frac{2}{3}$ in. high
7. drawing of garage is 3 in. by $3\frac{1}{2}$ in.
8. model truck is 8 in. long

Extra Practice

Set G (Lesson 9, pages 326–327)

Express each decimal as a percent. Then order from least to greatest.

1. 21% 0.5 2.1

2. 250% 2.4 27%

3. 0.05 0.01 20%

Write an equivalent percent or decimal for each.

4. 22%

5. 58%

6. 0.25

7. 1.3

8. 0.85

9. 40%

10. 15%

11. 0.33

12. 19%

13. 0.18

14. 0.05

15. 65%

16. 80%

17. 200%

18. 0.505

19. 1.05

Set H (Lesson 10, pages 328–329)

Write an equivalent percent or fraction in simplest form.

1. $\frac{1}{5}$

2. 25%

3. 45%

4. $\frac{30}{100}$

5. $\frac{3}{2}$

6. $\frac{1}{8}$

7. 125%

8. 200%

9. $\frac{3}{5}$

10. $\frac{9}{4}$

11. 11%

12. $\frac{38}{50}$

Set I (Lesson 11, pages 330–331)

Order the numbers in each group from greatest to least.

1. $\frac{35}{100}$ 0.7 $\frac{2}{3}$

2. $\frac{77}{100}$ 0.077 $\frac{7}{10}$

3. $\frac{3}{4}$ 0.65 $\frac{5}{8}$ 0.6

4. 1.2 $\frac{12}{100}$ 0.1 $\frac{1}{2}$

5. 0.042 $\frac{4}{10}$ $\frac{4}{5}$

6. $\frac{19}{100}$ 1.9 0.9

Extra Practice • Problem Solving

Write an equation and solve. *(Lesson 5, pages 314–315)*

1. Jim baby-sits four times a week, twice for the Kouba family and twice for the Jenkins family. If he earns \$9 each time he baby-sits for the Koubas and earns a total of \$42 per week, how much do the Jenkinses pay him each time he baby-sits?

2. On the map of Jennifer's city, the distance from her house to her best friend's house is $4\frac{1}{2}$ inches. If the map scale is 1 in.: $2\frac{1}{2}$ mi, what is the actual distance to her best friend's house?

3. Bruce spends $1\frac{1}{2}$ hours making cookies. How many batches of cookies does he make if it takes him 30 minutes to make each batch?

4. Fifty children are going to the art museum. Admission is \$2.50 per child. It costs \$75 to rent a bus for the trip. What will be the total cost for all of the children to attend the museum?

Solve. Think about whether each answer is reasonable. *(Lesson 8, pages 322–323)*

5. Corey and Felipe need to find the ratio of the length of their feet to the length of their hands. Corey calculates 7 : 2 and Felipe calculates 3 : 2. Are their results reasonable? Explain.

6. Abby is 12 years old. Her sister is 6 years old. Abby thinks that the ratio of her age to her sister's age is 1 : 2. Is this reasonable? Explain why or why not.

7. Three out of every four animals in a zoo were brought in from other zoos. The rest were born in the zoo. Jeff thinks that 4 bears were brought in from other zoos. Is this reasonable? Explain why or why not.

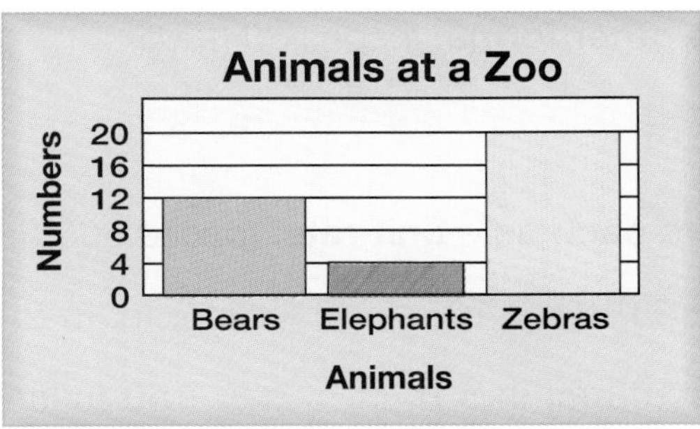

Solve. Use proportions. *(Lesson 12, pages 332–333)*

8. Ken can type 30 words per minute. Gloria can type 20 words per minute. After 1 hour, how many more words will Ken have typed than Gloria?

9. Hyun Soo can ride his bike 14 miles in 1 hour. His friend Mario can ride $\frac{6}{7}$ as fast. How many miles can Mario ride in 1 hour?

10. A job requires someone who can type 45 words per minute. José can currently type only 40 words per minute. In order to get the job, how many more words would he have to type in 30 minutes than he can now?

11. Margo, Anita, and Sam run the 50-yard dash in 12 s, 8 s, and 10 s. How long would it take for each of them to run the 100-yard dash, given that they run that race at the same pace as they run the 50-yard dash?

Chapter Review

Reviewing Vocabulary

Write *true* or *false* for each statement. Rewrite any false statements to make them true.

1. Ratios that are equivalent to each other are called equivalent ratios.

2. A proportion is a statement that shows that two ratios are equivalent.

3. You can use cross multiplication to find out if two proportions form a ratio.

4. A scale is a ratio of the measurements of an actual object to the corresponding measurements in a drawing of the object.

Match each word with its definition.

5. rate — **A** a ratio that compares a number with 100

6. percent — **B** a statement that shows that two ratios are equivalent

7. proportion — **C** a ratio that compares two quantities with different units of measure

Reviewing Concepts and Skills

Simplify each ratio if possible. Then express each in two other forms. *(pages 304-305)*

8. $\frac{10}{3}$ **9.** 3:7 **10.** 80 cups to 2 bowls

Write each as a unit rate. *(pages 306-307)*

11. \$3.12 for 12 **12.** $\frac{1}{2}$ in. in 2 weeks **13.** 12 pounds in 4 packages

14. 100 mi in 5 h **15.** 150 miles on 6 gallons **16.** \$1.50 for $\frac{1}{2}$ lb of ham

Find the missing term in each. *(pages 308-312)*

17. $\frac{4}{5} = \frac{20}{a}$ **18.** $\frac{4}{b} = \frac{2}{3}$ **19.** $\frac{7}{8} = \frac{c}{56}$

20. $\frac{3}{6} = \frac{e}{100}$ **21.** $\frac{8}{12} = \frac{12}{m}$ **22.** $\frac{8}{13} = \frac{y}{39}$

Find the speed (*s*) or the distance (*d*). *(pages 318-319)*

23. $s = ■$, $d = 18$ mi, $t = 3$ h **24.** $s = ■$, $d = 63$ mi, $t = 3$ h

25. $s = 12$ mi/h, $d = ■$, $t = 5\frac{1}{2}$ h **26.** $s = 40$ m/s, $d = ■$, $t = 25$ s

Use the scale of 1 in.:1 ft to find the measure(s) of the image in a scale drawing. *(pages 320-321)*

27. actual table is 8 ft long

28. actual room is 14 ft by 16 ft

Use the scale $\frac{1}{2}$ in. : 2 ft to find the actual measure(s) of each object. *(pages 320–321)*

29. room is 4 in. by 5 in.

30. height of dresser is $1\frac{1}{2}$ in.

31. door is 2 in. by 1 in.

Write an equivalent percent or decimal for each. *(pages 326-327)*

32. 18%

33. 0.05

34. 32%

35. 1.85

Write an equivalent percent or fraction in simplest form. *(pages 328-329)*

36. $\frac{3}{5}$

37. 30%

38. $\frac{5}{8}$

39. 150%

Order each set from the least to the greatest part of a unit. *(pages 330-331)*

40. 25% $\frac{3}{20}$ 0.16

41. $\frac{4}{7}$ 0.56 45%

42. $\frac{1}{3}$ 10% 0.18

Solve. *(pages 314-315, 322-323, 332-333)*

43. There are 650 grams in a box of crackers. Stephen eats 3 servings of the crackers. If there are 15 servings of crackers in one box, how many grams does Stephen eat?

44. Tony exercises for 25 minutes every weekday and 30 minutes every Saturday and Sunday. He calculates that in 2 weeks he exercises 435 minutes. Is his calculation reasonable? Explain.

Brain Teasers Math Reasoning

Something in Common

All of the following ratios are equivalent. Find each missing value.

0.25 $\frac{a}{100}$ $\frac{1}{b}$

$\frac{c}{8}$ 2:d $\frac{e}{16}$ 9 to f

Missing Digits

Put the digits 1, 2, 3, 4, 6, and 8 into the boxes to form equivalent ratios. Use each digit only once.

  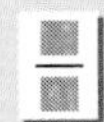

Internet Brain Teasers

Visit **www.eduplace.com/kids/mhm** for more *Brain Teasers.*

Chapter Test

Simplify each ratio if possible. Then express each in two other forms.

1. 15:5 **2.** 6 girls to 4 boys **3.** $\frac{8}{9}$ **4.** 4:20

Write each as a rate. Then write the unit rate.

5. \$2.70 for 9 beads **6.** 15 tests in 3 weeks

7. 25 mi in $\frac{1}{2}$ h **8.** 36 oz in 3 packs

Find the missing term in each.

9. $\frac{2}{5} = \frac{10}{a}$ **10.** $\frac{6}{b} = \frac{3}{5}$ **11.** $\frac{12}{8} = \frac{75}{c}$

12. $\frac{2.4}{1.2} = \frac{2}{d}$ **13.** $\frac{2}{9} = \frac{x}{81}$ **14.** $\frac{5}{4} = \frac{y}{20}$

15. $\frac{3}{m} = \frac{2}{14}$ **16.** $\frac{y}{25} = \frac{12}{10}$ **17.** $\frac{4}{8} = \frac{a}{26}$

Find the speed (*s*) or the distance (*d*).

18. $s = 18$ mi/h, $d = \blacksquare$, $t = 2$ h **19.** $s = \blacksquare$, $d = 240$ mi, $t = 4$ h

20. $s = \blacksquare$, $d = 10$ mi, $t = 5$ h **21.** $s = 55$ mi/h, $d = \blacksquare$, $t = 30$ min

Use the scale 1 in. : 2 ft to find the measure(s) of each image in a scale drawing.

22. actual room is 18 ft by 20 ft **23.** actual pole is 10 ft high

Use the scale $\frac{1}{2}$ in. : 1 ft to find the actual measure(s) of each object.

24. model chair is $1\frac{1}{2}$ in. high **25.** model table is 2 in. by 3 in.

Write an equivalent percent or decimal for each.

26. 0.23 **27.** 19% **28.** 69% **29.** 140%

30. 0.05 **31.** 1.34 **32.** 0.45 **33.** 84%

Write an equivalent percent or fraction in simplest form.

34. $\frac{2}{5}$ **35.** 60% **36.** $\frac{1}{10}$ **37.** 130%

38. 55% **39.** 1.5% **40.** $\frac{4}{1}$ **41.** $\frac{53}{25}$

Order each set from the least to the greatest part of a unit.

42. 0.45 $\frac{2}{5}$ 0.5 **43.** 0.08 $\frac{80}{100}$ 0.88 $\frac{5}{8}$ **44.** 0.67 $\frac{68}{100}$ $\frac{2}{3}$

45. 0.61 50% $\frac{2}{3}$ **46.** 0.11 $\frac{1}{11}$ 11.1% 0.101 **47.** $\frac{25}{10}$ 200% 2.10

Solve.

48. Perry can run 6 miles in 45 minutes. If he continuously runs at this same rate, how many miles can he run in 1 hour?

49. The ratio of the time Sandra spends studying each evening to the time she spends playing outside is 5:3. One evening, Sandra spends $2\frac{1}{2}$ hours studying. She thinks that she must have spent 6 hours outside playing. Is her estimate reasonable? Explain.

50. Stefan writes 5 pages in his journal every week. Lily writes 8 pages in her journal every week. How many more pages will Lily have written than Stefan after 6 weeks?

Write About It

Solve each problem. Use correct math vocabulary to explain your thinking.

1. Tisha solved the equation shown at the right.

a. Explain what she did wrong.

b. Show how to find the correct answer.

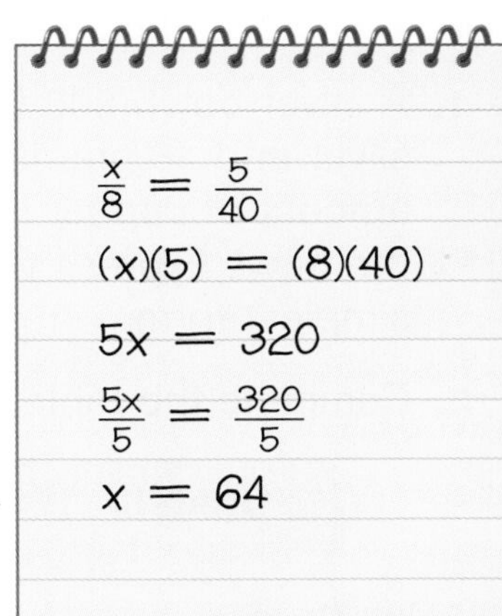

$$\frac{x}{8} = \frac{5}{40}$$
$$(x)(5) = (8)(40)$$
$$5x = 320$$
$$\frac{5x}{5} = \frac{320}{5}$$
$$x = 64$$

2. Alison bought 2 pencils and 3 notebooks for school. The pencils cost 25 cents each. If she spent a total of \$1.85, how much did each notebook cost?

a. Represent the problem with a drawing, with numbers, or in some other way.

b. Show your work.

c. Explain how you know that your answer is correct.

Another Look

Both gold and silver are precious metals. However, pure gold and pure silver are very soft. To make these metals harder, they are mixed with copper to form an alloy, or a mixture of two or more metals. The amount of pure silver or pure gold in an alloy can be shown by using different units.

FINENESS

Fineness is a measure of the amount of silver in an alloy. It is equal to 10 times the percentage of silver in the alloy. A silver alloy of 500 fineness contains 50% pure silver.
($10 \times 50 = 500$)

KARATS

A *karat* is a unit of proportion that measures how much of a gold alloy is pure gold. Pure gold is 24 karats. This means that $\frac{24}{24}$ is gold. Ten-karat gold is $\frac{10}{24}$ gold and $\frac{14}{24}$ copper.

Use the information given to solve Problems 1–4. Show your work.

1. A silver bowl (800 fineness) contains 192 grams of pure silver and 48 grams of copper. Use a ratio to compare the amount of copper in the bowl to the amount of pure silver in the bowl. Express your answer in three different ways using simplest form.

2. Complete the table.

Metal Object	Alloy	Percentage		Ratio of Gold or Silver to Copper
		Gold or Silver	Copper	
Gold ring	18 karats			
Gold watch	12 karats			
Silver coin	900 fine			
Sterling silver	925 fine			

3. **Look Back** What method did you use to find the ratio of gold or silver to copper? Describe another way to find these ratios.

4. **Analyze** How much gold is in a 20-karat gold ring? Express your answer as a fraction, as a decimal (round to the hundredths place), and as a percent (round to the tenths place).

Enrichment

World Currencies

Ratios can be used to determine the value of one currency with respect to another.

For example, here is how you would find out how many Japanese yen there are in 100 U.S. dollars.

Step 1 First, find out the current exchange rate for 1 U.S. dollar. For this example, we will assume that 1 U.S. dollar is worth 105 yen.

Step 2 Write a proportion that can be used to find the value of 100 dollars in yen. Then you need to set up a ratio showing the relationship of U.S. dollars to yen.

Step 3 Use cross products to solve.

$$\frac{1 \text{ U.S. dollar}}{100 \text{ U.S. dollars}} = \frac{105 \text{ yen}}{x \text{ yen}}$$

$$\frac{1}{100} \quad \frac{105}{x}$$

$$1x = (100)(105)$$

$$x = 10{,}500$$

In the example, 100 dollars is equivalent to 10,500 yen.

Determine the equivalent of 50 U.S. dollars for each of the following currencies. Use the information in the chart provided.

1. ▒ deutsche marks
2. ▒ francs
3. ▒ euros
4. ▒ pounds

1 U.S. dollar = 0.63 pound (United Kingdom)

1 U.S. dollar = 6.77 francs (France)

1 U.S. dollar = 2.02 deutsche marks (Germany)

1 U.S. dollar = 1.03 euros

Explain Your Thinking

► Cecilia says you cannot determine how many dollars are in one pound from the information given in the chart. Is Cecilia right? Explain your thinking.

CHAPTER 8

Applications of Percent

Why Learn About Applications of Percent?

Percents are used when people describe how something increases or decreases. Adding sales tax and calculating interest earned on savings are some of the many ways percents are used.

When you buy a T-shirt on sale for 20% off the regular price, you have to understand percent to figure out the sale price. Understanding percent can also help you figure out the sales tax.

This family has just bought a house. A bank lent them the money they needed. Now they will repay the bank with monthly payments at a specific rate of interest.

SALE
SOLD

Reviewing Vocabulary

Understanding math language helps you become a successful problem solver. Here are some math vocabulary words you should know.

equation a mathematical sentence using an equals sign to show that two expressions are equal

percent per hundred; hundredths written using a % sign instead of a decimal point

ratio a comparison of one number with another

proportion a mathematical sentence to show two equal ratios

Reading Words and Symbols

When you read mathematics, sometimes you read only words, sometimes you read words and symbols, and sometimes you read only symbols.

Each of the following looks at a single problem in a different way.

- What number is fifteen percent of eighty?
- 15 percent of 80 is equal to what number?
- 12 is what percent of 80?
- 15% of what number is 12?
- 15% of 80 = n
- $0.15 \times 80 = n$
- What is $\frac{15}{100}$ times 80?

68¢

12¢

80¢ total

Try These

1. Write each as a percent.

a. 0.75 **b.** 45 out of 100 **c.** $\frac{18}{100}$

2. Write *true* or *false* for each statement. If the statement is false, rewrite it to make it true.

a. A percent is a ratio.

b. You need only one number to make a ratio.

c. A ratio is a fraction whose value is always less than 1.

d. Percents can be written in fraction form or in decimal form.

3. Replace each variable *n* with the number that makes the equation true.

a. $5\% = \frac{n}{100}$ **b.** $\frac{25}{100} = n\%$ **c.** $n\% = \frac{99}{100}$ **d.** $\frac{18}{n} = 18\%$

4. Fill in the blanks with the correct words.

a. A ____ is two equal ratios.

b. Twenty-five is 25 ____ of 100.

c. A number sentence with two expressions separated by an equals sign is called an ____.

Upcoming Vocabulary

Write About It **Here are some other vocabulary words** you will learn in this chapter. Watch for these words. Write their definitions in your journal.

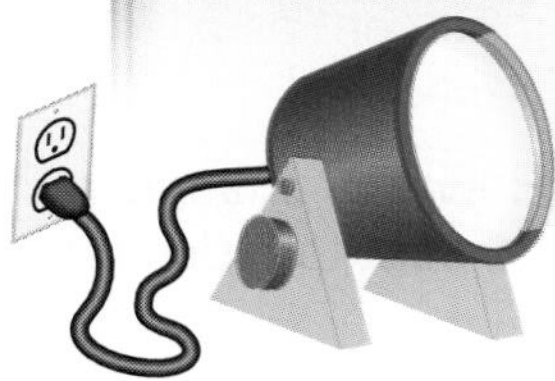

rate	**interest rate**
base	**simple interest**
percentage	**discount**
principal	

Find a Percent of a Number

You will learn how to find a percent of a number.

Review Vocabulary
percent
proportion

Learn About It

Sam notices a sign at the airport showing the **percent** of on-time flights for July. If 86% of flights were on time, then 100% minus 86%, or 14%, of flights were late. How many flights were late?

Fly with us!
86% of
1,650 total flights
were on time
in July!

Calculate. **14% of 1,650 = *n***

Different Ways to Find a Percent of a Number

You can write and solve a proportion.

Step 1 Write a **proportion**, using part-to-whole ratios.

$$\frac{14}{100} = \frac{n}{1{,}650}$$

part → 14; whole → 100; part (late flights) → n; whole (total flights) → 1,650

Step 2 Use cross multiplication to solve the proportion for n.

$$\frac{14}{100} \bowtie \frac{n}{1{,}650}$$

$$14 \times 1{,}650 = 100 \times n$$
$$23{,}100 = 100n$$
$$231 = n$$

You can write and solve an equation.

Step 1 Write an equation, using the decimal form of the percent.

$14\% = \frac{14}{100} = 0.14$ $\qquad n = 0.14 \times 1{,}650$

Step 2 Solve the equation for n.

$n = 231$

Check your work.

10% of 1,650 is 165.
5% of 1,650 is about 83.
So 15% of 1,650 is about 248.

Since 14% is close to 15% and 231 is close to 248, the answer is reasonable.

Solution: In July, 231 flights were late.

Explain Your Thinking

► Why can a ratio represent a percent?

Guided Practice

Use a proportion to find the percent of each number.

1. 70% of 100 **2.** 75% of 72 **3.** $6\frac{1}{2}$% of 88 **4.** 35% of 317

Use an equation to find the percent of each number.

5. 25% of 200 **6.** 1.8% of 50 **7.** 45% of 1 **8.** 250% of 18.5

Ask Yourself

- How do I represent a percent as a fraction?
- How do I change a percent to a decimal?

Independent Practice

Use a proportion to find the percent of each number.

9. 40% of 220 **10.** 20% of 66 **11.** 3.6% of 998 **12.** 99% of 1

13. 105% of 6 **14.** $33\frac{1}{3}$% of 123 **15.** 1% of 19 **16.** 23.5% of 48

17. 100% of 15 **18.** 4.4% of 112 **19.** 382% of 1,000 **20.** $17\frac{1}{2}$% of 34

Use an equation to find the percent of each number.

21. 60% of 150 **22.** 11.5% of 76 **23.** 90% of 210 **24.** 1% of 300

25. 10% of 189 **26.** 101% of 5 **27.** 18% of 18 **28.** 6% of 124

29. 115% of 200 **30.** 3.5% of 160 **31.** 10% of 212 **32.** 45% of 92

Find the percent of each number. Use either method.

33. 12.1% of 100 **34.** 15.6% of 47 **35.** 97.3% of 17 **36.** 56% of 143

Problem Solving • Reasoning

Use Data Use the bar graph for Problems 37 and 38.

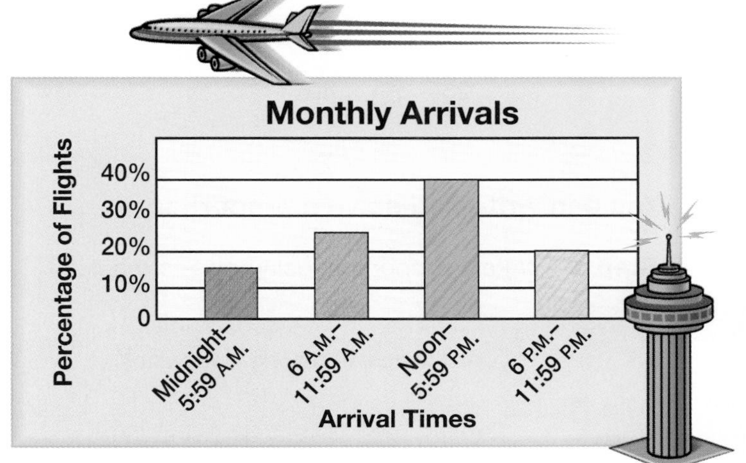

37. In January, 1,100 flights arrived at the airport. How many of those flights arrived between 6 P.M. and 11:59 P.M.?

38. If 1,980 flights arrived at the airport last month, about how many flights arrived between 6 A.M. and 5:59 P.M.?

39. **Analyze** In May the percent of on-time flights was 5% less than in April. In April the percent was 8% less than in March. If the percent of on-time flights in March was 87%, what was the percent in May?

40. **Write About It** Of a group of 125 tourists, 12 were on the tour for the second time. How could you use mental math to estimate the percent of tourists who were on the tour for the second time?

Mixed Review • Test Prep

Evaluate. Express your answer in simplest form. *(pages 168–169, 174–175)*

41. $\frac{5}{8} \times \frac{1}{4}$ **42.** $\frac{7}{10} \div \frac{3}{5}$ **43.** $16 \times \frac{2}{3}$ **44.** $\frac{1}{4} \div \frac{4}{10}$

45 Evaluate $73 \times (n + 3)$ for $n = 6$. *(pages 256–257)*

A 225 **B** 441 **C** 657 **D** 1,314

Find a Percent

You will learn how to find a percent.

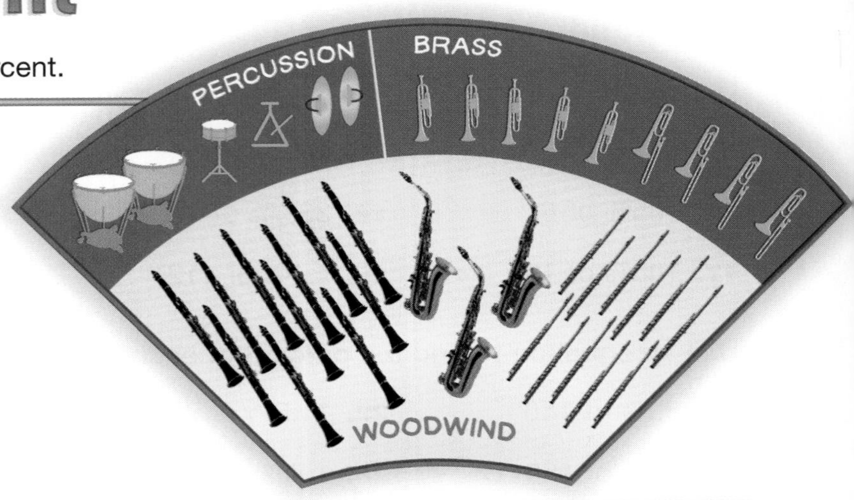

Learn About It

Of the 40 students in a school band, 25 play woodwind instruments, such as flutes, clarinets, and saxophones. What percent of the students play woodwind instruments?

Calculate. **$25 = n\%$ of 40**

Different Ways to Find a Percent

You can write and solve an equation.

Step 1 Write an equation.

$$25 = \frac{n}{100} \times 40$$

Step 2 Solve the equation for n.

$$\frac{25}{40} \times 100 = n$$
$$62.5 = n$$

You can write and solve a proportion.

Step 1 Write a proportion, using part-to-whole ratios.

$$\frac{n}{100} = \frac{25}{40}$$

part (students playing woodwinds)

whole (students playing woodwinds)

Step 2 Use cross multiplication to solve the proportion for n.

$$\frac{n}{100} \quad \frac{25}{40}$$

$$n \times 40 = 100 \times 25$$
$$40n = 2{,}500$$
$$n = 62.5$$

Solution: In the band, 62.5% of the students play woodwind instruments.

Check your work.

62.5% > 50%, or $\frac{1}{2}$. Since 25 is a little more than half of 40, the answer seems reasonable.

Another Example

Percent Greater Than 100

What percent of 600 is 672?

$$\frac{n}{100} = \frac{672}{600}$$
$$n \times 600 = 100 \times 672$$
$$600n = 67{,}200$$
$$n = 112$$

672 is 112% of 600.

Explain Your Thinking

- ► What information is needed to find a percent? Explain.
- ► Why does the first term of a ratio represent a percent if the second term of the ratio is 100?

Guided Practice

Use a proportion or an equation to find each percent.

1. What percent of 40 is 30?
2. 1.6 is what percent of 12.8?
3. $\frac{5}{6}$ is what percent of $3\frac{1}{3}$?
4. What percent of 300 is 24?

Ask Yourself

- Which number is the part and which is the whole?
- How do I express a decimal as a percent?

Independent Practice

Use a proportion or an equation to find each percent.

5. What percent of 80 is 24.4?
6. 96 is what percent of 120?
7. 44 is what percent of 44?
8. What percent of 200 is 45?
9. What percent of 80 is 88?
10. $1\frac{1}{2}$ is what percent of $3\frac{3}{4}$?
11. 15 is what percent of 125?
12. What percent of 90 is 63?
13. 4.6 is what percent of 0.8?
14. 2 is what percent of 1?
15. What percent of $3\frac{1}{3}$ is 3?
16. What percent of 65 is 13?

Problem Solving • Reasoning

17. Of 25 students who play violins, 8 have soft-sided instrument cases. What percent of the violinists have soft-sided cases?

18. **Analyze** Among 40 finalists in a music competition, 6 play trumpets, 4 play violins, and 1 plays tuba. The rest are singers. What percent of the finalists are singers?

19. **Write About It** There are 6 students in the band who play percussion instruments. Write an equation to find what percent of the 40 students in the band play percussion instruments. As you solve the equation, use words and symbols to explain each step.

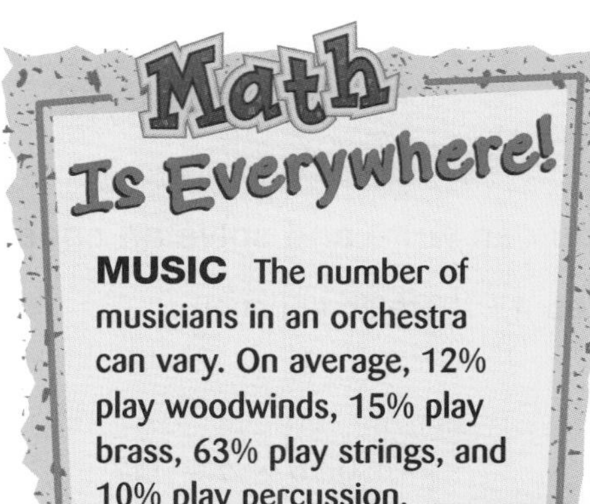

MUSIC The number of musicians in an orchestra can vary. On average, 12% play woodwinds, 15% play brass, 63% play strings, and 10% play percussion.

In an orchestra of 125 musicians, about how many play a woodwind instrument?

Mixed Review • Test Prep

Order from least to greatest. *(pages 208–209)*

20. $^{-}4$ $\quad ^{+}3$ $\quad ^{-}2$ $\quad ^{+}1$
21. $^{-}15$ $\quad ^{+}14$ $\quad 0$ $\quad ^{-}11$ $\quad ^{+}5$

22. How can 7 × 38 be rewritten, using the Distributive Property? *(pages 262–263)*

A (7 + 30) × (7 + 8)
B (8 × 7) + (8 × 30)
C (7 × 30) + (7 × 8)
D (7 × 30) + 8

Extra Practice See Set B on page 376.

Find a Number When a Percent Is Known

You will learn how to find a number when you know a percent.

Learn About It

Tropical Fish World has a total of 117 goldfish. Goldfish make up 18% of the fish in the store. How many fish, including goldfish, does the store have?

Calculate. **18% of n = 117**

Different Ways to Find a Number When a Percent Is Known

You can write and solve a proportion.

Step 1 Write a proportion.

$$\frac{117}{n} = \frac{18}{100}$$

Step 2 Use cross multiplication to solve the proportion for n.

$$\frac{117}{n} \bowtie \frac{18}{100}$$

$$117 \times 100 = n \times 18$$
$$11{,}700 = 18n$$
$$650 = n$$

You can write and solve an equation.

Step 1 Write an equation.

$$0.18 \times n = 117$$

Step 2 Solve the equation for n.

$$\frac{\overset{1}{\cancel{0.18}} \times n}{\underset{1}{\cancel{0.18}}} = \frac{117}{0.18}$$
$$n = \frac{117}{0.18}$$
$$n = 650$$

Check your work.

Estimate. 117 **rounds to** 120

0.18 **rounds to** 0.2

$120 \div 0.2 = 600$

Since 650 is close to 600, the answer is reasonable.

Solution: There are 650 fish in the store.

Explain Your Thinking

- ▶ Why is the variable the second term of the first ratio?
- ▶ How can you tell if your answer should be less than or greater than the given number?

Guided Practice

Use a proportion and an equation to find each number.

1. 75% of what number is 75?

2. 93 is $15\frac{1}{2}$% of what number?

Ask Yourself

- Are the proportion and the equation written correctly?

Calculator Option

Independent Practice

Use a proportion to find each number.

3. 220 is 110% of what number?

4. 80% of what number is 7.2?

5. 20.3 is 35% of what number?

6. $\frac{1}{2}$% of what number is 6?

7. 64% of what number is 24?

8. 9 is 15% of what number?

9. 25 is 125% of what number?

10. 2.5% of what number is 2.5?

Use an equation to find each number.

11. 112% of what number is 84?

12. 57 is 19% of what number?

13. 1% of what number is 6?

14. 92% of what number is 142.6?

15. 22 is 55% of what number?

16. 3.1 is 15.5% of what number?

17. 14% of what number is 56?

18. 90% of what number is 72.9?

Problem Solving • Reasoning

Use Data **Use the circle graph for Problems 19, 20, and 22.**

19. In June, Tropical Fish World's sales of African fish varieties totaled $2,790. What were the total sales in June?

20. Analyze Suppose total July sales were $34,600, but the percents stayed the same. What was the sum of sales of food, chemicals, aquariums, and other equipment in dollars?

21. In August, fish of all varieties represented 72% of total sales. Aquariums and equipment represented $\frac{1}{5}$ of total sales, and sales of all other products totaled $3,518. What were the total August sales in dollars?

22. Write Your Own Write a percent problem, using data from the circle graph. Have a classmate solve your problem.

June Sales

10%, 10%, 9%, 5%, 2%, 29%, 18%, 17%

- American Fish Varieties
- Goldfish
- Aquariums and Other Equipment
- Food and Chemicals
- South American Fish Varieties
- African Fish Varieties
- Aquarium Decorations
- Miscellaneous

Mixed Review • Test Prep

Solve for *n*. *(pages 280–281, 282–283, 284–285)*

23. $n + 19 = 37$

24. $n + \frac{2}{5} = \frac{7}{10}$

25. $(8 + n) - 32 = 27$

26. $n \times \frac{2}{5} = 3\frac{3}{5}$

27 Which expresses the ratio of 75 seeds to 25 flowers? *(pages 304–305)*

A $\frac{1}{3}$ **B** $\frac{5}{15}$ **C** $\frac{12}{5}$ **D** $\frac{3}{1}$

Extra Practice See Set C on page 377.

Percent Relationships

You will learn how you can use an equation to solve a percent problem.

New Vocabulary
rate
base
percentage

Learn About It

You have learned how to find any of the three parts of a percent problem: the percent, or **rate**; the original number, or **base**; and the percent of the number, or **percentage**. The relationship of percentage to rate and base can be written as an equation. You can use this equation to solve percent problems.

$$\text{Percent of a number} = \text{Percent} \times \text{Number}$$
$$\text{Percentage} = \text{Rate} \times \text{Base}$$
$$P = R \times B$$

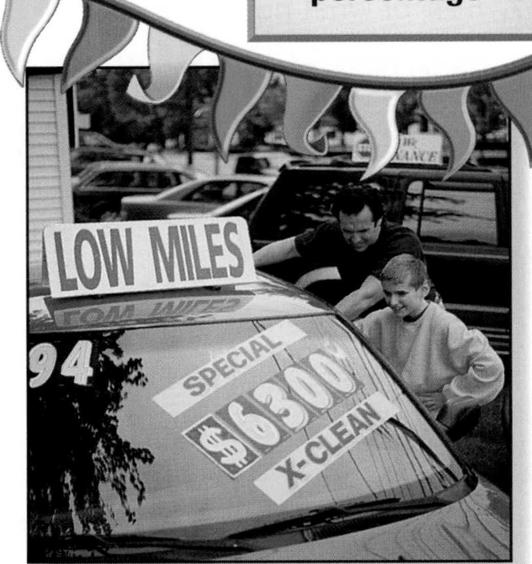

Toby's father bought a used car on sale for $6,300. The price he paid was 90% of the original price. What was the original price of the car?

Calculate. **90% of *n* = $6,300**

Find the original, or base, price of the car.

Step 1 Substitute the given values into the percent equation.

You know the sale price, or percentage, and the percent, or rate.

$$P = R \times B$$
$$6{,}300 = 0.90 \times B$$

↑ sale price ↑ percent of original price

Step 2 Solve the equation to find the original, or base, price.

$$6{,}300 = 0.90 \times B$$
$$\frac{6{,}300}{0.90} = B$$
$$7{,}000 = B$$

Check your work.

If he paid 90%, he got 10% off. Ten percent of $7,000 is $700. So he paid $7,000 minus $700, or $6,300.

Solution: The original price of the car was $7,000.

Other Examples

A. Find the Rate

$1,200 is what percent of $2,000?

$$P = R \times B$$
$$1{,}200 = R \times 2{,}000$$
$$\frac{1{,}200}{2{,}000} = R$$
$$R = 0.60 = 60\%$$

$1,200 is 60% of $2,000.

B. Find the Percentage

What is 85% of $3,000?

$$P = R \times B$$
$$P = 0.85 \times 3{,}000$$
$$P = 2{,}550$$

$2,550 is 85% of $3,000.

Explain Your Thinking

- ► When the rate is less than 100%, will the percentage be greater than or less than the base?
- ► What is true about the relationship between the percentage and the base for percents greater than 100?

Guided Practice

Solve, using the percent equation.

1. 12% of what number is $450?
2. What is 38% of $2,000?
3. $1,400 is what percent of $5,600?
4. $4,500 is 60% of what number?
5. What is 18% of $5,000?
6. $770 is what percent of $2,200?

Ask Yourself

- Where should the values be substituted in the percent equation?
- Is my answer reasonable?

Independent Practice

Solve, using the percent equation.

7. What is 15% of 2,300?
8. 48 is what percent of 320?
9. What percent of 220 is 55?
10. What is 75% of 4,000?
11. 10% of what number is 750?
12. 120 is what percent of 1,000?
13. What percent of 2,670 is 801?
14. What is 7% of 4,900?
15. 3,825 is 45% of what number?
16. $120 is what percent of $400?
17. What percent of $700 is $245?
18. What is 98% of $5,000?
19. $550 is what percent of $1,000?
20. $2,200 is 80% of what number?
21. What percent of $793 is $1,586?
22. What is 180% of $1,650?
23. $2,748 is 120% of what number?
24. 35% of what number is $664.65?

Algebra • Equations **Solve for *n*.**

25. $100 = n \times 200$
26. $n = 0.1 \times 150$
27. $5 = n \times 20$
28. $n = 0.75 \times 8$
29. $12 = 0.5 \times n$
30. $45 = 10 \times n$
31. $12 = n \times 60$
32. $0.35 \times 40 = n$
33. $n = 0.8 \times 25$

Problem Solving • Reasoning

Solve. Choose a method.

Computation Methods

• Mental Math • Estimation • Paper and Pencil • Calculator

34. An advertisement shows an upright piano that is on sale for 51% of its original price. If the original price was \$7,995, what is the sale price of the piano?

35. **Compare** A blue car is reduced to \$6,462 from \$8,975. A red car is reduced to \$7,007 from \$10,010. Which sale price is a greater percentage of the original price?

36. **Analyze** A car is on sale for 90% of its original price of \$8,000. The cost to add air conditioning has been reduced to 75% of the original price of \$800. Will the sale price of the car with air conditioning be less than \$7,700? Why?

37. **Patterns** In May a gallery painting was reduced from \$90.00 to \$88.50. In June the price was reduced to \$85.50. In July it was \$81.00, and in August it was \$75.00. If the pattern continues, what is the price likely to be in September?

Mixed Review • Test Prep

Solve for *n*. *(pages 252–254)*

38. $n + (27 + 4) = (5 + 27) + 4$ **39.** $^-54 + n = {^-54}$ **40.** $(13 + 29) + n = 88$

Choose the letter of the correct answer. *(pages 318–319, 330–331)*

41 About $\frac{1}{50}$ of California's trash is burned. What percentage of California's trash is burned?

A about 1% **C** about 25%
B about 2% **D** about 50%

42 The crabeater seal can travel 12 miles per hour on land. At that rate, how far can it travel in 10 minutes?

F 12 miles **H** 2 miles
G 10 miles **J** 1 mile

Logical Thinking

Percent Logic

43. Could a car be on sale for 105% of its original price? Why or why not?

44. Is 65% of a number always greater than 20% of another number? Explain.

45. How can you use mental math to find 50% of a number? 150% of a number?

▲ This 1934 Roadster originally cost \$785. It is now worth about \$18,500.

Extra Practice See Set D on page 377.

Practice Game

Three Tips

Practice finding percents of numbers by playing this game with your classmates. See who makes the most money.

What You'll Need

- *Two 1–6 number cubes*
- *Teaching Tool 7 or paper*

Players
2 or more

Here's What to Do

1. Each player uses Teaching Tool 7 or creates a record sheet like the one on the right.
2. Each player is a server in a restaurant and has 3 customers. One customer will leave a 15% tip, one will leave a 20% tip, and one will leave a 25% tip.
3. For each round, players take turns tossing the cubes, making a two-digit number that will be the bill amount in dollars, and choosing one of the tip rates. After calculating each tip, players enter the bill and tip on the record sheet.
4. Play until each player has earned 3 tips. The player who earns the greatest number of dollars for the 3 tips is the winner.

Tip Percent	Bill	Tip
15%		
20%		
25%		
	Total Tips:	

Share Your Thinking How did you decide which tip rate to choose each time?

Problem-Solving Skill: Choose a Computation Method

You will learn how to decide which computation method to use to solve a problem.

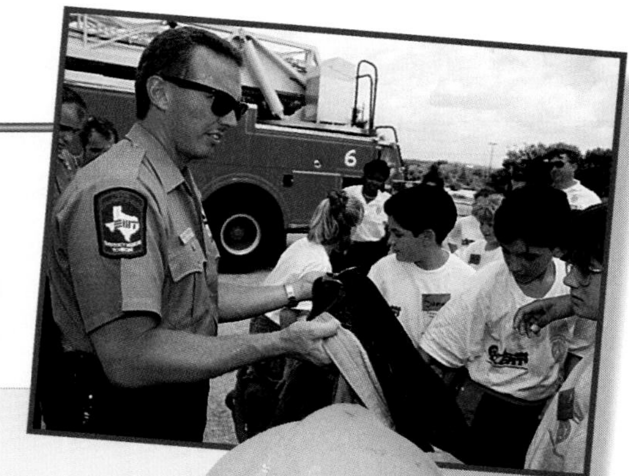

When you solve a problem, you need to decide which computation method is more appropriate to use.

Look at the situations below.

Sometimes you can use mental math.

Of 80 firefighters employed by a fire department, 50% have been employed for 5 years or less. How many firefighters have been employed 5 years or less?

Because fifty percent is equivalent to $\frac{1}{2}$, you can use mental math to find that $\frac{1}{2}$ of 80 is 40.

40 firefighters have been employed for 5 years or less.

Sometimes you need to use paper and pencil.

Of the 75 calls the fire department received last week, 18 were on Thursday. What percent of the calls were received on Thursday?

Since this problem cannot easily be solved mentally, use paper and pencil to solve it.

What percent of 75 is 18? $n = \frac{18}{75} = 18 \div 75 = 0.24$ or 24%

24% of the calls were received on Thursday.

Sometimes you can use estimation.

In July the fire department received calls from 193 locations. Of these locations, 22 were in the north end of town. About what percent of July's calls were from the north end of town?

Since this problem asks "About what percent . . . ?" you can use estimation to solve it.

What percent of 193 is 22? $\frac{22}{193}$ **rounds to** $\frac{20}{200}$; $\frac{20}{200} = \frac{10}{100} = 10\%$

About 10% of July's calls were from the north end of town.

Look Back How do you decide which computation method to use?

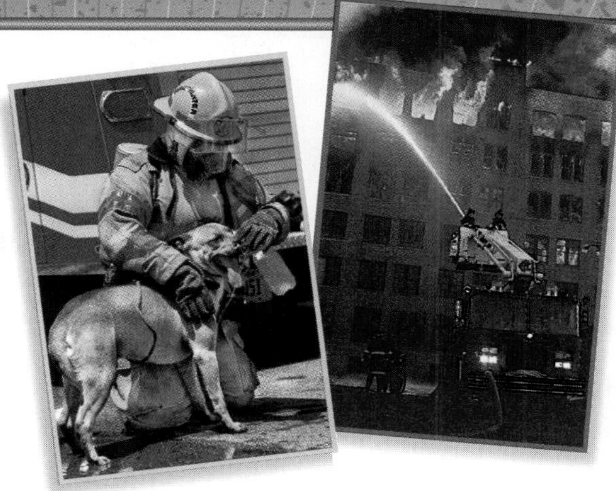

Firefighters need many skills for different situations. *Left*: rescuing a dog; *right*: fighting a building fire.

Guided Practice

Decide which computation method to use. Then solve.

1. There are 4 fire trucks at one of the fire stations. On Friday, 75% of the trucks were used. How many trucks were used on Friday?

    What computation method works best for the problem?

2. Of the 80 firefighters, 3 have been with the department for more than 20 years. What percent of the firefighters is this?

    What calculations are needed to solve the problem?

Choose a Strategy

Solve. Use these or other strategies. Tell what computation method you used.

Problem-Solving Strategies

- **Write an Equation**
- **Make a List**
- **Work Backward**
- **Use Logical Thinking**

3. A fire department spends about $275 each week on cleaning supplies. This is about 11% of what it spends on food for firefighters. About how much does the department spend on food each week?

4. Of the 80 firefighters at one fire station, about 19% are older than 35. At a second station about 27% of the 48 firefighters are older than 35. Which station has more firefighters older than 35?

5. Firefighters at one station own three dogs: Freckles, Lad, and Sparky. Freckles weighs 45 lb, and Lad weighs 60 lb. If Freckles and Lad together weigh 150% of Sparky's weight, how much does Sparky weigh?

6. Three ambulances traveled a total of 112 miles. Ambulance *A* was driven three times as many miles as Ambulance *B*. Together, the two ambulances traveled 50% of the 112 miles. How many miles was Ambulance *A* driven?

7. Ten percent of the residents surveyed never visited the public library, and 40% lived in the community more than 20 years. Of the residents who lived in the community more than 20 years, can you tell what percent never visited the library? Explain.

8. In 2000 the average police response time was 10 seconds less than in 1999. The response time in 1999 was 30 seconds less than in 1998. If the response time in 1998 was 280 seconds, what was the response time in 2000? What percent describes the improvement from 1998 to 2000?

Extra Practice See 1–4 on page 379.

Quick Check

Check Your Understanding of Lessons 1–5

Use a proportion or an equation to find the percent of each number.

1. 16% of 150 **2.** 7.5% of 64 **3.** 110% of 41

Use a proportion or an equation to find each percent.

4. What percent of 25 is $4\frac{1}{2}$? **5.** 118 is what percent of 50?

Use a proportion or an equation to find each number.

6. 9.1 is 13% of what number? **7.** 45% of what number is 63?

Solve, using the percent equation.

8. 15% of what number is $8.22? **9.** What is 129% of $31?

Solve. Tell what computation method you used.

10. Of the students at Chase Middle School, 25% are studying Spanish. If 200 students at the school are studying Spanish, how many students are there at Chase Middle School?

How did you do?

If you had difficulty with any items in the Quick Check, you can use the following pages for review and extra practice.

Items	Review These Pages	Do These Extra Practice Items
1–3	pages 350–351	Set A, page 376
4–5	pages 352–353	Set B, page 376
6–7	pages 354–355	Set C, page 377
8–9	pages 356–358	Set D, page 377
10	pages 360–361	1–4, page 379

Test Prep • Cumulative Review

Maintaining the Standards

Choose the letter of the correct answer.

1 Mr. Rodriguez finds a board in his workshop that is $8\frac{1}{2}$ feet long. He decides to cut the board into $1\frac{3}{8}$-foot pieces. How many $1\frac{3}{8}$-foot pieces can Mr. Rodriguez cut from the $8\frac{1}{2}$-foot board?

A 6

B 5

C 7

D 8

2 On Friday, three students were absent from Mrs. Zavala's mathematics class. If there are 30 students enrolled in the class, what percent of the class was absent on Friday?

F 0.3%

G 3%

H 3.3%

J 10%

3 Which of the following has the greatest quotient?

A $^{-}55 \div {}^{-}11$

B $55 \div {}^{-}1$

C $55 \div {}^{-}11$

D $^{-}55 \div 55$

4 Evaluate $2\frac{1}{2} \times a + \frac{5}{6}$, given $a = 9\frac{1}{3}$.

F $12\frac{2}{3}$

G $23\frac{1}{3}$

H $24\frac{1}{6}$

J $25\frac{5}{12}$

5 Marie made $\frac{1}{2}$ gallon of lemonade. If each glass holds $\frac{1}{2}$ cup of lemonade, how many glasses can Marie fill? (Hint: 1 gallon = 16 cups)

A $\frac{1}{2}$ glass

B 4 glasses

C 8 glasses

D 16 glasses

6 A western shop sells necklaces for \$29.95, straw hats for \$30.00, and leather belts for \$49.90. Linda buys three of each. Which expression represents the cost of Linda's purchase in dollars?

F $29.95 + 30.00 + 49.90$

G $2(29.95 + 30.00 + 49.90)$

H $3(29.95 + 30.00 + 49.90)$

J $3 \times 29.95 + 3 \times 30.00 + 49.90$

7 Use the factor tree to write the prime factorization of 36. Express your answer, using exponents when possible.

```
      36
     /  \
    4    9
   / \  / \
  2  2 3   3
```

Explain Tell how you can check your answer.

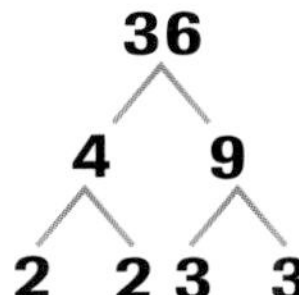

Internet Test Prep
Visit **www.eduplace.com/kids/mhm** for more *Test Prep Practice.*

Mental Math: Estimate With Percents

You will learn how to use mental math to estimate with percents.

Learn About It

John and Alex have just finished lunch at the Rainbow Cafe. Their total bill is $18.96, without a tip. They want to leave a tip of about 15%. How can they use mental math to estimate 15% of $18.96?

Estimate. **15% of $18.96 = ■**

Estimate 15% of $18.96.

Step 1 Round $18.96.

$18.96 **rounds to** $20.

Step 2 Find 15% of $20.

10% of $20 = $2
5% of $20 = $\frac{1}{2} \times \$2 = \$1$
15% of $20 = $2 + $1 = $3

Think: 5% is $\frac{1}{2}$ of 10%

Solution: Fifteen percent of $18.96 is about $3.

Other Examples

A. Round the Percent

Estimate 48% of $90.

48% **rounds to** 50%.

50% of $90 = $\frac{1}{2} \times \$90 = \$45$

B. Round the Percent and the Number

Estimate 11% of 147.

11% **rounds to** 10%.

147 **rounds to** 150.

10% of 150 = 15

Explain Your Thinking

► How can you decide what method to use to estimate a percent?

► How do you decide whether the estimate is reasonable?

Guided Practice

Estimate.

1. 120% of 400 **2.** 25% of 41 **3.** 9% of 106

4. 33% of 91 **5.** 21% of 99 **6.** 54% of 78

Ask Yourself

- Which do I round, the total or the percent?
- Is my answer reasonable?

Use mental math to estimate a 15% tip and a 20% tip for each amount.

7. $19.47 **8.** $32.14 **9.** $41.64

Independent Practice

Estimate.

10. 50% of 120 **11.** 33% of 60 **12.** 110% of 86 **13.** 40% of 10

14. 49% of 36 **15.** 16% of 58 **16.** 66% of 140 **17.** 150% of 61

18. 120% of 32 **19.** 25% of 103 **20.** 10% of 87 **21.** 20% of 77

Use mental math to estimate a 15% tip and a 20% tip for each amount.

22. \$59.43 **23.** \$7.95 **24.** \$16.40 **25.** \$38.44

26. \$12.31 **27.** \$28.99 **28.** \$30.75 **29.** \$21.40

Problem Solving • Reasoning

Use Data **Use the restaurant bill for Problems 30–33.**

GUEST CHECK
TABLE 9
SERVER 6
PERSONS 3
CHECK # 1771589
1 chef's salad \$6.50
1 tuna platter 7.95
1 vegetarian sandwich 5.95
2 iced teas 3.60
1 apple juice 1.95
subtotal \$25.95
tax 1.30
Total \$27.25

30. **Estimate** Monica and Terry are having lunch with their Aunt Judy at a cafe. Aunt Judy wants to leave a 15% tip. Use mental math to estimate a 15% tip for the cost of the meal, excluding the tax.

31. Monica ordered a chef's salad and an iced tea. Estimate her portion of the bill, including a 20% tip on her total bill. You can ignore the tax in your estimate.

32. **Analyze** What is the tax rate applied to the restaurant bill? Round the tax rate to the nearest whole percent.

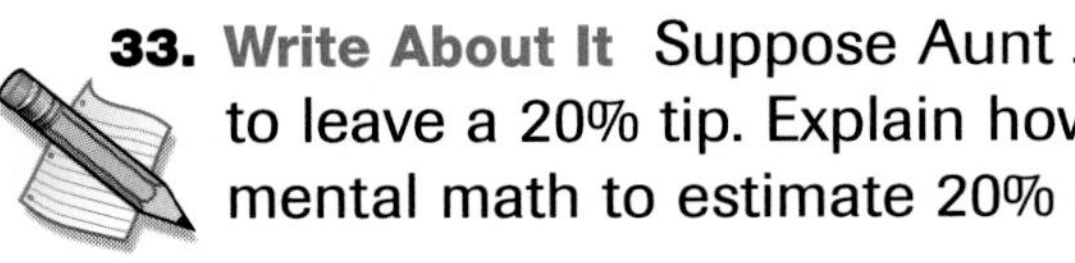

33. **Write About It** Suppose Aunt Judy decides to leave a 20% tip. Explain how she can use mental math to estimate 20% of the bill.

Mixed Review • Test Prep

Evaluate each expression, given $n = \frac{1}{2}$. *(pages 264–265)*

34. $(11 + 6 \times n - 2) \times \frac{1}{4}$ **35.** $(16 \times n) + 2$ **36.** $(\frac{7}{12} \times n) \times 3$

Choose the letter of the correct answer. *(pages 318–319, 320–321)*

37 A sailboat is 36 feet long. A scale model of the boat is 6 inches long. To what scale is the model built?

A 1 in. = 3 ft **C** 1 in. = 12 ft

B 1 in. = 6 ft **D** 1 in. = 36 ft

38 Suppose a plane flies at a constant rate of 480 miles per hour. At that rate, how far does it fly in 1 minute?

F 6 miles **H** 12 miles

G 8 miles **J** 16 miles

Extra Practice See Set E on page 378.

Simple Interest

You will learn how to calculate simple interest.

New Vocabulary
principal
interest rate
simple interest

Learn About It

Over the summer, Jenny earned $150 by pet sitting. The local bank pays 6.1% simple interest per year on money deposited. How much interest will Jenny earn in one year if she deposits her earnings in the bank? What will her total account balance be after one year if she does not withdraw any money?

Calculate the simple interest. Then add it to the principal.

Principal: The amount of money deposited or borrowed.

Interest Rates: The rate of interest paid over a given period of time, usually one year.

Simple Interest: An amount paid for the use of money. It is calculated only on the original principal.

Find the interest and the total of principal and interest.

Step 1 Calculate the simple interest.

Interest (I) = Principal (p) × rate (r) × time (t)
= $150 × 6.1% × 1 yr
= 150 × 0.061 × 1
= $9.15

Step 2 Find the total.

Total = Principal (p) + Interest (I)
= $150 + $9.15
= $159.15

Solution: Jenny will earn $9.15 in interest in one year. Her account balance will be $159.15 if she does not withdraw any money.

Another Example

Simple Interest for 6 Months

$I = p \times r \times t$

Interest = $100 × 6.1% × 0.5
= $100 × 0.061 × 0.5
Interest = $3.05

Explain Your Thinking

► Why was 6 months expressed as 0.5 year in the example?

► How would you express a time of 18 months? What time in months represents 2.25 years?

Guided Practice

Find the simple interest and the sum of the principal and the interest for each.

	Principal	Interest Rate	Time
1.	$150	4.0%	1 yr
2.	$500	12.0%	3 mo
3.	$3,000	8.5%	1 yr
4.	$80	3.9%	6 mo

Ask Yourself

- How do I change the percent to a decimal?
- How do I represent the months as a fraction of a year in decimal form?

Independent Practice

Find the simple interest and the sum of the principal and the interest for each.

	Principal	Interest Rate	Time
5.	$180	5.0%	1 yr
6.	$1,070	7.0%	1 yr
7.	$950	11.1%	4 mo
8.	$2,000	3.0%	3 mo
9.	$10,060	6.3%	6 mo
10.	$230	5.1%	1 yr
11.	$15,564	7.0%	9 mo
12.	$75	18.0%	6 mo

Problem Solving • Reasoning

13. Barry opens a bank account that earns simple interest at a rate of 3.2% a year. He deposits $900. After 5 months, he deposits another $360. At the end of one year, what will Barry's account balance be if he makes no withdrawals?

14. **Analyze** Maria deposits $800 in a savings account that earns simple interest at a rate of 5% a year. Suppose that at the end of the first year, the interest earned is added to the principal, and that the new amount is used to calculate the interest for the next year. At the end of the second year, what is the value of Maria's account?

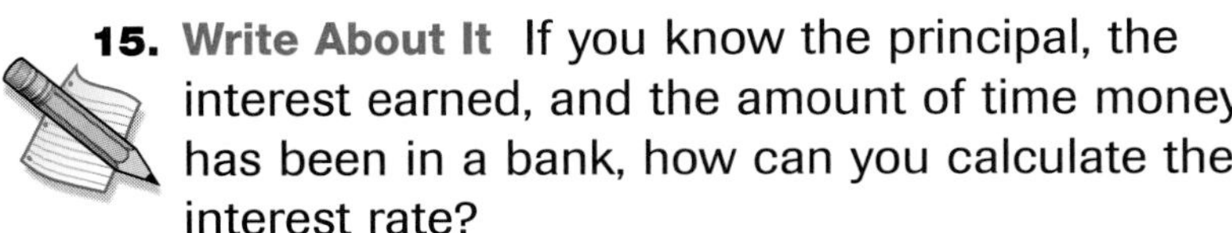

15. **Write About It** If you know the principal, the interest earned, and the amount of time money has been in a bank, how can you calculate the interest rate?

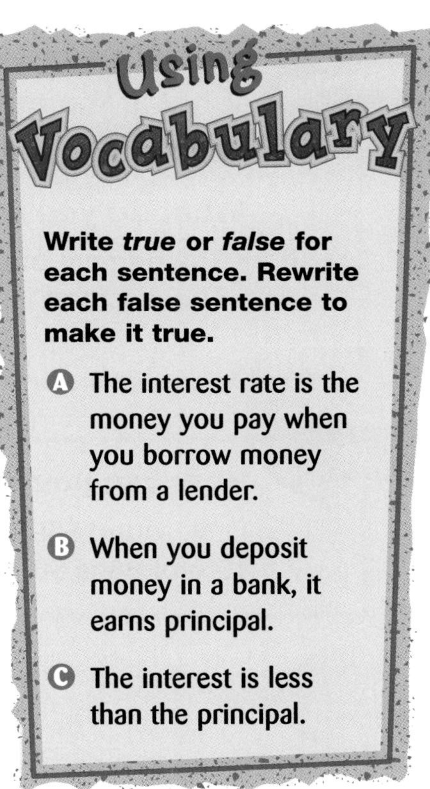

Using
Vocabulary
Write *true* or *false* for each sentence. Rewrite each false sentence to make it true.
A The interest rate is the money you pay when you borrow money from a lender.
B When you deposit money in a bank, it earns principal.
C The interest is less than the principal.

Mixed Review • Test Prep

Solve. *(pages 214–216, 218–220, 222–223, 224–225)*

16. $^{-}11 - {}^{+}7$ **17.** $^{-}18 \times {}^{-}3$ **18.** $^{+}14 + {}^{-}12$ **19.** $^{-}44 \div {}^{-}11$

Choose the letter of the correct answer. *(pages 304–305, 306–307)*

20 If 12 ounces (oz) of juice sell for $0.96, what is the unit rate?

A $0.06 per oz **C** $0.12 per oz
B $0.08 per oz **D** $0.32 per oz

21 Which does not express the ratio of 12 boys to 14 girls?

F 6 to 7 **H** 24 to 38
G 12 to 14 **J** 30 to 35

Extra Practice See Set F on page 378.

Problem-Solving Strategy: Find a Pattern

You will learn how to solve a problem by finding a pattern.

Sometimes you can use patterns to estimate percents.

Problem Sonia and her mother are shopping. Sonia's mother notices a jacket that is on sale at 40% off. The original price is $59.99. Sonia said, "I wonder what the sale price is." Her mother said, "The sale price is 60% of the original price. You can use a pattern to find the sale price."

Understand

What is the question?

What is the sale price of the jacket?

What do you know?

- The original price is $59.99.
- The discount is 40%. 100% − 40% = 60%, so the sale price will be 60% of the original price.

How can you solve the problem?

First, round $59.99 to $60. Then use a pattern to find 60% of $60. 10% of 60 is $6. Make a pattern that adds 10% until you reach 60%.

Solve

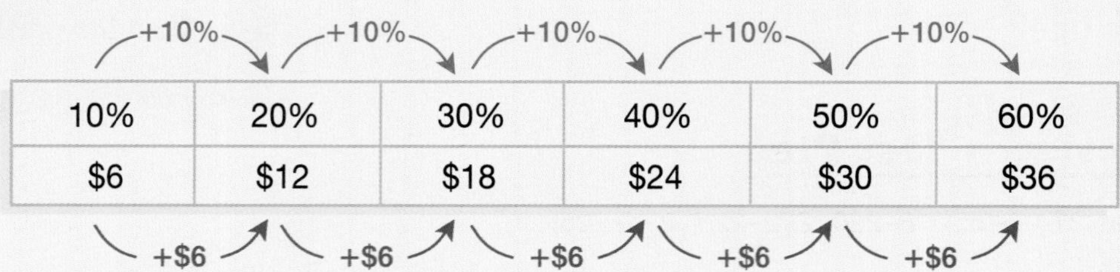

10%	20%	30%	40%	50%	60%
$6	$12	$18	$24	$30	$36

The sale price of the jacket is about $36.

Look Back

Look back at the problem.

What is another way that you could use a pattern to solve this problem?

Remember:
- ▶ Understand
- ▶ Plan
- ▶ Solve
- ▶ Look Back

Guided Practice

Solve these problems, using the Find a Pattern strategy.

1. Skirts that originally cost $39.95 are on sale at 45% off. How can you use a pattern and mental math to estimate the sale price?

   Think: What percentage of the original price is the sale price?

2. For the week of the sale, sales totaled 125% of the average weekly sales. If average weekly sales are $46,000, what was the total for the week of the sale?

   What pattern could you use to find 125% of a number?

Choose a Strategy

Solve. Use these or other strategies.

Problem-Solving Strategies

- **Find a Pattern**
- **Guess and Check**
- **Work Backward**
- **Write an Equation**

3. As part of a sale, a grocer reduces the price of melons each day for 5 days. The first day, melons are 10% off, the second day 12.5% off, and the third day 15% off. If the pattern continues, what is the percentage off on the fifth day?

4. Before a sale, an electronics store received a shipment of TVs. The first day, 27% of them were sold. The next day, 104 TVs were sold. The store then had 188 TVs left. How many TVs were in the shipment?

5. The cost of an item is reduced 10% for each week it is not sold. During the first week, the item was on sale for $240.00. How many weeks was the item on sale if it sold for $174.96?

6. To find 30% of 720, suppose one sixth grader solves $n = 0.3 \times 720$ for n. A second sixth grader solves $n = 30\% \times 720$ for n. Is each student correct? Explain.

7. One of the display cases in the store has a length equal to four times its width. The total perimeter of the case is 240 inches. What is the length of the display case in feet? What is its width in feet?

8. Of the customers that shop in a store, 45% spend $50 to $99, $\frac{1}{4}$ spend $100 to $199, and 10% spend $200 or more. The remaining customers spend less than $50. What percent spend less than $50?

Extra Practice See 5–7 on page 379.

Sales Tax and Discounts

You will learn how to use percents to calculate total cost with sales tax and sale prices.

New Vocabulary
discount

Learn About It

A **discount** is a decrease applied to the price of an item. The sale price is the price of the item after the discount.

Eddie's Toy Store is having a sale. Nathaniel wants to buy a model kit that was originally priced at $14.89. What is the sale price of the kit?

MODEL KITS
SALE
25% off
Original
Price $14.89
Street Rod
Model Kit
Sports Car
Model Kit

Find the sale price of the kit.

Step 1 Determine the discount. Round to the nearest cent.

Discount = 25% of $14.89
= 0.25 × $14.89
= $3.72

Step 2 Subtract the discount from the original price to find the sale price.

Sale price = Original price − Discount
= $14.89 − $3.72
= $11.17

Solution: The sale price of the kit is $11.17.

Other Examples

A. Find Total Cost With Sales Tax

Find the total cost of a $5.94 kite if sales tax is 6%.

Sales tax = 0.06 × $5.94
= $0.36

Total cost = $5.94 + $0.36
= $6.30

B. Subtract Percent First

Find the sale price of a $38.00 game with a discount of 20%.

100% − 20% = 80%

100% represents the original price.

Sale price = 80% of $38.00
= 0.8 × $38.00
= $30.40

Explain Your Thinking

- ► What information is needed to find the sale price? Explain.
- ► Which should you find first—the sales tax or the discount? Explain.

Guided Practice

Find each sale price or total cost with sales tax. Round your answer to the nearest cent.

1. 20% off $15.95

2. 35% off $13.35

3. $29.49 and 5% tax

4. $9.99 and 6.25% tax

Ask Yourself

- How do I use the discount to find the sale price?
- How do I find the total cost, including sales tax?

Calculator Option

Independent Practice

Find each sale price or total cost with sales tax. Round your answer to the nearest cent.

5. 15% off \$8.99 **6.** 50% off \$21.50 **7.** 30% off \$32.48

8. 75% off \$54.63 **9.** 20% off \$17.79 **10.** 20% off \$61.56

11. \$13.48 and 5% tax **12.** \$31.04 and 6% tax **13.** \$6.45 and 5.5% tax

14. \$15.75 and 4.5% tax **15.** \$7.99 and 5.5% tax **16.** \$5.00 and 7% tax

Algebra • Equations **Solve for *n*.**

17. $n = 0.30 \times \$15.40$ **18.** $\$16.34 = n \times \$32.68$

19. $\$1.59 = 0.20 \times n$ **20.** $n = 0.75 \times \$21.00$

Problem Solving • Reasoning

Use Data **Use the pictures for Problems 21 and 22.**

All MODEL KITS 25% OFF

21. **Estimate** Juan wants to buy a board game originally priced at \$12.95. About how much does the board game cost after the discount?

22. **Analyze** Alicia is buying a baseball glove on sale. The regular price of the glove is \$14.99. If Alicia pays 8% sales tax, what is the total cost of her purchase?

23. Use your understanding of percents and fractions to describe another way you could find the discounted price of an item that is on sale for 50% off. Write an equation. Write another equation for an item that is discounted 25%. Check your equations.

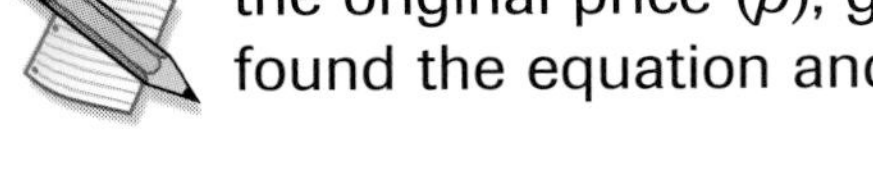

24. **Write About It** Write an equation that relates the sale price (*s*) to the original price (*p*), given the discount (*d*%). Explain how you found the equation and why you think it should work.

Mixed Review • Test Prep

Solve. *(pages 258–260)*

25. $3 + (2 + 3) - 1$ **26.** $42 \div (12 \div 2)$ **27.** $8 \div 2 + 6 \times 2$ **28.** $4 \times 5 - (4 + 5)$

Choose the letter of the correct answer. *(pages 272–273, 310–312)*

29 Which expression is equivalent to twenty-two times the sum of three and a number?

A $(22 + 3) \times n$ **C** $22 \times (3 + n)$

B $(22 \times 3) + n$ **D** $22 + (3 \times n)$

30 Duane weighs 126 pounds on Earth. If his weight on the moon is $\frac{1}{6}$ of that, how much does he weigh on the moon?

F 19 lb **H** 22 lb

G 21 lb **J** 23 lb

Extra Practice See Set G on page 378.

Problem-Solving Application: Use Percent

You will learn how to solve problems with percents.

To solve real-world problems, you must know how to apply percents to different situations.

Carmen and Sandra visit an art museum that has a collection of 3,500 art works. The circle graph below shows the percent of each kind of art in the museum's collection. How many paintings are in the collection?

Understand

What is the question?

How many paintings are in the museum's collection?

What do you know?

There are 3,500 art works in the entire collection.

Paintings make up 55% of the museum's art works.

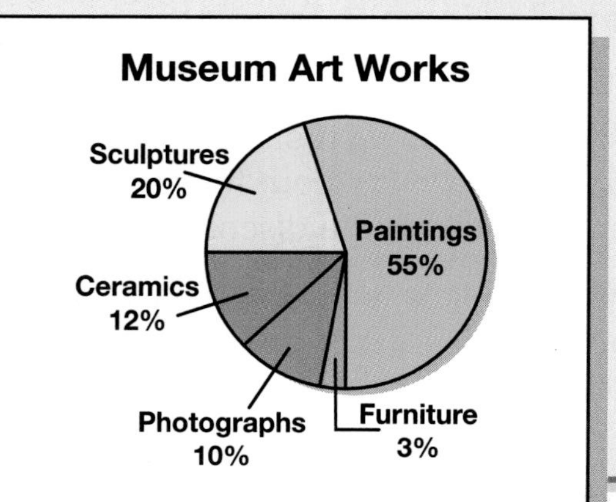

Plan

How can you find the answer?

Find 55% of 3,500.

Solve

Solve.

Let n represent the number of paintings in the collection.

$n = 55\%$ of 3,500

$n = 0.55 \times 3{,}500$

$n = 1{,}925$

There are 1,925 paintings in the museum's collection.

Look Back

Look back at the problem. Is your answer reasonable?

Explain how you can use estimation and the context of the situation to decide if your answer is reasonable.

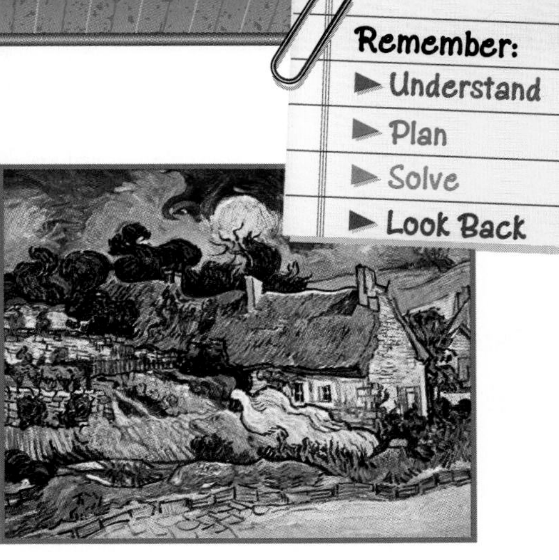

These paintings by the Dutch painter Vincent Van Gogh (1853–1890) are titled (*left*) *Still Life: Vase with Twelve Sunflowers* and (*right*) *Thatched Huts at Cordeville*.

Remember:
- Understand
- Plan
- Solve
- Look Back

Guided Practice

Solve.

1. A bank pays 4.5% simple interest annually on Sandra's savings account. If Sandra deposits $20 in the savings account and does not take from it or add to it, how much money will she have at the end of 1 year?

   Think: What is the interest for 1 year?

2. All museum calendars are 25% off. Desk calendars were originally $10.99 and wall calendars were $14.99. Address books are 30% off their original price of $13.50. If Carmen has $10 to spend, which of these items could she purchase?

   Think: What is each item's sale price?

Choose a Strategy

Solve. Use these or other strategies.

Problem-Solving Strategies

- **Write an Equation**
- **Draw a Diagram**
- **Use Logical Thinking**
- **Make a List**

3. After Joseph views the sculptures in the museum, he goes to the furniture gallery. Use the circle graph on page 372 to find the number of items in each of these collections.

4. The museum curator is hanging paintings on a wall as part of a new exhibit. She wants to hang 4 paintings in a row. In how many possible ways can the curator hang the paintings?

5. Joseph and his uncle decide to have lunch in the museum's cafe. The cost of the meal, not including tax is $12.95. If they want to leave a 15% tip, about how much money should they leave in all?

6. Joseph is buying a book of post cards for $2.95 and a set of acrylic paints for $14.50. The sales tax is 5.5%. What is the total cost of Joseph's purchase, including sales tax?

7. A mural in the museum has four panels that are equal in size and shape. The first panel is $\frac{1}{2}$ blue, the second panel is $\frac{1}{4}$ blue, the third panel is $\frac{1}{8}$ blue, and the fourth panel is $\frac{1}{16}$ blue. What percentage of the entire mural is blue?

8. Joseph's uncle buys a book about the museum's collections for $19.95. He also buys an art set that is on sale for 15% off the original price of $28.99. If the sales tax is 5.5%, what is the total cost of the purchase including the sales tax?

Extra Practice See 8–11 on page 379.

Quick Check

Check Your Understanding of Lessons 6–10

Estimate.

1. 53% of 84 **2.** 15% of $29.31 **3.** 41% of 108

Find the simple interest and the sum of the principal and the interest for each.

	Principal	Interest Rate	Time
4.	$250	6.0%	9 mo
5.	$1,570	3.5%	1 yr
6.	$600	12.9%	6 mo

Find each sale price or total cost with sales tax.

7. 20% off $28.70 **8.** $7.80 and 5.5% tax **9.** 40% off $10.49

Solve.

10. A book that originally cost $24.95 is on sale at 35% off. Use a pattern and mental math to estimate the sale price.

11. At a sports store, T-shirts are on sale at 20% off. The regular price of a T-shirt is $12.99. The sales tax is 5%. If Lana has $30 to spend, how many T-shirts can she buy? Explain.

How did you do?

If you had difficulty with any items in the Quick Check, you can use the following pages for review and extra practice.

Items	Review These Pages	Do These Extra Practice Items
1–3	pages 364–365	Set E, page 377
4–6	pages 366–367	Set F, page 377
7–9	pages 370–371	Set G, page 378
10	pages 368–369	5–7, page 379
11	pages 372–373	8–11, page 379

Test Prep • Cumulative Review

Maintaining the Standards

Choose the letter of the correct answer.

1. Write 34.5% in decimal form.

   A 0.0345
   B 0.3405
   C 0.345
   D 3.345

2. Joni is packaging meat to place in the freezer. She divides $10\frac{1}{2}$ pounds of meat into packages of $1\frac{1}{2}$ pounds each. How many packages of meat will Joni freeze?

   F 10
   G 9
   H 8
   J 7

3. To make a skirt, Mary needs $\frac{5}{8}$ yard of fabric. Mary cuts $\frac{5}{8}$ yard from a piece of fabric and has $\frac{1}{3}$ yard left. Write an equation to show the original length (b) of the piece of fabric.

   A $b + \frac{1}{3} = \frac{5}{8}$
   B $b + \frac{5}{8} = \frac{1}{3}$
   C $b - \frac{1}{3} = \frac{5}{8}$
   D $\frac{1}{3} - \frac{5}{8} = b$

4. At the Sunrise Stables, 24 riders take turns riding 10 horses. What is the ratio of horses to riders?

   F $\frac{24}{10}$ **H** $\frac{12}{5}$
   G $\frac{5}{12}$ **J** $\frac{14}{1}$

5. What are all the factors of 48?

   A 1, 2, 3, 4, 6, 8, 12, 16, 24, 48
   B 2, 3, 4, 6, 8, 12, 16, 24, 48
   C 1, 2, 3, 5, 6, 8, 12, 16, 24, 48
   D 1, 2, 4, 6, 8, 12, 16, 24, 48

6. The scale drawing below represents a living room. What is the area of the room?

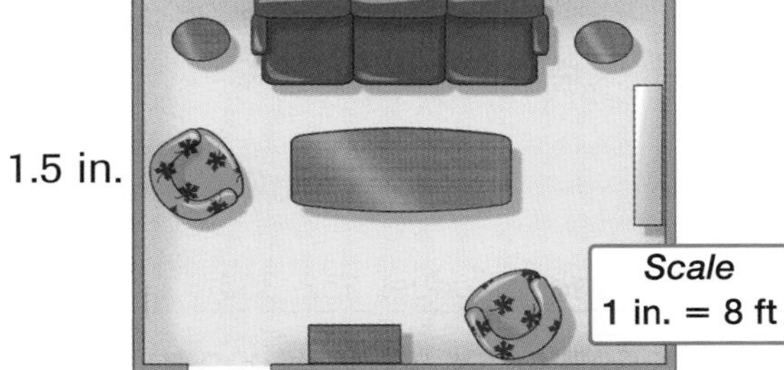

   F 480 ft^2 **H** 192 ft^2
   G 240 ft^2 **J** 60 ft^2

7. Audrey borrows $32 from her mother to buy plants for her room. To pay her mother back, Audrey works in the yard. For each hour she works, Audrey decreases her debt by $6. How much money will Audrey owe after working 4 hours?

   Explain Show how you found your answer.

Extra Practice

Set A (Lesson 1, pages 350–351)

Use a proportion or an equation to find the percent of each number.

1. 20% of 200
2. 50% of 150
3. 33% of 99
4. 140% of 75
5. 15% of 67
6. 95% of 89
7. 65% of 110
8. 5% of 10
9. 13% of 47.5
10. 23% of 50
11. $2\frac{1}{2}$% of $136
12. 12% of 75
13. 55% of 81
14. 10% of 320
15. 3% of 1,044
16. $\frac{1}{4}$% of 2,450
17. 71% of 29
18. 105% of $8
19. 1.8% of 513
20. 20.7% of 102
21. 51.3% of 98

Set B (Lesson 2, pages 352–353)

Use a proportion or an equation to find each percent.

1. What percent of 100 is 400?
2. 26 is what percent of 130?
3. 17 is what percent of 34?
4. What percent of 110 is 66?
5. What percent of 20 is 5?
6. 15 is what percent of 75?
7. 38 is what percent of 80?
8. What percent of 6.25 is 75?
9. What percent of 50 is 40?
10. 114 is what percent of 95?
11. 22 is what percent of 88?
12. What percent of 140 is 49?
13. What percent of 1.8 is 2.7?
14. 26.5 is what percent of 212?
15. 120 is what percent of 300?
16. What percent of 60 is 105?
17. 22 is what percent of 80?
18. What percent of 132 is 85.8?
19. What percent of 100 is 113?
20. 99 is what percent of 88?

Extra Practice

Set C *(Lesson 3, pages 354–355)*

Use a proportion or an equation to find each number.

1. 18 is 18% of what number?
2. 400% of what number is 20?
3. $6\frac{1}{4}$% of what number is 18?
4. 110 is 55% of what number?
5. 7% of what number is 9.1?
6. 28% of what number is 70?
7. 84 is 35% of what number?
8. 51 is 75% of what number?
9. 120% of what number is 90?
10. 64% of what number is 112?
11. 42 is 84% of what number?
12. 44 is 100% of what number?
13. 65% of what number is 26?
14. 6.3% of what number is 12.6?
15. 27 is 13.5% of what number?
16. $8\frac{1}{4}$% of what number is 198?
17. 135 is 450% of what number?
18. 2.4% of what number is 48?
19. 20% of what number is 112.5?
20. 55.5 is 15% of what number?

Set D *(Lesson 4, pages 356–358)*

Solve, using the percent equation.

1. What is 250% of 34?
2. $60.75 is what percent of $150?
3. 1.5 is 30% of what number?
4. What is 131% of 85?
5. What percent of 95 is 19?
6. $10\frac{1}{5}$% of what number is 35.7?
7. 36 is 180% of what number?
8. What percent of 500 is 110?
9. 50% of what number is $5\frac{3}{8}$?
10. What is $8\frac{1}{2}$% of $9.60?
11. What is 7% of $450?
12. 39 is 6.5% of what number?
13. 10.24 is 20% of what number?
14. 5.175 is what percent of 2.25?
15. $8\frac{1}{4}$ is what percent of 165?
16. 15% of what number is $1.86?
17. What percent of 29 is 87?
18. 8.37 is 46.5% of what number?
19. What is 88% of 45?
20. What percent of 1.25 is 1.7?

Extra Practice

Set E (Lesson 6, pages 364–365)

Estimate.

1. 15% of $19.62
2. 50% of 139
3. 10% of 289
4. 10% of $10.85
5. 24% of 399
6. 33% of 60
7. 15% of $27.82
8. 74% of 81
9. 12% of 63
10. 10% of $44.32
11. 66% of 121
12. 51% of 192
13. 10% of $15.64
14. 15% of $33.20
15. 20% of 52
16. 101% of $9.79

Set F (Lesson 7, pages 366–367)

Find the simple interest and the sum of the principal and the interest for each.

	Principal	Interest Rate	Time
1.	$125	3.0%	1 yr
2.	$1,000	4.2%	1 yr
3.	$8,000	4.0%	9 mo
4.	$112	10.9%	6 mo
5.	$5,500	7.9%	1 yr
6.	$1,200	19.0%	4 mo
7.	$20,000	5.7%	6 mo
8.	$2,800	3.5%	3 mo
9.	$750	21.0%	1 yr
10.	$300	12.9%	1 yr

Set G (Lesson 9, pages 370–371)

Find each sale price or total cost with sales tax. Round your answer to the nearest cent.

1. 25% off $8.50
2. 20% off $19.99
3. 10% off $40.75
4. $15.97 and 5% tax
5. $7.54 and 6% tax
6. 30% off $14.49
7. $4.01 and 5.5% tax
8. 50% off $21.90
9. 15% off $24.65
10. $30.00 and 6.25% tax
11. 15% off $55.69
12. 20% off $20.89
13. $22.22 and 5% tax
14. $57.21 and 6.5% tax

Extra Practice • Problem Solving

Solve. Tell what computation method you used. *(Lesson 5, pages 360–361)*

1. A petting zoo has 5 rabbits, 3 lambs, 1 goat, 1 pony, 4 ducks, 7 chickens, and 4 cats. What percent of the animals are rabbits?

2. Out of 180 school days last year, Marilyn walked to school on 45% of the days. How many days last year did she walk to school?

3. Seth is reading a book for English class. Out of the 128 pages in the book, Seth has read 32 pages. What percent of the book does Seth have left to read? Round your answer to the nearest whole percent.

4. The owner of Toy Land is ordering next month's shipment of toys. In this $15,108 order, 32% of the money is spent for toys for children under 10 years of age. About how much is spent for toys for this age group?

Solve these problems, using the Find a Pattern strategy. *(Lesson 8, pages 368–369)*

5. Chris is making a set of boxes that fit inside each other. The lengths of the boxes, from greatest to least, are 15.8 in., 13.6 in., 11.4 in., and 9.2 in. Find a pattern. If your pattern continues, what length will the next box likely be?

6. At Rick's Shoe Store, boots that originally cost $39.95 are now on sale at 45% off. Use a pattern and mental math to estimate the sale price.

7. Find a pattern in the sequence of percents below. If the pattern continues, what will the next percent likely be?

   112% 56% 28% 14%

Solve. *(Lesson 10, pages 372–373)*

8. Jessie and her friends have lunch at a restaurant. The cost of the meal is $45.78. If they want to leave a 15% tip, about how much money should they leave in all?

9. Ms. Clark borrows $5,000 from the bank. The interest rate on her loan is 8.7% per year. If she pays off the loan at the end of 1 year, how much interest will she pay on the loan?

10. Shin is collecting a series of books. At the local bookstore, the original price of each book is $6.95. The bookstore is having a 20% off sale. Sales tax is 8%. If Shin has $25, how many books can she buy?

11. Brad is buying a sweater that costs $15.99 and a vest that costs $21.99. Brad has a coupon for 15% off the cost of the sweater. If the sales tax is 7.5%, what is the total cost of Brad's purchase?

Chapter Review

Reviewing Vocabulary

Write *always, sometimes,* or *never* for each statement. Explain your answers.

1. Simple interest equals the principal in dollars multiplied by the time in years.

2. A percent must be less than or equal to 100.

3. In the percentage equation $P = R \times B$, the letter P stands for *principal.*

4. To change a percent to a decimal, multiply the percent by 100.

Reviewing Concepts and Skills

Use a proportion or an equation to find the percent of each number. *(pages 350–351)*

5. 30% of 210 **6.** 146% of 57 **7.** 62% of 19

Use a proportion or an equation to find each percent. *(pages 352–353)*

8. What percent of 310 is 62?

9. 31.5 is what percent of 70?

10. $2\frac{1}{4}$ is what percent of 18?

11. What percent of 29 is 43.5?

Use a proportion or an equation to find each number. *(pages 354–355)*

12. 55% of what number is 99?

13. 60 is 80% of what number?

14. 8.9% of what number is 6.23?

15. $4\frac{1}{2}$ is 15% of what number?

Solve, using the percent equation. *(pages 356–358)*

16. What is 35% of 170?

17. 15% of what number is 42?

18. 14.5 is what percent of 58?

19. What is 115% of 81?

20. 46 is 46% of what number?

21. What percent of $1\frac{3}{4}$ is 14?

Estimate. *(pages 364–365)*

22. 15% of \$19.82 **23.** 26% of 20 **24.** 10% of \$43.15

25. 47% of 118 **26.** 10% of \$26.29 **27.** 39% of 99

Find the simple interest and the sum of the principal and the interest for each. *(pages 366–367)*

	Principal	Interest Rate	Time
28.	$100	5%	1 yr
29.	$1,250	$7\frac{1}{2}$%	9 mo
30.	$248	3.5%	$\frac{1}{2}$ yr
31.	$1,111	11.1%	4 mo

Find each sale price or total cost with sales tax. *(pages 370–371)*

32. 35% off $36.19

33. 20% off $7.49

34. 70% off $42.35

35. $87.69 and 6.5% tax

36. $25.72 and 5% tax

37. $16.19 and 8.5% tax

Solve. Use the circle graph for Problems 38 and 39. *(pages 360–361, 368–369, 372–373)*

38. The circle graph on the right shows how Jenny spent her June allowance. If she spent $12.50 caring for her two cats, what was Jenny's June allowance?

39. About how much money did Jenny spend for magazines during June?

40. Find a pattern in the percents below. If the pattern continues, what will the next percent likely be?

100% 90% 81% 73%

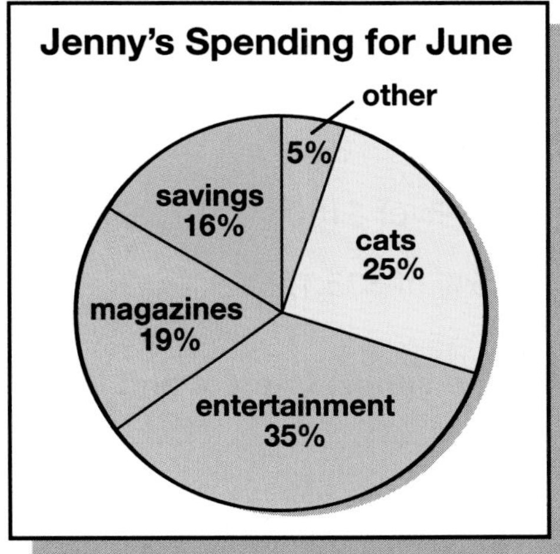

Brain Teasers Math Reasoning

Adding It Up

Which three fractions below have a sum of exactly $\frac{99}{100}$?

$\frac{1}{2}$ $\frac{1}{3}$ $\frac{1}{4}$

$\frac{3}{5}$ $\frac{7}{8}$ $\frac{6}{25}$ $\frac{1}{50}$

Double Discount

A suit was on sale at 30% off its original price of $250. Then the sale price was discounted by an additional 25%. What was the sale price after both discounts?

Internet Brain Teasers
Visit **www.eduplace.com/kids/mhm** for more *Brain Teasers.*

Chapter Test

Use a proportion or an equation to find the percent of each number.

1. 15% of 114

2. 6.8% of 500

3. 72% of 45

4. 120% of 60

Use a proportion or an equation to find each percent.

5. What percent of 250 is $7\frac{1}{2}$?

6. 54 is what percent of 40?

Use a proportion or an equation to find each number.

7. 4.9 is 70% of what number?

8. 25% of what number is 100?

Solve, using the percent equation.

9. 28 is what percent of 112?

10. What is $5\frac{1}{4}$% of 120?

Estimate.

11. 197% of $150

12. 10% of $29.57

13. 15% of $35.12

14. 21% of 93

Find the simple interest and the sum of the principal and the interest.

	Principal	Interest Rate	Time
15.	$90	12.1%	1 yr
16.	$348	4.5%	6 mo
17.	$1,200	7%	9 mo
18.	$57	9.9%	1 yr

Find each sale price or total cost with sales tax.

19. 45% off $45.16

20. 30% off $15.79

21. $6.08 and 7% tax

22. $112 and 8.25% tax

Solve.

23. A food bank has 400 cans of food to distribute. After the first day of distribution, there are 320 cans left; after the second day, 240 cans are left; and after the third day, 160 cans are left. Use the pattern to predict how many days it will likely take until the food bank has distributed all the cans.

24. The Sun and Fun Water Park is open certain days from April to September. If the water park was open 107 days last year, about what percent of the year was the park open?

25. May is buying a new dress. The dress was originally priced at $36.99, but is now discounted by 25%. If the sales tax is 7.5%, what is the total cost of the dress?

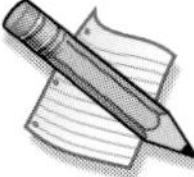

Write About It

Solve each problem. Use correct math vocabulary to explain your thinking.

1. Use the season pass prices on the right.

   a. If you buy a season pass two months or more before the park opens for the season, you save 10%. Three months before the park opens, Mr. Ramsey buys one season pass for an adult and two season passes for children. Explain why the total cost of Mr. Ramsey's passes is less than $200.

   b. How many season passes for children can Mrs. Ruiz get if she buys them two months before the park opens and pays with $350? How much change will she get?

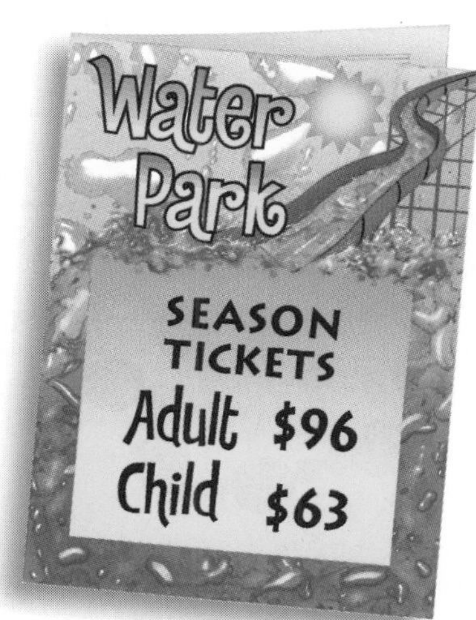

2. A 2-inch ribbon costs $5.95 per roll, a 1-inch ribbon costs $3.95 per roll, a $\frac{1}{2}$-inch ribbon costs $2.95 per roll, and a $\frac{1}{4}$-inch ribbon costs $2.45 per roll.

   a. If the pattern continues, what will the next size ribbon likely be? Show how you found the answer.

   b. If the pattern continues, what will the next cost likely be? Show how you found the answer.

   c. Explain why these patterns do not continue without end.

Another Look

Fiona makes and sells necklaces. She wants the price of each necklace to represent the cost of materials and the amount of time spent working on the necklace. She then adds 50% of that cost to the price of each necklace to make a profit.

The table below shows the average cost of materials and amount of time worked making short and long necklaces.

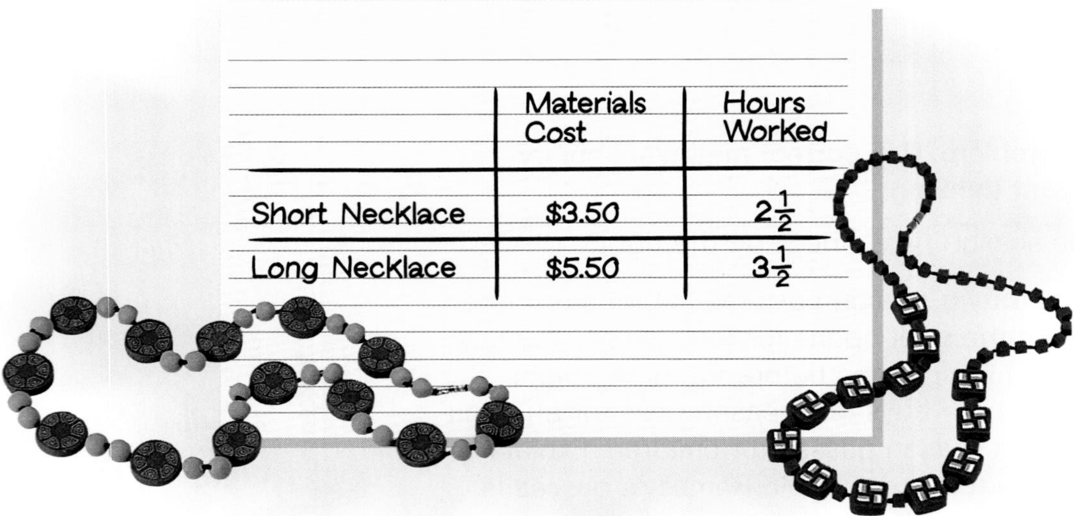

	Materials Cost	Hours Worked
Short Necklace	\$3.50	$2\frac{1}{2}$
Long Necklace	\$5.50	$3\frac{1}{2}$

1. If Fiona pays herself \$5 for each hour worked, what should the selling price of a short necklace be? What should the selling price of a long necklace be?

2. **Estimate** What is Fiona's profit on each necklace, expressed as a percent of the price?

3. Suppose Fiona sold $1\frac{1}{2}$ times as many long necklaces as short necklaces. If the sales of the necklaces totaled \$303, how many necklaces of each length did she sell?

4. **Analyze** A customer who buys two short necklaces gets 10% off the total price. Will Fiona's profit stay the same? Explain.

Enrichment

Percent of Change

When an amount changes, the percent of increase or decrease of that change is called the **percent of change**. The percent of change describes what percent of the original amount the change represents.

New Vocabulary
percent of change

Suppose a pair of hiking boots is on sale for $40. The original price was $50. What is the percent of change in price?

Step 1 Find the change in amount.

$50 − $40 = $10

Step 2 Write a ratio.

$$\frac{\$10}{\$50} = \frac{10}{50}$$

10 ← change in amount
50 ← original amount

Step 3 Write a proportion to find *p*, the percent of change.

$$\frac{10}{50} = \frac{p}{100}$$

Step 4 Solve the proportion for *p*.

$$10 \times 100 = 50 \times p$$
$$1{,}000 = 50p$$
$$20 = p$$

Solution: The percent of change in price is 20%.

A decrease of 20% is an example of a percent of decrease. A percent of increase is a change that causes an amount to increase. Taxes and growth are examples of percent of increase.

Find the percent of change for the following situations. Classify each as a percent of increase or a percent of decrease.

1. A tree grows from 20 ft to 25 ft.
2. The temperature changes from 45°F to 54°F.
3. A $120 guitar is on sale for $57.60.
4. The number of students in a school goes from 550 to 715.

Explain Your Thinking

When does a percent of change equal 100%? What is the relationship of the original amount to the amount of change?

Geometry of Plane Figures

Why Learn About the Geometry of Plane Figures?

Learning about the geometry of plane figures enables you to describe, classify, and measure plane figures and angles.

When you solve a tangram puzzle or draw a geometric design, you are using what you know about the geometry of plane figures.

In this picture, the architect is sharing his plans with the builder. In preparing his plans, the architect used geometric ideas to make the building both strong and attractive.

Reviewing Vocabulary

Understanding geometry vocabulary will help you understand and solve problems more easily. Here are some geometry vocabulary words you should know.

right angle	an angle that measures exactly 90°
acute angle	an angle that measures less than 90°
obtuse angle	an angle that measures more than 90° but less than 180°
straight angle	an angle that measures 180°
transformation	a change in the position but not the shape of a figure
translation	a transformation that slides a figure along a line from one position to another
rotation	a transformation that turns a figure around a given point
reflection	a transformation that flips a figure across a line

Reading Words and Symbols

When you read mathematics, sometimes you read words, sometimes you read words and symbols, and sometimes you read only symbols. In the examples below, each sentence has the same meaning.

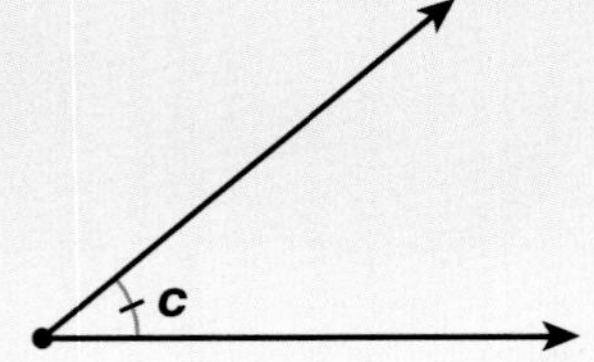

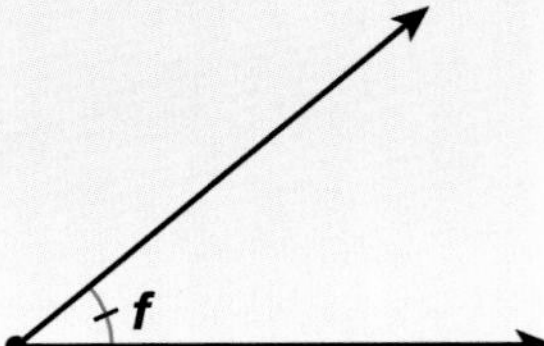

- $\angle c \cong \angle f$
- Angle *c* is congruent to angle *f*
- Angle *c* has the same degree measure as angle *f*

Try These

1. Write *true* or *false* for each statement.
   a. A change in the position of a figure by sliding it along a line is a translation.
   b. A rotation changes the position of a figure by flipping it across a line.
   c. A reflection is a type of geometric transformation.

2. Classify each angle measure as *right*, *acute*, *obtuse*, or *straight*.

   a. 180° b. 78° c. 20° d. 90° e. 122° f. 45°

3. Think about putting words and symbols together. Rewrite each statement in a different way.
   a. Angle p is congruent to angle r.
   b. $\angle j \cong \angle k$
   c. Angle w and angle v have the same degree measure.

Upcoming Vocabulary

Write About It **Here are some other vocabulary words** you will learn in this chapter. Watch for these words. Write their definitions in your journal.

complementary angles
supplementary angles
vertical angles
adjacent angles
interior of an angle
regular polygon
congruent
corresponding parts
diagonal
scale
chord
central angle

Plane Figures

You will learn how lines, points, planes, and angles can be found in many common objects.

New Vocabulary
interior of an angle

Learn About It

Did you know that geometry can be found in nature? Look at each of the snowflakes. Use the terms in the table below to describe geometric ideas you see in the snowflakes.

Geometric Ideas

Definition	Figure	Read/Write
Space is the collection of all points.		
A **point** is an exact location in space.	• A	**Read:** point *A* **Write:** •*A*
A **plane** is a collection of points that forms a flat, continuous, and unending surface.	P	**Read:** plane *P*
A **line** is a straight, continuous, and unending collection of points.	E F	**Read:** line *EF* or line *FE* **Write:** $\overleftrightarrow{EF}$ or $\overleftrightarrow{FE}$
A **line segment** is a part of a line with two endpoints.	G H	**Read:** line segment *GH* or line segment *HG* **Write:** $\overline{GH}$ or $\overline{HG}$
A **ray** is a straight, continuous, and unending set of points that has one endpoint.	I J	**Read:** ray *IJ* **Write:** $\overrightarrow{IJ}$
A **vertex** is the common endpoint of two rays or two line segments.	B	**Read:** vertex *B*
An **angle** consists of two rays that have a common endpoint. The part of a plane between the two rays is called **interior of the angle**.	m	**Read:** angle *m* **Write:** $\angle m$

Two rays with a common endpoint determine two different angles.

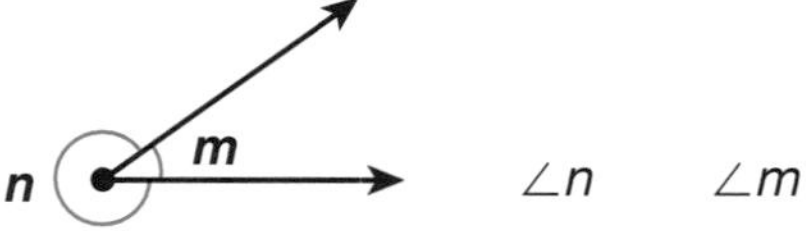

$\angle n$ $\angle m$

Sometimes an angle is named using three points, the vertex point, or a letter.

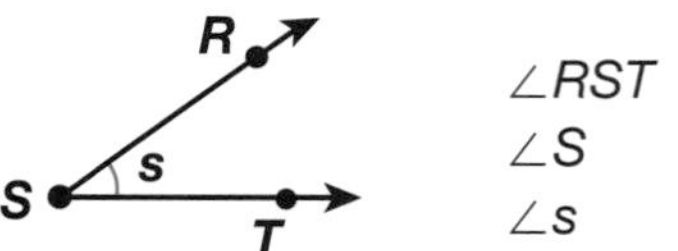

$\angle RST$
$\angle S$
$\angle s$

Explain Your Thinking

► Why must the letter for the vertex be in the middle when naming angles?

Guided Practice

Draw and label each geometric figure.

1. $\overrightarrow{MN}$ **2.** $\overline{PQ}$ **3.** $\angle n$ **4.** vertex R

Ask Yourself

- Did I remember that segments have two endpoints and rays have one endpoint?

Independent Practice

Draw and label each geometric figure.

5. $\overline{AB}$, $\overline{BC}$, and $\overline{AC}$ **6.** $\angle r$ **7.** $\overrightarrow{GJ}$ and $\overrightarrow{AK}$ **8.** $\overleftrightarrow{AB}$ and $\overleftrightarrow{AC}$

Write the name and symbol for each figure.

9. A B **10.** K L **11.** C D **12.** e **13.** Z

Problem Solving • Reasoning

Use Data Use the pictures on page 390 for Problems 14 and 15.

14. Draw a picture using segments to represent each snowflake shown.

15. **Analyze** Look at the snowflakes. Most snowflakes have six angles that are about the same size and share the same vertex. How many segments are necessary to form these six angles? What is the minimum number of endpoints necessary to describe a snowflake?

16. Draw one point on a sheet of paper. How many different lines can you draw that pass through the point? Now draw two points. How many different lines can you draw that pass through both points?

17. **Write About It** Suppose you are trying to cut out a snowflake from a round piece of paper. How would you fold the paper to end up with the proper number of angles? Explain.

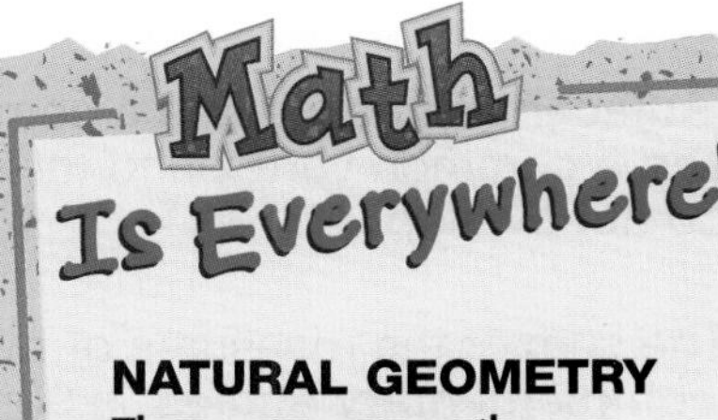

NATURAL GEOMETRY
There are many other examples of geometry in nature. Think of animals you see when you visit the beach or flowers you find in a flower garden. List five examples of geometry found in nature and describe a geometric idea found in each one.

Mixed Review • Test Prep

Solve. *(pages 354–355)*

18. 34% of what number is 11.9? **19.** 14% of what number is 16.8? **20.** 98% of what number is 122.5? **21.** 2% of what number is 2.4?

22 If 6 cartons of milk cost \$8.52, what is the cost of 1 carton? *(pages 306–307)*

A \$0.70 **B** \$1.42 **C** \$5.12 **D** \$14.20

Pairs of Angles

You will learn that when two straight lines intersect, two pairs of angles with special properties are formed.

New Vocabulary
vertical angles
adjacent angles
complementary angles
supplementary angles

Learn About It

When two lines cross each other, more than one angle is formed. Look at the map. How many angles are formed at the intersection of Lincoln and Cherry streets? You should be able to count four 90°, or right, angles. Use the map to find examples of adjacent angles and vertical angles.

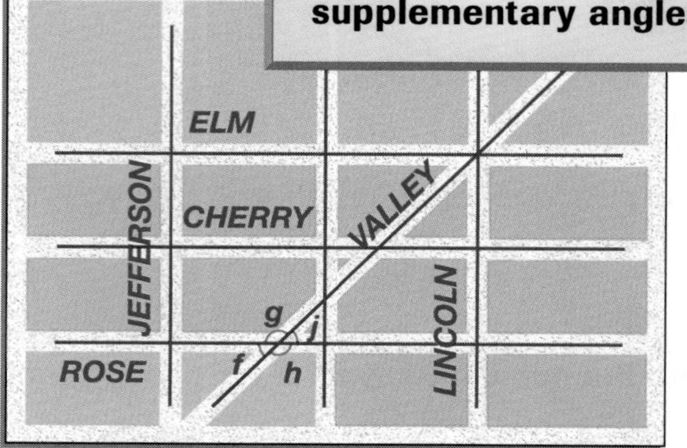

Pairs of Angles

When two straight lines intersect, two pairs of congruent **vertical angles** are formed.	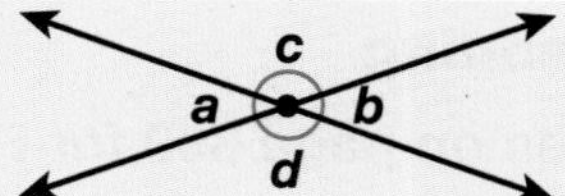	$\angle a \cong \angle b$ $\angle c \cong \angle d$
Adjacent angles share a common side and a common vertex and their interiors do not overlap.	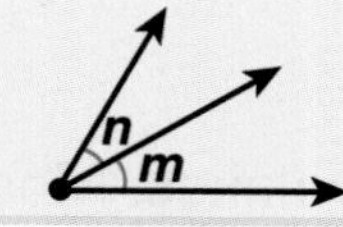	$\angle m$ and $\angle n$
The sum of the measures of two **complementary angles** is 90°.	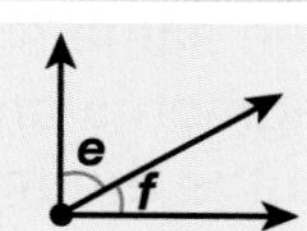	$\angle e$ and $\angle f$
The sum of the measures of two **supplementary angles** is 180°.	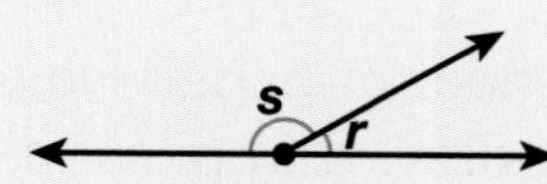	$\angle s$ and $\angle r$

Solution: Examples of vertical angles on the map are $\angle g$ and $\angle h$. Examples of adjacent angles are $\angle j$ and $\angle h$.

Other Examples

A. Supplementary Angles

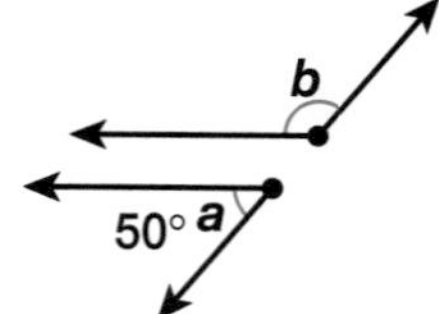

$\angle a$ and $\angle b$ are supplementary angles. Find the measure of $\angle b$.

$b + 50° = 180°$

$b + 50° - 50° = 180° - 50°$

$b = 130°$

measure of $\angle b = 130°$

A short way to write this is $m\angle b = 130°$.

Check: Is the sum of the measures of $\angle a$ and $\angle b$ equal to 180°?

B. Complementary Angles

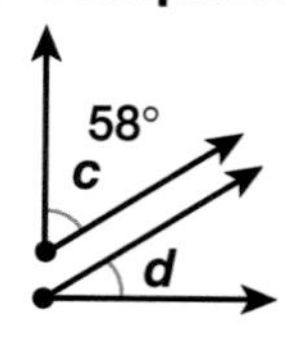

$\angle c$ and $\angle d$ are complementary angles. Find the measure of $\angle d$.

$d + 58° = 90°$

$d + 58° - 58° = 90° - 58°$

$d = 32°$

$m\angle d = 32°$

Check: Is the sum of the measures of $\angle c$ and $\angle d$ equal to 90°?

Explain Your Thinking

- ▶ Why are the adjacent angles formed by two intersecting lines always supplementary?
- ▶ Why are vertical angles equal in measure, or congruent?

Guided Practice

Use the diagram to give an example of a pair of angles that are:

1. supplementary **2.** vertical

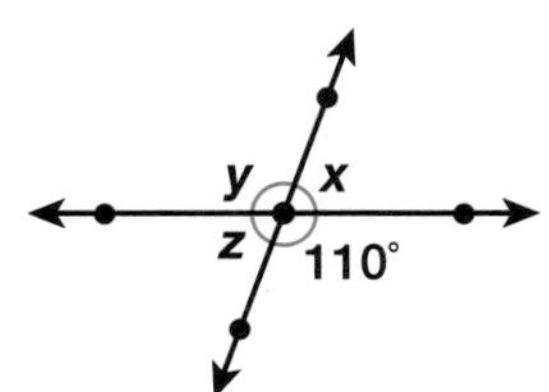

Ask Yourself

- Did I find the measure of one angle by subtracting the measure of its supplementary angle from 180°?

Find the degree measure of each angle.

3. $\angle x$ **4.** $\angle z$ **5.** $\angle y$

Independent Practice

Use the diagram to give two examples of a pair of angles that are:

6. complementary **7.** adjacent

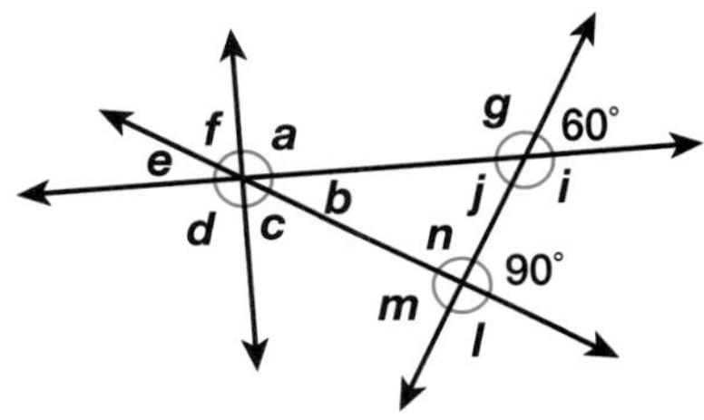

Find the measure in degrees of each angle.

8. $\angle n$ **9.** $\angle l$ **10.** $\angle j$ **11.** $\angle g$

Problem Solving • Reasoning

Use Data **Use the street map for Problems 12 and 13.**

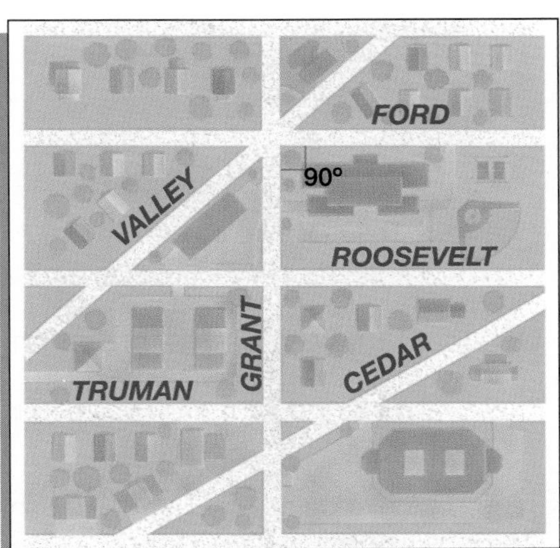

12. Logical Thinking There are four lots on the corner of Truman and Cedar. Two lots opposite each other each have sides that form 30° angles. What are the measures of the other two angles formed at the intersection?

13. Valley and Ford form a 42° angle. What is the degree measure of the angle between Grant and Valley?

14. Write About It Describe vertical angles, adjacent angles, supplementary angles, and complementary angles. Use drawings if they help.

Mixed Review • Test Prep

Solve. Simplify if necessary. *(pages 224–225, 284–285, 310–312)*

15. $\frac{6}{7} = \frac{e}{49}$ **16.** $n \times \frac{3}{2} = 5\frac{1}{4}$ **17.** $(\frac{3}{8} \times \frac{2}{3}) - (\frac{1}{6} \times \frac{3}{8})$ **18.** $^{-}72 \div {}^{-}9$

19 What percent is equivalent to $\frac{7}{8}$? *(pages 330–331)*

A 114.2% **B** 87.5% **C** 78% **D** 56%

Extra Practice See Set B on page 436.

Measure Angles

You will learn how to use a protractor to measure and compare angles.

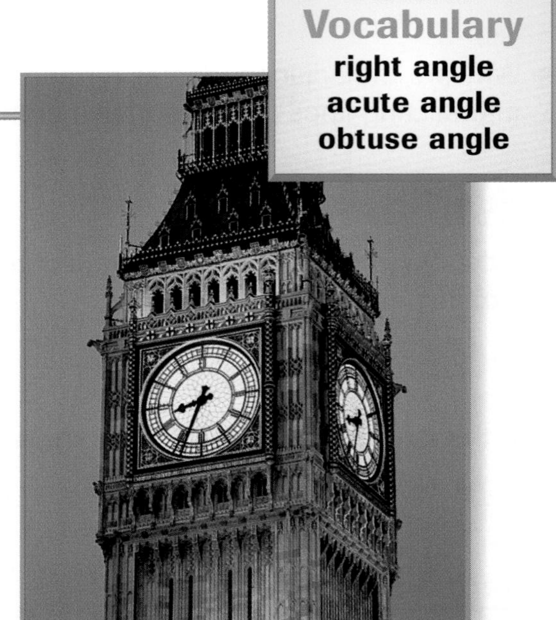

Review Vocabulary
- right angle
- acute angle
- obtuse angle

Learn About It

The hands of a clock are like two rays that form an angle at their endpoints. As the minute hand moves, or rotates, about its endpoint, the measure of the angle changes. In a fifteen-minute period, the minute hand rotates 90°, or one-quarter of a complete 360° rotation.

You can use a protractor to find the degree measure of an angle.

Find the degree measure of ∠*a* and ∠*b*.

Step 1 Place the center of the protractor at the vertex of the angle.

Step 2 Align the 0° mark on the protractor with one ray of the angle to be measured.

Step 3 Find where the other ray passes through the same scale. Read the measure of the angle on that scale.

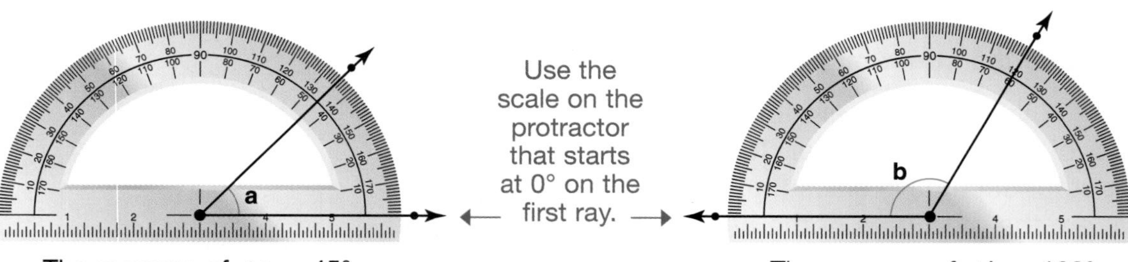
a
Use the scale on the protractor that starts at 0° on the first ray.
b

The measure of ∠*a* = 45°.

The measure of ∠*b* = 120°.

Once you know the measure of an angle, you can classify the angle.

Classifying Angles

The measure of a **right angle** is 90°.

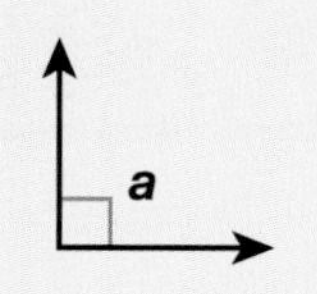
a

The measure of an **acute angle** is less than 90°.

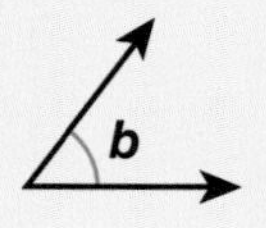
b

The measure of an **obtuse angle** is greater than 90° and less than 180°.

c

Explain Your Thinking

- ► Why does a protractor usually have two scales?
- ► When measuring an angle, why must you use the same scale for both rays of an angle?

Guided Practice

Estimate the measure of each angle. Then measure and classify each angle as acute, right, or obtuse.

1. $\angle c$ **2.** $\angle h$ **3.** $\angle d$

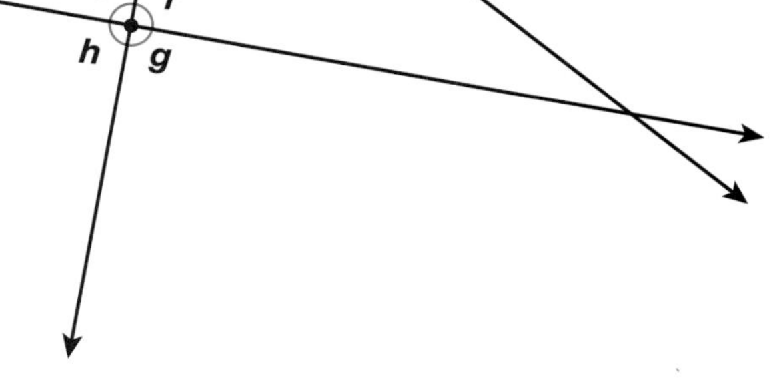

Ask Yourself

- Did I place the vertex of the angle at the 0° mark of the protractor?
- Did I read the correct scale on the protractor?

Independent Practice

Measure each angle. Then classify each angle as obtuse, right, or acute.

4. $\angle a$ **5.** $\angle b$ **6.** $\angle g$

Use >, <, or = to compare each pair of angles.

7. $\angle h$ and $\angle c$ **8.** $\angle c$ and $\angle a$

Problem Solving • Reasoning

Solve. Choose a method.

Computation Methods

- **Mental Math**
- **Estimation**
- **Paper and Pencil**
- **Calculator**

9. The sum of the measures of the angles of any quadrilateral is 360°. Three angles of a quadrilateral measure 95°, 72°, and 84°, respectively. Is the fourth angle an acute angle? Explain.

10. **Logical Thinking** Two lines intersect to form angles *a, b, c,* and *d*. The measure of $\angle a$ is 65°, $\angle a$ and $\angle b$ are supplementary, and $\angle a$ and $\angle c$ are vertical angles. What is the measure of $\angle d$?

11. Rhonda and Vic have just finished a 4-mi hike. Rhonda looks at her watch and notices it is 6:00 P.M. What is the measure of the angle formed by the minute hand and the hour hand on her watch?

12. **Analyze** The sum of the measures of vertical angles *h* and *j* is 140°. Angles *h* and *m* are supplementary angles. What are the angle measures of angles *h, j,* and *m*?

Mixed Review • Test Prep

Solve. Round to hundredths if necessary. *(pages 34–35, 350–351)*

13. 23% of 39 **14.** 4.15% of 88 **15.** 6.35 ÷ 0.42 **16.** 75.4 ÷ 7.9

17 The scale on a forest preserve map is 1 in.:3 mi. A ranger station and a campsite are 9.3 mi apart. What is this distance on the map? *(pages 320–321)*

A 0.3 in. **B** 3.1 in. **C** 9.3 in. **D** 27.9 in.

Extra Practice See Set C on page 436.

Draw Angles

You will learn how to use a protractor and a straightedge to draw angles.

Learn About It

Some cameras have zoom lenses, which can be adjusted. The angle measure of some zoom lenses can be adjusted from 15° to 140°. A nonadjustable camera lens might have an angle measure of 60°. You can use a protractor and a straightedge to draw any of these angles.

Draw a 60° angle.

Step 1 Use a straightedge to draw a ray.

Step 2 Place the center mark of the protractor on the endpoint of the ray. Align the ray with the 0° mark of one scale on the protractor.

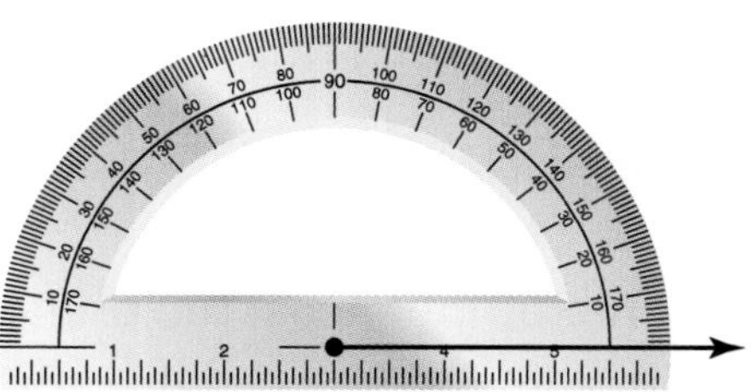

Step 3 Using the scale with the 0° mark, find the 60° mark. Place a point on your paper at that mark.

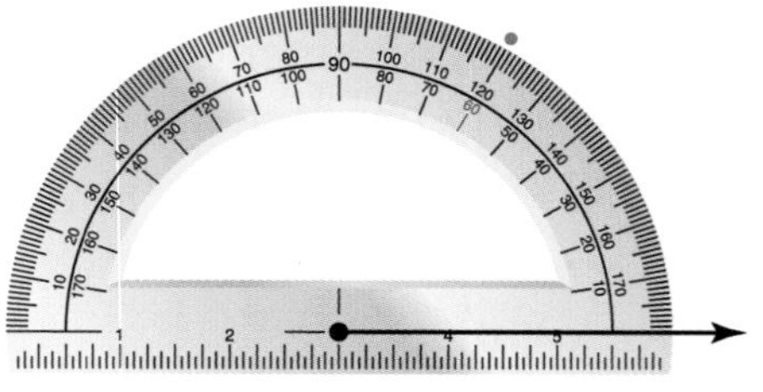

Step 4 Use a straightedge to connect this point with the endpoint of the first ray. Label the angle 60°.

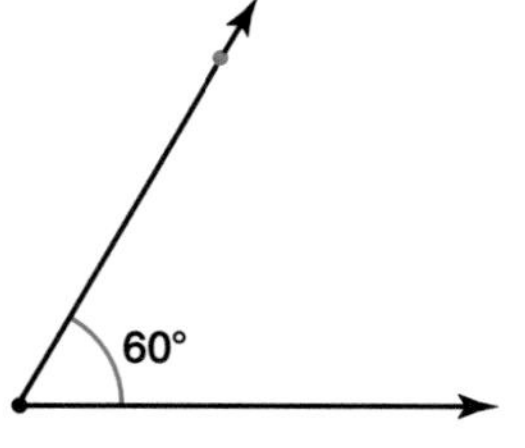

Check your work.

Use the protractor to measure the angle you have just drawn. Check to make sure the measure of the angle is correct.

Explain Your Thinking

- ► What happens if you align the first ray with the 0° mark, but use the scale that starts at 180° to draw the angle?
- ► How might you use a protractor to draw an angle greater than 180°?

Guided Practice

Use a protractor and a straightedge to draw each angle.

1. 35° **2.** 120° **3.** 68° **4.** 90°

5. 160° **6.** 32° **7.** 50° **8.** 200°

Ask Yourself

- Where should I line up the first ray?
- Did I use the correct scale on the protractor?

Independent Practice

Use a protractor and a straightedge to draw each angle.

9. 65° **10.** 135° **11.** 80° **12.** 170° **13.** 8°

14. 20° **15.** 142° **16.** 180° **17.** 210° **18.** 300°

Use a protractor and a straightedge to draw an example of each angle. Measure and label each angle with its degree measure.

19. a right angle **20.** an acute angle **21.** an obtuse angle

Problem Solving • Reasoning

22. Shelly is using a camera with a zoom lens. The lens can be adjusted from 28° to 80°. Draw these angles.

23. Jack drew an angle that measured 15°. Sari drew an angle of twice that measure. Toni drew an angle that was twice the measure of Sari's angle. Draw Sari's angle and tell whether it is obtuse or acute.

24. **Analyze** Margarite and Shannon photograph a landscape from the same location. Margarite uses a lens with an angle measure of 110°. Shannon uses a lens with a 45° angle. Whose picture will show more of the landscape?

25. **Logical Thinking** Michael has 40 pictures from his vacation. Suzy has half as many vacation pictures as Christopher. Christopher has 3 times as many vacation pictures as Michael. How many vacation pictures does Suzy have?

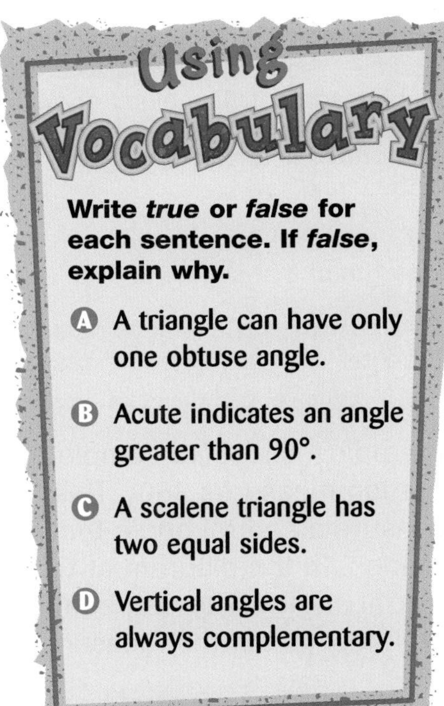

Using Vocabulary
Write *true* or *false* for each sentence. If *false*, explain why.
A A triangle can have only one obtuse angle.
B Acute indicates an angle greater than 90°.
C A scalene triangle has two equal sides.
D Vertical angles are always complementary.

Mixed Review • Test Prep

Compare. Write >, <, or = for each ●. *(pages 126–128, 168–171, 222–223)*

26. $^-4 \times 5$ ● $5 \times {}^-4$ **27.** $3\frac{5}{6} \times \frac{1}{4}$ ● $\frac{2}{3} \times 4\frac{3}{8}$ **28.** $\frac{4}{7}$ ● $\frac{2}{5}$

29 How much would a $65.99 dress cost after a 15% discount? *(pages 370–371)*

A $9.89 **B** $56.09 **C** $9.90 **D** $56.99

Circles and Central Angles

You will learn how to determine the measure of angles whose vertices are at the center of a circle.

New Vocabulary
chord
central angle

Learn About It

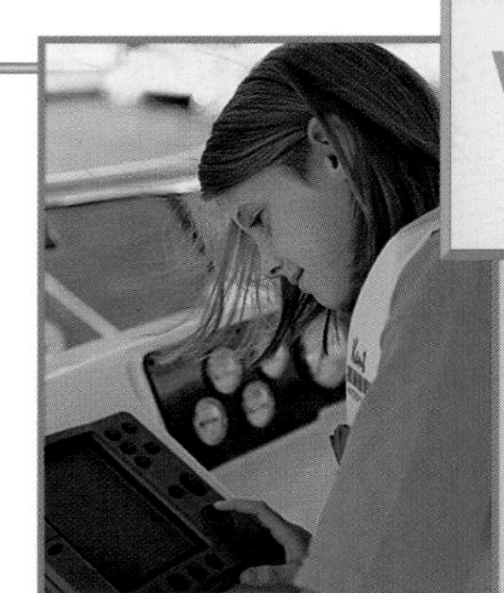

Radar is used on boats to help locate nearby objects, including other boats. Objects on a radar screen are shown within a circle. A circle is a geometric figure consisting of all points in a plane that are the same distance from a given point, called the center.

Circles

The **center** is the point that is the same distance from all points on the circle.

A **radius** is any segment that has one endpoint at the center of the circle and the other endpoint on the circle. The same word also describes the length of that segment. The plural of *radius* is *radii*.

A **chord** is any segment with both endpoints on the circle.

A **diameter** is any chord through the center or the length of that segment.

A **central angle** is any angle with its vertex at the center of the circle and sides that intersect the circle.

C
radius
chord
central angle
m
A
B
diameter
O
center

If a radius is rotated completely around a circle, the rotation measures 360°. This fact can help you measure a central angle that is less than a complete rotation. In the diagram at the right there are three central angles. The degree measures of two angles are known. Find the measure of the third angle.

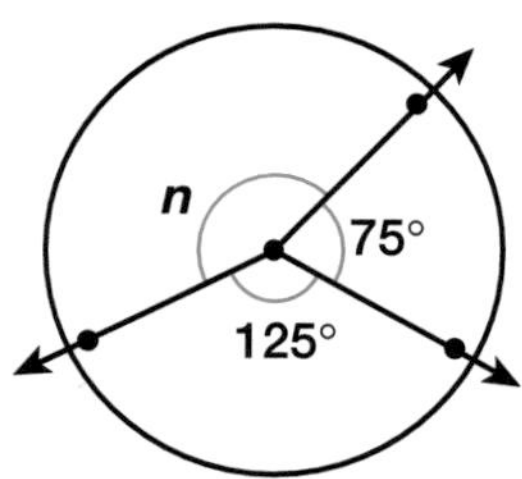

Find the measure of $\angle n$, m$\angle n$.

Step 1 Write an equation.	**Step 2** Add to simplify the expression at the left of the equals sign.	**Step 3** Subtract 200 from each side of the equation to find the measure of the unknown angle.
$125° + 75° + m\angle n = 360°$	$200° + m\angle n = 360°$	$m\angle n = 360° - 200° = 160°$

Solution: The measure of $\angle n$, $m\angle n = 160°$.

Explain Your Thinking

► Why must the sum of the degree measures of the central angles of a circle be 360°?

► What is the relationship between a radius and a diameter of the same circle?

Guided Practice

Use the diagram on the right to find the measure of each angle.

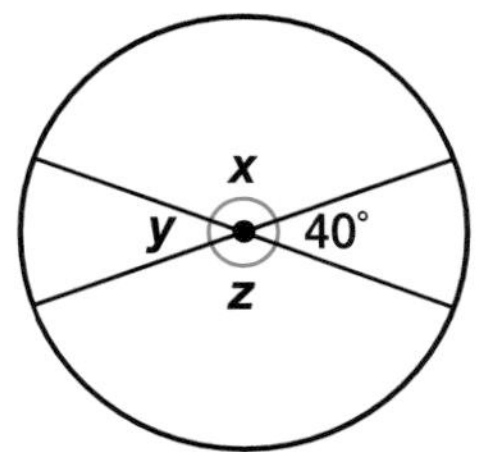

1. $\angle x$
2. $\angle y$
3. $\angle z$
4. $\angle x + \angle y$

Ask Yourself

- Is the sum of the central angles 360°?
- Did I remember that the diameter forms a 180° central angle?

Independent Practice

Use the diagram to find the measure of each angle.

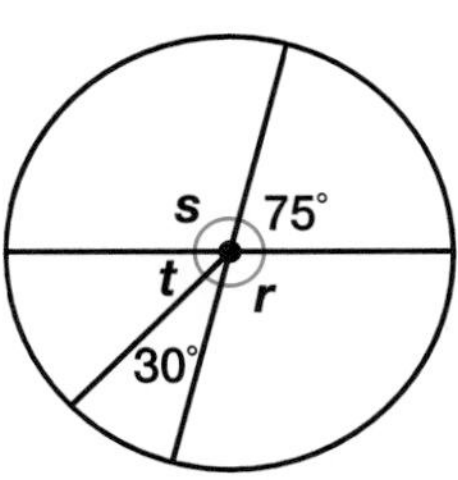

5. $\angle s$
6. $\angle r$
7. $\angle t$
8. $\angle s + \angle t$

Problem Solving • Reasoning

Use Data **Use the picture for Problem 9.**

9. The measure of the central angle determined by the cruise ship and the supply boat is 110°. What is the measure of the central angle with sides determined by the cruise ship and Captain Smith's boat?

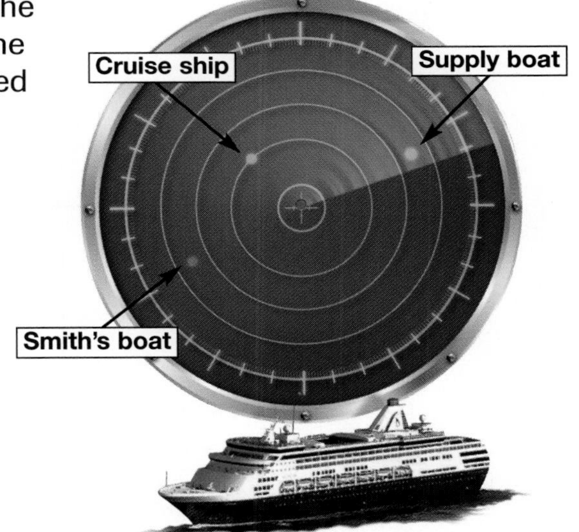

10. Logical Thinking Draw a line segment from a point on a circle that passes through the center and connects with another point on the circle. What is that line segment called? What would the line segment be called if it did not pass through the center?

11. Analyze Lizzy colors $\frac{1}{2}$ of a circle yellow. She then marks off a sector with a central angle of 40° and colors it blue. What is the measure of the central angle of the sector that is not yellow or blue?

Mixed Review • Test Prep

Find the reciprocal of each number. *(pages 172–173)*

12. $\frac{17}{13}$
13. $11\frac{4}{7}$
14. $25\frac{1}{3}$
15. $5\frac{3}{8}$

16. Evaluate $^{-}17 + 21 - {}^{-}5$. *(pages 214–216, 218–220)*

A $^{-}9$ **B** $^{-}1$ **C** 1 **D** 9

Problem-Solving Skill: Use a Circle Graph

You will learn how to make and use a circle graph to represent data.

When you have data that represent part of a whole, it is useful to display those data in a circle graph.

Problem William must create a visual display of the elements in Earth's crust. He decides to use a circle graph, since together these elements make a whole. To make a circle graph, you need to know what size to make each sector of the circle to represent the data accurately.

Find the measures of the central angles that represent each element.

Write a proportion to find the number of degrees for each central angle. Round your answers to the nearest degree.
Remember: The number of degrees in a circle is 360°.

Oxygen 47%

$\frac{47}{100} = \frac{■}{360°}$

$47 \times 360 = 100 \times ■$

$■ = 169.2 \approx 169°$

Silicon 28%

$\frac{28}{100} = \frac{■}{360°}$

$28 \times 360 = 100 \times ■$

$■ = 100.8° \approx 101°$

Aluminum 8%

$\frac{8}{100} = \frac{■}{360°}$

$8 \times 360 = 100 \times ■$

$■ = 28.8° \approx 29°$

All others 17%

$\frac{17}{100} = \frac{■}{360°}$

$17 \times 360 = 100 \times ■$

$■ = 61.2° \approx 61°$

Elements in Earth's Crust

Element	Percent
Oxygen	47%
Silicon	28%
Aluminum	8%
Other	17%

Draw your graph.

When you have calculated all the central angles, draw a circle and one radius. Use that radius as a side of one central angle. Measure and draw the second and third angles. Label your graph with the elements and the percents.

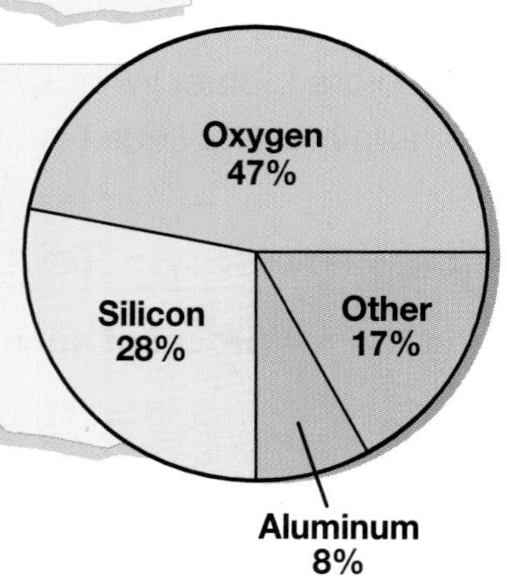

Look Back Why is a circle graph a good way to represent these data?

Guided Practice

Solve.

1. The circle graph shows the three gases that make up about 99.9% of Earth's atmosphere. Use a protractor to measure the central angles for the three sections of the graph.

   Think: How many angles do I have to actually measure?

2. Use the angle measures you found in Problem 1 to find the percentage of each gas in Earth's atmosphere.

   Think: What is the sum of all the central-angle measures in a circle?

Choose a Strategy

Solve. Use these or other strategies.

Problem-Solving Strategies

- **Write an Equation**
- **Work Backward**
- **Use Logical Thinking**
- **Draw a Diagram**

3. A circle graph shows that 36% of Mr. Smith's students prefer pizza for lunch. What is the measure of the central angle for this sector?

4. A circle graph is not labeled with percents. The central angles measure 90°, 45°, 180°, and 45°. What percents do these central angles represent?

5. Only 3% of Earth's water is fresh water. Of this fresh water, $\frac{2}{3}$ is frozen in glaciers and ice caps. What percent of Earth's fresh water is not in the form of ice?

6. About 720,000 species of insects have been identified. The table below shows the approximate number of species in five of the major insect groups. Make a circle graph to show these data.

Five Insect Groups	Number of Species
Beetles	350,000
Flies, Mosquitoes	120,000
Butterflies, Moths	120,000
Ants, Bees, Wasps	100,000
Grasshoppers, Crickets	20,000

7. Much of Earth's surface is covered by water. Of this surface water, the Atlantic Ocean makes up 23%, the Indian Ocean makes up 20%, the Arctic Ocean makes up 4%, and lakes and rivers make up about 7%. The rest of the water is in the Pacific Ocean. What percent of Earth's surface water is made up by the Pacific Ocean?

Extra Practice See 5–8 on page 439.

Quick Check

Check Your Understanding of Lessons 1–6

Draw each geometric figure.

1. $\overrightarrow{CD}$ **2.** $\overline{EF}$ **3.** $\overleftrightarrow{AC}$ and $\overrightarrow{BC}$

Use the diagram for Exercises 4–7.

4. Name one example of vertical angles, complementary angles, and supplementary angles.

Measure each angle in degrees. Then classify the angle as obtuse, right, acute, or straight.

5. $\angle p$ **6.** $\angle s$ **7.** $\angle c$

Use a protractor and a straightedge to draw each angle.

8. 45° **9.** 78° **10.** 150°

Use the diagram to find the measure of each angle.

11. $\angle j$ **12.** $\angle k$ **13.** $\angle l$

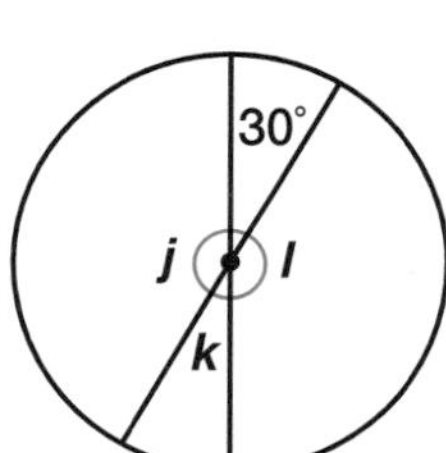

Solve.

14. A class votes on their favorite animal and makes a circle graph of the results. The section of the graph for horses has a central angle of 54°. What percent of the class voted for horses?

How did you do?

If you had difficulty with any items in the Quick Check, you can use the following pages for review and extra practice.

Items	Review These Pages	Do These Extra Practice Items
1–3	pages 390–391	Set A, page 436
4	pages 392–393	Set B, page 436
5–7	pages 394–395	Set C, page 436
8–10	pages 396–397	Set D, page 436
11–13	pages 398–399	Set E, page 437
14	pages 400–401	1–4, page 439

Test Prep • Cumulative Review

Maintaining the Standards

Choose the letter of the correct answer. If a correct answer is not here, choose NH.

1. Theo takes 2 gallons of lemonade to a picnic. How many pints of lemonade does he take?

   A 16 pints
   B 8 pints
   C 4 pints
   D 2 pints

2. Treya's school bus travels 15 miles in one half-hour. At what rate does the bus travel?

   F 35 mi/h
   G 30 mi/h
   H 25 mi/h
   J 7.5 mi/h

3. Which fraction is equivalent to $\frac{3}{7}$?

   A $\frac{7}{3}$
   B $\frac{5}{9}$
   C $\frac{12}{28}$
   D $\frac{6}{21}$

4. What is the value of w in this equation? $(36 - w) \times 4 = 100$

   F 133
   G 11
   H 1.4
   J NH

5. Which list of numbers is in order from least to greatest?

   A $^{-}0.6$, $^{+}\frac{3}{4}$, $^{-}5$, $^{+}11.4$
   B $^{-}5$, $^{-}0.6$, $^{+}\frac{3}{4}$, $^{+}11.4$
   C $^{-}0.6$, $^{-}5$, $^{+}\frac{3}{4}$, $^{+}11.4$
   D $^{+}11.4$, $^{+}\frac{3}{4}$, $^{-}5$, $^{-}0.6$

6. What is the mean number of points scored per game by the Spartans?

Points Scored per Game

	Raiders	Spartans
Game 1	56	51
Game 2	39	59
Game 3	64	37
Game 4	68	73

   F 65
   G 57
   H 55
   J 51

7. Daniel earned $68.00 selling tickets at the theater. If he saves 60% of his earnings, how much will he have left to spend?

   Explain How did you find your answer?

Safe Site

Internet Test Prep
Visit **www.eduplace.com/kids/mhm** for more *Test Prep Practice.*

Triangles and Angle Sums

You will learn to find the measure of one angle of a triangle if you know the measures of the other two angles.

Review Vocabulary
acute triangle
isosceles triangle
obtuse triangle
scalene triangle

Learn About It

If you look carefully at the house being constructed, you will notice a number of different familiar shapes, such as squares, rectangles, and triangles. Triangles, in particular, are widely used in construction. These three-sided figures provide strength and stability to many buildings, bridges, and other kinds of structures.

Classifying Triangles

By Side Measures	By Angle Measures
Equilateral All sides congruent	**Right** One 90° angle
Isosceles At least two sides congruent	**Acute** Three acute angles
Scalene No sides congruent	**Obtuse** One obtuse angle

As you can see, triangles come in many different shapes and sizes. But all triangles have one thing in common—the sum of the angle measures is always 180°.

You can see this for yourself by following the steps shown here.

1. Draw and cut out a triangle. Label the three angles.

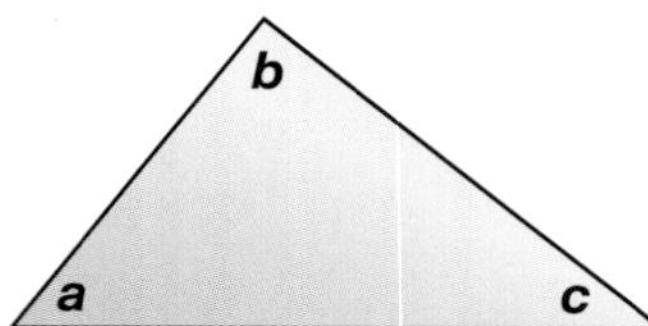

2. Tear off the three corners of the triangle.

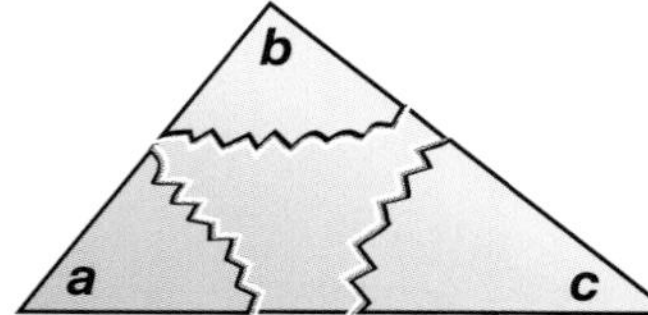

3. Arrange the pieces so that the three angles form a straight angle.

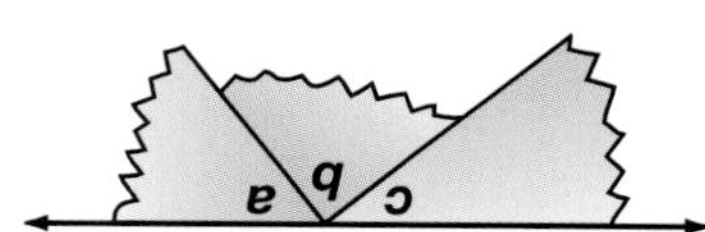

You can use what you know about the sum of the angle measures of any triangle and your knowledge of angles in general to find missing angle measures.

What are the measures of $\angle x$ and $\angle y$ in this triangle?

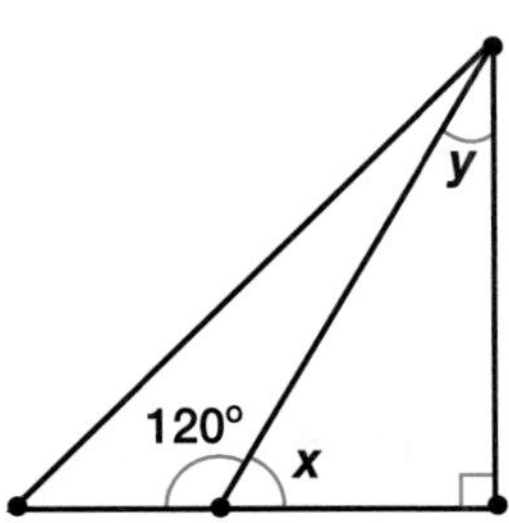

Find m$\angle x$ and m$\angle y$. **Remember:** m$\angle x$ means "the measure of $\angle x$."

Step 1 Write an equation to find m$\angle x$.

$m\angle x + 120° = 180°$ ← A straight angle measures 180°.
$m\angle x = 180° - 120°$
$m\angle x = 60°$

Step 2 Use the measure of $\angle x$ to find m$\angle y$.

$m\angle y + 60° + 90° = 180°$ ← The sum of the angle measures in a triangle is 180°.
$m\angle y = 180° - 150°$
$m\angle y = 30°$

Solution: $m\angle x = 60°$ and $m\angle y = 30°$.

Explain Your Thinking

- ► Why can't a triangle have two angles that each have a measure of 90°?
- ► When is a right triangle also an isosceles triangle?

Guided Practice

Classify each triangle by its sides and by its angles. Then find the measure of the angle *n* in each triangle.

1.
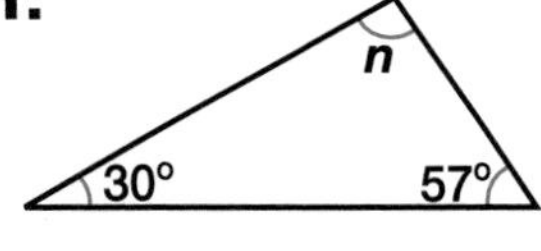

2.
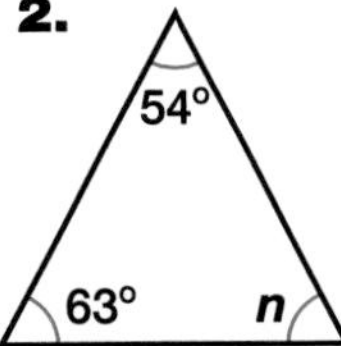

3.
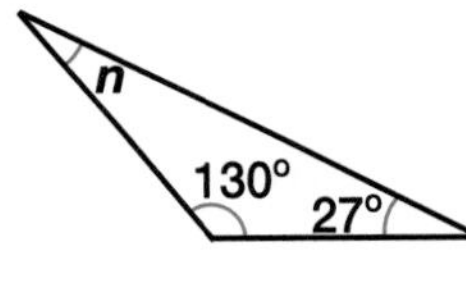

Ask Yourself

- Did I remember to find the sum of the two known angles before subtracting from 180°?
- Did I remember the difference between an obtuse angle and an acute angle?

Use the diagram to find the measure of each angle.

4. $\angle a$

5. $\angle b$

6. $\angle c$

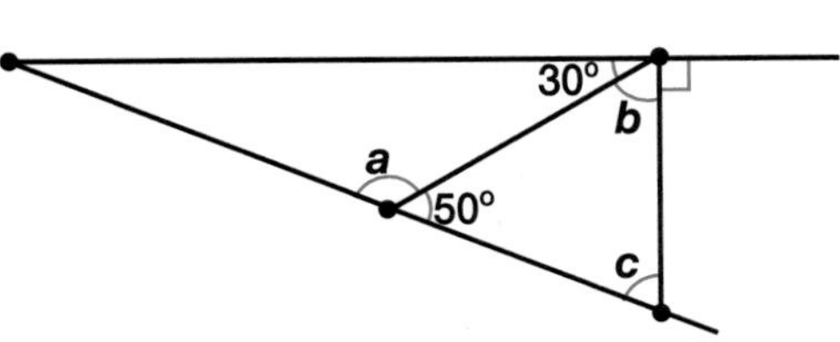

Independent Practice

Classify each triangle by its sides and by its angles. Then find the measure of angle *n* in each triangle.

7.
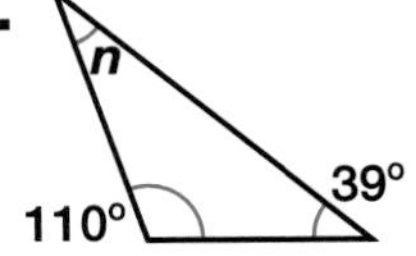

8.
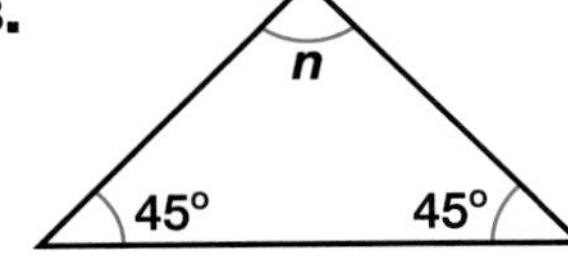

9.
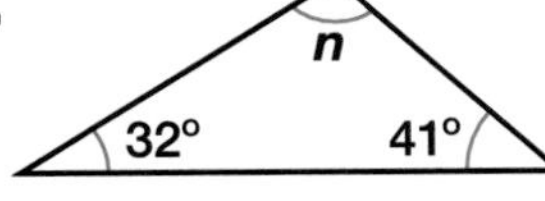

10.
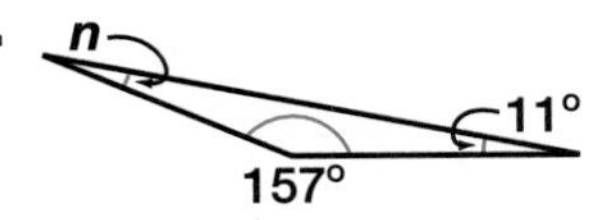

Use the diagram to find the measure of each angle.

11. $\angle r$ **12.** $\angle u$

13. $\angle s$ **14.** $\angle v$

15. $\angle t$ **16.** $\angle w$

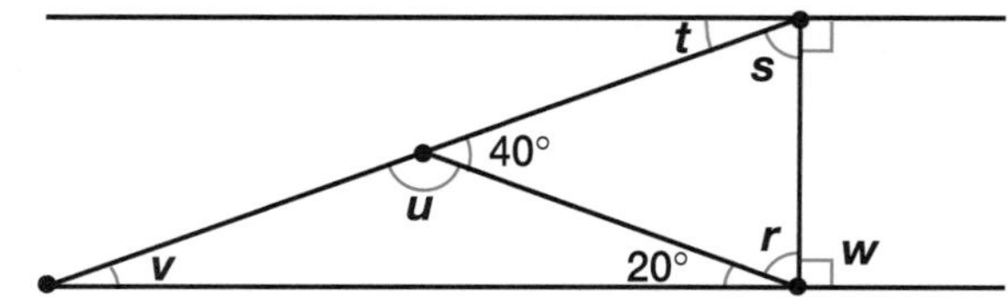

Algebra • Functions

Complete each table by following the rules.

Rule: Subtract input from 180.

	Input	Output
	70 + 80	30
17.	50 + 110	■
18.	90 + 45	■
19.	20 + 40	■

Rule: Subtract input from 360.

	Input	Output
	70 + 80 + 90	120
20.	45 + 45 + 170	■
21.	30 + 20 + 150	■
22.	170 + 170 + 10	■

Problem Solving • Reasoning

Use Data **Use the diagram for Problem 24.**

23. Analyze A house designer wishes to put solar panels on the roof of her house. To get the most solar energy, the part of the roof that faces south should be at an angle of 44° to the ground. The part of the roof that faces north should be at an angle of 60° to the ground. Draw this roof and label all of the angles with their correct measures.

24. A builder is considering this design for the roof of a new house. Find the missing angle measures in each triangle.

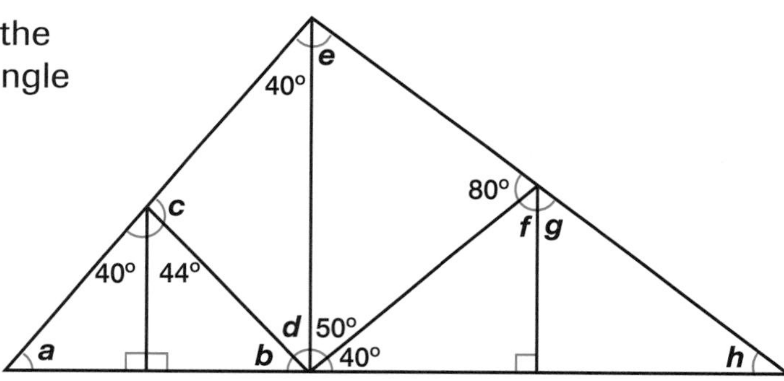

25. Write Your Own Draw a diagram similar to the one at the right. Measure and label about half of the angles. Challenge a classmate to find the missing angle measures.

Mixed Review • Test Prep

Find each unit rate. *(pages 306–307)*

26. \$14 in 7 days **27.** 144 ft in 16 s **28.** 35 mi in 40 min **29.** \$75 in 5 hr

30 What is the simple interest on \$140 for 12 months at 7.5% per year? *(pages 366–367)*

A \$10.50 **B** \$11.66 **C** \$124.44 **D** \$150.50

Extra Practice See Set F on page 437.

Practice Game

The Missing Angle

Practice finding the missing angle in a triangle.

What You'll Need

- *a piece of paper with many different triangles (Teaching Tool 8)*

Players
2

Here's What To Do

1. Player 1 starts by estimating the measure of one angle of any triangle and labeling it.
2. Player 2 then estimates the measure of and labels a second angle of the same triangle.
3. Player 1 has two choices:
   - Player 1 can decide that the measure written by Player 2 is impossible, indicate this, and receive the same number of points as the measure written by Player 2.
   - Player 1 can decide that the measure written by Player 2 is possible, indicate this, and label the third angle with a measure.
4. Player 2 checks the sum of the measures of the angles. If the sum is 180°, then Player 1 receives the same number of points as the measure of the third angle.
5. Play repeats with Player 2 starting. Players continue to take turns until all triangles have been used. The player with the most points is the winner.

Share Your Thinking Is it better to start with a large or small angle for the first angle? What strategy did you use to earn the most points during your turn?

Quadrilaterals and Angle Sums

You will learn about the properties of different types of quadrilaterals.

Learn About It

Flying High Company produces many kites that are quadrilaterals. A quadrilateral is a plane figure with four sides and four angles. Quadrilaterals are given names based on the properties of their angles and sides.

Properties of Quadrilaterals

Parallelogram

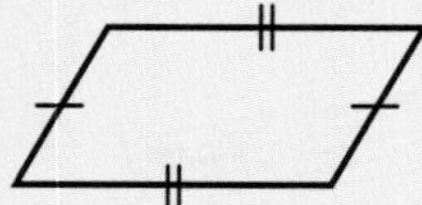

A quadrilateral with opposite sides parallel. The opposite sides and opposite angles are also congruent.

Rectangle

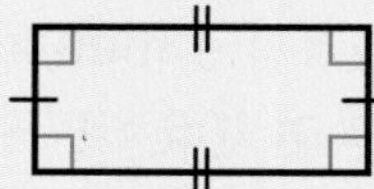

A quadrilateral with four right angles. A rectangle is also a parallelogram.

Square

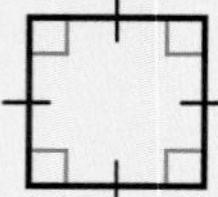

A rectangle with all sides congruent

Rhombus

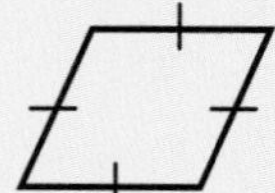

A quadrilateral with all sides congruent. A rhombus is also a parallelogram.

Trapezoid

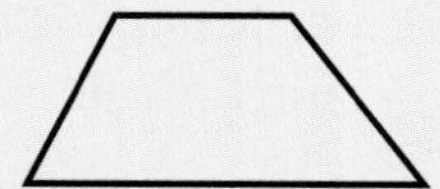

A quadrilateral with one pair of parallel sides

Any quadrilateral can be partitioned into two triangles, each of which has an angle sum of 180°. So, the angle sum of any quadrilateral is $2 \times 180°$, or 360°.

You can use this fact to find the measure in degrees of the missing angle in a parallelogram.

To find m∠*n*, write an equation.

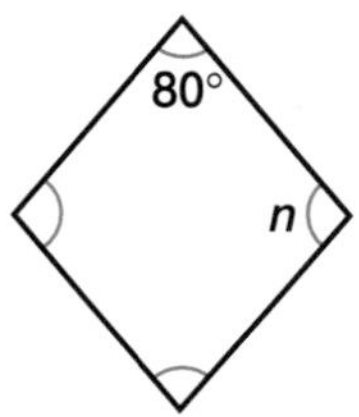

Since opposite angles of a parallelogram are congruent,

$2m\angle n + 2 \times 80° = 360°$

$2m\angle n + 160° = 360°$

$2m\angle n = 360° - 160° = 200°$

$m\angle n = 100°$

Explain Your Thinking

- ► Why is any square both a rhombus and a rectangle?
- ► Why is a rectangle also a parallelogram?

Guided Practice

Find each missing angle measure. Then classify each as quadrilateral, parallelogram, rectangle, rhombus, square, or trapezoid. List all classifications that apply.

> ### Ask Yourself
> - Are opposite angles of parallelograms always congruent?

1. 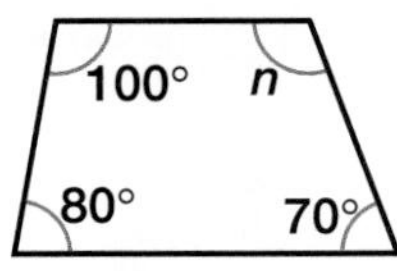

2. 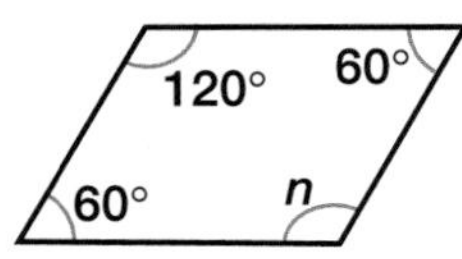

Independent Practice

Find each missing angle measure. Then classify each as quadrilateral, parallelogram, rectangle, rhombus, square, or trapezoid. List all that apply.

3. 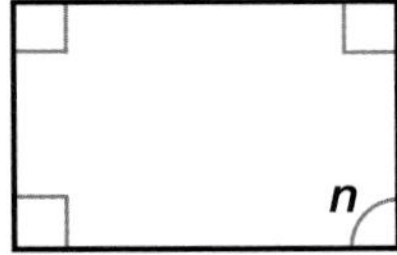

4. 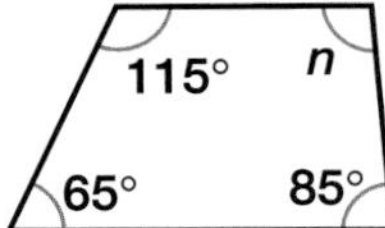

5. 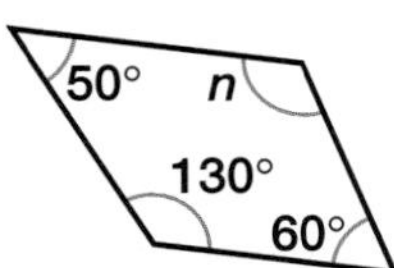

6. 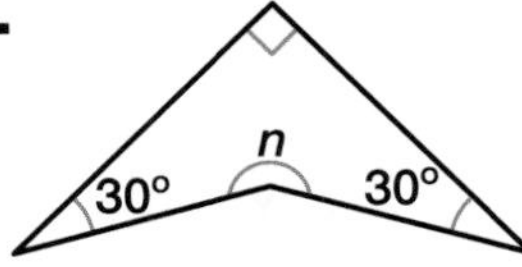

Problem Solving • Reasoning

Use Data **Use diagrams of Kites *A* and *B* for Problems 7–9.**

7. The measures of two angles of Kite *A* are shown in the diagram. If angles *y* and *z* are equal, what is the measure of each in degrees?

8. The kite manufacturer makes Kite *B* by sewing together two identical triangular pieces of cloth. Find the measure of the angles of the quadrilateral formed by the two triangles.

9. Flying High Kites produces the two kite designs shown. Classify each kite shape as quadrilateral, parallelogram, rectangle, square, rhombus, or trapezoid. Include all classifications that apply.

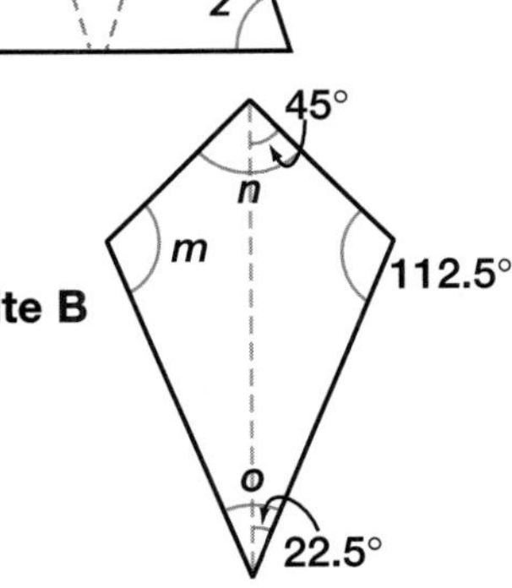

Mixed Review • Test Prep

Solve for *n*. *(pages 280–283)*

10. $(n - 36) \times 9 = 54$

11. $73.05 + n = 148.91$

12. $1{,}260.8 - n = 931.4$

13. $3(14 - n) = 20.4$

14 What is the simple interest rate if you pay $182 interest on $4,000 for one year? *(pages 366–367)*

A 2.2% **B** 4.55% **C** 7.28% **D** 21.98%

Extra Practice See Set G on page 437.

Draw Triangles and Quadrilaterals

You will learn how to draw triangles and quadrilaterals, given specific information.

You can use a ruler and a protractor to draw triangles and quadrilaterals.

Materials

For each group
ruler
paper
protractor
pencil

Drawing a Right Isosceles Triangle

Step 1 Use the ruler to draw a line segment of any length.

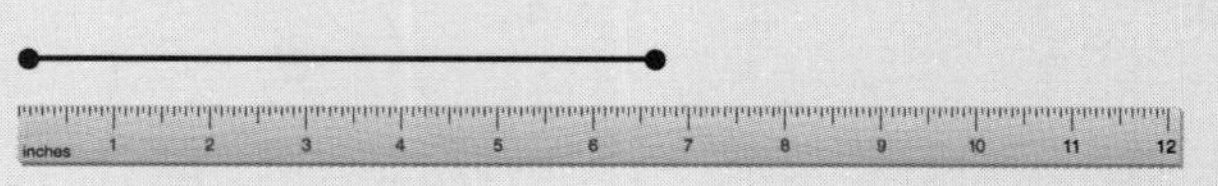

Step 2 Place the protractor on an endpoint of the segment. Make a pencil mark at 90°.

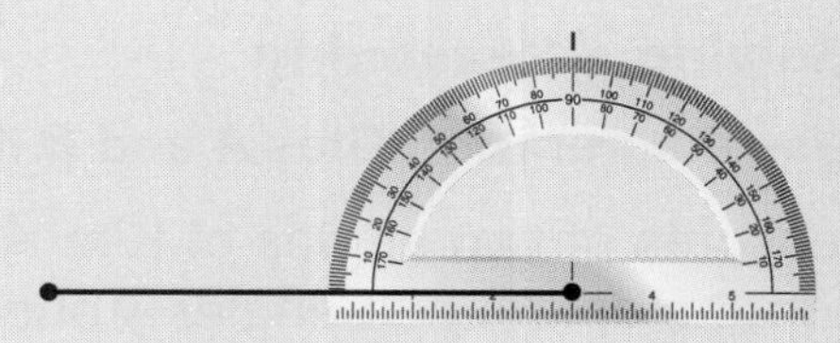

Step 3 Use the ruler to draw a second line segment equal in length to the first segment. The second line segment should extend from one endpoint of the first segment through the mark at 90°, forming a 90° angle.

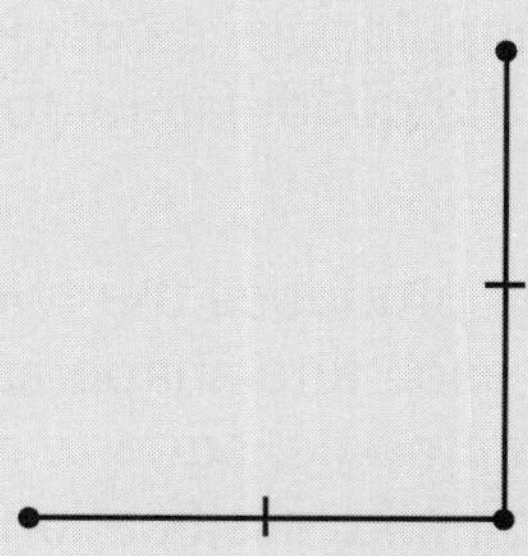

Step 4 Use the ruler to draw a third line segment connecting the endpoints of the line segments in Step 3.

- Why is this triangle a right triangle?
- How do you know the triangle you drew is an isosceles triangle?

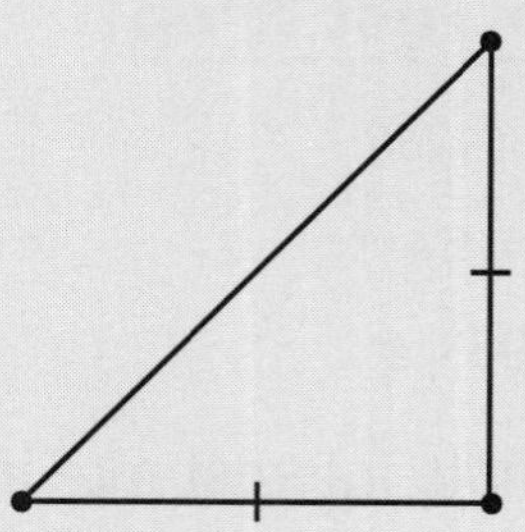

Drawing a Trapezoid

Step 1 Use the ruler to draw a line segment of any length.

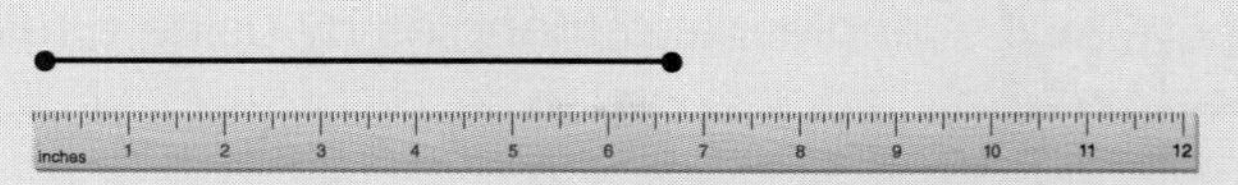

Step 2 Place the protractor on an endpoint of the segment. Make a pencil mark at an angle less than 90°. Use the ruler to draw a line segment extending from one end of the first segment through your angle mark.

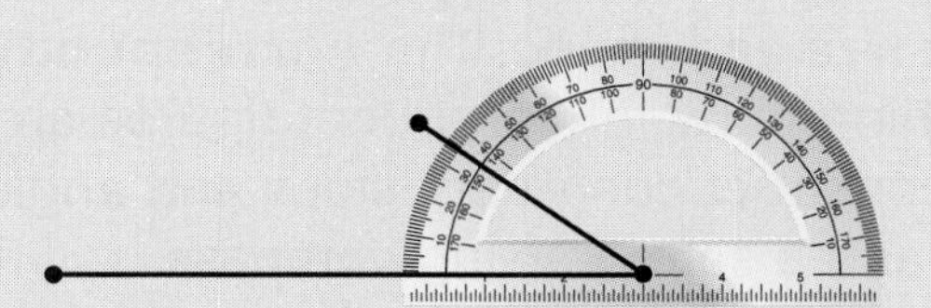

Step 3 Place the protractor on the second line segment. Mark off an angle that is the supplement of the first angle you drew.

Use the ruler to draw a side of the supplementary angle. This side will be parallel to the first segment and can be any length.

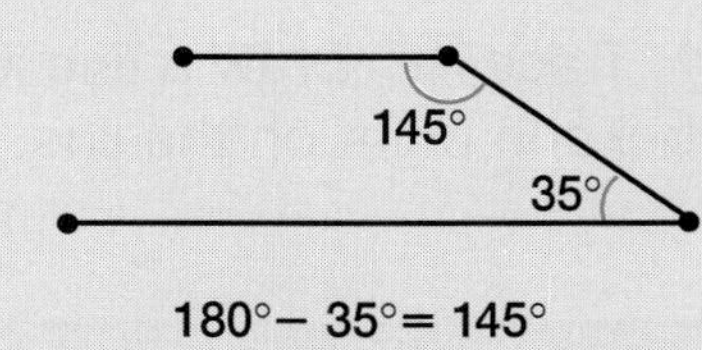

Step 4 Use the ruler to connect the endpoints of the parallel line segments.

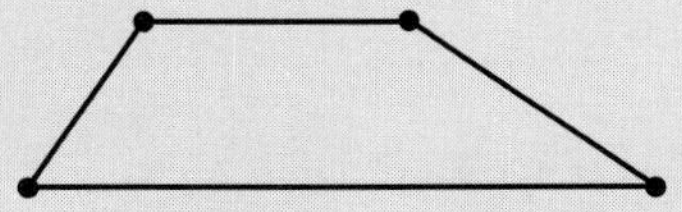

- Why do you need to draw the supplement of the angle in Step 3?
- In Step 3, what happens if the new side is equal in length to the side opposite it?

Try It Out

Draw an example of the triangles and quadrilaterals below.

1. an obtuse isosceles triangle

2. a scalene triangle with all acute angles

3. a quadrilateral with equal sides and no right angles

Use what you have learned to answer this question.

4. Can a triangle have more than one obtuse angle? Why or why not?

Extra Practice See Set H on page 438.

Congruence and Constructions

You will learn how to construct congruent line segments, angles, and triangles by using a ruler and compass.

New Vocabulary
congruent
corresponding parts

Learn About It

Two triangles are **congruent** if the triangles are the same size and shape. The **corresponding parts**, or matching parts, of congruent figures are congruent. You can construct congruent sides and angles by using a ruler and a safe drawing compass.

Materials
pencil
paper
ruler
safe drawing compass

Construct a line segment congruent to $\overline{AB}$.

Step 1 Trace $\overline{AB}$. Draw a line just below $\overline{AB}$. Label one point on the line, Point C.

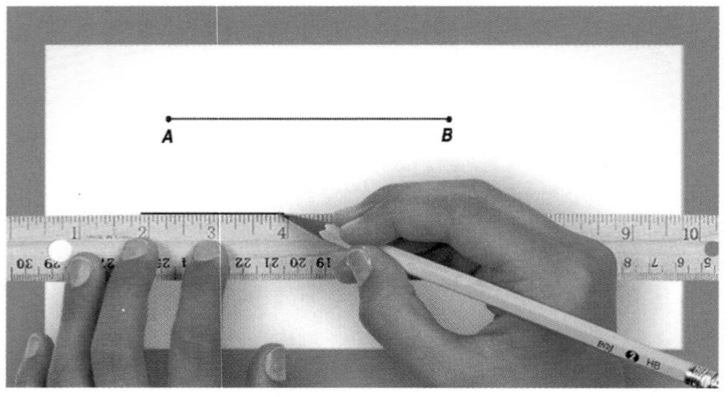

Step 2 Place the compass on Point A. Move the slider to measure the length of segment AB.

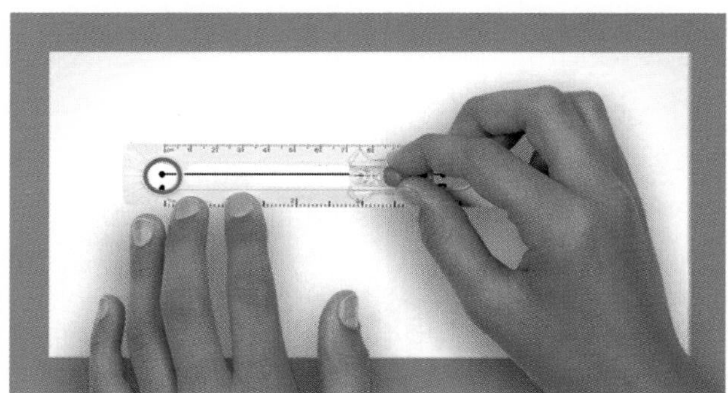

Step 3 Using this measure, place the compass on Point C.

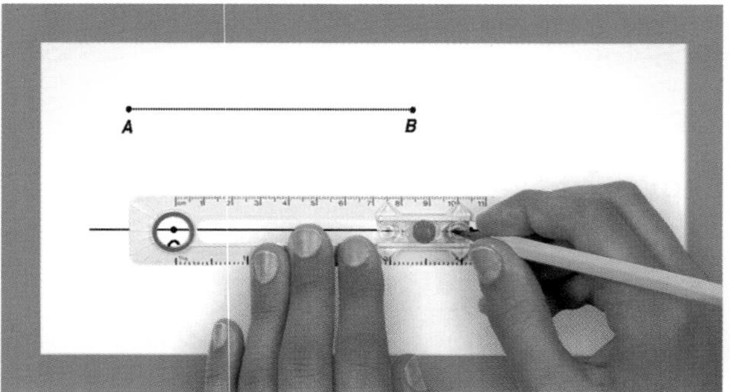

Step 4 Draw an arc from Point C. Label the intersection Point D.

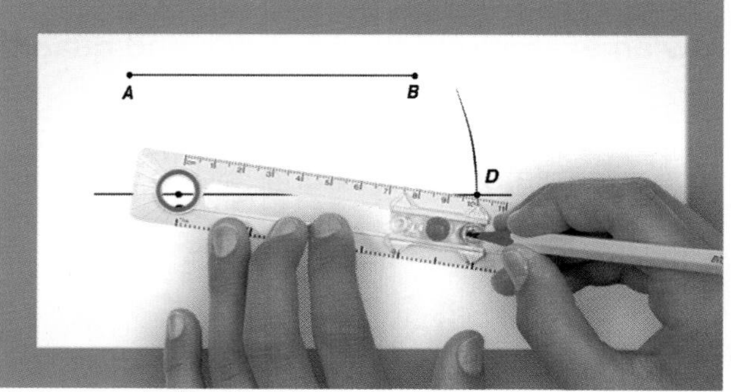

$\overline{CD}$ is congruent to $\overline{AB}$.

Check your work.

Use a ruler to measure the lengths of $\overline{CD}$ and $\overline{AB}$. If their lengths are the same, they are congruent.

Construct an angle congruent to ∠*M*, using Point *P* as the vertex.

Step 1 Trace ∠*M*. Draw a line below ∠*M*. Label one point on the line, Point *P*.

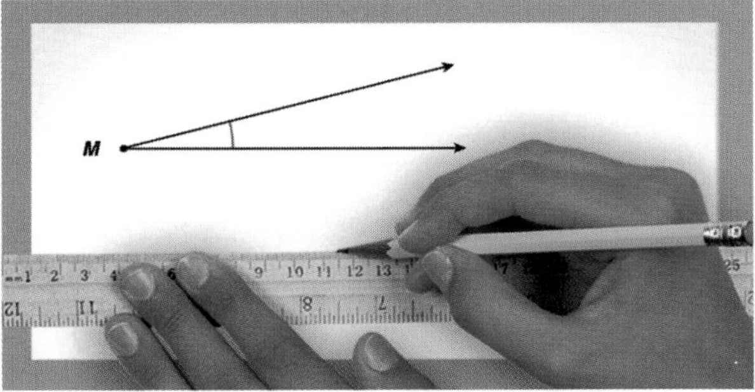

Step 2 Place the compass on Point *M* and draw an arc that intersects both rays. Label the intersections Points *X* and *Y*.

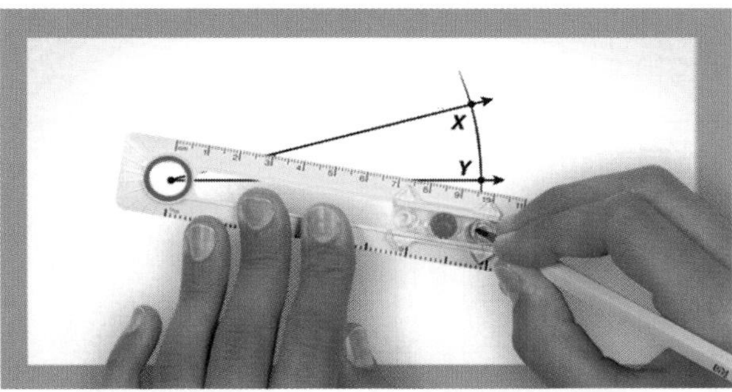

Step 3 Without changing the compass measure, place the compass on Point *P* and draw a similar arc that intersects the line. Label the intersection Point *Z*.

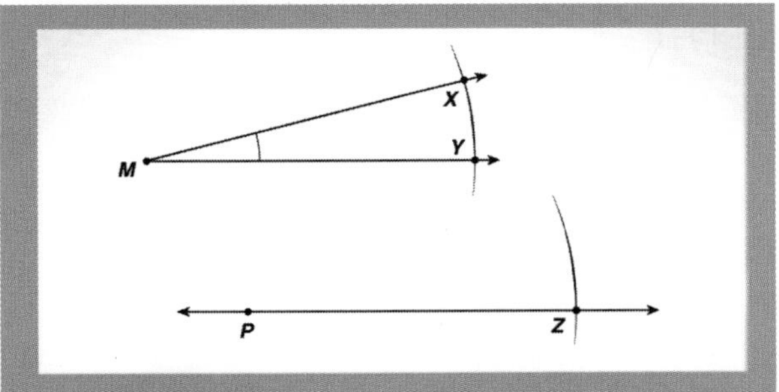

Step 4 Place the compass on Point *X* and measure the distance from *X* to *Y*.

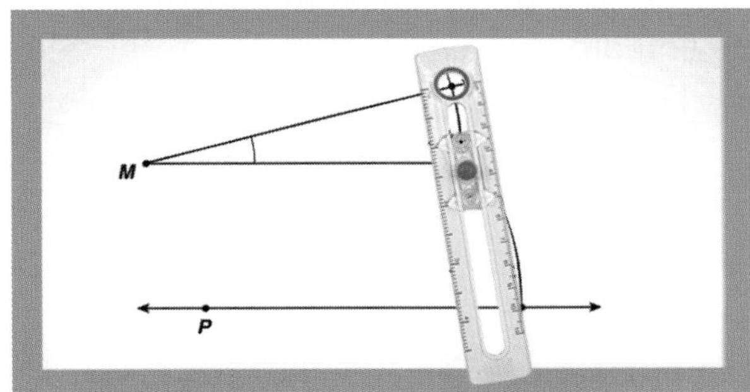

Step 5 Without changing the compass measure, place the compass at Point *Z*. Draw an arc that intersects the larger arc you drew earlier.

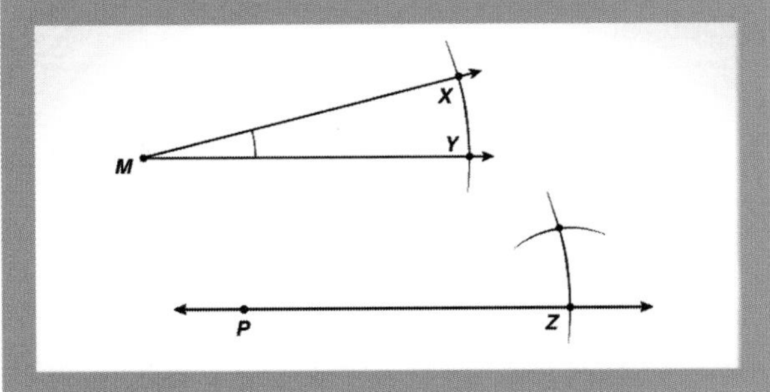

Step 6 Label the new Point *W*. Use a straightedge to draw Ray *PW*.

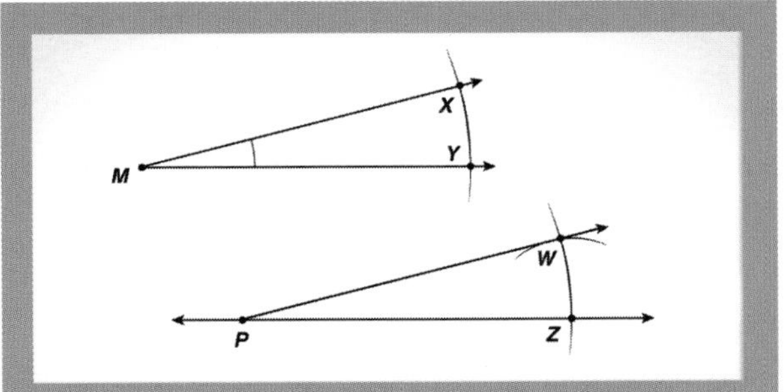

∠*P* is congruent to ∠*M* .

Check your work.

Use a protractor to measure ∠*M* and ∠*P*. If the angles have the same measure, they are congruent.

You can construct an equilateral triangle, using congruent line segments and congruent angles.

Construct equilateral △*GHI*.

Step 1 Draw a line. Label Points *G* and *H* on the line. Use a compass to measure the length of $\overline{GH}$.

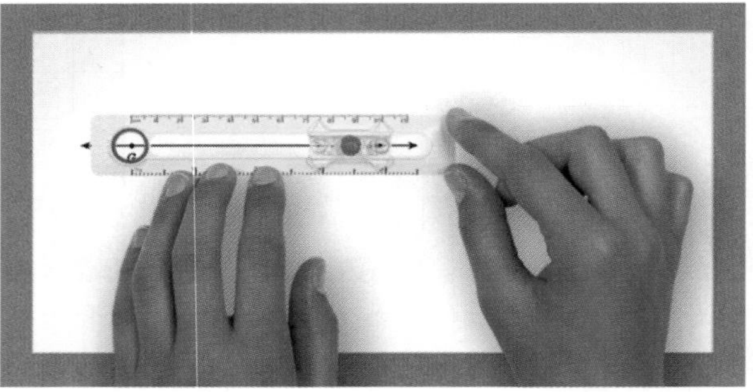

Step 2 Place the compass on Point *G*. Without changing the compass measure, draw an arc from Point *G*.

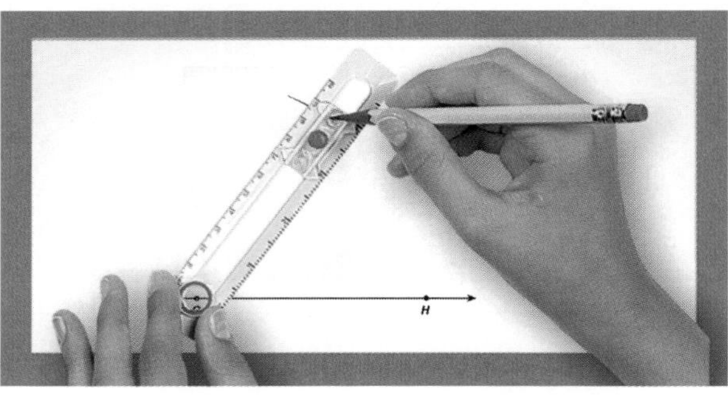

Step 3 Use the same measure to draw an arc from Point *H* that intersects the first arc.

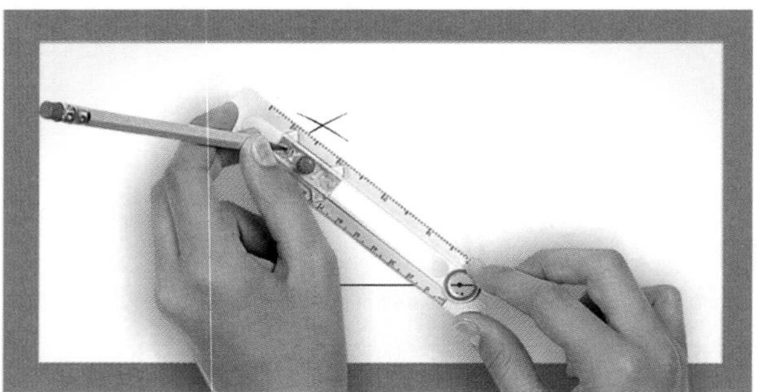

Step 4 Label the intersection Point *I* and use a straightedge to draw $\overline{GI}$ and $\overline{HI}$.

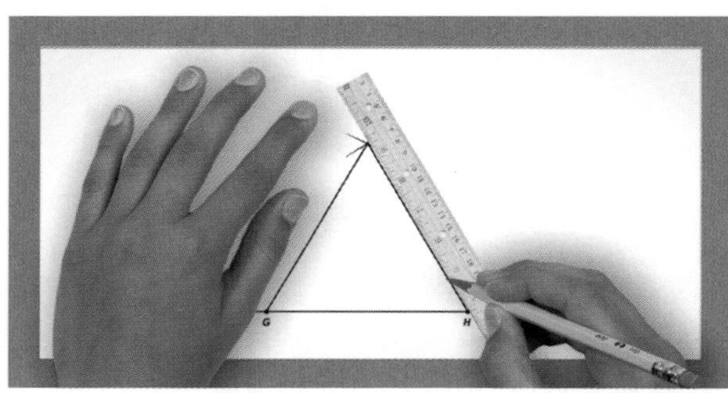

△*GHI* is an equilateral triangle.

Check your work.

Use a ruler to measure the length of each side of △*GHI*. If the lengths are the same, the triangle is equilateral.

Try It Out

Trace each figure. Use a compass and a straightedge to draw congruent figures.

1.

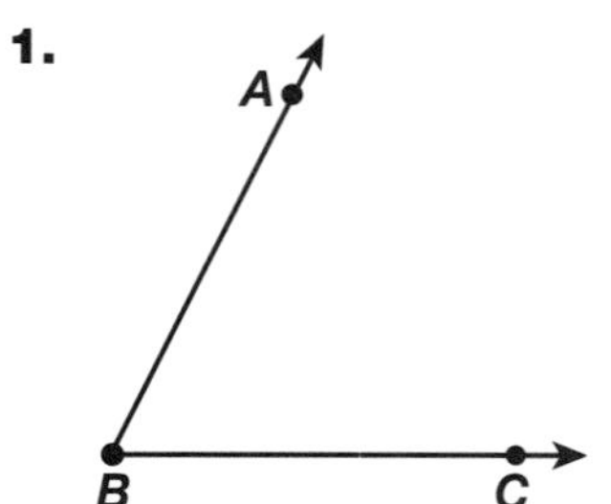

2.

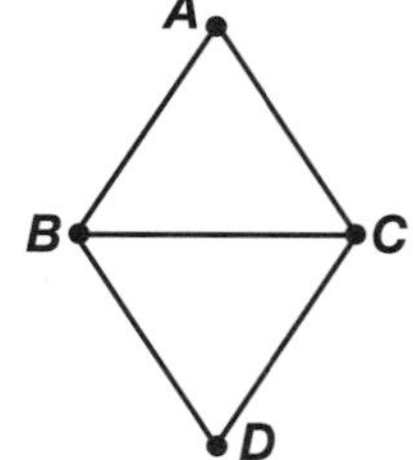

Draw each figure described.

3. an equilateral triangle whose sides are each 2 inches long

4. a square whose sides are each 3 inches long

Use the diagram at the right for Exercises 5–8.

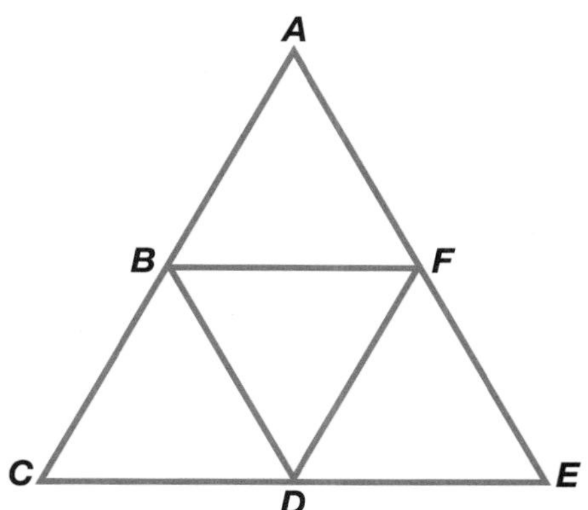

5. List all segments congruent to $\overline{AB}$.

6. List all the triangles you can find that are congruent to $\triangle ABF$.

7. Name two figures that are congruent to quadrilateral *BCEF*.

8. Trace triangle *BDF*. Construct equilateral triangle *PQR* congruent to triangle *BDF*. Hint: Begin by constructing a line segment congruent to $\overline{BD}$.

9. **Visual Thinking** Describe the steps of the following construction in your own words.

A

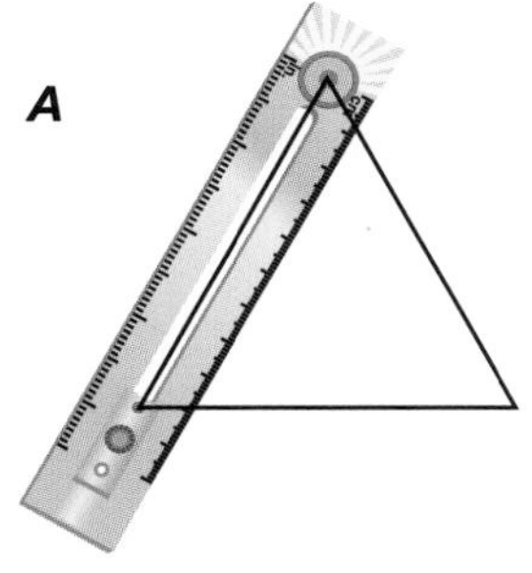

B

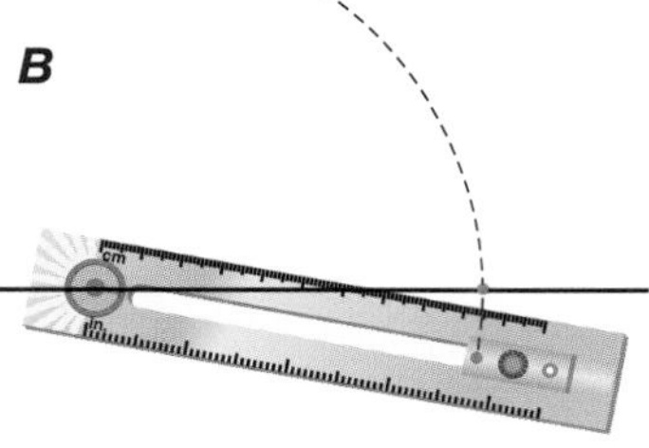

C

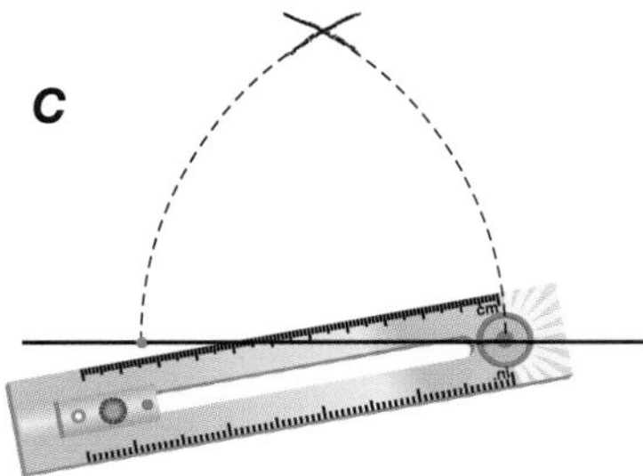

D

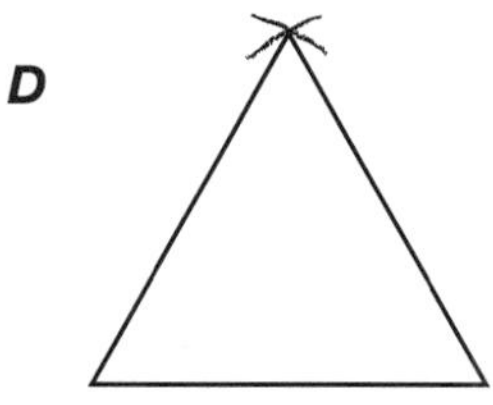

Write about it! Talk about it!

Use what you have learned to answer this question.

10. When constructing an equilateral triangle, why is it important not to change the compass setting to mark the lengths of the sides?

LESSON 11

Similar Figures

You will learn how to use similar figures to find measures of objects.

New Vocabulary
similar figures
scale

Learn About It

The buildings in the picture are scale models of real buildings in New York City. The models and the actual buildings are similar figures. **Similar figures** have the same shape, but they do not have to be the same size.

If figures are similar, the lengths of their corresponding sides are proportional and the measures of their corresponding angles are equal. Corresponding parts of real objects and their models have the same ratio. This ratio is called the **scale.**

The symbol ~ is read as "is similar to."

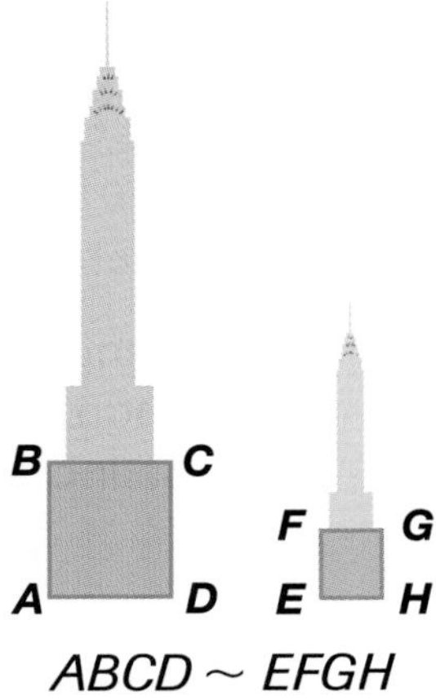

$ABCD \sim EFGH$

Find the width of rectangle *EFGH*.

Step 1 Label the corresponding sides of the similar figures.

$\overline{AB}$ and $\overline{EF}$ $\overline{CD}$ and $\overline{GH}$

$\overline{BC}$ and $\overline{FG}$ $\overline{AD}$ and $\overline{EH}$

Rectangle ABCD: BC = 28 in., AB = 32 in. Rectangle EFGH: FG = x, EF = 16 in.

Step 2 Write a proportion to represent the relationship between the pairs of corresponding sides, $\overline{AB}$, $\overline{EF}$, $\overline{BC}$, and $\overline{FG}$.

$$\frac{AB}{EF} = \frac{BC}{FG}$$

Rectangle ABCD: BC = 28 in., AB = 32 in. Rectangle EFGH: FG = x, EF = 16 in.

Step 3 Rewrite the proportion, using the corresponding measures of the figures. Then solve the proportion by cross-multiplying.

$$\frac{32}{16} = \frac{28}{x}$$

$$32x = 16 \times 28$$

$$x = \frac{\overset{1}{\cancel{16}} \times 28}{\underset{2}{\cancel{32}}} = \frac{28}{2}$$

$$x = 14 \text{ in.}$$

Solution: The width of rectangle *EFGH* is 14 in.

Another Example

Similar Triangles
$\triangle PQR \sim \triangle MNO$

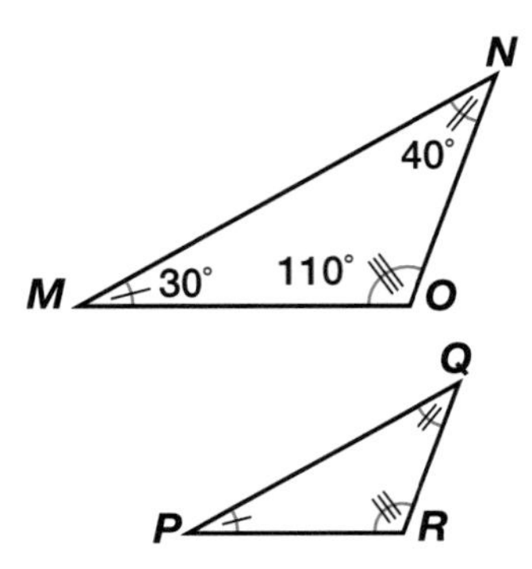

Find the measure of each angle of $\triangle PQR$.
$m\angle Q = 40°$
$m\angle R = 110°$
$m\angle P = 30°$

Explain Your Thinking

- Why is it important to identify the corresponding parts of similar figures when calculating side and angle measures?
- Why do corresponding angles of similar triangles have the same measure?

Guided Practice

Figure *ABCDE* ~ Figure *MNOPQ*. For each side and angle given for Figure *ABCDE*, name the corresponding part in Figure *MNOPQ*. Then find each measure.

1. $\overline{AB}$ **2.** $\overline{BC}$ **3.** $\overline{CD}$

4. $\overline{ED}$ **5.** $\angle A$ **6.** $\angle C$

> **Ask Yourself**
> - Which values should I use in a proportion?

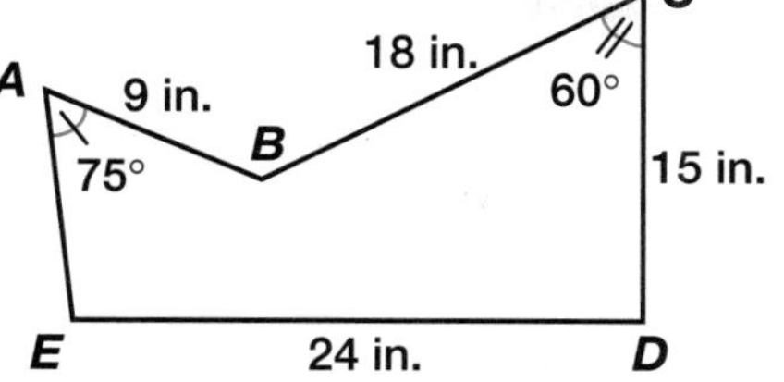

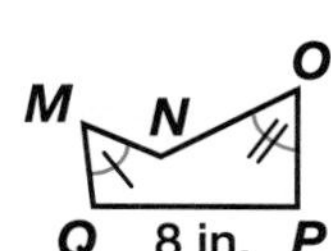

Independent Practice

In the figure at the right, $\triangle KHL \sim \triangle LFM$.

7. What side segment corresponds to $\overline{KL}$?

8. What angle corresponds to $\angle K$?

9. What is the length of $\overline{FL}$?

10. What is the measure of $\angle H$?

11. What is the length of $\overline{HL}$?

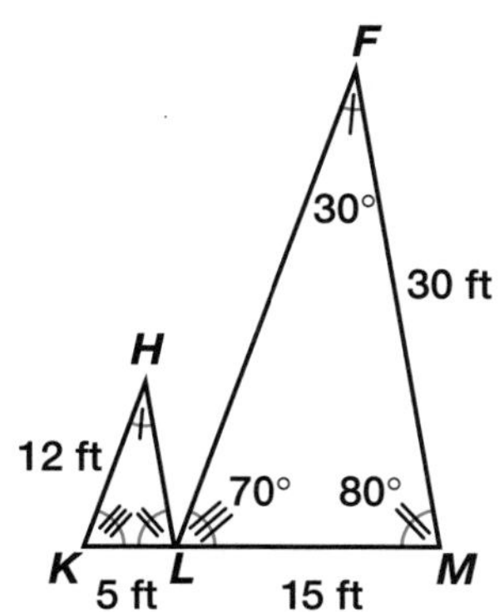

Problem Solving • Reasoning

Use Data **Use the figure for Problems 12–14.**

12. Compare The Smiths are building a summer cabin. The floor plan of the cabin is shown at the right. On the floor plan, the length of the living room is $1\frac{1}{2}$ inches. If the room is $\frac{2}{3}$ as wide as it is long, how wide (in inches) is the living room on the floor plan?

13. Analyze On the floor plan, segments representing the bathroom measurements are $\frac{3}{4}$ inch by $\frac{7}{8}$ inch. What will be the actual dimensions of the bathroom floor?

14. The Smiths bought a piece of property that already has a foundation. The foundation is 24 feet wide and 30 feet long. If you were to draw the foundation on the floor plan, what would its dimensions be?

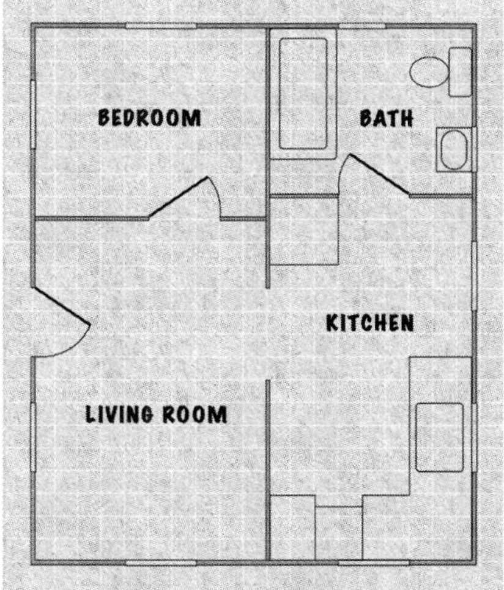

Scale: 1 in. = 10 ft

Mixed Review • Test Prep

Write each percent as an equivalent fraction. *(pages 330–331)*

15. 6.5% **16.** 36% **17.** 93.2% **18.** 52%

19 Which expression represents two times the sum of n and 5? *(pages 272–273)*

A $2 \times n + 5$ **B** $(2 \times n) + 5$ **C** $2 \times (n + 5)$ **D** $2n + 5$

Extra Practice See Set I on page 438.

Polygons

You will learn how to identify a polygon by the number of its sides.

New Vocabulary
regular polygon
diagonal

Learn About It

Many game boards have geometric designs. These figures are often polygons. A polygon is any simple closed plane figure formed by three or more line segments meeting only at their endpoints. The table includes some familiar polygons.

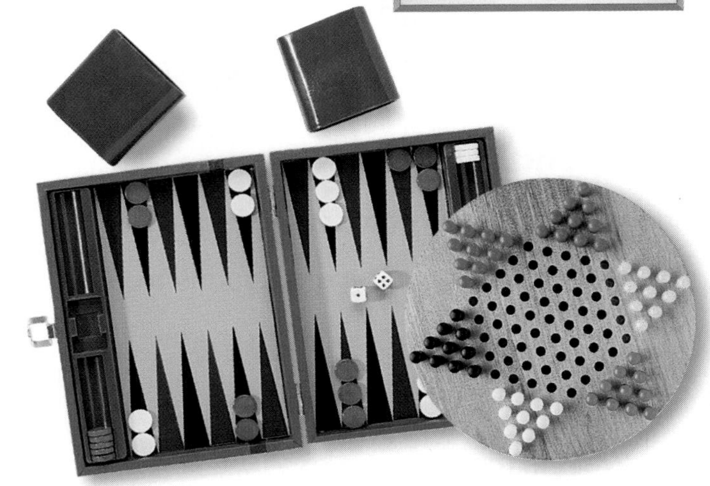

A **regular polygon** is a polygon with all sides congruent and all angles congruent.

Polygons

Name	Examples	Name	Examples
Triangle 3 sides		**Octagon** (8-gon) 8 sides	
Quadrilateral 4 sides		**Nonagon** (9-gon) 9 sides	
Pentagon (5-gon) 5 sides		**Decagon** (10-gon) 10 sides	
Hexagon (6-gon) 6 sides		**Undecagon** (11-gon) 11 sides	
Heptagon (7-gon) 7 sides		**Dodecagon** (12-gon) 12 sides	

A **diagonal** is a segment that joins two vertices of a polygon but is not a side. $\overline{AD}$ and $\overline{BE}$ are two diagonals of the hexagon.

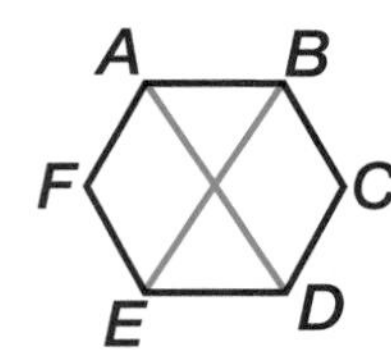

By drawing diagonals, you can calculate the sum of the angle measures in any polygon.

What is the sum of the angle measures of a regular pentagon?

Find the sum of the angle measures of a regular pentagon.

Step 1 Draw a regular pentagon, using a ruler.

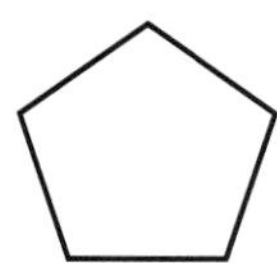

Step 2 Choose one vertex and draw all of the possible diagonals from this vertex.

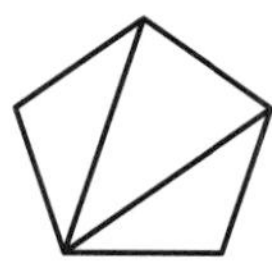

Step 3 Count the number of triangles formed. Each angle of the pentagon is an angle of one triangle or is formed by 2 or more adjacent angles from the triangles.

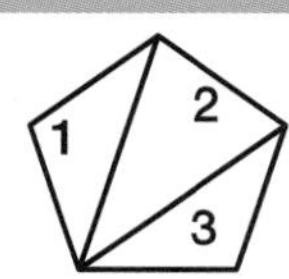

Step 4 Multiply the number of triangles in the pentagon by 180° to calculate the sum of all the angle measures.

$3 \times 180° = 540°$

Remember: The sum of the angle measures of any triangle is 180°.

Solution: The sum of the angle measures of a regular pentagon is 540°.

Another Example

Measure of Each Angle in a Regular Pentagon

The sum of all angle measures in a pentagon is 540°.

Since all angles in a regular polygon are congruent, divide by the number of angles in a pentagon.

$540° \div 5 = 108°$

Explain Your Thinking

► Why do you multiply the number of triangles in a polygon by 180° to find the sum of the angle measures?

Guided Practice

Find the sum of the angle measures in each regular polygon.

1. triangle **2.** hexagon **3.** nonagon

4. undecagon **5.** octagon **6.** quadrilateral

Find the measure of one angle in each polygon.

7. a regular octagon **8.** a regular heptagon

Ask Yourself

- Did I draw all the diagonals?
- Did I remember that the sum of all the angle measures in a triangle is 180°?

Independent Practice

Give the correct name for each polygon.

9. 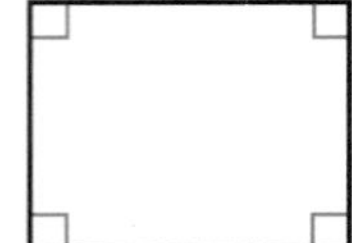

10. 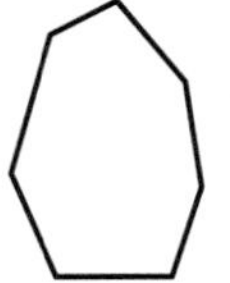

11. 9-sided figure

12. a 12-sided figure

Calculate the sum of the measures, in degrees, of the angles by dividing each figure into triangles.

13. Use the figure in Exercise 11.

14. Use the figure in Exercise 12.

Find the measure in degrees of one angle in each polygon.

15. a regular hexagon

16. a regular nonagon

Problem Solving • Reasoning

17. Bill and Sally plan to make a game board shaped like a regular decagon. What will be the measure of each angle on their board?

18. Analyze Alexa and Kalepa are creating a game board. Game pieces will move along diagonals to corners on a hexagon. How many diagonals must be on their board to connect all the corners of the hexagon?

19. Logical Thinking An airline wants to add a daily roundtrip between each pair of five cities. How many roundtrip flights will be added each day?

20. Write About It Designer Tile Company wants to introduce tiles that are in shapes other than squares. Is it possible to completely cover a square surface with equilateral triangles and leave no gaps? Draw a diagram to support your answer.

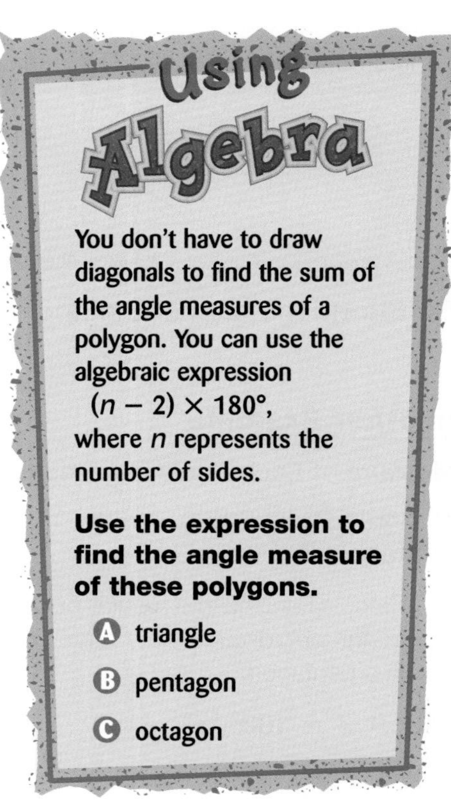

Using
Algebra
You don't have to draw diagonals to find the sum of the angle measures of a polygon. You can use the algebraic expression
(n − 2) × 180°,
where n represents the number of sides.
Use the expression to find the angle measure of these polygons.
A triangle
B pentagon
C octagon

Mixed Review • Test Prep

Order each group of numbers from least to greatest. *(pages 330–331)*

21. $\frac{7}{11}$ 0.06 2.5%

22. 44% 4.4 $\frac{4}{10}$

23. 0.83 $\frac{15}{7}$ 91%

24 Solve for n. $\frac{4}{9} + 5\frac{2}{3} = n$ *(pages 158–160)*

A $5\frac{6}{9}$ **B** $6\frac{1}{9}$ **C** $6\frac{1}{3}$ **D** $6\frac{1}{2}$

Extra Practice See Set J on page 438.

Show What You Know

Using Vocabulary

Write *true* or *false*.

1. All squares are parallelograms.

2. All trapezoids are quadrilaterals.

3. All parallelograms are rhombuses.

4. All rectangles are squares.

Math Expressions

Write an expression for the measure of angle *n*.

1. 105° 75° *n* 105°

2.

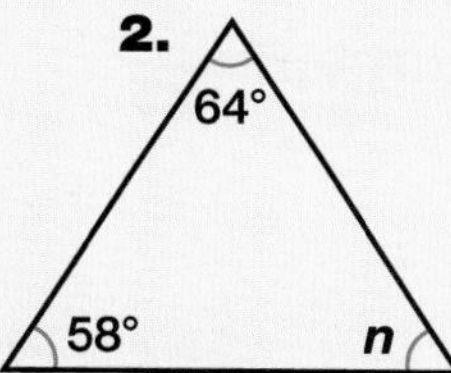

3.

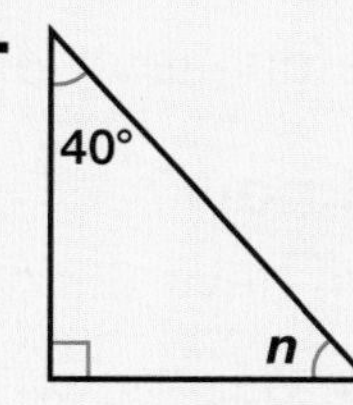

4.

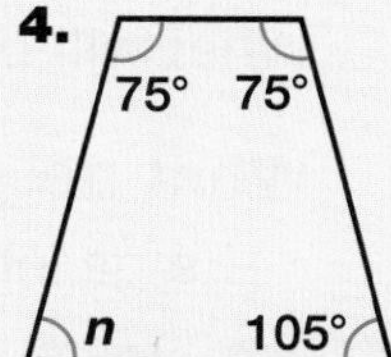

Angle Deductions

Use the information in the diagram below to find the measures of the unknown angles. Use your knowledge of the sums of the angles of triangles and quadrilaterals.

1. What is the measure of $\angle a$?

2. What is the measure of $\angle b$?

3. What is the measure of $\angle c$?

4. What is the measure of $\angle d$?

5. What is the measure of $\angle e$?

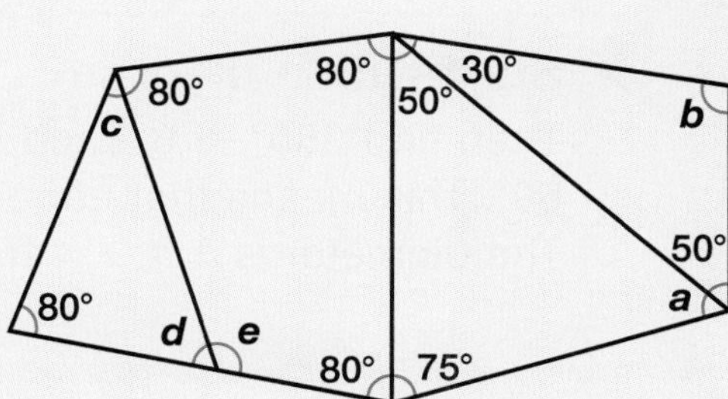

Problem-Solving Strategy: Draw a Diagram

You will learn how to solve a problem by drawing a diagram.

Sometimes when you are trying to solve a problem, it helps to make a diagram. Use the diagram and your knowledge of geometry to solve the problem.

Problem Juan and Seiko are designing a 6-sided gazebo for a contest. The floor will be divided into identical sectors. Each side will be 4 ft long. What will be the diameter of the gazebo?

Understand

What is the question?

What will be the diameter of the gazebo?

What do you know?

- The gazebo will have 6 sides.
- The floor of the gazebo will have 6 identical sectors.
- Each side will measure 4 ft.

Plan

How can you find the answer?

First, make a diagram of the floor.
Include all of the known information. Then use the diagram to find the diameter.

Solve

Start with a diagram.

Then find $360° \div 6$. Each central angle is $60°$. This means that each triangle is equilateral.
The diameter is $4 \text{ ft} + 4 \text{ ft} = 8 \text{ ft}$.

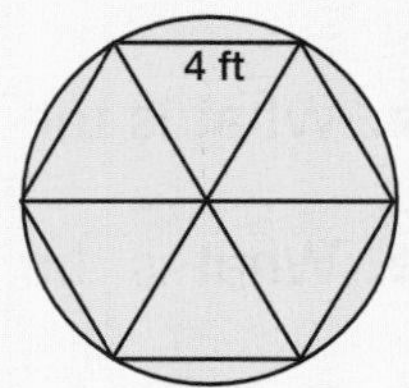

Look Back

Look back at the problem.

Does 8 ft seem reasonable compared to the drawing?

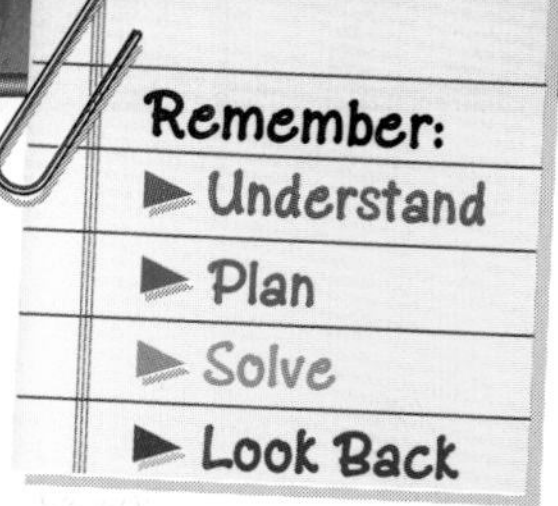

Guided Practice

Use a diagram to solve each problem.

1 Bianca is designing a flower garden in the shape of a half circle. Two sections of the garden will be planted with petunias. Each of these two sections has a central angle of 20°. What is the central angle of the section remaining?

Think: What do you know about the design of the garden?

2 Chiang is helping to build a gazebo at the local park. The round roof will need rafters that form central angles of 22.5° to support it. How many rafters in total will be needed around the roof of the gazebo?

Think: What do you know about the number of degrees in a circle?

Choose a Strategy

Solve. Use these or other strategies.

Problem-Solving Strategies

- **Write an Equation**
- **Use Logical Thinking**
- **Find a Pattern**
- **Draw a Diagram**

3 Sometimes time on an analog clock is used to indicate direction. Three o'clock is to the right, 6 o'clock is straight behind you, 9 o'clock is to the left, and 12 o'clock is straight ahead. If an object is located at 2 o'clock, what central angle is formed with the 12 o'clock direction?

4 Avenues *A*, *B*, and *C* originate at a common vertex. The angle formed by Avenues *A* and *B* and the angle formed by Avenues *C* and *B* are supplementary angles. Avenue *C* and Avenue *B* form an angle of 115°. What angle is formed by Avenue *A* and Avenue *B*?

5 Through how many degrees does a clock hand rotate as it moves from the 12 o'clock position to the 8 o'clock position?

6 If all 16 slices of two round pizzas are identical, what will be the degree measure of the central angle formed by each slice?

7 If any two paddles on a fan form an angle of 60°, how many paddles are on the fan?

8 Draw the next likely figure in the pattern.

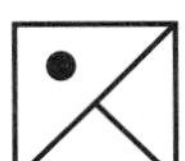 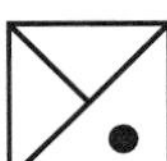 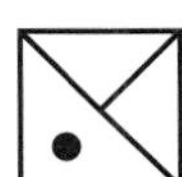 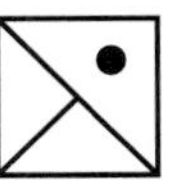 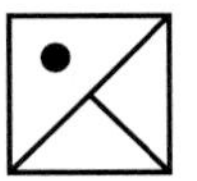

Extra Practice See 5–8 on page 439.

Quick Check

Check Your Understanding of Lessons 7–13

Find the measure of angle *n* in each polygon.
Then classify each polygon.
List all classifications that apply.

1. 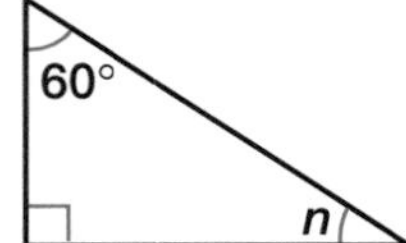

2. 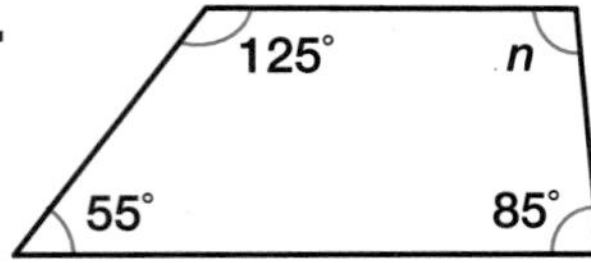

3. 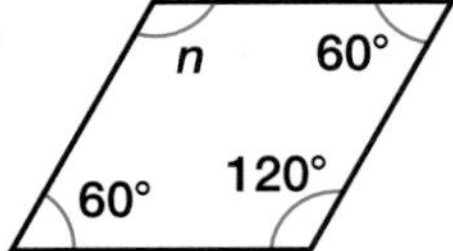

Use a protractor and a straightedge to draw each figure.

4. an obtuse scalene triangle

5. a parallelogram

Figure 1 is similar to Figure 2.

6. What is the degree measure of $\angle w$?

7. What is the length of the side corresponding to side *LO*?

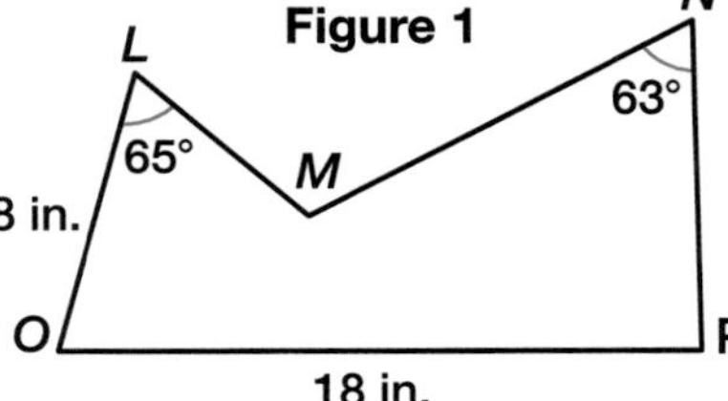

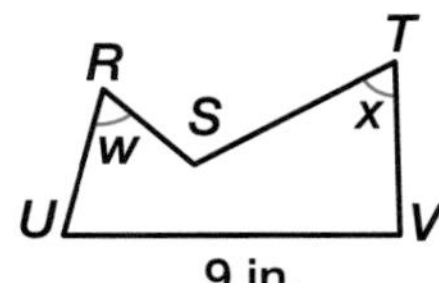

Find the sum of the angles in each regular polygon.

8. heptagon **9.** nonagon **10.** pentagon

Solve.

11. A circular game spinner is divided into equal sectors. Each sector has a central angle measure of 30°. How many sectors are there?

How did you do?

If you had difficulty with any items in the Quick Check, you can use the following pages for review and extra practice.

Items	Review These Pages	Do These Extra Practice Items
1–3	pages 404–409	Sets F and G, page 437
4–5	pages 410–411	Set H, page 438
6–7	pages 416–417	Set I, page 438
8–10	pages 418–420	Set J, page 438
11	pages 422–423	5–8, page 439

Test Prep • Cumulative Review

Maintaining the Standards

Choose the letter of the correct answer. If a correct answer is not here, choose NH.

1. Last week 13 flights were canceled due to bad weather. A total of 2,600 flights were scheduled. What percent of the total number of flights were canceled?

   A 50%
   B 5%
   C 0.5%
   D 0.05%

2. How can the expression $11 \times (4 + b)$ be rewritten using the Distributive Property?

   F $44 + b$
   G $(11 \times 4) + (11 \times b)$
   H $11 + 4 + b$
   J $(11 \times 4) \times (11 \times b)$

3. Which is another way to write the ratio of 4 cats to 5 dogs?

   A $\frac{5}{4}$ **C** 5:4
   B $\frac{4}{5}$ **D** $\frac{2}{3}$

4. Connie is sewing a border around a quilt. For each of two sides, she needs $3\frac{1}{2}$ feet of ribbon, and for each of the other 2 sides, she needs $4\frac{1}{2}$ feet of ribbon. What amount of ribbon will Connie have left if she has 18 feet of ribbon?

   F 5.5 ft **H** 8 ft
   G 10 ft **J** 2 ft

5. Which is the decimal equivalent of $\frac{5}{8}$?

   A 1.6
   B 1.5
   C 0.655
   D 0.625

6. The scale on a road map states that 1 in. = 50 mi. What distance does $2\frac{1}{2}$ inches on the map represent?

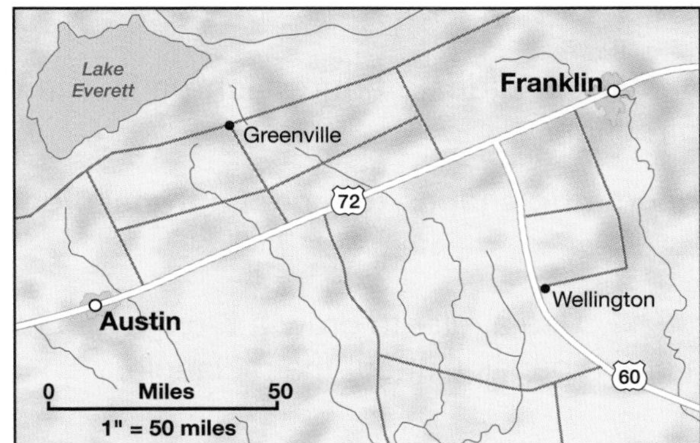

   F 200 miles
   G 150 miles
   H 125 miles
   J NH

7. Suzanne gets off the bus and walks 3 blocks south to a friend's house. Suzanne and her friend walk 6 blocks north to a park. Then Suzanne walks 8 blocks south to her own house. What is Suzanne's final position in relation to where she started?

   Explain What strategy did you use to solve the problem?

Internet Test Prep
Visit **www.eduplace.com/kids/mhm** for more *Test Prep Practice.*

Transformations

You will learn how geometric figures can be moved to create new figures.

Review
Vocabulary
transformation
translation
rotation
reflection

Learn About It

A geometric **transformation** changes the position of a figure. In the activity below, you will model transformations, such as translation, rotation, and reflection.

Maurits Escher was a Dutch artist who lived from 1898 to 1972. He is famous for creating designs in which congruent figures fit together to make interesting patterns. To create these designs, he used transformations.

Materials

graph paper
ruler
scissors
tape

A **translation** slides a figure along a line in one direction.

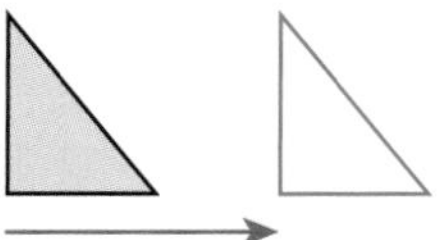

Use geometric shapes to model a translation.

Step 1 Use a ruler to draw a 7-cm by 5-cm rectangle on graph paper. Cut out the rectangle.

Step 2 Draw a polygon along the bottom edge of the rectangle. Cut out the polygon and slide it straight up so that its bottom edge lines up with the top edge of the square. Tape the two edges together.

Step 3 On a new sheet of graph paper, trace the pattern you just made as many times as needed to cover the entire sheet. Be sure the figures touch but do not overlap. Using different colored markers, color each new shape you outline.

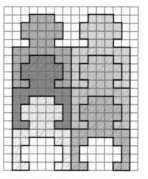

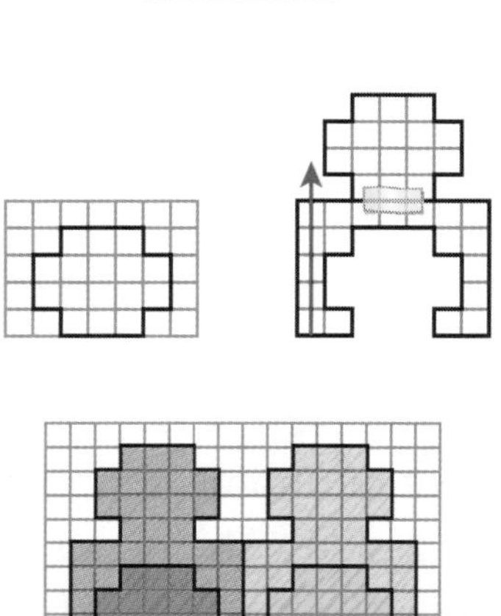

- Could you use a different design so that the pieces still fit together? Explain.

A **rotation** turns a figure about a given point.

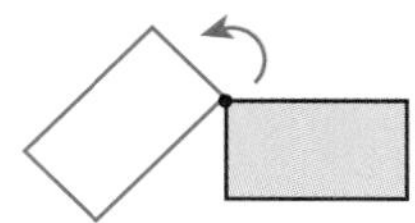

Use geometric shapes to model a rotation.

Step 1 Use a ruler to draw a trapezoid on one fourth of a sheet of graph paper. Cut out the trapezoid.

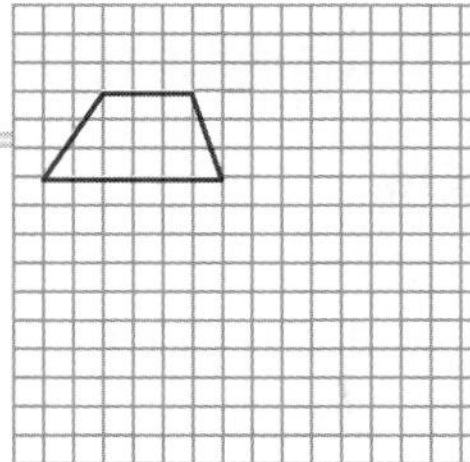

Step 2 On a new sheet of graph paper, draw an x-axis and a y-axis with the origin at the center of the paper. Place the trapezoid you just cut out in the upper right quadrant so that the longest side rests on the positive x-axis. Outline the trapezoid.

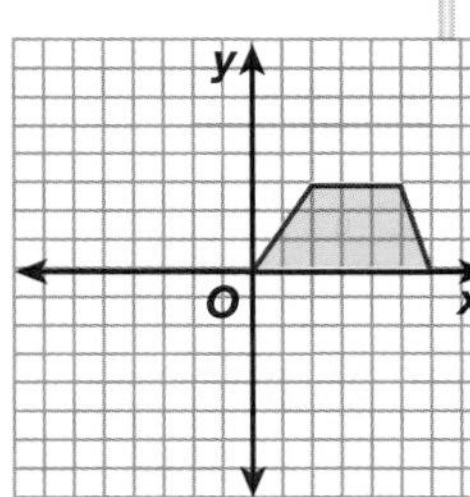

Step 3 Rotate the trapezoid about the origin so that its longest side rests on the positive y-axis. Outline the trapezoid again. The trapezoid has made a one-quarter turn, or 90° rotation, from its original position.

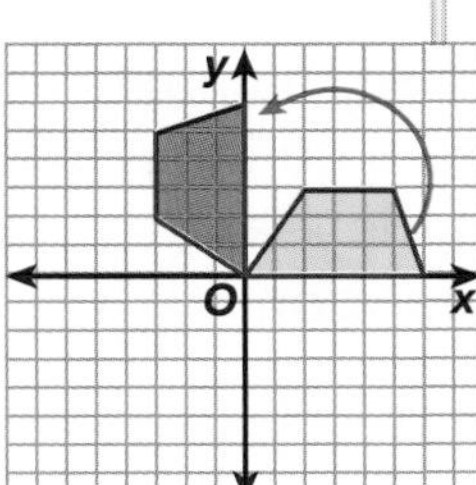

Step 4 Rotate the trapezoid again so that its longest side rests on the negative x-axis. Outline the trapezoid again. The trapezoid has now made a one-half turn, or 180° rotation, from its original position.

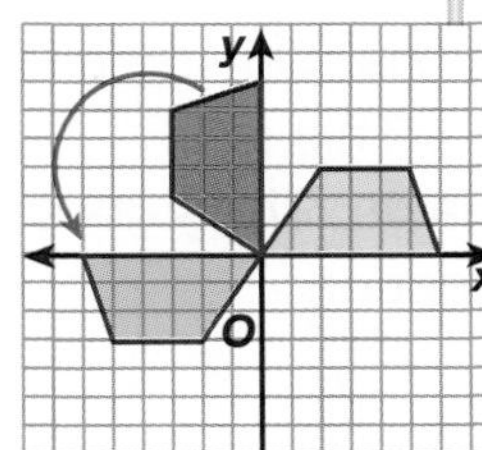

Step 5 Rotate the trapezoid once more so that its longest side rests on the negative y-axis. Outline the trapezoid. The trapezoid has now made a three-quarter turn, or 270° rotation, from its original position.

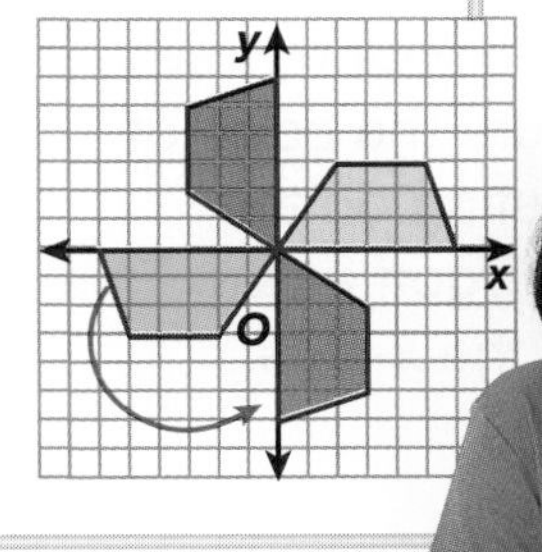

- Describe the location of the trapezoid if it is rotated one full turn, or 360°.

A **reflection** flips a figure across a line of reflection.

Use geometric shapes to model a reflection.

Step 1 Use a ruler to draw a polygon on one fourth of a sheet of graph paper. Cut out the polygon.

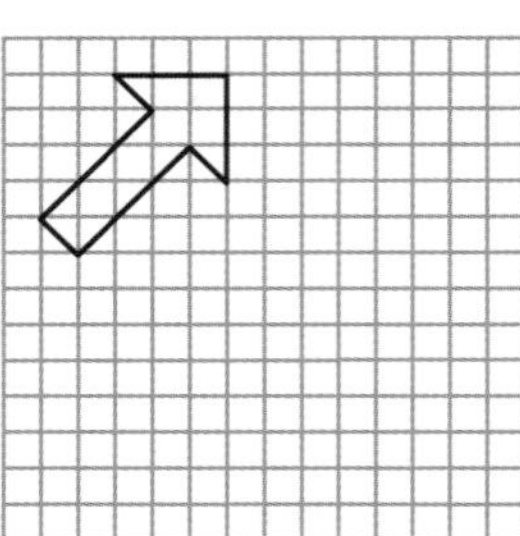

Step 2 On a new sheet of graph paper, draw an *x*-axis and a *y*-axis with the origin at the center of the paper. Place the polygon you just cut out in the upper left quadrant so that one edge of the polygon rests on the *y*-axis and one edge rests on the *x*-axis. Outline and color the polygon.

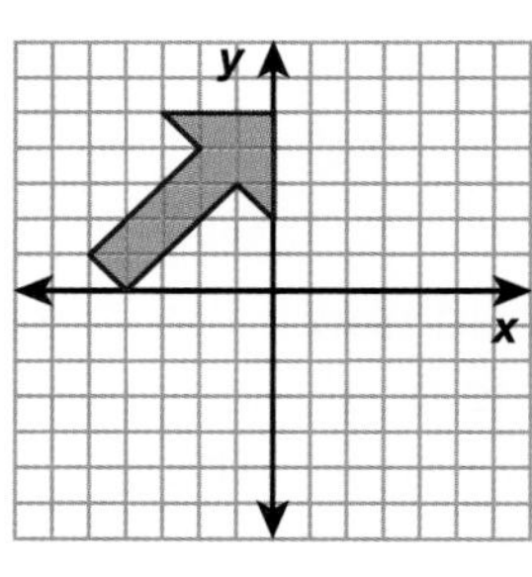

Step 3 Now flip the polygon over the *y*-axis. Be sure the edge of the polygon is still resting on the *y*-axis. Outline and color the polygon again. This is a reflection across the *y*-axis. The *y*-axis is called the line of reflection.

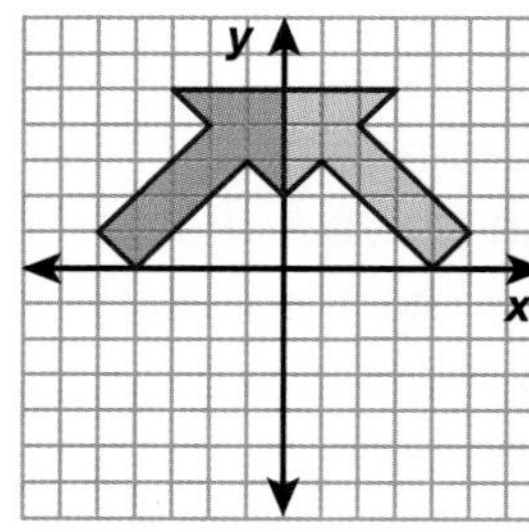

Step 4 Now flip the polygon down over the *x*-axis. Be sure the edge of the polygon is still resting on the *x*-axis. Outline the polygon again. This is a reflection across the *x*-axis.

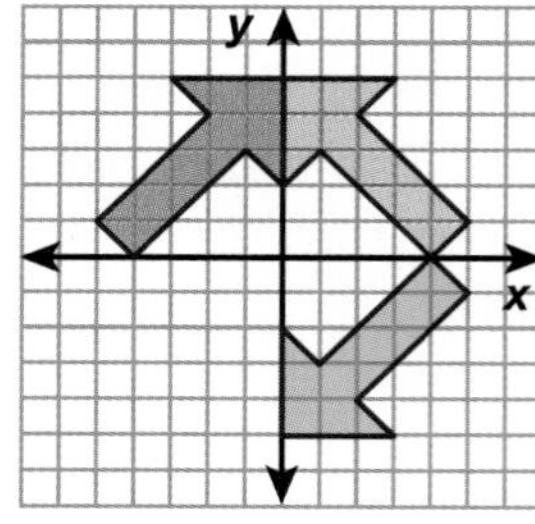

- What other transformation could be used to move the figure from the position in Step 2 to Step 4?

Try It Out

On graph paper, copy the image shown four times. Draw and label the figure in each new position for Exercises 1–4.

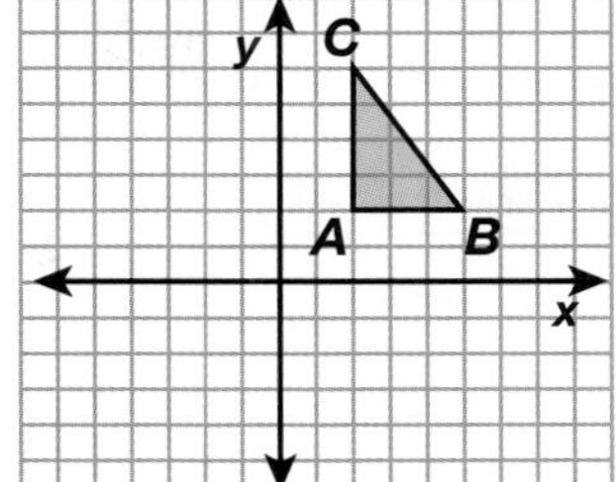

1. Translate the figure by moving each vertex 3 units to the right.
2. Translate the figure by moving each vertex 4 units down.
3. Rotate the figure 90° counterclockwise about the origin.
4. Reflect the figure across the *y*-axis.
5. Which figure represents the first image rotated 90° counterclockwise about the origin?

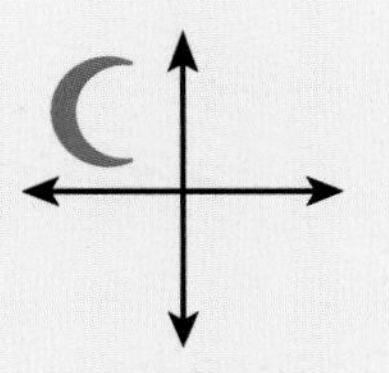

A 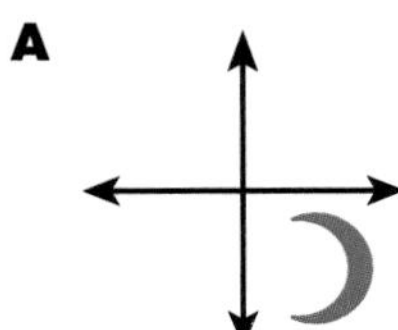 **B** 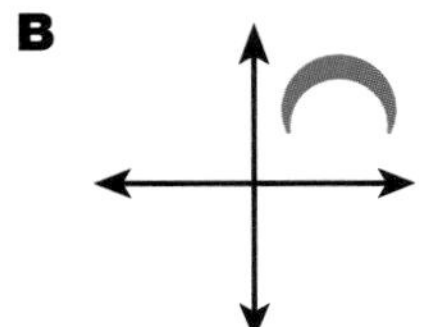 **C** 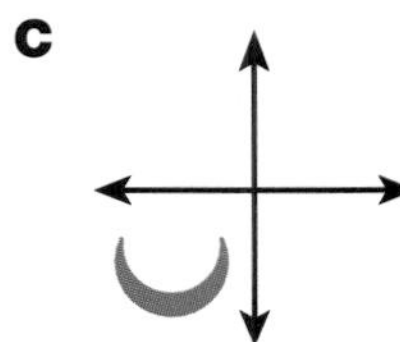

6. Which figure represents the first image reflected across the *x*-axis?

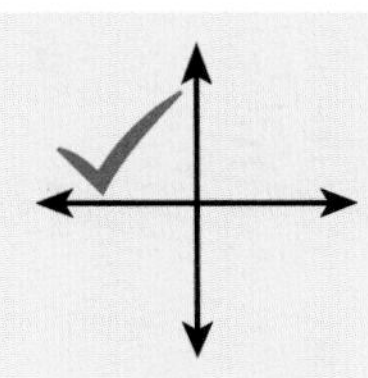

A 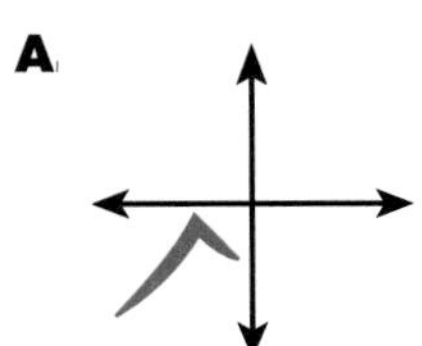 **B** 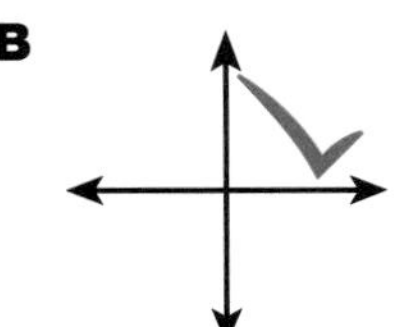 **C** 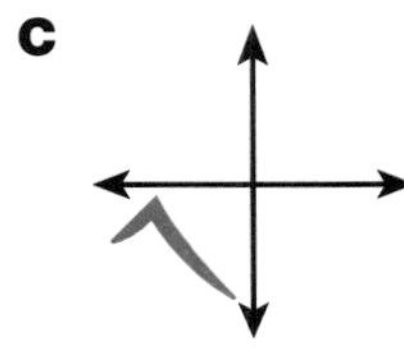

7. Which figure represents the first image translated?

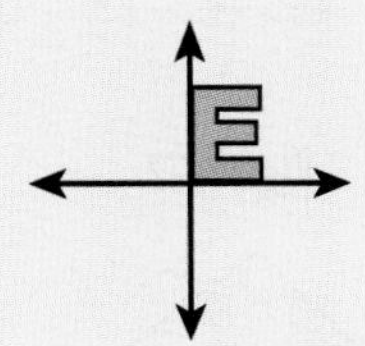

A 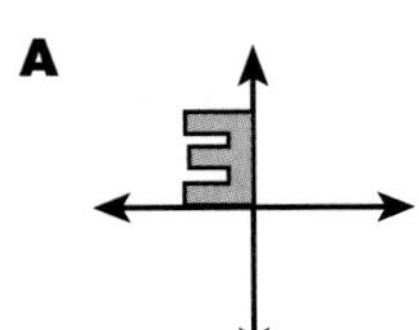 **B** 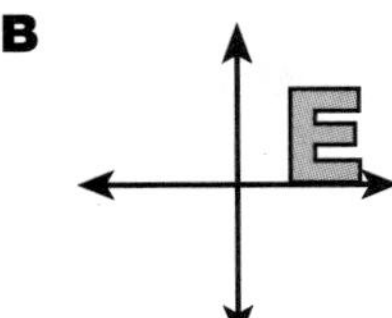 **C** 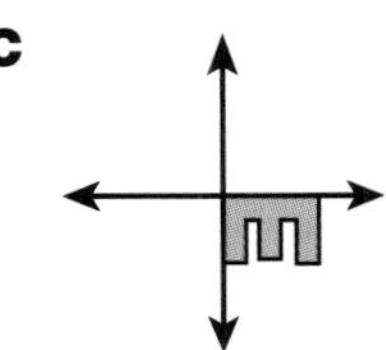

Write about it! Talk about it!

Use what you have learned to answer these questions.

8. Write your own definitions of translation, rotation, and reflection.
9. How is a rotation different from a translation?
10. How is a reflection different from both a translation and a rotation?
11. Why is it important to identify the point about which a figure is being rotated?

Corresponding Parts of Congruent Figures

You will learn how to find corresponding parts of congruent figures.

Review Vocabulary
congruent
corresponding parts

Learn About It

Two figures that have the same size and shape are **congruent**. When two figures are congruent, their **corresponding parts** are congruent. This means that corresponding sides are the same length and corresponding angles have the same measure.

$\triangle ABC$ and $\triangle DEF$ are congruent triangles. Their names are written so that corresponding vertices are in the same order.

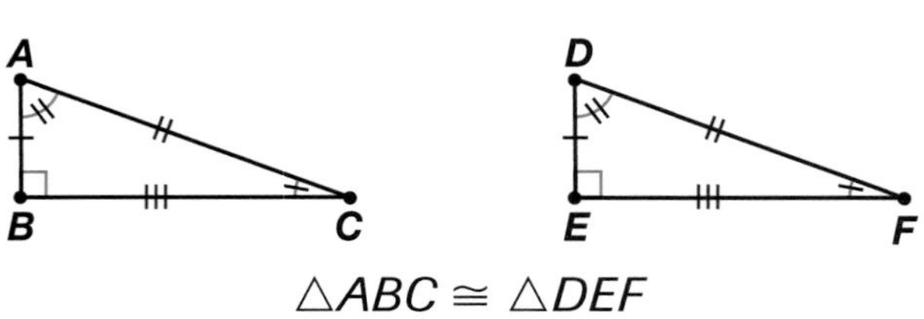

$\triangle ABC \cong \triangle DEF$

$\triangle ABC \cong \triangle DEF$

Corresponding angles	Corresponding sides
$\angle ABC \cong \angle DEF$	$\overline{AB} \cong \overline{DE}$
$\angle BCA \cong \angle EFD$	$\overline{AC} \cong \overline{DF}$
$\angle CAB \cong \angle FDE$	$\overline{BC} \cong \overline{EF}$

The symbol $\cong$ means "is congruent to."

One way to check if two figures are congruent is by moving one figure to see if it matches the other figure. Turning a figure over is allowed.

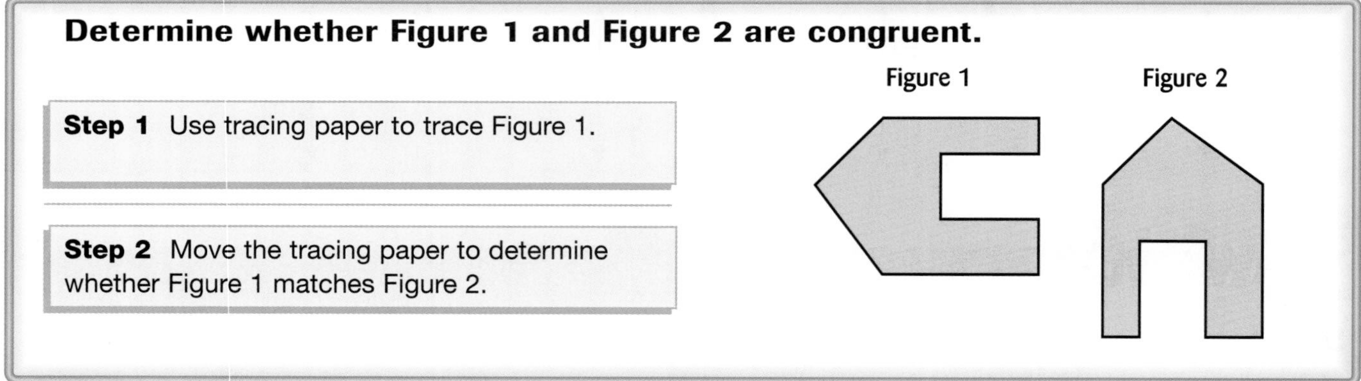

Determine whether Figure 1 and Figure 2 are congruent.

Step 1 Use tracing paper to trace Figure 1.

Step 2 Move the tracing paper to determine whether Figure 1 matches Figure 2.

Solution: By turning Figure 1 over, it can be made to match Figure 2, so Figure 1 is congruent to Figure 2.

Explain Your Thinking

► How would you describe the difference between similarity and congruence?

Guided Practice

Trace the first figure of each pair of figures. Determine whether the figures in each pair are congruent.

1. 

2. 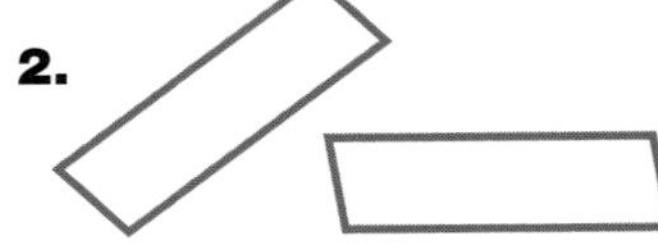

Ask Yourself

- Does my tracing of the first figure match the second figure?
- Did I write the vertices in the correct order?

Use the congruent triangles at the right to complete each statement.

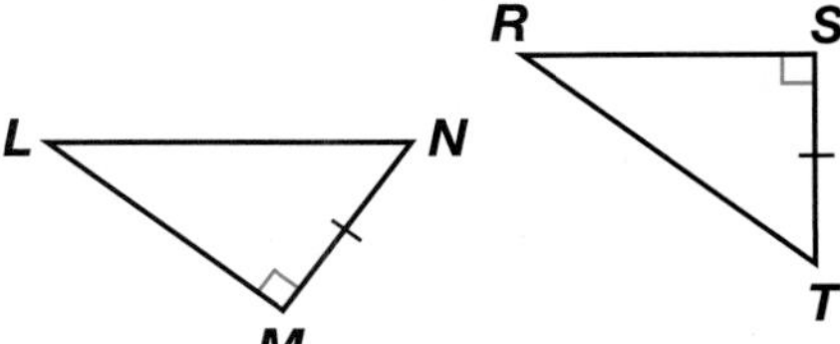

3. $\triangle LMN \cong$ ■ **4.** $\angle T \cong$ ■ **5.** $\overline{SR} \cong$ ■

Independent Practice

Trace the first figure of each pair of figures. Determine if the figures in each pair are congruent.

6. 

7. 

8. 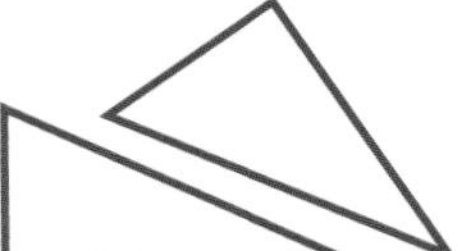

Use the congruent triangles at the right to complete each statement.

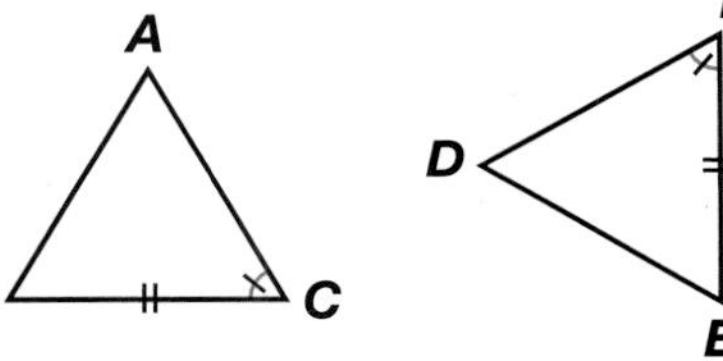

9. $\triangle ABC \cong$ ■ **10.** $\overline{CB} \cong$ ■ **11.** $\angle E \cong$ ■

12. $\overline{DE} \cong$ ■ **13.** $\angle D \cong$ ■ **14.** $\overline{CA} \cong$ ■

Problem Solving • Reasoning

Use Data **Use the figure at the right for Problems 15–17.**

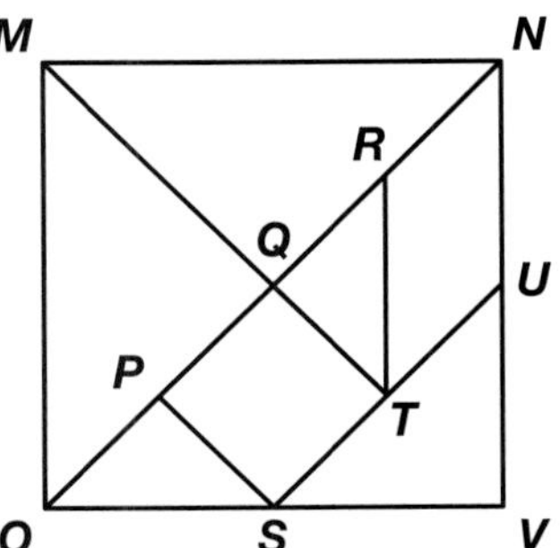

15. Given $\triangle OPS$ is congruent to $\triangle TQR$, name the corresponding sides and angles of the two triangles.

16. **Logical Thinking** Figures *MOVN* and *PSTQ* are squares. Are the two figures similar or congruent? Explain.

17. Is $\triangle MOQ$ congruent to $\triangle MNQ$, $\triangle NMO$, or both? Explain your answer.

Mixed Review • Test Prep

Solve for *n*. *(pages 310–312)*

18. $\frac{5}{9} = \frac{n}{54}$ **19.** $\frac{12}{18} = \frac{2}{n}$ **20.** $\frac{2}{7} = \frac{n}{28}$ **21.** $\frac{64}{100} = \frac{16}{n}$

22 Evaluate $(6 \times 2) + 20 \times (2.45 - 0.37)$. *(pages 258–260)*

A 53.60 **B** 60.72 **C** 66.56 **D** 78.03

Extra Practice See Set K on page 438.

Problem-Solving Application: Use Geometry

You will learn how to use visual thinking to solve geometry problems.

Visualizing an object in different positions sometimes helps to solve problems in geometry.

The Ferris wheel at the right has 12 carriages that rotate about a single point. How many times will the four-color pattern repeat itself during a 360° rotation of the Ferris wheel?

Understand

What is the question?

How many times will the four-color pattern be repeated during a 360° rotation of the Ferris wheel?

What do you know?

- The Ferris wheel has 12 carriages.
- The carriages are arranged in a repeating four-color pattern.

Plan

What can you do to find the answer?

Picture the Ferris wheel in your mind. Start with a specific color carriage. Mentally rotate the Ferris wheel clockwise, and count each time a carriage of the same color passes a fixed point. Stop when you get to the original carriage.

Solve

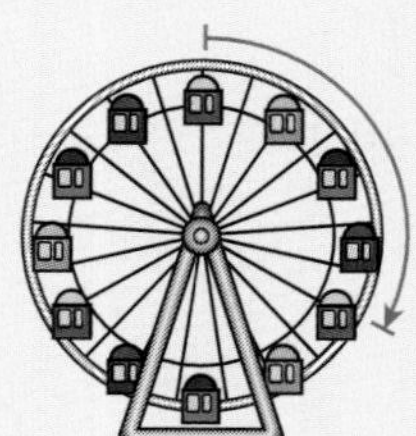

There are 4 colors of carriages. When you visualize the 360° rotation of the Ferris wheel, you will see the same color three times. The pattern repeats itself three times.

Look Back

Look back at the question. Is your answer reasonable?

Can you use the number of colors and the number of times the pattern repeats itself to check your answer?

At night the lighted Ferris wheel appears as a huge circle.

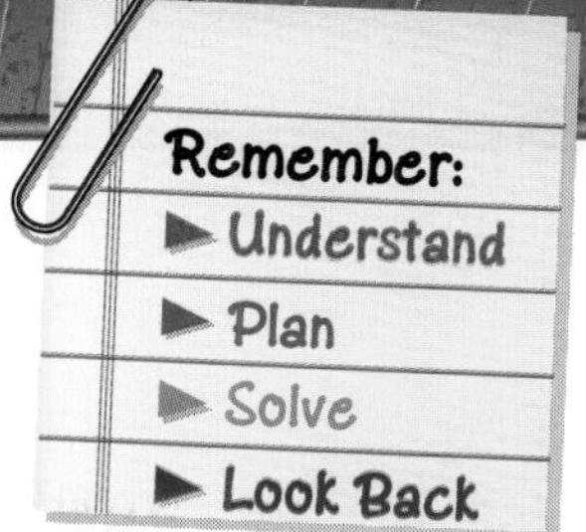

Guided Practice

Solve.

1. 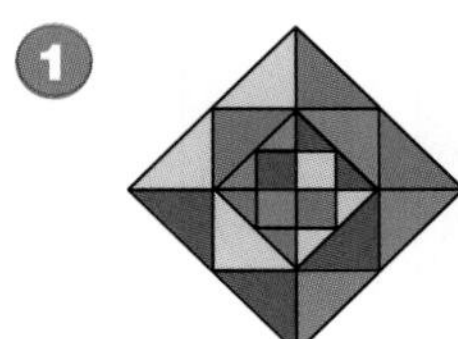 How many 90° rotations of the design are needed before the design appears as it does now?

   Think: Does the design have a pattern that repeats itself?

2. **ABCDEFGHIJKLMNOPQRSTUVWXYZ**
   Which of the capital letters can be reflected across a vertical line and still look the same?

   Think: Which direction should the capital letters be flipped?

Choose a Strategy

Solve. Use these or other strategies.

Problem-Solving Strategies

- **Draw a Diagram**
- **Make a List**
- **Use Logical Thinking**
- **Find a Pattern**

3. Which of the letters from Problem 2 can be rotated 90° around a point and still appear the same? Which letters appear the same after being rotated 180°?

4. How many squares are in the picture? (Hint: The answer is greater than 25.)

   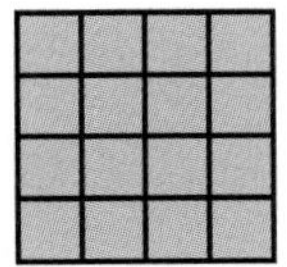

5. While at the fair, Harold rides once in an orange spinning teacup, twice in a red teacup, and once in a purple teacup. In what orders could Harold have ridden in the colored teacups? List all the possible choices.

6. The fairground is having a special on ride tickets. If you buy 5 tickets, you get a 5% discount. You get 7.5% off on 10 tickets, and 10% off on 15 tickets. If the pattern continues, how many tickets do you need to buy to get 15% off?

7. Elizabeth folded a sheet of paper once and drew the three shapes shown. Then she cut them out and unfolded them. Draw each unfolded shape.

   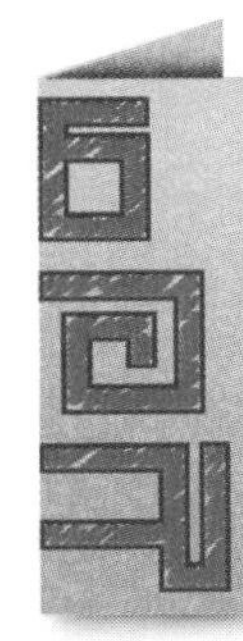

8. The bicycle wheel shown has 22 spokes. How many 90° rotations of the wheel are needed before the wheel appears as it does now?

Extra Practice See 9–11 on page 439.

Quick Check

Check Your Understanding of Lessons 14–16

Trace the first figure of each pair of figures. Determine whether the figures in each pair are congruent.

1. 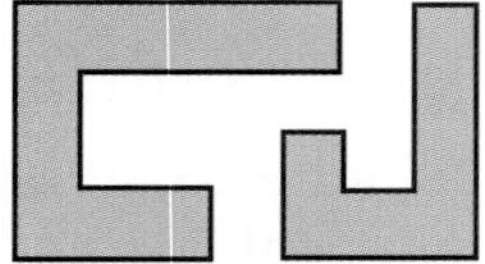

2. 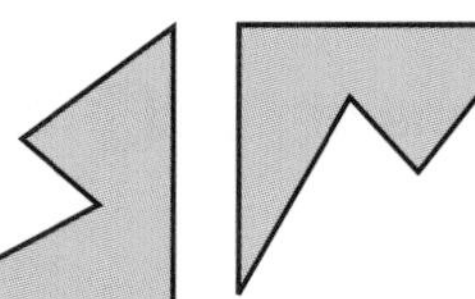

3. 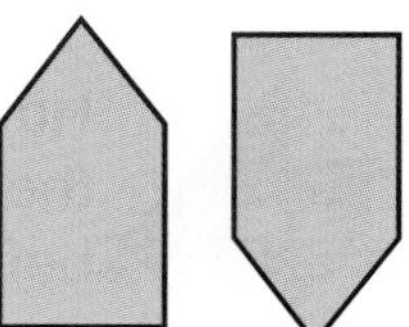

Use the congruent triangles at the right to complete each statement.

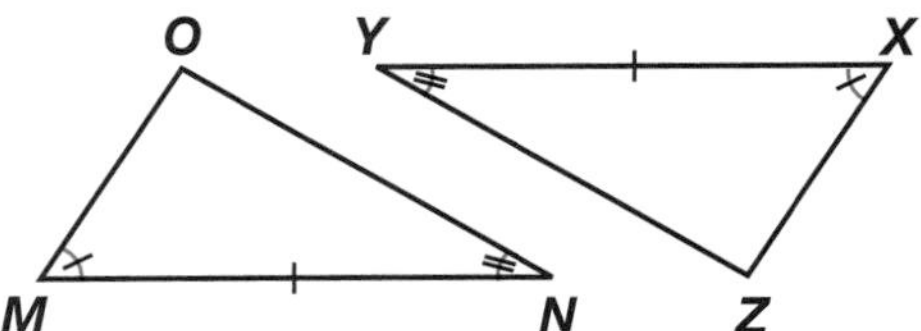

4. $\triangle MNO \cong$ ■

5. $\overline{XZ} \cong$ ■

6. $\angle O \cong$ ■

7. ■ $\cong \overline{XY}$

8. $\angle Z \cong$ ■

9. ■ $\cong \overline{MO}$

Solve.

10. Which figures can be reflected across a vertical line and still appear the same?

11. Which of the figures can be rotated 90° about its center and still appear the same?

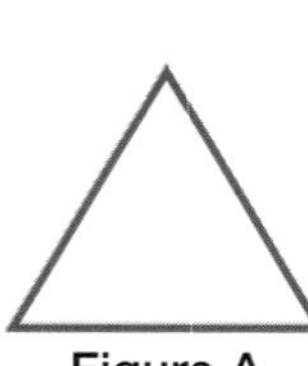
Figure A

Figure B

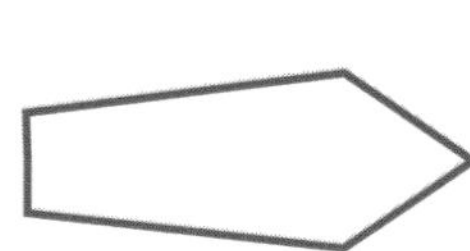
Figure C

Figure D

How did you do?

If you had difficulty with any items in the Quick Check, you can use the following pages for review and extra practice.

Items	Review These Pages	Do These Extra Practice Items
1–9	pages 430–431	Set K, page 438
10–11	pages 432–433	9–11, page 439

Test Prep • Cumulative Review

Maintaining the Standards

Choose the letter of the correct answer. If a correct answer is not here, choose NH.

1 Julian has saved \$30.25. If he buys two CDs that cost \$12.50 each, how much money will he have left?

- **A** \$25.00
- **B** \$17.75
- **C** \$4.25
- **D** NH

2 Lupé had lunch at a nearby café. She had chicken salad for \$6.95, iced tea for \$1.00, and a cookie for \$2.00. What percent of her bill was the iced tea?

- **F** about 40%
- **G** about 30%
- **H** about 10%
- **J** about 5%

3 Greg drove 292.5 miles at 65 mph. How long did it take him to drive 292.5 miles?

- **A** 2.5 hours
- **B** 4.5 hours
- **C** 5.5 hours
- **D** 6.5 hours

4 Use the order of operations to evaluate $(3 \times 12 - 8) \div 4 + 11$.

- **F** 55
- **G** 18
- **H** 14
- **J** 2.7

5 Which is the correct algebraic expression for the word phrase *the sum of one third of a number and 2 times the difference between 5 and 1?*

- **A** $\frac{1}{3}y + 2 \times (5 - 1)$
- **B** $\frac{1}{3}y - 2 \times (5 - 1)$
- **C** $\frac{1}{3}y + 2 \times (5 + 1)$
- **D** $\frac{1}{3}y - 2 \times (5 + 1)$

6 What is the measure of angle *n* in the triangle below?

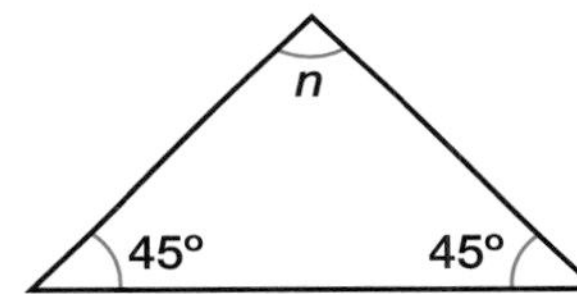

- **F** 40°
- **G** 90°
- **H** 180°
- **J** 200°

7 Phil deposited \$54 into a savings account. The bank pays 5.7% simple interest per year. How much money will Phil have in his account at the end of 1 year?

Explain How did you find your answer?

Safe Site

Internet Test Prep
Visit **www.eduplace.com/kids/mhm** for more *Test Prep Practice.*

Extra Practice

Set A (Lesson 1, pages 390–391)

Draw and label each geometric figure.

1. $\overrightarrow{ST}$ **2.** $\overline{GH}$ **3.** $\angle d$ **4.** $\overleftrightarrow{AB}$ with $\overrightarrow{BC}$

Write the name and symbol for each figure.

5.

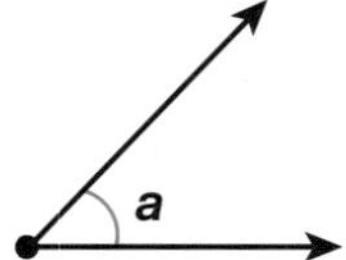

6.

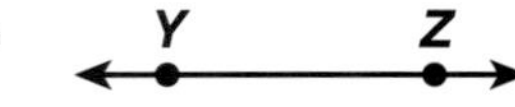

7. H I

Set B (Lesson 2, pages 392–393)

Find the degree measure of each angle.

1. $\angle a$ **2.** $\angle b$ **3.** $\angle c$

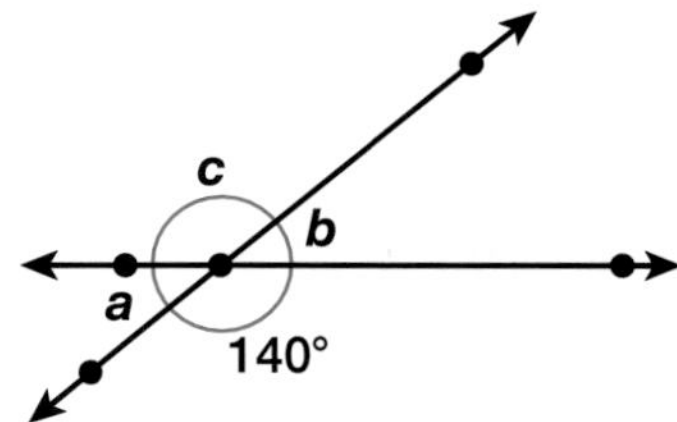

Use the diagram to give two examples of each pair of angles.

4. vertical **5.** supplementary **6.** adjacent

Set C (Lesson 3, pages 394–395)

Trace the figure shown. Measure each angle and then classify each as obtuse, acute, or right.

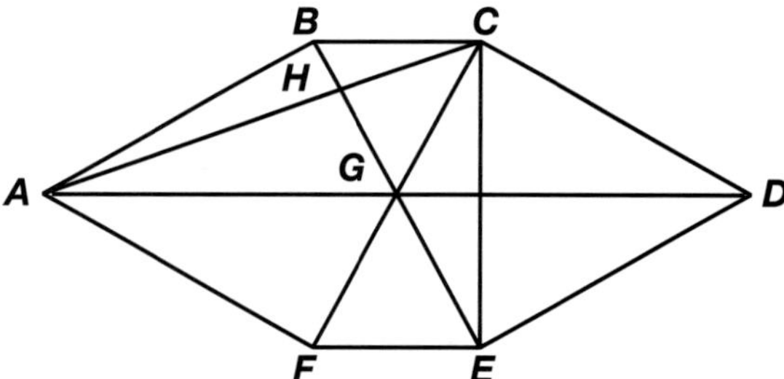

1. $\angle BAD$ **2.** $\angle BCD$

3. $\angle EGF$ **4.** $\angle EFG$

Use >, <, or = to compare each pair of angles.

5. $\angle ACD$ and $\angle ABE$ **6.** $\angle EGF$ and $\angle EFG$ **7.** $\angle BCE$ and $\angle CEF$

Set D (Lesson 4, pages 396–397)

Use a protractor and a straightedge to draw each angle.

1. 35° **2.** 72° **3.** 145° **4.** 110°

5. 22° **6.** 90° **7.** 165° **8.** 54°

Extra Practice

Set E (Lesson 5, pages 398–399)

Use the diagram to answer Exercises 1–4.

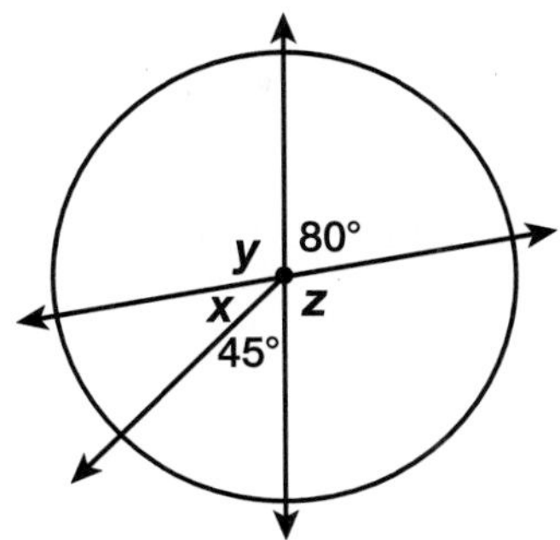

1. What is the measure of $\angle y$?
2. What is the measure of $\angle x$?
3. What is the measure of $\angle z$?
4. What is the measure of $\angle x + \angle y$?

Set F (Lesson 7, pages 404–406)

Classify each triangle by its sides and by its angles. Then find the measure of $\angle n$ in each triangle.

1. 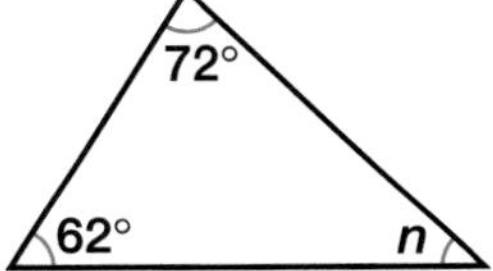

2. 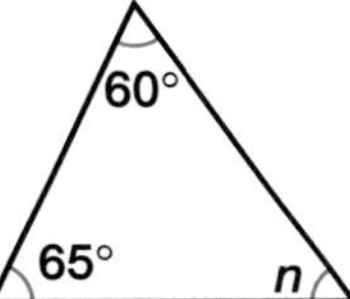

3. 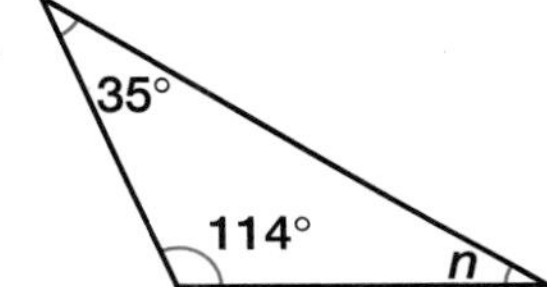

4. 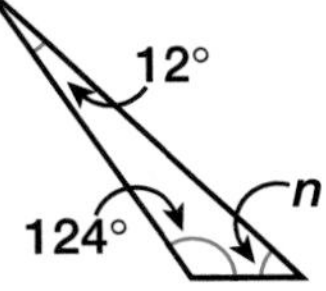

5. 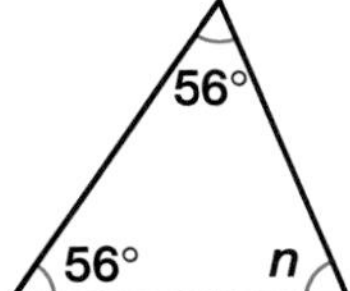

6. 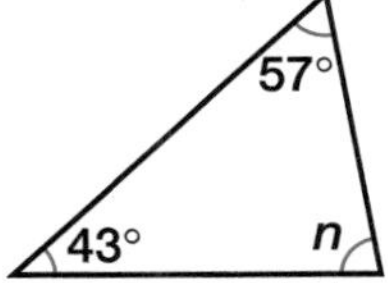

Set G (Lesson 8, pages 408–409)

Find each missing angle measure. Classify each as quadrilateral, parallelogram, rectangle, rhombus, square, or trapezoid. List all classifications that apply.

1. 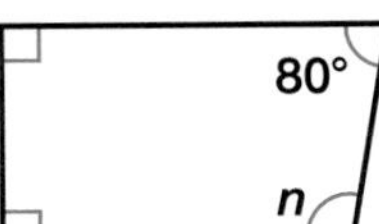

2. 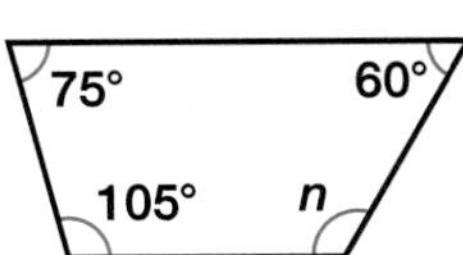

3. 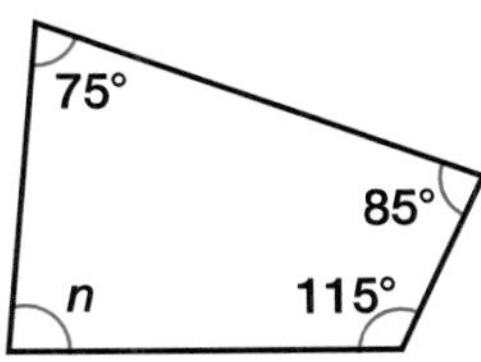

4. 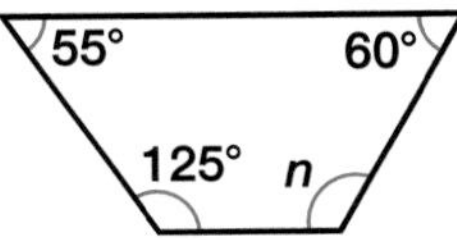

5. 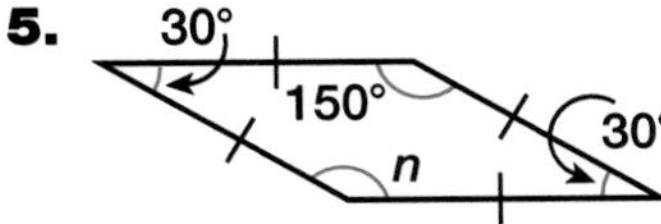

6. 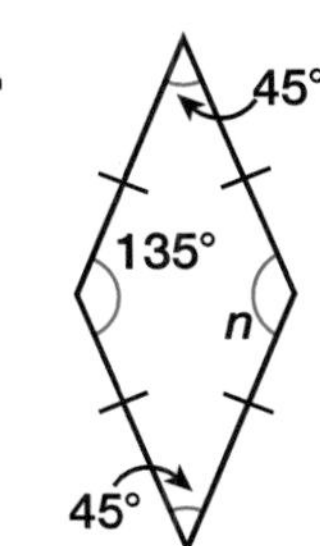

Extra Practice

Set H (Lesson 9, pages 410–411)

Use a protractor and ruler to draw each figure.

1. an equilateral triangle
2. a scalene triangle with one obtuse angle
3. a parallelogram with four right angles
4. a quadrilateral with equal sides but no right angles

Set I (Lesson 11, pages 416–417)

In the figure at the right, $\triangle JKL \sim \triangle MNO$.

1. Which side corresponds to $\overline{MN}$?
2. Which is the side corresponding to $\overline{NO}$?
3. What is the length of $\overline{NO}$?
4. What is the measure of $\angle NMO$?
5. What is the measure of $\angle JKL$?

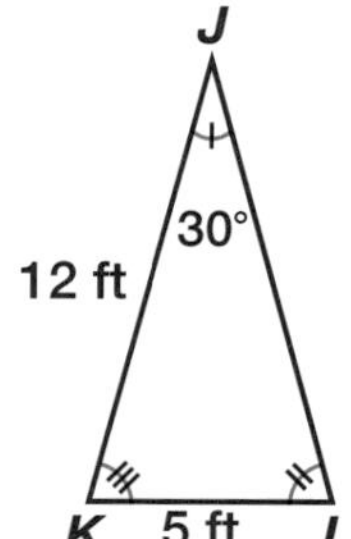

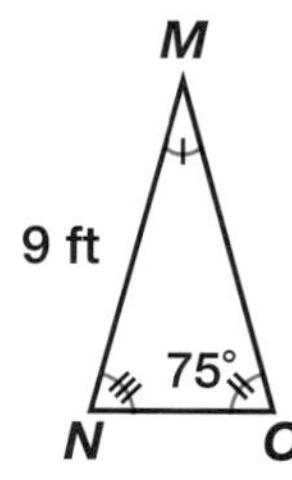

Set J (Lesson 12, pages 418–420)

Write the correct name for each polygon.

1. 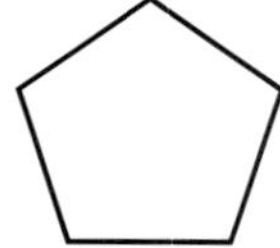
2. 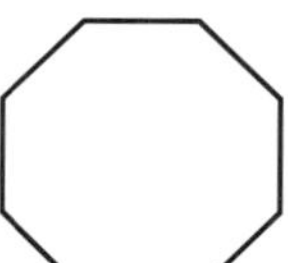
3. 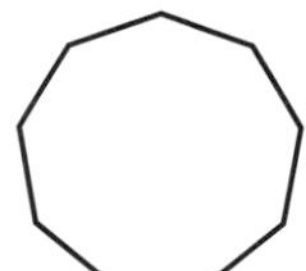
4. 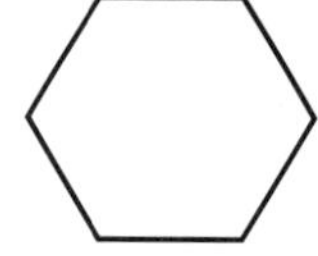

Find the sum of the angles and the measure of one angle in each regular polygon.

5. square
6. decagon
7. triangle
8. pentagon

Set K (Lesson 15, pages 430–431)

Four congruent pairs are shown.

1. Name a figure congruent to Figure *A*.
2. Name a figure congruent to Figure *B*.
3. Name a figure congruent to Figure *D*.
4. Name a figure congruent to Figure *G*.

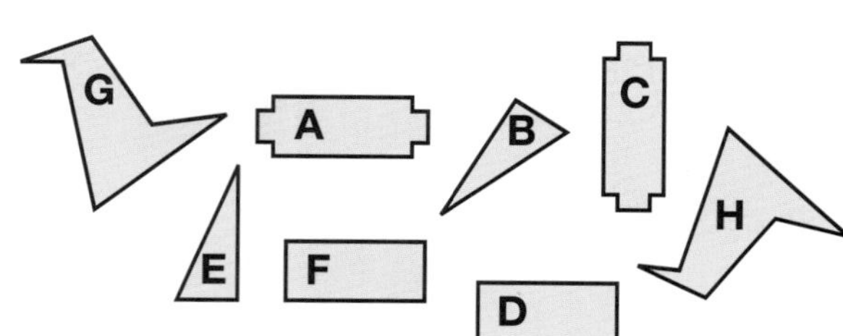

Extra Practice • Problem Solving

Solve. Show your calculations to find the central angles. *(Lesson 6, pages 400–401)*

1. John does yard work on many weekends. He spends 35% of his earnings on clothes, 10% on snack foods, and 25% on recreation. He saves 30%. Display these data in a circle graph.

2. Suppose you see a circle graph that is not labeled with percents. The angles measure 150°, 75°, 40°, and 95°. To the nearest whole percent, what percents do these central angles represent?

3. In an election for Mathematics Club president last week, William received 12 votes, Theresa received 6 votes, and Christopher received 2 votes. Display the election results in a circle graph.

4. Vivian spent 0.5 hour on the school bus, 2 hours doing homework, 0.5 hour eating dinner, 1.5 hours with her friends, and 0.5 hour using the computer. Display these data in a circle graph.

Solve these problems, using the Draw a Diagram strategy. *(Lesson 13, pages 422–423)*

5. The roof of a new outdoor concert stage is round. The roof has rafters that form central angles of 36°. How many rafters are there around the roof of the stage?

6. A wheel on a bicycle has 16 spokes. The spokes are spaced evenly on the wheel. What is the measure of the central angle formed by any two spokes that are next to each other?

7. Adjacent metal ribs in an umbrella form central angles that are less than 90°. Given this information, what is the least number of ribs an umbrella can have?

8. A revolving camera on the ceiling of a department store stops and takes a photograph 8 times during each complete revolution. What is the angle between any 2 camera stops?

Solve using visual thinking. *(Lesson 16, pages 432–433)*

9. A table fan has four blades colored alternately white and yellow. How many times will a white blade pass the base of the fan in three complete rotations of the blades?

10. The hour and minute hands on a clock move at different speeds. In the 12 hours it takes the hour hand to go completely around the clock, how many times will the minute hand have gone around the clock?

11. Look at the letters "BOB" in the diagram at the right. Which geometric transformation will result in the letters looking the same as in the diagram, a reflection across the *x*-axis or a reflection across the *y*-axis?

Chapter Review

Reviewing Vocabulary

Write *always*, *sometimes*, or *never* for each question. Give an example to support your answer.

1. Two similar triangles have corresponding angles of the same measure.
2. An octagon is a polygon with six sides.
3. The sum of the measures of complementary angles equals 180°.

Match each term with its definition.

4. reflection	**a.** two polygons that have the same shape but different sizes
5. congruent	**b.** a movement that involves flipping a figure across a line
6. similar	**c.** two polygons that have the same size and shape

Reviewing Concepts and Skills

Use a straightedge and a protractor to draw and label each figure. *(pages 390–391, 396–397, 410–411)*

7. $\overrightarrow{AB}$
8. an angle that measures 65°
9. a scalene triangle

Use the diagram at the right. *(pages 392–393)*

10. Name all angles adjacent to $\angle d$. Find their measures.
11. Name all pairs of vertical angles. Find their measures.

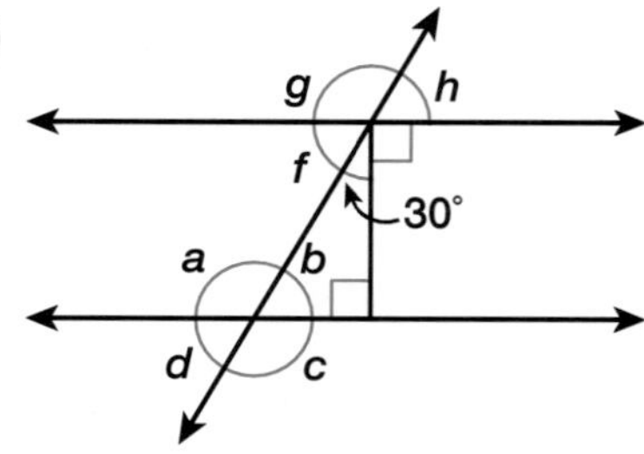

In the figure at the right, $\triangle ABC \sim \triangle FGH$. *(pages 404–406, 416–417)*

12. What is the length of $\overline{FG}$?
13. What is the measure of $\angle h$?
14. Classify the triangles by their sides and by their angles.

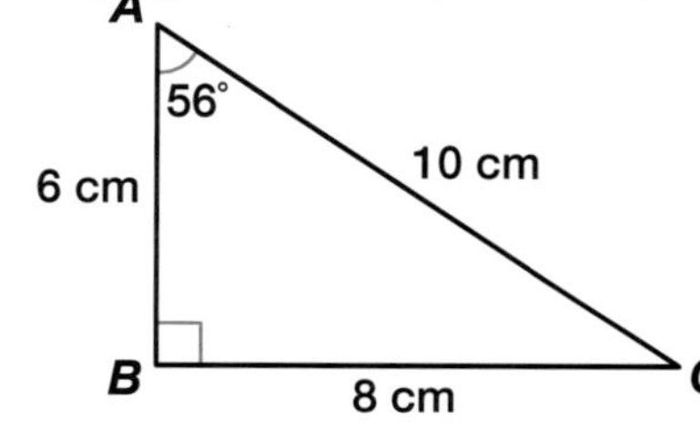

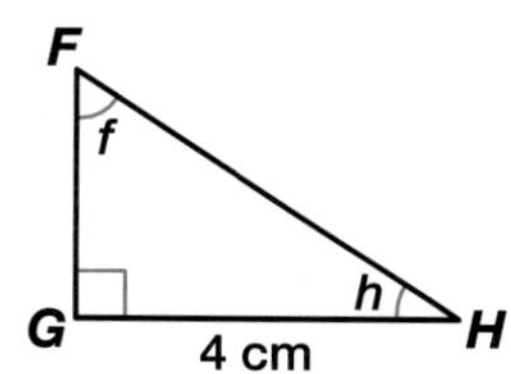

Find the sum of the angles in each polygon. Then find each missing angle measure. Classify each polygon as quadrilateral, parallelogram, rectangle, rhombus, square, or trapezoid. List all classifications that apply. *(pages 408–409, 418–420)*

15. 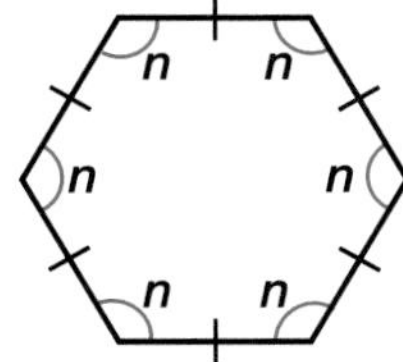

16. 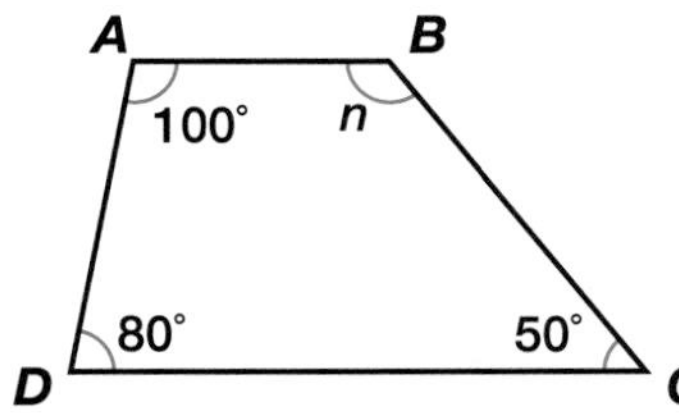

Determine whether the polygons are congruent. *(pages 430–431)*

17. 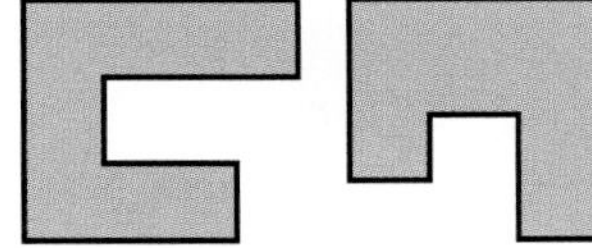

Solve. *(pages 400–401, 422–423, 432–433)*

18. A carnival ride called The Spider has 8 arms attached to a center point. What is the angle between each of the arms if they are spaced evenly?

19. At a local music store, 20% of sales are from cassette tapes, 75% of sales are from CDs, and 5% are from videotapes. Display these data in a circle graph.

20. Draw the design at the right as it would appear after it is rotated a three-quarter turn counterclockwise about Point *P* and then reflected across a vertical line.

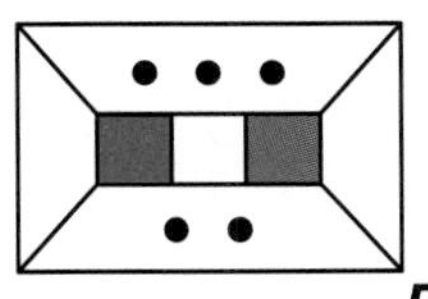

Brain Teasers Math Reasoning

Mystery Angle

Calculate the measure of angle *n*.

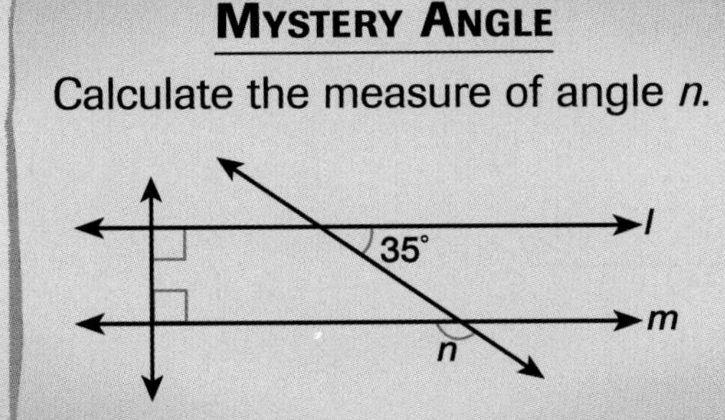

Polygon Puzzle

Which of the following are not polygons? Explain.

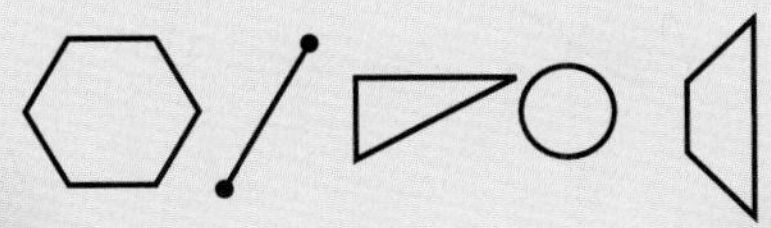

Internet Brain Teasers
Visit **www.eduplace.com/kids/mhm** for more *Brain Teasers.*

Chapter Test

Use a ruler and a protractor to draw each figure.

1. $\overleftrightarrow{AB}$
2. an angle that measures 115°
3. an equilateral triangle
4. a quadrilateral with two equal sides

Use the diagram to name an example for each item. Then find the degree measure of each angle you named.

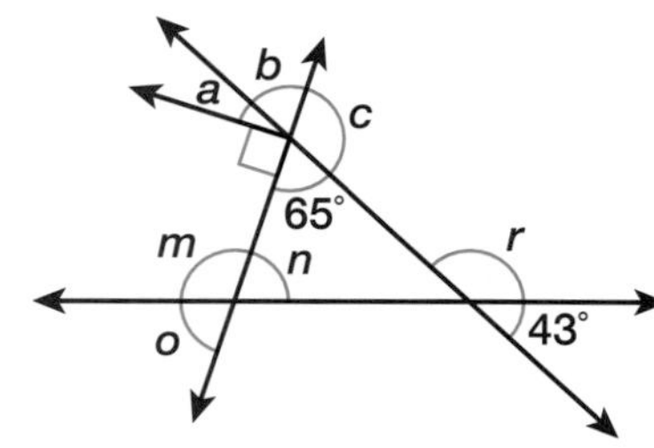

5. an angle adjacent to $\angle n$
6. two complementary angles
7. two supplementary angles
8. two vertical angles
9. an angle that is a supplement to $\angle n$
10. an angle that has the same measure as $\angle n$

In the figure at the right, $\triangle PQR \sim \triangle EFG$.

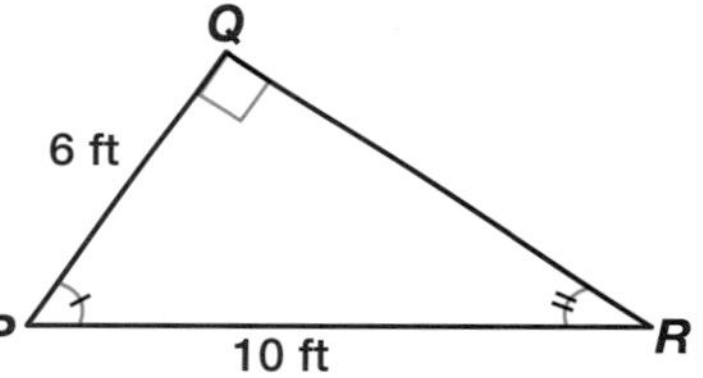

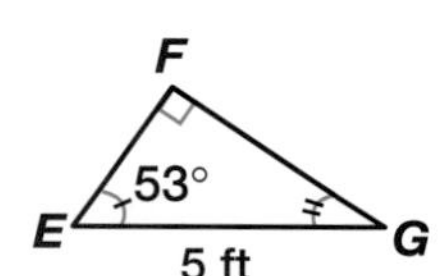

11. What is the length of $\overline{EF}$?
12. What is the degree measure of $\angle QPR$?
13. Classify the triangles by their side measures and by their angle measures.

Find the sum of the angles in each polygon. Then find each missing angle measure. Classify each polygon as quadrilateral, parallelogram, rectangle, rhombus, square, or trapezoid. List all classifications that apply.

14.

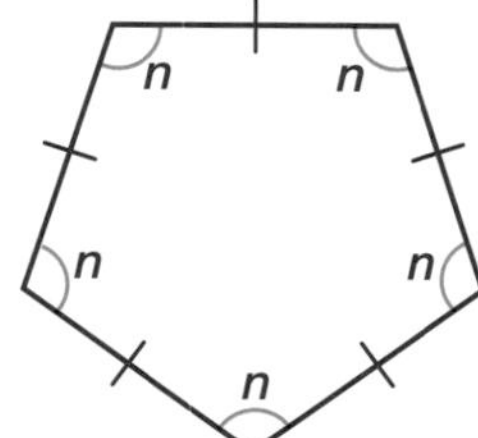

15.

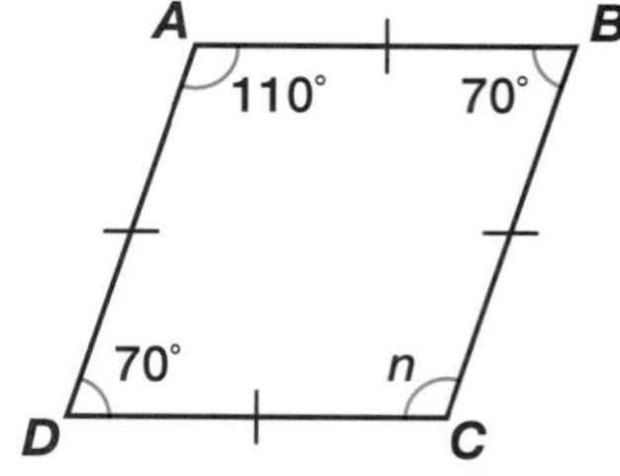

Determine whether the pairs of polygons are congruent.

16.

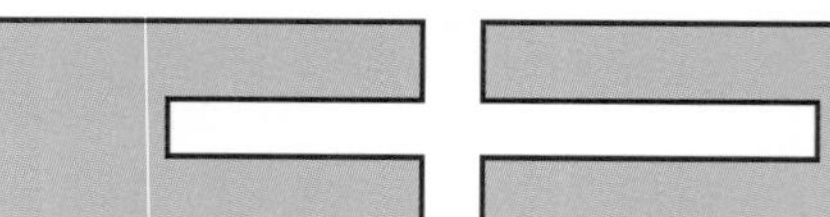

17.

18. A clothing store has collected the following information about the shirts sold.

All cotton	30% of all sales
All polyester	20% of all sales
Cotton/polyester blends	25% of all sales
Other	25% of all sales

Display these data in a circle graph.

19. The petals of a flower are distributed equally in a circle around the flower's center. If the petals are spaced 30° apart, how many petals does the flower have?

20. Draw the design at the right as it would appear after it is rotated one-quarter turn counterclockwise about Point *X*.

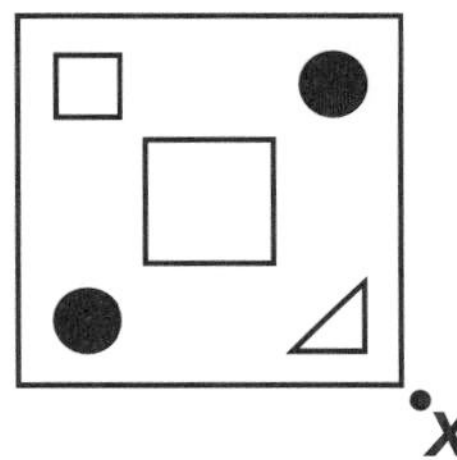

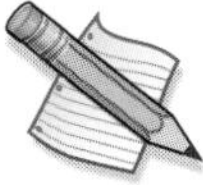

Write About It

Solve each problem. Use correct math vocabulary to explain your thinking.

1. Name one instance in which it might be helpful to use similar figures. Explain why.

2. Describe the relationship of corresponding angles in similar triangles.

3. Gary was asked to reflect the shape in Figure 1 across the *y*-axis. Figure 2 shows his answer. Is the transformation correct? If not, how might you correct it?

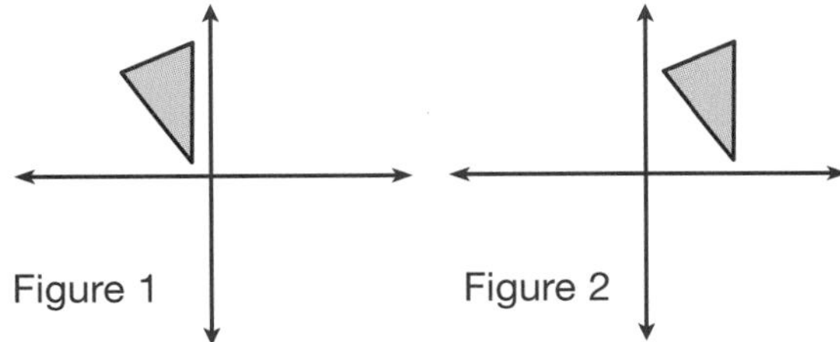

Another Look

Brad and Elyse created a game board that is in the form of a bus route. To advance, players solve problems. Use the game board of the No. 99 city bus route and the facts to solve each problem.

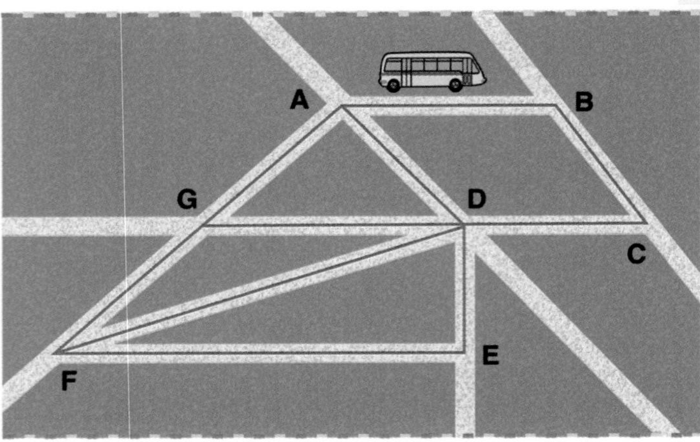

Facts About the No. 99 Bus Route

- The bus route forms a right isosceles triangle between stops *A*, *D*, and *G*.
- The route forms an isosceles triangle between stops *G*, *F*, and *D*.
- The route makes a 90° turn at stops *D* and *E*.

1. The cost to take the No. 99 bus on any part of the route that forms a triangle is \$0.50. The cost for any quadrilateral route is \$0.75. List the streets and stops for each part of the route that costs \$0.50 and for each part that costs \$0.75.
2. Parts of the route that form obtuse angles must be checked by the city safety inspector. List the streets and stops on each part of the route that the safety inspector must check.
3. **Analyze** Start with $\triangle AGD$. Name the angle measures in $\triangle AGD$. Next, use what you know about angles and triangles to name the angle measures in $\triangle GFD$. Then name the angle measures in $\triangle DEF$.

Enrichment

Finding Patterns in Regular Polygons

There are many number patterns in geometry.

Look at the number of diagonals from any one vertex of different polygons.

Regular Polygon	Number of Sides	Number of Diagonals from Any One Vertex
Triangle	3	0
Quadrilateral	4	1
Pentagon	5	2
Hexagon	6	3
Heptagon	7	?
Octagon	8	?

The number pattern for the diagonals from any one vertex is

0, 1, 2, 3, . . .

If you know the number of sides in a regular polygon, you can find the number of diagonals from any one vertex by subtracting 3 from the number of sides. A 50-sided polygon would have 47 diagonals from each vertex.

Practice finding the number of diagonals from any one vertex in each polygon.

1. a 15-sided polygon

2. a 33-sided polygon

3. a 58-sided polygon

4. a 70-sided polygon

5. a 100-sided polygon

Now look at the total number of diagonals.

Regular Polygon	Number of Sides	Total Number of Diagonals
Triangle	3	0
Quadrilateral	4	2
Pentagon	5	5
Hexagon	6	9
Heptagon	7	14
Octagon	8	?

The number pattern for the total number of diagonals is

0, 2, 5, 9, . . .

To find the total number of diagonals in a regular polygon, first subtract 3 from the number of sides. Then multiply by the number of sides and divide the product by 2. A hexagon will have $6 \times (6 - 3) \div 2 = 9$ diagonals.

Practice finding the total number of diagonals in each polygon.

6. a 13-sided polygon

7. a 15-sided polygon

8. a 20-sided polygon

9. a 25-sided polygon

10. a 30-sided polygon

Explain Your Thinking

► How can number patterns be used to solve problems in geometry? Explain your thinking.

Geometry and Measurement

Why Learn About Geometry and Measurement?

You use geometry and measurement to find and compare the perimeter, area, and volume of different figures.

When you and your family want to buy carpeting for a room in your home, you use geometry and measurement to figure out how much carpeting to buy.

Look at the circle that is formed by the Ferris wheel. If you know the distance from the center to the outside, you can find the distance around the circle.

RAND WHEEL

Reviewing Vocabulary

Understanding math language helps you become a successful problem solver. Here are some math vocabulary words you should know.

congruent figures figures that have the same size and shape

plane a flat surface made up of a continuous and unending collection of points

polygon a closed plane figure made up of three or more line segments meeting only at endpoints

quadrilateral a four-sided polygon

right angle an angle that measures 90° and corresponds to one quarter of a complete revolution

Reading Words and Symbols

In mathematics, many words have symbols to represent them. The word and the symbol mean the same thing.

- perimeter P
- area A
- length l
- width w
- height h
- base b
- volume V
- radius r
- diameter d
- circumference C
- surface area SA
- pi π
- approximately equal to $\approx$
- square, as in 5 square inches 5 in.^2
- cubic, as in 8 cubic meters 8 m^3
- right angle ⊾

Try These

1. Rewrite each measurement using the appropriate symbol.

   a. 24 cubic feet
   b. 15 square yards
   c. 32 square meters
   d. 83 square inches
   e. 27 cubic centimeters
   f. 10 square miles

2. Rewrite the following, substituting a symbol listed on the previous page or any other symbol you know.

   a. The area of the triangle is 26 square inches.
   b. The perimeter of the square is 10 meters.
   c. To find the area of the rectangle, multiply its length by its width.
   d. The volume of the cube is 40 cubic inches.
   e. The circle's circumference is 14.5 centimeters.

3. Write *true* or *false* for each statement. Rewrite false statements to make the statements true.

   a. Two right triangles each with sides of 3 inches, 4 inches, and 5 inches are congruent.
   b. A right angle measures 180°.
   c. 7.895 ft $\approx$ 8 ft
   d. A ball is a plane figure.
   e. A polygon is a closed figure consisting of three line segments.

Upcoming Vocabulary

Write About It **Here are some other vocabulary words** you will learn in this chapter. Watch for these words. Write their definitions in your journal.

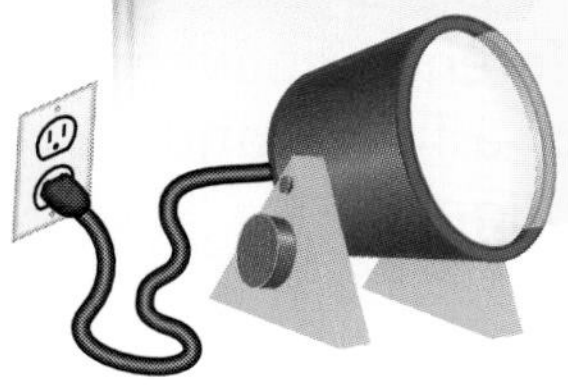

perimeter
area
circumference
pi
prism
pyramid
solid figure
cylinder
cone
net
surface area
volume

LESSON 1

Perimeter and Area

You will learn how to find the perimeter and the area of a rectangle.

New Vocabulary
perimeter
area

Learn About It

Among the many uses of geometry is its use in measuring land. People want to know the distance around their property and its area.

The distance around a figure is called its **perimeter**. Perimeter is measured in units of length, such as feet. The **area** of a figure is the number of square units the figure contains. How can you find the perimeter and area of this rectangle?

Different Ways to Find the Perimeter of a Rectangle

Add the sides of the figure.

5 in. + 3 in. + 5 in. + 3 in. = 16 in.

Use the formula.

$P = 2l + 2w$
$= (2 \times 5) + (2 \times 3)$
$= 10 + 6$
$= 16$ in.

l = length
w = width
P = perimeter

Solution: The perimeter of the figure is 16 inches.

Different Ways to Find the Area of a Rectangle

Count the number of 1-inch squares.

1	2	3	4	5
6	7	8	9	10
11	12	13	14	15

3 in.
5 in.

Use the formula.

$A = l \times w$
$= 5 \text{ in.} \times 3 \text{ in.}$
$= 15 \text{ in.}^2$

l = length
w = width
A = area

Solution: The area of the figure is 15 square inches.

Another Example

Area of Complex Figures

Divide the figure into two rectangles.

$A_1 = 10 \times 8 = 80 \text{ ft}^2$

$A_2 = 6 \times 4 = 24 \text{ ft}^2$

$A_1 + A_2 = 80 + 24$

Total area $= 104 \text{ ft}^2$

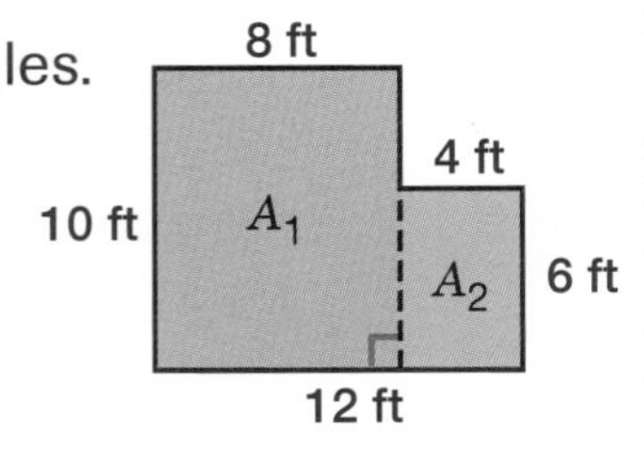

Explain Your Thinking

- Can you think of another way to divide the figure at the left? Explain.
- What is the difference between the perimeter of a figure and the area of the figure?

Guided Practice

Find the perimeter and area of each figure.

1. Rectangle $ABCD$

$l = 5$ m

$w = 2$ m

2. Rectangle $QRST$

$l = \frac{3}{4}$ in.

$w = \frac{7}{2}$ in.

3.

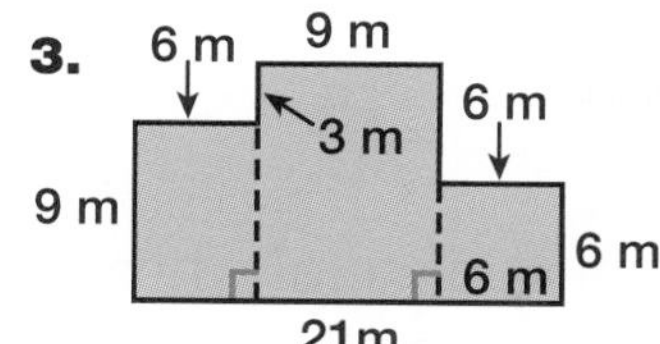

Ask Yourself

- Did I find the distance around the figure to find the perimeter?

Independent Practice

Find the perimeter and area of each rectangle.

4. $l = 12$ ft
$w = 8$ ft

5. $l = 16$ m
$w = 7$ m

6. $l = 12.4$ ft
$w = 15.6$ ft

7. $l = \frac{9}{5}$ yd
$w = \frac{5}{3}$ yd

Find the perimeter and area of each figure.

8.

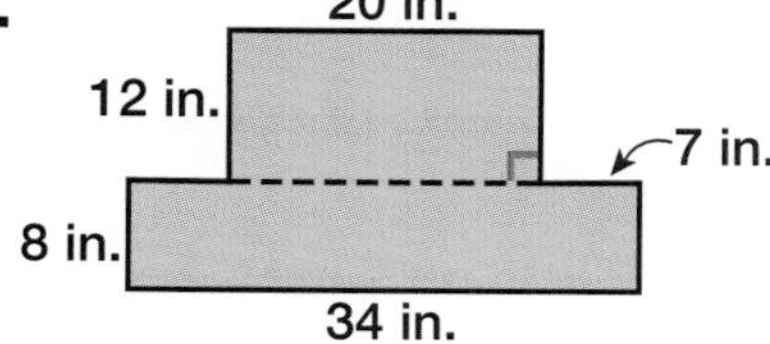

9.

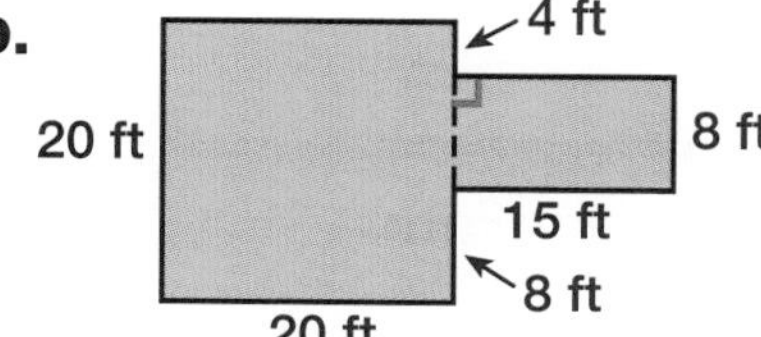

10.

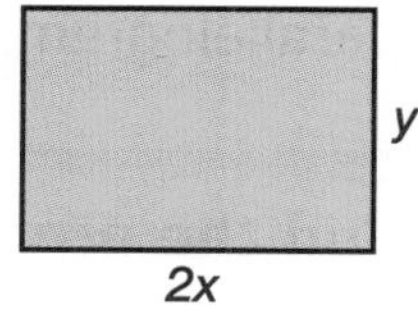

Problem Solving • Reasoning

11. Analyze Pam wants to carpet a room that is $6\frac{1}{2}$ yards long by 5 yards wide. The carpet costs $12 per square yard. If there is no waste, how much will it cost Pam to carpet the room?

12. Logical Thinking The length of a department store window is twice its width. The area of the window is 72 square feet. Find the width and length of the window.

13. Find the area of a rectangular field if the field's perimeter is 500 feet and its width is 80 feet.

14. Estimate Estimate the width of a rectangle if the length is 12.37 meters and the area is 59.85 square meters.

15. A rectangle has a 40-in. perimeter. What is the greatest possible area the rectangle could have? Explain.

16. Write Your Own Write a problem in which the area of one rectangle is twice the area of another.

Mixed Review • Test Prep

Solve each equation. *(pages 282–283)*

17. $c \times 7 = 49$

18. $p \div 24 = 3$

19. $2 + h \times 5 = 27$

20. $s \div 6 \div 2 = 3$

21 The number 36 is 60% of what number? *(pages 354–355)*

A 0.006 **B** 0.016 **C** 60 **D** 167

Extra Practice See Set A on page 482.

LESSON 2

Area of a Parallelogram

You will learn how to find the area of a parallelogram.

Review Vocabulary
parallelogram

Learn About It

A **parallelogram** is a quadrilateral whose opposite sides are parallel. The opposite sides are also congruent. A rectangle is a special type of parallelogram that has four right angles.

Parallelogram

h = height

b = base

The height is the length of a line segment that is perpendicular to both bases.

You know how to find the area of a rectangle. If you cut a right triangle from one end of a parallelogram and attach it to the other end, the rectangle obtained has the same area as the area of the parallelogram. So the formula for the area of a parallelogram is also $A = bh$.

Parallelogram

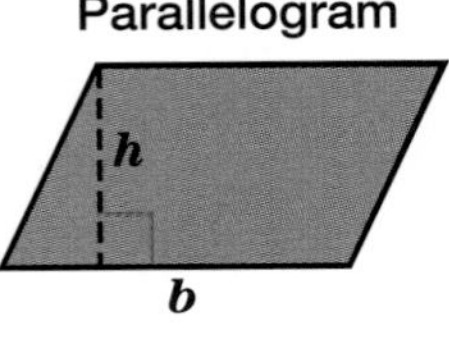

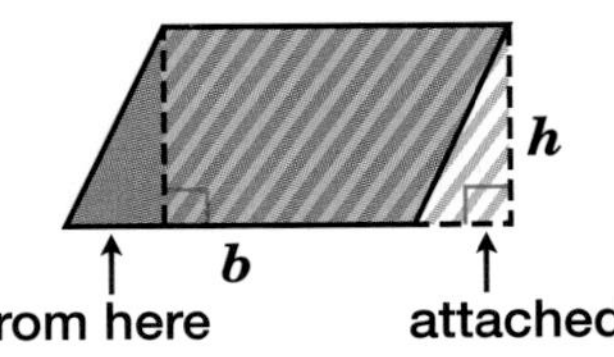

Rectangle

h

b

Find the area of this parallelogram.

Step 1 Identify the length of the base and the perpendicular height.

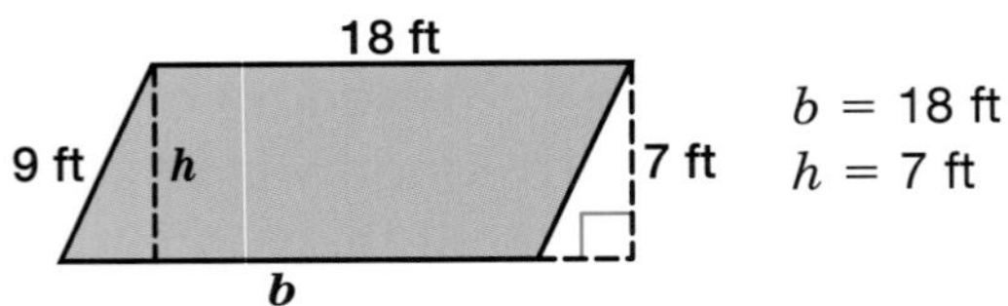

$b = 18$ ft
$h = 7$ ft

Step 2 Use the formula to find the area.

$A = bh$
$= 18 \times 7$
$= 126$

Solution: The area of the parallelogram is 126 square feet.

Check your work.
18 ft is almost 20 ft.
$20 \times 7 = 140$, so 126 ft^2 is reasonable.

Explain Your Thinking

► Does it matter where or how you draw the line segment to measure the height?

Guided Practice

Find the missing measure for each parallelogram, given base b, height h, or area A.

1. $b = 25$ m
$h = 30$ m
$A = ■$

2. $b = 8.2$ yd
$h = 1.25$ yd
$A = ■$

3.

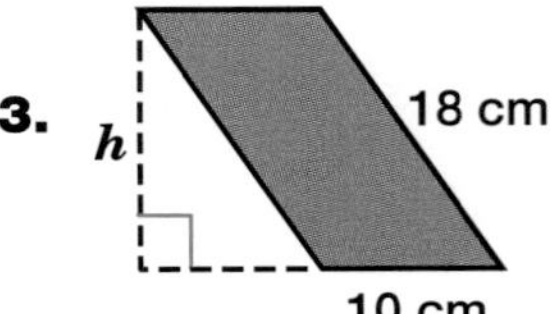

$A = 150\ cm^2$

Ask Yourself

- Did I use the correct numbers in the formula?

Independent Practice

Find the missing measure for each parallelogram or combination of parallelograms.

4. $b = 1{,}000$ ft
$h = 2.5$ ft
$A = ■$

5. $b = 6$ ft
$h = 5$ ft
$A = ■$

6. $b = 5\frac{1}{4}$ in.
$h = 7\frac{3}{7}$ in.
$A = ■$

7. $b = 6.32$ m
$h = 2.85$ m
$A = ■$

8. $b = 8$ in.; 6 in.; $h = 5$ in.

$A = ■$

9. 22 ft; h; 16 ft

$A = 320\text{ ft}^2$ $h = ■$

10.

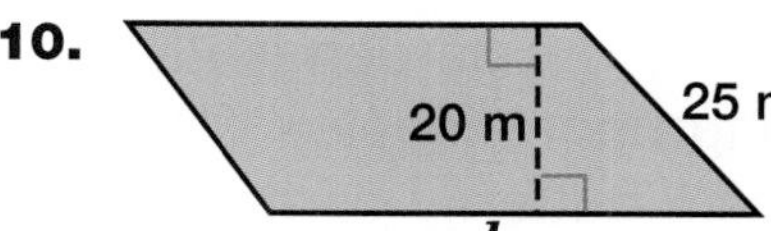

$A = 1{,}000\text{ m}^2$ $b = ■$

11.

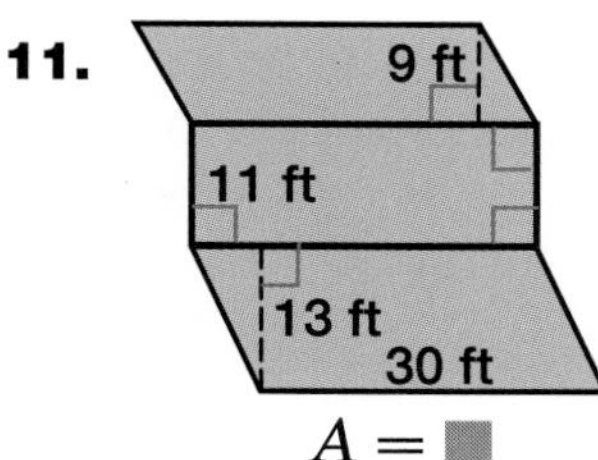

$A = ■$

12.

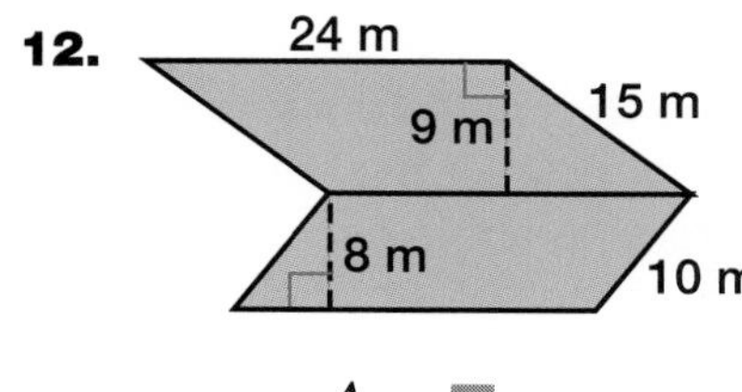

$A = ■$

13.

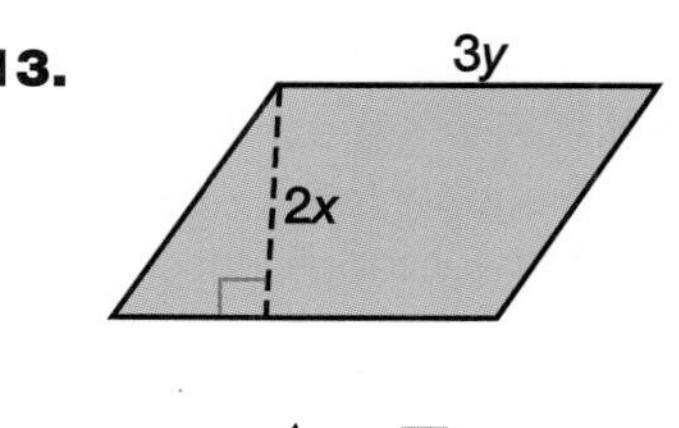

$A = ■$

Problem Solving • Reasoning

Use Data **Use the image to answer Problems 14 and 15.**

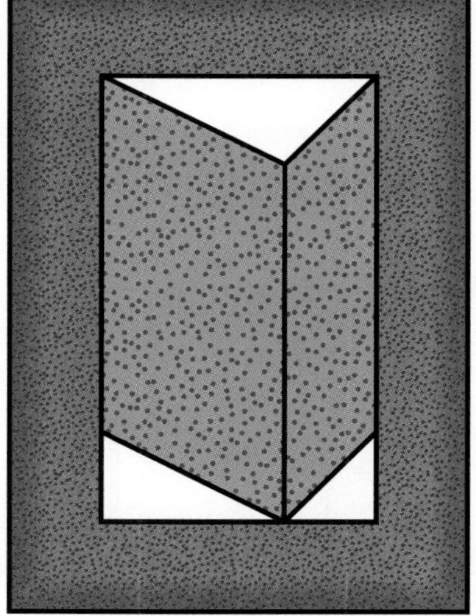

14. A stained-glass pattern includes two blue parallelograms. Measure the base and height of each parallelogram in centimeters. Find the total area of the two parallelograms.

15. The parallelograms are surrounded by 3 triangles and a red border. Find the area of the red border.

16. **Compare** The length of the base of parallelogram *ABCD* is 4 times the length of the base of parallelogram *QRST*. The height of *ABCD* is $\frac{2}{3}$ the height of *QRST*. Which parallelogram has the smaller area?

17. **Write About It** The base b of a parallelogram is 3 times its height h. Find b and h if the area is 300 cm². Explain your answer.

Mixed Review • Test Prep

Round each number to the underlined place. *(pages 8–9)*

18. 5<u>6</u>.894 **19.** 4.0<u>7</u>7 **20.** 1<u>2</u>3.12 **21.** 0.05<u>3</u>7

22 Evaluate $(p + 2.5) \times 0$, given $p = 17$. *(pages 256–257)*

A 0 **B** 2.5 **C** 17 **D** 42.5

LESSON 3

Area of a Triangle

You will learn how to find the area of a triangle.

Learn About It

In the schoolyard, the sixth-grade science class marked off a parallelogram-shaped garden with a base of 20 ft and a height of 6 ft. The garden is divided into two congruent triangles. One triangular part was a butterfly garden. How can you find the area of the butterfly garden?

Find the area of a triangle.

Step 1 Draw the parallelogram. Draw a diagonal to divide the figure into two congruent triangles.

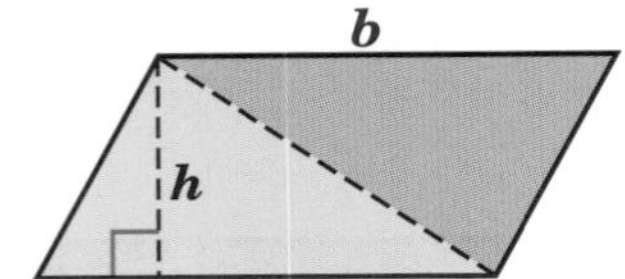

The area of each triangle is one half the area of the parallelogram.

Step 2 Use the drawing and the formula for the area of a parallelogram to find a formula for the area of a triangle.

Let b = base

Let h = perpendicular height

A of the parallelogram $= bh$

A of the triangle $= \frac{1}{2}bh$

Step 3 Use the formula to find the area of the triangular garden where $b = 20$ and $h = 6$.

$A = \frac{1}{2}bh$

$= \frac{1}{2}(20 \times 6)$

$= \frac{1}{2}(120)$

$= 60$ ft^2

Solution: The area of the butterfly garden is 60 square feet.

Another Example

Find the Height of a Triangle

$A = 54$ ft^2

$A = \frac{1}{2}bh$

$54 = \frac{1}{2}(12h)$

$54 = 6h$

$9 = h$

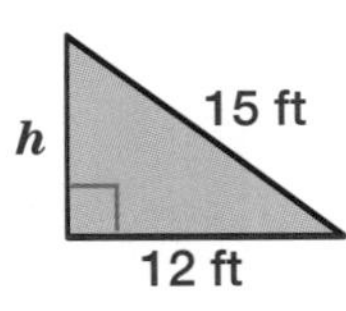

The height is 9 ft.

Explain Your Thinking

- ▶ Draw a parallelogram and one of its diagonals. Explain how you know that two congruent triangles are formed.
- ▶ Why is the area of any triangle half the area of a parallelogram with the same lengths of the base and height?

Guided Practice

Find the missing measure for each triangle.

1. $A = ■$
$b = 20$ ft
$h = 12$ ft

2. $A = 28$ m^2
$b = 8$ m
$h = ■$

3. $A = 60.16$ in.^{2}
$b = ■$
$h = 9.4$ in.

4. $A = 7\frac{1}{2}$ in.^{2}
$b = 5$
$h = ■$

Find the area of each figure.

5. 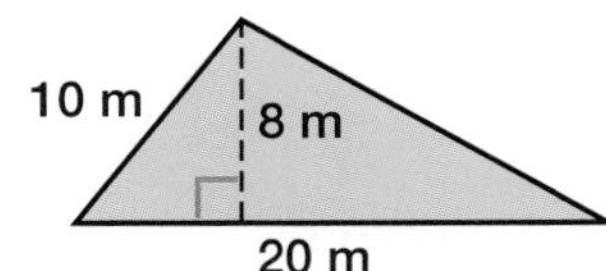

6. 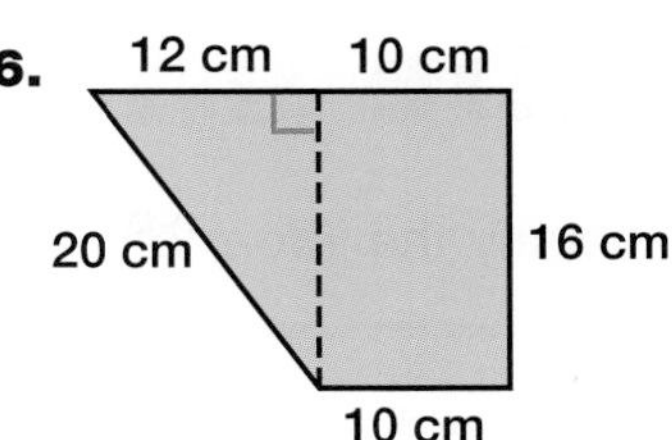

> **Ask Yourself**
> - Did I use the correct formula?
> - Did I use the correct values for b, h, and A?

Independent Practice

Find the missing measure for each triangle.

7. $A = \blacksquare$
   $b = 15$ cm
   $h = 18$ cm

8. $A = 156.16$ ft^2
   $b = 12.2$ ft
   $h = \blacksquare$

9. $A = \frac{180}{40}$ in.^{2}
   $b = \blacksquare$
   $h = 2\frac{1}{2}$ in.

10. $A = \blacksquare$
    $b = 4$ yd
    $h = 2$ yd

Find the area of each figure.

11. 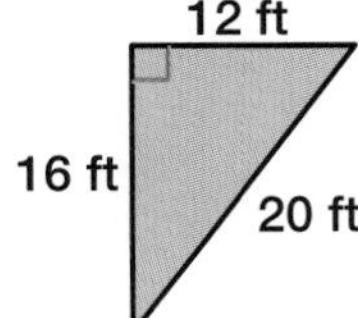

12. 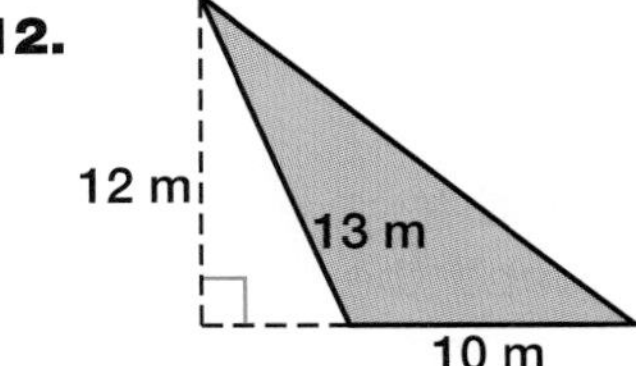

13. 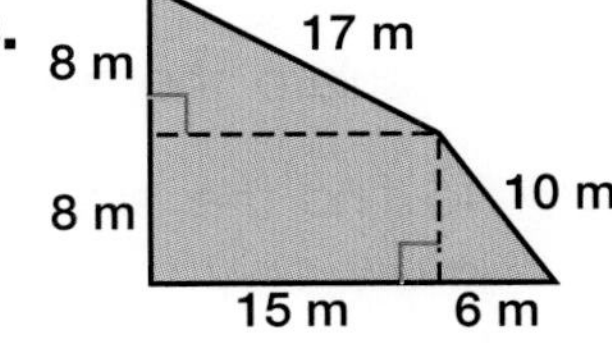

Problem Solving • Reasoning

14. Next to each plant in the garden there is a triangular label stating the plant's name. The base of each label is 8 in., and the area is 24 in.^{2} What is the height of each label?

15. **Logical Thinking** The banner that hangs over the garden entrance is a triangle whose height is 3 times its base. The area of the banner is 54 square meters. What is its height?

16. **Compare** The height of triangle *DEF* is 4 times as great as the height of triangle *ABC*. The bases of the triangles are equal. How does the area of triangle *DEF* compare with the area of triangle *ABC*?

17. **Analyze** Cindy and Eric each drew a triangle with an area of 120 ft^2. The base of Cindy's triangle is half as long as the base of Eric's triangle. Compare the heights.

Mixed Review • Test Prep

Order these integers from least to greatest. *(pages 208–209)*

18. $^+6$ $^-7$ 0 $^+4$

19. $^+3$ $^-3$ $^-9$ $^+4$

20. $^-8$ $^+2$ $^-1$ 0

21. What is the distance between two towns if they are 4.5 inches apart on a map with a scale of 0.5 in. = 75 mi? *(pages 320–321)*

A 16.67 mi **B** 168.75 mi **C** 337.5 mi **D** 675 mi

Problem-Solving Skill: Too Much or Too Little Information

You will learn how to identify the information you need to solve a problem.

Sometimes you have too much information, and sometimes you have too little, or missing, information.

When a problem has more information than you need, you must decide what information is important. When a problem does not have enough information, you must decide what information is missing. Sometimes you can find the missing information.

Sometimes there is too much information.

Sid and Angel are building a model sailboat. The triangular sail for their model has the measurements shown at right. Do they have enough information to calculate the area of the sail?

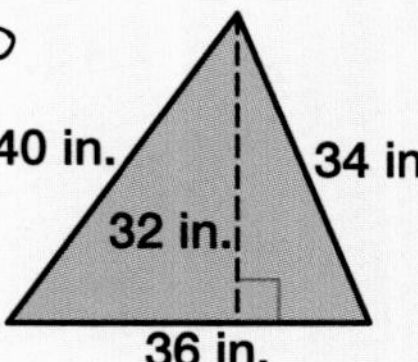

$$A = \frac{1}{2}bh$$
$$= \frac{1}{2} \times 36 \times 32$$
$$= 576 \text{ in.}^2$$

To find the area, Sid and Angel need to know only the length of the base and the perpendicular height. Therefore, Sid and Angel have enough information to find the area.

Sometimes there is too little information.

Sid and Angel want to buy trim to sew around the edge of the emblem shown at right. They are having trouble finding the emblem's perimeter. Why?

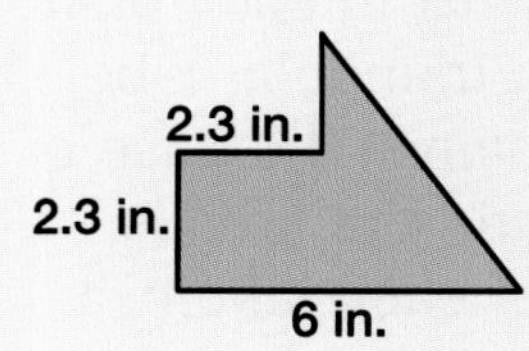

Sid and Angel cannot determine the lengths of the unlabeled segments, based on the information in the figure.

Sometimes you need to find the missing information.

Sid and Angel cut a piece of brass trim for their sailboat. Can they calculate the perimeter of the piece of trim?

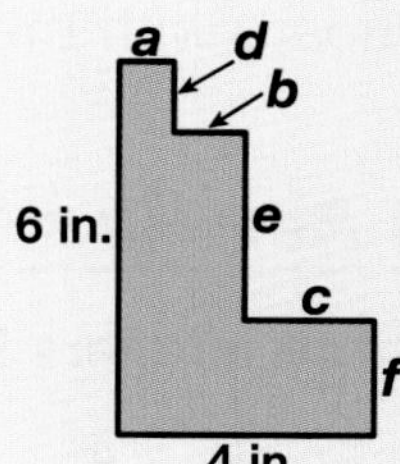

At first, they think they cannot find the perimeter. Then they realize that the sum of *a*, *b*, and *c* must be 4 inches and the sum of *d*, *e*, and *f* must be 6 inches.

$P = 6 + 4 + 6 + 4 = 20$ in.

Look Back How much information do you need to find both the area and the perimeter of a rectangle?

Sails for boats and ships are made from triangular and rectangular pieces of material.

Remember:
- ▶ Understand
- ▶ Plan
- ▶ Solve
- ▶ Look Back

Guided Practice

Solve. If there is not enough information to solve, tell what information is missing.

1. Part of the deck on a model ship is a rectangle with an area of 60 square inches. The rectangle's height is 10 inches. Find the perimeter of the rectangle.

   Think: What information do I need to calculate the perimeter?

2. A triangular sail on Mrs. Henderson's new sailboat has two sides that are each 12 meters long. If the perimeter of the sail is 32 meters, what is the area of the sail?

   Think: Is it possible to find the triangle's height?

Choose a Strategy

Solve. If there is not enough information to solve, tell what information is missing.

Problem-Solving Strategies

- **Work Backward**
- **Draw a Diagram**
- **Use Logical Thinking**
- **Make a List**

3. Find the area of this figure.

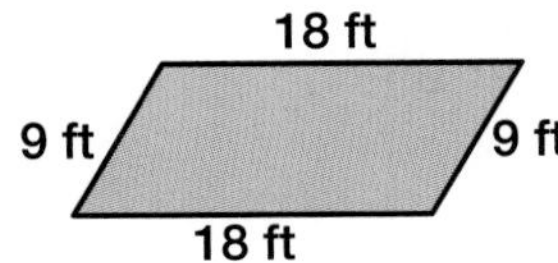

4. Sid is making two triangular flags. The smaller flag has a base of 4 inches and a height of 3 inches. The larger one has a base of 4 inches and a height of 4 inches. How much greater is the area of the larger flag?

5. Find the area of a rectangular poster whose length is 3 times its width. How would the area of this poster compare with the area of a rectangular poster whose width is 3 times its length?

6. Angel is spreading bark chips on her mother's garden. One bag of bark chips will cover 50 square feet. If the chips are spread in a layer 2 inches deep, how many bags of bark chips will Angel need?

7. Sid is sewing two right triangles together to make flags. If each right triangle has a 4-inch base and a 6-inch height, how many flags can he make from a piece of 24-inch by 48-inch cloth?

8. A parallelogram has a height of 4.2 feet and an area of 14.7 square feet. A triangle has the same height as the parallelogram and a base of 6 feet. What is the area of the triangle?

Extra Practice See 1–4 on page 485.

Quick Check

Check Your Understanding of Lessons 1–4

Find the perimeter and area of each figure.

1.

2.

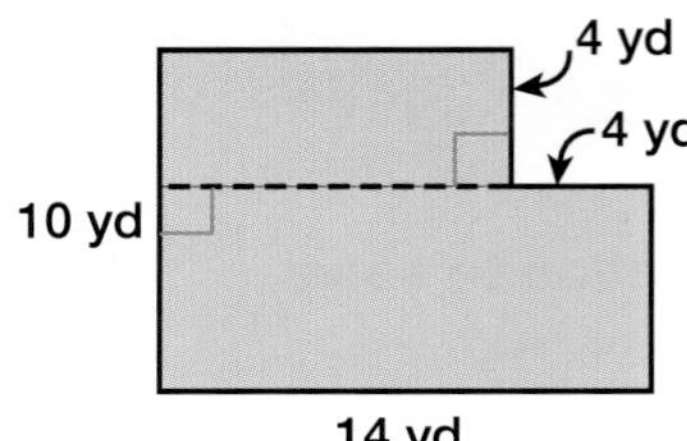

Find the missing measure for each parallelogram.

3. $b = 12$ cm
$h = 4$ cm
$A = ■$

4. $b = 30$ in.
$h = ■$
$A = 660 \text{ in.}^2$

5. $b = ■$
$h = 13$ yd
$A = 247 \text{ yd}^2$

Find the missing measure for each triangle.

6. $A = 90 \text{ in.}^2$
$b = 12$ in.
$h = ■$

7. $A = ■$
$b = 20$ cm
$h = 9$ cm

8. $A = 60 \text{ m}^2$
$b = ■$
$h = 8$ m

Solve. If there is not enough information to solve, tell what information is missing.

9. The length of a rectangle is 12 cm and its perimeter is 42 cm. Find the area of the rectangle.

10. The height of a triangle is 15 ft and its area is 90 ft^2. Find the length of the base of the triangle.

How did you do?

If you had difficulty with any items in the Quick Check, you can use the following pages for review and extra practice.

Items	Review These Pages	Do These Extra Practice Items
1–2, 9	pages 450–451	Set A, page 482
3–5	pages 452–453	Set B, page 482
6–8, 10	pages 454–455	Set C, page 482
9–10	pages 456–457	1–4, page 485

Test Prep • Cumulative Review

Maintaining the Standards

Choose the letter of the correct answer.

1. A triangle has one angle with a measure of 42° and one angle with a measure of 103°. What is the measure of the third angle?

   A 35°
   B 77°
   C 138°
   D 215°

2. Rebecca baby-sits every weekend. In 4 weeks she earned $180. If she earned the same amount each weekend, how much did she earn each weekend?

   F $25
   G $45
   H $176
   J $720

3. Marsha drove 248 miles in 4 hours. What was her average speed?

   A 40 miles per hour
   B 60 miles per hour
   C 62 miles per hour
   D 70 miles per hour

4. Lana is cooking spaghetti sauce. The recipe calls for $1\frac{3}{4}$ pounds of meat. How much meat will Lana need if she is making 5 times the amount of sauce in her recipe?

   F $8\frac{3}{4}$ pounds
   G $8\frac{1}{2}$ pounds
   H $6\frac{3}{4}$ pounds
   J $2\frac{6}{7}$ pounds

5. Brett bought a CD player for $169. It was on sale for 20% off the original price. What was the original price of the CD player?

   A $211.25
   B $155.48
   C $135.20
   D $33.80

6. Order these numbers from least to greatest.

   $0.4 \quad 0.31 \quad ^{-}\frac{5}{4} \quad 2\frac{1}{2}$

   F $^{-}\frac{5}{4}$, 0.4, 0.31, $2\frac{1}{2}$
   G $2\frac{1}{2}$, $^{-}\frac{5}{4}$, 0.31, 0.4
   H 0.4, 0.31, $^{-}\frac{5}{4}$, $2\frac{1}{2}$
   J $^{-}\frac{5}{4}$, 0.31, 0.4, $2\frac{1}{2}$

7. What is the value of $3n + {}^{-}2$ given $n = {}^{-}4$?

   A $^{-}14$ **C** 10
   B $^{-}10$ **D** 14

8. What is the measure in degrees of $\angle a$?

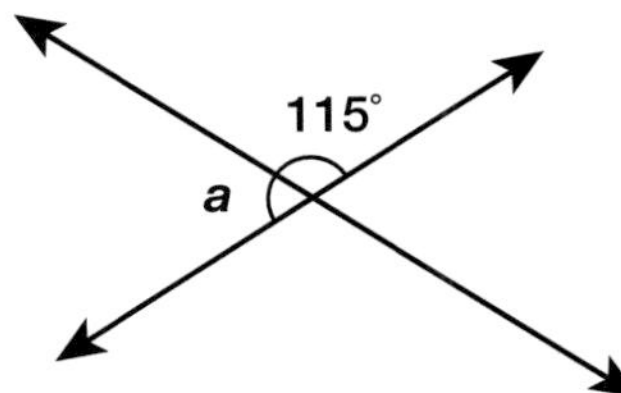

   Explain How did you find your answer?

Internet Test Prep
Visit **www.eduplace.com/kids/mhm** for more *Test Prep Practice.*

Circumference

You will learn how to find the circumference of a circle using the ratio π.

Review Vocabulary
circumference
diameter
pi (π)
radius

Learn About It

The distance around a circle is called the **circumference**. The ratio of the circumference, C, to the **diameter,** d, of any circle is always the same. This constant is slightly greater than 3. The Greek letter π (**pi**)is used to name this ratio $\frac{C}{d}$. An approximation of π can be written in fraction or decimal form. We use $\pi \approx 3.14$ or $\pi \approx \frac{22}{7}$. The symbol $\approx$ means "is approximately equal to."

Since $\pi = \frac{C}{d}$, you can use $C = \pi d$ to find circumference. Since the diameter of a circle is twice its **radius**, $C = 2\pi r$ can also be used to find circumference.

The circumference C is the distance around a circle.

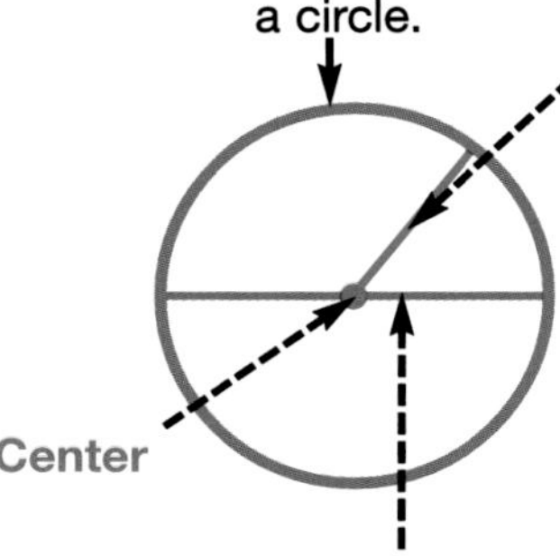

The word radius is used to describe both a line segment from the center of a circle to any point on the circle and the length of that line segment.

The word diameter is used to describe both a line segment through the center of a circle with endpoints on the circle and the length of that line segment.

Different Ways to Approximate Circumference With $\pi \approx \frac{22}{7}$

You can use the formula $C = 2\pi r$.

The radius of the circle is 7 inches. Find the circumference C.

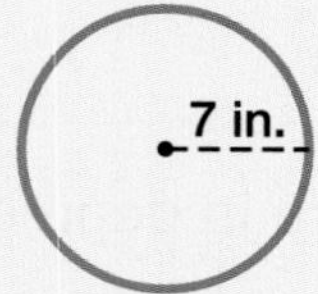

$$C = 2\pi r$$
$$= 2\pi \times 7$$
$$= 2 \times 7 \times \pi$$
$$\approx 14 \times \frac{22}{7}$$
$$\approx 44$$

You can use the formula $C = \pi d$.

The diameter of the circle is 14 inches. Find the circumference C.

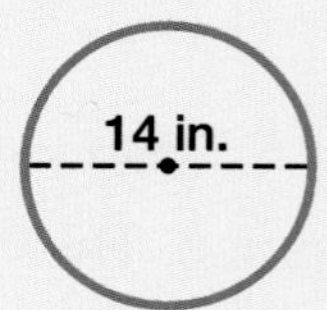

$$C = \pi d$$
$$= 14\pi$$
$$\approx 14 \times \frac{22}{7}$$
$$\approx 44$$

Solution: The circumference is approximately 44 inches.

Measure to check.

Draw and cut out a circle with a radius of 7 inches. Measure its circumference with a measuring tape. Compare your answer with your measurement.

Different Ways to Approximate Circumference With $\pi \approx 3.14$

You can use the formula $C = 2\pi r$.

The radius of the circle is 5 inches. Find the circumference C.

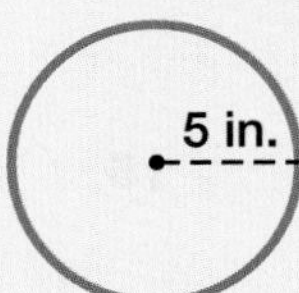

$$C = 2\pi r$$
$$= 2\pi \times 5$$
$$= 10\pi$$
$$\approx 10 \times 3.14$$
$$\approx 31.4$$

You can use the formula $C = \pi d$.

The diameter of the circle is 10 inches. Find the circumference C.

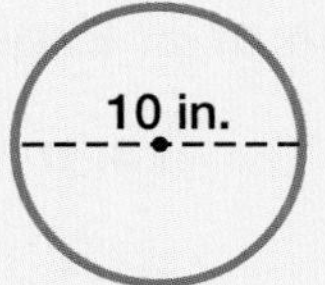

$$C = \pi d$$
$$= 10\pi$$
$$\approx 10 \times 3.14$$
$$\approx 31.4$$

Measure to check.

Draw and cut out a circle with a diameter of 10 inches. Measure its circumference with a measuring tape. Compare your answer with your measurement.

Solution: The circumference is approximately 31.4 inches.

Another Example

Find the Radius of a Circle

Given $C = 18.84$ in.

$$C = 2\pi r$$
$$\frac{C}{2\pi} = r$$
$$\frac{18.84}{2 \times 3.14} \approx r$$
$$3 \text{ in.} \approx r$$

The radius is about 3 inches.

Explain Your Thinking

- ▶ When is using $\frac{22}{7}$ a better choice than using 3.14 as an approximation of π?
- ▶ Why are all circles similar?

Guided Practice

Find the circumference or missing measure for each circle. Use 3.14 or $\frac{22}{7}$ as an approximation of π.

Ask Yourself

- Which formula should I use?
- Which value for π is best to use?

1.

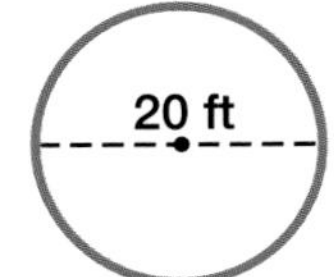

2.

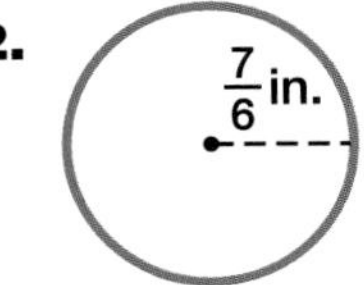

3.

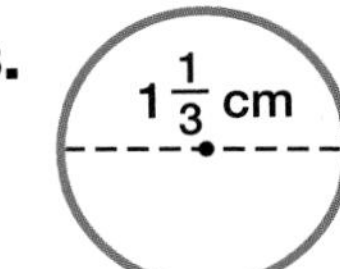

4. $r = 70$ m
$C \approx$ ■

5. $r = 15$ in.
$C \approx$ ■

6. $d = 0.35$ ft
$C \approx$ ■

7. $C = d^2$
$d =$ ■

Independent Practice

Find the circumference. Use 3.14 or $\frac{22}{7}$ as an approximation of π.

8. 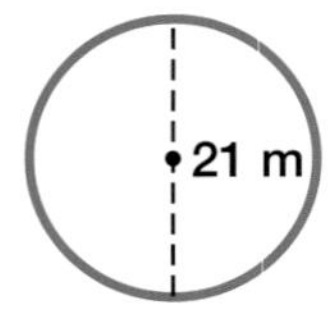

9. 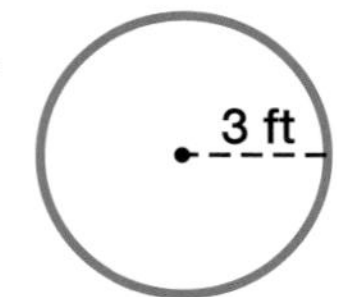

10. 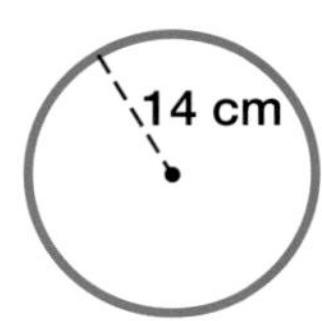

11. 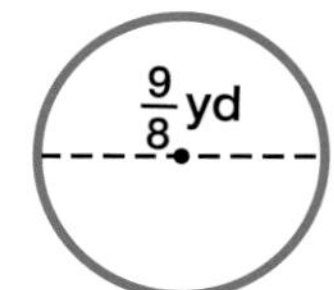

Find the missing measure for each circle. Use 3.14 or $\frac{22}{7}$ as an approximation of π. Explain your choice.

12. $r = 35$ ft
$C \approx$ ■

13. $d = 28.7$ yd
$C \approx$ ■

14. $r = 3\frac{3}{4}$ m
$C \approx$ ■

15. $C = 110$ cm
$d \approx$ ■

16. $d = 3$ m
$C \approx$ ■

17. $r = \frac{7}{11}$ yd
$C \approx$ ■

18. $d = 67$ in.
$C \approx$ ■

19. $C \approx$ ■
$r = \frac{1}{2}$ m

Problem Solving • Reasoning

Solve. Estimate to check your answers.

20. Sam is building a fence for a circular pen with a diameter of 40 feet. If fencing costs $3.50 per foot, how much will it cost Sam to enclose the pen? Round your answer to the nearest dollar.

21. **Logical Thinking** When Dave rides his bicycle 100 yards, the bike's front wheel makes 50 complete revolutions. What is the circumference of the wheel in inches? What is the wheel's diameter rounded to the nearest inch?

22. **Analyze** The wheel of a bicycle has a diameter of 24 inches. How many times will the wheel revolve if the bicycle is ridden 100 yards? Round your answer to the nearest whole revolution.

23. **Write About It** If the diameter of one circle is twice the diameter of a second circle, why is the circumference of the first circle twice the circumference of the second?

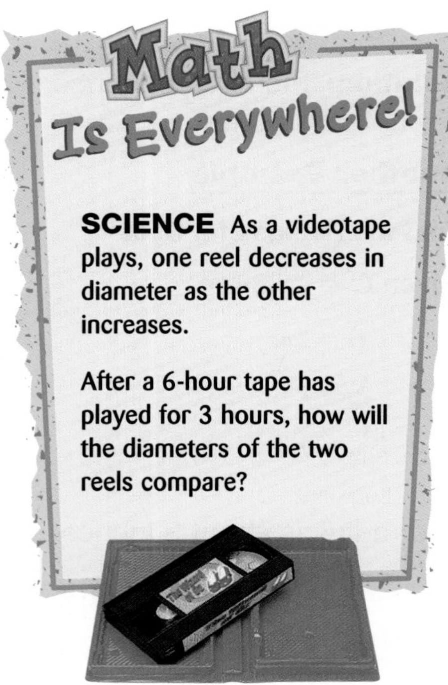

SCIENCE As a videotape plays, one reel decreases in diameter as the other increases.

After a 6-hour tape has played for 3 hours, how will the diameters of the two reels compare?

Mixed Review • Test Prep

Find each sum. *(pages 214–216)*

24. $^{-}14 + ^{+}8$

25. $^{-}5 + ^{-}5$

26. $^{+}18 + ^{-}20$

27. $^{-}3 + ^{+}3$

28 27 is what percent of 12? *(pages 352–353)*

A 324% **B** 225% **C** 44.4% **D** 22.5%

Extra Practice See Set D on page 483.

Practice Game

Competing Circles

Practice calculating the circumference of a circle by playing this game with a partner. Try to win your partner's cards!

What You'll Need

- *5 "diameter" cards (Teaching Tool 9)*
- *5 "radius" cards (Teaching Tool 10)*

Players
2

Here's What to Do

1. Shuffle the cards and deal five cards to each player.
2. Each player places one card faceup.
3. Each player calculates the circumference of a circle with the radius or diameter listed on his or her card. Use 3.14 or $\frac{22}{7}$ as an approximation of π. The player with the circle having the greater circumference takes both cards.

Repeat Steps 2 and 3. The player with the most cards after five turns wins.

Share Your Thinking Is there a way to know which circumference is greater without actually doing the calculation? Explain.

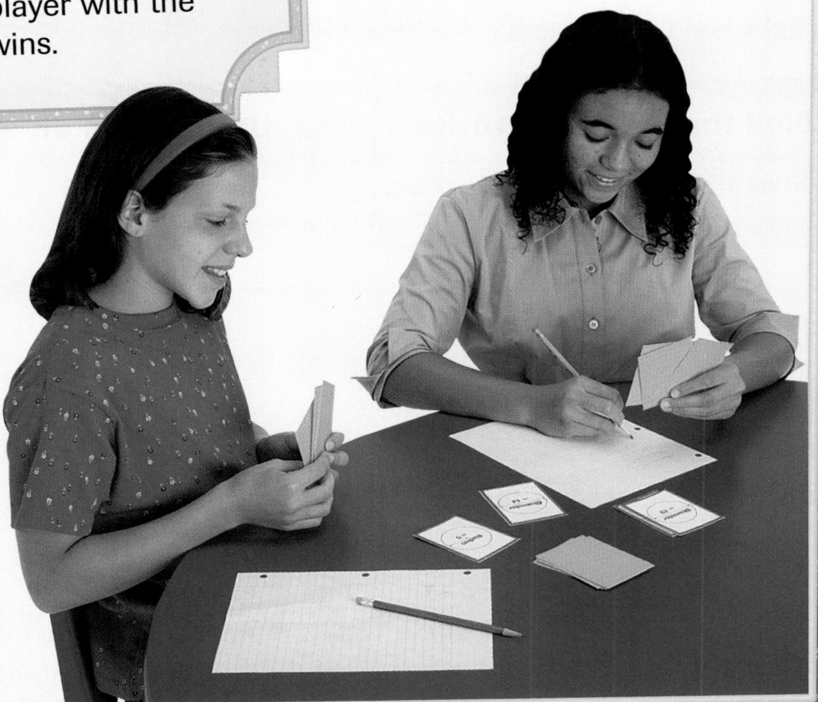

LESSON 6

Area of a Circle

You will learn how to calculate the area of a circle.

Learn About It

The formulas for circumference of a circle and area of a parallelogram can help you find the formula for the area of a circle.

Find the area of a circle.

Step 1 Divide a circle into 8 equal sectors. Shade half the sectors.

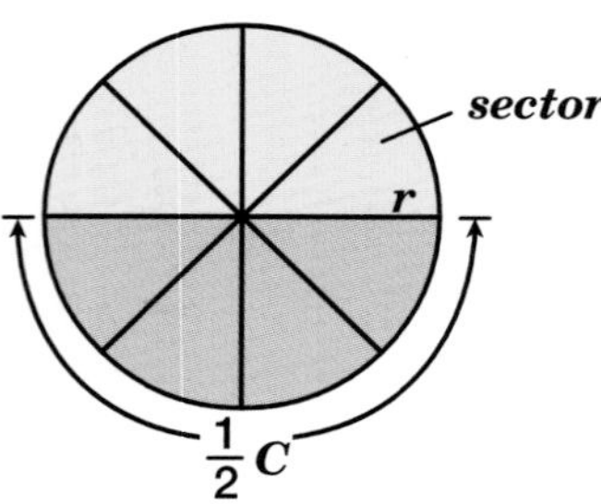

Think: If $C = 2\pi r$, then $\frac{1}{2}C = \pi r$.

Step 2 Separate the sectors and arrange them side by side. The arrangement resembles a parallelogram.

The radius r of the circle is approximately equal to the height h of the parallelogram.

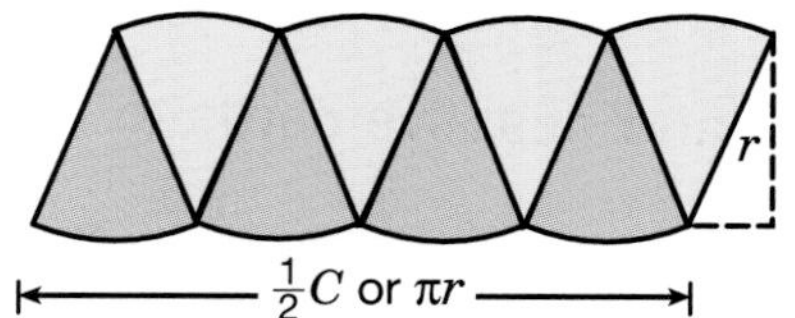

One half the circumference C of the circle is approximately equal to the base b of the parallelogram.

The greater the number of sectors, the closer the approximation will be to πr^2.

The area of a parallelogram $= b \times h$,
so the area of a circle $= (\pi r) \times r$, or πr^2.

$$A = \pi r^2$$

What would be the area of a 16-inch pizza?

Find the area of a 16-inch pizza. Use 3.14 as an approximation of π.

Step 1 Find the radius of the pizza.

$$r = \frac{1}{2}d$$
$$= \frac{1}{2} \times 16$$
$$= 8 \text{ in.}$$

Step 2 Use the formula to find the area.

$$A = \pi r^2$$
$$= \pi \times 8^2$$
$$\approx 3.14 \times 64$$
$$A \approx 200.96 \text{ in.}^2$$

Solution: The area of the pizza is about 201 square inches.

Explain Your Thinking

- Calculate the area of a circle with a 3 in. radius. Draw one and divide it into 16 equal sectors. Use them to form a parallelogram. Measure its area and compare with the area you calculated.

Guided Practice

Find the area of each circle. Use 3.14 or $\frac{22}{7}$ for π.

1. $r = 5$ in. **2.** $r = \frac{3}{4}$ cm **3.** $d = 24$ yd **4.** $d = 4\frac{1}{2}$ m

5. $r = 4$ ft **6.** $d = 21$ in. **7.** $d = 40$ ft **8.** $r = 6.7$ cm

Ask Yourself

- Did I use the correct formula?

Independent Practice

Find the area of each circle. Use 3.14 or $\frac{22}{7}$ for π.

9. $r = 28$ cm **10.** $d = 30$ ft **11.** $r = 5\frac{2}{3}$ in. **12.** $d = 64.2$ m

13. $r = 84$ ft **14.** $r = 7$ m **15.** $d = 25$ yd **16.** $d = 3{,}500$ cm

Find the area of each figure. Use 3.14 for π. Round to the nearest tenth.

17.

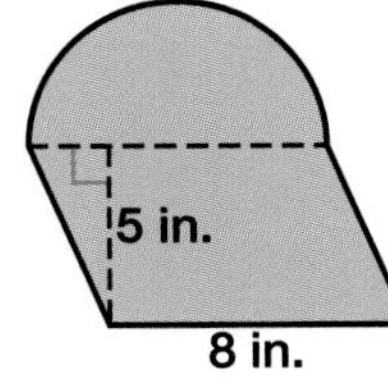

18.

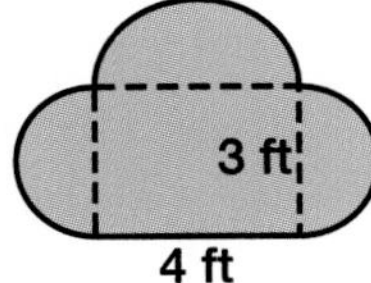

19.

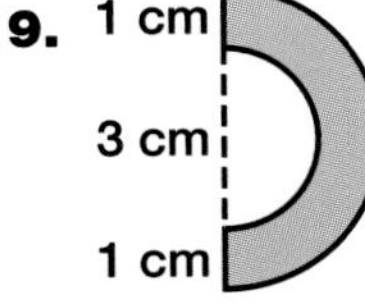

20.

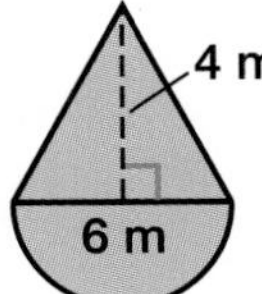

Problem Solving • Reasoning

Use Data **Use the pizza menu to answer Problems 23–24.**

21. Pizza Palace has free delivery within a 10-mile radius of the restaurant. How large is the free-delivery area?

22. **Analyze** If one sixth-grader can eat an 8-in. pizza, how many sixth-graders will it take to eat a 16-in. pizza?

23. **Compare** How many more square inches of pizza would you get if you ordered a 16-inch pizza instead of a 12-inch pizza? Which pizza costs more per square inch?

24. **Write About It** Terri wants to order a healthier kind of pizza. If she orders a 12-inch pizza with mushrooms and broccoli, how much will the pizza cost? Explain your answer.

PIZZA • PALACE

CHEESE PIZZA

	12"	14"	16"
Price	$7.99	$9.99	$11.99
Each Topping	$1.00	$1.25	$1.50

—EXTRA TOPPINGS—

Onions Peppers Broccoli Mushrooms

Mixed Review • Test Prep

25. Look at the triangles at the right. If $\triangle ABC \sim \triangle DEF$, what is the length of $\overline{DF}$? *(pages 416–417)*

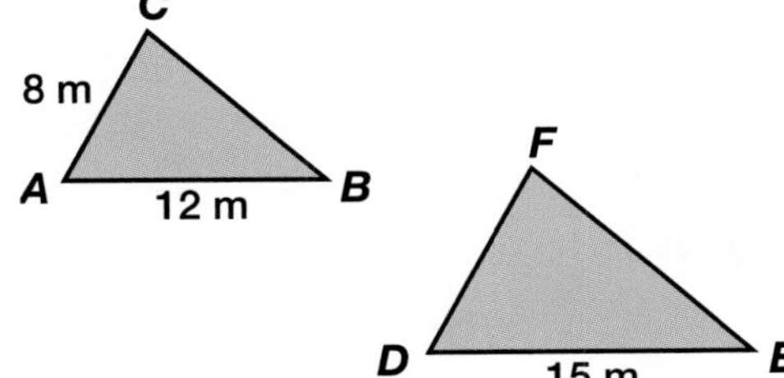

26 What is another way of writing the ratio $\frac{3}{4}$? *(pages 304–305)*

A 4:3 **B** 3:4 **C** $\frac{1}{4}$ **D** $\frac{4}{3}$

Extra Practice See Set E on page 483.

Problem-Solving Strategy: Choose a Strategy

You will learn how to solve problems by choosing a strategy.

When solving more difficult problems, trying different strategies can help you.

Problem Mr. Jenkin's lawn is a 30-foot square. He uses a rotating sprinkler to water his lawn. The sprinkler waters a circular region with a radius of 15 feet. If Mr. Jenkin puts the sprinkler at the center of his lawn, about what area of the lawn is not watered by the sprinkler?

Understand

What is the question?
What area of the lawn is not watered by the sprinkler?

What do you know?
The lawn is a 30-foot by 30-foot square, and the area watered is a circle with a 15-foot radius.

Plan

How can you find the answer?
You can use the Draw a Diagram and the Write an Equation strategies.

Solve

Draw a Diagram
First, find the area of the whole lawn. Next, find the area of the watered part of the lawn. Then subtract to find the area of the lawn that is not watered by the sprinkler.

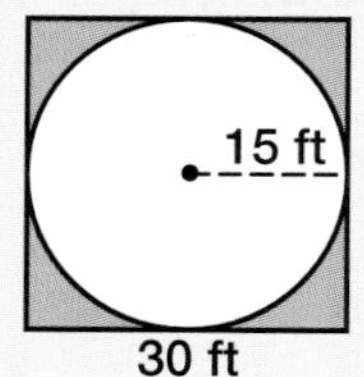

Write an Equation
Write an equation to find the area of the lawn that is not watered by the sprinkler.

A_1 = area of the square
A_2 = area of the circle
A_3 = area of the lawn not watered

$$A_3 = A_1 - A_2$$
$$A_3 = s^2 - \pi r^2$$
$$\approx 30^2 - 3.14 \times 15^2$$
$$\approx 900 - 706.5$$
$$\approx 193.5$$

An area of about 194 ft^2 is not watered by the sprinkler.

Look Back

Look back at the problem.
Is your answer reasonable? Is the area not watered less than the total area of the lawn?

Remember:
- ► Understand
- ► Plan
- ► Solve
- ► Look Back

Guided Practice

Use the Draw a Diagram or the Write an Equation strategy to solve each problem.

1. Mr. Smith has a 36-square-foot flower bed. He plants petunias in a circular area with a radius of 3 feet. In the rest of the bed he plants marigolds. What area of the bed is planted with marigolds? Use 3.14 for π.

   Think: What formulas are necessary to solve this problem?

2. Evan's rectangular patio is 3 yards wide and 6 yards long. Evan is helping his mother put up two circular tables on the patio. The diameters of the tables are 4 feet and 5 feet. What area of the patio is not covered by the tables?

   Think: What information should be used first?

Choose a Strategy

Solve. Use these or other strategies. If there is not enough information to solve, tell what information is missing.

Problem-Solving Strategies

- **Work Backward**
- **Use Logical Thinking**
- **Write an Equation**
- **Draw a Diagram**

3. Every afternoon Danny jogs around his block 10 times. The block is a rectangle 280 yards long. How far does Danny jog each afternoon?

4. Look at the expressions below. Find a pattern. What is the next expression in the pattern likely to be?

   $2 \times 3 \qquad 5 \times 5 \qquad 8 \times 7 \qquad 11 \times 9$

5. A company's logo is being painted on a building. The logo consists of a red circle inside a blue rectangle. The rectangle is 12 feet wide and 18 feet high. The circle has a radius of 5 feet. What area of the logo is painted blue?

6. The radius of a circular fountain is 3 feet. What is the area of the smallest rectangular flower bed that could hold two rows of three circular fountains? What area of the flower bed is left to plant flowers in?

7. An archery target has a radius of 4 feet. The bull's-eye of the target has a radius of 0.5 feet. To the nearest hundredth, what is the area of the target not covered by the bull's-eye?

8. A circle is placed inside a square so that all four sides of the square just touch the circle. What is the relationship between the radius of the circle and a side of the square?

Extra Practice See 5–8 on page 485.

Quick Check

Check Your Understanding of Lessons 5–7

Find the circumference of each circle.
Use 3.14 or $\frac{22}{7}$ as an approximation of π.

1.

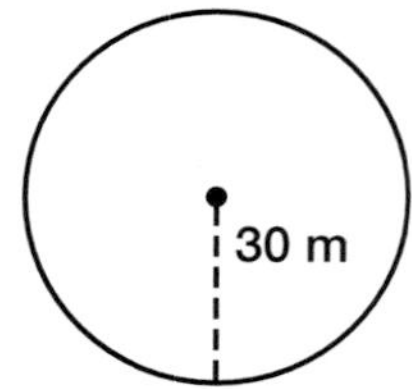

2.

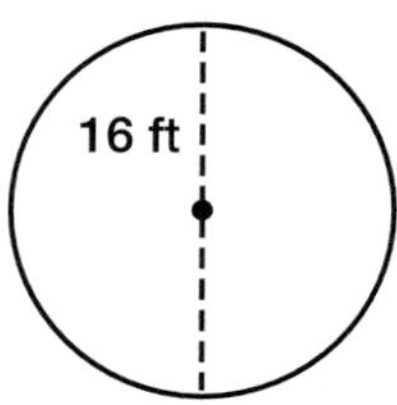

3.

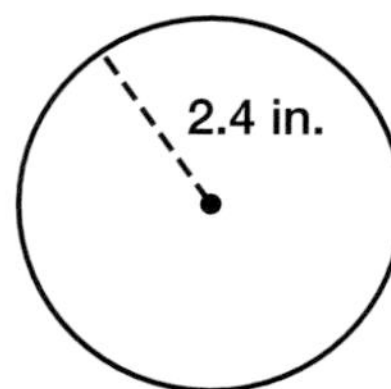

Find the missing measure for each circle. Use 3.14 or $\frac{22}{7}$ as an approximation of π. Explain your choice.

4. $r = 21$ m
$C \approx$ ■

5. $d = 70$ ft
$C \approx$ ■

6. $d \approx$ ■
$C = 22$ in.

Find the area of each figure. Use 3.14 for π.

7.

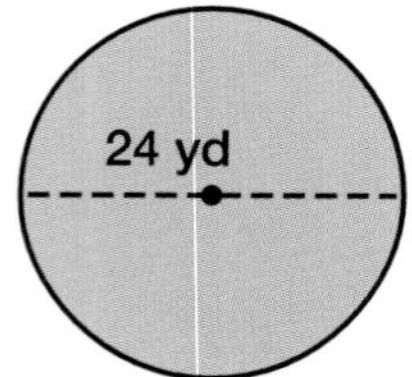

8.

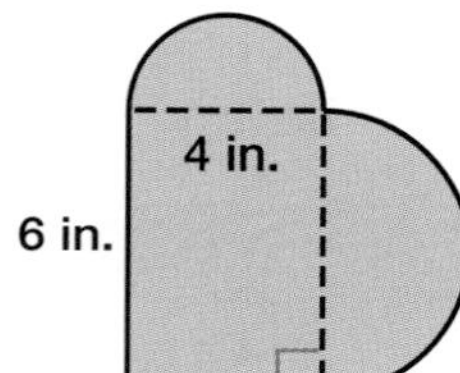

9.

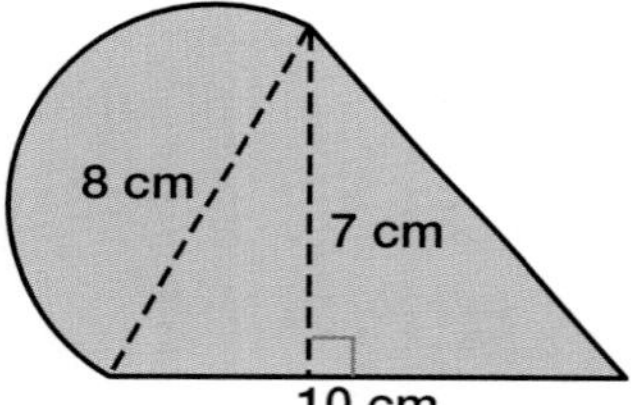

10. A round tablecloth hangs 1.5 feet over the edge of a round table with a diameter of 4.5 feet. What is the area of the tablecloth?

11. What is the area of the smallest rectangular shelf that could hold a row of 3 flowerpots if each flowerpot is 6 inches in diameter?

How did you do?

If you had difficulty with any items in the Quick Check, you can use the following pages for review and extra practice.

Items	Review These Pages	Do These Extra Practice Items
1–6	pages 460–463	Set D, page 483
7–9	pages 464–465	Set E, page 483
10–11	pages 466–467	5–8, page 485

Test Prep • Cumulative Review

Maintaining the Standards

Choose the letter of the correct answer.

1 What is the circumference of a circle that has a radius of 6 feet? Use 3.14 as an approximation of π.

A 12 feet
B 18.84 feet
C 37.68 feet
D 113.04 feet

2 A restaurant bill is $34.50. What is a reasonable estimate for a 15% tip?

F $6.50
G $6.00
H $5.00
J $4.50

3 A submarine descends to a depth of 156 feet below the surface. It then ascends 44 feet before descending another 90 feet. At what depth is the submarine?

A 22 feet below the surface
B 110 feet below the surface
C 202 feet below the surface
D 290 feet below the surface

4 A sweater is on sale for 25% off the original price. If the original price is $56, what is the sale price?

F $70
G $42
H $40
J $14

5 What is the measure of $\angle c$?

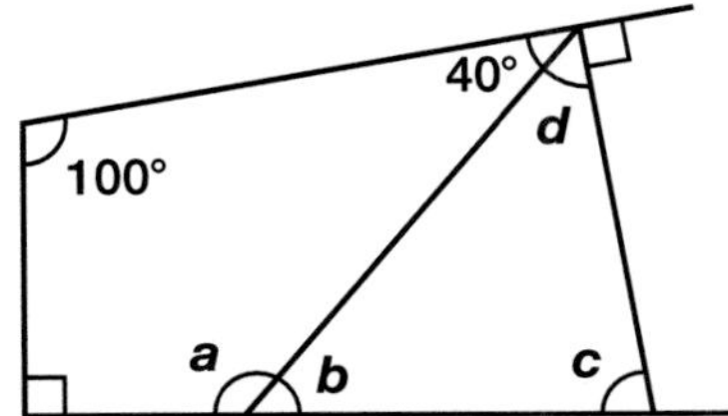

A 50°
B 80°
C 90°
D 100°

6 Mr. Glen invests $4,125 in an account with a simple interest rate of 6.2%. How much interest will he earn in 9 months?

F $191.81
G $255.75
H $4,144.81
J $4,380.75

7 Which of the following ratios is equivalent to $\frac{4}{7}$?

A $\frac{7}{4}$ **C** $\frac{4}{14}$
B $\frac{8}{14}$ **D** $\frac{1}{4}$

8 A circular window has an area of 50.24 square feet. What is the radius of the window? Use 3.14 as an approximation of π.

Explain Describe the method you used to solve the problem.

Safe Site

Internet Test Prep
Visit **www.eduplace.com/kids/mhm** for more *Test Prep Practice.*

Solid Figures

You will learn how to relate three-dimensional figures to two-dimensional figures.

New Vocabulary
solid figure
polyhedron
prism
pyramid
cylinder
cone
net

Learn About It

Most of the objects in the world around you are solid figures.

Solid Figures

Solid figures occupy a portion of space.

A **polyhedron** is a solid figure enclosed by polygons.

A **prism** is a polyhedron with two congruent parallel bases joined by rectangular faces.

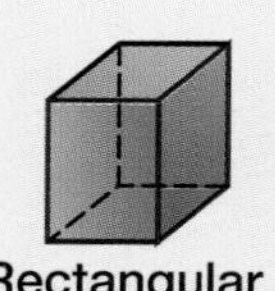
Rectangular prism

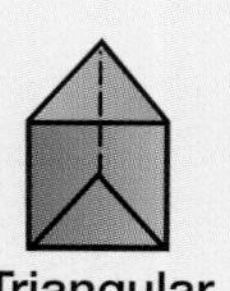
Triangular prism

A **pyramid** is a polyhedron whose base is a polygon and whose other faces are triangles that share a common vertex. A pyramid is named for the shape of its base.

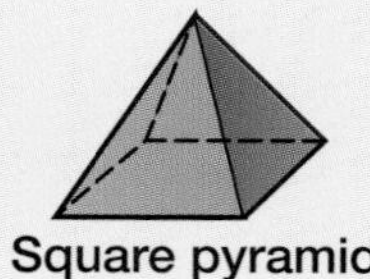
Square pyramid

Cylinders and **cones** are solid figures with curved surfaces. They are not polyhedra (plural of *polyhedron*). A cylinder has two congruent bases. A cone has only one base.

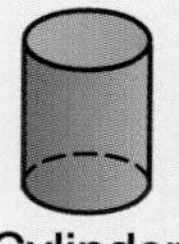
Cylinder

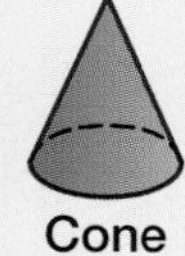
Cone

Parts of a Solid Figure

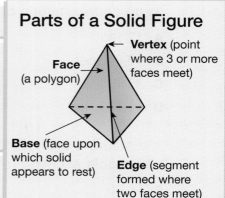

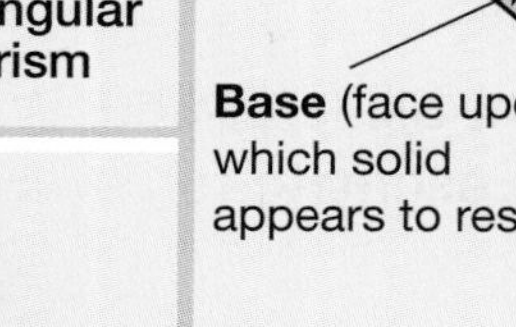

A **net** is a plane pattern that can be folded to make a solid figure.

Ali designs packaging for companies. She works with nets to develop her designs. What package shape has Ali designed?

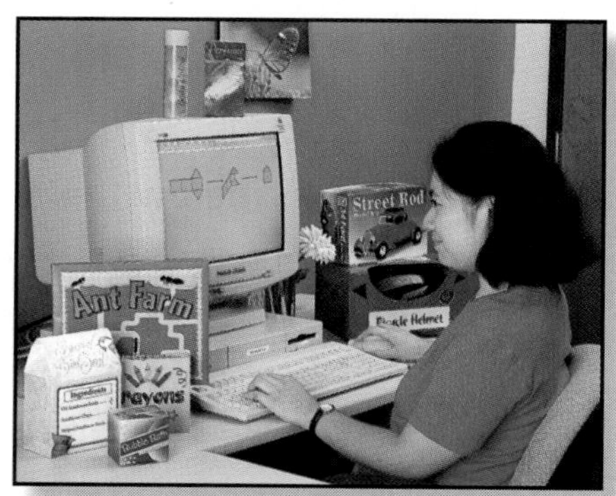

Find the package shape by visualizing Ali's net.

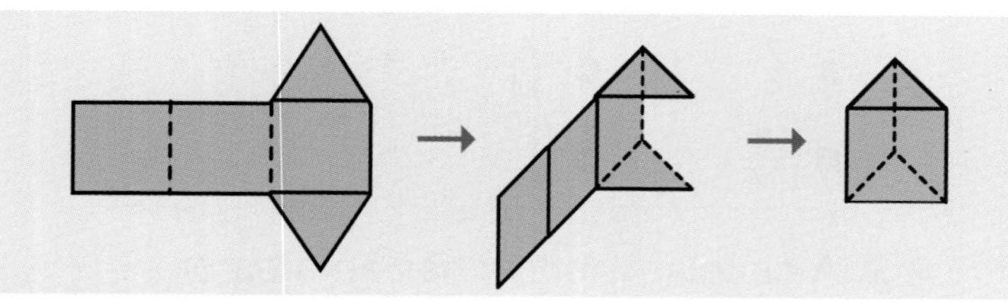

Solution: Ali has designed a triangular prism.

Another Example

Cylindrical Net

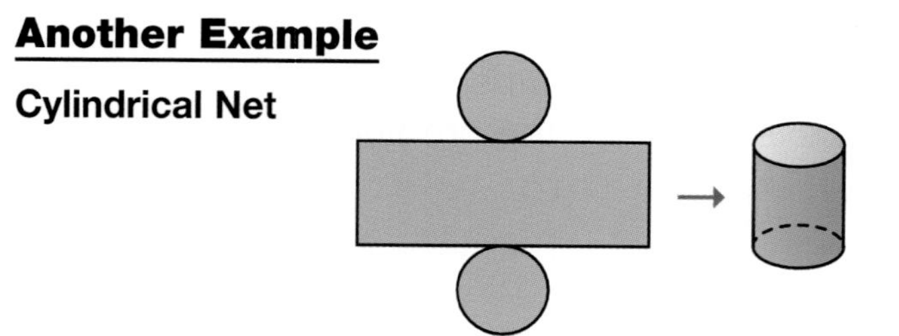

Explain Your Thinking

- ► Why does folding transform a net into a solid?
- ► The two bases of a solid figure are congruent pentagons. Which type of solid figure is this? How do you know?

Guided Practice

Draw a net for each solid figure or identify the solid figure each net represents.

1. 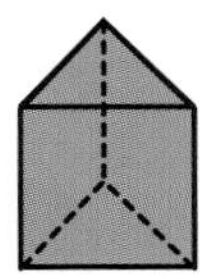

2. 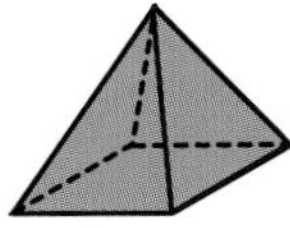

3. 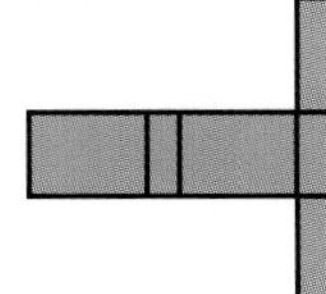

> **Ask Yourself**
>
> - Did I include all of the faces and bases in my net?

Independent Practice

Draw a net for each solid figure or identify the solid figure each net represents.

4. 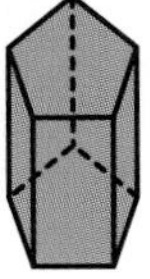

5. 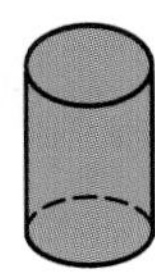

6. 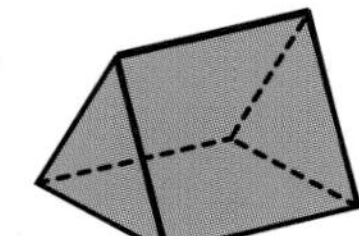

7. 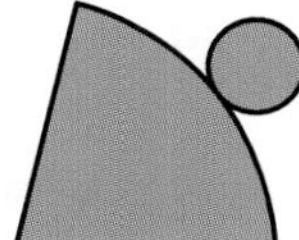

Problem Solving • Reasoning

Use Data **Use Figures A–D for Problem 9.**

8. Melissa and Melody were to make a net of a triangular pyramid. Melissa's net was made of 4 triangles. Melody's net was made of 2 triangles and 3 rectangles. Who made the correct net?

9. **Patterns** Make a chart listing the number of edges, faces, and vertices for each solid figure at the right. Write an equation to describe the relationship between the number of edges and the sum of the vertices and faces.

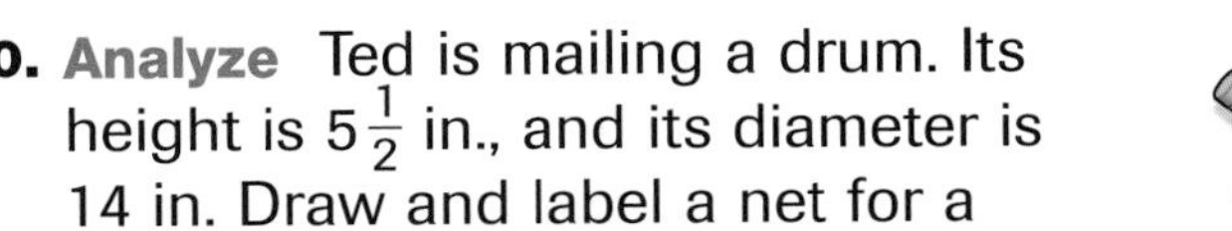

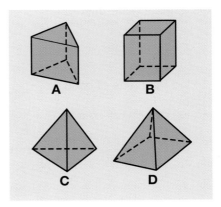

10. **Analyze** Ted is mailing a drum. Its height is $5\frac{1}{2}$ in., and its diameter is 14 in. Draw and label a net for a rectangular box to hold the drum.

11. **Write Your Own** Write a problem in which you draw a net. Then have a classmate identify the solid figure that the net represents.

Mixed Review • Test Prep

Multiply. Write each product in simplest form. *(pages 168–171)*

12. $\frac{4}{9} \times \frac{5}{6}$ **13.** $2\frac{1}{3} \times \frac{3}{4}$ **14.** $\frac{2}{5} \times 7$ **15.** $1\frac{1}{2} \times 2\frac{1}{4}$

16 Which is the correct expression for the difference between y and the sum of 3 and x? *(pages 270–271)*

A $y - (x + 3)$ **B** $y - 3 + x$ **C** $x + 3 + y$ **D** $y + 3 - x$

Extra Practice See Set F on page 483.

Surface Area

You will learn to find the surface area of a rectangular prism and a square pyramid.

New Vocabulary
surface area

Learn About It

Surface area (SA) is the sum of the areas of all the surfaces of a solid figure. José and Martin want to cover the mystery box they are making for the school carnival. The box is a rectangular prism with dimensions of (l) 18 inches, (w) 14 inches, and (h) 10 inches. To find the amount of paper they will need, José and Martin must find the surface area of the box.

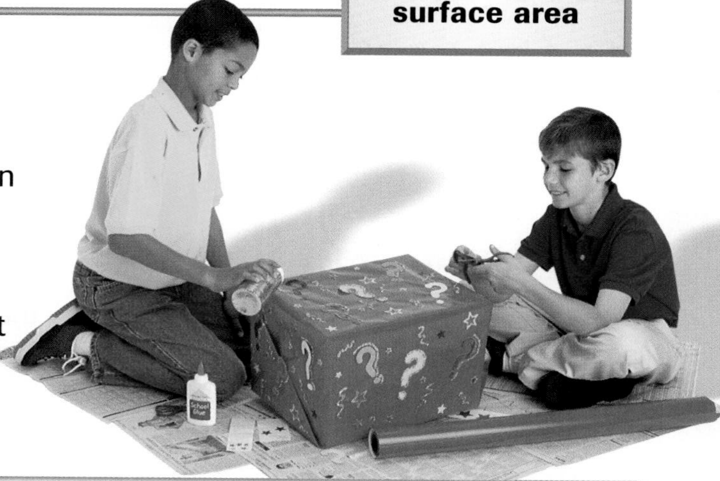

Find the surface area of the mystery box.

Step 1 Draw a diagram of the box and label its dimensions. The box is a rectangular prism.

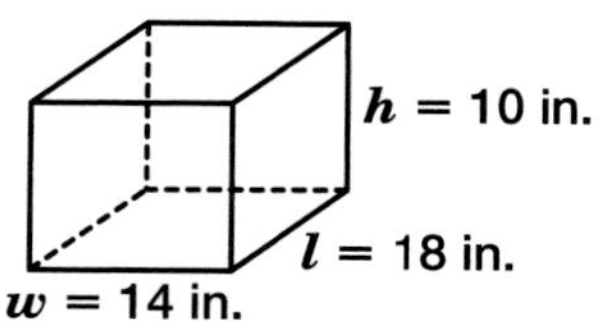

Step 2 Find the areas of each pair of opposite faces.

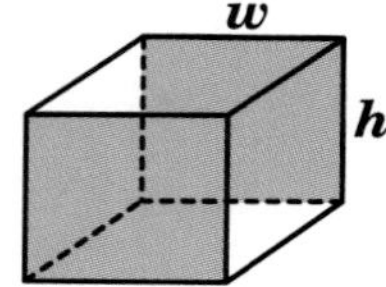

Front and Back

$A = 2wh$
$= 2(14 \text{ in.} \times 10 \text{ in.})$
$= 280 \text{ in.}^2$

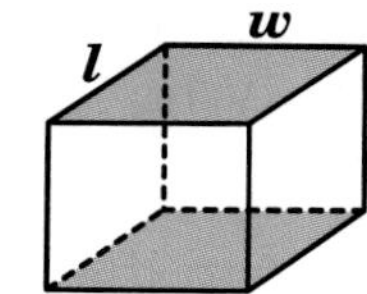

Top and Bottom

$A = 2lw$
$= 2(18 \text{ in.} \times 14 \text{ in.})$
$= 504 \text{ in.}^2$

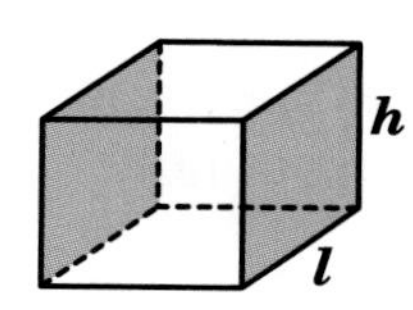

Two Sides

$A = 2lh$
$= 2(18 \text{ in.} \times 10 \text{ in.})$
$= 360 \text{ in.}^2$

Step 3 Find the total surface area of the rectangular prism.

$SA = 2wh + 2lw + 2lh$
$= 280 \text{ in.}^2 + 504 \text{ in.}^2 + 360 \text{ in.}^2$
$= 1{,}144 \text{ in.}^2$

Solution: The surface area of the box is 1,144 square inches.

Another Example

Surface Area of a Square Pyramid

SA = area of base + areas of triangular faces
$= s^2 + 4(\frac{1}{2}bh)$
$= (10 \times 10) + 4(\frac{1}{2} \times 10 \times 12)$
$= 340 \text{ cm}^2$

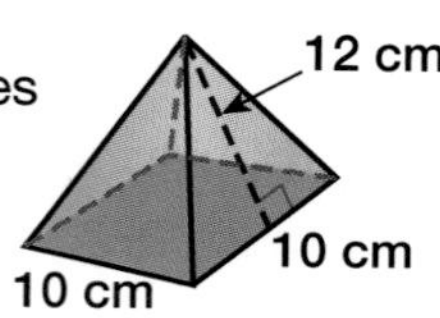

Explain Your Thinking

► How are finding the surface area of a rectangular prism and finding the surface area of a square pyramid alike?

Guided Practice

Find the surface area of each figure.

1. 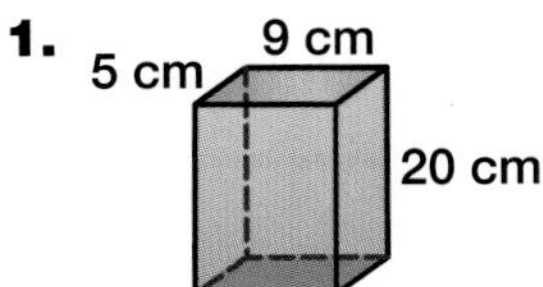

2.

3. 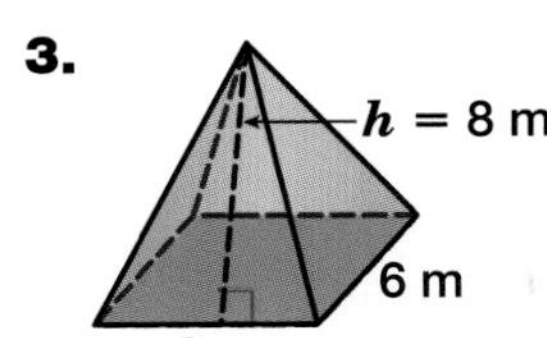

Ask Yourself

- Did I include the areas of all the surfaces?

Independent Practice

Find the surface area of each figure.

4. 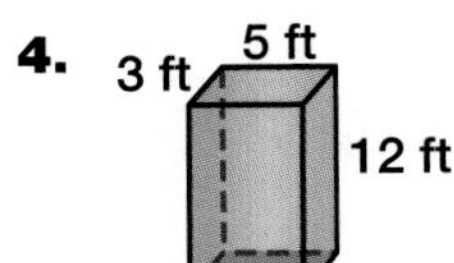

5. 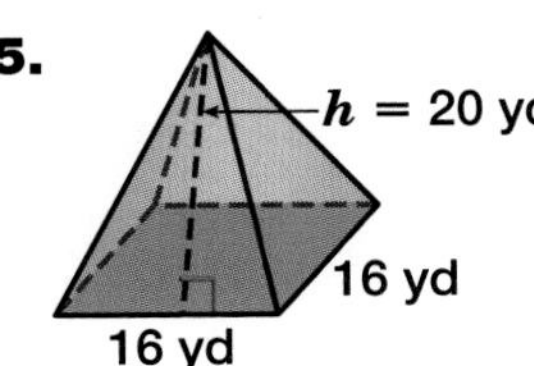

6. 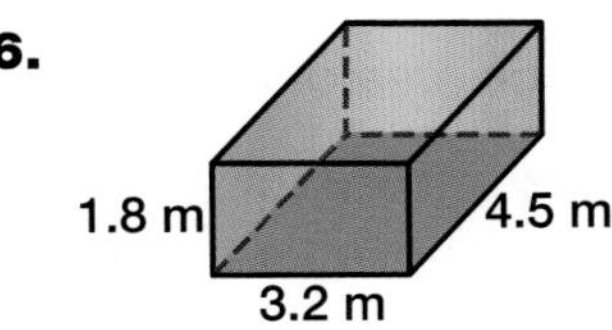

7. 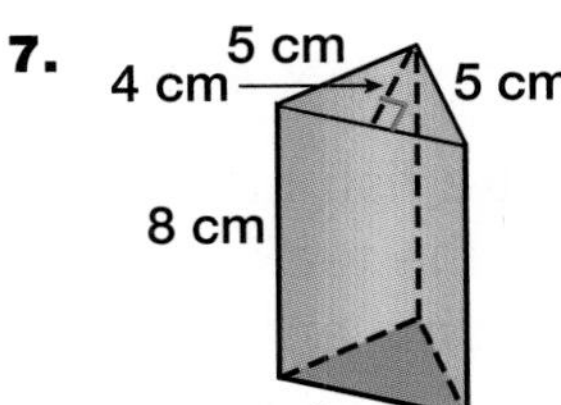

Algebra • Equations **Find each surface area.**

8. Suppose the edge of a number cube is *n* centimeters long. What is the surface area of the number cube?

9. If all of the dimensions of the cube in Problem 8 are doubled, what is the surface area of the new number cube?

Problem Solving • Reasoning

10. **Logical Thinking** Some 2-ft-wide cubes will be used in a carnival game. The class is painting the cubes bright colors. One can of paint will cover 200 ft^2. Each cube will need two coats of paint. How many cubes can be completely painted with one can of paint?

11. **Estimate** The edges of a square pyramid are each 7.89 cm. The perpendicular height of each triangular face is 6.83 cm. Estimate the surface area if the lengths of each edge and the height are tripled. Support your answer.

12. **Analyze** If a cube has a surface area of 24 square inches, what is the length of one edge?

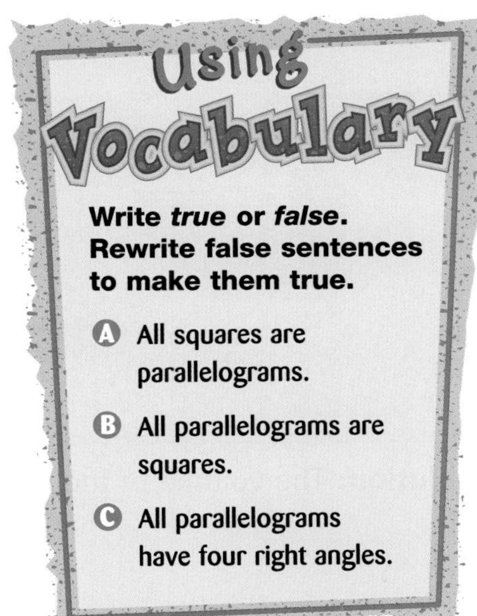

Write *true* or *false*. Rewrite false sentences to make them true.

A. All squares are parallelograms.

B. All parallelograms are squares.

C. All parallelograms have four right angles.

Mixed Review • Test Prep

Complete each expression. *(pages 252–254, 256–257)*

13. $\frac{3}{4} \times \frac{5}{3} = \frac{5}{3} \times$ ■

14. $(\frac{1}{2} + 4) + \frac{1}{3} =$ ■ $+ (4 +$ ■$)$

15. $9 +$ ■ $= 0$

16 What is the sale price of an $18.00 item that is 6% off? *(pages 370–371)*

A $16.85 **B** $16.92 **C** $17.20 **D** $19.08

Extra Practice See Set G on page 484.

Volume of Rectangular Prisms

You will learn how to find the volume of a rectangular prism.

New Vocabulary
volume
unit cube

Learn About It

The **volume** V of a solid figure is a measure of the space enclosed by the figure. Volume is measured in unit cubes. A **unit cube** is a cube with an edge length of 1. The formula for the volume of any rectangular prism is

V = length $\times$ width $\times$ height

$V = (l \times w) \times h = Bh$ since area of the base $B = l \times w$.

At a fish hatchery, Clark is surprised at the size of some of the tanks. He sees that the tanks are rectangular prisms and wonders how much water one of the smaller tanks holds. To find out, he needs to calculate the tank's volume. What is the volume of a rectangular prism with a length of 4 ft, a width of 4 ft, and a height of 3 ft?

Find the volume of the rectangular prism in cubic feet.

Step 1 Find the area of the base in square feet.

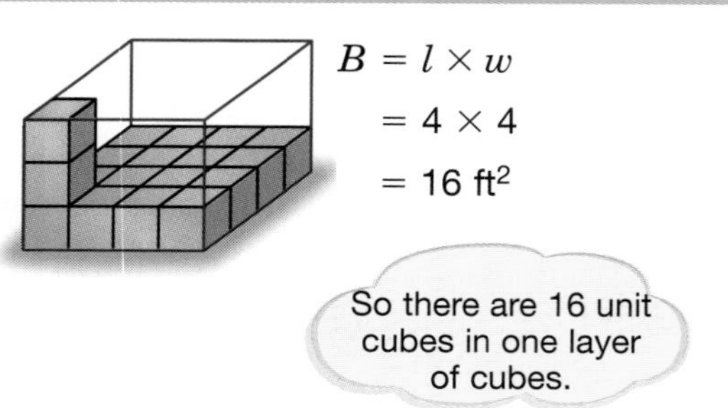

$B = l \times w$
$= 4 \times 4$
$= 16 \text{ ft}^2$

So there are 16 unit cubes in one layer of cubes.

Step 2 Find the total number of unit cubes in the rectangular prism. There are 3 layers of cubes with 16 cubes in each layer.

$V = Bh$
$= 16 \times 3$
$= 48 \text{ ft}^3$

This is the same as:
$V = lwh$
$= 4 \times 4 \times 3$
$= 48 \text{ ft}^3$

ft^3 means "cubic feet."

Solution: The volume of the rectangular prism is 48 ft^3.

Another Example

Volume of a Cube

$V = s \times s \times s = s^3$
$= 8 \times 8 \times 8$
$= 512 \text{ in.}^3$

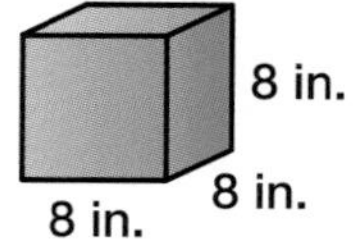

Explain Your Thinking

► Does it matter which dimension of a rectangular prism is used as the height? Explain why or why not?

Guided Practice

Find the volume of each rectangular prism.

1. 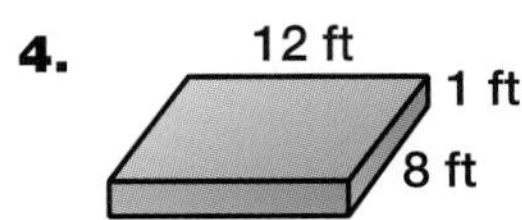

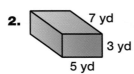

2. 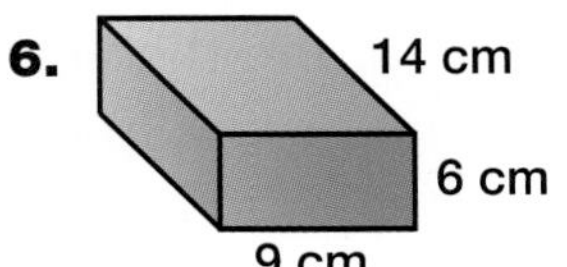

3. $l = 8$ ft
$w = 2$ ft
$h = 13$ ft

Ask Yourself

- Did I express my answer with the correct cubic units?

Independent Practice

Find the volume of each figure.

4. 12 ft, 1 ft, 8 ft

5. 12 ft, 12 ft, 12 ft

6. 14 cm, 6 cm, 9 cm

7. $l = 16$ cm
$w = 10$ cm
$h = 8$ cm

Algebra • Reasoning

8. What would happen to the volume V of a rectangular prism if the length l became $2l$ and w and h are unchanged?

9. What would happen to the volume V of a rectangular prism if l, w, and h become $3l$, $3w$, and $3h$?

Problem Solving • Reasoning

Solve. Choose a method.

Computation Methods

- Mental Math
- Estimation
- Paper and Pencil
- Calculator

10. A rectangular aquarium is 12 in. wide by 14 in. long by 12 in. high. What is the volume of water needed to fill the aquarium?

11. **Compare** Use a ratio to compare the volumes of a rectangular box of fish food that is 3 in. by 4 in. by 2 in. and a container that is 4 in. by 5 in. by 3 in.

12. **Estimate** A number cube has an edge of 5.89 centimeters. Estimate the volume of this number cube. About how much greater is this volume than the volume of a number cube with an edge of 4.22 centimeters?

13. **Logical Thinking** Candles in the shape of rectangular prisms are 4 in. by 4 in. by 15 in. tall. How many candles can you pack in a box with inside dimensions of 40 in. by 18 in. by 15 in. and still be able to close the lid?

Mixed Review • Test Prep

Write an equivalent ratio for each. *(pages 308–309)*

14. 12:3 **15.** $\frac{3}{4}$ **16.** 1 to 4 **17.** $\frac{5}{6}$ **18.** 15 to 3

19 Two of the angles in a triangle measure 27° and 50°. What is the measure of the third angle? *(pages 404–406)*

A 180° **B** 103° **C** 77° **D** 33°

Extra Practice See Set H on page 484.

Volumes of Other Solids

You will learn how to use formulas to find the volumes of other solids.

Learn About It

The prism at the right has a base as shown and a height of 3 cm. Each unit square of the base is 1 cm by 1 cm, so the area of the base is 10 cm^2. Each unit square in the base is also the base of a stack of 3 unit cubes. Therefore, the volume V of the prism is 30 cubic centimeters (30 cm^3).

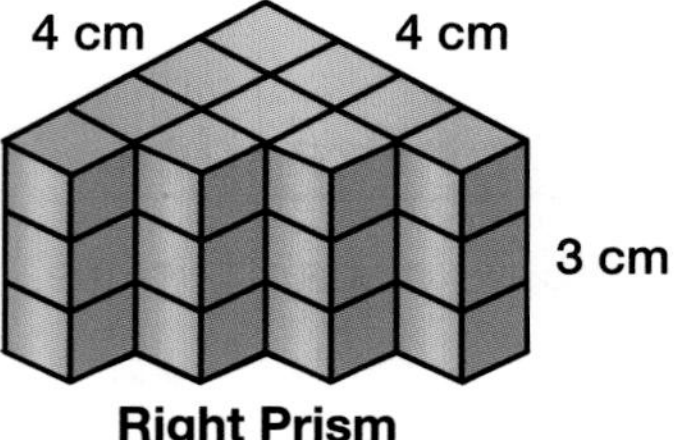

Right Prism

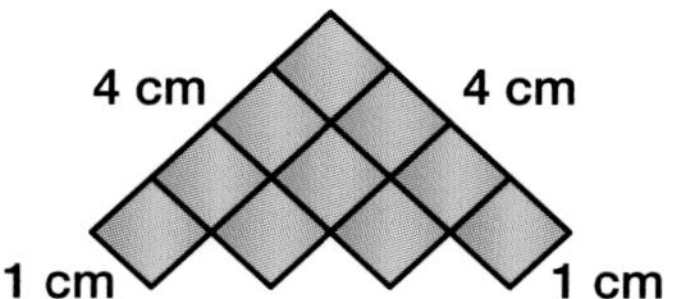

$$V = 10 \times 3 = 30 \text{ cm}^3$$

For solids like prisms and cylinders with congruent bases,

$$V = \text{area of base } (B) \times \text{height } (h)$$

Volumes of Triangular Prisms and Cylinders

Triangular Prism

V = area of base (B) × height

$= \frac{1}{2} bh_1 \times h_2$

$= \frac{1}{2} \times 12 \times 8 \times 10$

$V = 480$ m^3

Cylinder

V = the area of base (B) × height

$= \pi r^2 \times h$

$\approx 3.14 \times 4^2 \times 14$

$V \approx 703.36$ m^3

The formula for the volume of a pyramid or a cone is related to the formula for the volume of a prism or a cylinder.

$$V = \frac{1}{3} Bh$$

Volumes of Pyramids and Cones

Square Pyramid

$V = \frac{1}{3} \times$ area of base (B) × perpendicular height (h)

$= \frac{1}{3} \times s^2 \times h$

$= \frac{1}{3} \times 10 \times 10 \times 9$

$V = 300$ m^3

Cone

$V = \frac{1}{3} \times$ area of base (B) × perpendicular height (h)

$= \frac{1}{3} \times \pi r^2 \times h$

$\approx \frac{1}{3} \times 3.14 \times 6^2 \times 16$

$V = 602.88$ m^3

Explain Your Thinking

► What is similar about the formulas for volume of a triangular prism and volume of a cylinder? Compare these formulas to the formula for volume of a rectangular prism.

Guided Practice

Find the volume of each figure. Use 3.14 as an approximation of π.

1. 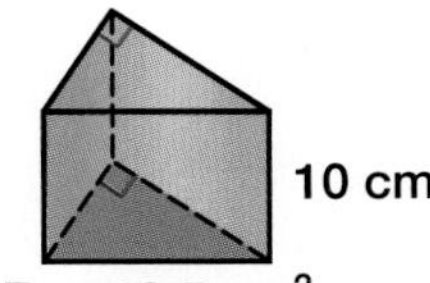

2. 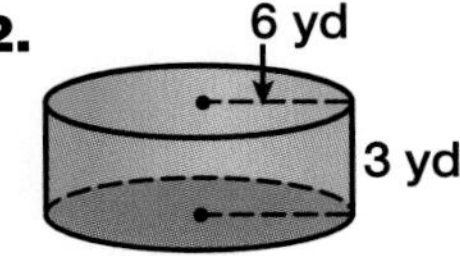

3. 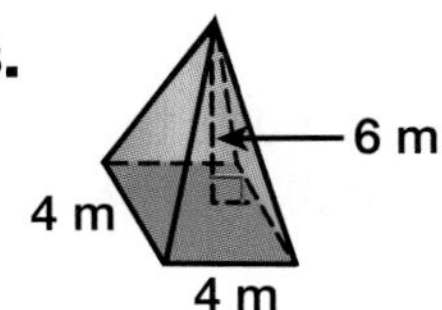

Ask Yourself

- Did I choose the correct formula?
- Did I find the area of the base first?

Independent Practice

Find the volume of each figure. Use 3.14 as an approximation of π.

4. 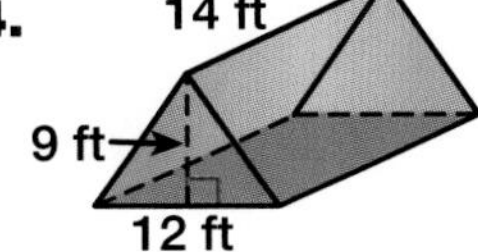

5. 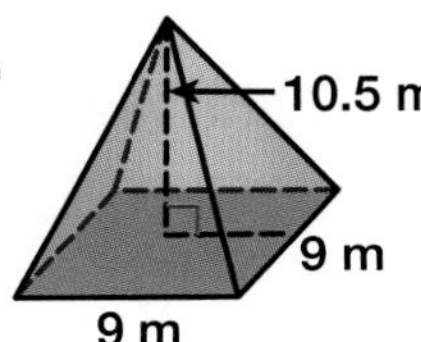

6. 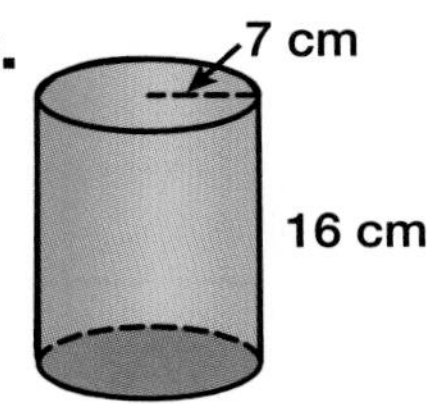

7. 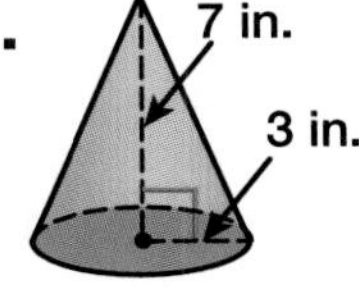

Problem Solving • Reasoning

8. Rose has a circle that is 10 inches in diameter. She uses it as the base for a cone with a height of 9 inches. Find the volume of the cone.

9. **Analyze** A square pyramid has a volume of 1,200 cm^3. If the base has sides 15 cm in length, what is the height of the pyramid?

10. **Write About It** Carlos has a rectangular bar of modeling clay. How would he cut the clay to form two congruent triangular prisms? What would the relationship of the volume of each triangular prism to the rectangular prism be? Explain your answer.

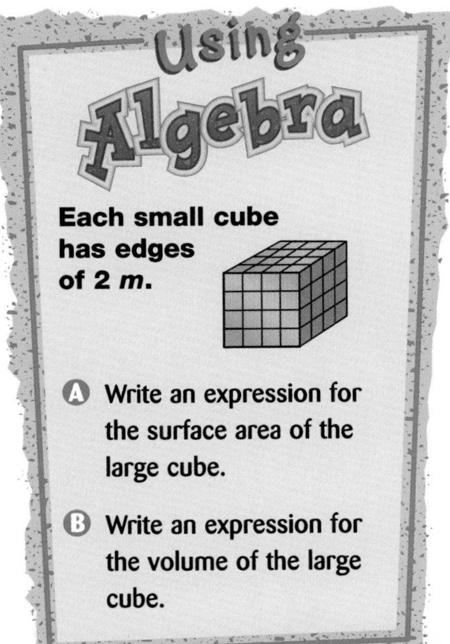

Using Algebra
Each small cube has edges of 2 m.
A Write an expression for the surface area of the large cube.
B Write an expression for the volume of the large cube.

Mixed Review • Test Prep

Subtract. *(pages 12–13, 218–220)*

11. $^{+}6 - {}^{-}5$ **12.** $^{-}8 - {}^{+}3$ **13.** 209,001 − 99,871

14 What is the LCM of 12 and 18? *(pages 116–117)*

A 6 **B** 36 **C** 108 **D** 336

Extra Practice See Set I on page 484.

Problem-Solving Application: Use a Formula

You will learn how to use a formula to solve a problem.

You often need to use formulas to solve problems.

Kurt is helping his father paint the silo on their farm. The silo's top is a circular dome with a diameter of 10 ft. The silo is 30 ft tall. The silo will be painted red. The dome will not be painted. What is the area that Kurt and his father will paint red?

Understand

What is the question?
What is the area Kurt and his father will paint red?

What do you know?
- the dimensions of the silo
- the formulas for circumference and area

Plan

What can you do to find the answer?
Draw a diagram of the silo and label its dimensions. Find the area of its curved surface.

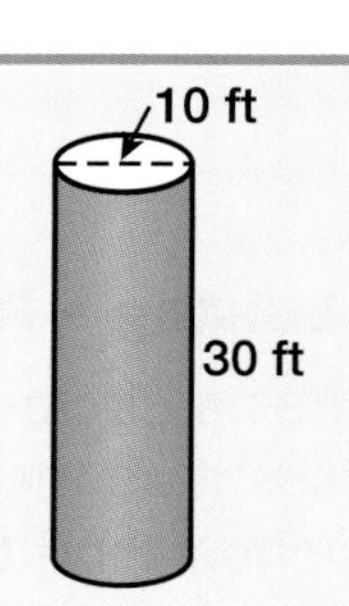

Think: If I make a net to represent the silo, the curved surface becomes a rectangle with a base equal to the silo's circumference (πd) and a height equal to the silo's height (30 feet).

Remember:
Kurt will not paint the top or bottom of the silo.

Solve

Area of Curved Surface (Lateral Area)

A = circumference of the base × height

$= \pi dh$

$A \approx 3.14 \times 10 \times 30$ or 942 ft^2

The area to be painted red is about 942 ft^2.

Look Back

Look back at the question. Is your answer reasonable?
How can you use estimation to check your answer?

On some farms, all members of the family learn to complete various chores.

Guided Practice

Solve by applying a new formula.

1. Kurt's mother built a feed box for the cattle. The feed box is a rectangular prism and holds 45 cubic feet of feed. It is 10 feet long and 3 feet wide. What is the height of the feed box?

   Think: Should I use the formula for surface area or volume?

2. Kurt's sister Samantha painted the outside of the feed box mentioned in Problem 1. She painted the outside of each side and the bottom of the box. Find the area she painted.

   Think: Do I want to find the surface area or volume?

Choose a Strategy

Solve. Use these or other strategies. If there is not enough information to solve, tell what information is missing.

Problem-Solving Strategies

- **Write an Equation**
- **Use Logical Thinking**
- **Draw a Diagram**
- **Find a Pattern**

3. Kurt's family is buying a heater for the barn. The heating company needs to know the volume of air that must be heated. If the barn is 120 feet long, 70 feet wide, and 30 feet tall, estimate the volume of air in the building.

4. Kurt's father is drilling holes in the ground for a windmill. One hole is to be 3 meters deep and have a radius of 0.5 meters. Kurt must remove the earth from the hole. Find the volume of the earth that Kurt must remove.

5. A cardboard box holds one piece of a pie. The box is a triangular prism that is $1\frac{1}{2}$ inches high. The base of the prism is an isosceles triangle with a base of 3 inches and a height of 4 inches. Find the volume of the box.

6. The formula for the area of a trapezoid is $A = \frac{1}{2}h(b_1 + b_2)$. The height of the trapezoid is h, and b_1 and b_2 are the lengths of the bases. Find the area of a trapezoid with a height of 6 meters and bases of 14 meters and 16 meters.

7. Diana is constructing several cones to protect tomato plants from the cold. If the height of each cone is 2.4 feet, what is the volume of each cone?

8. At the right is the plan for a garden. Find the area of the garden.

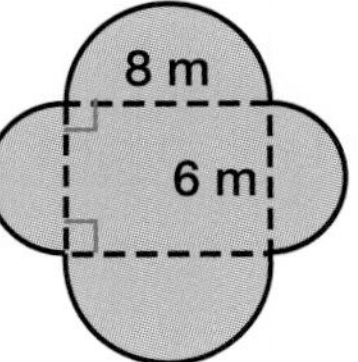

Extra Practice See 9–11 on page 485.

Quick Check

Check Your Understanding of Lessons 8–12

Draw a net for each solid figure or identify the solid figure each net represents.

1. 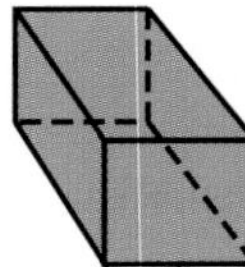

2. 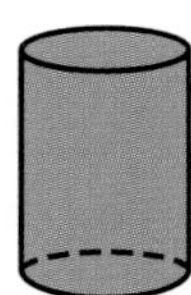

3. 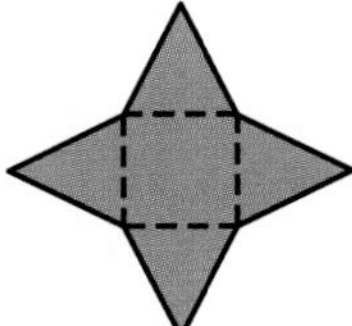

Find the surface area and volume of each figure.

4. 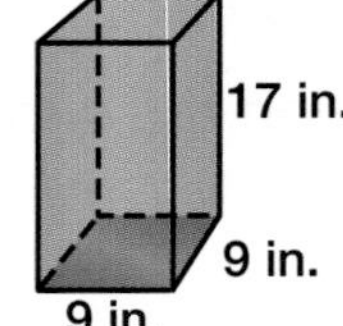

5. 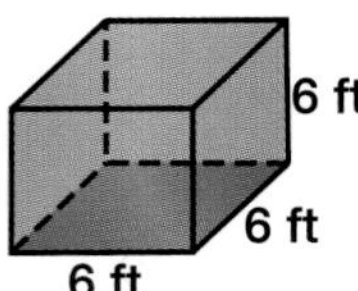

6. 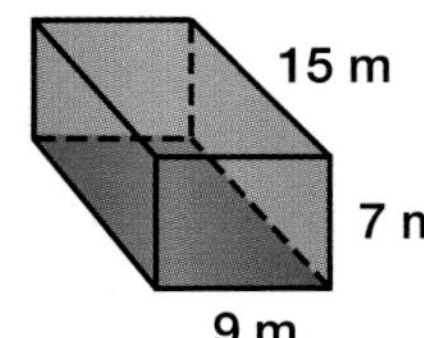

Find the volume of each figure. Use 3.14 or $\frac{22}{7}$ for π.

7. 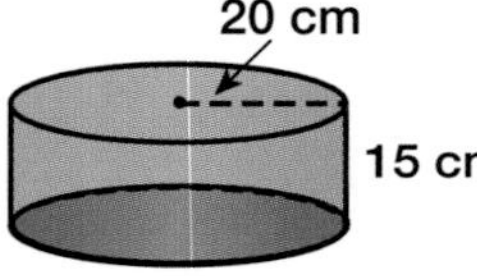

8. 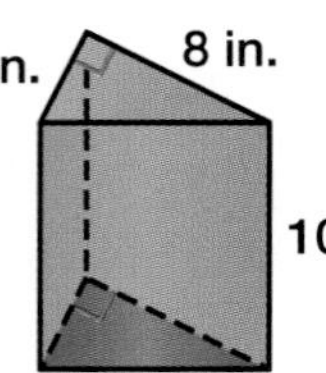

9. 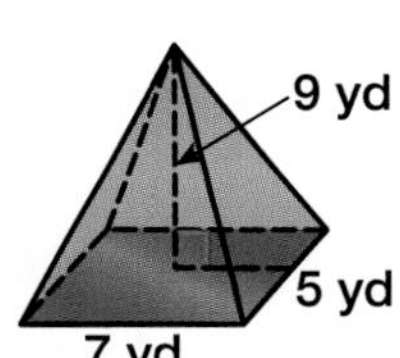

10. 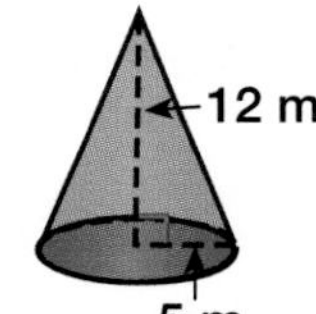

11. A cylindrical paper cup has a radius of 2 inches and a height of 5 inches. How many times can this cup be filled from a cone-shaped paper cup with a height of 3 inches and a diameter of 4 inches?

How did you do?

If you had difficulty with any items in the Quick Check, you can use the following pages for review and extra practice.

Items	Review These Pages	Do These Extra Practice Items
1–3	pages 470–471	Set F, page 483
4–6	pages 472–475	Sets G and H, page 484
7–10	pages 476–477	Set I, page 484
11	pages 478–479	9–11, page 485

Test Prep • Cumulative Review

Maintaining the Standards

Choose the letter of the correct answer.

1. Chantal bought 2 shirts that cost \$15 each. There was an 8.5% sales tax on her purchase. What was the total cost of Chantal's purchase?

   A \$16.28
   B \$30.00
   C \$32.55
   D \$55.50

2. What is the length of $\overline{XZ}$?

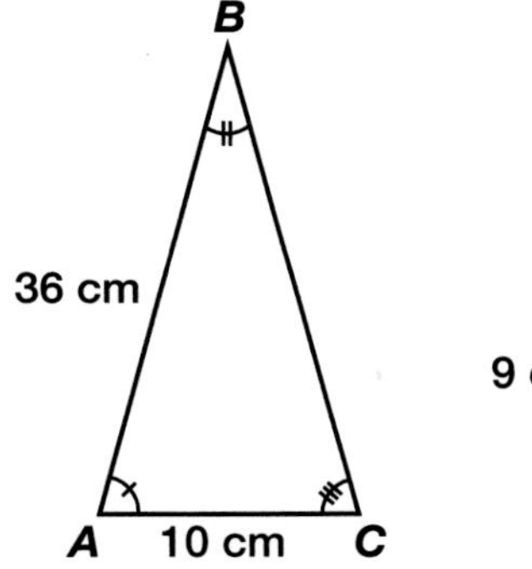

$\triangle ABC \sim \triangle XYZ$

   F 1 centimeter
   G 2.5 centimeters
   H 32.4 centimeters
   J 40 centimeters

3. Shannon bought $7\frac{1}{3}$ yards of cloth. She gave Andrea $\frac{3}{4}$ yard. How much cloth does Shannon have left?

   A $3\frac{1}{3}$ yards
   B $6\frac{5}{12}$ yards
   C $6\frac{7}{12}$ yards
   D $8\frac{1}{12}$ yards

4. What is the value of r in this equation?

$$r + 195 = 276$$

   F 1.4
   G 81
   H 90
   J 471

5. Each of 50 problems on a history test is worth 2 points. There are two extra-credit problems, each worth 1 point. What is Jared's test score if he misses three problems but answers one extra-credit problem correctly?

   A 99
   B 95
   C 93
   D 91

6. What is the measure in degrees of $\angle n$?

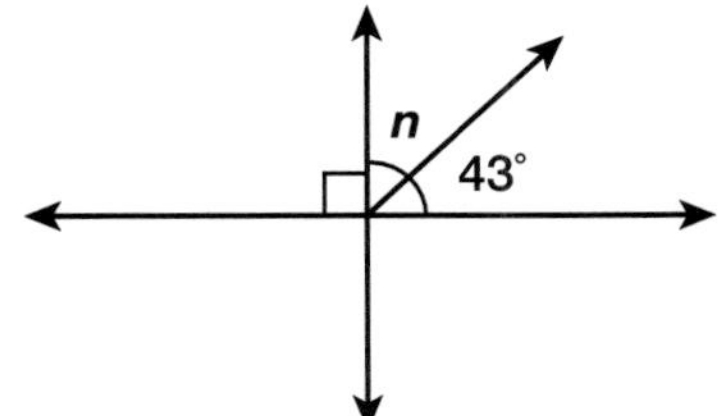

   F 43° **H** 90°
   G 47° **J** 137°

7. Order these numbers from least to greatest.

$$0.6 \quad \frac{65}{100} \quad 7.8 \quad 3\frac{1}{2} \quad 3.4$$

   Explain What method did you use? Tell why.

Internet Test Prep
Visit **www.eduplace.com/kids/mhm** for more *Test Prep Practice.*

Extra Practice

Set A (Lesson 1, pages 450–451)

Find the perimeter and area of each rectangle.

1. 6 ft; 20 ft

2. l = 15 in.
w = 7 in.

3. l = 11 m
w = 18 m

Find the perimeter and area of each figure.

4.

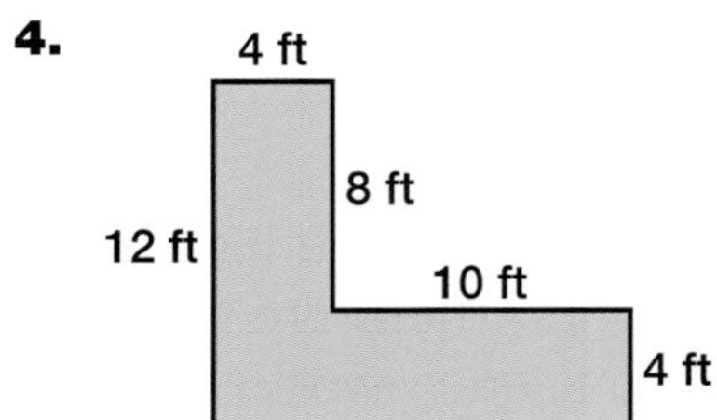

5. 7 m; 6 m; 15 m; 9 m; 6 m

6.

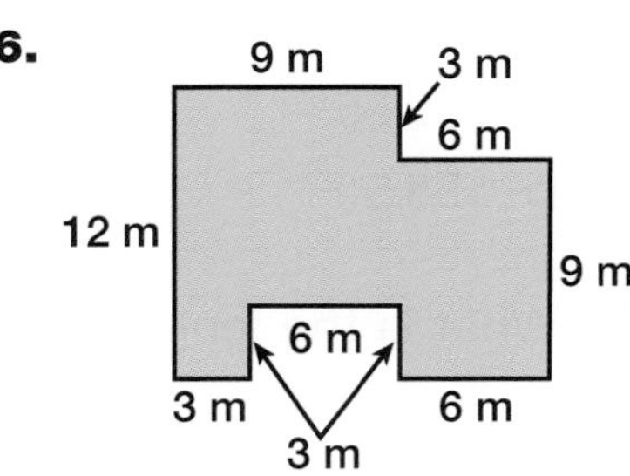

Set B (Lesson 2, pages 452–453)

Find the area of each parallelogram.

1. 14 ft; 8 ft; 6 ft

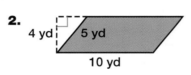

2. 4 yd; 5 yd; 10 yd

3. 17 m; 21 m

4. b = 19 in.
h = 8 in.

5. b = 15 ft
h = 8 ft

6. b = 12 cm
h = 15 cm

Set C (Lesson 3, pages 454–455)

Find the area of each triangle.

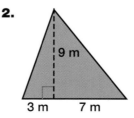

1. 30 ft; 24 ft; 18 ft

2. 9 m; 3 m; 7 m

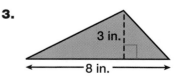

3. 3 in.; 8 in.

4. b = 10 m
h = 7 m

5. b = 8 ft
h = 7 ft

6. b = 14 in.
h = 15 in.

Extra Practice

Set D (Lesson 5, pages 460–463)

Find the circumference or missing measure for each circle. Use 3.14 or $\frac{22}{7}$ for π.

1. 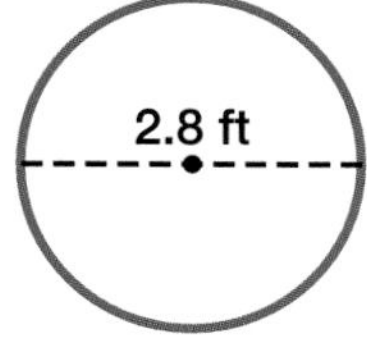

2. 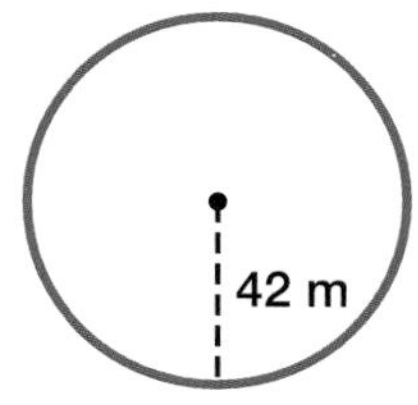

3. 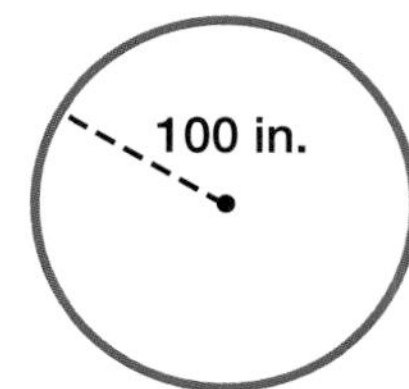

4. $d = 6.5$ ft
$C \approx$ ■

5. $r \approx$ ■
$C = 25.12$ in.

6. $d \approx$ ■
$C = 44$ ft

Set E (Lesson 6, pages 464–465)

Find the area of each figure. Use 3.14 or $\frac{22}{7}$ for π.

1. 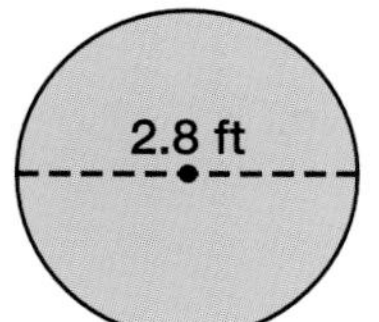

2. 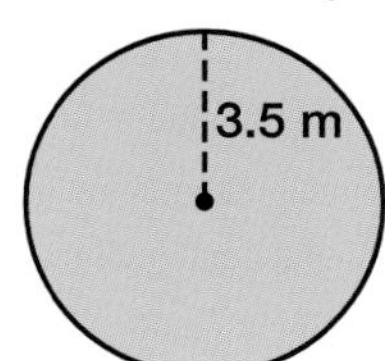

3. 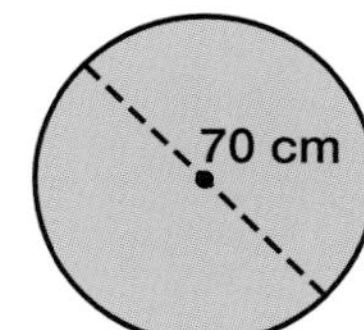

4. 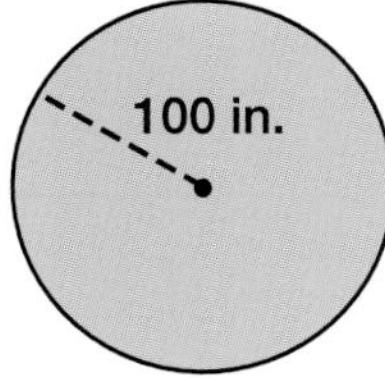

5. 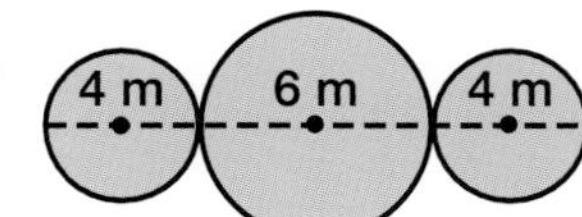

6. 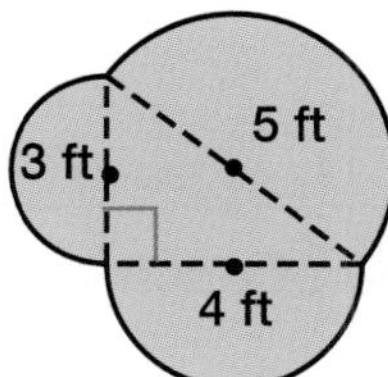

Set F (Lesson 8, pages 470–471)

Draw a net for each solid figure or identify what solid figure each net represents.

1. 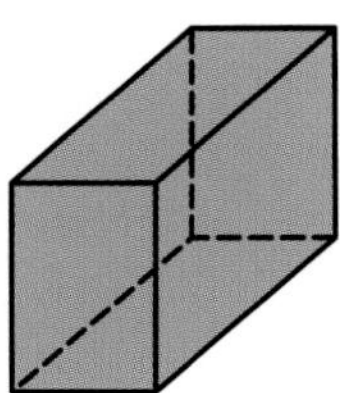

2. 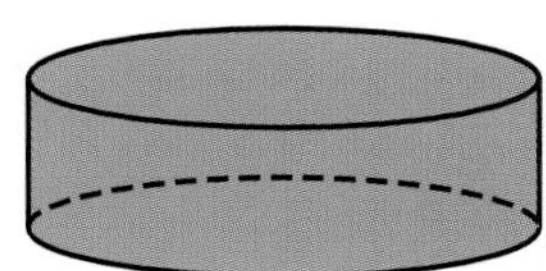

3. 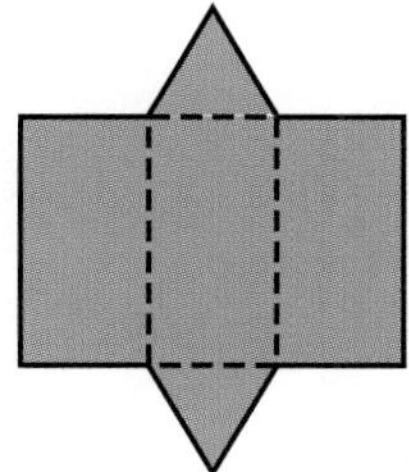

Extra Practice

Set G (Lesson 9, pages 472–473)

Find the surface area of each figure.

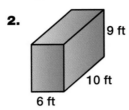

1. 10 ft, 25 ft, 10 ft

2. 9 ft, 10 ft, 6 ft

3. 8 in., 8 in., 8 in.

4. A rectangular prism with a length of 20 in., a width of 40 in., and a height of 10 in.

Set H (Lesson 10, pages 474–475)

Find the volume of each figure.

1. 10 ft, 25 ft, 10 ft

2. 9 ft, 10 ft, 6 ft

3.

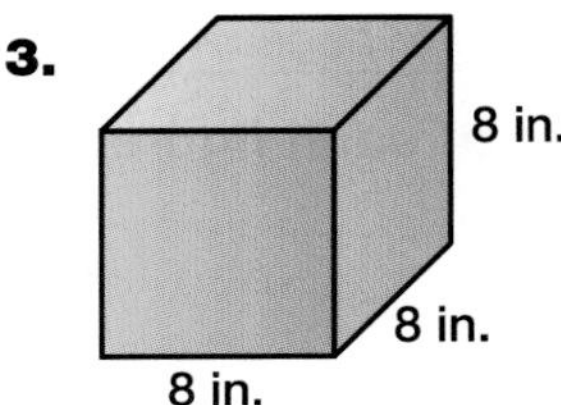

4. A cube with edges of 10 ft.

5. A cube with edges of 100 ft.

Set I (Lesson 11, pages 476–477)

Find the volume of each figure. Use 3.14 for π.

1.

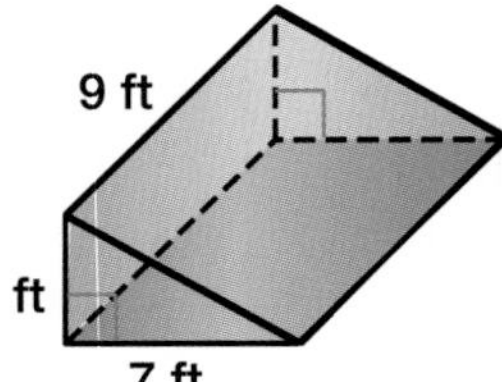

2.

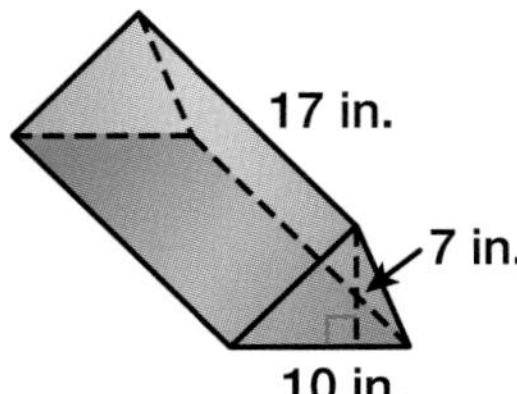

3.

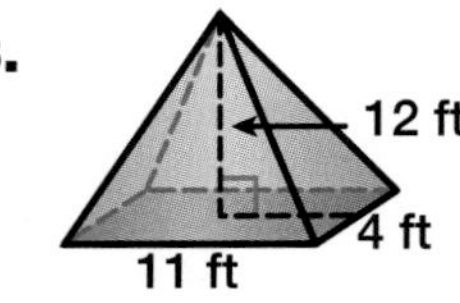

4.

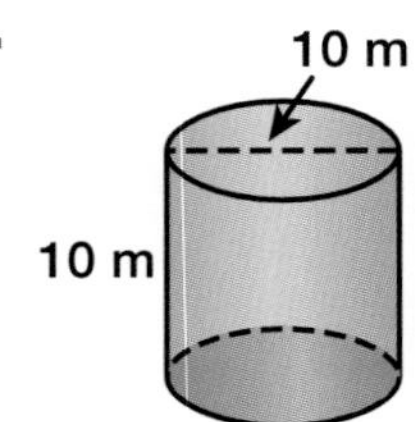

5.

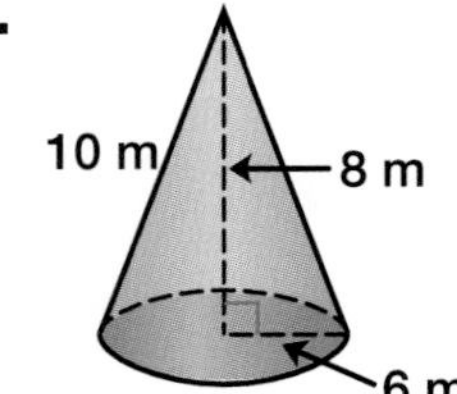

6.

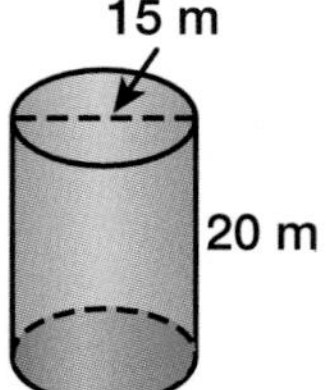

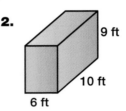

Extra Practice • Problem Solving

Solve each problem. If there is not enough information to solve, tell what is missing. *(Lesson 4, pages 456–457)*

1. Rafael has a rectangular map. The map is folded into 4 congruent rectangles, each with a length of 5 in. and a width of 3 in. Find the area of the original unfolded map.

2. Leah plans to put a border around a rectangular bulletin board that is 3 feet long and 2.5 feet wide. The border costs $0.59 per foot. How much will the border cost?

3. Irene is making a flag in the shape of a parallelogram. Two sides are 5 yards long. The other two sides are 14 yards long. Find the area of the flag that Irene is making.

4. Clarence made a triangular mirror with an area of 48 square inches. The base of the mirror is 8 inches long. What is the height of the mirror that Clarence made?

Solve. Use any problem-solving strategies you have learned. *(Lesson 7, pages 466–467)*

5. Erica's basketball team made a square poster 5 feet by 5 feet. On the poster, they drew a basketball with a diameter of 2 feet. What area of the poster is not covered by the drawing of the basketball?

6. Theo made a drawing of a traffic light as a prop for the school play. The drawing had a row of three circles inside a rectangle. What was the smallest area the rectangle could have been if each circle has a diameter of 5 inches?

7. Tori is walking around a circular track with a diameter of 140 feet. How many feet will Tori walk if she walks around the track 5 times?

8. A circular window in the state capitol building has a circumference of 25.12 feet. Find the diameter and area of the window.

Solve. Use a formula. *(Lesson 12, pages 478–479)*

9. Mrs. Froelich's sixth-grade class is planning to build a large square pyramid. The base of the pyramid will have sides of 12 feet. The height of the pyramid will be 8 feet. Find the volume of the pyramid that the class plans to build.

10. Deep River Nursery built a greenhouse in the shape of a rectangular prism. The greenhouse has a width of 7 feet and a length of 20 feet. The volume of the greenhouse is 1,400 cubic feet. What is the height of the greenhouse?

11. Deep River Nursery stores seedling plants in a greenhouse shaped like the figure at the right. The base of a triangle is 11 feet, and its height is 8 feet. The height of the greenhouse is 12 feet. What is the volume of the greenhouse?

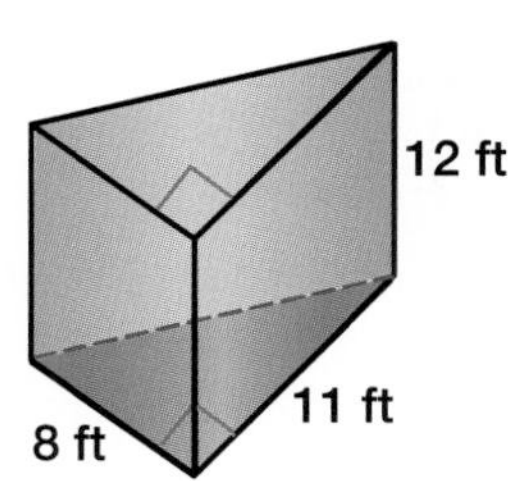

Chapter Review

Reviewing Vocabulary

Match each word with the proper definition.

1. **perimeter** — **A** the amount of space enclosed by a solid figure
2. **area** — **B** the distance around a plane figure
3. **circumference** — **C** area of the surface of a solid figure
4. **surface area** — **D** the distance around a circle
5. **volume** — **E** the number of square units a figure contains

Use one of the following terms to identify each figure: *cylinder, prism, cone, pyramid.* *(pages 470-471)*

6. 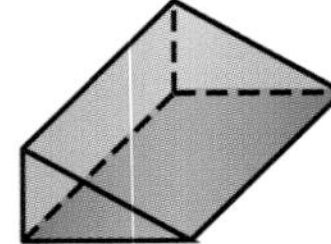

7. 

8. 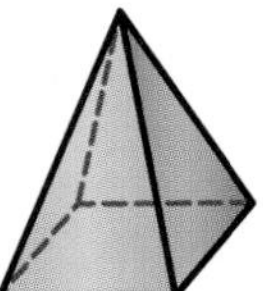

9. 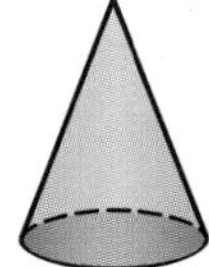

Reviewing Concepts and Skills

Find the perimeter and area of each figure. *(pages 450-451, 452-453, 454-455)*

10. 3.5 cm, 5 cm

11. 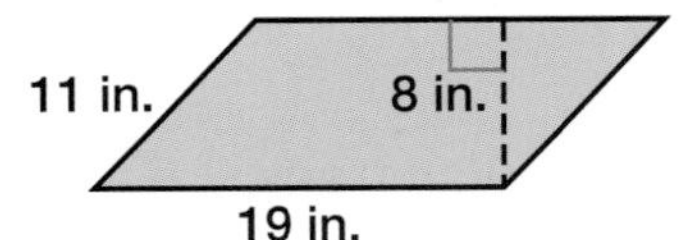

12. 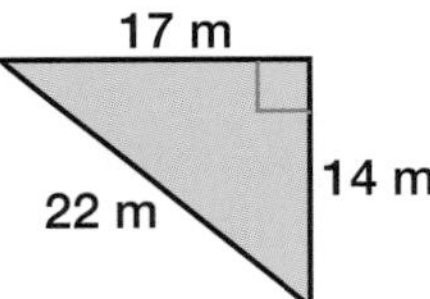

Find the area of each figure. *(pages 450-451, 452-453, 454-455)*

13. 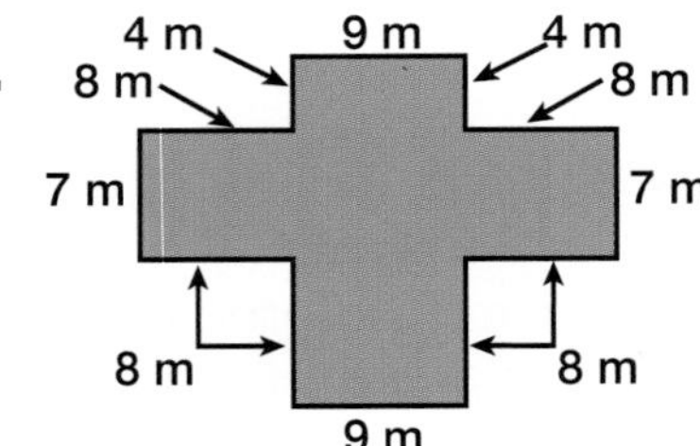

14. 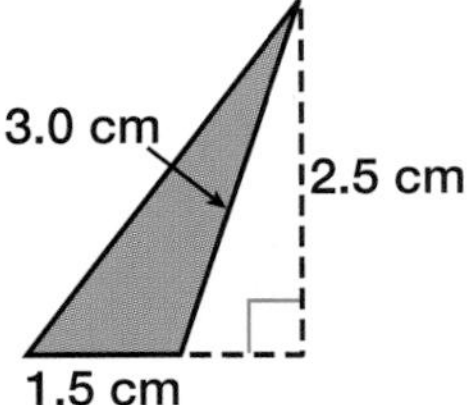

15. 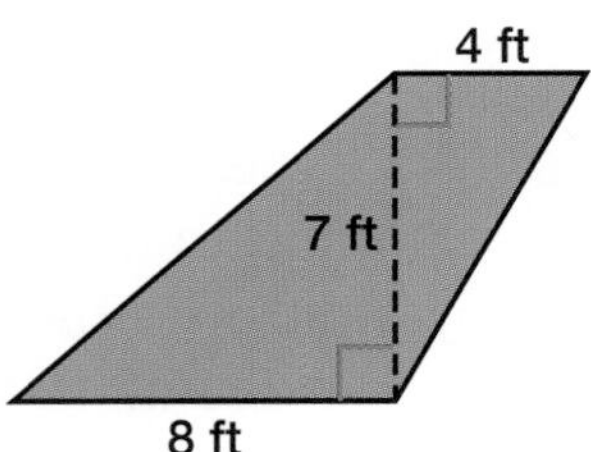

Find the missing measure of each circle. Use 3.14 for π. *(pages 460-462)*

16. 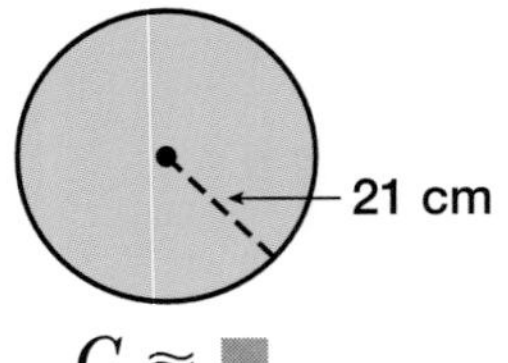

$C \approx$ ■

17. $d \approx$ ■

$C = 62.8$ in.

18. $r \approx$ ■

$C = 31.4$ m

Find the area. Use 3.14 for π. *(pages 464-465)*

19. 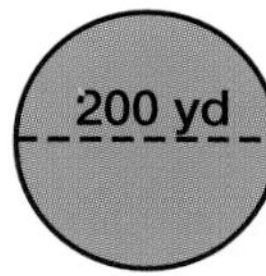

20. 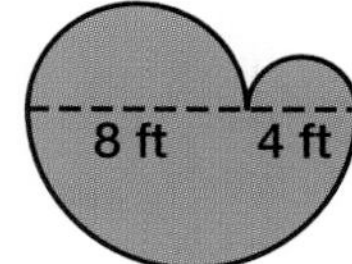

21. 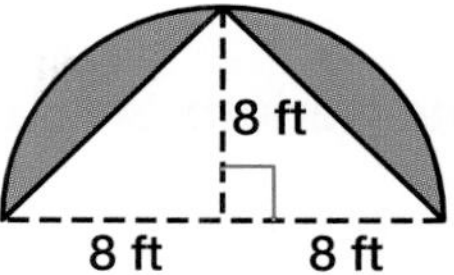

Draw a net for each figure. Then find the surface area. *(pages 470-471, 472-473)*

22. 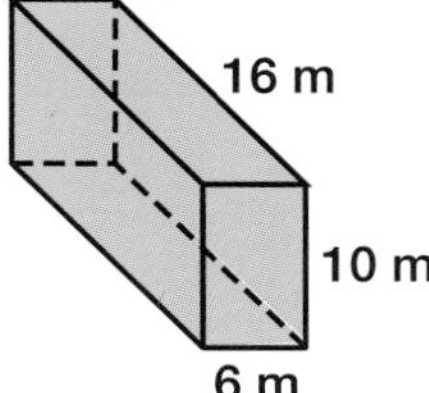

23. 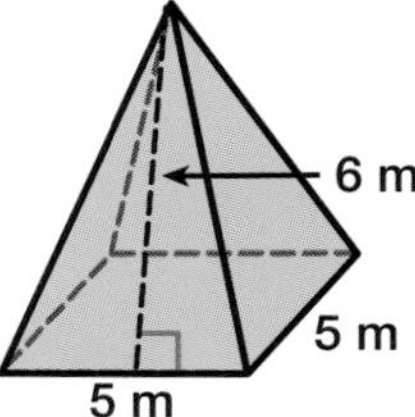

24. 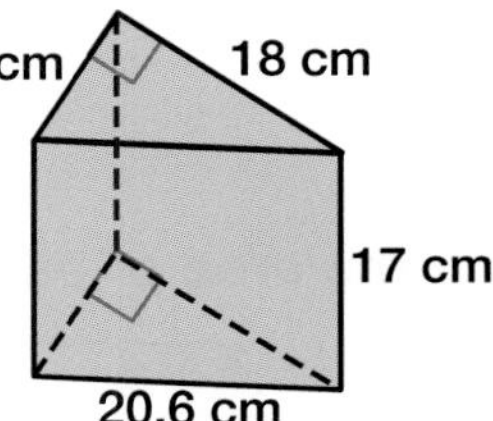

Find the volume of each figure. Use 3.14 for π. *(pages 474-475, 476-477)*

25. 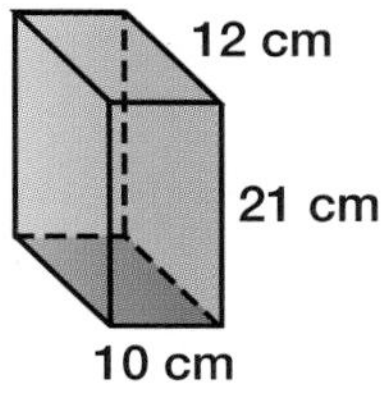

26. 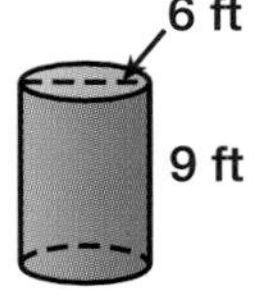

27. 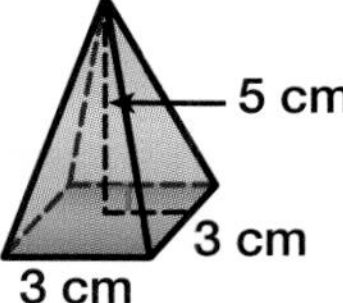

Solve. *(pages 456-457, 466-467, 478-479)*

28. The length of a rectangle is 3 times its width. Its area is 108 m^2. Find the length and width or explain what additional information is needed to find them.

29. Bert is analyzing a painting that shows an 8 in. blue circle within a 10 in. red circle. Write a formula that shows how to find the area that is red. Then find the area that is red.

30. Jan wants to make some concrete rectangular prisms to use in a garden sculpture. The cast she will use measures 6 ft by 10 ft by 8 ft. What volume of concrete will Jan need to cast four prisms?

Brain Teasers Math Reasoning

Similar Circles?

The circumference of one circle is 9 times the circumference of another. What must be true about the diameters?

Simply Double?

Two cones of equal height have bases with diameters x and $2x$. How will the volumes of the two cones compare?

Internet Brain Teasers
Visit **www.eduplace.com/kids/mhm** for more *Brain Teasers.*

Chapter Test

Find the perimeter and area of each figure.

1. Rectangle *ABCD*
   $l = 8.5$ yd
   $w = 3.4$ yd

2. 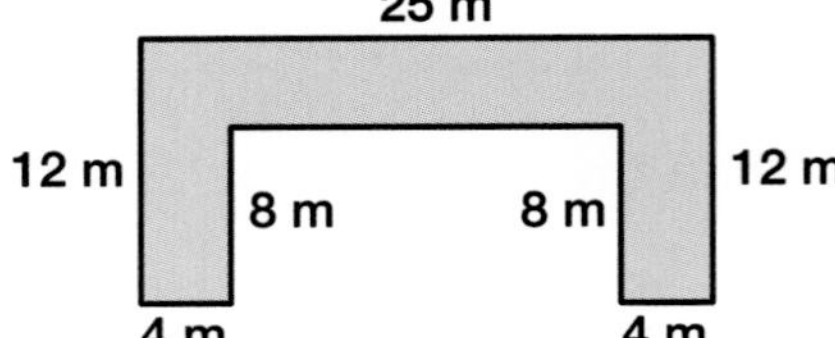

3. 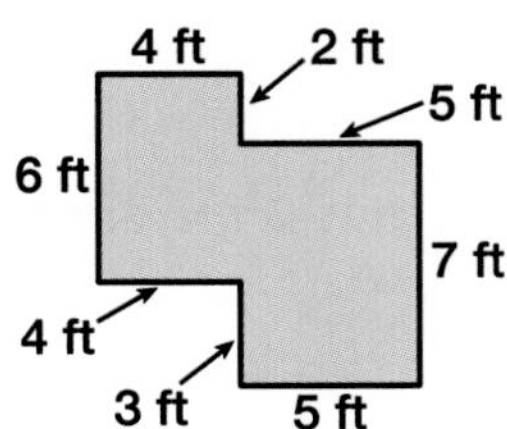

Find the area of each figure.

4. 9 cm, 7 cm, 18 cm

5. 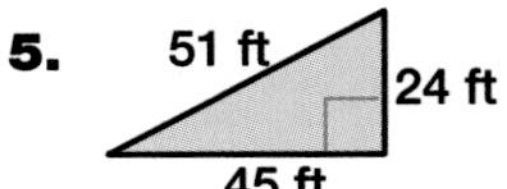

6. 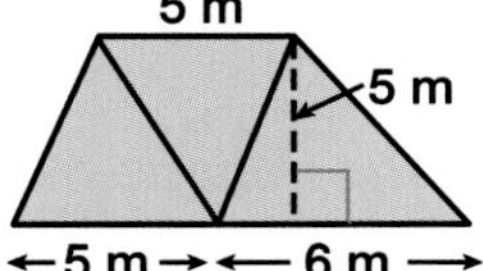

Find the missing measure for each circle. Use 3.14 for π.

7. $r = 3.2$ m
   $C \approx$ ■

8. $d \approx$ ■
   $C = 131.88$ cm

9. $r \approx$ ■
   $C = 75.36$ in.

Find the area of each figure. Use 3.14 for π.

10. 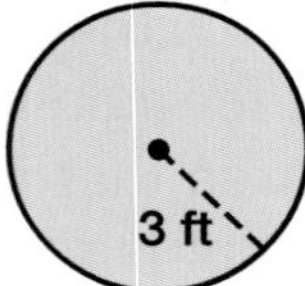

11. 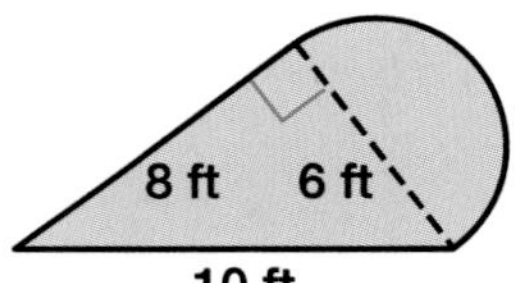

Make a net for each figure. Then find the surface area. Use 3.14 for π.

12. 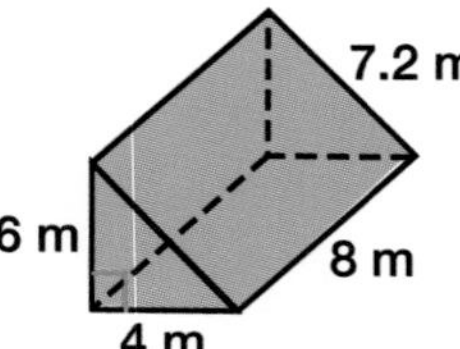

13. 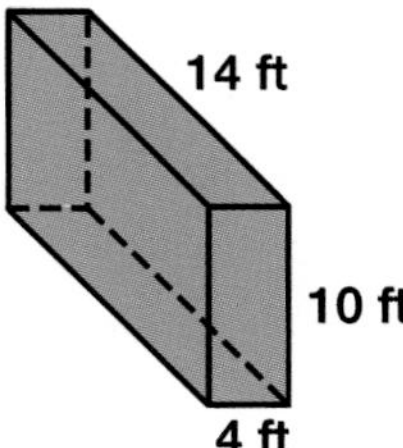

14. 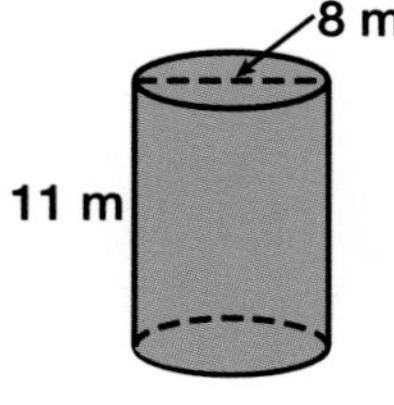

Find the volume of each figure.

15. 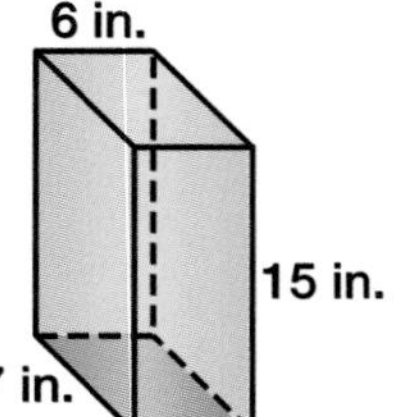

16. 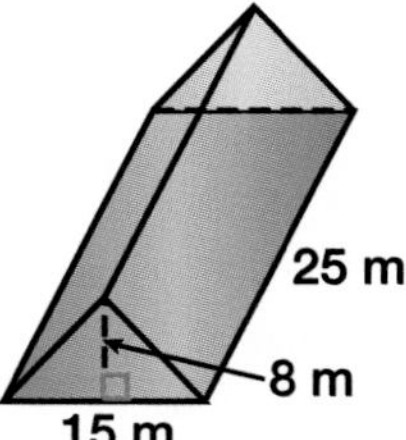

17. 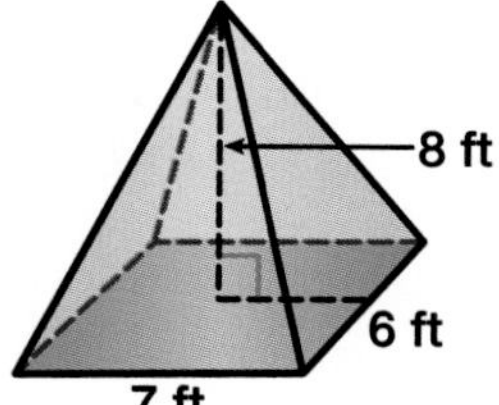

18. A group of students in Mrs. Figueroa's math class decides to bury a time capsule. The capsule is in the shape of a cylinder with a radius of 1.5 ft and a height of 5 ft. Find the surface area and volume of the time capsule. Use 3.14 for π.

19. Todd's class is making a mobile. Todd made a piece for the mobile by gluing the bases of two square pyramids together. If the sides of each base are 6 inches and each pyramid has a height of 7 inches, what is the volume of the piece Todd made for the mobile?

20. Triangle *NMO* shown at the right is similar to triangle *RST*. The ratio of the corresponding parts of the triangles is 1:4. The height of triangle *RST* is 28 inches, and the area is 784 square inches. How long is the base of triangle *NMO*?

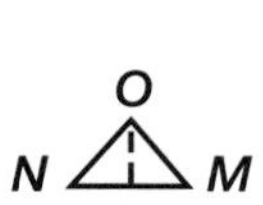

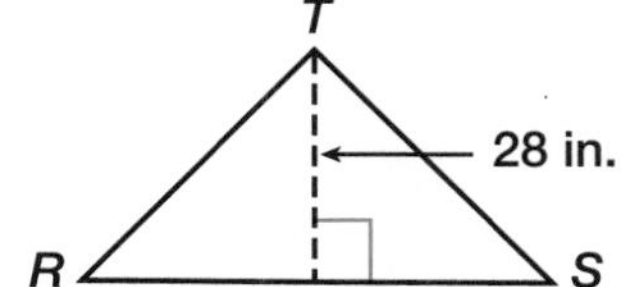

Write About It

Solve each problem. Use correct math vocabulary to explain your thinking.

1. Use the geometric figures found in this chapter.

a. Name six geometric figures you studied.

b. For each figure you listed, give one or more examples of a real-world object that has the same shape.

c. Explain why each object you listed is a good example. For example, a can is a cylinder. The top and the bottom of the can represent the bases. The curved surface of the can represents the curved surface of a cylinder.

2. Olivia's driveway is 20 feet long and 6 feet wide. Olivia draws a circular design in the middle of her driveway. The radius of the circle is 3 feet.

a. Draw a picture that represents Olivia's driveway and her design.

b. Write an equation to represent the area of Olivia's driveway that is not covered by her design.

c. Use the equation to find the area of the driveway that is not covered by the design.

Another Look

Use the diagram to solve each problem. Show all your work.

r = 2 ft
d = 6 ft
r = 4 ft
soil strip 1 ft wide
1 ft
1 ft

1. Volunteers built three circular fountains in front of the Hometown Community Center. Each fountain is surrounded by a strip of soil that is 1 foot wide. The volunteers would like to plant flowers inside each soil strip around the fountains. If they plant 2 flowers in every square foot of area, about how many flowers will they plant around each fountain? Use 3.14 as an approximation for π.

2. If the walls of each fountain are 3 inches thick, how much water is needed to fill all three fountains to a depth of 1.2 feet?

3. **Look Back** Would using $\frac{22}{7}$ as an approximation for π make the calculations in Problem 2 easier or more difficult? Explain.

4. **Analyze** The walls of each fountain are 1.8 feet tall. As a final task, the volunteers paint the outside walls of each fountain. If one gallon of paint covers approximately 250 square feet, about how many gallons of paint do they need?

Enrichment

Obelisks

An obelisk is a four-sided solid figure that slants inward, or tapers, as it rises to its top, which is usually a pyramid. The base of an obelisk is a square, and the faces up to its top section are trapezoids.

You have probably seen a picture of the Washington Monument. The monument is designed as a classical Egyptian obelisk—tall and slender with a pyramid-shaped top. The monument is about 10 times as tall as it is wide at the base.

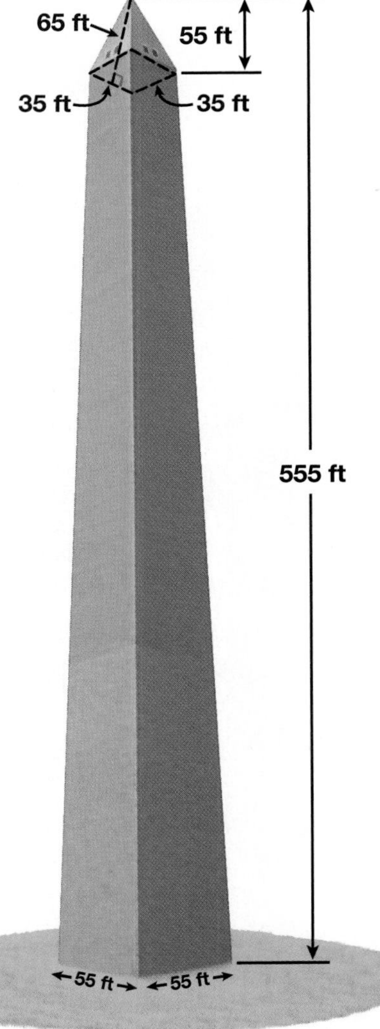

Look at the diagram of the Washington Monument at the right.

1. Can you separate the structure into two or more solid figures? Explain your answer, using vocabulary from the chapter.
2. How can you find the surface area of the obelisk? Is any information missing? Explain.
   Hint: The area of a trapezoid is $A = \frac{1}{2}h(b_1 + b_2)$.
3. How does the base of the pyramid at the top compare to the base of the monument?

Explain Your Thinking

► If the Washington Monument were a rectangular prism with a square pyramid at the top, would its volume be greater than or less than the volume of the actual monument? Explain your thinking.

CHAPTER 11

Statistics and Probability

Why Learn About Statistics and Probability?

Learning about statistics helps you to read and interpret data. Understanding probability helps you predict the likelihood that an event will happen.

When you survey your classmates about their favorite type of music and display the data on a graph, you are using statistics. A weather forecaster uses probability to describe the likelihood that it will rain tomorrow.

This man is banding young peregrine falcons in Alaska. After the banding, the birds will be released. The banding will help ecologists track the birds and gather statistical data about them.

Reviewing Vocabulary

Understanding math vocabulary helps you become a successful problem solver. Here are some math vocabulary words you should know.

data	numbers that provide information
outcome	a result of a probability experiment
probability	a measure of the likelihood that an event will occur
statistics	numbers that describe the characteristics of a set of data
tree diagram	a diagram showing the possible results of an activity

Reading Words and Symbols

When you read mathematics, sometimes you read only words, sometimes you read words and symbols, and sometimes you read only symbols.

Probability can be expressed as a fraction, a decimal, or a percent. All of these represent the probability that the ball will land on red.

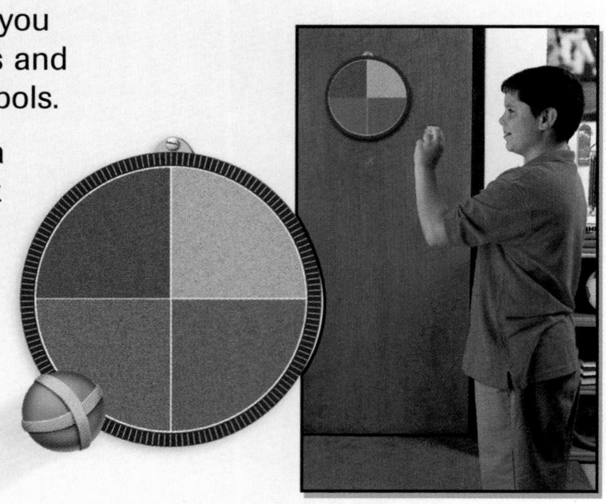

- The probability of landing on red is 1 out of 4.
- P(red) = $\frac{1}{4}$
- P(red) = 0.25
- P(red) = 25%

Try These

1. Write *true* or *false* for each statement.

a. A tree diagram is the only way to show all the outcomes of an experiment.

b. Data can be used to determine probability.

c. Outcomes are the results of probability experiments.

d. Statistics describe the characteristics of a set of data.

e. Data are always numbers.

2. Fill in the blanks with the following words: *data, outcome, probability, statistics, tree diagram.* Use each word only one time.

____ are the numbers that provide information.

____ describe the numbers in a set of data.

The ____ is the result of a ____ experiment

and can be shown in a ____.

Upcoming Vocabulary

Write About It **Here are some other vocabulary words** you will learn in this chapter. Watch for these words. Write their definitions in your journal.

sample	**survey**
biased sample	**disjoint events**
random sample	**theoretical probability**
fundamental counting principle	**representative sample**
experimental probability	**independent events**
dependent events	**population**

Use Samples to Predict

You will learn how to use data from a sample to predict data for an entire population.

New Vocabulary
population
sample
representative sample

Learn About It

All individuals that fit a particular description are called a **population**. Often researchers poll a small part of a population to make predictions about the whole group. This small group is called a **sample**. A sample is said to be a **representative sample** if it has characteristics similar to the entire population. A sample is used when it is not practical to survey an entire population.

Suppose 100,000 Americans were asked if they thought their president was doing a good job and 55,000 said yes. Predict about how many of the 280 million Americans would say that the president was doing a good job if all were surveyed.

Step 1 Set up a proportion.

sample population → $\frac{55{,}000 \text{ people}}{100{,}000 \text{ people}} = \frac{n \text{ million people}}{280 \text{ million people}}$ ← total population

Simplify where possible. $\frac{55}{100} = \frac{n}{280}$

Step 2 Solve for n.

$$100 \times n = 55 \times 280$$
$$100n = 15{,}400$$
$$n = 154$$

Remember
n is in millions.

Solution: Out of 280 million Americans, about 154 million would say the president is doing a good job.

Explain Your Thinking

- ► Would a sample be needed for a population of 50 people? Why or why not?
- ► Does using a sample to predict provide an exact answer or an estimate?

Guided Practice

Decide whether you would use a sample to learn something about each group. Explain.

1. the students in your math class
2. the residents of a city
3. all the employees of a very large company

Ask Yourself
- Could I poll or survey each member of this population?

Predict the number of *yes* responses from the total population.

4. total population: 200 students
   sample population: 50 students
   yes responses from sample: 10

5. total population: 300 women
   sample population: 50 women
   yes responses from sample: 36

Independent Practice

Decide whether you would use a sample to learn about each group. Explain.

6. the account holders at a local bank
7. the players on your sports team
8. all the students in a high school
9. the teachers in your school

Predict the number of *yes* responses from the total population.

10. total population: 1,000 students
    sample population: 250 students
    yes responses from sample: 175

11. total population: 500 residents
    sample population: 20 residents
    yes responses from sample: 8

Problem Solving • Reasoning

12. **Predict** It is estimated that a lake has a fish population of 900. In a sample, 10 out of 50 fish are trout. Based on this sample, predict about how many fish in the lake are trout.

13. One day 62 of 93 visitors to the White House were United States citizens. Use those visitors as a sample to predict about how many of every 1,200 visitors would be United States citizens.

14. **Write About It** In a sample, 2 out of 20 students said they brush their teeth more than three times a day. If the sample was taken from 520 students, is it sensible to make conclusions from this sample? Tell why or why not.

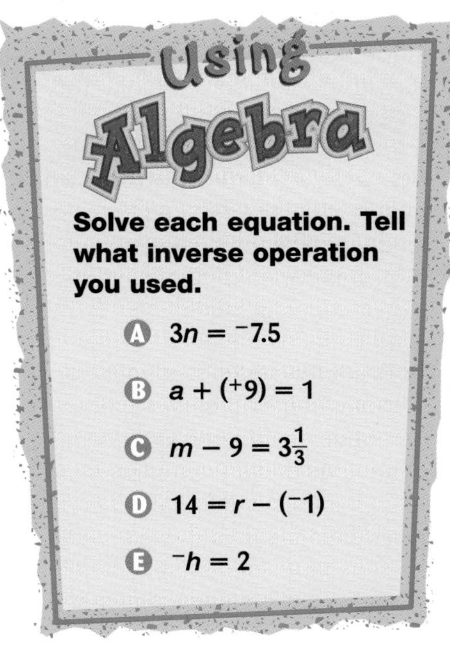

Solve each equation. Tell what inverse operation you used.

A. $3n = {}^{-}7.5$

B. $a + ({}^{+}9) = 1$

C. $m - 9 = 3\frac{1}{3}$

D. $14 = r - ({}^{-}1)$

E. ${}^{-}h = 2$

Mixed Review • Test Prep

Find the number of diagonals and the sum of the angles for each regular polygon. *(pages 418–420)*

15. pentagon
16. triangle
17. quadrilateral
18. octagon

19. Which is an algebraic expression for 12 less than the sum of p and q? *(pages 270–271)*

A $p + 12 + q$ **B** $p + q - 12$ **C** $12 - p + q$ **D** $q - 12 - p$

Extra Practice See Set A on page 534.

Select a Sample

You will learn how to select a representative sample.

New Vocabulary
- **survey**
- **convenience sample**
- **biased sample**
- **random sample**

Learn About It

A representative sample has no bias. Bias is the difference between the way the selected sample responds and the way the population would really respond. A sample can be biased in many ways.

Nadia, Alex, and Cy want to know how many of their school's 600 students would buy breakfast in the cafeteria if it were offered. They each used a different sampling method to poll a sample of students. Which method provides a representative sample?

Sampling Methods	Analysis of Methods
Nadia makes 600 copies of a written **survey** and distributes them to all homeroom teachers. Students return 40 surveys with *yes* circled and 10 with *no* circled to Nadia. (80% *yes* responses)	Nadia has polled a **biased sample**, because students who want breakfast are more likely to respond to her survey.
Alex uses a **convenience sample**. He asks his friends if they would buy breakfast at school and records their answers: 2 *yes* and 18 *no* responses. (10% *yes* responses)	Alex has polled a biased sample, because he only asks his small group of friends, whose interests may not be representative of the whole school.
Cy randomly asks students coming into the school whether they would buy breakfast at school or not. Twenty students say *yes*, and 60 say *no*. (25% *yes* responses)	Cy's sample is more representative. The students polled are a **random sample**, and each student's response is collected.

The homeroom teachers then asked all the students the question and 126 students, or 26%, said *yes*. The results of Nadia's and Alex's surveys were not the same as the survey of the whole population, but Cy's random sample was close.

Solution: Of the 3 methods used, the random sample provides the most representative sample.

Explain Your Thinking

- ► When is a sample representative? not representative?
- ► How is a sample from a survey affected when only a small percentage are returned?

Guided Practice

Give a reason why each sample may not be representative.

1. A written survey is mailed to addresses at random.
2. People are called at home between 3 P.M. and 4 P.M.

Ask Yourself

- Is the sample too small?
- What group of people are not included in this sample?

Independent Practice

Give a reason why each sample may not be representative.

3. Students at a high school football game are randomly asked questions.
4. Five people are asked for whom they would vote for president.

Use the table for Exercises 5–6.

5. How may Sample A be biased? Give an example of a way in which that bias may be eliminated.
6. Which sample may be the least biased? Explain.

Sample	How Selected
A	Every 25th number in a phone book is called.
B	Every 25th address in a phone book is mailed a questionnaire.
C	People walking by a bank are randomly chosen and asked questions.

Problem Solving • Reasoning

Use Data **Use the table at right for Problem 7.**

7. Predict Out of 250 sixth-graders, 50 were asked what kinds of breakfast foods they would like the cafeteria to offer. Predict how many of the 250 sixth-graders want granola and fruit and how many would not want omelets.
8. Estimate A survey reported that one out of every five students would buy breakfast at school. About how many of the 621 middle-school students would buy breakfast at school?

Breakfast Choices

Food	Responses
Pancakes	22
Omelet	8
Oatmeal	11
Granola and Fruit	9

9. Write About It How would you gather information to determine what the players on your school's soccer team think about student attendance at their games?

Mixed Review • Test Prep

Find the missing number in each proportion. *(pages 310–312)*

10. $\frac{3}{m} = \frac{6}{24}$
11. $\frac{f}{20} = \frac{4}{5}$
12. $\frac{36}{k} = \frac{4}{1}$
13. $\frac{5}{2} = \frac{g}{12}$

14. What is the area of a parallelogram with a base of 12 in. and a height of 5 in.? *(pages 452–453)*

A 17 in.^{2} **B** 34 in.^{2} **C** 60 in.^{2} **D** 124 in.^{2}

Extra Practice See Set B on page 534.

Problem-Solving Skill: Multistep Problems

You will learn how to solve problems that involve more than one step.

You may encounter word problems that require more than one step to reach a solution. To solve these problems, you need to decide what steps are required.

In a random survey of 50 students, 58% said they ride the bus to school. Based on this sample, predict how many of the 350 students in the school do not ride the bus to school.

Determine what information you know.

Out of 50 students, 58% ride the bus to school. The total number of students in the school is 350.

Decide what information you need.

You need to find how many of the 350 students might ride the bus to school and then subtract to find how many students do not ride the bus.

Decide how to solve the problem.

First, find 58% of 350, since 58% of the students surveyed said they ride the bus to school.

$$58\% \text{ of } 350 = n$$
$$0.58 \times 350 = n$$
$$203 = n$$

Of the 350 students, about 203 ride the bus to school.

Then subtract to find how many of the 350 students do not ride the bus to school.

$$350 - n = x$$
$$350 - 203 = x$$
$$147 = x$$

Of the 350 students, about 147 students do not ride the bus to school.

Look Back Why does it help to identify what you know and what you need to know before you begin making calculations?

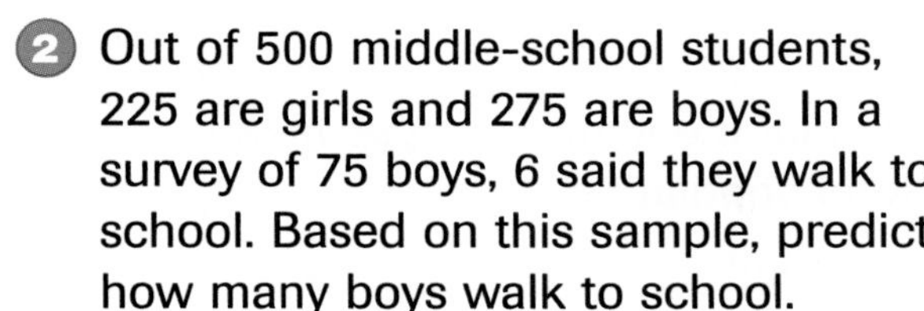

Left: In northern Maine, children may snowshoe to school in winter.

Right: In Malaysia, some children ride in a rickshaw to go to school.

Guided Practice

Solve.

1. In a sample of 150 high-school students, sixty students said they ride to school with a friend. Based on this sample, predict how many of 900 high-school students do not ride to school with a friend.

Think: What fraction of the 150 students ride to school with a friend?

2. Out of 500 middle-school students, 225 are girls and 275 are boys. In a survey of 75 boys, 6 said they walk to school. Based on this sample, predict how many boys walk to school.

Think: What information is necessary to solve this problem?

Choose a Strategy

Solve. Use these or other strategies.

Problem-Solving Strategies

- **Draw a Diagram**
- **Work Backward**
- **Find a Pattern**
- **Use Logical Thinking**

3. In a random survey of 80 students at Parker School, 30% said they have been late to their first-period class. Based on this sample, decide how many of 550 students at Parker School have been late to a first period class.

4. Last year, 16 out of 200 students surveyed rode their bikes to school every day. This year, three fourths as many students surveyed ride their bikes. Based on this sample, how many of 500 students ride their bikes this year?

5. Sixteen students made a school safety bulletin board. The area of the bulletin board was 22 square feet. The perimeter of the bulletin board was 19 feet. The height was greater than the width. What was the height of the bulletin board?

6. One ninth of the students in Mr. Dodd's sixth-grade class walk to school. Eight students in the class ride in a car. The other sixteen students in the class ride the bus. How many students are in Mr. Dodd's class?

7. In a sample of high-school students, 30 students said yes and 20 students said no when asked if they drive to school. Based on this sample, predict how many high-school students there are if 90 students drive to school.

8. On Monday, 14 students were tutored. On Wednesday, 5 more students were tutored than on Monday. On Thursday, 2 fewer students were tutored than on Wednesday. How many students were tutored on Thursday?

Extra Practice See 1–4 on page 537.

Check Your Understanding of Lessons 1–3

Decide whether you would use a sample to learn something about each group. Explain.

1. the fans of professional baseball
2. the cellists in a local orchestra
3. members of a relay team
4. your best friends

Predict the number of *yes* responses from the total population.

5. total population: 10,000
   sample population: 250
   yes responses from sample: 100

Give a reason why each sample may not be representative.

6. A store sends an e-mail to 1 out of every 100 people randomly chosen from its database of 100,000 e-mail addresses.
7. One out of every 10 people who donated to the library fund is telephoned.

Solve.

8. Out of 1,200 high-school students, 575 are boys and 625 are girls. In a survey of 50 girl students, 38 said they own a bicycle. Based on this sample, predict how many girls at that school own a bicycle.

How did you do?

If you had difficulty with any items in the Quick Check, you can use the following pages for review and extra practice.

Items	Review These Pages	Do These Extra Practice Items
1–5	pages 496–497	Set A, page 534
6–7	pages 498–499	Set B, page 534
8	pages 500–501	1–4, page 537

Test Prep • Cumulative Review

Maintaining the Standards

Choose the letter of the correct answer.

1. Saul buys a bag of dog food that weighs $25\frac{1}{2}$ lb. Because the bag is so heavy, he pours $6\frac{1}{4}$ lb into a smaller bag. How much dog food is left in the original bag?

   A $18\frac{3}{4}$ lb **C** $19\frac{1}{2}$ lb
   B $19\frac{1}{4}$ lb **D** $31\frac{3}{4}$ lb

2. David has a table in the shape of a hexagon. His sister has a pentagonal table. What is the ratio of the number of sides of David's table to the number of sides of his sister's table?

   F 5:7 **H** 6:5
   G 5:6 **J** 6:7

3. Millie needs to find the volume of the cereal box shown below. Which number represents the volume of Millie's cereal box?

   A 32 in.^{3}
   B 40 in.^{3}
   C 120 in.^{3}
   D 240 in.^{3}

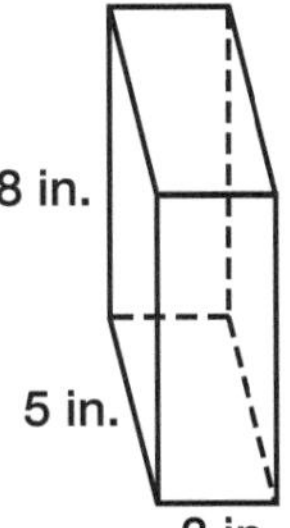

4. Solve $\frac{67}{80} = \frac{a}{320}$ for a.

   F 67 **H** 134
   G 80 **J** 268

5. What is the area of this parallelogram?

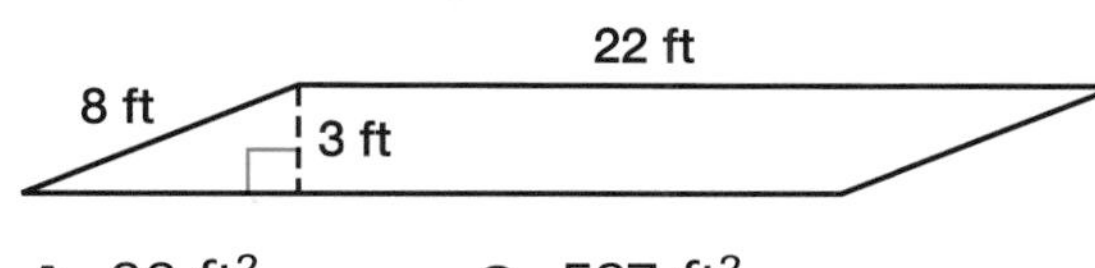

   A 66 ft^2 **C** 527 ft^2
   B 176 ft^2 **D** 528 ft^2

6. Mr. Kohl ordered $56\frac{1}{3}$ yards of window trim. The perimeter of his window is 2,040 inches. Which statement describes Mr. Kohl's situation?

   F He needs 2 yards more trim.
   G He needs 12 inches more trim.
   H He needs $\frac{1}{3}$ foot more trim.
   J He needs $\frac{2}{3}$ yard more trim.

7. What is the surface area of this rectangular prism?

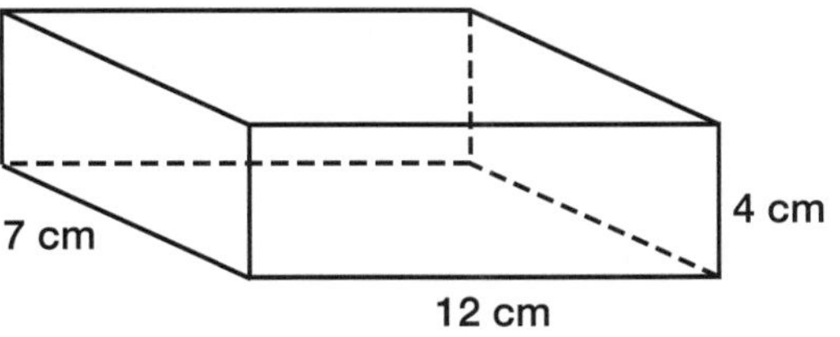

   A 168 cm^2 **C** 336 cm^2
   B 320 cm^2 **D** 672 cm^2

8. If the diameter of a circle is doubled, by what factor is the area of the circle increased?

   Explain How did you find your answer?

Internet Test Prep
Visit **www.eduplace.com/kids/mhm** for more *Test Prep Practice.*

Misleading Statistics

You will learn how statistics can be misleading.

Learn About It

The Middletown City Council is going to vote on whether to allow skateboarders on city park walkways. Two citizen groups use surveys to get the opinions of the local population. They plan to display the results. Many sixth-graders are concerned that the surveys or displays may not be fair.

How can the wording of the question and display methods cause bias?

Wording the Survey Question

Should skateboarders be allowed to endanger people by doing stunts on city park walkways?

- shows bias by emphasizing possible danger

Should our children be allowed to use skateboards for transportation to and from school on city park walkways?

- shows bias by suggesting benefit to parents

Displaying the Results

The results of one survey were very close, with 48% answering *yes* and 52% answering *no.*

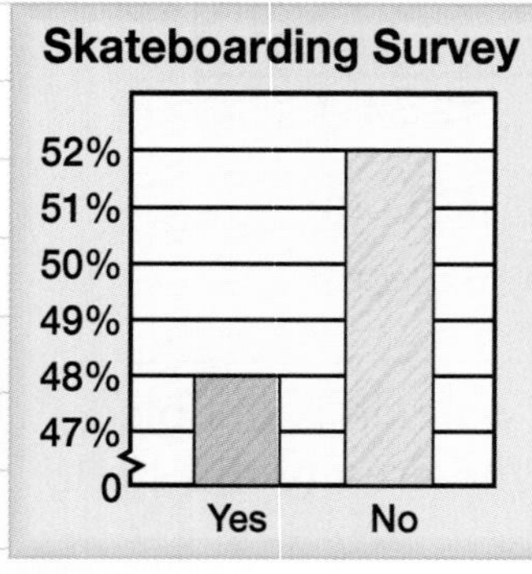

- shows bias by using a scale to make it look as if many more people answered *no*

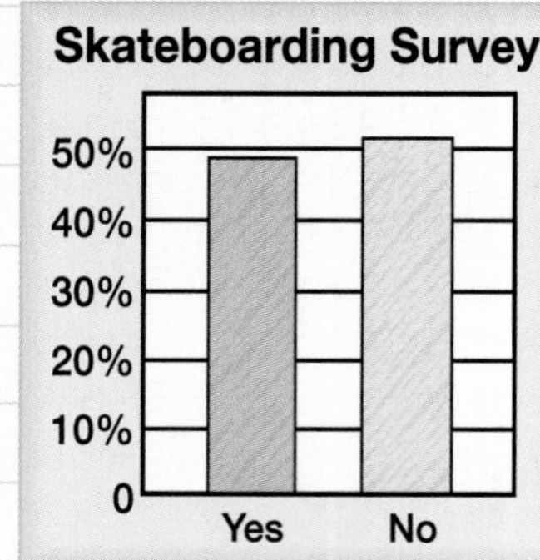

- displays the same survey results, but in a fair way

Explain Your Thinking

▶ What other factors could cause the results to be misleading?

▶ How would you word an unbiased question for the survey?

Guided Practice

Identify each source of bias.

1. Parents are asked, "Should children waste their time visiting the Internet?"

2. Parents of young children are asked, "Do you think all public rest rooms should have changing tables?"

> **Ask Yourself**
> - Did I look at the wording of the survey question?

Independent Practice

Identify each source of bias.

3. Parents are asked, "Should we develop hand-eye coordination by teaching our children how to play computer games?"

4. The president of a large company asks her employees, "Do you agree with my opinion each time I make a decision about our company?"

For Exercises 5 and 6, refer to Exercises 3 and 4 above.

5. Reword the question in Exercise 3 to remove bias.

6. Reword the question in Exercise 4 to remove bias.

7. Write an unbiased question for a survey of parents with young children about speed limits on city streets.

8. Write an unbiased question for a survey of fifth-graders' opinions about the value of learning mathematics.

Problem Solving • Reasoning

Use Data **Use the graph at the right for Problem 9.**

9. Analyze A reporter made this graph to support his story titled "Skateboarders Stopped by Huge Vote Against Using City Parks." Do the graph and headline display bias? Explain.

10. A member of the Fly High skateboard club stands outside a local sports shop to hand out surveys about permitting skateboarding on all streets. Identify the bias.

Mixed Review • Test Prep

Solve. *(pages 280–281)*

11. $12 + 4 + j = 28$ **12.** $w - 11 = 50$ **13.** $h + 32 = 54 - 8$ **14.** $p - 9 + 16 = 24$

Choose the letter of the correct answer. *(pages 350–351, 352–353)*

15 What is 80% of 445?

A 55.6 **C** 356
B 3.56 **D** 5.56

16 328 is what percent of 820?

F 40% **H** 2.49%
G 91% **J** 35%

Extra Practice See Set C on page 534.

Interpret Data Displays

You will learn how to interpret data displays and draw accurate conclusions.

Learn About It

Many advertisements attempt to persuade people to buy products or services. However, to avoid making incorrect conclusions, people must be careful to interpret the data correctly. Both of these building companies claim to have built the most new homes in 3 months.

Quickly look at the number of houses built in June by both companies. What incorrect conclusion might you draw? Which company has a valid claim?

Count the number of symbols for each company in June.

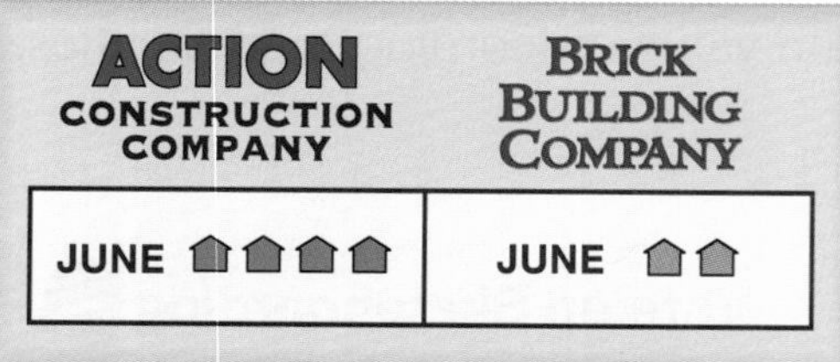

What might you conclude from just a glance at the symbols?

Action has 4 symbols. Brick has 2 symbols. It appears that Action built twice as many houses as Brick in June.

Use the keys to find the total number of houses each company built in June.

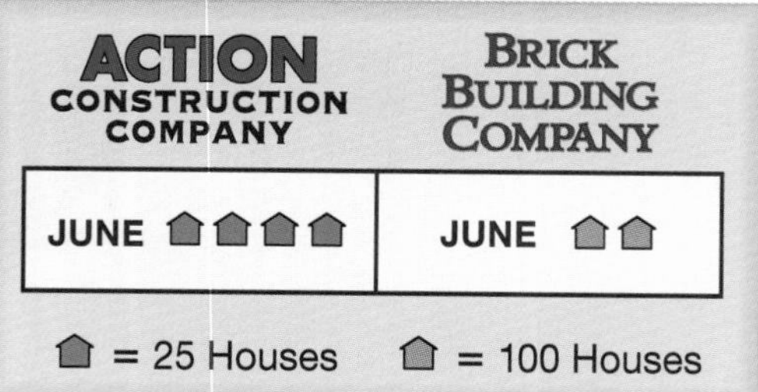

Action: Since each symbol represents 25 houses, Action built 100 houses in June.

Brick: Since each symbol represents 100 houses, Brick built 200 houses in June.

Compare the actual number of houses to the conclusions you made earlier.
In June, Action built half as many houses as Brick, not twice as many. Brick actually built twice as many houses as Action.

Solution: A quick comparison of only symbols suggesting that Action built twice as many houses as Brick is not accurate. When reading graphs, you need to interpret all of the symbols, including the key, carefully.

Explain Your Thinking

- Name ways to display data so that each display looks different.
- What do you need to look at when you read a graph?

Guided Practice

Use the graph for Exercises 1–2.

1. What might you conclude when you look at the bar graph? What influenced your conclusion?

2. Draw a graph that shows the difference in preferences more fairly.

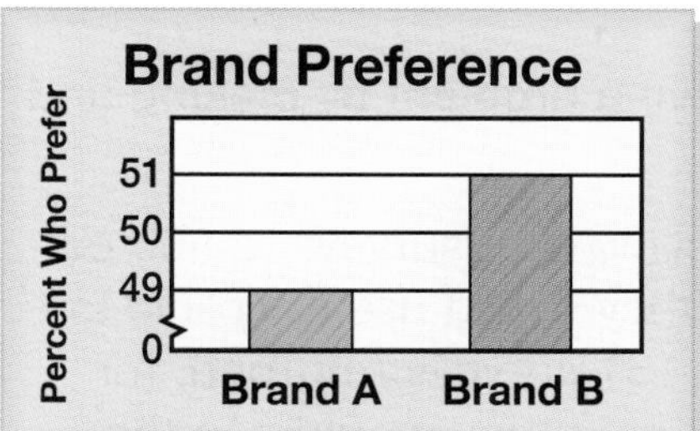

Ask Yourself

- How might the scale change the presentation of data?

Independent Practice

Use the graph for Exercises 3–4.

3. What might you conclude when you look at the bar graph? What influenced your conclusion?

4. Draw a graph that shows the difference in the cost of a small ad more fairly.

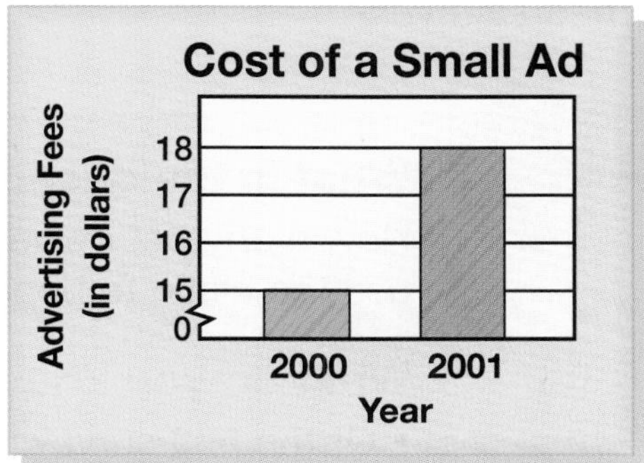

Problem Solving • Reasoning

Use Data **Use the graph for Problem 5.**

5. In 3 years the average length of a local radio commercial increased from 35 seconds to 37 seconds and then to 40 seconds. Redraw the graph in a way that makes it appear that the lengths of commercials have increased greatly.

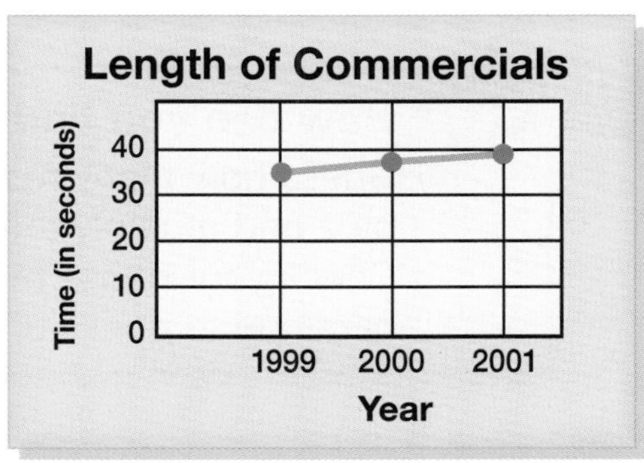

6. Write Your Own Draw a graph that may be misinterpreted and see if a classmate can describe the bias presented.

Mixed Review • Test Prep

Solve. *(pages 354–355)*

7. 120% of what number is 106.8?

8. 150 is 60% of what number?

9 What is the area of a triangle with a base of 14 in. and a height of 6 in.? *(pages 454–455)*

A 42 in.^{2} **C** 168 in.^{2}

B 84 in.^{2} **D** 21 in.^{2}

Extra Practice See Set D on page 535.

Problem-Solving Strategy: Guess and Check

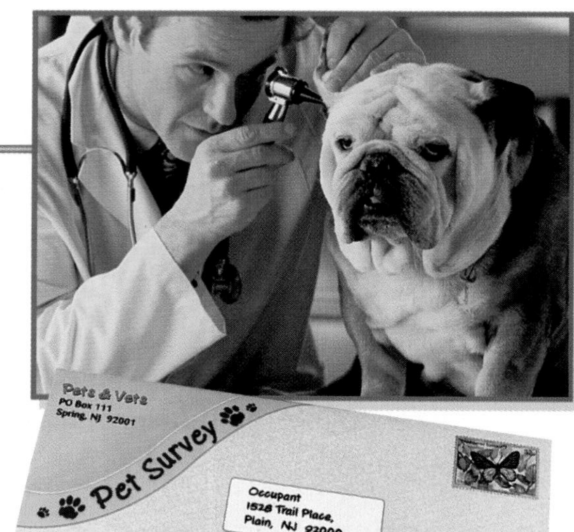

You will learn how to solve a problem using the Guess and Check strategy.

Sometimes you can solve a problem by making and checking guesses.

Problem A veterinary clinic sent surveys to 500 pet owners asking whether they would use the clinic to board their pets. Of the 161 surveys returned, for every 5 pet owners that said they would use the clinic there were 2 that said they would not. Based on this sample, how many of the surveys that were returned said *yes*?

Understand

What is the question?

How many pet owners would use the clinic to board their pets?

What do you know?

- Of the 500 surveys, 161 were returned.
- For every 5 *yes* responses, there were 2 *no* responses.

Plan

How can you find the answer?

Guess how many responses were *no*. Divide that number by 2 and multiply the result by 5 to find the *yes* responses. Check your guess by adding. Revise your guess and continue to guess until the sum is 161.

Solve

Guess	*Yes* Responses	Sum	Check
50 *no* responses	125	175	too high
40 *no* responses	100	140	too low
48 *no* responses	120	168	too high
46 *no* responses	115	161	correct

The number of *yes* responses is 115.

Look Back

Look back at the problem.

When is guessing and checking useful?

Remember:
- Understand
- Plan
- Solve
- Look Back

Guided Practice

Solve each problem, using the Guess and Check strategy.

1. Stephanie brought her dogs, Skipper and Spot, to the clinic. The product of the dogs' ages was 117. The sum of their ages was 22. Spot was older than Skipper. What was the age of each dog?

   Think: How many ways do the guesses need to be checked?

2. Another survey showed that out of 138 responses, twice as many people would board their dog as would board their cat. How many people would board their dog?

   Think: How do the number of dogs and cats relate?

Choose a Strategy

Solve. Use these or other strategies.

- **Write an Equation**
- **Work Backward**
- **Use Logical Thinking**
- **Guess and Check**

3. Last week, 70% of the kennels were full for the entire week. If the veterinary clinic has 18 kennels for cats and 22 kennels for dogs, how many kennels were not full last week?

4. In a sample of 50 cat owners, 14 said they bathed their cat at home. Based on this sample, tell how many of 275 cat owners would bathe their cat at home.

5. Last year the clinic's monthly electricity bills were $110, $115, $118, $120, $130, $117, $155, $185, $201, $117, $120, $132. The average monthly electricity bill was four times as much as the average monthly water bill. What was the average monthly water bill last year?

6. The veterinary clinic treated 3 dogs and 4 cats on Monday, 5 dogs and 5 cats on Tuesday, 6 dogs and 1 cat on Wednesday, 3 dogs and 8 cats on Thursday, and 5 dogs and 5 cats on Friday. What is the mean number of animals treated on each of those days?

7. Ms. Anderson spends $132 boarding her dog and her cat for 6 days. The cost of boarding her cat is $10 a day. How much does it cost to board her dog per day?

8. The clinic gave rabies shots to twice as many dogs in July as it did in June. In June it gave twice as many shots as it did in May. If 9 dogs got rabies shots in May, how many dogs got them in July?

Extra Practice See 5–7 on page 537.

Quick Check

Check Your Understanding of Lessons 4–6

Identify each source of bias.

1. Citizens are asked, "Do you believe the local government should continue to waste money on sidewalk repairs?"
2. Twelfth-graders are asked, "Should the school reserve parking places for all high-school seniors?"

Refer to Exercises 1 and 2 above.

3. Reword the question in Exercise 1 to remove bias.
4. Reword the question in Exercise 2 to remove bias.

Use the graph for Exercises 5–7.

5. What conclusion might you make from the data displayed by the bar graph?
6. What influenced your conclusion?
7. Draw a graph that shows less drastically the difference between the number of missions for each spacecraft.

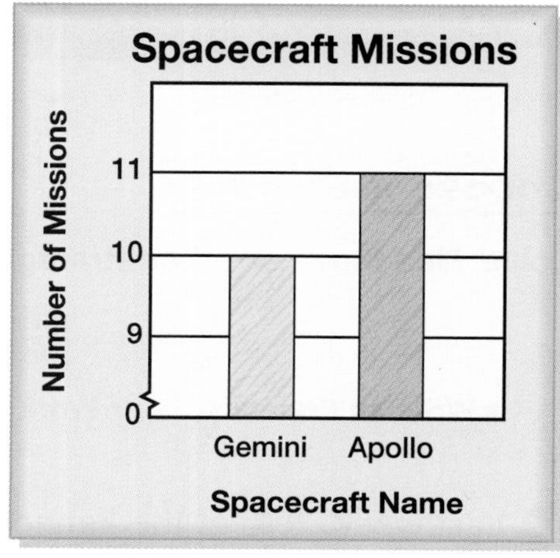

Solve.

8. Bethany is buying clay flowerpots to use in her back yard. Small flowerpots cost $1.50 each and large flowerpots cost $4.00 each. If Bethany spends $22.50 for flowerpots, how many of each size does she buy?

How did you do?

If you had difficulty with any items in the Quick Check, you can use the following pages for review and extra practice.

Items	Review These Pages	Do These Extra Practice Items
1–4	pages 504–505	Set C, page 534
5–7	pages 506–507	Set D, page 535
8	pages 508–509	5–7, page 537

Test Prep • Cumulative Review

Maintaining the Standards

Choose the letter of the correct answer.

1 What is an appropriate unit to use to measure the capacity of a swimming pool?

A ounces
B cups
C gallons
D tons

2 Suppose 88% of the student body attend an assembly. There are 450 students in school. How many students attend the assembly?

F 39,600 students
G 396 students
H 400 students
J 54 students

3 What is the area of this figure?

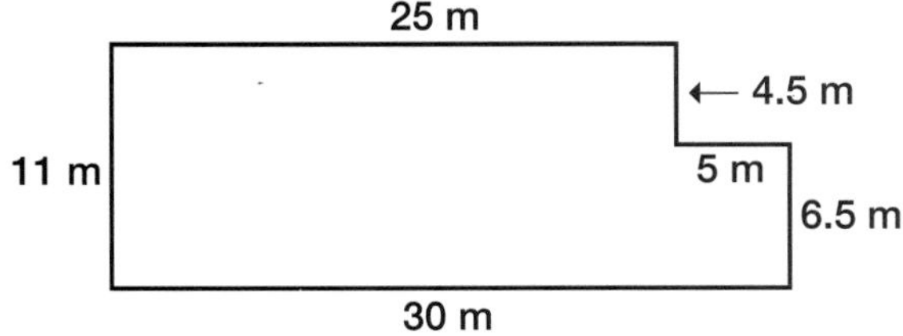

A 82 m^2
B 275 m^2
C 307.5 m^2
D 307.6 m^2

4 6.01% of what number is 33.3555?

F 200 **H** 555
G 550 **J** 688

5 On Monday, 97 books were returned to the library. On Tuesday, 114 books were returned. How many more books were returned on Tuesday than on Monday?

A 13 **C** 17
B 14 **D** 19

6 Which pair of figures are congruent?

F 
G
H
J

7 What is the correct name of the given angle?

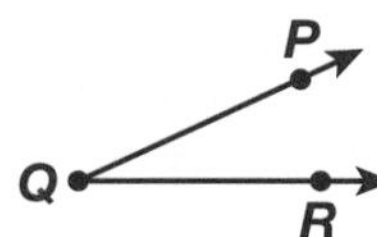

A $\angle QPR$ **C** $\angle PQR$
B $\angle R$ **D** $\angle P$

8 Write a mathematical expression for this statement.

The product of 9.6 and a number, *x*, is divided by the difference of 64 and a number, *y*.

Explain Tell how you found your answer.

Safe Site

Internet Test Prep
Visit **www.eduplace.com/kids/mhm** for more *Test Prep Practice.*

Possible Outcomes

You will learn how to find all of the possible results, or outcomes, of a multistep problem or experiment.

New Vocabulary
fundamental counting principle

Learn About It

For some problems you may need to know all of the possible outcomes. Using a systematic approach helps you list all of the possibilities.

Janet is planning her class schedule. What are the possible schedules that Janet can plan for her first two classes?

First Period
Spanish, French, or German

Second Period
drawing or pottery

Different Ways to Find All Possibilities

You can make a table.

For each language, list each art choice.

Language	Art
Spanish	drawing
Spanish	pottery
French	drawing
French	pottery
German	drawing
German	pottery

You can use a grid.

Write each different pair of choices.

	drawing	pottery
Spanish	Spanish, drawing	Spanish, pottery
French	French, drawing	French, pottery
German	German, drawing	German, pottery

You can draw a tree diagram.

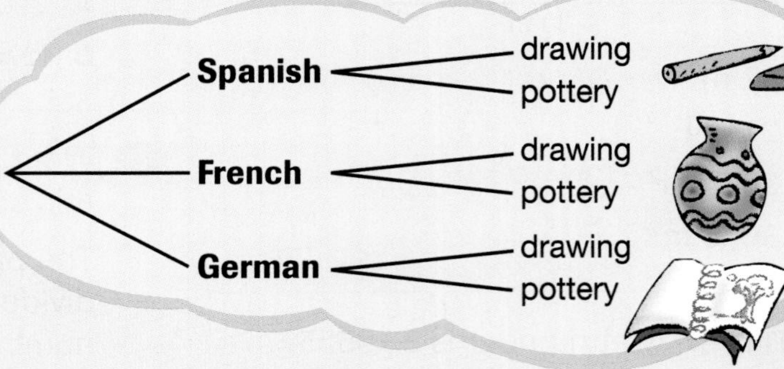

Trace each path from left to right.

Solution: Janet has these choices: Spanish and drawing, Spanish and pottery, French and drawing, French and pottery, German and drawing, or German and pottery.

Sometimes you do not need to know the specific outcomes. If you only need to know the number of possible outcomes, you can use the **fundamental counting principle**.

If an experiment or problem has two steps with m different ways to do the first step and n different ways to do the second step, the total number of possible outcomes for both steps is $m \times n$. Janet has 3 language choices (m ways to choose) and 2 art choices (n ways to choose).

$$\begin{aligned}\text{Total number of possible schedules} &= m \times n \\ &= 3 \times 2 \\ &= 6\end{aligned}$$

Another Example

Three Categories of Choices
6 shirts, 3 pairs of shorts, 4 hats
$6 \times 3 \times 4 = 72$ possible outfits

Explain Your Thinking

► What is an advantage of each method of finding all possible choices?

Guided Practice

Make a grid, a table, and a tree diagram to show all possible outcomes. The first few entries in the grid for Exercise 1 are shown.

Ask Yourself

- Did I include all possibilities?
- Did I duplicate anything?

1. Toss a 1–6 number cube. Then toss a second 1–6 cube.

Second Cube

First Cube	1	2	3	4	5	6
1	1, 1	1, 2	1, 3	1, 4	1, 5	1, 6
2	2, 1	2, 2				
3	3, 1					
4						
5						
6						

2. Spin this spinner and then flip a coin.

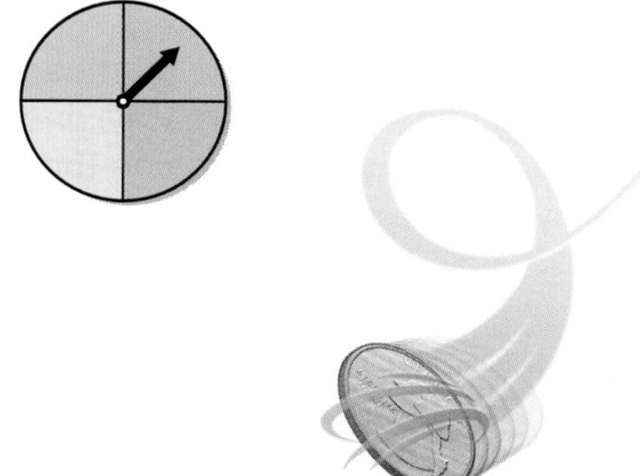

Use the fundamental counting principle to find the number of possible choices of one item from each group.

3. 3 sizes, 4 colors

4. 5 flowerpots, 8 kinds of plants

5. 6 projects, 3 kinds of wood

6. 3 soups, 4 main dishes, 6 desserts

Independent Practice

Make a grid, a table, and a tree diagram to show all possible outcomes.

7. Flip a coin, then pick a card.

8. Toss a number cube, then spin this spinner.

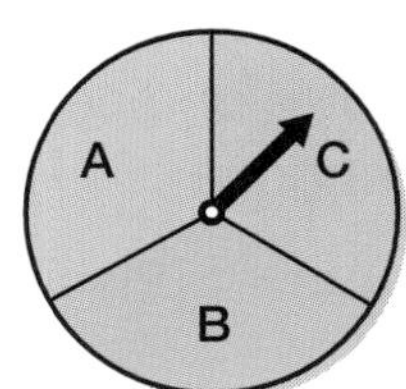

Use the fundamental counting principle to find the number of possible choices when you combine one item from each category.

9. 3 salads, 7 dressings

10. 4 pastas, 5 sauces

11. 3 cars, 5 colors, 2 options

12. 6 shirts, 5 ties, 2 jackets

Problem Solving • Reasoning

Use Data **Use the lists for Problems 13–15.**

13. **Predict** The sixth-graders at Appleton Middle School are planning a dance. They must make one choice from each category shown. How many possible choices are there?

14. **Analyze** The dance committee wants to add more choices to the list of themes. If they want the total number of possible choices to be 120, how many new themes do they need to add?

15. **Write About It** The new themes were not added, but for the first weekend in May, one location will not be available. How will choosing the first weekend in May change the number of possible choices?

Theme
- 1950s
- Carnival
- Beach

Dates
- May 4
- May 12
- May 25

Location
- Gym
- Cafeteria
- Youth Club
- Roller Rink

Mixed Review • Test Prep

Find the circumference for each circle. Use 3.14 for π. *(pages 460–462)*

16. $r = 16$ ft

17. $d = 120$ yd

18. $r = 4$ m

19. $d = 80$ in.

Choose the letter of the correct answer. *(pages 328–329)*

20 Which decimal is equivalent to 1%?

A 10.0 **C** 1.0
B 0.01 **D** 0.10

21 Which list of numbers is ordered from least to greatest?

F 95% 0.45 0.97
G 0.97 95% 0.45
H 0.45 95% 0.97
J 0.45 0.97 95%

Extra Practice See Set E on page 535.

Show What You Know

Check It Out

Bart decides that there are 10 different choices that include one shirt, one pair of shorts, and one hat. Is he correct? Explain.

Using Vocabulary

Identify each experiment as having one step or two steps. If it has only one step, add a second step. Then decide the number of different outcomes that are possible.

1. Spin a 1–6 spinner. Then pick a card from 20 different cards.
2. Pick one color of paint from a set containing 12 different colors.
3. Flip a coin and then toss a 1–6 number cube.
4. Pick one sock from twenty different socks.

Mental Math

Which two-step experiment gives the greatest number of possibilities?

A.

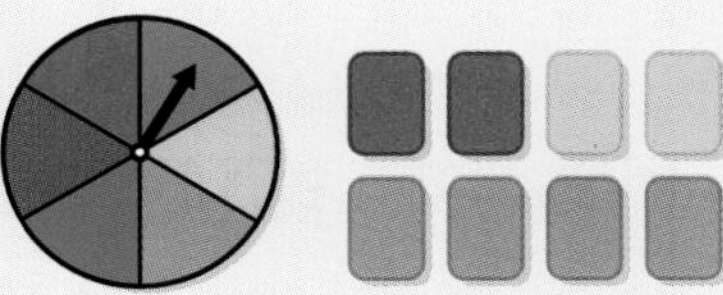

B.

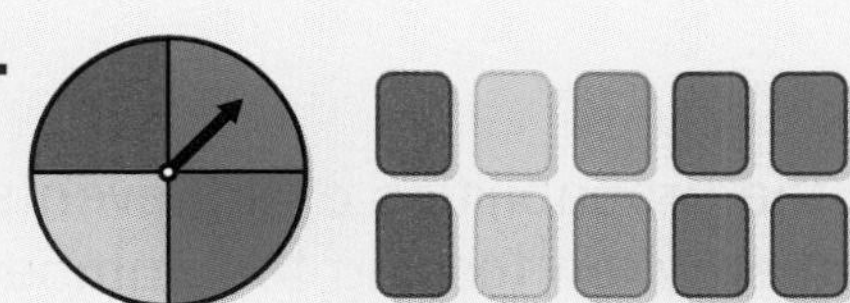

C.

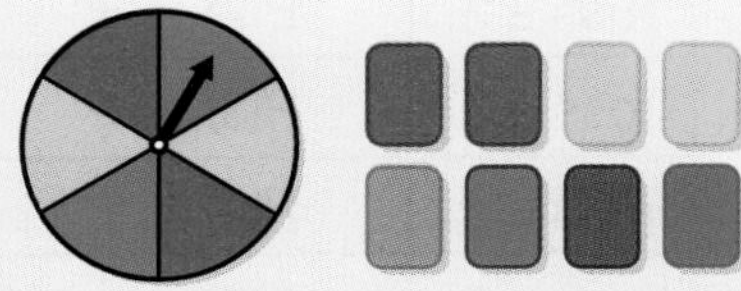

D.

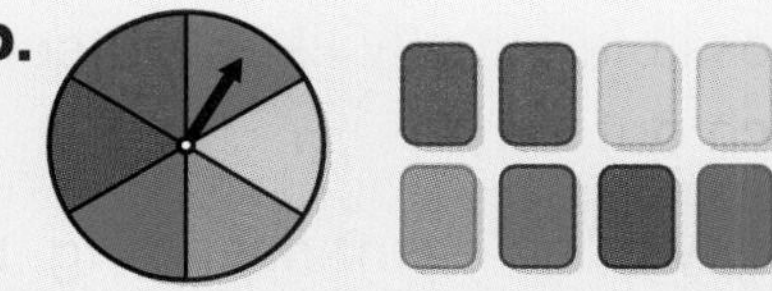

Theoretical Probability

You will learn how to find probabilities if each outcome of an experiment has the same chance of occurring.

New Vocabulary
experiment
event
theoretical probability
experimental probability
sample space

Learn About It

You have learned that a result of an experiment is called an outcome. A probability **experiment** is one way of collecting data. One or more outcomes of an experiment make up an **event**. The probability of an event is a measure of the likelihood that the event will occur

The probability of an event is a number from 0 through 1. It can be written as a fraction, a decimal, or a percent.

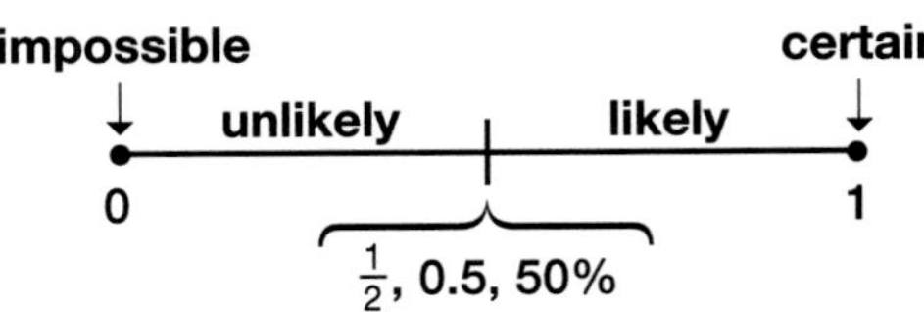

Probabilities can be theoretical or experimental. To find a **theoretical probability**, you use mathematical reasoning to calculate the expected result for an experiment. To find an **experimental probability**, you do an experiment to collect data. This lesson is about theoretical probability.

The outcomes for tossing this number cube are equally likely. You have the same chance of tossing 1, 2, 3, 4, 5, or 6.

If each outcome is equally likely, the probability of an event is the ratio of the number of possible outcomes in the event to the total number of possible outcomes.

$$P(A) = \frac{\text{number of outcomes in the event}}{\text{total number of possible outcomes}}$$

To read P(A), say "The probability of event A."

This table shows the probabilities of the events of tossing each number when tossing the number cube shown above.

Event	Probability
Toss a 1.	$P(1) = \frac{1}{6}$
Toss a 2.	$P(2) = \frac{1}{6}$
Toss a 3.	$P(3) = \frac{1}{6}$
Toss a 4.	$P(4) = \frac{1}{6}$
Toss a 5.	$P(5) = \frac{1}{6}$
Toss a 6.	$P(6) = \frac{1}{6}$

When there are *m* possible equally likely outcomes, the probability of each outcome is $\frac{1}{m}$.

If P(A) is the probability of an event occurring, the probability that the event does not occur is $1 - P(A)$.

Suppose there are 4 marbles of identical size—1 red, 1 blue, 1 green, and 1 yellow. Len picks 1 marble without looking.

a. What is the probability that he picks a blue marble?
b. What is the probability that he does not pick a blue marble?

Step 1 Find all the possible outcomes. This is called the **sample space**.

red
blue
green
yellow

Step 2 Use a ratio to find each probability.

a. P(blue) $= \frac{1}{4}$ ⟵ $\frac{\text{outcomes in event}}{\text{possible outcomes}}$

b. P(not blue) $= \frac{3}{4}$ ⟵ $\frac{\text{outcomes in event}}{\text{possible outcomes}}$

Solution: The probability of Len picking a blue marble is $\frac{1}{4}$. The probability of Len picking a marble that is not blue is $\frac{3}{4}$.

Other Examples: 4 Red Marbles in a Jar

A. Probability of 0
Drawing a Purple Marble

P(purple) $= \frac{0}{4}$ ⟵ outcomes in event / ⟵ possible outcomes

P(purple) = 0

B. Probability of 1
Drawing a Red Marble

P(red) $= \frac{4}{4}$ ⟵ outcomes in event / ⟵ possible outcomes

P(red) = 1

Explain Your Thinking

- ► Why can you find the probability of an event not happening by subtracting the probability of that event happening from 1?
- ► Can a probability be less than 0? Can a probability be greater than 1? Explain why or why not.

Guided Practice

Of 20 pennies in a jar, 2 were minted in 1996, 5 in 1998, 4 in 1999, 8 in 2000, and 1 in 2001. A penny is drawn at random and its date checked. Find each probability.

1. P(1998) **2.** P(1996) **3.** P(not 2001)

4. P(2000) **5.** P(1997) **6.** P(not 1997)

Ask Yourself

- How many outcomes are there in the event?
- How many possible outcomes are there?

List the sample space to find all possible outcomes for flipping three coins. Use your list to find each probability.

7. P(three heads) **8.** P(1 heads, 2 tails) **9.** P(no heads)

Independent Practice

A jar contains marbles that are all the same size. It contains 6 blue, 5 yellow, and 9 red marbles. Find each probability.

10. P(blue)
11. P(red)
12. P(yellow)
13. P(green)
14. P(not red)
15. P(not blue)
16. P(not yellow)
17. P(not white)
18. P(white)

List the sample space to find all possible outcomes for flipping four identical coins at once. Use your list to find each probability.

19. P(4 heads)
20. P(1 head, 3 tails)
21. P(2 tails, 2 heads)

Problem Solving • Reasoning

Solve. Choose a method.

Computation Methods

- Mental Math
- Estimation
- Paper and Pencil
- Calculator

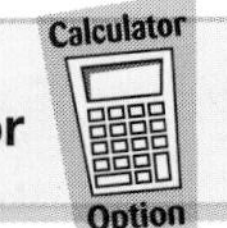

22. **Explain** Joshua tossed 3 identical coins. Kay tossed 4 identical coins. Who has the better chance of having more coins land with heads than tails? Explain your answer.

23. Ellie bought prizes for a party. She had $150 to spend. She bought 144 small prizes at $5 per dozen and 20 large prizes at 2 for $7. How much money did Ellie have left?

24. **Analyze** Drawing randomly from a jar of purple, red, and orange marbles, there is a $\frac{2}{5}$ chance of drawing a purple marble and an $\frac{8}{25}$ chance of drawing a red marble. How many of the 25 marbles in the jar are orange?

25. Drawing at random from a jar filled with white and black marbles, drawing a black marble is 3 times more likely than drawing a white marble. If there are 60 marbles in the jar, how many marbles are black?

Mixed Review • Test Prep

Find the total with simple interest for each situation. *(pages 366–367)*

26. $180 with 7% interest for 3 years

27. $556 with 2.5% interest for 2 years

28 A train travels 488 miles in 8 hours. What is its rate of travel? *(pages 318–319)*

A 80 mi/h **B** 61 mi/h **C** 60 mi/h **D** 10 mi/h

Extra Practice See Set F on page 535.

Practice Game

Which Is the Winning Cube?

Practice working with probabilities by teaming up with a partner. Try to be the first team in the class to determine which number cube wins more often.

What You'll Need

- *number cube A with sides labeled 1, 1, 1, 1, 6, 6*
- *number cube B with sides labeled 2, 2, 2, 5, 5, 5*

Players
Teams of 2

Here's What to Do

Predict which cube will roll a greater number and win more often. Then test your prediction.

1. Make a table like the one shown.
2. Each player chooses a number cube.
3. Players roll their number cubes at the same time. The greater number wins the round.
4. Make a check mark in the correct column of the chart for the winning cube.
5. Repeat Steps 3 and 4 until you can determine which number cube wins more often. Try to be the first team in the class to identify the winning cube.
6. Play a new game. Repeat steps 1–5 except that each player rolls the number cube twice. The greater sum wins each round.

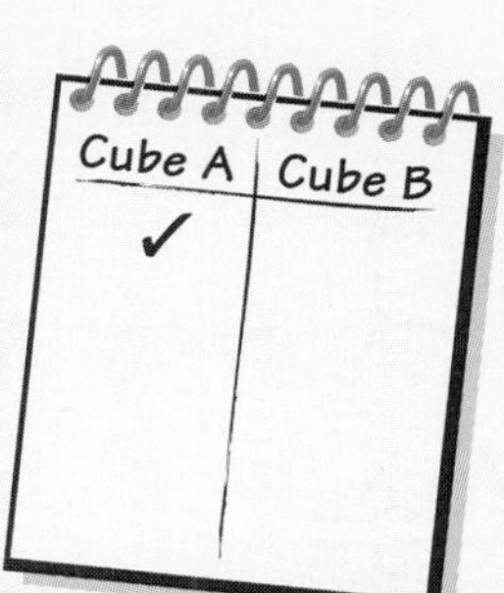

Share Your Thinking Explain how your predictions were made. Was each prediction correct?

Experimental Probability

You will learn the difference between experimental probability and theoretical probability.

Review Vocabulary
experimental probability

Learn About It

You have been learning about theoretical probability. This tells what *should* happen during an experiment with a very large number of trials. When you do an experiment, you may not get the results predicted by the theoretical probability.

To find **experimental probability**, you use the ratio of the number of times the outcomes in the event actually occur to the total number of completed trials.

You can use a table to record the results of experiments. Suppose you tossed a coin 10 times and heads landed up 6 times. Your table for P(heads) would look like this.

Materials
2 number cubes

Theoretical Probability	Number of Trials	Expected Results	Actual Results	Experimental Probability
$\frac{1}{2}$ 0.5 50%	10	$\frac{x}{10} = \frac{1}{2}$ $2x = 10$ $x = 5$	heads 𝍸 I	$\frac{6}{10} = \frac{3}{5}$ 0.6 60%

Note:
Record only the number of times the outcomes in the event occur.

Collect Data

Make a table like the one below. Complete 50 tosses of two number cubes. Record your results in the table. Find the experimental probability of getting a sum greater than 7 when you toss two number cubes, P(sum $>$ 7).

Theoretical Probability	Number of Trials	Expected Results	Actual Results	Experimental Probability
$\frac{15}{36} = \frac{5}{12}$ $0.41\overline{6}$ $41\frac{2}{3}\%$	50		sum $>$ 7	

Try It Out

Copy and complete the table for each probability experiment. Record each probability as a ratio, a decimal, and a percent.

1. Toss 2 coins and get heads both times, P(heads, heads).

Theoretical Probability	Number of Trials	Expected Results	Actual Results	Experimental Probability
$\frac{1}{4}$	50		heads, heads	

2. Roll 2 number cubes and get a sum of 7, P(sum of 7).

Theoretical Probability	Number of Trials	Expected Results	Actual Results	Experimental Probability
$\frac{6}{36} = \frac{1}{6}$	50		sum of 7	

3. Toss 2 number cubes and get an even sum, P(even sum).

Theoretical Probability	Number of Trials	Expected Results	Actual Results	Experimental Probability
$\frac{18}{36} = \frac{1}{2}$	20		even sum	

4. Repeat Exercise 3, but complete 100 trials.

Theoretical Probability	Number of Trials	Expected Results	Actual Results	Experimental Probability
$\frac{18}{36} = \frac{1}{2}$	100		even sum	

Write about it! Talk about it!

Use what you have learned to answer these questions.

5. In your own words, explain the difference between experimental probability and theoretical probability.

6. Use your results from Exercises 3 and 4. Does the experimental probability get closer to or farther from the theoretical probability as the number of trials increases? Add your results to others' results and compare the experimental and theoretical probabilities.

Quick Check

Check Your Understanding of Lessons 7–8

Make a grid, table, or tree diagram to show all the possible outcomes. Use a different method for each problem.

1. Toss this 1–6 number cube. Then spin this spinner.

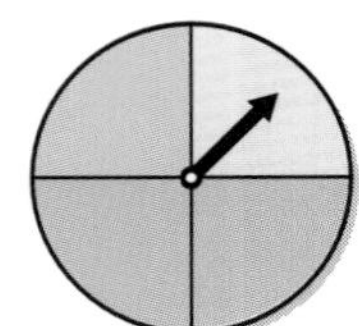

2. Choose a size and then choose a flavor.

Size	Flavor
Small	Strawberry
Medium	Orange
Large	Lemon
	Lime

Use the fundamental counting principle to find the number of possible choices of one item from each group.

3. 5 blouses, 3 skirts

4. 11 styles, 7 colors

5. 3 soups, 6 main dishes, 7 desserts

6. 4 jeans, 5 shirts, 2 hats

A jar contains 5 blue marbles, 2 orange marbles, 4 white marbles, and 7 red marbles. Suppose you draw out a marble without looking. Find the theoretical probability of each event.

7. P(white)

8. P(not orange)

9. P(green)

10. P(not purple)

How did you do?

If you had difficulty with any items in the Quick Check, you can use the following pages for review and extra practice.

ITEMS	REVIEW THESE PAGES	DO THESE EXTRA PRACTICE ITEMS
1–6	pages 512–514	Set E, page 535
7–10	pages 516–519	Set F, page 535

Test Prep • Cumulative Review

Maintaining the Standards

Choose the letter of the correct answer.

1. What is the simple interest earned for a deposit of \$300 at 8.4% for 2 years?

   A \$25.20
   B \$50.40
   C \$2,520.00
   D \$5,040.00

2. Kenzie purchased new softball cleats for \$36. If the cleats were on sale for 40% off, how much did they originally cost?

   F \$36.40
   G \$45.00
   H \$60.00
   J \$140.00

3. What is the measure of angle *x*?

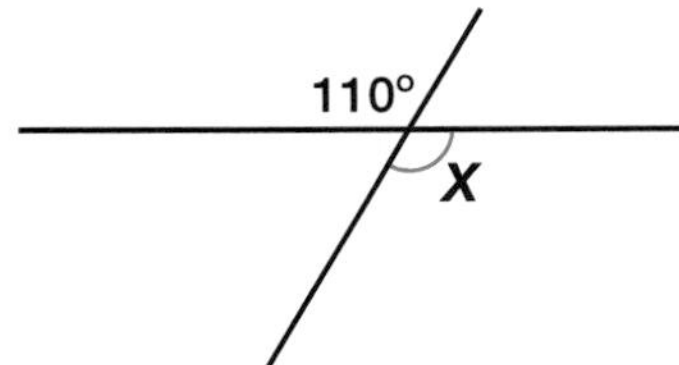

   A 40°
   B 70°
   C 110°
   D 180°

4. Determine the circumference of a circle with a radius of 280 cm.

   F ≈ 880 cm
   G ≈ 1,760 cm
   H ≈ 246,176 cm
   J ≈ 984,704 cm

5. What is the area of the triangle?

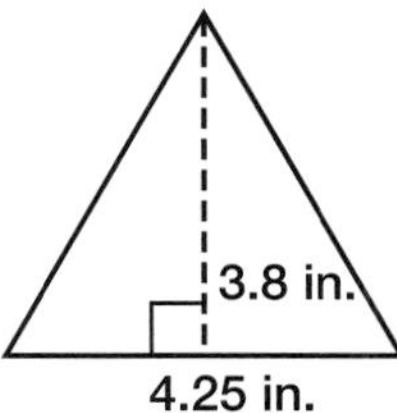

   A 8.075 in.^{2}
   B 12.750 in.^{2}
   C 16.150 in.^{2}
   D 32.305 in.^{2}

6. If the volume of a cylinder is 785 ft^3 and the diameter of its base is 10 ft, what is the height of the cylinder?

   F 2.5 ft
   G 10 ft
   H 12.5 ft
   J 25 ft

7. What is the mean of the following data?

   2, 4, 4, 5, 6, 6, 7, 7, 7, 12

   A 5
   B 6
   C 7
   D 8

8. What value is an outlier in the following data set?

   3, 5, 7, 8, 8, 10, 13, 37

   Explain How does the outlier in the data set affect the mean?

Internet Test Prep
Visit **www.eduplace.com/kids/mhm** for more *Test Prep Practice.*

LESSON 10 Disjoint Events

You will learn about disjoint events and how to calculate the probability for disjoint events.

New Vocabulary
disjoint events

Learn About It

Suppose Eli tosses two 1–6 number cubes and records the results of 2 events: the event that the sum is less than 7 and the event that the sum is greater than 7. The events in Eli's experiment have no outcome in common because it is impossible for a sum to be less than 7 and greater than 7 at the same time.

If A and B are events with no outcome in common, then A and B are said to be **disjoint events**.

When A and B are disjoint events, the probability of either event occurring is the sum of the individual probabilities of both events.

P(A or B) = P(A) + P(B).

In Eli's experiment, what is the probability that the sum is less than 7 or greater than 7?

Results of Tossing 2 Number Cubes

Second Number Cube \ First Number Cube	1	2	3	4	5	6
1	(1, 1)	(2, 1)	(3, 1)	(4, 1)	(5, 1)	(6, 1)
2	(1, 2)	(2, 2)	(3, 2)	(4, 2)	(5, 2)	(6, 2)
3	(1, 3)	(2, 3)	(3, 3)	(4, 3)	(5, 3)	(6, 3)
4	(1, 4)	(2, 4)	(3, 4)	(4, 4)	(5, 4)	(6, 4)
5	(1, 5)	(2, 5)	(3, 5)	(4, 5)	(5, 5)	(6, 5)
6	(1, 6)	(2, 6)	(3, 6)	(4, 6)	(5, 6)	(6, 6)

Find the probability that the sum is less than 7 or greater than 7.

Think of a sum < 7 as event A.
Think of a sum > 7 as event B.

$$P(A \text{ or } B) = P(A) + P(B)$$
$$= P(< 7) + P(> 7)$$
$$= \frac{15}{36} + \frac{15}{36} = \frac{5}{12} + \frac{5}{12}$$
$$= \frac{10}{12} = \frac{5}{6}$$

Hint:
In the table above are 36 ordered pairs of results. Count the number of ordered pairs shown in the red tint. What is each sum? Use this information to help solve the problem.

Solution: The probability that the sum is less than 7 or greater than 7 is $\frac{5}{6}$.

Explain Your Thinking

► Describe how finding the probability of disjoint events could be related to the formula for finding probability.

$$P(A) = \frac{\text{number of outcomes in the event}}{\text{total number of possible outcomes}}$$

Guided Practice

Use the lists below for Exercises 1–7. The experiment is to toss two 1–6 number cubes and determine the sum.

1. List the outcomes of each event A–J.

Probabilities	
$P(A) = \frac{5}{12}$	$P(F) = \frac{1}{2}$
$P(B) = \frac{5}{12}$	$P(G) = \frac{1}{36}$
$P(C) = \frac{5}{6}$	$P(H) = \frac{1}{18}$
$P(D) = \frac{1}{6}$	$P(I) = \frac{1}{12}$
$P(E) = \frac{1}{2}$	$P(J) = \frac{1}{9}$

Events	
A : Sum is less than 7.	F : Sum is even.
B : Sum is greater than 7.	G: Sum is 2.
C : Sum is not 7.	H: Sum is 3.
D : Sum is 7.	I : Sum is 4.
E : Sum is odd.	J : Sum is 5.

Ask Yourself

- Can I find a common outcome shared by each event?
- Can I use 1 − P for the probability of an event not happening?

Determine whether the pairs of events are disjoint. If the pairs are disjoint, find the probability of the disjoint events.

2. B and I **3.** A and G **4.** H and J **5.** E and F **6.** I and F **7.** F and J

Independent Practice

Use the lists at right for Exercises 8–19. The experiment is to toss four identical coins at the same time and record the number of heads *n*. P(*n*) is the probability of getting exactly *n* heads.

8. List the outcomes of each event, R, S, T and U.

P(*n*)
$P(0) = \frac{1}{16}$
$P(1) = \frac{1}{4}$
$P(2) = \frac{3}{8}$
$P(3) = \frac{1}{4}$
$P(4) = \frac{1}{16}$

Events
R : Number of heads is even.
S : Number of heads is odd.
T : Number of heads is less than 2.
U : Number of heads is greater than 2.

Determine whether the following pairs of events are disjoint. If not, name a common outcome.

9. R and S **10.** R and T **11.** T and U **12.** S and T **13.** S and U **14.** R and U

Find the probabilities.

15. P(0 or 1 or 2 or 3) **16.** P(R) **17.** P(S) **18.** P(T) **19.** P(U)

Mixed Review • Test Prep

Solve. *(pages 280–285)*

20. $b \times 1\frac{3}{4} = 7$ **21.** $3 \times n = 2$ **22.** $k \div 15 = 6$ **23.** $\frac{1}{2} + (e - 5) = 1$

24 How would you classify a triangle that has three congruent sides? *(pages 404–405)*

A scalene **B** right **C** isosceles **D** equilateral

Independent Events

You will learn how to find the probability of two independent events.

New Vocabulary
compound event
independent events

Learn About It

A **compound event** consists of the outcomes of two or more events. Sometimes the events that make up a compound event are independent events.

Events that have no effect on each other are called **independent events**. To find the probability of both of two independent events occurring, you multiply the individual probabilities.

P(A and B) = P(A) × P(B)

Events	Description
G	Student is a girl.
B	Student is a boy.
W	Student won a prize.
L	Student did not win a prize.

At the Vance School, 60 of the 90 students are girls. During the Spring Carnival, 40 of the students are chosen at random to win a prize. What is the probability that a single student chosen at random is both a girl *and* a prize winner?

Step 1 Decide if the events are independent.

G and W are independent events. Knowing that the chosen student is a girl does not help you know if the student won a prize.

Step 2 Determine the theoretical probability of each event.

$$P(G) = \frac{60}{90}$$
$$P(W) = \frac{40}{90}$$

Step 3 Simplify the theoretical probability of each event, if possible.

$$P(G) = \frac{60}{90} \text{ or } \frac{2}{3}$$
$$P(W) = \frac{40}{90} \text{ or } \frac{4}{9}$$

Step 4 Find the product of the theoretical probabilities. Simplify the product, if necessary.

$$P(G \text{ and } W) = P(G) \times P(W)$$
$$= \frac{2}{3} \times \frac{4}{9} = \frac{8}{27}$$

Solution: The probability that the student chosen is both a girl *and* a prize winner is $\frac{8}{27}$.

Another Example

Probabilities with *Not*

Flip a coin and toss a 1–6 number cube. Find the probability of the outcome heads and a number that is not 4.

$$P(H \text{ and not } 4) = P(H) \times P(\text{not } 4)$$
$$= \frac{1}{2} \times \left(1 - \frac{1}{6}\right) = \frac{1}{2} \times \frac{5}{6}$$
$$= \frac{5}{12}$$

Explain Your Thinking

- Are flipping a coin and tossing a number cube independent events? Why or why not?
- For independent events X and Y, why is P(X or Y) always greater than P(X and Y)?

Guided Practice

For tossing the cube and spinning the spinner, find each probability.

1. P(1 and blue)
2. P(yellow and an odd number)
3. P(4 and not blue)

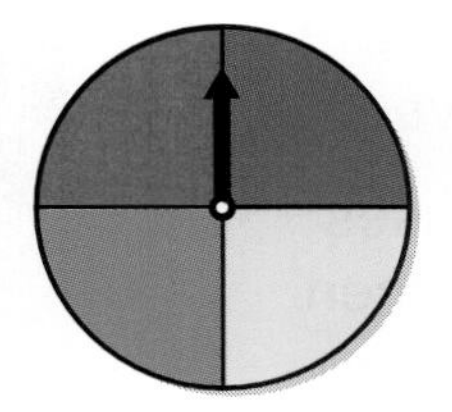

Ask Yourself

- Did I subtract from 1 to find probabilities with *not*?

Independent Practice

For tossing the cube and spinning the spinner, find each probability.

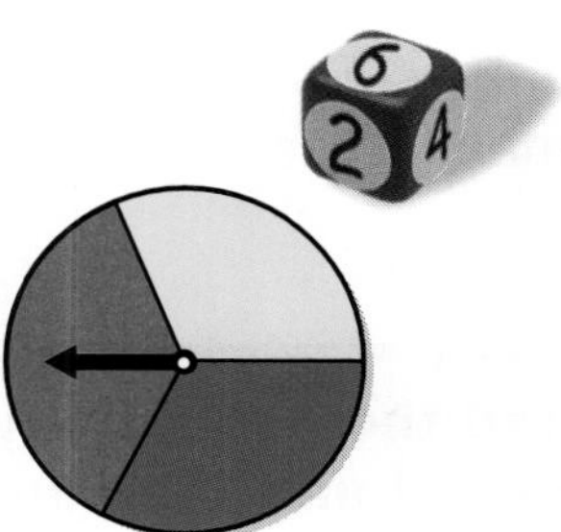

4. P(6 and red)
5. P(1 and yellow)
6. P(yellow and an even number)
7. P(1 and orange)
8. P(an even number and not red)
9. P(blue and 15)

Problem Solving • Reasoning

10. **Analyze** Fredrico flipped a coin and spun a spinner. He said that P(heads and red) $= \frac{1}{12}$. The spinner has equal sections, each of a different color. How many colors are on the spinner?

11. Design and describe a situation involving independent events such that the theoretical probability of a specific outcome is $\frac{1}{4}$. Show any calculations that you used.

12. Suzy's batting average was 0.450. Then she had 20 official at bats. How many hits did she get if her batting average did not change?

13. **Write About It** Describe a situation in which you would add probabilities. Then describe a situation in which you would multiply probabilities.

Mixed Review • Test Prep

Estimate. *(pages 364–365)*

14. 25% of 102
15. 49% of 240
16. 20% of 156
17. 66% of 180

Choose the letter of the correct answer. *(pages 464–465, 470–471)*

18. About what is the area of a circle with a diameter of 12 in.?

 A 38 in.^{2}
 B 452 in.^{2}
 C 113 in.^{2}
 D 19 in.^{2}

19. Which of the following is a solid figure with only one base?

 F prism
 G pyramid
 H cylinder
 J net

Extra Practice See Set H on page 536.

LESSON 12

Dependent Events

You will learn how to find the probability of dependent events.

New Vocabulary
dependent events

Learn About It

Sometimes the events that make up a compound event are dependent. **Dependent events** are events in which the outcome of the first event *does* affect the outcome of the second event.

Frank and Julia are playing a game that uses four 8s. Frank picks a card, keeps it, and then Julia picks a card. Find the probability of the compound event that both the cards are red if Frank keeps his card and Julia picks from the remaining cards.

Find the probability if Frank draws and keeps a card and then Julia picks a card.

If Frank keeps his card, then the possible outcomes for Julia are different.

Step 1 Find the probability of each event.

$P(A) = \frac{2}{4}$ ← number of red cards before Frank picks / ← total number of cards before Frank picks

Frank draws a red card and keeps it, so

$P(B) = \frac{1}{3}$ ← number of red cards left after Frank picks a red card / ← total number of cards left after Frank picks

Step 2 Find the product of the probabilities.

P(A and B) = P(A) × P(B if A has occurred)

$P(\text{A and B}) = \frac{\overset{1}{\cancel{2}}}{\underset{2}{\cancel{4}}} \times \frac{1}{3} = \frac{1}{6}$

Solution: The probability that both cards are red is $\frac{1}{6}$.

Another Example

Picking Two Cards in Order

Find P(blue, red) if the first card is not returned.

$P(\text{blue}) = \frac{2}{6} = \frac{1}{3}$

$P(\text{red}) = \frac{3}{5}$ ← one fewer cards

$P(\text{red, blue}) = \frac{1}{3} \times \frac{3}{5} = \frac{3}{15} = \frac{1}{5}$

Explain Your Thinking

► Explain how the events that make up a compound event can be either dependent or independent.

Guided Practice

Determine whether each event is independent or dependent. Explain your reasoning.

1. Clara and Emilio each spin a spinner.
2. Gerard picks a card from a deck and keeps it. Then Margeaux picks a card.

Ask Yourself

- Does the outcome of the first event affect the outcome of the second event?

Use the cards to find the probability of each compound event. The first card is not returned before the second card is chosen.

3. P(blue, yellow)
4. P(red, blue)
5. P(yellow, yellow)

Independent Practice

Use the cards to find the probability of picking two cards in the order and colors listed. The first card is not returned before the second card is chosen.

6. P(blue, yellow)
7. P(red, blue)
8. P(blue, not yellow)
9. P(green, not red)

Problem Solving • Reasoning

Use Data **Use the table for Problems 10 and 11.**

10. Carla and Hannah are the first two people to pick prizes from the treasure bag. What is the probability that they both pick spiders?
11. Analyze After 5 spiders and 8 stickers have been picked, Brian picks two prizes. What is the probability that both are key rings?

12. Write About It You and 3 friends are drawing straws. Three straws are long and one straw is short. Hal draws first and picks a long straw. You draw second. Are your chances of getting the short straw greater or less than Hal's chances?

Contents of the Treasure Bag

Type of Boxed Prize	Number in Bag
Plastic spider	25
Glow-in-the-dark sticker	21
Key ring	3
$20 bill	1
Total Number of Prizes	**50**

Mixed Review • Test Prep

Find the volume of each figure. *(pages 474–477)*

13. cube with 4 in. edges
14. cylinder: $d = 6$ in., $h = 10$ in.

15. Find the area of a triangle with $b = 9$ ft and $h = 6$ ft. *(pages 454–455)*

A 27 ft^2 **B** 54 ft^2 **C** 27 ft^3 **D** 54 ft^3

Extra Practice See Set I on page 536.

Problem-Solving Application: Use Data to Predict Future Events

You will learn how to use data to estimate probability.

You can use what you know about probability to make predictions.

Data for Joan's town for the month of June show that in the past 3 years, there have been 72 sunny days out of 90. Joan's coach wants to estimate the probability of having 3 sunny days in a row in June. He will assume that each day's weather is not affected by the weather from the day before.

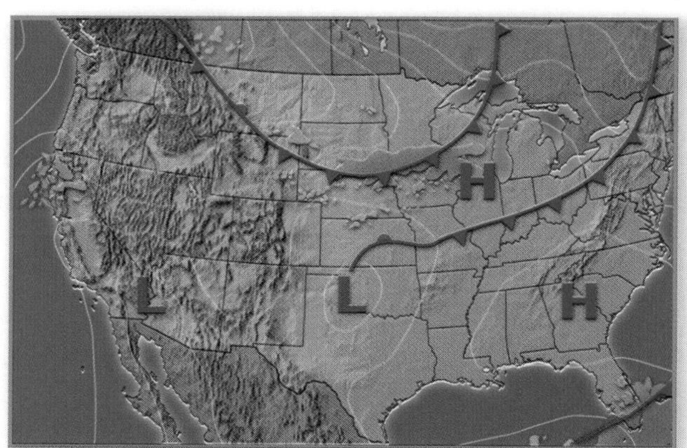

What is the question?

What is the probability of having 3 sunny days in a row in June?

What do you know?

72 out of 90 days were sunny. You can assume that the weather each day is independent of the previous day's weather.

How can you find the answer?

First, estimate the probability that any given day will be sunny. Then use the formula for the probability of independent events.

Find the probability of events A, B, and C when each event represents a sunny day.

$$P(\text{A and B and C}) = P(A) \times P(B) \times P(C)$$
$$= \frac{4}{5} \times \frac{4}{5} \times \frac{4}{5}$$
$$= \frac{64}{125} \text{ or } 0.512 \approx 50\%$$

Event	Description	Probability
A	First day is sunny.	$\frac{72}{90} = \frac{4}{5}$
B	Second day is sunny.	$\frac{72}{90} = \frac{4}{5}$
C	Third day is sunny.	$\frac{72}{90} = \frac{4}{5}$

The probability of 3 sunny days in a row is about 50%.

Look back at the problem. Is your answer reasonable?

Yes. Since a high percentage of the days in June have been sunny, there should be a reasonable chance of 3 sunny days in a row.

Remember:
- Understand
- Plan
- Solve
- Look Back

Guided Practice

Solve.

1. Joan's batting average is $\frac{9}{30}$, or 0.300. What is a reasonable prediction of the probability of Joan having no hits in her next 3 at bats?

   Think: What events make up the compound events?

2. What is a reasonable prediction of the probability of Joan having exactly one hit in 3 times at bat? having exactly two hits in 3 times at bat?

   Think: Are the events disjoint, independent, or dependent?

Choose a Strategy

Solve. Use these or other strategies.

Problem-Solving Strategies

- **Use Logical Thinking**
- **Guess and Check**
- **Solve a Simpler Problem**
- **Make a List**

3. Use the data given on this page to estimate the approximate probability of Joan having 5 hits in a row.

4. Paulo has a batting average of 0.200. Predict how many hits Paulo will get if he bats 10 times.

5. A tree diagram used to represent a probability experiment shows eight possible outcomes. For each trial of the experiment, a coin is tossed and a spinner is spun. How many outcomes does the spinner have? Are all of the outcomes equally likely? Explain.

6. In a classroom, seven chairs are arranged in a row. How many different ways can seven students arrange themselves in the chairs if Devan must always sit in a chair at either end of the row and Tika must always sit in the chair in the middle of the row?

7. In Rob's county, 20,000 drivers each drive about 10,000 miles in a year. The number of accidents per mile driven is 0.000002. About how many accidents occur there in a year?

8. A bag holds 3 white marbles and 1 red marble. Estimate the probability of drawing out, without replacing, the marbles in this order: white, white, white, red.

Extra Practice See 8–11 on page 537.

Quick Check

Check Your Understanding of Lessons 10–13

Answer each question.

1. List the possible outcomes of tossing two coins.
2. Two coins are tossed. Are the events (all heads) and (1 head, 1 tail) disjoint?
3. Find P(all heads or all tails) if two coins are tossed.

For tossing this 1–6 number cube and spinning this spinner, find each probability.

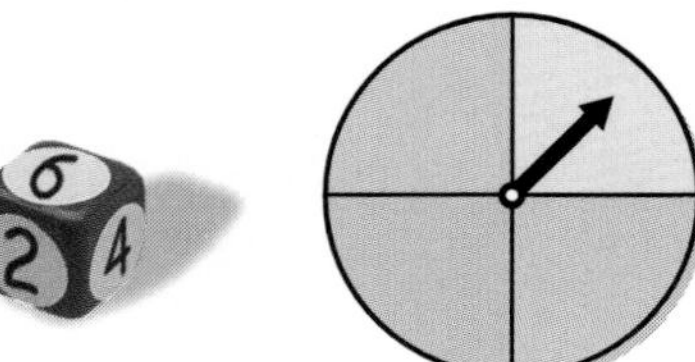

4. P(blue and 5)
5. P(prime number and not blue)
6. P(yellow and not an odd number)

Use the cards to find the probability of picking two cards in the order and colors listed. The first card is not returned before the second card is drawn.

7. P(green, then orange)
8. P(orange, then not blue)

Solve.

9. Ralph's batting average is $\frac{8}{25}$ or 0.320. What is a reasonable prediction of the probability of Ralph getting exactly two hits in 3 times at bat?

How did you do?

If you had difficulty with any items in the Quick Check, you can use the following pages for review and extra practice.

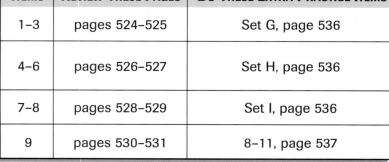

Items	Review These Pages	Do These Extra Practice Items
1–3	pages 524–525	Set G, page 536
4–6	pages 526–527	Set H, page 536
7–8	pages 528–529	Set I, page 536
9	pages 530–531	8–11, page 537

Test Prep • Cumulative Review

Maintaining the Standards

Choose the letter of the correct answer.

1 What is the height of a triangle with a base of 24 m and an area of 216 m^2?

A 9 m
B 18 m
C 36 m
D 72 m

2 Susan puts $89 in a savings account. The bank's rate of simple interest is 5.5%. How much money is in Susan's account at the end of 2 years if Susan makes no withdrawals?

F $99.06
G $93.90
H $91.90
J $9.79

3 What is the volume of this cylinder?

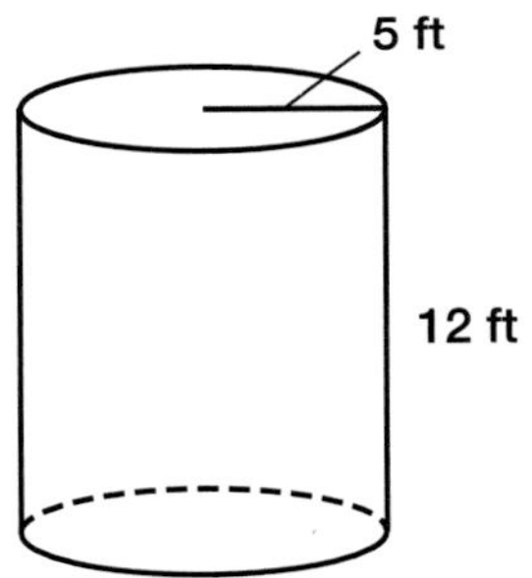

A 3,600 ft^3
B 942 ft^3
C 282 ft^3
D 60 ft^3

4 In Mike's school, $\frac{1}{3}$ of the fifth graders (f) take art and $\frac{3}{4}$ of the sixth graders (s) take a foreign language. Which expression describes the total number of fifth graders who take art and sixth graders who take a foreign language?

F $\frac{1}{3}f + s$
G $\frac{1}{3}f + \frac{3}{4}s$
H $f + \frac{3}{4}s$
J $\frac{3}{4}f + \frac{1}{3}s$

5 Kenna bikes 1.5 miles in 12 minutes. At that rate, what is her speed in miles per hour?

A 0.125 mi/h
B 7.5 mi/h
C 8 mi/h
D 12 mi/h

6 Determine the volume of a pyramid that has a rectangle for a base. The sides of the rectangle measure 3 cm and 4 cm, and the height of the pyramid is 8 cm.

F 8 cm^3
G 32 cm^3
H 48 cm^3
J 96 cm^3

7 What is the surface area of this pyramid?

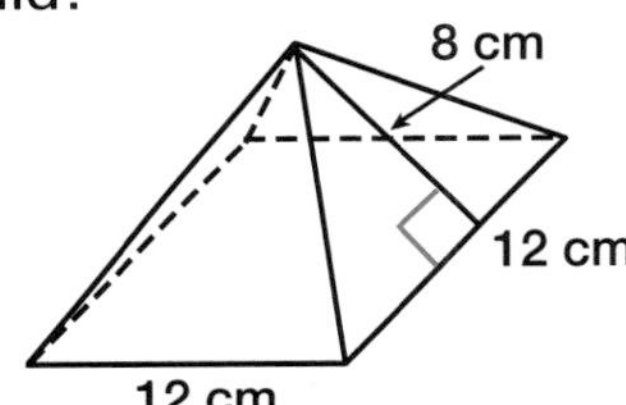

A 60 cm^2
B 144 cm^2
C 336 cm^2
D 1,152 cm^2

8 What is the measure of $\angle BOC$?

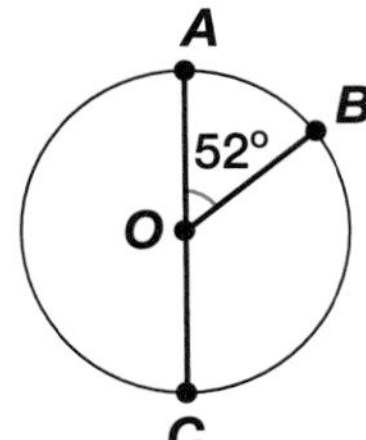

Explain Tell how you found your answer.

Internet Test Prep
Visit **www.eduplace.com/kids/mhm** for more *Test Prep Practice.*

Extra Practice

Set A (Lesson 1, pages 496–497)

Predict the number of *yes* responses from the total population.

1. total population: 500 students
   sample population: 50 students
   yes responses from sample: 25

2. total population: 800 voters
   sample population: 100 voters
   yes responses from sample: 30

Predict.

3. Suppose you ask 50 of the 300 students at a school what their favorite subject is, and 40 name math. Predict the number of students in the entire school who like math best.

4. In a sample of 100 mice, 10 mice are found to be carrying a disease. If the population of mice is estimated to be 1,000, how many disease-carrying mice would you predict there to be?

Set B (Lesson 2, pages 498–499)

Give a reason why each sample may not be representative.

1. A swim coach asks students what their favorite sport is.

2. A student asks her friends about their favorite teacher.

3. A busing survey is sent to all homes within one mile of a school.

4. One out of every 100 people is randomly chosen and sent a survey.

5. Five people are asked their opinion about what their favorite food is.

6. Ten people at a bus stop are asked what public transportation they use.

Set C (Lesson 4, pages 504–505)

Identify each source of bias.

1. People are asked, "Should your hard-earned tax dollars be wasted on that useless and unneeded road project?"

2. People are asked, "Will you vote for Bill Jones, the candidate with the sensible, money-saving programs?"

3. Students are asked, "Do you agree with your parents that this is a cool song?"

4. Students are asked, "Do you agree with 95% of the nation's teenagers that this is a cool song?"

Refer to Exercises 1 and 2 above.

5. Reword the question in Exercise 1 to remove bias.

6. Reword the question in Exercise 2 to remove bias.

Extra Practice

Set D (Lesson 5, pages 506–507)

Use the graph for Exercises 1–2.

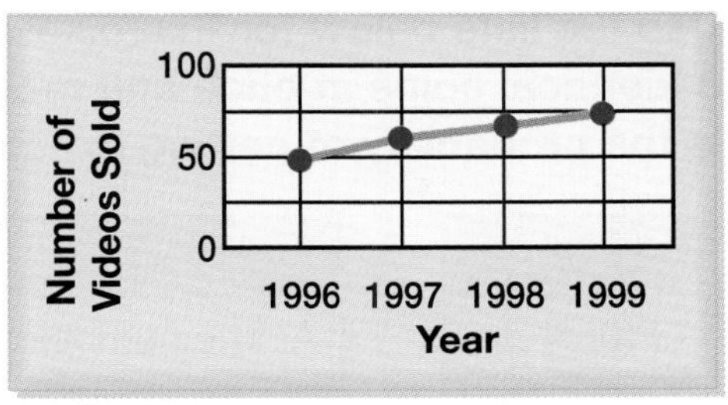

1. What might you conclude when you look quickly at the line graph? What influenced your conclusion?
2. Draw another graph that suggests the number of videos sold has increased dramatically.

Use the graph for Exercises 3–4.

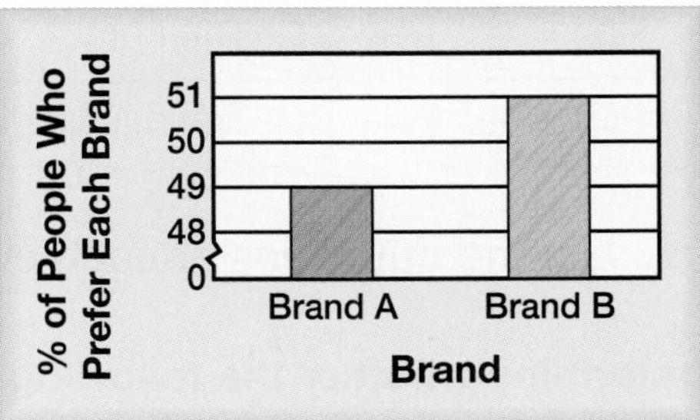

3. What might you conclude when you look at the bar graph? What influenced your conclusion?
4. Draw another graph that shows the difference of brand preferences more fairly.

Set E (Lesson 7, pages 512–514)

Make a grid, table, and tree diagram to show all possible outcomes.

1. Randomly select a season of the year. Then flip a coin.
2. Roll a 1–6 number cube. Then randomly select a geographical direction (N, S, E, W).

Use the fundamental counting principle to find the number of possible choices of one item from each group.

3. 4 shirts, 5 pants
4. 6 classes first period, 4 classes second period
5. 6 colors, 2 kinds of paint
6. 3 choices for president, 4 choices for secretary

Set F (Lesson 8, pages 516–518)

A jar contains 5 purple marbles, 12 blue marbles, 8 red marbles, 7 green marbles, and 3 yellow marbles. Suppose you draw a marble out without looking. Find each probability.

1. P(blue)
2. P(yellow)
3. P(green)
4. P(not purple)
5. P(not red)
6. P(not blue)
7. P(purple or blue)
8. P(purple or red)
9. P(red or green)

Extra Practice

Set G *(Lesson 10, pages 524–525)*

Use the lists below for Exercises 1–8. The experiment is to toss 3 identical coins at once and record the number of tails *n*. P(*n*) is the probability of getting exactly *n* tails.

P(*n*)
$P(0) = \frac{1}{8}$
$P(1) = \frac{3}{8}$
$P(2) = \frac{3}{8}$
$P(3) = \frac{1}{8}$

Events
A: The number of tails is even.
B: The number of tails is odd.
C: The number of tails is greater than 1.
D: The number of tails is less than 1.

1. List the outcomes of each event, A–D.

Determine whether the following pairs of events are disjoint. If the events are not disjoint, name a common outcome.

2. A and B **3.** A and C **4.** B and C **5.** C and D

Find each probability.

6. P(0 or 2) **7.** P(B) **8.** P(C)

Set H *(Lesson 11, pages 526–527)*

Find the probability of each event.

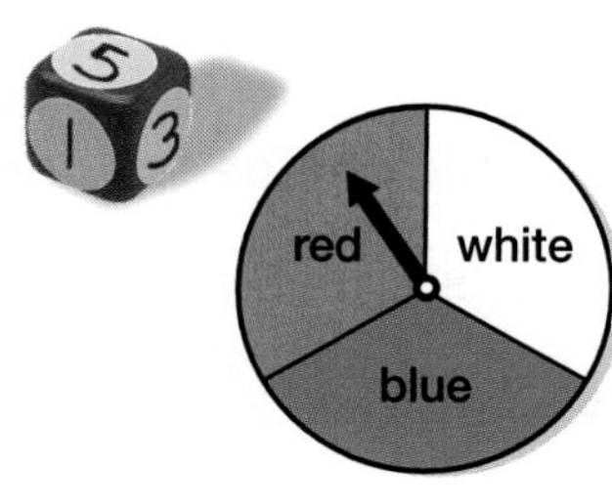

1. P(1 and blue) **2.** P(red and an even number)

3. P(5 and red) **4.** P(white and an odd number)

5. P(3 and not white) **6.** P(6 and not blue)

Set I *(Lesson 12, pages 528–529)*

Use the cards to find the probability of choosing two cards in the order and shapes listed. The first card is not returned before the second card is chosen.

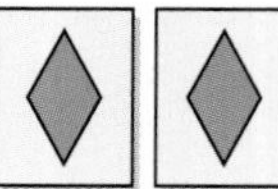

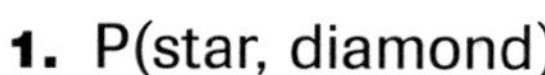

1. P(star, diamond)

2. P(diamond, not diamond)

3. P(happy face, happy face)

Extra Practice • Problem Solving

Solve. Use the skills you have learned to solve these multistep problems. *(Lesson 3, pages 500–501)*

1. The student newspaper reports that in a sixth grade, 56 students have traveled to another state, while 30% of the students have not traveled outside their state. How many students are in the sixth grade?

2. Last year, 75 out of 300 students favored a dress code. This year, $\frac{2}{3}$ as many students out of 300 favor one. Based on this sample, predict how many of 500 students would be in favor of a dress code this year.

3. One third of the students in John's class eat lunch in the cafeteria. One third of the students and 4 additional students bring their lunch to school. The other 4 students in the class go home for lunch. How many students are in John's class?

4. On Wednesday, 12 students were late to school. On Thursday, $\frac{3}{4}$ as many students were late. On Friday, $\frac{2}{3}$ of the number of students who were late on Thursday were late. How many students were late on Friday?

Solve. Use the Guess and Check strategy or another strategy. *(Lesson 6, pages 508–509)*

5. William is mixing yellow and blue paint in art class to make 2 cups of green paint. If he uses 3 times as much yellow paint in the mixture as blue paint, how much blue paint does he use?

6. When making sandwiches, Timmy uses 3 times as much peanut butter as jelly. In one year, he uses 51 jars of peanut butter. How many same-size jars of jelly does he use during this time period?

7. Petra shopped for school supplies and paid $10.25 for 9 notebooks. How many of each type of notebook did she buy?

Notebook Prices

Kind	Price
Widerule	$1.00
Narrowrule	$1.25

Solve. For Problems 9 and 10, assume that the weather on any day is independent of the weather the day before. *(Lesson 13, pages 530–531)*

8. Dennis has a batting average of 0.250. Estimate the probability that Dennis will get 2 hits in his next 2 times at bat.

9. In a city it rains an average of 1 out of 10 days. Estimate the probability that it will rain there 3 days in a row.

10. Margo lives in a place where it rains an average of 3 out of every 5 days. Estimate the probability that it will rain 2 out of the next 3 days.

11. Jason has a softball batting average of 0.350. Estimate the number of hits he will get if he bats 20 times during games this week.

Chapter Review

Reviewing Vocabulary

Write *always, sometimes,* or *never* to answer each statement. Give an example to support your answer.

1. A sample is a representative sample.
2. A convenience sample may contain bias.
3. An experimental probability of an event is the same as the theoretical probability of that event.
4. Dependent events have no effect on each other.

Reviewing Concepts and Skills

Predict the number of *yes* responses from the total population. *(pages 496–497)*

5. total population: 1,200 students
sample population: 100 students
yes responses from sample: 75

6. total population: 200 teachers
sample population: 30 teachers
yes responses from sample: 12

Reword each question to remove bias. *(pages 498–499, 504–505)*

7. People are asked, "Do you think it is fair that we are being charged such outrageous amounts for the gasoline we need to drive to work?"

8. People are asked, "Are you going to vote to build a new highway that will increase pollution and destroy several neighborhoods?"

Make a grid, table, or tree diagram to show each sample space. Use a different method for each problem. *(pages 512–514)*

9. Toss a 1–6 cube and randomly select a season of the year.

10. Randomly select a direction (N, S, E, W) and flip a coin.

Use the fundamental counting principle to find the number of possible choices when you combine one item from each group. *(pages 512–514)*

11. 3 skirts, 5 blouses

12. 12 flavors of ice cream, 3 kinds of cones

A jar contains 5 red marbles, 7 blue marbles, 6 yellow marbles, and 12 green marbles. Suppose you draw a marble out without looking. Find each probability. *(pages 516–518, 524–525)*

13. P(blue)

14. P(red or blue)

15. P(not red)

For tossing this 1–6 number cube and randomly selecting a direction (N, S, E, or W), find each probability. *(pages 526–527)*

16. P(1, W)

17. P(3, N)

18. P(an even number, S)

19. P(2 not E)

Find each probability for choosing two shape cards in the given order. The first card is not returned before the second card is chosen. *(pages 528–529)*

20. P(moon, sun)

21. P(heart, sun)

22. P(moon, not heart)

23. P(sun, sun)

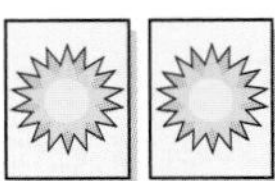

Solve. *(pages 500–501, 508–509, 530–531)*

24. In a survey of parents last year, 40 out of 90 parents said they would prefer year-round school for their children. This year, 10 percent more parents would prefer year-round school. Based on this sample, how many parents this year would prefer year-round school?

25. Each student in Jim's class plays on one sports team. One fourth play on the soccer team. One fourth and 6 more play on the basketball team. The remaining 6 students are on the track team. How many students are in Jim's class?

26. Alejandro's batting average is 0.300. If he bats 20 times during the next week, how many hits would you expect him to get?

27. Corey has a batting average of 0.400. Estimate the probability that he will get at least one hit in his next 2 times at bat.

Brain Teasers Math Reasoning

Take a Spin

Label a spinner so that the probability of landing on a prime factor of 165 is $\frac{5}{8}$ and the probability of landing on a prime factor of 84 is $\frac{1}{2}$.

Marble Logic

Jar 1 has 4 red and 4 blue marbles. Jar 2 has 5 red and 5 blue marbles. In which jar is the probability of picking two marbles of the same color greater?

Internet Brain Teasers
Visit **www.eduplace.com/kids/mhm** for more *Brain Teasers.*

Chapter Test

Predict the number of *yes* responses from the total population.

1. total population: 12,000 voters
   sample population: 100 voters
   yes responses from sample: 30
2. total population: 700 students
   sample population: 140 students
   yes responses from sample: 58

Identify each source of bias.

3. Students are asked, "Don't you think that a 4.6 percent tuition increase is overly excessive?"
4. Parents are asked, "Do you agree that students today don't work as hard as students did when you went to school?"
5. Reword the question in Exercise 3 to remove bias.
6. Reword the question in Exercise 4 to remove bias.

A jar contains 4 red marbles, 3 white marbles, and 7 blue marbles. Suppose you draw a marble outwithout looking. List the sample space. Find each probability.

7. P(blue)
8. P(not red)
9. P(not white)
10. P(blue or red)

Suppose you toss a coin and spin this spinner. Find each probability.

11. P(tails, green)
12. P(not heads and white)
13. P(heads and not white)
14. P(not tails and not blue)

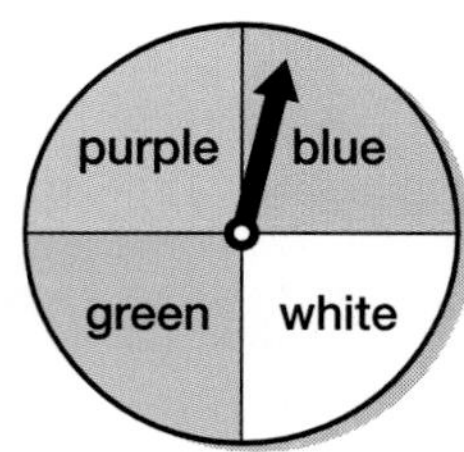

Use the cards to find the probability of choosing two shape cards in the given order. The first card is not returned before the second card is chosen.

15. P(apple, orange)
16. P(orange, banana)
17. P(apple, not banana)
18. P(banana, not banana)

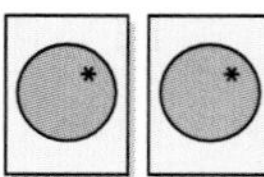

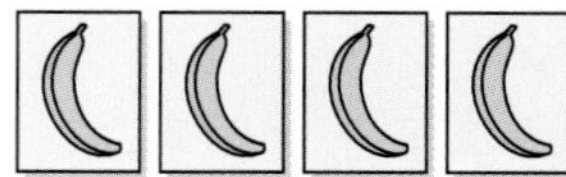

Solve.

19. Fred always makes his sandwiches a certain way. He always puts 3 slices of ham and 2 slices of cheese on each sandwich. During the past 2 months, he has used 45 pieces of ham for sandwiches. How many pieces of cheese did Fred use for those sandwiches?

20. Alexa lives in a place where it is sunny an average 7 out of every 8 days. If the weather each day is independent of the previous day's weather, what is the probability it will be sunny 3 days in a row?

Write About It

Solve each problem. Use correct math vocabulary to explain your thinking.

1. Liz studied this graph and concluded that Yummy O's must be tastier than Fruity Nuggets.

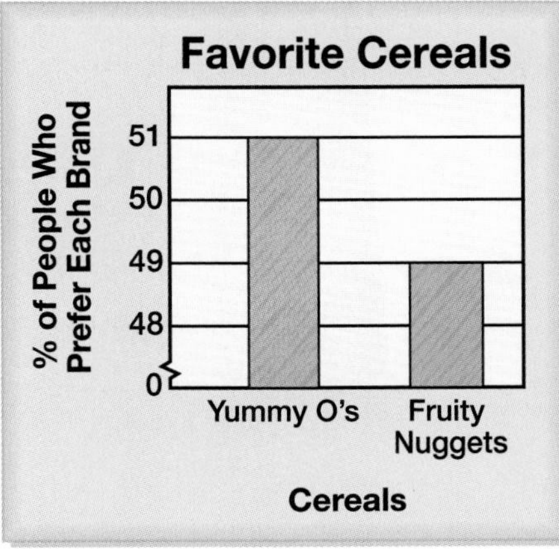

a. Do you agree with Liz's conclusion? Why or why not?

b. Redraw the graph to present the data fairly.

2. Of the 9 pennies in Nicola's pocket, 3 were minted in 1999, 4 in 2000, and 2 in 2001. If Nicola chooses 2 pennies at random, what is the probability that she will choose a 1999 and a 2001 penny?

a. Represent the problem with a drawing, with numbers, or in some other way.

b. Show your work and find the answer.

c. Explain how you know that your answer is correct.

3. In a random survey of 50 students, 20% said they attended a school sports event during the past 2 weeks.

a. If there are 450 students in the school, tell about how many may have attended a school sporting event during the past 2 weeks.

b. Estimate the probability that a single student selected at random would have attended a school sports event during the past 2 weeks.

Another Look

Use the information from the catalog page to solve each problem. Show your work.

SALE! Buy one, get one free!
Mastodon $11.95
Agate $11.95
Keychain
$11.95
Box $11.95
Wooden Cat
$11.95

1. The museum gift shop is having a sale. If you buy one item from this page of the museum catalog, you get a different item free. How many combinations of one purchased item and one free item are possible?
2. The first 75 customers are entered in a drawing to win a free item. The museum shop is giving away 6 CDs and 9 posters. What is the probability of winning a CD? What is the probability of winning a poster?
3. **Look Back** What is the probability of winning a CD or a poster?
4. **Analyze** If the museum shop has already given away 1 CD and 4 of the posters, what is the probability of winning one of the remaining CDs or posters?

Enrichment

Strategies

New **Vocabulary**
strategy

An understanding of probabilities can be used to develop strategies. Look at the following example.

A bag has three discs in it. One disc is colored blue on both sides (blue-blue). One disc is colored red on both sides (red-red). One disc is colored blue on one side and red on another (blue-red).

A disc is drawn from the bag, and you see the color of only one side. Your task is to guess the color on the other side of the disc.

You can develop a **strategy** or a plan, for guessing the color on the other side, even though you do not know the color that was drawn.

What is your strategy?

Step 1 Determine how many ways the color on the side you cannot see is the SAME color as the side that you can see. Red-red and blue-blue are the two ways.

Step 2 Determine the total possibilities. Red-red, blue-blue, blue-red are the only possibilities.

Step 3 Determine the probability that the color is the same color as the side you see.

$$P = \frac{2}{3}$$

Step 4 Determine the probability that the color is different from the color you see.

$$P = \frac{1}{3}$$

Solution: Because $\frac{2}{3}$ is greater than $\frac{1}{3}$, you will be right more often by using the strategy of guessing that the color on the back is the same as the color you see.

Determine a strategy for similar games, but with different numbers of discs in the bag.

1. The bag has 5 discs in it: 3 that are blue-red, 1 that is red-red, and 1 that is blue-blue.
2. The bag has 4 discs in it: 2 that are blue-red, 1 that is red-red, and 1 that is blue-blue.

Coordinate Graphing, Equations, and Integers

Why Learn About Coordinate Graphing, Equations, and Integers?

You can use coordinate graphing, equations, and integers to understand and display the relationship between two variables.

If you earn $5.00 an hour when you baby-sit, you make a graph to show the relationship between the number of hours you baby-sit and the amount of money you earn.

Many cities, like the one shown in this aerial photograph, are laid out in a grid. When people look at a map of the city, they use coordinates to locate a specific place on the map.

Reviewing Vocabulary

Understanding math vocabulary helps you become a successful problem solver. Here are some math vocabulary words you should know.

evaluate find the value of an expression by substituting a number for the variable

expression a way of writing operations on numbers and variables, using symbols

linear equation an equation like $y = 2x + 3$. The ordered pairs that are solutions to this equation all lie along the same line.

order of operations
1. Complete any operation(s) inside parentheses.
2. Evaluate any terms with exponents.
3. Multiply and divide in order from left to right.
4. Add and subtract in order from left to right.

quadrant one of four parts into which a plane is separated by the *x*-axis and the *y*-axis. The axes are not parts of the quadrant.

Reading Words and Symbols

When you read mathematics, sometimes you read only words, sometimes you read words and symbols, and sometimes you read only symbols.

Quadrants are represented by Roman numerals.

You can determine the quadrant placement of any point to be graphed.

- (1, 4) consists of two positive numbers. This point will lie in Quadrant I.
- ($^-5$, $^-4$) consists of two negative numbers. This point will lie in Quadrant III.
- ($^-1$, 5) and (2, $^-5$) each consists of one positive and one negative number. The first point will lie in Quadrant II and the second point will lie in Quadrant IV.

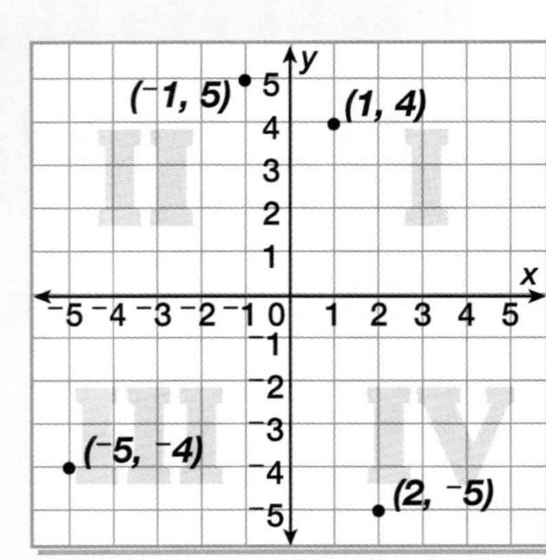

Try These

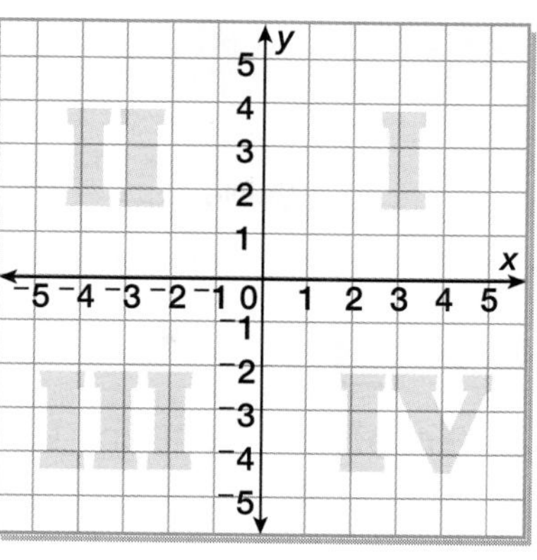

1. Name the quadrant in which each point lies.

   a. (⁻4, 4) **b.** (3, ⁻1)

   c. (5, 5) **d.** (⁻3, ⁻2)

   e. (6, 2) **f.** (⁻10, 3)

   g. (4, ⁻8) **h.** (⁻9, 2)

2. Write *true* or *false* for each statement.

   a. An expression consists only of variables.

   b. The first step in the order of operations is to complete what is in parentheses.

   c. Some coordinate planes may have more than four quadrants.

3. Indicate which operation should be performed first in simplifying the following expressions.

   a. $(5 + 3) \times 2$ **b.** $5 + 3 \times 2$ **c.** $5 + 3^2 \times 2$ **d.** $5 + 3 - 2$

   e. $3 - 2 + 5$ **f.** $5 \times 2 - 3$ **g.** $2 - 3 \times 5$ **h.** $5 - (3 \div 2)$

Upcoming Vocabulary

Write About It **Here are some other vocabulary words** you will learn in this chapter. Watch for these words. Write their definitions in your journal.

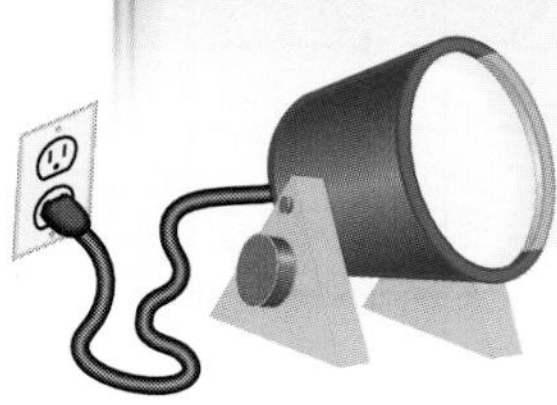

coordinate plane
origin
ordered pair
function
***x*-coordinate**
***y*-coordinate**

Graph Points in the Coordinate Plane

You will learn how to identify and graph points in a coordinate plane.

Review Vocabulary
coordinate plane
origin
ordered pair
x-coordinate
y-coordinate

Learn About It

A **coordinate plane** contains a horizontal number line called the *x*-axis and a vertical number line called the *y*-axis. The point where the two axes intersect is called the **origin**. The number pair (0, 0) gives the coordinates of the origin. The axes divide the coordinate plane into four quadrants, I, II, III, and IV.

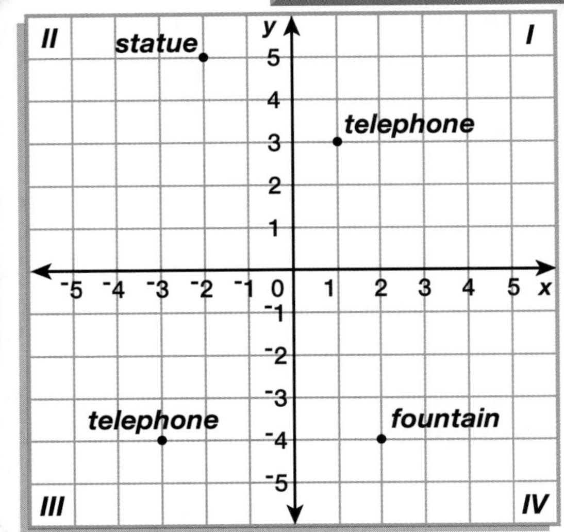

Find the coordinates for the fountain.

Step 1 Locate the fountain on the coordinate plane above. — The fountain is in Quadrant IV.

Step 2 Find the distance left or right of the origin. Find the distance above or below the origin. — The point for the fountain is 2 units to the right of the origin. The point for the fountain is 4 units below the origin.

Solution: The fountain is located at (2, ⁻4).

(2, ⁻4) is called an **ordered pair**. The number 2 is the first number, or ***x*-coordinate**, and the number ⁻4 is the second number, or ***y*-coordinate**, in the ordered pair.

Name the point located at (⁻3, ⁻2).

Step 1 Begin at the origin. Since ⁻3 is a negative integer, move three units to the left.

Step 2 Next, since ⁻2 is a negative integer, move down two units.

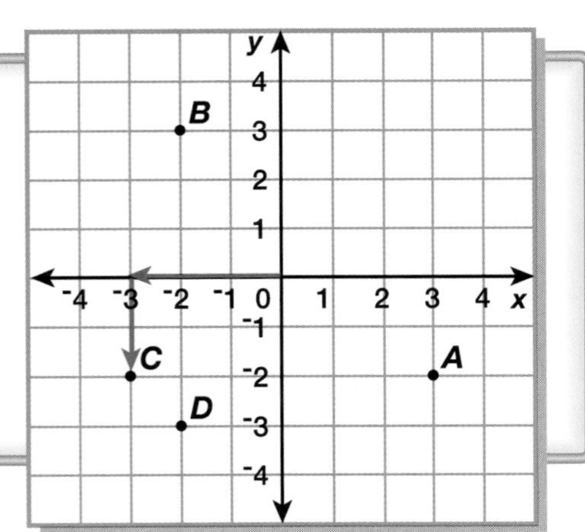

Solution: Point *C* is located at (⁻3, ⁻2).

Explain Your Thinking

- Which axis is used to find the first coordinate of an ordered pair? Which axis is used to find the second coordinate?
- In which quadrant is the point ($^-1$, 3)? How do you know?

Guided Practice

> **Ask Yourself**
> - Did I count along the *x*-axis to find the first coordinate?
> - Did I count along the *y*-axis to find the second coordinate?

Use the graph on the right. Write the coordinates of each point.

1. *A* **2.** *L* **3.** *J* **4.** *F*

Use the graph on the right. Name the point for each ordered pair. Tell in which quadrant or on which axis the point lies.

5. (1, $^-3$) **6.** (3, $^-1$) **7.** ($^-1$, $^-3$)

8. (3, 1) **9.** (0, $^-2$) **10.** (2, 0)

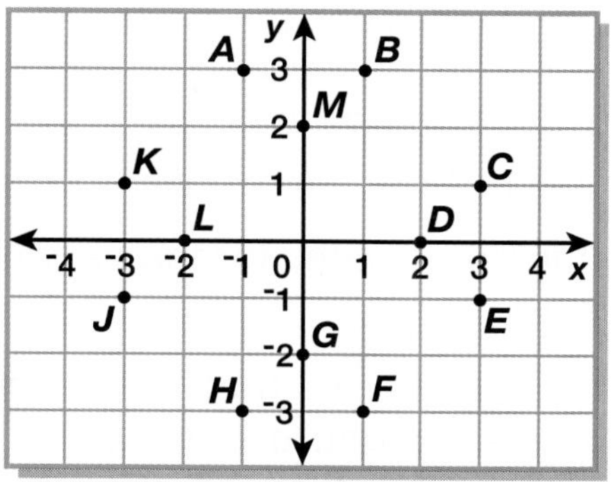

Independent Practice

Use the graph on the right. Write the coordinates of each point.

11. *A* **12.** *B*

13. *C* **14.** *D*

15. *E* **16.** *F*

17. *G* **18.** *H*

Use the graph on the right. Name the point for each ordered pair.

19. (2, 5) **20.** ($^-2$, $^-3$)

21. ($^-4$, 3) **22.** (0, 4)

23. (4, $^-1$) **24.** ($^-2$, 3)

25. (5, 2) **26.** ($^-1$, 0)

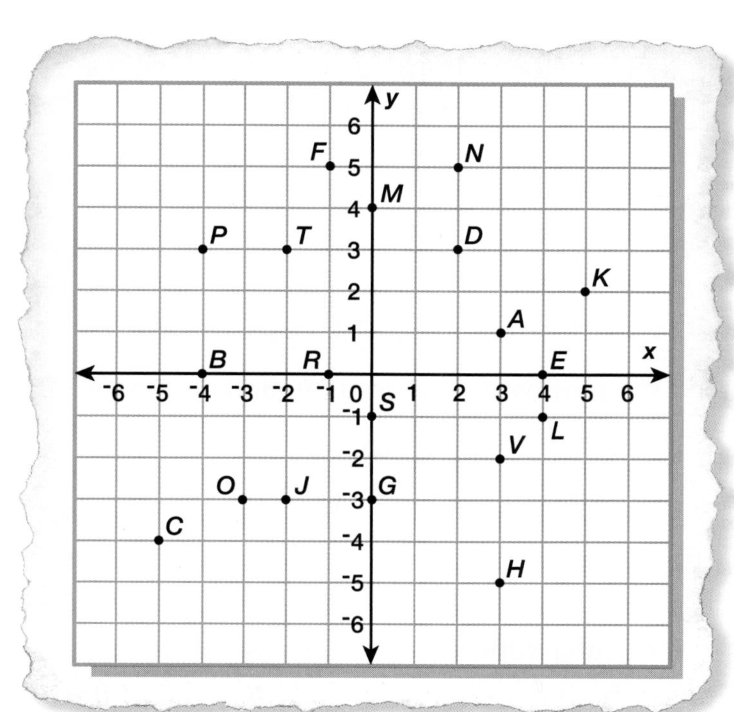

Graph each ordered pair. Label the point with the given letter. Tell in which quadrant or on which axis the point lies.

27. Point A (1, 5)

28. Point B (3, $^-6$)

29. Point C (0, $^-2$)

30. Point D ($^-4$, $^-6$)

31. Point E ($^-5$, 4)

32. Point F ($^-2$, $^-5$)

33. Point G (5, $^-2$)

34. Point H (0, 3)

35. Point J ($^-6$, 0)

Answer each question.

36. A point is in Quadrant IV. What is the sign of the first coordinate? What is the sign of the second coordinate?

37. A point is in Quadrant III. What is the sign of the first coordinate? What is the sign of the second coordinate?

38. The first coordinate of a point is negative, and the second coordinate is positive. In which quadrant does the point lie?

39. Both coordinates of a point are positive. Neither coordinate is 0. In what quadrant does the point lie?

Problem Solving • Reasoning

Use Data **Use the map for Problems 40–42.**

40. Name the coordinates for the entrance to the zoo.

41. **Analyze** The point that locates which animals has a negative x-coordinate and a positive y-coordinate? In which quadrant does this point lie?

42. **Predict** Akiko leaves the lions and walks left 5 units and up 1 unit. What animals are there? Write the coordinates of the point.

43. **Write About It** Give a real-world example of how you would use a coordinate plane. Explain.

Mixed Review • Test Prep

Find the perimeter and area of each rectangle. *(pages 450–451)*

44. $l = 4$ in.
$w = 6$ in.

45. $l = 7$ ft
$w = 2$ ft

46. $l = 1\frac{1}{2}$ yd
$w = \frac{1}{2}$ yd

47. $l = 3.5$ in.
$w = 2.9$ in.

48 Aaron picks a card from a deck and keeps it. Then Margo picks a card. What kind of event is Margo's pick compared to Aaron's? *(pages 528–529)*

A independent

B both dependent and independent

C dependent

D none of the above

Extra Practice See Set A on page 582.

Practice Game

Recycle That Newspaper

Practice graphing ordered pairs by playing this game.

What You'll Need

- *Decimal Grid or Fraction Grid for each player (Teaching Tool 11)*

Players
2

Here's What to Do

1. The object of the game is to find the other player's newspaper and recycling center.
2. Each player marks the location of a newspaper (1 point) and a recycling center (3 points in a row) on his or her grid without letting the other player see the points.
3. First, take turns naming the coordinates of a point to try to locate the other player's newspaper. After each try, the other player will tell whether it was found or give a hint telling whether it is above, below, to the right of, or to the left of the named point.
4. After finding the newspaper, each player tries to locate all 3 points of the other player's recycling center. The first player to find the newspaper and recycling center is the winner.

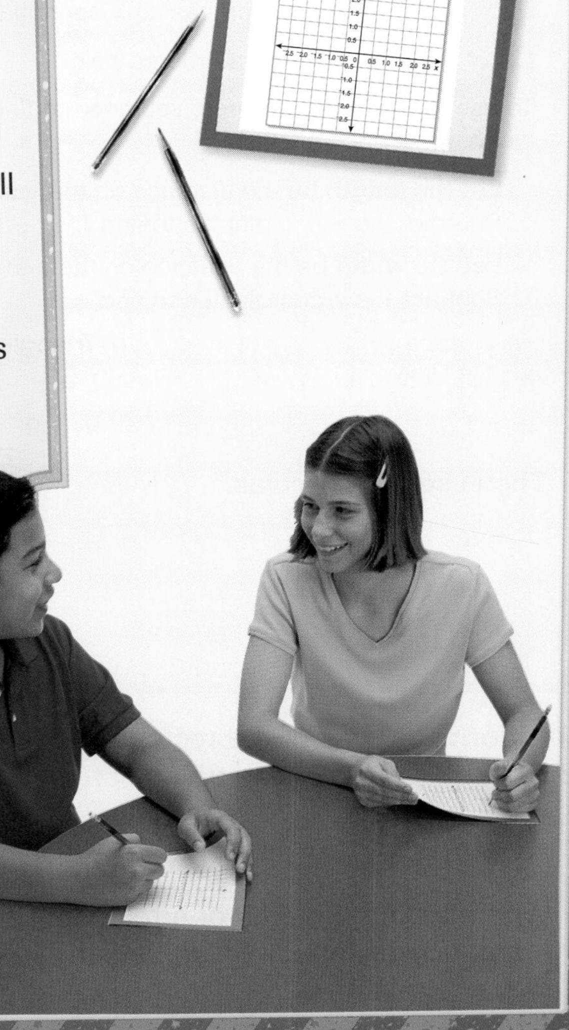

Share Your Thinking What strategy did you use for placing your newspaper and recycling center on your grid? What strategy did you use for guessing?

Geometric Figures and the Coordinate Plane

You will learn how to find the area of geometric figures on a coordinate plane.

Learn About It

Ms. Whitley volunteered at an excavation site in Utah. Her album contains pictures of the archaeologists and volunteers excavating different sections of the site. What is the area of the sections that Ms. Whitley helped excavate?

Finding Area in a Coordinate Plane

First, find the distances.

Each vertex of the section has an *x*-coordinate and a *y*-coordinate.

Label each vertex with its ordered pair.

To use the formulas for area, you need to find the length, l, and width, w, of each section.

Let the length be the distance on the *x*-axis. Subtract the *x*-coordinates to find l.

Let the width be the distance on the *y*-axis. Subtract the *y*-coordinates to find w.

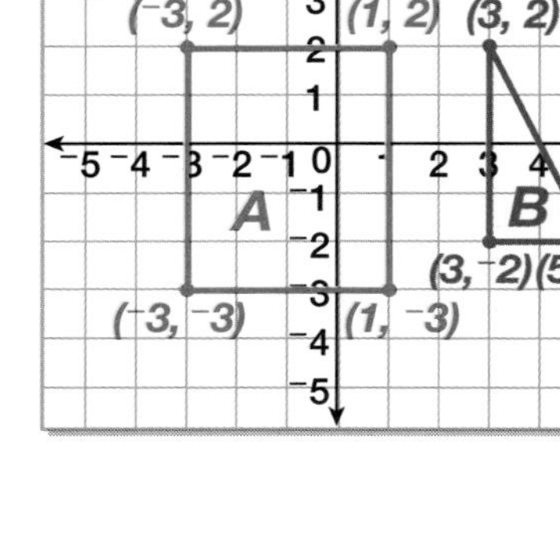

Rectangle A

$l = 1 - {}^{-}3 = 4$

$w = 2 - {}^{-}3 = 5$

Triangle B

$l = 5 - 3 = 2$

$w = 2 - {}^{-}2 = 4$

Then use the formulas.

Rectangle A:

$A = lw$

$= 4 \times 5$

$= 20$ square units

Triangle B:

$A = \frac{1}{2}lw$

$= \frac{1}{2} \times 2 \times 4$

$= 4$ square units

Solution: The area of the rectangular site is 20 square units and the area of the triangular site is 4 square units.

Explain Your Thinking

► When finding the area of a rectangle or triangle, does it matter which measure is the length and which is the width? Explain.

Guided Practice

Find the area of each figure.

1. Rectangle *A*
2. Triangle *D*

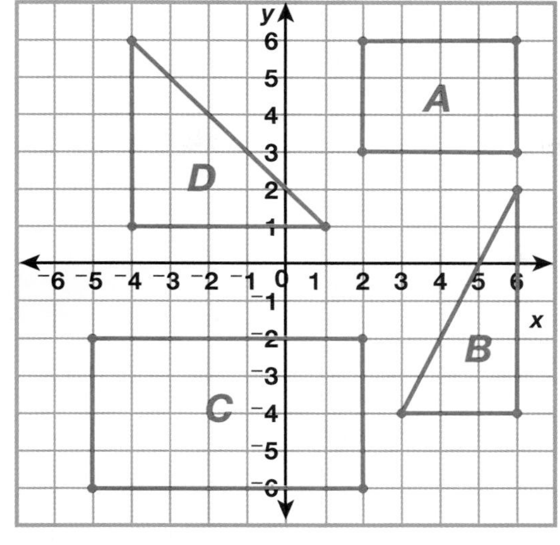

Ask Yourself

- Which coordinates do I subtract to find the length and width of the figure?

Independent Practice

Find the area of each figure.

3. Rectangle *C*
4. Triangle *B*

Graph each point. Connect the points in order and connect the last point to the first. Find the area of each figure.

5. (4, ⁻2), (10, ⁻2), (10, ⁻5), (4, ⁻5)
6. (⁻3, 2), (⁻7, 2), (⁻7, 3), (⁻3, 3)
7. (3, ⁻2), (7, ⁻2), (7, ⁻8)
8. (⁻3, 2), (⁻3, ⁻4), (6, 2)

Problem Solving • Reasoning

9. **Predict** Archaeologists rope off a rectangular excavation site that is located on a coordinate grid. The vertices of the site are (5, 3), (17, 3), (5, ⁻11), and (17, ⁻11). If the units are in meters, how many meters are the length and the width of the site? What is the area of the site?
10. **Analyze** A triangle has an area of 96 ft^2. The length of the triangle is 3 times its width. What are the length and the width of the triangle?
11. An excavation site has vertices (⁻12, ⁻4), (⁻12, ⁻21), (7, ⁻4), and (7, ⁻21), with units in feet. A test plot within the site has been excavated. The area of the test plot is 16 ft^2. What area has not been excavated?

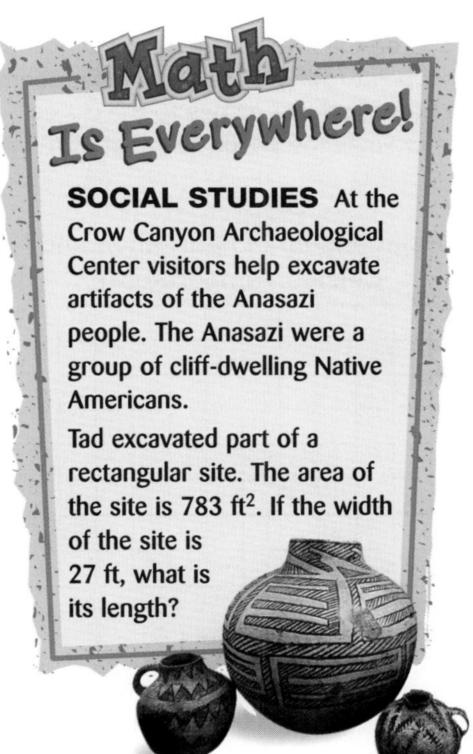

Math Is Everywhere!
SOCIAL STUDIES At the Crow Canyon Archaeological Center visitors help excavate artifacts of the Anasazi people. The Anasazi were a group of cliff-dwelling Native Americans.
Tad excavated part of a rectangular site. The area of the site is 783 ft^2. If the width of the site is 27 ft, what is its length?

Mixed Review • Test Prep

Find the area of each triangle. *(pages 454–455)*

12. base = 10 ft, height = 16 ft
13. base = 9 ft, height = $7\frac{1}{2}$ ft
14. Which is the best estimate of a 15% tip for a $21.35 bill at a restaurant? *(pages 364–365)*
    A $2 **B** $3 **C** $1 **D** $5

LESSON 3

Graphs and Measurement

You will learn how to convert between customary and metric units.

Learn About It

For his science-fair project, Pierre must cool a solution to a temperature of 15°C. Pierre has a Fahrenheit thermometer. How can he convert 15°C into a Fahrenheit temperature? What would that temperature be?

Convert. **15°C = ■°F**

Different Ways to Convert Temperatures

You can use a graph.

Find 15°C on the *x*-axis. Draw a vertical line from this point to the graph. From this point, draw a horizontal line across to the *y*-axis. The line crosses the *y*-axis at about 60°F.

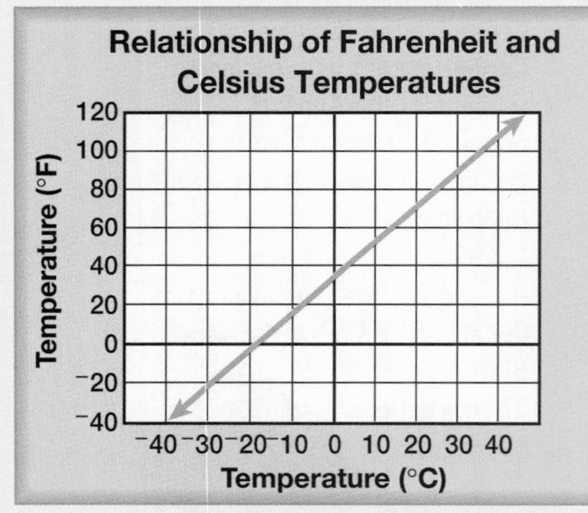

You can use a conversion formula.

The relationship between Fahrenheit (*F*) and Celsius (*C*) temperatures is expressed by this formula.

$$F = \frac{9}{5}C + 32$$

Convert 15°C to degrees in Fahrenheit.

$$\begin{aligned} F &= \frac{9}{5}C + 32 \\ &= \frac{9}{\cancel{5}_1}(\cancel{15}^3) + 32 \\ &= 9 \times 3 + 32 \\ &= 27 + 32 \\ &= 59 \end{aligned}$$

You can also use a quick estimate.

$$\begin{aligned} F &\approx 2C + 30 \\ &\approx 2(15) + 30 \\ &\approx 30 + 30 \\ &\approx 60 \end{aligned}$$

15°C ≈ 60°F

Solution: Pierre's thermometer would read about 60°F.

Explain Your Thinking

► If Pierre needs to know an exact temperature in degrees Fahrenheit, which method should he use? Explain.

Guided Practice

Complete. Check your answers with a quick estimate.

1. Use the graph.
   27°C ≈ ■°F

2. Use the formula.
   −25°C = ■°F

> **Ask Yourself**
> - Which axis shows Fahrenheit temperatures?
> - Did I calculate correctly?

Independent Practice

Use the graph on page 554 to approximate each temperature in °F.

3. 24°C ≈ ■°F **4.** 13°C ≈ ■°F **5.** 40°C ≈ ■°F **6.** 35°C ≈ ■°F

Use the formula $F = \frac{9}{5}C + 32$ to convert each Celsius temperature. Check your answers with a quick estimate.

7. 20°C = ■°F **8.** 35°C = ■°F **9.** 25°C = ■°F **10.** 3.3°C = ■°F

11. 9.1°C = ■°F **12.** 100°C = ■°F **13.** −10°C = ■°F **14.** −40°C = ■°F

Problem Solving • Reasoning

Use Data **Use the chart or the graph for Problems 15 and 16.**

15. On Sunday, Paul walked three times as far as he did on Saturday. On Saturday, he walked half as far as he did on Friday. If Paul walked 2.5 kilometers on Friday, about how many miles did he walk altogether?

16. **Estimate** Suppose you extend the *x*-axis of the graph to include values greater than 50 centimeters. Approximate the number of inches in 60 centimeters.

17. Roy, Pam, Bill, and Grace have one marker each. The markers are red, blue, green, and purple. No one has a color that begins with the same letter as their name. Grace does not have blue or purple. Bill does not have red or purple. What color marker does Roy have?

Converting Between Customary and Metric Lengths

1 in. = 25.4 mm	3.28 ft ≈ 1 m
1 in. = 2.54 cm	1.09 yd ≈ 1 m
1 ft = 30.48 cm	1 mi ≈ 1.6 km

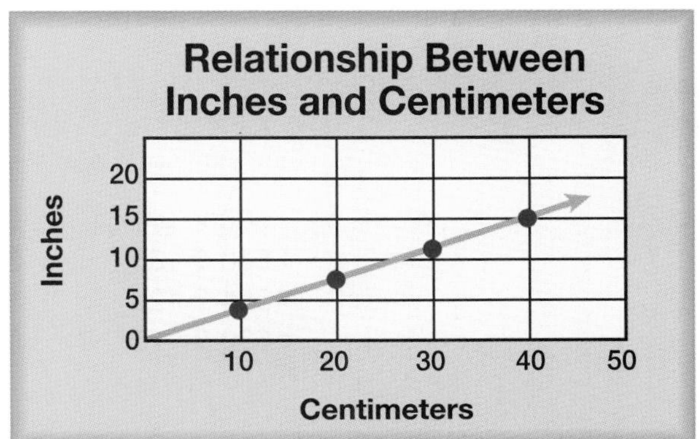

Mixed Review • Test Prep

Find the circumference of each circle. *(pages 460–462)*

18. $r = 5$ ft **19.** $d = 1\frac{1}{2}$ yd **20.** $r = 6.8$ ft **21.** $d = 100$ in.

22 Darian has 4 scarves and 6 hats. What is the number of possible combinations? *(pages 512–514)*

A 10 **B** 24 **C** 64 **D** 48

Problem-Solving Strategy: Find a Pattern

You will learn how to find a pattern and write an equation using variables.

Sometimes it is helpful to identify a pattern in a problem. If you can write an equation describing the pattern, then you can use the equation to find new numbers in the pattern.

Problem The manager at Pat's Bakery records the amount of flour and cheese used each week to make cheese bread. Look at the table on the right. Find a pattern relating the amounts of flour and cheese used each week. Write an equation describing the pattern.

Flour and Cheese Use Each Week

	Amount of Flour	Amount of Cheese
Week 1	600 cups	150 cups
Week 2	660 cups	165 cups
Week 3	504 cups	126 cups
Week 4	692 cups	173 cups

Understand

What is the question?

What is the relationship between the amounts of cheese and flour?

What do you know?

The data in the table are the given information.

How can you find the answer?

Look for a pattern. Then express the pattern using variables.

Think
Analyze the data by comparing numbers. You might try subtraction and division.

Solve

Find the pattern.

	Try subtraction.	Try division.
Week 1 → 600 **?** 150	$600 - 150 =$ **450**	$600 \div 150 =$ **4**
Week 2 → 660 **?** 165	$660 - 165 =$ **495**	$660 \div 165 =$ **4**
Week 3 → 504 **?** 126	$504 - 126 =$ **378**	$504 \div 126 =$ **4**
Week 4 → 692 **?** 173	$692 - 173 =$ **519**	$692 \div 173 =$ **4**
	There is no pattern.	**The pattern is *divide by 4.***

Write an equation.

$f =$ amount of flour $\quad c =$ amount of cheese $\quad f \div 4 = c$

Look Back

Look back at the problem

Is your answer reasonable? Is the amount of cheese $\frac{1}{4}$ the amount of flour?

Remember:
- Understand
- Plan
- Solve
- Look Back

Guided Practice

Solve each problem, using the Find a Pattern strategy. Use the information on page 556 for Problem 1.

1. The manager of Pat's Bakery is planning a sale next week. She hopes to sell more cheese bread than usual. If she buys 840 cups of flour for cheese bread, how much cheese should she buy?

   Think: Which equation can be used to solve the problem?

2. One loaf of raisin bread is made with $3\frac{1}{2}$ c flour and 1 c raisins. Two loaves use 7 c flour and 2 c raisins. Four loaves use 14 c flour and 4 c raisins. Find a pattern and express it with variables.

   Think: What is the pattern relating flour and raisins?

Choose a Strategy

Solve. Use these or other strategies.

Problem-Solving Strategies

- **Guess and Check**
- **Use Logical Thinking**
- **Work Backward**
- **Find a Pattern**

3. Darlene is making iced tea. The proportions she uses are shown in the table at the right. Find a pattern. Then write an equation expressing the relationship. Use the equation to find how much tea is needed when 8 cups of water are used.

Ingredients for Iced Tea

Water	Tea
1 cup	2 teaspoons
2 cups	3 teaspoons
5 cups	6 teaspoons
10 cups	11 teaspoons

4. At Matthew's last party, 12 guests drank 36 glasses of tea. One glass holds two cups of tea. How many cups of tea will he probably need for six guests at his next party?

5. The number of spoons, s, and forks, f, used at Matthew's party follows the pattern $s = 2f + 3$. Make a table to show how many spoons would be used with 5, 10, 15, and 20 forks.

6. The number of pounds of butter, b, and pecans, p, used for pecan muffins follows the pattern $p = \frac{2}{3}b + 3$. You have 10 lb of pecans and 10 lb of butter. How many pounds of pecans would be left if you made as many muffins as possible?

7. For every three muffins Kimberly buys, she gets one free. Write an equation to describe this pattern. Use the equation to find how many muffins Kimberly must buy in order for her to get six muffins free.

Extra Practice See 1–2 on page 585.

Quick Check

Check Your Understanding of Lessons 1–4

Use the graph on the right. Write the coordinates of each point.

1. *C* **2.** *D* **3.** *E*

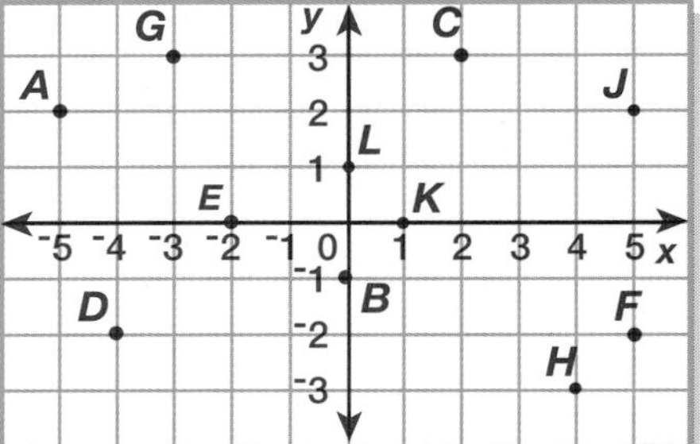

Use the graph on the right. Name the point for each ordered pair. Tell in which quadrant or on which axis the point lies.

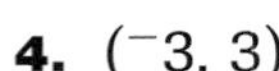

4. (−3, 3) **5.** (0, −1) **6.** (5, −2)

7. (1, 0) **8.** (5, 2) **9.** (−5, 2)

Use the graph on the right. Find the area of each figure.

10. Rectangle *A* **11.** Triangle *B*

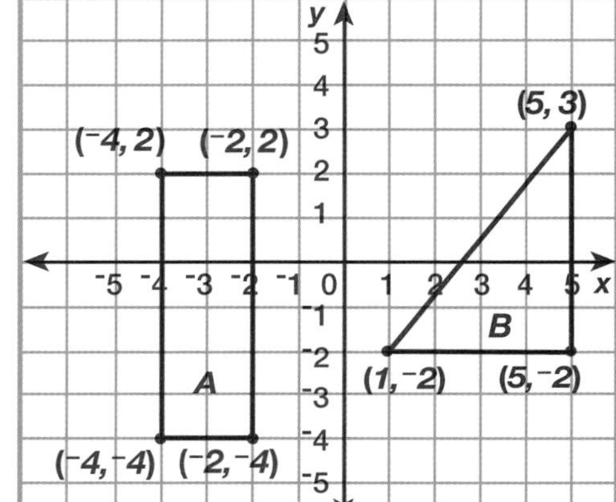

Use the formula $F = \frac{9}{5}C + 32$ to convert each Celsius temperature.

12. 15°C = ■°F **13.** 9.5°C = ■°F **14.** 29.5°C = ■°F

Solve.

15. At a restaurant, the chef knows that she needs 3 pounds of rib roast for 5 people, 6 pounds for 10 people, and 9 pounds for 15 people. Write an equation to describe the pattern. Use the equation to find how many people can be served by 24 pounds of rib roast.

How did you do?

If you had difficulty with any items in the Quick Check, you can use the following pages for review and extra practice.

Items	Review These Pages	Do These Extra Practice Items
1–9	pages 548–550	Set A, page 582
10–11	pages 552–553	Set B, page 582
12–14	pages 554–555	Set C, page 582
15	pages 556–557	1–2, page 585

Test Prep • Cumulative Review

Maintaining the Standards

Choose the letter of the correct answer.

1 Sarah has a choice of mathematics, art, science, or music for her first period class. For her second period class she has a choice of physical education, Spanish, or history. How many different possible schedules for her first two classes does she have to choose from?

A 15

B 12

C 4

D 3

2 A triangle has an area of 42 square feet. If the base is 14 feet long, what is the height of the triangle?

F 3 ft

G 6 ft

H 9 ft

J 588 ft

3 Sasha is drawing a marble out of a jar without looking. There are 4 red, 5 yellow, and 3 blue marbles. What is the probability that Sasha will draw a blue marble?

A $\frac{4}{5}$ **C** $\frac{1}{4}$

B $\frac{5}{12}$ **D** $\frac{1}{3}$

4 Which number represents the angle formed by 2 complementary angles?

F 30°

G 90°

H 180°

J 360°

5 Henry has an above-ground swimming pool that has a radius of 10 feet. Which number represents the circumference of the pool? Use $\pi = \frac{22}{7}$.

A $62\frac{6}{7}$ feet

B $31\frac{3}{7}$ feet

C $15\frac{5}{7}$ feet

D $5\frac{5}{7}$ feet

6 Find the perimeter of the figure shown below.

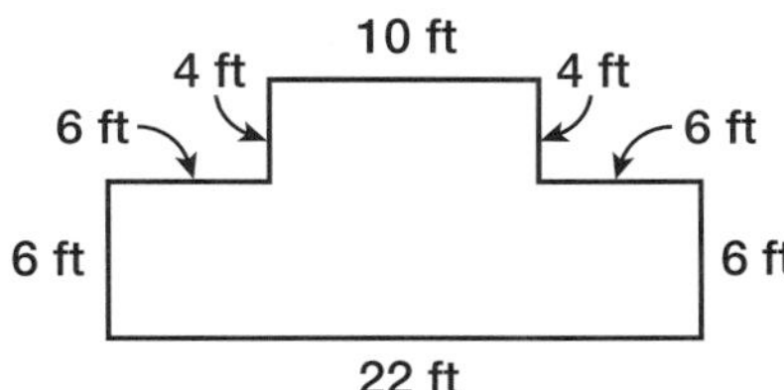

F 172 ft

G 66 ft

H 65 ft

J 64 ft

7 The price of a reference book was \$24.95. In addition, the sales tax was 8%. The next day Carl discovered the same reference book was discounted 25%. How much would Carl have paid for the book on sale, including tax?

Explain How did you find your answer?

Safe Site

Internet Test Prep
Visit **www.eduplace.com/kids/mhm** for more *Test Prep Practice.*

Functions

You will learn about functions and how to write and solve equations with two variables.

New Vocabulary
functions

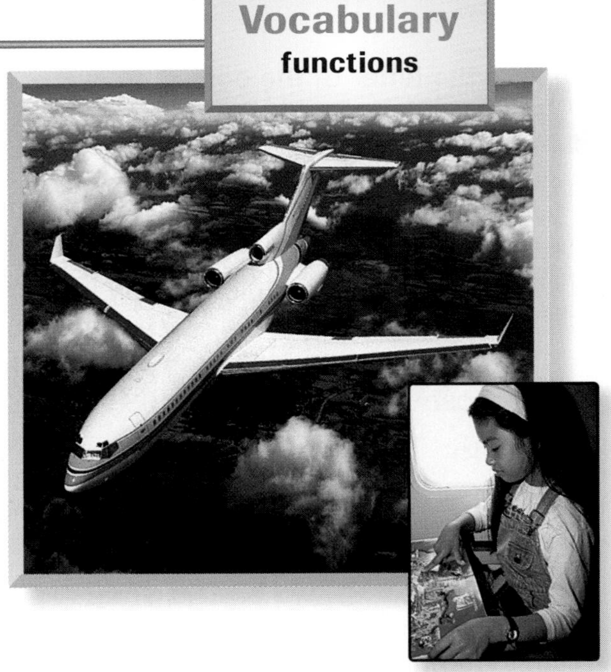

Learn About It

A **function** is a rule that associates one and only one value of one variable with each value of another variable. The function $d = 400t$ expresses d in terms of t. For each value of t, there is one and only one value of d. In this case, d represents distance and t represents time. For the function $d = 400t$, *distance is expressed as a function of time*. Notice that the function $d = 400t$ is an equation with 2 variables.

Pilar is a passenger in an airplane traveling at a speed of 400 miles per hour. Use the function $d = 400t$ to find how far the plane will travel in 2 hours, 3 hours, and 5 hours.

Different Ways to Record Solutions to an Equation With Two Variables

You can use substitution.

$d = 400t$, when $t = 2$
$d = 400(2)$
$= 800$

$d = 400t$, when $t = 3$
$d = 400(3)$
$= 1{,}200$

$d = 400t$, when $t = 5$
$d = 400(5)$
$= 2{,}000$

You can use a function table.

t (h)	d (mi)
2	800
3	1,200
5	2,000

function: $d = 400t$
$d = 400(2) = 800$
$d = 400(3) = 1{,}200$
$d = 400(5) = 2{,}000$

For each value in the first column, there is only one value in the second column. Based on these values, d is a function of t.

Solution: The plane can travel 800 miles in 2 hours, 1,200 miles in 3 hours, and 2,000 miles in 5 hours.

Explain Your Thinking

► Based on these values, decide whether each table at the right is a function table for y as a function of x. Explain.

A.

x	y
1	3
1	8
2	9
4	20

B.

x	y
1	6
2	7
3	8
4	7

Guided Practice

Copy and complete each table of values.

1. $y = x + 7$

x	y
3	
5	
7	
9	

2. $y = 50x$

x	y
0	
1	
2	
3	

3. $b = a - 10$

a	b
10	
20	
30	
40	

Ask Yourself

- What value is given?
- Should I use mental math or inverse operations?

Independent Practice

Copy and complete each table of values.

4. $y = x + 5$

x	y
4	
8	
12	
16	

5. $y = 2x$

x	y
1	
2	
5	
10	

6. $y = \frac{2}{3}x$

x	y
0	
3	
6	
9	

7. $b = 2 - a$

a	b
3	
0	
$^-3$	
$^-5$	

8. $y = 3x$

x	y
10	
5	
0	
$^-5$	

9. $c + d = 0$

c	d
5	
2	
0	
$^-2$	

To escape Earth's gravity, a rocket must reach a speed of 7 mi/sec. Use this information to solve Exercises 10–11.

10. Make a function table for $d = 7t$. Use these values for t: 1, 5, 10, 60.

11. Show how to express 7 miles per second in miles per hour.

Based on these values, tell whether each table is a function table for the second variable as a function of the first variable.

12.

x	y
2	0
2	1
2	2
2	3

13.

r	s
0	2
1	2
2	2
3	2

14.

a	b
1	1
5	5
5	10
10	10

15.

u	v
0	8
5	17
10	25
20	8

16.

m	n
0	0
1	3
2	4
0	6

Problem Solving • Reasoning

Solve. Choose a method.

Computation Methods

- Mental Math
- Estimation
- Paper and Pencil
- Calculator

17. The function $d = 350t$ shows the relationship between the distance d in miles that a certain airplane can travel in a given amount of time t in hours. How far will this plane travel in 3.5 hours?

18. A movie theater charges $7 per ticket. The manager says there are 198 people in the theater. If every person in the theater bought a ticket, about how much did the theater take in from ticket sales?

19. You are making a pyramid. The base layer of the pyramid is a square with 10 rows of 10 cans each. Each layer above will have 1 less row and 1 less can in each row. The top layer will have 1 can. How many cans will be used?

20. Jet A's distance and time are shown by the function $d = 560t$. Jet B's distance and time are shown by the function $d = 650t$. Jet A flies for 2.5 hours and Jet B flies for 2 hours. Which jet flies farther? How much farther?

Mixed Review • Test Prep

Multiply. *(pages 170–171)*

21. $1\frac{1}{8} \times \frac{3}{4}$ **22.** $6\frac{1}{2} \times 3$ **23.** $2\frac{1}{4} \times 1\frac{2}{3}$ **24.** $\frac{2}{5} \times 3\frac{1}{5}$

Choose the letter of the correct answer. *(pages 392–393, 472–473)*

25 What is the surface area of a rectangular prism with $l = 6$ in., $w = 4$ in., and $h = 7$ in.?

A 168 in.^{2} **C** 188 in.^{2}
B 38 in.^{2} **D** 96 in.^{2}

26 How are two angles whose sum is 180° classified?

F supplementary **H** vertical
G complementary **J** adjacent

See how the first pair is related. Choose the letter of the word that forms a similar relationship for the second pair.

27. Add is to subtract as multiply is to

A square **C** graph
B divide **D** distribute

28. x is to variable as $x = 3t$ is to

F expression **H** reciprocal
G equation **J** function table

Extra Practice See Set D on page 583.

Number Sense

Solving Two-Step Equations

Some equations involve more than one operation, such as $2x - 3 = 4$. To solve this type of equation, you need to isolate the variable. Use inverse operations and reverse the usual order of operations for evaluating mathematical expressions.

Inverse Operations

- Addition and Subtraction
- Multiplication and Division

Solving the Equation

$2x - 3 = 4$	Addition is the inverse of subtraction. Do that first.
$2x - 3 + 3 = 4 + 3$	Add 3 to both sides of the equation.
$2x = 7$	Division is the inverse of multiplication. Do that next.
$\frac{2x}{2} = \frac{7}{2}$	Divide both sides by 2. Simplify.
$x = 3\frac{1}{2}$	

Try These

Tell what is done in each step to solve the equation.

1.
$$3n + 2 = 11$$
$$3n + 2 - 2 = 11 - 2$$
$$3n = 9$$
$$\frac{3n}{3} = \frac{9}{3}$$
$$n = 3$$

2.
$$7c + 2 = 2$$
$$7c + 2 - 2 = 2 - 2$$
$$7c = 0$$
$$\frac{7c}{7} = \frac{0}{7}$$
$$c = 0$$

3.
$$9y - 3 = 6$$
$$9y - 3 + 3 = 6 + 3$$
$$9y = 9$$
$$\frac{9y}{9} = \frac{9}{9}$$
$$y = 1$$

Solve each equation.

4. $2t + 3 = 5$

5. $8r - 14 = 10$

6. $3x = 8 + 1$

7. $5e - 5 = 10$

8. $4m + 4 = 4$

9. $\frac{1}{2}s + 3 = 5$

Graph Linear Equations

You will learn how to use a table of values to graph linear equations.

Review Vocabulary
linear equation

Learn About It

In the coordinate plane, the graph of a **linear equation** is a line. The coordinates of every point on this line are solutions to the linear equation. To graph a linear equation, first make a table of values for x and y. Then plot the ordered pairs and draw a line through the points.

Graph the equation $y = x + 5$.

First, make a table of values. Choose easy x-values to work with, such as $^-1$, 0, and 1. In the equation $y = x + 5$, substitute the value of x to find the value of y.

x	y
$^-2$	
$^-1$	
0	
1	
2	

$y = (^-2) + 5$, so $y = 3$
$y = (^-1) + 5$, so $y = 4$
$y = (0) + 5$, so $y = 5$
$y = (1) + 5$, so $y = 6$
$y = (2) + 5$, so $y = 7$

x	y
$^-2$	**3**
$^-1$	**4**
0	**5**
1	**6**
2	**7**

Now plot each ordered pair in a coordinate plane. Use a ruler to draw a line that connects the points.

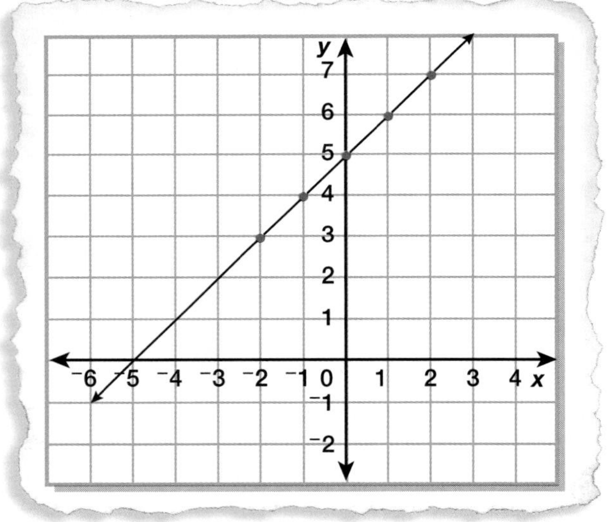

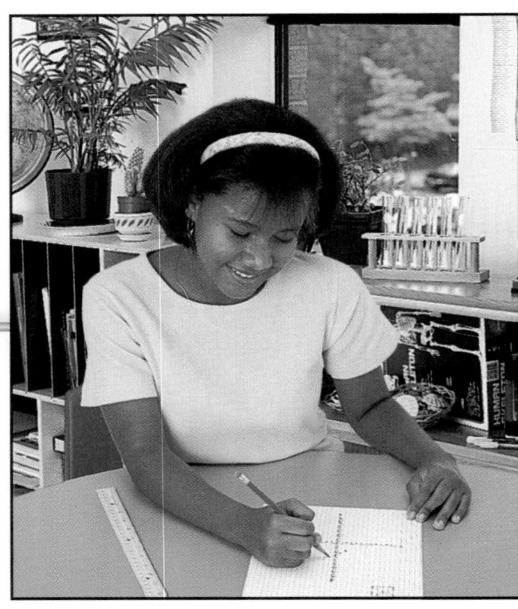

Explain Your Thinking

► Is the point $(^-5, 0)$ on the graph of the linear equation $y = x + 5$? How else can you check that $(^-5, 0)$ is a solution to that equation?

Guided Practice

For each equation, copy and complete a table of values like the one on the right. Use grid paper to graph the equation.

x	y
$^{-}2$	
$^{-}1$	
0	
1	
2	

1. $y = x + 3$ **2.** $y = x + 1$

3. $y = x$ **4.** $y = 3x$

5. $y = x - 1$ **6.** $y = {}^{-}2x$

> **Ask Yourself**
>
> - Did I use the horizontal axis for the x-values and the vertical axis for the y-values?
> - Do the points for each graph lie in a straight line?

Independent Practice

For each equation, copy and complete a table of values like the one above. Use grid paper to graph the equation.

7. $y = x - 2$ **8.** $y = {}^{-}5x$ **9.** $y = x + 2$ **10.** $y = 2x$

11. $y = 2x - 1$ **12.** $y = x - 3$ **13.** $y = {}^{-}x$ **14.** $y = 3x + 2$

Problem Solving • Reasoning

15. **Patterns** Look at the three graphs on the right. Each graph is identified by its equation. What patterns do you see in the graphs and in the equations? Without graphing, describe what the graph of $y = x + 3$ would look like and where it would be located.

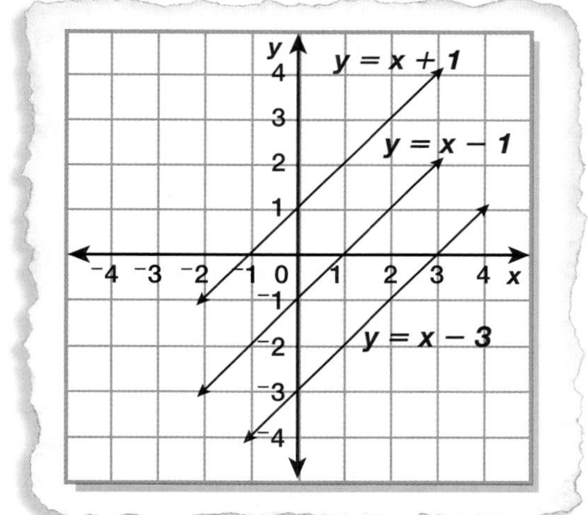

16. **Analyze** On grid paper, draw the graph of $y = 4x$ and the graph of $y = {}^{-}4x$ on the same set of axes. How are the graphs alike? How are they different?

17. **Write Your Own** Write your own linear equation, using the variables x and y. Make a table of values, and then graph your equation.

Mixed Review • Test Prep

Find the missing term that makes the ratios equivalent.
(pages 308–309)

18. $\frac{3}{15} = \frac{w}{5}$ **19.** $\frac{9}{7} = \frac{27}{s}$ **20.** $\frac{21}{7} = \frac{n}{1}$ **21.** $\frac{24}{48} = \frac{2}{p}$

22 What is the total price of a \$24.50 item with 6.5% sales tax? *(pages 370–371)*

A \$40.43 **C** \$26.09

B \$26.20 **D** \$22.91

Problem-Solving Skill: Is the Answer Reasonable?

You will learn how to use a line graph to check whether your answer is reasonable.

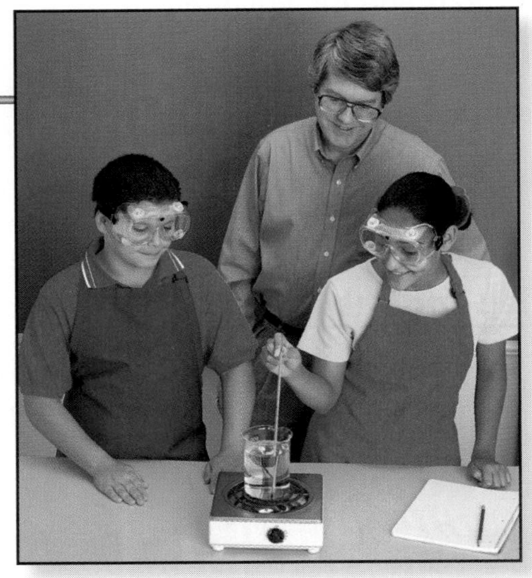

When you graph data on a line graph, you can use that graph to check whether your answer is reasonable.

The students in Mr. Stanton's class are heating water, using the middle setting on a hot plate. Each minute they record the temperature of the water. Mr. Stanton has done this experiment before and shows his results with a line graph. How do the students' results compare with his?

Sometimes the value is on the line.

Stacy and Magdalena measure a temperature of 75°C after 5 minutes. Point *A* (5, 75) is on the line, so the value is reasonable.

Sometimes the value is close to the line.

Rafael and Joe measure a temperature of 72°C after 5 minutes. Point *B* (5, 72) is close to the line. If the point is close to the line, the value is reasonable.

Sometimes the value is far from the line.

Shawna and Randy measure a temperature of 61°C after 5 minutes. Point *C* (5, 61) is far from the line. Based on the graph, the value is not reasonable.

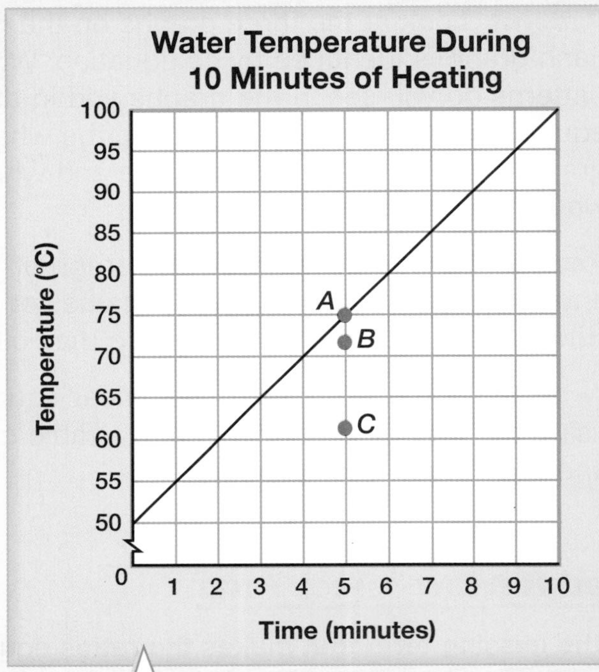

On Mr. Stanton's graph, the temperature rose the same number of degrees for each minute of time that passed. Therefore, the graph is linear.

Look Back How can you use a line graph to determine if an answer is reasonable? Explain.

Glass blowers make whimsical as well as practical glass items.

Guided Practice

Solve. Use the graph on page 566.

1. While doing the experiment, Stacy and Magdalena did not notice that their hot plate did not stay hot. After 8 minutes, their thermometer read 75°C. Was that a reasonable value?

   Think: What point does this data represent?

2. The graph only shows the temperature for the first 10 minutes of heating. Using an equation, Mr. Stanton predicts that the temperature will be 99.8°C after 10 minutes. Is this value reasonable?

   Think: Is the value close to the graphed line?

Choose a Strategy

Solve. Use the graph on page 566 for Problems 3–4.
Use these or other strategies.

Problem-Solving Strategies

- **Find a Pattern**
- **Guess and Check**
- **Write an Equation**
- **Use Logical Thinking**

3. Rafael and Joe cannot read the temperature they recorded after 2 minutes. It is either 63°C or 68°C. If their experiment is fairly accurate, which value is probably correct?

4. According to the graph, the temperature of the water increases 5°C each minute. Write an equation to show the water temperature after x minutes. Remember, the starting temperature is 50°C.

5. Meg works in laboratory. One type of testing she does takes 90 minutes per test. How can Meg complete 6 such tests in one 7-hour day? Explain.

6. Sam is 2 years older than Liz. Liz is twice as old as Chris. Geraldo is half as old as Sam. Chris is 10 years old. How old is Sam? How old is Liz? How old is Geraldo?

7. A glass blower sells small glass balls for $14 each plus a shipping charge of $9 no matter how many balls are ordered. Write an equation and find how much 24 glass balls will cost, including shipping.

8. One store sells small glass animals for $15 and larger glass animals for $27. Maria bought 8 glass animals for $180. How many small glass animals did Maria buy? How many larger glass animals did she buy?

Extra Practice See 3–5 on page 585.

Quick Check

Check Your Understanding of Lessons 5–7

Copy and complete each table of values.

1. $y = 3x$

x	y
$^{-}2$	■
0	■
2	■
4	■

2. $x + y = 5$

x	y
■	2
$^{-}2$	■
■	$^{-}5$
$3\frac{1}{2}$	■

3. $b = a - 2$

a	b
■	9
■	$^{-}1$
0	■
$^{-}8$	■

For each equation, copy and complete a table of values like the one below. Use grid paper to graph the equation.

4. $y = x - 4$

5. $y = 2x$

6. $y = {}^{-}x + 5$

7. $y = {}^{-}3x$

x	y
$^{-}2$	■
$^{-}1$	■
0	■
1	■
2	■

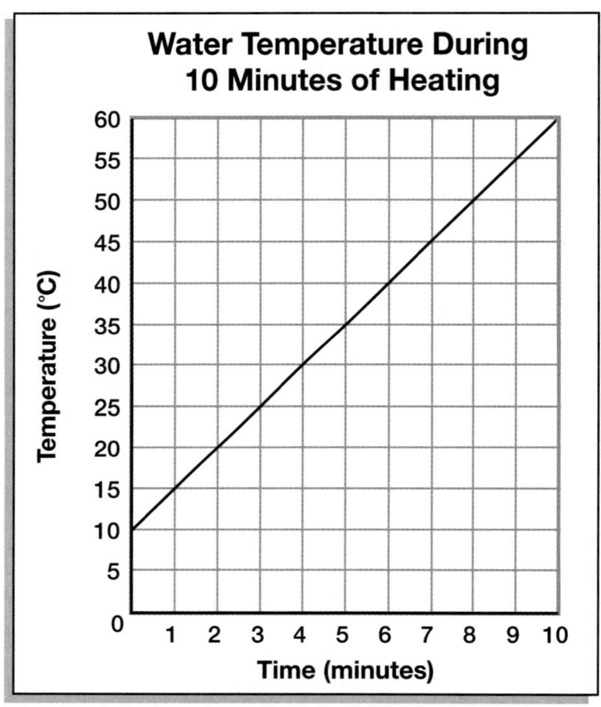

Solve.

8. You are performing an experiment in science class. After 5 minutes, you measure a temperature of 45°C. Based on the graph on the right, is this value reasonable? Explain.

How did you do?

If you had difficulty with any items in the Quick Check, you can use the following pages for review and extra practice.

Items	Review These Pages	Do These Extra Practice Items
1–3	pages 560–562	Set D, page 583
4–7	pages 564–565	Set E, page 583
8	pages 566–567	3–5, page 585

Test Prep • Cumulative Review

Maintaining the Standards

Choose the letter of the correct answer.

1. What figure does the given net represent?

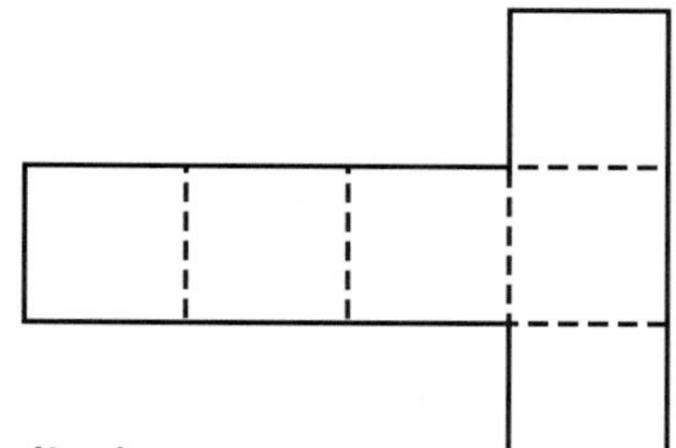

   A cylinder
   B circle
   C square
   D cube

2. Which is the measure of a straight angle?

   F 90°
   G 160°
   H 180°
   J 360°

3. A number cube with sides numbered 1–6 is rolled. What is the probability of rolling a 2?

   A $\frac{2}{3}$
   B $\frac{1}{6}$
   C $\frac{1}{4}$
   D $\frac{1}{3}$

4. A jar contains 5 red marbles, 8 blue marbles, 10 green marbles, and 2 white marbles. A marble is chosen without looking. Find *P* (not blue).

   F 0.32
   G 0.44
   H 0.68
   J 0.88

5. Which group would you use as a *sample* to learn about the total population?

   A all the students in choir classes
   B members of your family
   C all your brothers and sisters
   D 45 students in a school of 250 students

6. Gary has a bicycle wheel that is 14 inches in diameter. What is the circumference of Gary's bicycle wheel? Use $\frac{22}{7}$ for π.

   F 22 inches
   G 44 inches
   H 154 inches
   J 616 inches

7. What is the volume of the rectangular solid?

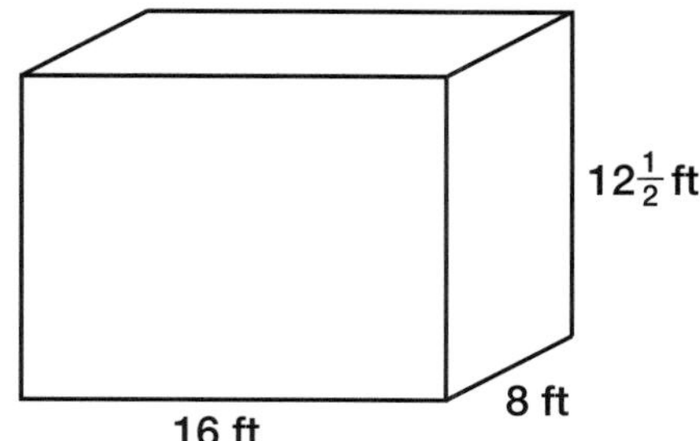

   Explain How did you find your answer?

Safe Site

Internet Test Prep
Visit **www.eduplace.com/kids/mhm** for more *Test Prep Practice.*

LESSON 8 Order of Operations With Integers

You will learn how to use the order of operations to simplify expressions with integers.

Review Vocabulary
expression

Learn About It

When a numerical **expression** has more than one operation, simplify the expression by following the order of operations.

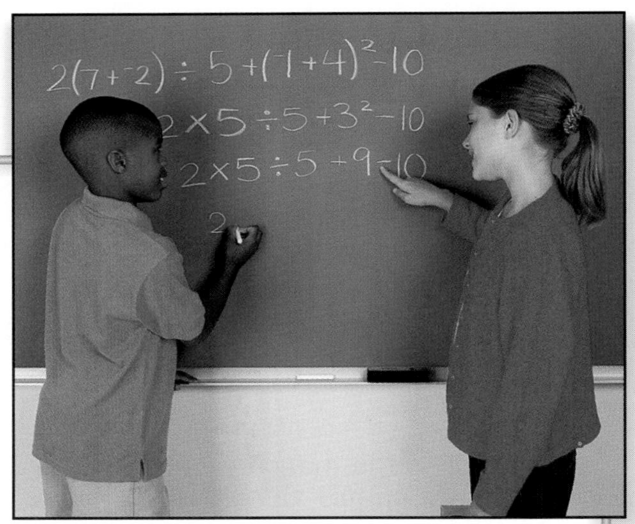

Simplify. $\mathbf{2(7 + {}^{-}2) \div 5 + ({}^{-}1 + 4)^2 - 10}$

$2(7 + {}^{-}2) \div 5 + ({}^{-}1 + 4)^2 - 10$

Complete operations within parentheses.

$2 \times 5 \div 5 + 3^2 - 10$

Evaluate powers.

$2 \times 5 \div 5 + 9 - 10$

Multiply and divide in order from left to right.

$10 \div 5 + 9 - 10$

$2 + 9 - 10$

Add and subtract in order from left to right.

$11 - 10$

1

Solution: $2(7 + {}^{-}2) \div 5 + ({}^{-}1 + 4)^2 - 10 = 1$

Explain Your Thinking

- ▶ Why is it necessary to follow the order of operations when simplifying an expression?
- ▶ Why can you consider the expression in parentheses as one number?

Guided Practice

Simplify each expression.

1. $(17 + 3) \div {}^{-}2$

2. $(2)(3) - (4)({}^{-}8)$

3. $(2 - 4)^2 - 4 - 3$

4. ${}^{-}6 - 3(7 + 8) \div 5 + 4$

Has each expression been simplified correctly? Write *yes* or *no*. If not, give the correct value.

5. ${}^{-}4 - 6 + 8 = {}^{-}12$

6. $5(3 + 15) \div 3 = 20$

7. $9 + (4 - 3) - 4 = 6$

8. ${}^{-}5 - 2(5 - 1) = {}^{-}16$

Ask Yourself

- Which operation do I complete first?
- Which sign do I use when I multiply or divide?

Independent Practice

Simplify each expression.

9. $5 - 10 + 4 - 1$
10. $6(2 - 1) - 6$
11. $3(^{-}6 - 3) - 8$
12. $5 + (^{-}1 - 3) \div 2$
13. $^{-}8 - (4 - 5)$
14. $^{-}1 - 4(1 + 2)^2$
15. $^{-}2(2 + 6) \div (^{-}8)$
16. $9(3 - 4)^2$
17. $^{-}11 + 4(2 - 3) + 16$
18. $(^{-}1 + 9)^2 - (^{-}9 - 1)^2$
19. $^{-}6(^{-}5 - 1) - 3$
20. $^{-}7(^{-}6 + 6) - 2(20)$

Has each expression been simplified correctly? Write *yes* or *no*. If not, write the correct value.

21. $^{-}9(2 - 4) - 17 = {}^{-}39$
22. $(^{-}4 - 5)2 - 4 = {}^{-}60$
23. $(3)(10) \div 5 = 2$
24. $5(6 - 3) \div 3 = 29$
25. $(9 - 3)2 - 6 = 6$
26. $10 - 4 - 6 + 7 = {}^{-}1$

Problem Solving • Reasoning

27. **Explain** Which two of the expressions $(^{-}4 + 1)^2$, $(^{-}1 - 4)^2$, $3(^{-}4 + 1)$, $(^{-}1 + 4)^2$, and $^{-}4^2 + 1^2$ have the same value?

28. **Predict** Bob has a piece of paper with an area of 1,200 cm^2. He folds it in half 3 times. Predict the area of the top of the folded piece of paper after the third fold. Check your prediction. What is the actual area?

29. Tana's age is 5 years more than twice Mark's age. In two years Tana will be three times as old as Mark. How old is Tana now?

30. **Write About It** Neil says $(2 - 1)^2$ and $2^2 - 1^2$ have the same value. Tim says they do not. Who is correct? Explain.

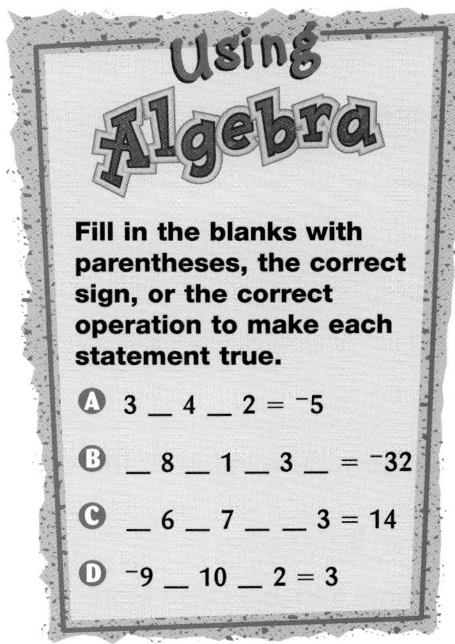

Fill in the blanks with parentheses, the correct sign, or the correct operation to make each statement true.

Ⓐ 3 _ 4 _ 2 = $^{-}5$
Ⓑ _ 8 _ 1 _ 3 _ = $^{-}32$
Ⓒ _ 6 _ 7 _ _ 3 = 14
Ⓓ $^{-}9$ _ 10 _ 2 = 3

Mixed Review • Test Prep

Find the area of each circle. Use 3.14 for π. *(pages 464–465)*

31. $r = 10$ in.
32. $d = 200$ cm
33. $r = 0.1$ m
34. $c = 314$ ft

35 A $75.00 purchase totaled $85.50 with tax. What percent was the tax? *(pages 370–371)*

A 25%
B 15%
C 14%
D 1.5%

LESSON 9

Evaluate and Simplify Expressions With Integers

You will learn how to use properties to make evaluating expressions easier.

Review Vocabulary
evaluate
expression

Learn About It

To **evaluate** an algebraic **expression** you must substitute given values for variables. You use the order of operations and other mathematical properties to evaluate expressions.

Evaluate $7(^{-}x) + 19y + 101$, given $x = 19$ and $y = 7$.

Step 1 Substitute the given values for x and y. You can now simplify the expression or look for ways to apply addition or multiplication properties to make the calculations easier.

$7(^{-}19) + 19(7) + 101$

Step 2 Use the Commutative Property of multiplication, $ab = ba$.

$7(^{-}19) + 19(7) + 101$
$7(^{-}19) + 7(19) + 101$

Step 3 Use the Distributive Property, $ab + ac = a(b + c)$.

$7(^{-}19) + 7(19) + 101$
$7(^{-}19 + 19) + 101$
$7(0) + 101$
101

Solution: The value of the expression is 101.

Other Examples

A. Same Variable Used More Than Once
Evaluate $6n + 5 + 4n$, given $n = {}^{-}8$.

$6n + 5 + 4n$
$6n + 4n + 5$ ← Commutative Property
$(6 + 4)n + 5$ ← Distributive Property
$(10)n + 5$
$(10 \times {}^{-}8) + 5$ ← Substitution
$^{-}80 + 5$
$^{-}75$

B. Expressions Using Multiplication
Evaluate $2n \times 3 + 4n$, given $n = 5$.

$2n \times 3 + 4n$
$6n + 4n$ ← Multiply first.
$(6 + 4)n$ ← Distributive Property
$10n$
$10(5)$ ← Substitution
50

Explain Your Thinking

► What happens if you simplify $7(^{-}19) + 19(7) + 101$ without using the Distributive Property? Which way do you like better?

Guided Practice

Evaluate each expression for the given values.

1. $^{-}x - 7$, given $x = 6$ **2.** $8(x - y)$, given $x = 5$ and $y = 5$

3. $x \div 2$, given $x = {}^{-}2$ **4.** $x^2 + y$, given $x = 4$ and $y = {}^{-}8$

> **Ask Yourself**
> - Did I use the correct signs?
> - Did I consider that the product is zero when one of the factors is zero?

Independent Practice

Evaluate each expression.

5. $7 + x - y$, given $x = {}^{-}7$ and $y = 10$ **6.** $10x + 3(^{-}y)$, given $x = {}^{-}1$ and $y = 1$

7. $x^2 + 10$, given $x = {}^{-}3$ **8.** $x + y - 2x$, given $x = {}^{-}2$, $y = {}^{-}20$

Evaluate each expression, given $a = 3$, $b = {}^{-}2$, and $c = 5$.

9. $3b + 5b$ **10.** $(a + b + c) \times 0$ **11.** $a + b^2 - c$

12. $a(b + c)$ **13.** $5 + a - b - c$ **14.** $a + 2(b - c)$

Algebra • Properties **Evaluate. Tell what properties you used.**

15. $x^2 + 7 + y$, given $x = {}^{-}4$ and $y = {}^{-}16$

16. $7x + 78y - 5$, given $x = {}^{-}78$ and $y = 7$

Problem Solving • Reasoning

17. Explain Jeff evaluated the expression on the right for $x = 2$ and $y = {}^{-}2$. What did he do wrong? What answer should he have had?

$8(^{-}x) - 5y + 2$
$8(^{-}2) - 5(2) + 2$
$^{-}16 - 10 + 2$
$^{-}24$

18. Analyze Marcia says that $(x + y)^2 = x^2 + y^2$, when $x = 2$ and $y = 0$. Max says that is true when $x = 2$ and $y = {}^{-}2$. Who is correct? Show your work to justify your answer.

19. Carla earns \$8 per hour in take-home pay. Last week she worked 19 hours. She saves 10% of her take-home pay. How much should she have put in savings last week?

Mixed Review • Test Prep

Solve. *(pages 282–283)*

20. $4 \times d = 48$ **21.** $y \div 4 = 120$ **22.** $(n + 3) \times 2 = 8$ **23.** $p \div (16 - 8) = 16$

24 How is a triangle with sides of 3 different lengths classified? *(pages 404–406)*

A isosceles **B** right **C** scalene **D** equilateral

Extra Practice See Set G on page 584.

Write Expressions With Integers

You will learn how to write expressions with integers.

Learn About It

You can translate word descriptions into algebraic expressions to help you understand what is happening.

Word Description	Algebraic Expression
• $^-10$ less than some number	$x - (^-10)$
• two times some number	$2r$
• two times the sum of two different numbers	$2(b + c)$
• six less than the sum of three numbers	$f + g + h - 6$
• a number of marbles shared equally among six people	$a \div 6$
• the cost of three shirts of equal value	$s + s + s$ or $3s$
• five times the quantity x minus y	$5(x - y)$

Explain Your Thinking

► What is the difference between "five times the quantity x minus y" and "five times x minus y"?

Guided Practice

Write an expression. Tell what each variable represents.

1. the sum of two numbers divided into three equal parts
2. grow by the same amount for four days, then shrink by a different amount
3. negative seven increased by three times a number
4. Ted bought the same number of shares of stock each day for 4 days. Then he sold a different number of shares on the 5th day. How many shares of stock does he have now?
5. A stock is worth $350 per share. The price decreases by a certain amount and then increases by half that amount. What is the stock now worth?
6. Another stock is worth $65 and climbs two dollars every day. What is the value of the stock after n days?

Ask Yourself

- Did I use the correct operation?
- Did I use variables for numbers that change?

Independent Practice

Write an expression. Tell what each variable represents.

7. a number times the difference between that number and seven

8. split the sum of twelve and a number into another number of equal parts

9. four times the sum of a gain of one amount and the loss of a different amount

Problem Solving • Reasoning

10. During part of one year, William saves \$20 every month and his sister spends \$20 every month. Write an expression for the difference between the amounts of money William and his sister have after x months.

11. Heather has \$150 in her savings account. She withdraws \$5 every month. She deposits nothing in her savings account. Write an expression for the amount of money she will have in her savings account in x months.

12. **Analyze** Pamela saved \$50. Every time she goes to a movie she spends \$4. Every time she goes ice skating she spends \$4. Does the expression $50 - 4(x + y)$ describe her saving and spending habits? What do x and y represent?

13. George earns \$15 per day on his paper route. He spends \$120 for a new CD player and \$4 every time he visits the ice-cream parlor. Write an expression that describes the money he earns and spends. Tell what each variable represents.

14. Paul sold 5 more raffle tickets than Francine. Francine sold twice as many tickets as Anna. Bill sold 6 more tickets than Paul. Anna sold 12 tickets. How many tickets did the 4 students sell?

15. Jon raises chickens and sheep. In one field he counted 39 heads and 122 legs. How many chickens and how many sheep were in that field on that day? Explain how you found your answer.

Mixed Review • Test Prep

Martin earned \$35 one week. He made the circle graph on the right to show how he earned the money. Round each answer to the nearest dollar. *(pages 354–355)*

How much money did Martin get from

16. lawn mowing?

17. dog sitting?

18. his allowance?

19. running errands?

Martin's Earnings

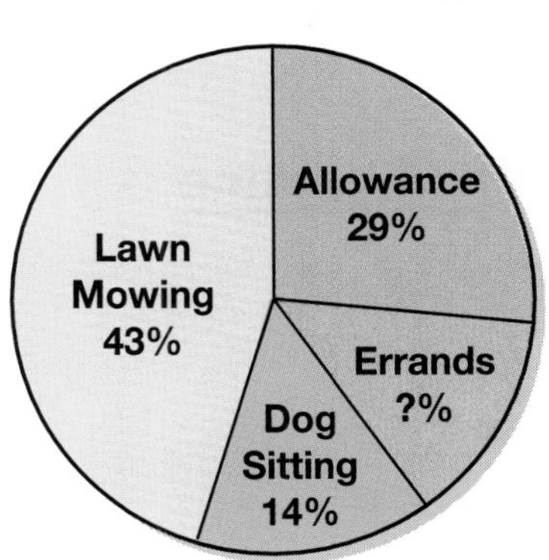

20 What is $1,673 \div 10^4$? *(pages 36–37)*

A 16.73 **B** 1.673 **C** 0.1673 **D** 0.01673

Extra Practice See Set H on page 584.

LESSON 11

Equations With Integers

You will learn how to solve equations with integers.

Learn About It

Maria and Luis live in the city. A peregrine falcon has built its nest on a ledge of the building that is opposite theirs. Maria and Luis watch from their kitchen window as the falcon swoops 475 feet from its nest to prey that is 175 feet below their window. How far above their kitchen window is the falcon's nest?

Step 1 Let h stand for the height of the falcon's nest above the kitchen window.	**Step 2** Write a subtraction equation to represent the distance between the falcon's nest and the falcon's prey.	**Step 3** Add $^-175$ to each side of the equation and simplify.
h = height in feet of nest above kitchen window	$h - (^-175) = 475$	$h - {}^-175 + {}^-175 = 475 + {}^-175$ $h = 300$

Solution: The falcon's nest is 300 feet above the kitchen window.

Another Example

Use Division

Solve. $^-3h = 540$

$$^-3h = 540$$
$$\frac{^-3h}{^-3} = \frac{540}{^-3}$$
$$h = {}^-180$$

Explain Your Thinking

► If you subtract the same number from each side of an equation, will you still have an equation?

► If you multiply both sides of an equation by the same number, will you still have an equation?

Guided Practice

Solve.

1. $2 + x = 4$

2. $^-10 + x = {}^-20$

3. $2x = 6$

4. $^-4x = {}^-8$

5. $^-3x = 9$

6. $^-x = 10$

7. $x - 61 = 32$

8. $x - {}^-81 = {}^-31$

Ask Yourself

- Which signs do I use?
- Which inverse operations do I use?

Independent Practice

Solve.

9. $x + 4 = {}^-3$ **10.** $x - ({}^-1) = 4$ **11.** ${}^-4 + x = {}^-3$

12. $h - 4 = {}^-4$ **13.** $t + 8 = {}^-8$ **14.** $x - {}^-4 = 4$

15. $3x = 9$ **16.** $2x = {}^-4$ **17.** $x \div 2 = 2$

18. $5x = {}^-10$ **19.** $x \div 16 = {}^-2$ **20.** $4x = 4$

21. $x \div 3 = 7$ **22.** $5 + x = {}^-13$ **23.** $x \div {}^-8 = {}^-16$

Problem Solving • Reasoning

24. **Analyze** A pelican is hovering above the water. It dives 180 inches to catch a fish swimming 30 inches below the surface of the water. How many inches above the water is the pelican? Write an equation using integers.

25. A shark dives from the surface of the water to a school of fish 10 feet below. Then the shark dives to the bottom of the ocean, which is 27 feet below the surface of the water. What is the distance of the school of fish to the bottom of the ocean?

26. **Explain** Suppose you earn 1¢ on May 1, 2¢ on May 2, 4¢ on May 3, and 8¢ on May 4. If this pattern continues, how much will you earn on May 14? How much will you have earned from May 1 through May 14? Explain how you found your answers.

Write *true* or *false*. If a sentence is false, rewrite it to make it true.

A The x-coordinate at the origin is less than the y-coordinate.

B The x-axis and y-axis in a coordinate plane are perpendicular.

C If both coordinates in an ordered pair are negative, that point is in Quadrant IV.

Mixed Review • Test Prep

Tell whether you would use a sample to learn about each group. Explain. *(pages 496–497)*

27. parents of the students in your class **28.** people who watch TV

29. people who use the Internet **30.** members of a chess club

31 Which algebraic expression represents growing by the same amount for 3 days and then shrinking? *(pages 574–575)*

A $x + 3 - y$ **C** $3x - y$

B $3 + x - y$ **D** $y - 3 \times x$

Extra Practice See Set I on page 584.

Problem-Solving Application: Use a Graph

You will learn how to use graphs to solve problems.

You can solve some problems by interpreting a line graph.

Don's family is driving to a state park to go camping. Their car uses 1 gallon of gas for every 27.5 miles they drive on the highway. The graph below shows the relationship between the number of miles driven and the amount of gas used. About how much gas do they need to drive 90 miles?

Gasoline Mileage

Miles: 0, 30, 60, 90, 120, 150

Gallons of Gasoline: 1, 2, 3, 4, 5

Understand

What is the question?

How many gallons of gas do they need to drive 90 miles?

What do you know?

The line graph relates the number of miles and the number of gallons. Don's family drives 90 miles.

Plan

What can you do to find the answer?

Locate the number of miles they drive on the *y*-axis. Then find the corresponding number of gallons on the *x*-axis.

Solve

Locate 90 on the *y*-axis. Look across the graph to where the line of the graph crosses the grid line for this *y*-coordinate. Then look down to find the *x*-coordinate for this point. The *x*-coordinate is between 3 and 4. Don's family needs about $3\frac{1}{3}$ gallons of gas to drive 90 miles.

Look Back

Look back at the question. Is your answer reasonable?

Explain how you can use a proportion to check your answer.

Remember:
- ► Understand
- ► Plan
- ► Solve
- ► Look Back

Guided Practice

Use the information on page 578 for Problems 1–2.

1. Don's family has 130 more miles to drive before they reach the park. If they have 4 gallons of gas left, will they have to stop for gas before they get there?

   Think: How many miles can they drive on 4 gallons of gas?

2. Use the graph to estimate the number of miles Don's family can drive using 2.5 gallons of gas. Check your answer using the equation of the graph, $y = 27.5x$.

   Think: On which axis is the value 2.5 gallons located?

Choose a Strategy

Solve. Use these or other strategies.

Problem-Solving Strategies

- **Work Backward**
- **Solve a Simpler Problem**
- **Use Logical Thinking**
- **Guess and Check**

3. The data on the right show the relationship between the number of nights and the camping cost. How much will it cost a family to camp for 6 nights?

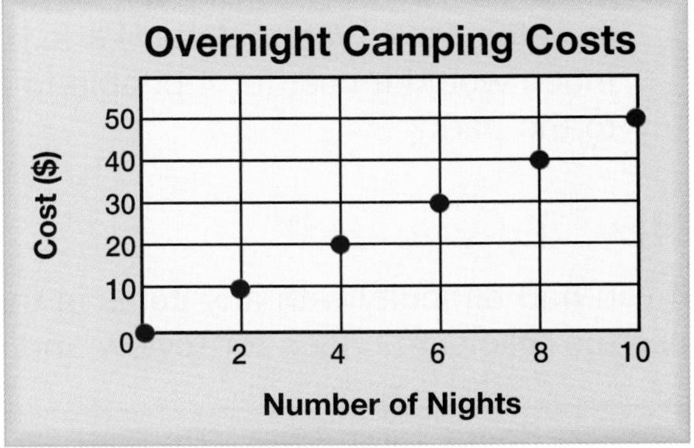

4. After 6 nights, one family decides to camp 2 more nights. They have already paid for the first 6 nights. Using the data on the right, how much more do they need to pay for the 2 extra nights?

5. Cal earns $254 each week. He saves 20% of his earnings. How much does he save each week?

6. Meghan saves $32.50 each week. How much does Meghan earn each week if she saves 10% of her earnings?

7. **Analyze** Box *A* weighs 10 pounds. Together Boxes *B* and *C* weigh twice as much as Box *D*. Together all 4 boxes weigh 55 pounds. How much does Box *D* weigh?

8. Sue gave half of the pears she picked to Ed. Then she gave half of what she had left to Dale. Next she gave Ken 3 pears. Then she had 2 pears left. How many pears did Sue start with?

Extra Practice See 6–7 on page 585.

Quick Check

Check Your Understanding of Lessons 8–12

Evaluate each expression.

1. $3 - 2(^{-}8 + 7)$

2. $(^{-}4)(4) \div 2(^{-}1 + 6)$

3. $(9 - 6)^2 + 5(^{-}1)$

4. $x - 3y$, given $x = 7$ and $y = 4$

5. $b(a + b)$, given $a = {}^{-}10$ and $b = 3$

6. $y^2 + 5x$, given $x = 2$ and $y = {}^{-}3$

Write an expression. Tell what each variable represents.

7. the difference between four times some number and 5

8. a number is divided into 7 equal parts, then increased by 4 times another number

Solve.

9. $x + 3 = 8$

10. $^{-}x - 2 = {}^{-}6$

11. $4x = 16$

12. $x \div 2 = {}^{-}8$

Solve.

13. The data on the right show the admission price for a number of people to enter Wavy Waters Water Park. How much would it cost for 4 people to go to the park?

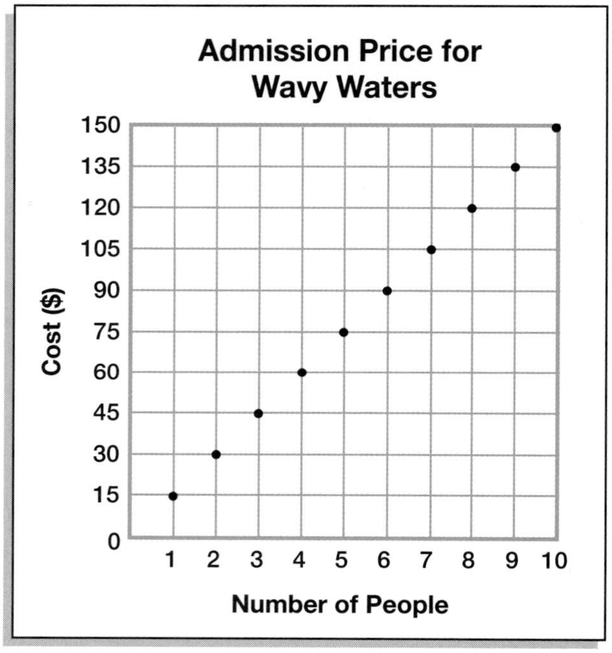

Admission Price for Wavy Waters

Cost ($): 0, 15, 30, 45, 60, 75, 90, 105, 120, 135, 150

Number of People: 1, 2, 3, 4, 5, 6, 7, 8, 9, 10

How did you do?

If you had difficulty with any items in the Quick Check, you can use the following pages for review and extra practice.

Items	Review These Pages	Do These Extra Practice Items
1–3	pages 570–571	Set F, page 583
4–6	pages 572–573	Set G, page 584
7–8	pages 574–575	Set H, page 584
9–12	pages 576–577	Set I, page 584
13	pages 578–579	6–7, page 585

Test Prep • Cumulative Review

Maintaining the Standards

Choose the letter of the correct answer.
If a correct answer is not here, choose NH.

1. Diana and David work at a flower shop. At the beginning of the day they had 3 times as many roses in stock as ever before. They sold 156 before the end of the day. Which expression shows how many roses they have left?

   A $3m + 156$

   B $3m - 156$

   C $3m - {}^{-}156$

   D $3 - 156$

2. Rankin surveyed 100 students about their movie preferences. The results showed that 20 students only liked action movies and 15 only liked comedies. Ten students liked both comedies and action movies. What is the probability that a student likes action movies or likes comedies?

   F $\frac{7}{20}$ **H** $\frac{1}{2}$

   G $\frac{9}{20}$ **J** $\frac{11}{20}$

3. Neal has 18 cards for magic tricks. Five cards are marked with a star. Shana picks a card with a star and keeps it. Then Vicki picks a card and keeps it. What is the probability that both Shana and Vicki pick a card with a star?

   A $\frac{5}{18}$ **C** $\frac{23}{153}$

   B $\frac{10}{153}$ **D** $\frac{157}{306}$

4. 1.35% of what number is 645.3?

   F 4,780

   G 871.16

   H 490

   J NH

5. Mrs. Hall is serving juice to her class. She has large glasses that each hold $1\frac{1}{2}$ cups of liquid. If she served 32 students, how many cups of juice did she serve?

   A 12 cups

   B 24 cups

   C 32 cups

   D 48 cups

6. What is the measure of the missing angle in the rhombus?

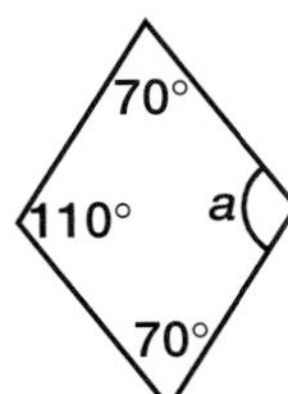

   F 110° **H** 220°

   G 140° **J** 250°

7. Simplify the expression by following the order of operations.

   $$(12 \times 9) \div 3 + 4(7 - 15)$$

   Explain Show how you found your answer.

Internet Test Prep
Visit **www.eduplace.com/kids/mhm** for more *Test Prep Practice.*

Extra Practice

Set A (Lesson 1, pages 548–550)

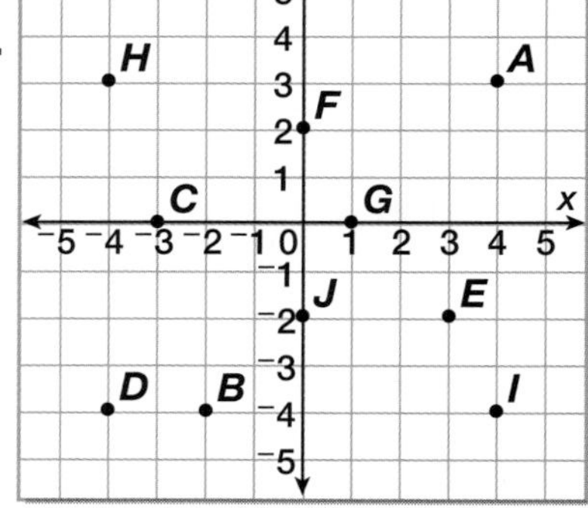

Use the graph on the right. Write the coordinates of each point.

1. *A* **2.** *B* **3.** *C* **4.** *D* **5.** *E*

6. *F* **7.** *G* **8.** *H* **9.** *I* **10.** *J*

Graph each ordered pair. Label the point with the given letter. Tell in which quadrant or on what axis the point lies.

11. *A* (5, 1) **12.** *B* (⁻2, 3) **13.** *C* (4, ⁻2)

14. *E* (0, 5) **15.** *F* (⁻5, ⁻2) **16.** *G* (3, 0)

Set B (Lesson 2, pages 552–553)

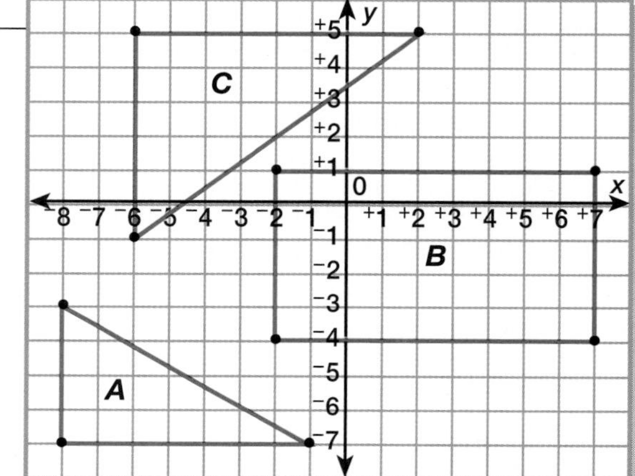

Use the graph on the right.

1. Find the area of triangle *A*.

2. Find the area of rectangle *B*.

3. Find the area of triangle *C*.

Graph each point in Exercises 4–13. Connect the points in order and connect the last to the first. Find the area of each figure.

4. (⁻2, 4), (⁻2, 10), (⁻5, 10), (⁻5, 4)

5. (⁻3, ⁻1), (⁻3, ⁻5), (⁻7, ⁻5)

6. (4, ⁻2), (4, 3), (6, 3)

7. (4, 2), (4, 7), (⁻6, 7), (⁻6, 2)

8. (⁻2, ⁻4), (⁻2, 1), (⁻6, 1)

9. (⁻5, ⁻1), (⁻5, 3), (2, 3), (2, ⁻1)

10. (⁻1, 7), (1, 7), (1, ⁻4), (⁻1, ⁻4)

11. (⁻6, ⁻4), (5, ⁻4), (5, 2)

12. (3, 3), (⁻2, 3), (⁻2, 10)

13. (2, ⁻3), (2, ⁻7), (3, ⁻7), (3, ⁻3)

Set C (Lesson 3, pages 554–555)

Use the formula $F = \frac{9}{5}C + 32$ to convert each Celsius temperature. Check your answers with a quick estimate.

1. 60°C = ■°F **2.** 5°C = ■°F **3.** 20°C = ■°F **4.** ⁻20°C = ■°F

5. 0°C = ■°F **6.** 8.5°C = ■°F **7.** ⁻15°C = ■°F **8.** 100°C = ■°F

Extra Practice

Set D (Lesson 5, pages 560–562)

Copy and complete each table of values.

$y = x + 1$

	x	y
1.	2	■
2.	4	■
3.	6	■
4.	8	■

$y = 3x$

	x	y
5.	0	■
6.	5	■
7.	10	■
8.	15	■

$b = {}^{-}2a$

	a	b
9.	■	2
10.	■	$^{-}5$
11.	0	■
12.	■	4

$f = \frac{d}{3}$

	d	f
13.	$^{-}15$	■
14.	■	0
15.	■	$-\frac{2}{3}$
16.	9	■

Set E (Lesson 6, pages 564–565)

For each equation, copy and complete the table of values. Use grid paper to graph the equation.

1. $y = x - 2$ **2.** $y = x + 1$ **3.** $y = x + {}^{-}3$

4. $y = 4x$ **5.** $y = {}^{-}2x$ **6.** $y = x - 1$

7. $y = x - {}^{-}2$ **8.** $y = x + {}^{-}4$ **9.** $y = {}^{-}3x$

10. $y = \frac{x}{3}$ **11.** $y = {}^{-}x + 4$ **12.** $y = \frac{x}{2}$

13. $y = x$ **14.** $y = x \div {}^{-}2$ **15.** $y = {}^{-}x$

x	y
$^{-}2$	■
$^{-}1$	■
0	■
1	■
2	■

Set F (Lesson 8, pages 570–571)

Simplify each expression.

1. $5 + 2({}^{-}3 + 7)$ **2.** $14 - (8 - 6)^2$ **3.** $7 + 20 \div 4 - ({}^{-}5 + 9)^2$

4. $(3)(7) + ({}^{-}5)(2)$ **5.** $45 \div (30 \div 2)$ **6.** $8(2 + 11) - 3(5)(6)$

7. $^{-}9 + 5 - (2)(6)$ **8.** $(3)(9) - 39 \div 3$ **9.** $(9 - 4)^2 - 3(5 - 8)$

Has each expression been simplified correctly? Write *yes* or *no*. If not, write the correct value.

10. $7 + (9 - 5) + 12 = 22$ **11.** $^{-}2 - 8(3 + 5) = {}^{-}66$

12. $36 - 17 + 21 = 40$ **13.** $^{-}6(13 - 4) + (3)(7) = {}^{-}35$

14. $5(2 + 7) - 3^2 = 39$ **15.** $(6 - 2)^2 + 4(15 - 6) = 52$

16. $^{-}8(14 - 11) \div (2 \times 4) = {}^{-}4$ **17.** $72 \div 9 - 3(10 - 4) = 30$

Extra Practice

Set G (Lesson 9, pages 572–573)

Evaluate each expression.

1. $8 - x$, given $x = 10$
2. $5(a + c)$, given $a = {}^{-}8$ and $c = 2$
3. $p^2 - 6q$, given $p = 9$ and $q = 7$
4. $7k + 11m$, given $k = {}^{-}9$ and $m = 3$
5. $3x^2 + 5$, given $x = {}^{-}2$
6. $m + 2n - 8$, given $m = 14$ and $n = {}^{-}3$
7. $7m - 12n$, given $m = 4$ and $n = {}^{-}2$
8. $39 - x + 4z$, given $x = 21$ and $z = {}^{-}3$

Evaluate, given $m = {}^{-}5$, $n = 4$, and $p = 8$.

9. $p - m \times n$
10. $5m + n + p$
11. $p(m + n)$
12. $2(p + m) \div 3$
13. $15 + m + p$
14. $(p \times m) \div n$
15. $n^2 - p$
16. $(p + m)^2 - 3n$

Set H (Lesson 10, pages 574–575)

Write an expression. Tell what each variable represents.

1. nine more than twice a number
2. eight less than half a number
3. a number divided into 4 equal parts
4. the sum of 5 times a number and twelve
5. three times the difference of two numbers
6. seven less than the square of a number
7. the product of two numbers decreased by six
8. the square of a number increased by three times another number
9. the quotient of the sum of three numbers and ten
10. the square of the sum of two different numbers

Set I (Lesson 11, pages 576–577)

Solve.

1. $x - 3 = 2$
2. ${}^{-}3 + x = {}^{-}3$
3. $2x = 8$
4. $h - 5 = 8$
5. $b + 3 = {}^{-}6$
6. $x \div 3 = 5$
7. ${}^{-}2y = 12$
8. $2x = 9$
9. $x \div 4 = {}^{-}2$
10. $t + 4 = 12$
11. $8 - x = {}^{-}8$
12. ${}^{-}3x = {}^{-}6$

Extra Practice • Problem Solving

Solve, using the Find a Pattern strategy. *(Lesson 4, pages 556–557)*

1. Corey claims that the perfect peanut butter, p, and jelly, j, sandwich follows the pattern $p = \frac{3}{2}j$. If he has 3 lb of peanut butter and 3 lb of jelly, how many pounds of jelly would be left if he makes as many sandwiches as possible?

2. One batch of cookies is made with $4\frac{1}{2}$ c of flour and 1 c of chocolate chips. Two batches are made with 9 c of flour and 2 c of chips. Four batches are made with 18 c of flour and 4 c of chips. Find this pattern and express it with variables.

Solve. Use the graph on the right. *(Lesson 7, pages 566–567)*

3. David and Mary are heating water for a science experiment. After 3 minutes, they record a temperature of 36°C. Is this value reasonable? Explain.

4. If David and Mary start with water that is 26°C, how long would you expect it to take for the temperature to become 32°C?

5. Suppose the time for the experiment was extended. What would be a reasonable temperature for a time of 20 minutes?

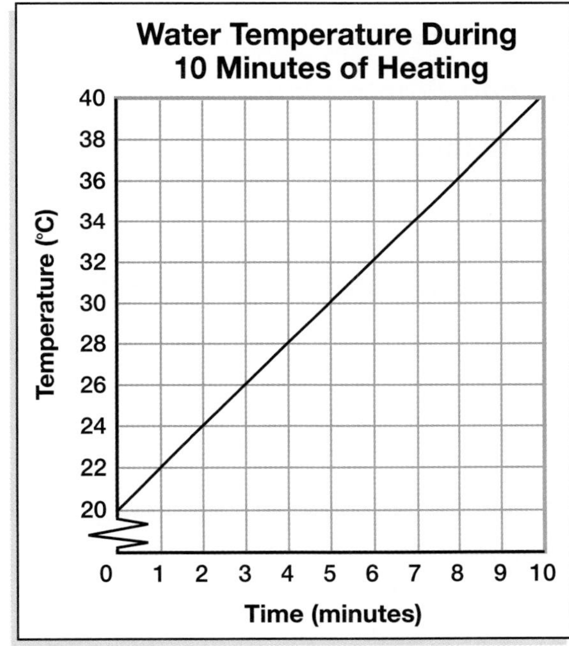

Solve. Use a graph. *(Lesson 12, pages 578–579)*

6. The graph shows the relationship between the number of hours a DJ plays and the cost of hiring the DJ. How much will it cost the Henninger family to hire a DJ for 4 hours?

7. The Henninger family later rehired the same DJ to play at their daughter's Sweet 16 party. If the DJ was hired to play for $2\frac{1}{2}$ hours, about how much will it cost the family?

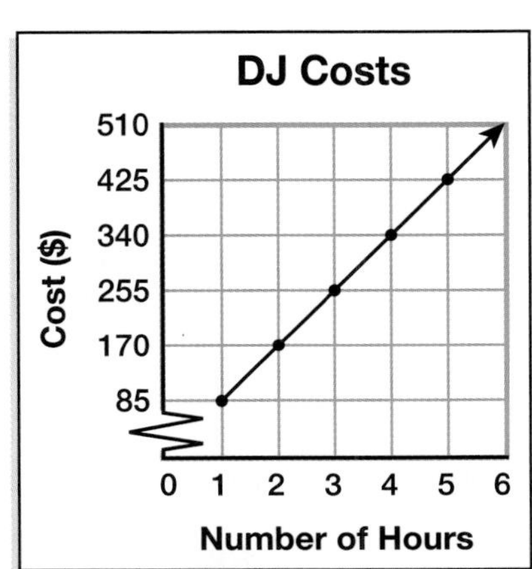

Chapter Review

Reviewing Vocabulary

Write *true* or *false*. If false, rewrite the sentence to make it true.

1. The origin on a coordinate plane has coordinates $(^-1, ^-1)$.
2. The graph of a linear equation is a straight line.
3. A point in the fourth quadrant has two negative coordinates.
4. The y-axis is the horizontal axis on a coordinate plane.

Match each word with a definition.

5. **ordered pair**
6. **expression**
7. **coordinate plane**
8. **evaluate**

A substitute a value for the variable to find a value of the expression

B a grid on a plane with two perpendicular number lines

C contains numbers, operations, and variables

D a pair of numbers in which the order shows the location of a point on the grid

Reviewing Concepts and Skills

Use the graph on the right. Write the coordinates of each point. *(pages 548–550)*

9. P 10. Q 11. R 12. S

Graph each ordered pair. Label the point with the given letter. Tell in which quadrant or on which axis the point lies. *(pages 548–550)*

13. $A\ (^-4, ^-3)$ 14. $B\ (3, ^-2)$ 15. $C\ (^-1, 0)$

Graph each point in Exercises 16–17. Connect the points in each set in order and connect the last points to the first. Find the area of each figure. *(pages 552–553)*

16. $(^-2, 6), (4, 6), (4, 1), (^-2, 1)$ 17. $(^-3, 2), (^-3, ^-2), (4, ^-2)$

Use the formula $F = \frac{9}{5}C + 32$ to convert each Celsius temperature. *(pages 554–555)*

18. 30°C = ■°F 19. $^-10$°C = ■°F 20. 0°C = ■°F

Use grid paper to graph each equation. *(pages 564–565)*

21. $y = x + 2$ 22. $y = {^-3}x$ 23. $y = x - 1$ 24. $y = x \div 3$

Simplify each expression. *(pages 570–571)*

25. $3(14 - 5)^2 - 5^2 + 12 \div 3$

26. $^-7 + 5(10 - 2) \div 2 - 6$

Evaluate each expression, given $x = {}^-3$, $y = 18$, and $z = 8$. *(pages 572–573)*

27. $x + y - z$

28. $4(z - x) - y$

29. $2y + 5x$

30. $x^2 + 3z - y$

Write an expression. Tell what each variable represents. *(pages 574–575)*

31. three times the difference between a number and eight

32. the quotient of a number and the square of another number

Solve. *(pages 576–577)*

33. $x + 3 = 5$

34. $2p = 7$

35. $x - {}^-3 = 8$

36. $x - 8 = {}^-10$

Solve. *(pages 556–557, 566–567, 578–579)*

37. Meg charges a base fee plus an hourly rate as shown in the graph on the right. How much would the labor costs be if it took $3\frac{1}{2}$ hours for Meg to fix your car?

38. Spike used 2 cups of cereal to make 5 packages of trail mix. He used 4 cups of cereal to make 10 packages of mix and 6 cups to make 15 packages. Find the pattern and express it with variables.

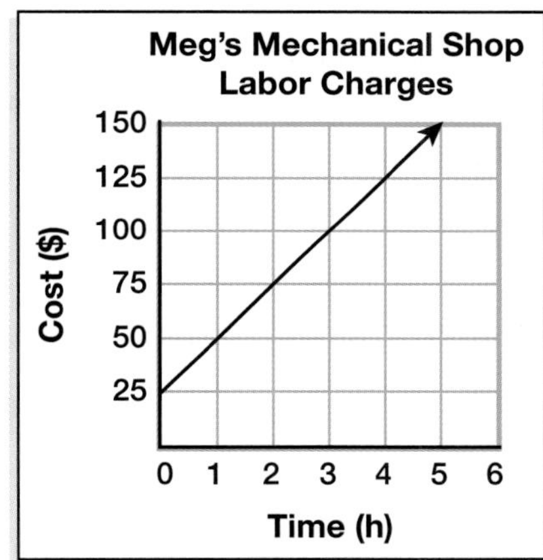

Brain Teaser Math Reasoning

Max's robot can cross a yard by walking on stepping stones.

- It can only move forward 3 stones or back 2 stones at a time.
- It cannot move forward more than 3 times without moving backward at least once.
- It starts on the first stone and cannot step on the ninth stone.

What is the least number of moves the robot can make to land on the fifteenth stone?

Internet Brain Teasers
Visit **www.eduplace.com/kids/mhm** for more *Brain Teasers.*

Chapter Test

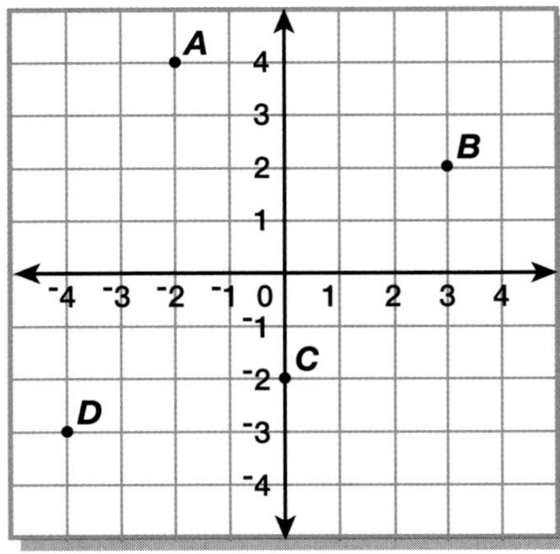

Use the graph on the right. Write the coordinates of each point.

1. *A** **2.** *B* **3.** *C* **4.** *D*

Graph each point in Exercises 5–8. Connect the points in each set in order and connect the last point to the first. Find the area of each figure.

5. $(4, 7), (^-1, 7), (^-1, ^-1), (4, ^-1)$

6. $(^-4, ^-5), (^-4, 3), (^-1, 3), (^-1, ^-5)$

7. $(6, ^-1), (^-1, ^-1), (^-1, 2)$

8. $(10, 4), (2, 4), (2, ^-3)$

Use the formula $F = \frac{9}{5}C + 32$ to convert each Celsius temperature.

9. 100°C = ■°F **10.** 30°C = ■°F **11.** 50.5°C = ■°F **12.** $^-25$°C = ■°F

Use graph paper to graph each equation.

13. $y = x - 4$ **14.** $y = {^-2}x$ **15.** $y = x + 1$

Simplify each expression.

16. $4^2 + 2(8 + 4) \div 12$ **17.** $5(6 - 15) + 7$

18. $(11)(4) - 3^2 + 5$ **19.** $24 \div (^-3 + 5) + 14$

Simplify, given $a = {^-2}$, $b = 8$, and $c = 5$.

20. $a + c - b$ **21.** $(c - a)^2 + b$ **22.** $3b - 4a - c^2$ **23.** $7(b + c) \div a$

Write an expression. Tell what each variable represents.

24. the square of a number decreased by 7

25. twice the sum of two different numbers

26. the quotient of 9 and the difference between a number and 4

27. the product of 5 and the sum of three and a number

Solve.

28. $x - 6 = {^-2}$ **29.** $a \div 4 = 2$ **30.** $x + 3 = 9$ **31.** $2s = {^-8}$

Solve.

32. The graph on the right shows the relationship between the number of miles driven and the number of gallons of gasoline used. If Jeremy has used 6 gallons of gasoline on his trip, how many miles has he driven?

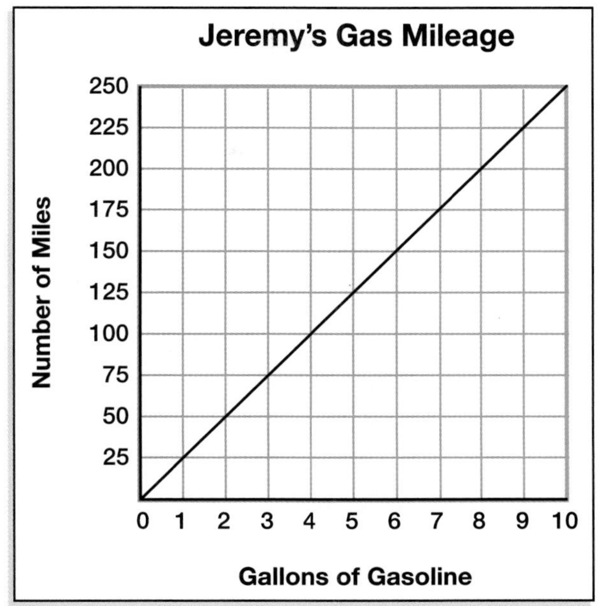

33. To cook sandwiches in the microwave, Matt uses this chart.

Number of Sandwiches	2	4	8
Time (min)	$1\frac{1}{2}$	3	6

Find the pattern and use variables to express it. How many sandwiches is Matt making if he microwaves them for $4\frac{1}{2}$ minutes?

Write About It

Solve each problem. Use correct math vocabulary to explain your thinking.

Stuart bought some boneless chicken at the supermarket to cook this evening for his family. His cookbook says to bake the chicken at 350°F for 45 minutes. He doesn't have that much time to prepare dinner. He heard that for every 50° you increase the oven temperature, the amount of time to bake is decreased by 10 minutes.

1. Complete the chart so that it represents the problem.

a. Create a linear graph that compares baking time to oven temperature (°F).

b. Create a linear graph that compares the oven temperature (°F) to baking time.

c. How are these graphs similar? How are they different?

Oven Temperature (°F)	Baking Time (min)
350°	
400°	

2. How long would it take at 575°F? Does this make sense?

3. Over what range of temperatures do you think this model is useful?

Another Look

Use the information from the table to help solve each problem.

ES/UCLA
Time (in hours)
Total Distance (in miles)
1
1½
2
3½
4

1. Heather, Amber, Troy, and Sierra go hiking. The distance, d, that they hike in a specific amount of time, t, can be represented by the equation $d = 2.75t$. Make a copy of the table and use this equation to complete the table.

2. Use graph paper to graph the equation $d = 2.75t$.

3. **Look Back** Use the graph to find out how many miles Heather, Amber, Troy, and Sierra hiked in 3 hours.

4. **Analyze** On their next hiking trek, Heather, Amber, Troy, and Sierra plan to start hiking at 10 A.M. and be back at 5 P.M. They plan to take three 20-minute breaks and a 30-minute lunch break. If they walk at the same rate as on the hike in Exercise 1, how many miles can they walk on this hike?

Enrichment

New Vocabulary
slope
rise
run

Slope of a Line

The **slope** of a line is a measure of the steepness or slant of the line. Slope is a ratio of the form $\frac{\text{rise}}{\text{run}}$.

The **rise** is the vertical difference between any two points on the line and the **run** is the horizontal difference between those same two points. If the origin is one of the points, it is easy to find the difference.

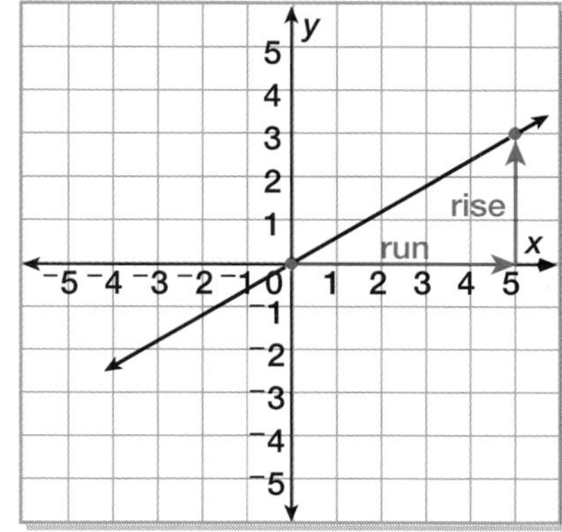

Find the slope of the line $y = \frac{3}{5}x$.

Step 1 Graph the equation and choose two points on the graph. Label the coordinates of the points.

Step 2 Find the slope. Subtract the y-coordinates to find the rise. Subtract the x-coordinates to find the run. Write the ratio of $\frac{\text{rise}}{\text{run}}$.

rise: $3 - 0 = 3$ run: $5 - 0 = 5$

slope: $\frac{3}{5}$

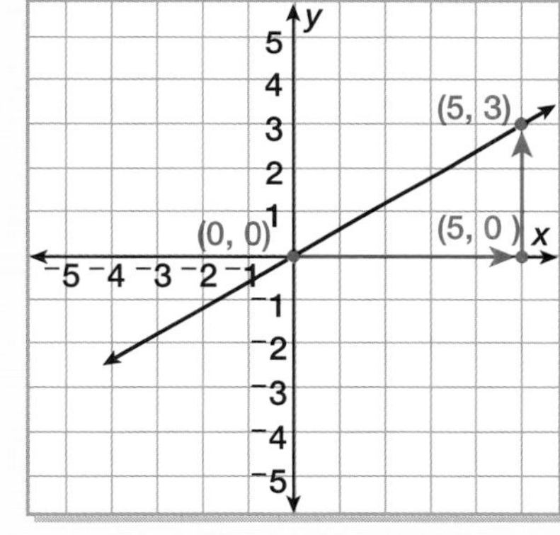

Solution: The slope of the line $y = \frac{3}{5}x$ is $\frac{3}{5}$.

Try These

Graph each line. Then find the slope of each line.

1. $y = x$ **2.** $y = 2x$ **3.** $y = 4x$ **4.** $y = {}^{-}2x$ **5.** $y = {}^{-}4x$

Explain Your Thinking

- What happens if you choose two different points?
- What connection do you see between the equations and their slopes?

Table of Measures

Customary Units of Measure

Length

1 foot (ft) = 12 inches (in.)
1 yard (yd) = 36 inches
1 yard = 3 feet
1 mile (mi) = 5,280 feet
1 mile = 1,760 yards

Capacity

1 cup (c) = 8 fluid ounces (fl oz)
1 pint (pt) = 2 cups
1 quart (qt) = 2 pints
1 quart = 4 cups
1 gallon (gal) = 4 quarts
1 gallon = 8 pints

Weight

1 pound (lb) = 16 ounces (oz)
1 ton (T) = 2,000 pounds

Metric Units of Measure

Length

1 meter (m) = 1,000 millimeters (mm)
1 meter = 100 centimeters (cm)
1 meter = 10 decimeters (dm)
1 kilometer (km) = 1,000 meters
1 decimeter = 10 centimeters
1 centimeter = 10 millimeters

Capacity

1 liter (L) = 1,000 milliliters (mL)
1 liter = 10 deciliters (dL)

Mass

1 kilogram (kg) = 1,000 grams (g)
1 metric ton (t) = 1,000 kilograms

Units of Time

1 minute (min) = 60 seconds (s)
1 hour (h) = 60 minutes
1 day (d) = 24 hours
1 week (wk) = 7 days
1 year (yr) = 12 months (mo)

1 year = 52 weeks
1 year = 365 days
1 leap year = 366 days
1 decade = 10 years
1 century = 100 years
1 millennium = 1,000 years

Glossary

absolute value The distance of a number from zero on a number line.

acute angle An angle with a measure less than that of a right angle.

acute triangle A triangle in which each of the three angles is acute.

addend A number to be added in an addition expression. In $7 + 4 + 8$, the numbers 7, 4, and 8 are addends.

additive inverse The opposite of a number. The sum of a number and its additive inverse is always zero.

adjacent angles Angles that share a common side and a common vertex. Their interiors do not overlap.

algebraic expression An expression that consists of one or more variables. It could contain some constants and some operations.

Example: $2x + 3y + 6$

angle An angle is formed by two rays with the same endpoint.

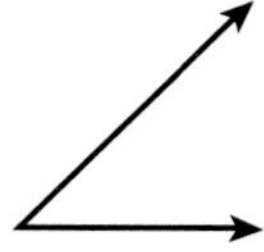

area The number of square units in a region.

array An arrangement of objects, pictures, or numbers in columns and rows.

Associative Property of Addition The property which states that the way in which addends are grouped does not change the sum. It is also called the Grouping Property of Addition.

Associative Property of Multiplication The property which states that the way in which factors are grouped does not change the product. It is also called the Grouping Property of Multiplication.

average The number found by dividing the sum of a group of numbers by the number of addends.

bar graph A graph in which information is shown by means of rectangular bars.

base of a geometric figure A bottom side or face of a geometric figure.

base of a power A factor that is repeated a number of times in a product.

bias The difference between what the responses of a sample are and what the actual responses from the entire population would be.

box-and-whisker plot A data representation that shows the extremes, the median, and the first and third quartiles in a simple and clear diagram.

Glossary

capacity The amount a container can hold.

Celsius The metric temperature scale.

center A point lying in the middle of a circle that is the same distance from all points on the circle.

centimeter (cm) A metric unit used to measure length.

100 centimeters = 1 meter

central angle An angle with a vertex at the center of a circle.

chord A segment that connects two points on a circle.

circle A closed figure in which every point is the same distance from a given point called the center of the circle.

circle graph A graph used for data that are parts of a whole.

circumference The distance around a circle.

cluster In a data display, a group of points that are close to each other.

common denominator Any common multiple of the denominators of two or more fractions.

common factor A number that is a factor of two or more numbers.

Commutative Property of Addition The property which states that the order of addends does not change the sum. It is also called the Order Property of Addition.

Commutative Property of Multiplication The property which states that the order of factors does not change the product. It is also called the Order Property of Multiplication.

complementary angles Two angles for which the sum of the angle measures is 90°.

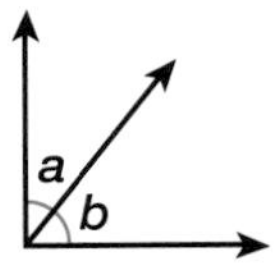

composite number A whole number that has more than two factors.

compound event In probability, an event that is made up of two or more events.

cone A solid that has a circular base and a surface from a boundary of the base to the vertex.

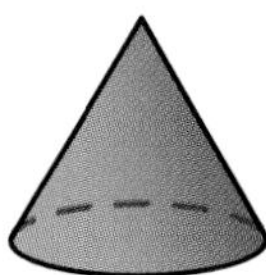

congruent figures Figures that have the same size and the same shape.

convenience sample In statistics, a sample that is easy to survey. A convenience sample allows results to be obtained quickly.

coordinate plane A plane formed by two perpendicular number lines in which every point is assigned an ordered pair of numbers.

coordinates An ordered pair of numbers that locates a point in the coordinate plane with reference to the *x*- and *y*-axes.

corresponding parts In geometry, matching sides and angles of polygons.

cube A solid figure that has six square faces of equal size.

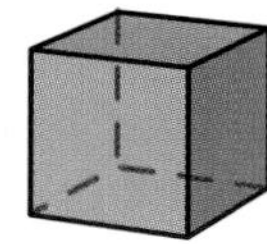

cubic centimeter A metric unit for measuring volume. It is the volume of a cube with each edge 1 centimeter long.

cylinder A solid with two circular faces that are congruent and a cylindrical surface connecting the two faces.

data In statistics, a set of individual numbers or pieces of information.

decagon A polygon with 10 sides.

regular irregular

decimal A number with one or more digits to the right of a decimal point.

deciliter (dL) A metric unit used to measure capacity.

10 dL = 1 L

decimeter (dm) A metric unit used to measure length.

10 dm = 1 m

denominator The number below the bar in a fraction.

dependent event An event that is affected by the outcome of another event.

diagonal A line segment that connects two vertices of a polygon and is not a side.

diameter of a circle A segment that connects two points on the circle and passes through the center.

difference The result of subtraction.

discount A decrease in the price of an item.

disjoint events Two or more events with no outcomes in common.

Distributive Property The property which states that when two addends are multiplied by a factor the product is the same as if each addend was multiplied by the factor and those products were added.

dividend The number that is divided in a division problem.

divisible One number is divisible by another if the quotient is a whole number and the remainder is 0. For example, 10 is divisible by 2, since $10 \div 2 = 5$ R0.

divisor The number by which a number is being divided. In $6 \div 3 = 2$, the divisor is 3.

Glossary

dodecagon A polygon with 12 sides.

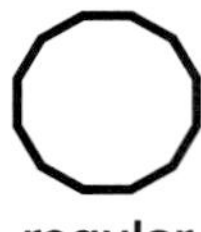
regular

irregular

double bar graph A graph in which data are compared by means of pairs of rectangular bars drawn next to each other.

double line graph A graph that is used to show data by means of two broken lines.

E

edge The segment where two faces of a solid figure meet.

endpoint The point at either end of a line segment. The beginning point of a ray.

equation A mathematical sentence with an equals sign.

Examples: $3 + 1 = 4$ and $2x + 5 = 9$ are equations.

equilateral triangle A triangle that has three congruent sides.

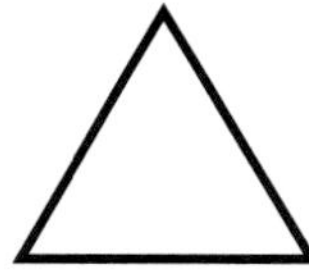

equivalent fractions Fractions that show different numbers with the same value.

Example: $\frac{1}{2}$ and $\frac{4}{8}$ are equivalent fractions.

estimate A number close to an exact amount. An estimate tells *about* how much or *about* how many.

evaluating an expression Substituting the values given for the variables and performing the operations to find the value of the expression.

even number A whole number that is a multiple of 2. The ones digit in an even number is 0, 2, 4, 6, or 8. The numbers 56 and 48 are examples of even numbers.

event In probability, a collection of possible outcomes of an experiment.

experimental probability The actual results of a probability experiment.

exponent The number in a power that tells how many times a factor is repeated in a product.

expression A number, a variable, or any combination of numbers, variables, operation signs, and grouping symbols.

F

face A flat surface of a solid figure.

fact family Facts that are related, using the same numbers.

Examples: $1 + 4 = 5$, $4 + 1 = 5$, $5 - 1 = 4$, $5 - 4 = 1$; $3 \times 5 = 15$, $5 \times 3 = 15$, $15 \div 3 = 5$, $15 \div 5 = 3$

factor One of two or more numbers that are multiplied to give a product.

factorization A number written as a product of its factors.

factor of a number A number that divides evenly into a given number.

Fahrenheit The customary temperature scale.

first quartile (Q1) The median of the lower set of numbers obtained when a median divides data into a lower set of numbers and a higher set of numbers.

fraction A number that names a part of a whole, a part of a collection, or a part of a region.

Examples: $\frac{1}{2}$, $\frac{3}{4}$, and $\frac{2}{3}$.

frequency table A way of summarizing data that shows the frequency, or total, for each group or type of data.

function A rule that gives exactly one value of y for every value of x.

fundamental counting principle If a two-step situation or experiment has m ways to do the first step and n ways to do the second step, then the total number of possible outcomes for both steps is $m \times n$.

gallon (gal) A customary unit used to measure capacity.

4 quarts = 1 gallon

gap In a data display, a large space between data points.

gram (g) A metric unit used to measure mass.

1,000 milligrams = 1 gram

greatest common divisor The greatest whole number that is a common factor of two or more numbers. It is also called the greatest common factor.

greatest common factor The greatest whole number that is a common factor of two or more numbers. It is also called the greatest common divisor.

heptagon A polygon with 7 sides.

regular

irregular

hexagon A polygon with 6 sides.

regular

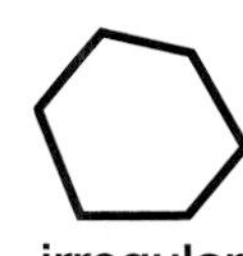

irregular

histogram A graph in which bars are used to display how frequently data occurs within equal intervals.

horizontal axis The x-axis in a coordinate system. It is a number line that locates points to the left or to the right of the origin.

Identity Property For addition, the sum of any number and 0 is that number; for multiplication, the product of any number and 1 is that number.

Glossary

improper fraction A fraction that is greater than or equal to 1. The numerator in an improper fraction is greater than or equal to the denominator.

inch (in.) A customary unit used to measure length.
12 inches = 1 foot

independent event In probability, an event that is not affected by another event.

inequality A sentence that contains > (is greater than) or < (is less than).

Examples: 8 > 2, 5 < 6

integers The set of positive whole numbers and their opposites (negative numbers) and 0.

..., $^-3$, $^-2$, $^-1$, 0, $^+1$, $^+2$, $^+3$,...

interest rate The rate of interest paid for a given period of time.

intersecting lines Lines that meet or cross at a common point.

inverse operations Two operations that undo each other, such as addition and subtraction or multiplication and division.

isolate the variable In algebra, to work with an equation until the variable stands alone on one side of the equation.

isosceles triangle A triangle that has two congruent sides.

K

kilogram (kg) A metric unit used to measure mass.

1 kilogram = 1,000 grams.

kilometer (km) A metric unit used to measure length.

1 kilometer = 1,000 meters.

L

least common denominator (LCD) For two or more fractions, the least common multiple of the denominators.

least common multiple The least number that is a multiple of two or more numbers.

Example: 12 is the least common multiple of 3 and 4.

like denominators Denominators in two or more fractions that are the same.

line A straight, continuous, and unending set of points in a plane.

line graph A graph that uses a broken line to show changes in data.

line of symmetry The line along which a figure can be folded so that the two halves match exactly.

line plot A diagram that organizes data using a number line.

line segment A part of a line that has two endpoints.

line symmetry A figure has line symmetry if it can be folded in half and the two halves are congruent.

linear equation An equation that represents the graph of a straight line.

Example: $y = x + 3$

liter (L) A metric unit used to measure capacity.

1 liter = 1,000 milliliters

maximum The greatest value in a set of numbers.

mean Arithmetic mean, also called *average*. The number found by dividing the sum of a group of numbers by the number of addends.

measures of central tendency The mean, median, and mode.

median The middle number when a set of numbers is arranged in order from least to greatest.

Examples: The median of 2, 5, 7, 9, and 10 is 7. For an even number of numbers, it is the average of the two middle numbers. The median of 2, 5, 7, and 12 is $\frac{(5+7)}{2}$, or 6.

meter (m) A metric unit used to measure length.

1 meter = 100 centimeters

mile (mi) A customary unit used to measure length.

5,280 feet = 1 mile

milligram (mg) A metric unit used to measure mass.

1,000 milligrams = 1 gram

milliliter (mL) A metric unit used to measure capacity.

1,000 milliliters = 1 liter

millimeter (mm) A metric unit used to measure length.

1,000 millimeters = 1 meter

minimum The least value in a set of numbers.

mixed number A number that is the sum of a whole number and a fraction.

mode The number or numbers that occur most often in a set of data.

multiple A number that is the product of the given number and a number.

negative integer An integer less than 0.

Examples: $^-4$, $^-7$, $^-100$

negative number A number that is less than 0.

Examples: $\frac{^-7}{8}$, $^-5$, and $^-2.8$ are negative numbers.

net A flat pattern that can be folded to make a solid.

nonagon A polygon with 9 sides.

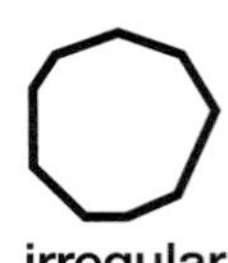

number line A line on which numbers are assigned to points.

numerator The number above the bar in a fraction.

obtuse angle An angle with a measure greater than that of a right angle and less than 180°.

obtuse triangle A triangle that has one obtuse angle.

octagon A polygon with 8 sides.

odd number A whole number that is not a multiple of 2. The ones digit in an odd number is 1, 3, 5, 7, or 9. The numbers 67 and 493 are examples of odd numbers.

opposite of a number The same number but of opposite sign. Examples of opposite numbers are $^{+}2$ and $^{-}2$, $^{-}7$ and $^{+}7$, and $^{-}12$ and $^{+}12$. The opposite of a number is also called its additive inverse.

order of operations The order in which operations in an expression to be evaluated are carried out. Do the operation in parentheses first; next evaluate exponents; then multiply and divide from left to right; and finally add and subtract from left to right.

ordered pair A pair of numbers in which one number is considered to be first and the other number second.

origin A point assigned to zero on the number line or the point where the *x*-axis and *y*-axis intersect in a coordinate system.

outcome A result in a probability experiment.

outlier A number or numbers that are at one or the other end of a set of data, arranged in order, where there is a gap between the end numbers and the rest of the data.

parallel lines Lines that lie in the same plane and do not intersect. They are everywhere the same distance apart.

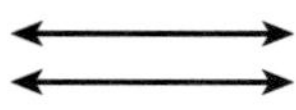

parallelogram A quadrilateral in which both pairs of opposite sides are parallel.

pentagon A polygon with 5 sides.

regular

irregular

percent Per hundred. Ratio of a number to 100.

Example: 7% means 7 out of 100 or $\frac{7}{100}$.

perimeter The distance around a figure.

period In a multidigit number, a group of three digits set off by commas.

perpendicular Two lines or line segments that cross or meet to form right angles.

pi (π) A number defined by the ratio of the circumference of any circle to its diameter. Two common approximations used for pi are $\frac{22}{7}$ and 3.14.

plane A flat surface made up of a continuous and unending collection of points.

point An exact location in space, represented by a dot.

polygon A simple closed plane figure made up of three or more line segments.

population In statistics, all the individuals that fit a given description.

Examples: all the residents of a state or all the fish in a lake

positive numbers Numbers that are greater than zero.

pound (lb) A customary unit used to measure weight.

1 pound = 16 ounces

prime factorization Factoring a number into its prime factors only.

Example: the prime factorization of 30 is $2 \times 3 \times 5$.

prime number A whole number, greater than 1, that has exactly two factors.

principal An amount of money invested or borrowed.

prism A solid figure that has two parallel congruent bases and rectangles and parallelograms for faces.

probability The chance of an event occurring. A probability can be any number from 0 through 1.

product The answer in a multiplication problem.

proper fraction A fraction in which the numerator is less than the denominator.

Example: $\frac{4}{7}$

proportion An equation showing that two ratios are equal.

pyramid A solid figure whose base can be any polygon and whose faces are triangles.

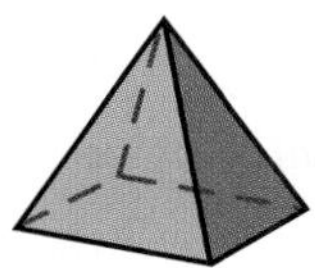

Glossary

quadrant Each of the four parts into which a plane is separated by the *x*-axis and the *y*-axis. The axes are not parts of the quadrant.

quadrilateral A polygon with four sides.

quart (qt) A customary unit to measure capacity.

4 quarts = 1 gallon

quotient The answer in a division problem.

radius A segment that connects the center of a circle to any point on the circle.

random sample In statistics, a sample in which every individual in the population has the same chance of being included.

range The difference between the greatest and least numbers in a set of data.

rate A comparison by a ratio of two quantities using different kinds of units.

ratio A comparison of two numbers by division.

ray Part of a line that starts at an endpoint and goes on without end in one direction.

reciprocal The product of a number and its reciprocal is 1.

Example: $\frac{2}{3} \times \frac{3}{2} = 1$, so $\frac{2}{3}$ and $\frac{3}{2}$ are reciprocals of each other.

rectangle A polygon with opposite sides parallel and four right angles.

rectangular prism A solid figure with six faces that are rectangles.

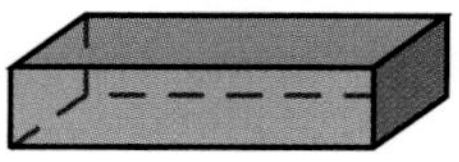

rectangular pyramid A solid figure whose base is a rectangle and whose faces are triangles.

reflection A transformation that involves a flipping movement of a figure over a line.

regular polygon A polygon with all sides having the same length and all angles having the same measure.

remainder The number that is left after one whole number is divided by another.

repeating decimal A decimal quotient that contains a repeating block of digits.

representative sample A sample for which the results from the sample can be considered the same as the results from the entire population.

rhombus A parallelogram with all four sides the same length.

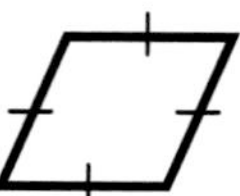

right angle An angle that measures 90°.

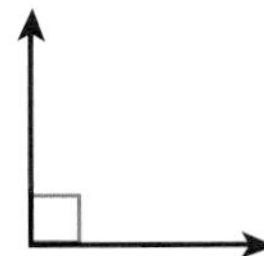

right triangle A triangle that has one right angle.

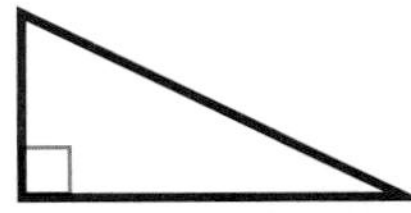

rotation A transformation that involves a turning movement of a figure about a point.

rotational symmetry A figure has rotational symmetry if, after the figure is rotated about a point, the figure is the same as when in its original position.

rounding To find about how many or how much by expressing a number to the nearest ten, hundred, thousand, and so on.

sale price The price of an item after the discount is subtracted.

sample In statistics, a smaller group used to gather data about a population.

scalene triangle A triangle with all sides of different lengths.

scale The ratio of the size in a drawing or model to the actual size of an object.

side of a polygon One of the line segments that make up a polygon.

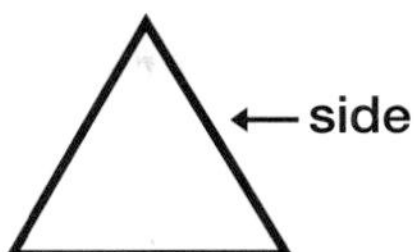

similar figures Figures that have the same shape but not necessarily the same size.

simple interest The amount of money a bank pays to use money or the amount paid to borrow money calculated once a year.

simplest form of a fraction A fraction whose numerator and denominator have the number 1 as the only common factor.

simplest form of an algebraic expression An algebraic expression is in simplest form if no terms can be combined.

slope A measure of the slant or steepness of a line. Slope is a ratio in the form $\frac{\text{rise}}{\text{run}}$.

solution of an equation A number or numbers that, when substituted for the variable or variables in an equation, give a true statement.

solid figure A three-dimensional figure in space.

space figure A figure with three dimensions: length, width, and height.

speed A ratio of distance per unit of time.

Glossary

sphere A solid figure that is shaped like a round ball.

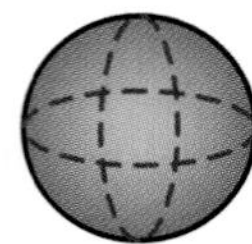

square A polygon with four right angles and four congruent sides.

stem-and-leaf plot A frequency distribution that arranges data in order of place value. The last digits of the number are the leaves. The digits to the left of the leaves are the stems.

substitute To put in place of.

supplementary angles Two angles for which the sum of the angle measures is 180°.

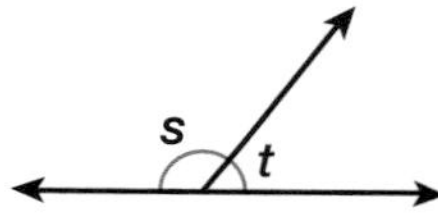

surface area The total area of the surface of a solid.

survey In statistics, a method used to gather information.

symmetric figure A figure that has symmetry.

symmetry (line symmetry) A figure has line symmetry if it can be folded along a line so that the two parts match exactly.

terminating decimal A decimal quotient that terminates or stops because the repeating block of digits consists only of zeros.

terms of a ratio The numerator and denominator of a ratio expressed as a fraction. The numerator is the first term, and the denominator is the second term.

theoretical probability For a single event, the probability calculated by dividing the number of outcomes in the event by the total number of outcomes

third quartile (Q3) The median of the higher set of numbers obtained when a median divides data into a lower set of numbers and a higher set of numbers.

ton (T) A customary unit used to measure weight.

2,000 pounds = 1 ton

translation A transformation that involves a sliding movement of a figure in any direction.

trapezoid A quadrilateral with exactly one pair of parallel sides.

tree diagram A diagram that shows combinations of outcomes of an event.

triangle A polygon with three sides.

triangular prism A prism whose bases are triangles.

triangular pyramid A pyramid whose base is a triangle.

two-variable equation An equation that has two different variables.

undecagon A polygon with 11 sides.

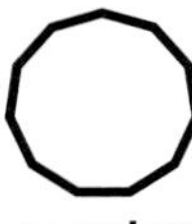

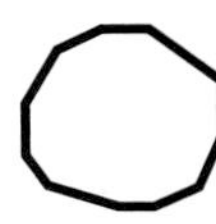

unit cost The cost of a single item.

unit fraction A fraction in which the numerator is 1.

Example: $\frac{1}{5}$

unit rate A rate expressed with a denominator of 1.

variable A letter or a symbol that represents a number in an algebraic expression.

vertex of an angle A point common to the two sides of an angle.

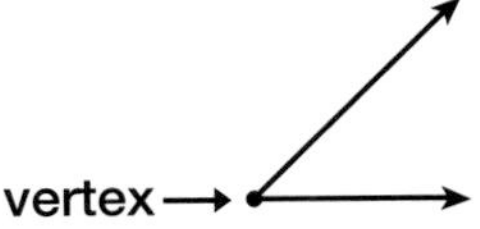

vertex of a polygon A point common to two sides of a polygon.

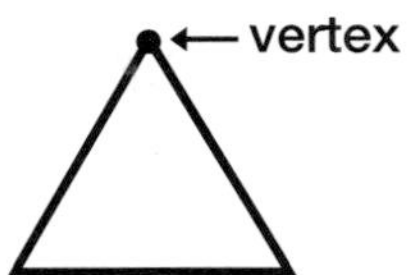

vertex of a prism A point common to three edges of a prism.

vertical angles Angles formed by intersecting lines. Vertical angles are always equal in size, or congruent.

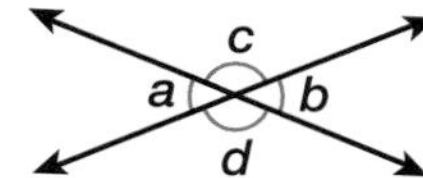

$\angle a$ and $\angle b$
$\angle c$ and $\angle d$

vertical axis The *y*-axis in the coordinate system. It is a number line that locates points up or down from the origin.

volume The number of cubic units that make up a solid figure.

weight The measure of how heavy something is.

***x*-axis** The horizontal number line in a coordinate system.

***x*-coordinate** The first number of an ordered pair of numbers that names a point in a coordinate system.

Glossary

yard A customary unit used to measure length.

3 feet = 1 yard

***y*-axis** The vertical number line in a coordinate system.

***y*-coordinate** The second number of an ordered pair of numbers that names a point in a coordinate system.

***y*-intercept** The *y*-intercept of a line is the point on a graph where the line crosses the *y*-axis.

Z

Zero Property of Addition The property which states that the sum of any number and 0 is that number.

Zero Property of Multiplication The property which states that the product of any number and 0 is 0.

Index

B

Index

Index

Index

Index

Index

P

Index

Index

Credits

PHOTOGRAPHY

All photographs by Houghton Mifflin Company (HMCo.) unless otherwise noted.

Coin photography by Mike Tesi for HMCo. xi: *t.l.* © J. Cochin/Photo Researchers, Inc.; *t.r.* Peter Kaplan/Bruce Coleman Inc. xii: *b.* Lawrence Migdale/Pix. xiv: *b.l.* VCG/FPG International; *b.r.* Bill O'Connor/Peter Arnold, Inc. xv: *t.* Reed/Williams/Animals Animals/Earth Scenes. xvi: *t.* Ken Sherman/Bruce Coleman Inc.; *b.l.* Bob Daemmrich Photography; *b.r.* David Madison Photography. xviii: *t.* Vladimir Pcholkin/FPG International. xx: *t.* The Image Bank. xxi: *b.* Frank Siteman/Stock Boston. xxii–1: © David Nunuk/Science Photo Library/Photo Researchers, Inc. 4: Richard Pasley/Stock Boston. 5: © US Geological Survey/Science Photo Library/Photo Researchers, Inc. 8: *t.* Mike Tesi for HMCo. 12: *t.* Superstock; *b.* Russ Gutshall/Dembinsky Photo Associates. 15: *l.* Kim Robbie/The Stock Market; *r.* Lawrence Migdale/Pix. 18: Richard Hutchings for HMCo. 22: Owen Franken/Corbis. 30: *l.* Novastock/PhotoEdit. 32: *t.* Arthur Tilley/FPG International. 36: *l.* Alex Rakosy/Dembinsky Photo Associates; *r.* © Corbis. 37: *l.* © M.I. Walker/Photo Researchers, Inc.; *r.* © Eric Grave/Photo Researchers, Inc. 40: *l.* Adam Jones/Dembinsky Photo Associates; *m.l.* M.C. Chamberlain/DRK Photo; *m.r.* Barbara Gerlach/Dembinsky Photo Associates; *r.* © Harold Hoffman/Photo Researchers, Inc. 43: *l.* Alan Pitcairn/Grant Heilman Photography, Inc. 56–57: Bob Daemmrich Photography. 60: Andy Sacks/Tony Stone Images. 64: Corbis. 66: Joseph Nettis/Stock Boston. 68: Dick Durrance/The Stock Market. 69: *l.* © J. Cochin/Photo Researchers, Inc.; *r.* Peter Kaplan/Bruce Coleman Inc. 71: Alan Scheim/The Stock Market. 72: © 2000 Newsweek, Inc. All rights reserved. Reprinted by permission. 73: *l.* Jose L. Pelaez/The Stock Market; *m.l.* Bob Daemmrich/Stock Boston; *m.r.* Stephen Simpson/FPG International; *r.* Chuck Savage/The Stock Market. 76: Bob Daemmrich Photography. 77: Dave Rosenberg/Tony Stone Images. 78: *l.* Bettmann/Corbis; *r.* Myrleen Ferguson/PhotoEdit. 82: Ken Biggs/Tony Stone Images. 85: © Francois Gohier/Photo Researchers, Inc. 98: *t.* © David Weintraub/Photo Researchers, Inc.; *b.* Glen Allison/Tony Stone Images. 100–101: Richard Hutchings for HMCo. 104: *l.* Archivo Iconografico, S.A./Corbis; *m.* Araido de Luca/Corbis; *r.* Bettmann/Corbis. 107: © David Parker/Science Photo Library/Photo Researchers, Inc. 110: Lawrence Migdale/Pix. 112: Randi Anglin/The Image Works. 114: Joe Viesti/The Viesti Collection. 118: Patrick Olear/PhotoEdit. 122: *t.* Bob Daemmrich/Stock Boston. 126: Michael Gaffney for HMCo. 130: *t.* Painet Inc. 131: *r.* Brian Bailey/Stone/Getty Images. 134: *inset* Steve Chenn/Corbis. 137: *l.* Owen Franken/Corbis. 138: *t.* Stuart Westmorland/Corbis; *b.* Color-Pic, Inc. 139: *l.* Steve Simonsen/Marine Scenes; *r.* © G. Carleton Ray/Photo Researchers, Inc. 152–153: David Young-Wolff/PhotoEdit. 156: Uniphoto Pictor. 162: *r.* Michael Gaffney for HMCo. 165: *l.* M.K. Denny/PhotoEdit; *r.* Bob Daemmrich/Stock Boston. 171: Carol Mazloomi/Women of Color Quilters Network. 174: *l.* Michael Gaffney for HMCo.; *r.* Richard Hutchings Photography. 178: Dennis MacDonald/PhotoEdit. 185: *l.* Peter Vandermark/Stock Boston; *r.* Myrleen Ferguson/PhotoEdit. 186: *r.* Michelle Bridwell/PhotoEdit. 188: Michael Newman/PhotoEdit. 189: *l.* David Lassman/The Image Works; *r.* Steve Rubin/The Image Works. 200: Dennis Gottlieb/FoodPix/Getty Images. 202–203: Nigel Francis/The Stock Market. 204: William Johnson/Stock Boston. 208: *l.* Harvey Lloyd/FPG International; *r.* Telegraph Colour Library/FPG International. 211: Stephen Frink/The Stock Market. 214: VCG/FPG International. 222: David Young-Wolff/PhotoEdit. 223: Chuck Savage/The Stock Market. 226: *r.* C Squared Studios/PhotoDisc, Inc. 227: *l.* ©1993 Mel Fisher Maritime Heritage Society, Key West, FL. Photo By Dylan Kibler; *m.* Dick Luria/FPG International; *r.* Victor R. Boswell/National Geographic Society. 233: Bob Daemmrich/Stock Boston. 234: *t.* VCG/FPG International. 235: Bill O'Connor/Peter Arnold, Inc. 246: Chromosohm/Sohm/Stock Boston. 248–249: Stephen Simpson/FPG International. 254: Rudi Von Briel/PhotoEdit. 267: © Corbis. 270: © Ulrike Welsch. 274: R. Kopfle/Bruce Coleman Inc. 275: The Maritime Museum and the Warship Wasa/FPG International. 280: *r.* Tom Bean/Tom & Susan Bean, Inc. 282: David Bailey/David Bailey Images. 283: Mark Gallup/Uniphoto Pictor. 284: Mitsuaki Iwago/Minden Pictures. 285: Reed/Williams/Animals Animals/Earth Scenes. 287: *l.* Bettman/Corbis; *r.* AT&T Media Relations. 304: *inset* David Young-Wolff/PhotoEdit. 306: Bob Daemmrich/The Image Works. 308: Arthur Tilley/FPG International. 309: Michael Keller/The Stock Market. 310: NASA. 312: NASA/StockTrek/PhotoDisc, Inc. 314: Richard Hutchings for HMCo. 318–319: NASA. 322: Bob Daemmrich/The Image Works. 323: *l.* Bob Daemmrich Photography; *r.* David Madison Photography. 326: Superstock. 328: *l.* Bob Daemmrich/Stock Boston. 329: Ken Sherman/Bruce Coleman Inc. 330: © Joseph Sohm/ChromoSohm Inc./Corbis. 333: *l.* FPG International; *r.* Burke & Triolo/Artville/Picture Quest Network International/PNI. 346–347: Paul Barton/The Stock Market. 350: Patti McConville/Dembinsky Photo Associates. 352: PhotoSpin/Artville Stock Images. 353: Jack Vartoogian Photography. 354: J.D. Carton/Bruce Coleman Inc. 355: *bkgd.* J.D. Carton/Bruce Coleman Inc.; *inset* Michael Simpson/FPG International. 356: Richard Hutchings for HMCo. 358: Ron Kimball Photography. 360: *t.* Bob Daemmrich/Stock Boston. 361: *l.* © Greg Lovett/The Palm Beach Post; *r.* Jim Regan/The Stock Market. 372: Tom Stewart/The Stock Market. 373: *l.* Philadelphia Museum of Art/Corbis; *r.* Leonard de Selva/Corbis. 386–387: Steve Leonard Photography. 390: © Nuridsany et Perennou/Science Source/Photo Researchers, Inc. 391: Joe McDonald/Corbis. 394: Vladimir Pcholkin/FPG International. 396: © Matthew Phillips/Photo Network/Picture Quest Network. 398: Laura Reyes/Fran Heyl Associates. 400: © Soames Summerhays/Photo Researchers, Inc. 401: Richard Price/FPG International. 404: Meinrad Faltner/The Stock Market. 408: John Neubauer/Picture Quest Network International/PNI. 416: Michael S. Yamashita. 426: Symmetry Drawing E118 by M.C. Escher. ©2000 Cordon Art-Baarn-Holland. All rights reserved. 428: *t.* VCG/FPG International; *b.* Tom Walker/Stock Boston. 433: Cosmo Condina/Tony Stone Images. 446–447: Mark E. Gibson/Mark and Audra Gibson Photography. 450: Frank Siteman/Stock Boston. 454: Dwight Cendrowski/Focusing Group Photography. 457: *l.* Harvey Lloyd/FPG International; *r.* Stock Boston. 460: Strauss/Curtis/The Stock Market. 464: Burke & Triolo/Artville Stock Images. 466: Laura

Credits

Reyes/Fran Heyl Associates. 474: Kevin R. Morris/Corbis. 477: Mike Tesi for HMCo. 478: Larry Lefever/Grant Heilman Photography, Inc. 479: Ariel Skelley/The Stock Market. 491: Rob Crandall/Stock Boston. 492–493: Stephen J. Krasemann/DRK Photo. 496: *bkgd.* Comstock; *inset* The White House. 498: Associated Press/AP. 500: *t.* Paul Grebliunas/Tony Stone Images; *b.* Bob Daemmrich/Stock Boston. 501: *l.* Jock Montgomery/Bruce Coleman Inc.; *r.* Bob Krist/Corbis. 504: Ellen Senisi/The Image Works. 505: The Image Bank. 508: *t.* LWA/Dann Tardif/The Stock Market. 512: Jeff Baker/FPG International. 514: *b.* Richard Hutchings Photography. 515: *t.l.* PhotoDisc, Inc.; *t.m.l.* PhotoDisc, Inc.; *t.m.m.* PhotoDisc, Inc.; *b.l.* PhotoDisc, Inc.; *b.m.l.* PhotoDisc, Inc.; *b.m.m* PhotoDisc, Inc. 531: *l.* Jeff Kaufman/FPG International; *r.* Ed Bock/The Stock Market. 544–545: Barrie Rokeach/Aerial/Terrestrial Photography. 548: Dennie Cody/FPG International. 550: PhotoDisc, Inc. 552: Frank Siteman/Stock Boston. 553: Scott S. Warren Photography. 557: *l.* Painet Inc. 560: *l.* Lester Lefkowitz/The Stock Market; *r.* Jeff Greenberg/PhotoEdit. 561: Frank Rossotto/The Stock Market. 567: *m.l.* © 1991 Chad Ehlers/International Stock Photography Ltd. 574: Jose L. Pelaez/The Stock Market. 576: Randall Hyman Photography. 578: Bob Daemmrich//The Image Works. 590: David Young-Wolff/PhotoEdit.

ILLUSTRATIONS
xiii: Leah Palmer. xviii: Scott Fray. 66: *t.* Bryon Thompson; *b.* Joe and Kathy Heiner. 10: Russel Benfanti. 20–21: Margo De Paulis. 24: Rob Schuster. 25: Garry Colby. 28: Gary Hallgren. 29: John Kovaleski. 40: Patrick Gnan. 54: Doug Horne. 72: Tom Barrett. 81: Bob Kayganich. 84: Walter Stuart. 86–87: Margo De Paulis. 104–105: Art Thompson. 116: David Preiss. 119: Dave Joly. 124: John Youssi. 126: Art Thompson. 128: Art Thompson. 136: Gary Antonetti. 157: Stephen Wagner. 163: Leah Palmer. 168: Walter Stuart. 178: Garry Colby. 195: Doug Horne. 200: Deborah Drummond. 210: Walter Stuart. 214: Joe and Kathy Heiner. 226: Leah Palmer. 230: Doug Horne. 245: Walter Stuart. 258: Doug Horne. 264: Doug Horne. 266: Gary Antonetti. 270: Chris Lensch. 272: John Youssi. 274: Philip Scheuer. 275: Dan Fell. 276–277: David Schultz. 282: Art Thompson. 285: Doug Horne. 286: Garry Colby. 298: Doug Horne. 299: Rob Schuster. 302: Joe Taylor. 308: Janos Maffly. 310: Janos Maffly. 312: Janos Maffly. 313: Dave Joly. 315: Dave Joly. 350–351: Doug Horne. 352: Ken Batelman. 355: Rob Schuster. 356: Doug Horne. 366: Bob Kayganich. 369: Guy Smalley. 371: Dan Clyne. 375: Barbara Cousins. 383: Dave Hile. 392–393: Stephen Wagner. 394: Ken Batelman. 396: *t.* Doug Horne; *b.* Ken Batelman. 399: Jon Watson. 410–411: Ken Batelman. 415: Ken Batelman. 417: Patrick Gnan. 422–423: Scott Fray. 425: Gary Antonetti. 433: Doug Horne. 444: Doug Horne. 462: Rob Schuster. 465: Doug Horne. 466: Art Thompson. 467: Leah Palmer. 477: Wayne Watford. 490: Neverne Covington. 491: Patrick Gnan. 494: Art Thompson. 509: Guy Smalley. 512: Paul Sharp. 513: Doug Horne. 521: Doug Horne. 524: Doug Horne. 530: Gary Antonetti. 532: Doug Horne. 576: Gary Hallgren. 579: Manuel King. 590: Joe Taylor.